THE REVIVAL

OF

PRAGMATISM

Duke University Press   Durham and London, 1998

The Revival of Pragmatism

Edited by Morris Dickstein

NEW ESSAYS
ON SOCIAL
THOUGHT, LAW,
AND CULTURE

Typeset in Minion by Keystone Typesetting, Inc.
Library of Congress Cataloging-in-Publication Data
appear on the last printed page of this book.

Contents

Acknowledgments

This book originated in a conference on the revival of pragmatism that took place at the Graduate School of the City University of New York on November 3–4, 1995. It was organized by the Center for the Humanities and cosponsored by the New York Council for the Humanities, the Jacob Burns Institute for Advanced Legal Studies at the Benjamin N. Cardozo School of Law of Yeshiva University, and the Simon Rifkind Center for the Humanities at City College. I am especially grateful for the constant and unremitting support of President Frances Degen Horowitz, Provost Geoffrey Marshall, and Dean Alan Gartner of the CUNY Graduate School. The conference could not have taken place without help from Professors David Gray Carlson, Michael Herz, Michel Rosenfeld, and Richard H. Weisberg of the Cardozo School of Law, Jay Kaplan of the New York Council for the Humanities, and Dean Martin Tamny and Paul Sherwin of City College. Jeffrey Kittay and *Lingua Franca* hosted a festive dinner for all the participants.

At the CUNY Graduate School the conference was first proposed by Charles Molesworth and planned by a committee that also included John Patrick Diggins, Charles Landesman, Louis Menand, and Joan Richardson. Their deep interest in pragmatism and advice in shaping the conference proved most valuable. Elizabeth Rosen offered some timely assistance in seeking funding. My assistants at the Center for the Humanities, especially Micki Grover and Pati Cockram, worked hard to make the conference a success.

Most of the essays included here are revised versions of papers originally presented at the conference, but this volume also includes additional essays by Richard J. Bernstein, Ray Carney, John Patrick Diggins, Giles Gunn, James T. Kloppenberg, Ross Posnock, Michel Rosenfeld, and Alan Wolfe, as well as Richard Rorty's response to the papers on legal pragmatism. Some of the conference participants were also generous with advice in planning it, especially Richard Rorty, Stanley Fish, Michel Rosenfeld, Thomas Grey, Alan Wolfe, and Richard J. Bernstein. Louis Menand gave me some helpful comments on my introduction. I am especially grateful for Richard Rorty's courtesy and encouragement and Stanley Fish's early and unflagging enthusiasm for publishing this volume.

With meticulous care, good humor, and attention to detail, Mary-Jo Haronian gave invaluable assistance in the preparation of this book. Mark Noonan and Vincent Bissonette provided much additional help in preparing the manuscript for publication.

Introduction: Pragmatism Then and Now

MORRIS DICKSTEIN

The revival of pragmatism has excited enormous interest and controversy in the intellectual community over the past two decades. By the middle of the twentieth century, pragmatism was widely considered a naively optimistic residue of an earlier liberalism, discredited by the Depression and the horrors of the war, and virtually driven from philosophy departments by the reigning school of analytic philosophy. Now once again it is recognized not only as the most distinctive American contribution to philosophy but as a new way of approaching old problems in a number of fields. As the present volume shows, pragmatism has become a key point of reference around which contemporary debates in social thought, law, and literary theory as well as philosophy have been unfolded. It has appealed to philosophers moving beyond analytic philosophy, European theorists looking for an alternative to Marxism, and postmodernists seeking native roots for their critique of absolutes and universals. The revival has not only drawn new attention to the original pragmatists but altered our view of writers as different as Emerson and Frost, Nietzsche and Wittgenstein, Santayana and Stevens, Du Bois and Ellison, all of whom have been reconsidered in the light of a broader conception of pragmatist thinking.

Pragmatism as a branch of philosophy is exactly a hundred years old. The term was first brought forward by William James in a lecture in Berkeley in 1898, published as "Philosophical Conceptions and Practical Results." In developing pragmatism as a critique of abstractions and absolutes and as a philosophy oriented toward practice and action, James insisted that he was only building on thoughts developed by his friend Charles Sanders Peirce in Cambridge more than twenty years earlier. But the cantankerous Peirce was far from pleased with what James did with his ideas. Pragmatism's early years were as filled with controversy as its recent career. James plunged into the fray with his usual zest, and the lectures published as *Pragmatism* in 1907 became one of his most widely read

1

books. In part because they were so clearly yet provocatively formulated, James' lectures created something of a scandal. James had targeted rationalists and idealists of every stripe, and pragmatism was widely attacked as an extreme form of relativism that undermined any notion of objective truth.

As it is used in common speech, the qualities associated with "pragmatism" generally win our enthusiastic assent. Politicians and pundits see pragmatism as the essence of American politics—the art of the possible, rooted in our aversion to ideology and our genius for compromise. Those who take a pragmatic approach to diplomacy and foreign policy—or those who craft legislation and strike political deals—pride themselves in negotiating differences and achieving incremental results rather than holding out for unbending moral absolutes. Others condemn this kind of pragmatism as policy without principle, goal-oriented but lacking a moral anchor. When presidents like Franklin Roosevelt, John Kennedy, or Bill Clinton are described as the ultimate pragmatists, this may mean that they got something done, or that their behavior, for better or worse, differed from their rhetoric, or that they were cunning and pliable men with few consistent values or ideals. "I'm a pragmatist, a problem solver," said one recent presidential advisor to explain his seemingly contradictory approach to two different issues.

As a philosophical position, pragmatism seems at first to have little in common with this widespread usage. John Dewey's ideas were radical and dynamic rather than limited to practical considerations. His emphasis on "creative intelligence," especially in education, stressed the transformation of the given rather than the acceptance of the status quo. Despite the value it places on doing and practice, in some ways it was more utopian than practical. This is why Dewey repeatedly criticizes empiricism, to which his work otherwise shows a strong kinship. "Empiricism is conceived of as tied up to what has been, or is, 'given,' " Dewey wrote. "But experience in its vital form is experimental, an effort to change the given; it is characterized by projection, by reaching forward into the unknown; connection with a future is its salient trait."[1] For pragmatists the upshot of thought comes not in logical distinctions or intellectual systems but in behavior, the translation of ideas into action. As Peirce wrote in "How to Make Our Ideas Clear," one of pragmatism's founding texts,

> The essence of belief is the establishment of a habit, and different beliefs are distinguished by the different modes of action to which they give rise. . . . Imaginary distinctions are often drawn between

beliefs which differ only in their mode of expression. . . . [T]he whole function of thought is to produce habits of action. . . . To develop its meaning, we have, therefore, simply to determine what habits it produces, for what a thing means is simply what habits it involves.[2]

Within the American tradition, this practical, result-oriented side of Peirce, James, and Dewey places their work in a line that goes back at least to Benjamin Franklin, while the pragmatists' commitment to creative self-transformation shows the influence of Emerson. "The world stands really malleable, waiting to receive its final touches at our hands," says James near the end of *Pragmatism*. He goes on to describe a world that "suffers human violence willingly," that is "still in the making, and awaits part of its complexion from the future."[3] A bit disingenuously, James presents pragmatism not as philosophy but as a way of doing philosophy, "a method of settling metaphysical disputes that otherwise might be interminable" (42). Pragmatism provides a practical test but "it does not stand for any special results," he claimed. "It is a method only" (46). Yet its consequences were far-reaching.

James himself was exhilarated by the controversy that surrounded his lectures on pragmatism. Just as Marx saw his materialist version of Hegel as a Copernican turn in philosophy, James quite seriously compared pragmatism to the Protestant Reformation, which augmented the authority of the individual conscience against the power of the Church.[4] He also suggested that his account of truth, once it was definitively settled, would "mark a turning-point in the history of epistemology, and consequently in that of general philosophy" (196). Yet in the subtitle of his book, James described pragmatism as "a new name for some old ways of thinking," perhaps to deflect the charges of outrageous novelty and irresponsibility that were already being leveled against him.

In the first decade of the century James's pragmatism was under sharp attack from adherents of philosophical and religious idealism. Pragmatism had a considerable tradition behind it, yet it was also part of a larger modern turn marked by the inexorable growth of science, secularism, and the historical consciousness in American thinking. In Dewey's hands especially, it reflected an evolutionary perspective that showed the influence of both Hegelian historicism and Darwinian naturalism. Darwin's work undercut not only traditional religious belief but also the sense of an unchanging, essential nature. As Hegel (and Marx) fostered a dynamic view of history, Darwin legitimized a genetic approach to animal and human behavior. Social Darwinists took this as a justification of the harsh struggle for life under unregulated capitalism, but for progressive thinkers it meant that the sources of social inequality, far from being a given, could be traced empirically and altered by changes in education and public policy. In Dewey's work as an active reformer and prolific theorist, pragmatism became part of the surge of liberalism, progressivism, and social reform in the first decades of the twentieth century.

Yet even apart from questions of social policy, pragmatism also had its cultural dimension. Though pragmatism and modernism often diverge, and the early pragmatists themselves had mixed feelings about modern art, the moment of pragmatism was also the moment of Picasso's and Braque's cubism, Einstein's theory of relativity, and a new wave of advanced literature. Realism and naturalism, which had sought an objective standpoint on man and society, gave way to experiments that tried to capture the flow of the individual consciousness. William James' focus on the stream of consciousness in his *Principles of Psychology* (1890), his admired friend Henri Bergson's studies of *durée,* or experienced time, in his *Time and Free Will* (1899), and Freud's explorations of the unconscious in his *Interpretation of Dreams* (1900) ran parallel to these literary experiments, including the close attention to point of view in the difficult late novels of Henry James. The James brothers were often impatient with each others' work, but they achieved a momentary convergence in 1907 when Henry, after reading *Pragmatism,* wrote that "I was lost in the wonder of the extent to which all my life I have . . . unconsciously pragmatised,"[5] and the easily exasperated William yielded conditionally to the prismatic hall of mirrors he saw with some astonishment in *The American Scene.* Together and separately, James, Bergson, and Freud had an incalculably large influence on the forms and outlook of modern art.

Pragmatism, like modernism, reflects the break-up of cultural and religious authority, the turn away from any simple or stable definition of truth, the shift from totalizing systems and unified narratives to a more fragmented plurality of perspectives. In modern literature this would be epitomized by Joyce's shaping of the interior monologue, Ford Madox Ford's use of the unreliable narrator, Gertrude Stein's flow of verbal association, and Faulkner's overlay of multiple perspectives in *The Sound and the Fury* and *As I Lay Dying.* Literary modernism displaces the omniscient narrator in fiction as religious liberalism unseats the omniscient deity. But where many modernists, especially after World War I—the *Waste Land* generation—would portray the fragmentation of the modern world with an acrid nostalgia for earlier hierarchies, the pragmatists tend to be exuberant and constructive rather than pessimistic. The dark and apocalyptic strain of modernism held little appeal for them; the rupture with past certainties opened up new horizons. They saw "the quest for certainty" as the futile and misguided remnant of an outworn metaphysics, and they take the new, contingent, human-centered world as source of opportunity and possibility. For the pragmatists, truth is provisional, grounded in history and experience, not fixed in the nature of things. In the words of historian John P. Diggins, "pragmatism offered uncertainty and plurality as an answer to the exhausted past ideas of authority."[6]

Yet the break with the past would also involve a new emphasis on history. The edifice of the law especially came to be seen as an evolving process rather than a set of fixed principles. As Oliver Wendell Holmes, Jr., wrote near the beginning of *The Common Law,* "It is something to show that the consistency of a system requires a particular result, but it is not all. The life of the law has not been logic: it has been experience. The felt necessities of the time, the prevalent moral and political theories, institutions of public policy, avowed or unconscious, even the prejudices which judges share with their fellow-men, have had a good deal more to do than the syllogism in determining the rules by which men should be governed."[7]

Such an empirical outlook offended formalists, rationalists, philosophical idealists, and traditional moralists alike. Pragmatism became a new chapter in the struggle between defenders of the ancients and the moderns that went back to Aristophanes and Euripides. In 1915 Walter Lippmann was still the young progressive, not yet the expounder of natural law he became in later works like *The Public Philosophy* (1955). As a gifted undergraduate at Harvard, he had attracted the notice of William James, whom he immensely admired. But in a *New Republic* essay of 1915 he initially expressed concern that Dewey, with his radical experimentalism, was "urging us to do something never done before by any other people. He is urging us consciously to manufacture our philosophy." It would be hard to imagine a better description of what Emerson or Whitman were propounding for the new American nation: a genuinely fresh start, an escape from the heavy hand of European tradition, an emancipation by self-definition. "The whole value of philosophies up to the present," says Lippmann, "has been that they found support for our action in something outside ourselves. We philosophized in order to draw sanction from God, or nature or evolution."[8] A few years later Lippmann's Harvard classmate, T. S. Eliot, objected to "a certain meanness of culture" in the philosophy of William Blake, which he compared to "an ingenious piece of home-made furniture: we admire the man who has put it together out of the odds and ends about the house."[9] For Eliot, too, philosophy was something you inherited, something externally sanctioned, not ideas and beliefs that could be shaped to your own needs.

But the Lippmann of 1915 quickly reversed field and went on to argue that in fact philosophers had always done what Dewey (and Freud) described: projected general ideas out of their own temperament and needs. "Most philosophy is not a revelation of absolute principles, but a human being's adjustment of his desires to his limitations." Lippmann's sympathy for pragmatism would not endure, but for now he puts an eloquent spin on Dewey's views:

> All philosophies are experiments, but they are unconscious ones. They all represent an attempt to make ourselves better at home in the world. . . . Instead of spinning our thoughts blindly and calling them absolute truth, let us spin them deliberately and be ready to change them. Let us continue to write autobiographies, but let us be sure we know they are autobiographies. Let us recognize that the true use of philosophy is to help us to live.[10]

Dewey could not have been entirely pleased to see himself defended in such a spongy, subjective vein. Just as Blake tried to escape Romantic subjectivity by creating an immense, eclectic mythology, the pragmatists hoped to avoid relativism by developing an evolutionary outlook in social and intersubjective rather than merely subjective terms. Working from a scientific model like the one later developed by Thomas Kuhn, Dewey envisioned a self-correcting community of enquirers who would proceed experimentally according to fallibilistic norms of "warranted assertability," instead of claiming to discover timeless truths that corresponded to the way the world actually is. Richard Rorty has described this as "a search for the widest possible intersubjective agreement," adding that "objectivity is not a matter of corresponding to objects but of getting together with other subjects."[11]

As Rorty would be drawn to literature, especially the novel, for its concrete portrayal of intersubjectivity, James evoked a Whitmanesque version of truth still grounded in "the muddy particulars of experience," a truth whose claims were "conditional" and constantly evolving rather than abstract and absolute (149, 150). In an arresting passage in *Pragmatism,* James also turned to the common law to describe this process of accretion and transmutation. The key metaphor here is a biological one:

> Distinctions between the lawful and the unlawful in conduct, or between the correct and incorrect in speech, have grown up incidentally

among the interactions of men's experiences in detail; and in no other way do the distinctions between the true and the false in belief ever grow up. Truth grafts itself on previous truth, modifying it in the process, just as idiom grafts itself on previous idiom, and law on previous law. . . .

All the while, however, we pretend that the eternal is unrolling, that the one previous justice, grammar or truth are simply fulgurating and not being made. . . . These things *make themselves* as we go. (158)

Such parallels between law and language, language and truth, all seen as part of an evolving historical process, were prophetic of the later directions of pragmatism, as the essays in the present volume make clear. James sees laws and languages, if not truth itself, as "man-made things." "Human motives sharpen all our questions, human satisfactions lurk in all our answers, all our formulas have a human twist" (159).

When James says that the pragmatist turns away from abstraction and absolutes "towards facts, towards action and towards power," when he adds that this empiricist temper "means the open air and the possibilities of nature, as against dogma, artificiality, and the pretence of finality in truth" (45), he is expressing his own robust temperament, his love of the outdoors, of risk and adventure, but also a typical American preference for action over reflection, for facts over theories, and above all for results. "Pragmatism unstiffens all our theories, limbers them up and sets each one to work" (46–47). What made pragmatism so embattled in its original form was also what made it strikingly American: its practical, situational, problem-solving emphasis.

James puts all this in an inflammatory way as a foil to idealism, metaphysics, and popular notions about what philosophy is and what philosophers do. Instead of words like God, matter, and reason that play an almost magical, incantatory role in metaphysics, the pragmatic method prevents you from looking "on any such word as closing your quest. You must bring out of each word its practical cash-value, set it at work within the stream of your experience" (46). James insists that truth or meaning is a process, an action leading to a pay-off, a verb rather than a noun. "The truth of an idea is not a stagnant property inherent in it. Truth *happens* to an idea. It *becomes* true, is *made* true by events. . . . Its validity is the process of its *validation*" (196). "It is the nature of truths to be validated, verified. It pays for our ideas to be validated. Our obligation to seek truth is part of our general obligation to do what pays" (149–50). Truth is the outcome of experience. "Men's beliefs at any time are so much experience *funded*" (146).

James' aim with these and other pointed metaphors is to ground ideas in lived experience—to see them as emerging from a living subject and issuing in real consequences, to see them as made rather than given. He uses loaded words like "power" or "cash-value" not to ally pragmatism with force or business—two major American preoccupations during Teddy Roosevelt's presidency, when he wrote his book—but as a way of jolting his audience, appealing to them almost too vividly in terms of the forces that were really running the world.

By stating his case polemically in such charged language, James opened pragmatism to the charge that it was philistine, a methodology without a moral compass, an epistemology with a merely tactical sense of truth. Pragmatism is always contextual. It sees things not in isolation, not as essences existing in and of themselves, but as belonging to contexts that shape their meaning and value. It is concerned about the *production* of meaning, the production of truth, because it sees them as dynamic, always in formation. To its detractors, this emphasis on the situation and the "cash" payoff revealed a method that could be used to justify anything. Had not James himself said that "the true, to put it very briefly, is only the expedient in the way of our thinking, just as the right is only the expedient in our way of our behaving"? (196).

The most damning attack on pragmatism as expediency came not from metaphysicians or traditional moralists but from one of Dewey's most gifted admirers, Randolph Bourne. In "Twilight of Idols" (1917), Bourne argued that Dewey's pragmatic justification for the America's entry into World War I, which shocked many of his followers, showed up his concern with technique and efficiency at the expense of consistent values, and revealed the limits of Dewey's instrumentalism: it was a narrowly expedient philosophy of "adaptation" and "adjustment" bereft of ultimate goals. (Dewey's educational views were often attacked in the same terms.) Bourne was appalled that a pragmatist approach could be made to serve repugnant ends. He complained that Dewey's young disciples—like the "best and brightest" who would prosecute a later American war—"have absorbed the secret of scientific method as applied to political administration. They are liberal, enlightened, aware. . . . They are making themselves efficient instruments of the war-technique, accepting with little question the ends as announced from above. . . . To those of us who have taken Dewey's philosophy almost as our American religion, it never occurred that values could be subordinated to technique."[12] If the social conscience that led to progressive reforms showed Dewey's break with tradition in the best light, the war revealed its darker side.

Bourne's critique became the template for subsequent attacks on pragmatism from both left and right. The date alone, 1917, was momentous: even more than America's entry into the war, the Russian Revolution would energize and divide the left while terrifying and galvanizing the right. Soon cultural critics like Van Wyck Brooks and Lewis Mumford would develop Bourne's attack. To later Marxist critics like Theodor Adorno, pragmatism was hopelessly wedded to the status quo; they saw it as little more than a rationale for America's ruthless and amoral business civilization. Conservatives would be just as offended by its relativism and optimism, its critique of moral absolutes and foundational values. Near the end of the essay Bourne places himself among the young "malcontents" created by the war, who reject "a philosophy of adjustment" and react with "robust desperation" to "the continual frustrations and aridities of American life."[13] He thus became the prototype of the disillusioned modernist intellectual who would turn against pragmatism during the next two decades, looking instead toward Europe, toward modern art, and eventually toward Marxism and revolution.

The war discredited the kind of enlightened planning with which pragmatism had become identified. The reaction against progressivism after 1920 also became a reaction against pragmatism, among conservatives who celebrated America's exceptionalism and achievements and as well as among radicals who castigated its abuses and inequalities. The reaction against pragmatism became even more marked after World War II, abetted by a variety of new influences including existentialism, crisis theology, the cold war, psychoanalysis, European modernism, and a cultural conservatism bred of growing prosperity and the fear of Communism. Part of this story was told many years ago in Morton White's 1949 book *Social Thought in America: The Revolt Against Formalism,* where White points to "the submersion of a certain style of thinking which dominated America for almost half a century—an intellectual pattern compounded of pragmatism, institutionalism, behaviorism, legal realism, economic determinism, and the 'new history.'" "It might be argued," he writes in his introduction, "that these movements are not dead, but one cannot avoid the feeling that they are past the peak of their influence. These are days in which Dewey's views are being replaced by Kierkegaard's in places where once Dewey was king."[14]

Other versions of this narrative of liberalism in decline can be found in Lionel Trilling's *The Liberal Imagination* (1950), where socially oriented naturalists like Dreiser and Sherwood Anderson give way before modernists like Faulkner and Hemingway, or in Richard Hofstadter's books on the

Age of Reform and the Progressive Historians, which ratified the decline of progressive historiography. Trilling complained of liberalism in exactly the same terms Bourne and Van Wyck Brooks had used in attacking pragmatism: it lacked imagination, it was spiritually empty, it lacked a sense of tragedy, it had become identified with bureaucracy and social engineering—the "organizational impulse."[15] Yet the eclipse of pragmatism was never complete. Trilling's and Niebuhr's critiques of moral absolutes—a key part of their attack on utopian and totalitarian thinking—were deeply influenced by the spirit of pragmatism. Writing as self-described realists skeptical of progressive idealism, they turned instinctively to pragmatism as a supple and concrete form of critical thinking, a refuge from abstraction.[16]

At the same time Kierkegaard and Niebuhr displaced Dewey, just when the lively ghost of Henry James can be said to have displaced William James, at the very moment Trilling's version of "tragic realism" became canonical for critics and legal realism was under withering assault in the law schools, the beginnings of a revival of pragmatism could already be seen among analytic philosophers like W. V. Quine. This would later be brought to the attention of a wider audience by Richard Rorty in *Philosophy and the Mirror of Nature* (1979) and the essays collected in *Consequences of Pragmatism* (1982). Meanwhile, a handful of other philosophers like Richard J. Bernstein, John E. Smith, and John McDermott kept pragmatism alive in the schools. During the very period when it seemed least fashionable, the pragmatist renewal was already under way.

The current revival of pragmatism is a varied and complex phenomenon involving many crosscurrents. But a few broad patterns suggest themselves.

—After the chill of the postwar years, which put progressive ideas into cold storage, the 1960s provided a new impetus to radical thinking beyond the exhausted Marxism of the Old Left. Dewey's ideas about democracy in works like *The Public and Its Problems* (1927), particularly his defense of a town-meeting model of participatory democracy against the authority of elites and the reign of experts, found their way into the Port Huron Statement (1962), the founding document of the Students for a Democratic Society (largely written by Tom Hayden), and into the work of widely read social critics and educational theorists like C. Wright Mills and Paul Goodman.

—The subsequent collapse of the New Left shifted these critical currents into the university. This contributed to the rising influence of European theory, first with the neo-Marxism of the Frankfurt School, then in linguistically based forms of deconstruction and poststructuralism. As postmodern theorists announced the exhaustion of the "grand narratives," Americans discovered that the pragmatists had been there first, developing a skeptical theory of knowledge and a well-articulated critique of essentialism and foundationalism that did not devolve into nihilism but emphasized the contingencies of language and context.

—As the Marxism of the 1970s and 1980s once again became the God that failed, intellectuals searched for an incremental, democratic alternative: the French rediscovered liberalism, the Germans discovered empiricism, Americans rediscovered pragmatism. Apocalyptic thinking, the grand narratives of earlier systems, began to go out of fashion in all three countries. The work of Richard Rorty formed a bridge between a Deweyan faith in liberal democracy and a postmodern antifoundationalism. As James and Dewey had attacked formalism, "intellectualism," and metaphysics, Rorty attacked philosophy itself, deriding its Platonic quest for a truth beyond appearances, its self-described position as an arbiter of knowledge, and insisting that its traditional debates were simply part of an ongoing process of linguistic redescription.

Dewey himself had said that old philosophical problems were never resolved; they simply stopped mattering. Rorty had emerged from the analytical tradition, which had developed its own version of the "linguistic turn" and the critique of metaphysics. Focusing on language rather than on experience as the basis of all our understanding, he forged a synthesis between Dewey and James on the one hand, Heidegger and Derrida on the other—freely discarding what he did not like, such as Dewey's faith in science. To Rorty science had its own metaphysical assumptions; far from being provisional and experimental, it was another form of the quest for certainty, the faith in an objective order of truth. If pragmatism began with James's strong misreading of Peirce, it came to life again with Rorty's strong misreading of Dewey, whom he described as "a postmodernist before his time."[17]

Rorty's strikingly contemporary versions of Dewey and James led to equally vigorous rejoinders by other students of the original pragmatists, including Richard Bernstein, Robert Westbrook, and Hilary Putnam. Putnam has devoted much of his recent work, including the new essay published here, to a defense of philosophical realism. As these controversies heated up, pragmatism became a broad terrain of ongoing debate rather than a musty historical legacy. The present volume shows up the major fault lines in that contested ground. This book is not primarily concerned with philosophy, or indeed with the classical pragmatists, although they figure repeatedly in these pages. Instead it focuses on the cultural impact of the pragmatist revival in different yet overlapping regions of contemporary thought.

A major issue that emerges in the discussion of the law is whether legal pragmatism is "freestanding," perhaps simply common-sensical, or depends on adherence to some form of pragmatist philosophy. Both Richard Posner and Thomas Grey find pragmatism so intrinsic to the way legal decisions are actually made that they paradoxically need no philosophical justification. As Grey writes: "Pragmatist jurisprudence is a theoretical middle way between grand theorizing and anti-intellectual business as usual." He connects basic legal reasoning to two of the main lines of pragmatic thinking.

> Law is contextual: it is rooted in practice and custom, and takes its substance from existing patterns of human conduct and interaction. To an equal degree, law is instrumental, meant to advance the human good of those it serves, hence subject to alteration to achieve this end. Law so conceived is a set of practical measures for cooperative social life, using signals and sanctions to guide and channel conduct. ("Freestanding Legal Pragmatism")

From this viewpoint, most jurists, like the happily surprised Henry James, have been unconsciously pragmatizing all their lives, with little need for theoretical scaffolding. They are likely to agree with Grey that "more precise and determinate general theories of the nature and function of law should be viewed with suspicion, at least when put forward to control practice." Legal theory, it is said, has value only as a description of legal practice or as an independent inquiry into it, not as a ground or justification for it. (This is very much like what Rorty says of philosophy in general.) Grey points to a friend who, unlike him, is a religious believer and foundationalist but shares his legal views and agrees with him that "law itself imposes no absolute moral claims." David Luban complicates this argument that legal pragmatism is "freestanding" by introducing another distinction: between philosophical pragmatism, which (he argues) *does* provide a useful basis for judicial thinking, and the kind of post-philosophical pragmatism associated with Rorty, which generally does not.

The parallel debate among social theorists and historians centers on the question of whether pragmatism provides a rationale for democracy and community, as Dewey clearly thought it did, or is simply a method that presupposes no particular politics, social views, or religious views. "If pragmatism is true it has nothing to say to us," says Stanley Fish in his afterword to this volume; "no politics follows from it or is blocked by it; no morality attaches to it or is enjoined by it." Rorty has always insisted that his liberal democratic views are completely independent of his pragmatism, while some acute students of Dewey's work, including Westbrook, Bernstein, James Kloppenberg, and Hilary Putnam, have tried to reinforce the connections between democratic practice and a pragmatic theory of knowledge.

In his searching essay "A Reconsideration of Deweyan Democracy" (in *Renewing Philosophy*), Putnam finds in Dewey an "epistemological justification of democracy," which "rests at every point on arguments which are not at all transcendental, but which represent the fruit of our collective experience."[18] Bernstein stresses Dewey's view that "regarded as an idea, democracy is not an alternative to other principles of associated life. It is the idea of community life itself." This belief forms the kernel of *The Public and Its Problems*, Dewey's only work of political theory, but Dewey himself adds realistically that "democracy in this sense is not a fact and never will be." His aim is to approach the problem more pragmatically: "Only when we start from a community as a fact, grasp the fact in thought so as to clarify and enhance its constituent elements, can we reach an idea of democracy which is not utopian."[19] This is precisely what critics like Alan Wolfe and John P. Diggins maintain that Dewey and pragmatism are unable to do. Both insist that Deweyan ideas of community are utopian and future-oriented, and are therefore of little help in describing communities as they actually exist or have existed in the past.

In his important new essay for this volume, Rorty, criticizing Nietzsche's contempt for democracy (and for John Stuart Mill) as "an adventitious extra, inessential to his overall philosophical outlook," comes much closer to identifying pragmatism with democracy—at least with the kind of democracy he finds in Mill's *On Liberty*. For Rorty, Mill's conception of liberty—the freedom to pursue private happiness without impinging on others—is virtually identical with Nietzsche's sparkling meditation on polytheism in *The Gay Science* as a "*plurality of norms*" in which "one god was not considered a denial of another god, nor blasphemy against him." Joined to Isaiah Berlin's pluralist argument that different people live with incommensurable values, this polytheism in turn becomes a strong metaphor for Rorty's pragmatism. It leads him to say that "you are a polytheist if you think there is no actual or possible object of knowledge which would permit you to commensurate and rank all human needs."

Once one sees no way of ranking human needs other than playing them off against one another, human happiness becomes all that matters. Mill's *On Liberty* becomes all the ethical instruction you need—all the philosophical advice you are ever going to get about your responsibilities to other human beings. For human perfection becomes a private concern, and our responsibility to others becomes a matter of permitting them as much space to pursue these private concerns—to worship their own gods, so to speak—as is compatible with granting an equal amount of space to all. The tradition of religious toleration is extended to moral toleration. ("Pragmatism as Romantic Polytheism")

Rorty has always been extraordinarily resourceful in finding new metaphors for his pragmatism and antirepresentationalism; the notion of "romantic polytheism" is one of the most suggestive. But the metaphor has powerful implications of its own. Rorty has been accused of an implacable antitheism—"proscribing god talk," as Eugene Goodheart puts it[20]—but Rorty's expansion of this new metaphor is at least rhetorically more sympathetic to religion than anything he has previously written. He positions his essay as a rejoinder to "those who think that pragmatism and religion do not mix." A critic might argue that "ranking human needs" is at best a reductive description of ethical and religious values. But by identifying polytheism with toleration and monotheism with intolerance and absolutism, Rorty creates a bridge from religion and ethics, as he understands them, to democracy. The multiplicity of gods becomes a metaphor for the multiplicity of ethical goals and private needs in a democratic society. This becomes a version of the "negative liberty," the freedom from unnecessary constraint, that Berlin saw as the essence of Mill's liberalism. But as Rorty's religion offers little comfort to believers, dissolving God into a "personal symbol of ultimate concern," it offers even less to those who feel that "democratic politics" must involve more than what he calls "a free consensus about how much space for private perfection we can allow each other." They are likely to feel, as Giles Gunn does, that Rorty sacrifices the public sphere for private life and, unlike Dewey, purchases individual liberty at the expense of community.

Rorty's emphasis on personal happiness, his agnosticism about social theory except as a gloss on social practice, may explain why his work has been more warmly received by literary critics than by historians or social scientists. The literary side of the revival of pragmatism has been much concerned with critical method, more skeptical of any specific social goals, more postmodernist, and hence more closely allied with Rorty than with Putnam or Bernstein. At one extreme, a recent collection of essays draws pragmatism into the orbit of new work on rhetoric, and especially on the sophists; pragmatism becomes another name for radically detaching the sign from its referent.[21] Closer to the mainstream of literary thinking are those who see pragmatism as a way out of the cul-de-sac of theory, much as Giovanni Papini once called pragmatism a philosophy for getting along without philosophy.[22] Stanley Fish, in *Is There a Text in This Class?*, and Barbara Herrnstein Smith, in *Contingencies of Value*, have adapted Dewey's idea of the community of enquirers into a pragmatic view of the "interpretive community," which makes critical interpretation and evaluation contingent on the changing assumptions of different reading communities at different times and places. From this viewpoint, statements about the world or judgments of value are always provisional: constructions of language that belong to a particular context. Such arguments, like similar ones in legal interpretation, have drawn outrage from critics upholding a more stable or objective view of linguistic meaning and literary judgment.

The work of Richard Poirier in *The Renewal of Literature* (1987) and *Poetry and Pragmatism* (1992) represents yet another strand of literary pragmatism. Like Harold Bloom and Stanley Cavell, Poirier identifies a tradition of "Emersonian linguistic skepticism" which undermines the once-dominant way of reading American literature through the prism of modernism or New Critical formalism. That kind of formalist modernism had been integral to F. O. Mattheissen's work on the American Renaissance and much of the criticism that followed. Using Emerson and William James—and poets like Frost and Stevens—as touchstones of American writing, Poirier emphasizes the layered, dynamic, self-undoing complexity of literary language, with its residues of historical meaning and individual effort. "When used in the intensely self-reflecting way that literature uses them," Poirier writes in *The Renewal of Literature*, "words not only continuously modify but actually tend to dissolve one another." When language reaches this "point of incandescence," he says, "it marks the disappearance of individuality on the occasion of its triumph." We can feel a kind of amazement "that any one person, any author (or reader), can be responsible for what we see and hear going on."[23] Poirier picks up this theme in *Poetry and Pragmatism*, referring to "the responsibilities to words which reading entails, an obligation to all the barely audible cultural inheritances carried within them."[24]

Poirier gives a dynamic Emersonian turn to the New Critical emphasis on the irony and complexity of poetic language, disengaging it from the formalism that sees literary works as static, self-contained objects. Poetry, like pragmatism, is provisional, contextual. In contrast to most New Critics, who saw in literature a principle of order, and to more recent cultural conservatives, who cast it a stable source of virtues or values, Poirier sees the twists and turns of literary language as an endless self-remaking, very much in the spirit of William James or of Emerson's "Circles," with its ecstatic, Whitmanesque peroration:

> Do not set the least value on what I do, or the least discredit on what I do not, as if I pretended to settle any thing true or false. I unsettle all things. No facts are to me sacred; none are profane; I simply experiment, an endless seeker with no Past at my back. . . . In nature every moment is new; the past is always swallowed and forgotten; the coming only is sacred. Nothing is secure but life, transition, the energizing spirit.[25]

"I simply experiment." Emerson is too protean to be entirely identified with pragmatism, but this is one strand of Emerson that is central to both the American tradition and the recent revival of pragmatism. It also helps explain why pragmatism remains as controversial today as it was in James' and Dewey's day. Whether we see pragmatism in terms of the flux of the moment, the orientation toward the future, or what Holmes describes as the residue of past experience, to its critics it remains a dangerous and irresponsible form of moral and epistemological relativism.

Today's debate takes place in a different world from Emerson's or James', though many of the same criticisms have surfaced. Despite the conservative nostalgia of bestselling books like Allan Bloom's *The Closing of the American Mind,* the current orthodoxy in academic life arises not from a dominant idealism or an array of traditional moral absolutes but out of a mixture of European theories from Marxism to poststructuralism. Within this context, pragmatism has come to be seen as an American alternative, an escape from the abstraction of theory and the abyss of nihilism. We might describe it as a constructive skepticism. If liberal politicians and intellectuals share one thing at this moment, it is the loss of old certainties. Pragmatism today is less an attack on the foundations of knowledge, as it was portrayed by its early critics, than a search for method when the foundations have already crumbled.

Just as each generation reshapes the classics to its own needs, each generation resurrects earlier thinkers and reconfigures them in its own image. The decline of pragmatism belonged to a moment of deep pessimism in American thought, the moment of the Holocaust, of original sin, of global cold war and nuclear stand-off. But the tragic realism and fashionable dark theology of the 1940s and 1950s proved as perishable as the progressive liberalism that preceded it. They were anchored in their cultural moment. Sartre himself turned against an existentialism that was entirely conditioned by the war experience. The 1960s, which made Emerson and Whitman readable, even inspiring, to a new generation, also contributed to the revival of pragmatism. To everyone's surprise, Dewey returned not only to replace Kierkegaard but to jostle Derrida, Lacan, and Foucault. One would hardly say that it is the same Dewey the second time around, but a Dewey unexpectedly compatible with main currents of American thinking from Emerson to postmodernism. For Americans, at least, always suspicious of abstractions, pragmatism has been the perennial philosophy, one that has become contemporary again in today's post-ideological climate.

Notes

1 John Dewey, "The Need for a Recovery of Philosophy," in *John Dewey: The Essential Writings,* ed. David Sidorsky (New York: Harper & Row, 1977), p. 71. First published in a collection of essays edited by John Dewey, *Creative Intelligence: Essays in the Pragmatic Attitude* (1917).

2 Charles Sanders Peirce, "How to Make Our Ideas Clear," in *Pragmatism: A Contemporary Reader,* ed. Russell B. Goodman (New York: Routledge, 1995), pp. 42–43.

3 William James, *Pragmatism and Four Essays from the Meaning of Truth,* ed. Ralph Barton Perry (Cleveland: Meridian Books, 1955), p. 167. Page numbers of further references are in parentheses in the text.

4 *Letters of William James,* ed. Henry James, Jr. (Boston: Little, Brown, 1920), vol. 2, p. 279.

5 Quoted in R. W. B. Lewis, *The Jameses: A Family Narrative* (New York: Farrar, Straus and Giroux, 1991), p. 565.

6 John P. Diggins, *The Promise of Pragmatism: Modernism and the Crisis of Knowledge and Authority* (Chicago: University of Chicago Press, 1994), p. 342.

7 Quoted in *Ibid.,* pp. 352–53.

8 Walter Lippmann, "The Footnote," in *Early Writings,* ed. Arthur Schlesinger Jr. (New York: Liveright, 1970), p. 307. First appeared in *The New Republic* (July 17, 1915). Also quoted in Diggins, *Promise of Pragmatism,* p. 341.

9 T. S. Eliot, "William Blake," in *Selected Essays* (London: Faber and Faber, 1951), p. 321.

10 Lippmann, *Early Writings,* pp. 308, 309.

11 Richard Rorty, "Does Academic Freedom Have Philosophical Presuppositions?" in *The Future of Academic Freedom,* ed. Louis Menand (Chicago: University of Chicago Press, 1996), pp. 21, 29.

12 Randolph Bourne, "Twilight of Idols," in *The Radical Will: Selected Writings, 1911–1918,* ed. Olaf Hansen (New York: Urizen Books, 1977), pp. 342–43.

13 *Ibid.*, pp. 345–46.
14 Morton White, *Social Thought in America: The Revolt Against Formalism* (Boston: Beacon Press, 1957), p. 3.
15 Lionel Trilling, *The Liberal Imagination: Essays on Literature and Society* (New York: Viking Press, 1950), p. xiv.
16 Trilling, for example, writes of a would-be revolutionary in Henry James's *The Princess Casamassima* that she "cannot but mistake the nature of reality, for she believes it is a thing, a position, a finality, a bedrock. She is, in short, the very embodiment of the modern will which masks itself in virtue, . . . that despises the variety and modulations of the human story and longs for an absolute humanity" (*The Liberal Imagination*, pp. 91–92). And Niebuhr's great admirer, Arthur M. Schlesinger, Jr., describes how "the penetrating critic of the Social Gospel and of pragmatism . . . ended up, in a sense, the powerful reinterpreter and champion of both. . . . [T]he resources of democratic pragmatism turned out to be greater than many people—including Niebuhr himself in certain moods—had imagined" (*The Politics of Hope*, Boston: Houghton Mifflin, 1963, pp. 123–24).
17 Quoted in Diggins, *Promise of Pragmatism*, p. 453.
18 Hilary Putnam, "A Reconsideration of Deweyan Democracy," in his book *Renewing Philosophy* (Cambridge: Harvard University Press, 1992), pp. 183, 195.
19 John Dewey, *The Public and Its Problems* (Denver: Alan Swallow, 1954), pp. 148–49.
20 Eugene Goodheart, "The Postmodern Liberalism of Richard Rorty," in Goodheart, *The Reign of Ideology* (New York: Columbia University Press, 1997), p. 52. Goodheart focuses his criticism of Rorty for extruding religion from the liberal commonwealth on statements like the following: "In its ideal form, the culture of liberalism would be one which was enlightened, secular, through and through. It would be one in which no trace of divinity remained, either in the form of a divinized world or a divinized self. Such a culture would have no room for the notion that there are nonhuman forces to which human beings should be responsible. It would drop, or drastically reinterpret, not only the idea of holiness but those of 'devotion to truth' and of 'fulfillment of the deepest needs of the spirit'" (Richard Rorty, *Contingency, Irony, and Solidarity,* Cambridge: Cambridge University Press, 1989, p. 45).
21 See Steven Mailloux (ed.), *Rhetoric, Sophistry, Pragmatism* (Cambridge: Cambridge University Press, 1995).
22 See Diggins, *Promise of Pragmatism*, p. 408. John Ashbery develops a philosophy for living without philosophy in an amusing but serious poem, "My Philosophy of Life," in *Can You Hear, Bird* (New York: Farrar, Straus and Giroux, 1995), pp. 73–75. First trying to live "the way philosophers live, / according to a set of principles," he soon wonders: "What was the matter with how I acted before?" By the end he discovers that "there's a lot of fun to be had in the gaps between ideas. / That's what they're made for!"
23 Richard Poirier, *The Renewal of Literature: Emersonian Reflections* (New York: Random House, 1987), p. 45.
24 Richard Poirier, *Poetry and Pragmatism* (Cambridge: Harvard University Press, 1992), p. 175.
25 Ralph Waldo Emerson, "Circles," in *The Complete Essays and Other Writings of Ralph Waldo Emerson*, ed. Brooks Atkinson (New York: Modern Library, 1940), pp. 288, 289.

WHAT DIFFERENCE
DOES PRAGMATISM
MAKE? THE VIEW
FROM PHILOSOPHY

Pragmatism as Romantic Polytheism

RICHARD RORTY

In 1911 a book appeared in Paris with the title *Un Romantisme Utilitaire: Étude sur le Mouvement Pragmatiste.* This was the first of three volumes on the subject by René Berthelot. Berthelot had been struck by the resemblances between the views of William James, John Dewey, Nietzsche, Bergson, Poincaré, and certain Catholic Modernists. He was the first to treat them as belonging to the same intellectual movement. A convinced Cartesian, Berthelot disliked and distrusted all these thinkers, but he wrote about them with acuity and verve. He traced the romantic roots of pragmatism back behind Emerson to Schelling and Hoelderlin, and the utilitarian roots to the influence of Darwin and Spencer.[1] But he thought that the difference between these two modes of thought was too great to permit synthesis. "In all its different forms," Berthelot said, "pragmatism reveals itself to be a romantic utilitarianism: that is its most obviously original feature and also its most private vice and its hidden weakness."[2]

Berthelot was probably the first to call Nietzsche "a German pragmatist," and the first to emphasize the resemblance between Nietzsche's perspectivism and the pragmatist theory of truth. This resemblance—frequently noted since, notably in a seminal chapter of Arthur Danto's book on Nietzsche—is most evident in the *The Gay Science.* There Nietzsche says "We do not even have any organ at all for *knowing,* for 'truth'; we 'know' . . . just as much as may be *useful* in the interest of the human herd."[3] This Darwinian view lies behind James' claim that "thinking is for the sake of behavior" and his identification of truth as "the good in the way of belief."

That identification amounts to accepting Nietzsche's claim that human beings should be viewed, for epistemological purposes, as what Nietzsche called "clever animals." Beliefs are to be judged solely by their utility in fulfilling these animals' varied needs. James and Nietzsche did for the word "true" what John Stuart Mill had done for the word "right." Just as

Mill says that there is no ethical motive apart from the desire for the happiness of human beings, so James and Nietzsche say that there is no will to truth distinct from the will to happiness. All three philosophers think that the terms "true" and "right" gain their meaning from their use in evaluating the relative success of efforts to achieve happiness.

Nietzsche, to be sure, had no use for Mill, but this was a result of arrogant ignorance, which resulted in a failure to grasp the difference between Mill and Bentham. James, on the other hand, dedicated his first philosophical treatise to Mill's memory, and tried to cultivate not only the debunking, Benthamite strain in Mill's thought but also the romantic, Coleridgean strain. The latter led Mill to choose an epigraph from Wilhelm von Humboldt for *On Liberty:* "The grand, leading principle, towards which every argument unfolded in these pages directly converges, is the absolute and essential importance of human development in its richest diversity." As a romantic utilitarian, Mill wanted to avoid Benthamite reductionism, and to defend a secular culture against the familiar charge of blindness to higher things.

This led him, as M. H. Abrams has pointed out, to share Arnold's view that literature could take the place of dogma. Abrams quotes Alexander Bain as saying of Mill that "he seemed to look upon Poetry as a Religion, or rather as Religion and Philosophy in One." Abrams also quotes a letter of Mill's which says that "the new utilitarianism"—his own as opposed to Bentham's—holds "Poetry not only on a par with, but the necessary condition of, any true and comprehensive Philosophy." Abrams argues that Mill and Arnold, despite their differences, drew the same moral from the English Romantics: that poetry could and should take on "the tremendous responsibility of the functions once performed by the exploded dogmas of religion and religious philosophy."[4] The exploded dogmas included the claim that, whereas there can be many great poems, there can be only one true religion, because only one true God. Poetry cannot be a substitute for a monotheistic religion, but it can serve the purposes of a secular version of polytheism.

The substitution of poetry for religion as a source of ideals, a movement that began with the Romantics, seems to me usefully described as a return to polytheism. For if, with the utilitarians, you reject the idea that a nonhuman authority can rank human needs, and thus dictate moral choices to human beings, you will favor what Arnold called "Hellenism" over what he called "Hebraism." You will reject the idea, characteristic of the evangelical Christians whom Arnold thought of as "Hebraist," that it suffices to love God and keep his commandments. You will substitute what

Arnold called the idea of "a human nature perfect on all its sides."[5] Different poets will perfect different sides of human nature, by projecting different ideals. A romantic utilitarian will probably drop the idea of diverse immortal persons, such as the Olympian deities, but she will retain the idea that there are diverse, conflicting, but equally valuable forms of human life.

A polytheism of this sort is recommended in a famous passage near the end of *The Varieties of Religious Experience* at which James says

> If an Emerson were forced to be a Wesley, or a Moody forced to be a Whitman, the total human consciousness of the divine would suffer. The divine can mean no single quality, it must mean a group of qualities, by being champions of which in alternation, different men may all find worthy missions. Each attitude being a syllable in human nature's total message, it takes the whole of us to spell the meaning out completely.[6]

James' loose use of the term "the divine" makes it pretty much equivalent to "the ideal." In this passage he is doing for theology what Mill had done for politics when he cited von Humboldt's claim that "human development in its richest diversity" is the aim of social institutions.

There is a passage in Nietzsche in praise of polytheism that complements the one I have just quoted from James. In section 143 of *The Gay Science* he argues that morality—in the wide sense of the need for acceptance of binding laws and customs—entails "hostility against the impulse to have an ideal of one's own." But, he says, the pre-Socratic Greeks provided an outlet for individuality by permitting human beings "to behold, in some distant overworld, a *plurality of norms:* one god was not considered a denial of another god, nor blasphemy against him." In this way, Nietzsche says, "the luxury of individuals was first permitted; it was here that one first honored the rights of individuals." For in pre-Socratic polytheism "the free-spiriting and many-spiriting of man attained its first preliminary form—the strength to create for ourselves our own new eyes."[7]

Here is a definition of "polytheism" that covers both Nietzsche and James. You are a polytheist if you think that there is no actual or possible object of knowledge that would permit you to commensurate and rank all human needs. Isaiah Berlin's well-known doctrine of incommensurable human values is, in my sense, a polytheistic manifesto. To be a polytheist in this sense you do not have to believe that there are nonhuman persons with power to intervene in human affairs. All you need do is to abandon the idea that we should try to find a way of making everything hang together, which will tell all human beings what to do with their lives, and tell all of them the same thing.

Polytheism, in the sense I have defined it, is pretty much coextensive with romantic utilitarianism. For once one sees no way of ranking human needs other than playing them off against one another, human happiness becomes all that matters. Mill's *On Liberty* provides all the ethical instruction you need—all the philosophical advice you are ever going to get about your responsibilities to other human beings. For human perfection becomes a private concern, and our responsibility to others becomes a matter of permitting them as much space to pursue these private concerns—to worship their own gods, so to speak—as is compatible with granting an equal amount of space to all. The tradition of religious toleration is extended to moral toleration.

This privatization of perfection permits James and Nietzsche to agree with Mill and Arnold that poetry should take over the role that religion has played in the formation of individual human lives. They also agree that nobody should take over the function of the clergy. For poets are to a secularized polytheism what the priests of a universal church are to monotheism. Once you become polytheistic, you will turn away not only from priests but from such priest-substitutes as metaphysicians and physicists—from anyone who purports to tell you how things *really* are, anyone who invokes the distinction between the true world and the apparent world that Nietzsche ridiculed in *Twilight of the Idols*. Both monotheism and the kind of metaphysics or science that purports to tell you what the world is *really* like are replaced with democratic politics. A free consensus about how much space for private perfection we can allow each other takes the place of the quest for "objective" values, the quest for a ranking of human needs that does not depend upon such consensus.

So far I have been playing along with Berthelot's emphasis on the similarities between Nietzsche and the American pragmatists. Now I want to turn to the two most obvious differences between them: their attitude toward democracy and their attitude toward religion. Nietzsche thought democracy was "Christianity for the people"—Christianity deprived of the nobility of spirit of which Christ himself, and perhaps a few of the more strenuous saints, had been capable. Dewey thought of democracy as Christianity cleansed of the hieratic, exclusionist elements. Nietzsche thought those who believed in a traditional monotheistic God were foolish weaklings. Dewey thought of them as so spellbound by the work of one poet as to be unable to appreciate the work of other poets. Dewey thought that the sort of "aggressive atheism" on which Nietzsche prided himself is unnecessarily intolerant. It has, he said, "something in common with traditional supernaturalism."[8]

I want first to argue that Nietzsche's contempt for democracy was an adventitious extra, inessential to his overall philosophical outlook. Then I shall get down to my main task in this paper—defending Dewey's tolerance for religious belief against those who think that pragmatism and religion do not mix.

Nietzsche was a utilitarian only in the sense that he saw no goals for human beings to pursue other than human happiness. He had no interest in the greatest happiness of the greatest number, but only in that of a few exceptional human beings—those with the capacity to be *greatly* happy. Democracy seemed to him a way of trivializing human existence. By contrast, James and Dewey took for granted, as Mill had, the ideal of universal human fraternity. Echoing Mill, James wrote, "Take any demand, however slight, which any creature, however weak, may make. Ought it not, for its own sole sake, to be desired?"[9]

Romantic utilitarianism, pragmatism, and polytheism are compatible with both wholehearted enthusiasm and whole-hearted contempt for democracy. The frequent complaint that a philosopher who holds the pragmatic theory of truth cannot give you a reason not to be a fascist is perfectly justified. But neither can that person give you a reason to be a fascist. For once you become a polytheist in the sense I just defined, you have to give up on the idea that philosophy can help you choose among the various deities and the various forms of life offered. The choice between enthusiasm and contempt for democracy becomes more like a choice between Walt Whitman and Robinson Jeffers than between competing sets of philosophical arguments.

Those who find the pragmatist identification of truth with what is good to believe morally offensive often say that Nietzsche, rather than James and Dewey, drew the proper inference from the abandonment of the idea of an object of knowledge that tells one how to rank human needs. Those who think of pragmatism as a species of irrationalism, and of irrationalism as selling the pass to fascism, say that James and Dewey were blind to the antidemocratic consequences of their own ideas, and naive to think that one can be both a good pragmatist and a good democrat.

Such critics make the same mistake that Nietzsche made. They think that the idea of fraternity is inextricable from Platonism. Platonism, in this sense, is the idea that the will to truth is distinct from the will to happiness—or, to be a bit more precise, the claim that human beings are divided between a quest for a lower, animal form of happiness and a higher, God-like form of happiness. Nietzsche mistakenly thought that once (with Darwin's help) you had given up this idea, and had gotten used to the idea that you are just a clever animal, you could have no reason to wish for the happiness of all human beings. He was so impressed by the fact that Christianity would have seemed ludicrous to the Homeric heroes that he was unable, except at occasional fleeting moments, to think of Christianity as the work of strong poets. So Nietzsche assumed that once poetry had replaced religion as the source of ideals, there would be no place for either Christianity or democracy.

Nietzsche would have done better to ask himself whether the Christian emphasis on human fraternity—the idea that for Christians there is neither Jew nor Greek, and the related idea that love is the only law—might have been only accidentally, for contingent historical reasons, associated with Platonism. This ideal might have gotten along nicely without the logocentrism of the Gospel of John, and without Augustine's unfortunate suggestion that Plato had prefigured Christian truth. In a different, but possible, world, some early Christian might have anticipated James' remark about Emerson and Wesley by writing "If Caesar were forced to be Christ, the total human consciousness of the divine would suffer."

A Christianity that was merely ethical—the sort Jefferson and other Enlightenment thinkers commended and was later propounded by theologians of the social gospel—might have sloughed-off exclusionism by viewing Jesus as one incarnation of the divine among others. The celebration of an ethics of love would then have taken its place within the relatively tolerant polytheism of the Roman Empire, having disjoined the ideal of human brotherhood from the claim to represent the will of an omnipotent and monopolistic Heavenly Father (not to mention the idea that there is no salvation outside the Christian Church).

Had they preached such a merely moral and social gospel, the Christians would never have bothered to develop a natural theology. So thirteenth-century Christians would not have worried about whether the Scriptures could be reconciled with Aristotle. Seventeenth-century believers would not have worried about whether they could be reconciled with Newton, nor those in the nineteenth century about whether they could be reconciled with Darwin. These hypothetical Christians would have treated Scripture as useful for purposes for which Aristotle, Newton, and Darwin were useless, and as useless for purposes of prediction and control of the environment. As things stood, however, the Christian churches remained obsessed by the Platonic idea that both Truth and God are One. So it was natural, when physical science began to make some progress, that its practitioners should take over this rhetoric, and thereby stir up a war between science and theology, between Scientific Truth and Religious Faith.

I have imagined such a non-Platonic and nonexclusivist form of Christianity in order to emphasize that no chain of inference links the ideal of human fraternity to the ideal of escaping from a world of appearance inhabited by animals to a real world in which humans will become as gods. Nietzsche and contemporary critics who see Nietzsche and Dewey as holding similarly dangerous "irrationalist" doctrines have been tricked by Plato into believing that, unless there is such a real world, Thrasymachus, Callicles, and Hitler are unanswerable. But they are unanswerable only in the sense that, *pace* Habermas, there are no premises to which they must assent simply by virtue of being rational, language-using animals. *A fortiori,* there are no such premises that would lead them to agree that they should treat all other human beings as brothers and sisters. Christianity as a strong poem, one poem among many, can be as socially useful as Christianity backed up by the Platonist claim that God and Truth are interchangeable terms.

Although I do not think that there is an inferential path that leads from the antirepresentationalist view of truth and knowledge common to Nietzsche, James, and Dewey either to democracy or antidemocracy, I do think there is a plausible inference from democratic convictions to such a view. Your devotion to democracy is unlikely to be wholehearted if you believe, as monotheists typically do, that we can have knowledge of an "objective" ranking of human needs that can overrule the result of democratic consensus. But if your devotion is wholehearted, then you will welcome the utilitarian and pragmatist claim that we have no will to truth distinct from the will to happiness.

So much for the disagreement between Nietzsche and his American colleagues about the value of democracy. I turn now to the other big difference between Nietzsche on the one hand and James and Dewey on the other. Nietzsche thinks religious belief is intellectually disreputable; James and Dewey do not.

In order to defend James and Dewey's tolerance for theism against Nietzsche, I shall sketch a pragmatist philosophy of religion in five brief theses. Then I shall try to relate these theses to what James and Dewey actually said about belief in God.

First, it is an advantage of the antirepresentationalist view of belief that

James took over from Bain and Peirce—the view that beliefs are habits of action—that it frees us from the responsibility to unify all our beliefs into a single worldview. If our beliefs are all parts of a single attempt to represent a single world, then they must all hang together fairly tightly. But if they are habits of action, then, because the purposes served by action may blamelessly vary, so may the habits we develop to serve those purposes.

Second, Nietzsche's attempt to "see science through the optic of art, and art through that of life," like Arnold's and Mill's substitution of poetry for religion, is an attempt to make more room for individuality than can be provided either by orthodox monotheism, or by the Enlightenment's attempt to put science in the place of religion as a source of Truth. So the attempt, by Tillich and others, to treat religious faith as "symbolic," and thereby to treat religion as poetic and poetry as religious, and neither as competing with science, is on the right track. But to make it convincing we need to drop the idea that some parts of culture fulfill our need to know the truth and others fulfill lesser aims. The pragmatists' romantic utilitarianism does drop this idea: if there is no will to truth apart from the will to happiness, there is no way to contrast the cognitive with the noncognitive, the serious with the nonserious.

Third, pragmatism does permit us to make another distinction, one that takes over some of the work previously done by the old distinction between the cognitive and the noncognitive. The new distinction is between projects of social cooperation and projects of individual self-development. Intersubjective agreement is required for the former projects, but not for the latter. Natural science is a paradigmatic project of social cooperation: the project of improving man's estate by taking account of every possible observation and experimental result in order to facilitate the making of predictions that will come true. Law is another such paradigm. Romantic art, by contrast, is a paradigmatic project of individual self-development. Religion, if it can be disconnected from both science and morals—from the attempt to predict the consequences of our actions and the attempt to rank human needs—may be another such paradigm.

Fourth, the idea that we should love Truth is largely responsible for the idea that religious belief is "intellectually irresponsible." But there is no such thing as the love of Truth. What has been called by that name is a mixture of the love of reaching intersubjective agreement, the love of gaining mastery over a recalcitrant set of data, the love of winning arguments, and the love of synthesizing little theories into big theories. It is never an objection to a religious belief that there is no evidence for it. The only possible objection to it can be that it intrudes an individual project into a social and cooperative project, and thereby offends against the teachings of *On Liberty*. Such intrusion is a betrayal of one's responsibilities to cooperate with other human beings, not of one's responsibility to Truth or to Reason.

Fifth, the attempt to love Truth, and to think of it as One, and as capable of commensurating and ranking human needs, is a secular version of the traditional religious hope that allegiance to something big, powerful, and nonhuman will persuade that powerful being to take your side in your struggle with other people. Nietzsche despised any such hope as a sign of weakness. Pragmatists who are also democrats have a different objection to such hope for allegiance with power. They see it as a betrayal of the ideal of human fraternity that democracy inherits from the Judeo-Christian religious tradition. That ideal finds its best expression in the doctrine, common to Mill and James, that every human need should be satisfied unless doing so causes too many other human needs to go unsatisfied. The pragmatist objection to religious fundamentalists is not that fundamentalists are *intellectually* irresponsible in disregarding the results of natural science. Rather it is that they are *morally* irresponsible in attempting to circumvent the process of achieving democratic consensus about how to maximize happiness. They sin not by ignoring Mill's inductive methods, but by ignoring his reflections on liberty.

I turn now to the question of how the view of religious belief epitomized in my five theses accords with the views of James and Dewey. It would not, I think, have been congenial to James. But I think it might have suited Dewey. So I shall argue that it is Dewey's rather unambitious and half-hearted *A Common Faith*, rather than James' brave and exuberant "Conclusion" to *Varieties of Religious Experience*, that coheres best with the romantic utilitarianism which both accepted.

James says, in that chapter of *Varieties*, that "the pivot round which the religious life revolves . . . is the interest of the individual in his private personal destiny." By "repudiating the personal point of view," however, science gives us a picture of nature that "has no distinguishable ultimate tendency with which it is possible to feel a sympathy." The "driftings of the cosmic atoms" are "a kind of aimless weather, doing and undoing, achieving no proper history, and leaving no result."[10] On the view I have just outlined, he should have followed this up by saying "But we are free to describe the universe in many different ways. Describing it as the drifting of cosmic atoms is useful for the social project of working together to control our environment and improve man's estate. But that description leaves us entirely free to say, for example, that the Heavens proclaim the glory of God."

Sometimes James seems to take this line, as when, with obvious approval, he quotes James Henry Leuba as saying

> *God is not known, he is not understood, he is used*—sometimes as meat-purveyor, sometimes as moral support, sometimes as friend, sometime as an object of love. If he proves himself useful, the religious consciousness can ask no more than that. Does God really exist? How does he exist? What is he? are so many irrelevant questions. Not God, but life, more life, a larger, richer, more satisfying life, is, in the last analysis, the end of religion.

Unfortunately, however, almost immediately after quoting Leuba James says "we must next pass beyond the point of view of merely subjective utility and make inquiry into the intellectual content itself." He then goes on to argue that the material he has gathered together in *Varieties* provides empirical evidence for the hypothesis that "the conscious person is continuous with a wider self through which saving experiences come." He calls this "a positive content of religious experience which, it seems to me, is literally and objectively true as far as it goes."[11]

On the view I have been suggesting, this claim to literal and objective truth is unpragmatic, hollow, and superfluous. James should have rested content with the argument of "The Will to Believe." As I read that essay, it says that we have a right to believe what we like when we are, so to speak, on our own time.[12] But we abandon this right when we are engaged in, for example, a scientific or a political project. For when so engaged it is necessary to reconcile our beliefs, our habits of action, with those of others. On our own time, by contrast, our habits of action are nobody's business but our own. A romantic polytheist will rejoice in what Nietzsche called the "free-spiritedness and many-spiritedness" of individuals, and see the only constraint on this freedom and this diversity as the need not to injure others.

James wobbled on the question of whether what he called "the religious hypothesis" was something to be adopted on "passional" or on "intellectual" grounds. This hypothesis says that "the best things are the more eternal things, the overlapping things, the things in the universe that throw the last stone, so to speak, and say the final word."[13] In "The Will to Believe" this is put forward as a hypothesis to which considerations of evidence are irrelevant, and must therefore be turned over to our emotions. But in the "Conclusion" to *Varieties of Religious Experience,* the hypothesis that "God's existence is the guarantee of an ideal order that shall be permanently preserved" is one for which he has accumulated evidence. There he also says that the least common denominator of religious beliefs is that "The solution [to the problem presented by a 'sense that there is something wrong about us as we naturally stand'] is that we are saved from the wrongness by making proper connection with the higher powers." Again, he says that "the conscious person is continuous with a wider self from which saving experiences come."[14]

James should not have made a distinction between issues to be decided by intellect and issues to be decided by emotion. If he had not, he might have wobbled less. What he should have done instead was to distinguish issues that you must resolve cooperatively with others and issues that you are entitled to resolve on your own. The first set of issues are about conciliating your habits of action with those of other human beings. The second set are about getting your own habits of action to cohere with each other sufficiently so that you acquire a stable, coherent, self-image. But such a self-image does not require monotheism, or the belief that Truth is One. It is compatible with the idea that you have many different needs, and that the beliefs that help you fill one set of needs are irrelevant to, and need not be made to cohere with, those that help you to fill another set.

Dewey avoided James' mistakes in this area. One reason he did so is that he was much less prone to a sense of guilt than was James. After he realized that his mother had made him unnecessarily miserable by burdening him with a belief in original sin, Dewey simply stopped thinking that, in James' words, "there is something wrong about us as we naturally stand." He no longer believed that we could be "saved from the wrongness by making proper connection with the higher powers." He thought that all that was wrong with us was that the Christian ideal of fraternity had not yet been achieved—society had not yet become pervasively democratic. That was not a problem to be solved by making proper connection with higher powers, but a problem of men to be solved by men.

Dewey's steadfast refusal to have any truck with the notion of original sin, and his suspicion of anything that smacked of such a notion is bound up with his lifelong distaste for the idea of authority—the idea that anything could have authority over the members of a democratic community save the free, collective, decisions of that community. This anti-authoritarian motif is perhaps clearest in his "Christianity and Democracy"—an early essay to which Alan Ryan has recently called our attention, saying that it is "a dazzling and dazzlingly brave piece of work."[15] Indeed it is. It must have seemed strange to the University of Michigan's Christian Students Association to be told, in 1892, that "God is essentially and only the self-revealing" and that "the revelation is complete only as men come to realize him."

Dewey spelled out what he meant by going on to say, "Had Jesus Christ made an absolute, detailed and explicit statement upon all the facts of life, that statement would not have had meaning—it would not have been revelation—until men began to realize in their own action the truth that he declared—until they themselves began to *live* it."[16] This amounts to saying that even if a nonhuman authority tells you something, the only way to figure out whether what you have been told is true is to see whether it gets you the sort of life you want. The only way is to apply the utilitarian test for whether the suggestion made proves to be "good in the way of belief." Granted that hearing what such a being has to say may change your wants, you nevertheless test those new wants and that purported truth in the same way: by living them, trying them out in everyday life, seeing whether they make you and yours happier.

Suppose that a source you believe to be nonhuman tells you that all men are brothers, that the attempt to make yourself and those you cherish happier should be expanded into an attempt to make all human beings happy. For Dewey, the source of this suggestion is irrelevant. You might have heard it from a god or a guru, but you might just as well have found it carved out by the waves on a sandy beach. It has no validity unless it is treated as an hypothesis, tried out, and found successful. The good thing about Christianity, Dewey is saying, is that it has been found to work.

More specifically, what has been found to work is the idea of fraternity and equality as a basis for social organization. This worked not just as a Thrasymachian device for avoiding pain—what Rawls calls a "mere modus vivendi"—but as a source of the kind of spiritual transfiguration that Platonism and the Christian churches have told us would have to wait upon a future intersection of time with eternity. It makes possible precisely the sort of nobility of spirit that Nietzsche mistakenly thought could be had only by the exceptional few—those who were capable of being greatly happy.

"Democracy," Dewey says, "is neither a form of government nor a social expediency, but a metaphysic of the relation of man and his experience in nature."[17] The point of calling it a metaphysic is not, of course, that it is an accurate account of the fundamental relation of reality, but that if one shares Whitman's sense of glorious democratic vistas stretching on indefinitely into the future one has everything which Platonists hoped to get out of such an account. For Whitman offers what Tillich called "a symbol of ultimate concern," of something that can be loved with all one's heart and soul and mind.

Plato's mistake, in Dewey's view, was having identified the ultimate object of *eros* with something unique, atemporal, and nonhuman rather than with an indefinitely expansible pantheon of transitory temporal accomplishments, both natural and cultural. This mistake lent aid and comfort to monotheism. Dewey might well have agreed with Nietzsche that "Monotheism, this rigid consequence of the doctrine of one normal human type—the faith in one normal god beside whom there are only pseudo-gods—was perhaps the greatest danger that has yet confronted humanity."[18]

When Christianity is treated as a merely social gospel, it acquires the advantage which Nietzsche attributes to polytheism: it makes the most important human achievement "creating for ourselves our own new eyes," and thereby "honors the rights of individuals." As Dewey put it, "Government, business, art, religion, all social institutions have . . . a purpose[:] . . . to set free the capacities of human individuals. . . . [T]he test of their value is the extent to which they educate every individual into the full stature of his possibility."[19] In a democratic society, everybody gets to worship his or her personal symbol of ultimate concern, unless worship of that symbol interferes with the pursuit of happiness by his or her fellow-citizens. Accepting that utilitarian constraint, the one Mill formulated in *On Liberty*, is the only obligation imposed by democratic citizenship, the only exception to democracy's commitment to honor the rights of individuals.

This means that nobody is under any constraint to seek Truth, nor to care, any more than Sherlock Holmes did, whether the earth revolves around the sun or conversely. Scientific theories become, as do theological and philosophical ones, optional tools for the facilitation of individual or social projects. Scientists thereby lose the position they inherited from the monotheistic priesthood, as the people who pay proper tribute to the authority of something "not ourselves."

"Not ourselves" is a term that tolls like a bell throughout the text of Arnold's *Literature and Dogma*, and this may be one of the reasons Dewey had a particular dislike for Arnold.[20] Once he got out from under his mother's Calvinism, Dewey distrusted nothing more than the suggestion that there was a nonhuman authority to which human beings owed respect. He praised democracy as the *only* form of "moral and social faith" that does *not* "rest upon the idea that experience must be subjected at some point or other to some form of external control: to some 'authority' alleged to exist outside the process of experience."[21]

This passage in an essay of 1939 echoes one written forty-seven years earlier. In "Christianity and Democracy" Dewey had said that "The one claim that Christianity makes is that God is truth; that as truth He is love and reveals Himself fully to man, keeping back nothing of Himself; that man is so one with the truth thus revealed that it is not so much revealed *to* him as *in* him; he is its incarnation."[22] For Dewey God is in no way Kierkegaard's Wholly Other. Nor is he One. Rather, he is all the varied sublimities human beings come to see through the eyes that they themselves create.

If atheism were identical with antimonotheism, then Dewey would have been as aggressive an atheist as has ever lived. The idea that God might have kept something back, that there might be something not ourselves that it was our duty to discover, was as distasteful to him as was the idea that God could tell us which of our needs took priority over others. He reserved his awe for the universe as a whole, "the community of causes and consequences in which we, together with those not born, are enmeshed." "The continuing life of this comprehensive community of beings," he said, "includes all the significant achievement of men in science and art and all the kindly offices of intercourse and communication."

Notice, in the passages I have just quoted, the phrase "together with those not born" and also the adjective "continuing." Dewey's distaste for the eternity and stability on which monotheism prides itself is so great that he can never refer to the universe as a whole without reminding us that the universe is still evolving—still experimenting, still fashioning new eyes with which to see itself.

Wordsworth's version of pantheism meant a great deal to Dewey, but Whitman's insistence on futurity meant more. Wordsworth's pantheism saves us from what Arnold called "Hebraism" by making it impossible to treat, as Dewey put it, "the drama of sin and redemption enacted within the isolated and lonely soul of man as the one thing of ultimate importance." But Whitman does something more. He tells us that nonhuman nature culminates in a community of free men, in their collaboration in building a society in which, as Dewey said, "poetry and religious feeling will be the unforced flowers of life."[23]

Dewey's principal symbol of what he called "the union of the ideal and the actual" was the United States of America treated as Whitman treated it: as a symbol of openness to the possibility of as yet undreamt of, ever more diverse, forms of human happiness. Much of what Dewey wrote consists of endless reiteration of Whitman's caution that "America . . . counts, as I reckon, for her justification and success, (for who, as yet, dare claim success?) almost entirely on the future. . . . For our New World I consider far less important for what it has done, or what it is, than for results to come."[24]

Notes

1 René Berthelot, *Un Romantisme Utilitaire: Étude sur le Mouvement Pragmatiste*, vol. 1 (Paris: F. Alcan, 1911), pp. 62–63. Berthelot also looked back behind Darwin and Spencer to Hume, whom he regarded as "la transition entre la psychologie utilitaire et intellectualiste d'Helvétius et la psychologie vitaliste de l'instinct que nous rencontrons chez les Ecossais." He views Lamarck as "la transition entre cette conception vitaliste de la biologie et ce qu'on peut appeler l'utilitarisme mécanique de Darwin" (vol. 1, p. 85).

2 Berthelot, *Romantisme Utilitaire*, vol. 1, p. 128.

3 Friedrich Nietzsche, *The Gay Science*, section 354: Wir haben eben gar kein Organ fuer das *Erkennen*, fuer die 'Wahrheit'; wir 'wissen' . . . gerade so viel, als es im Interesse der Menschen-Herde, der Gattung, *nuetzlich* sein mag.

4 M. H. Abrams, *The Mirror and the Lamp* (New York: Oxford University Press, 1953; quotes on pp. 334–35, 333 (quoting a letter to Lytton Bulwer), and 335 respectively.

5 Matthew Arnold, *Culture and Anarchy*, ed. Samuel Lipman (New Haven: Yale University Press, 1994), p. 37.

6 William James, *Varieties of Religious Experience* (Cambridge: Harvard University Press, 1985), p. 384.

7 "Aber ueber sich and ausser sich, in einer fernen Ueberwelt, durfte man eine *Mehrzahl von Normen* sehen; der eine Gott war nicht die Leugnung oder Laesterung des anderen Gottes. . . . Hier erlaubte man sich zuerst Individuen, hier ehrte man zuerst das Recht von Individuen. . . . In Polytheismus lag die Freigeisterei und Vielgeisterei des Menschen vorgebildet; die Kraft, sich neue und eigne Augen zu schaffen" (Nietzsche, *The Gay Science*, sec. 143).

8 John Dewey, "A Common Faith," in *Later Works of John Dewey*, ed. Jo Ann Boydston (Carbondale: Southern Illinois University Press, 1986), vol. 9, p. 36.

9 William James, *The Will to Believe* (Cambridge: Harvard University Press, 1979), p. 149.

10 James, *Varieties of Religious Experience*, pp. 387–88.

11 *Ibid.*, pp. 399 and 405, respectively.

12 See my "Religious Faith, Intellectual Responsibility, and Romance," in *The Cambridge Companion to William James*, ed. Ruth Anna Putnam (Cambridge: Cambridge University Press, 1997).

13 James, *The Will to Believe*, p. 29.

14 James, *Varieties of Religious Experience*, pp. 407, 400, 405 respectively.

15 Alan Ryan, *John Dewey and the High Tide of American Liberalism* (New York: Norton, 1995), p. 102.

16 John Dewey, *Early Works of John Dewey* (Carbondale: Southern Illinois University Press, 1969), vol. 3, pp. 6–7.

17 Dewey, "Maeterlinck's Philosophy of Life," *The Middle Works of John Dewey*, vol. 6. Dewey says that Emerson, Whitman, and Maeterlinck are the only three to have grasped this fact about democracy.

18 Nietzsche, *The Gay Science*, section 143: "Der Monotheismus . . . diese starre Konsequenz der Lehre von einem Normalmenschen—also der Glaube an einen Normalgott,

neben dem es nur noch falsche Luegengoetter gibt—war vielleicht die groesste Gefahr der bisherigen Menscheit."

19 Dewey, *Reconstruction in Philosophy,* in *Middle Works,* vol. 12, p. 186.

20 See Dewey, *A Common Faith,* in *Later Works,* vol. 9, p. 36, and also Dewey's early essay "Poetry and Philosophy." In the latter Dewey says that "the source of regret which inspires Arnold's lines is his consciousness of a twofold isolation of man—his isolation from nature, his isolation from his fellow-man" (*Early Works,* vol. 3, p. 115).

21 "Creative Democracy—The Task Before Us" (1939). The passage cited is in *Later Works,* vol. 14, p. 229. Dewey says that he is here "stating briefly the democratic faith in the formal terms of a philosophic position."

22 Dewey, *Early Works,* vol. 4, p. 5.

23 Dewey, *Reconstruction in Philosophy,* in *Middle Works,* vol. 12, p. 201.

24 Walt Whitman, *Democratic Vistas,* in *Complete Poetry and Selected Prose* (New York: Library of America, 1982), p. 929.

Pragmatism and Realism

HILARY PUTNAM

Let me begin by asking what will undoubtedly seem to many if not all of my readers a most peculiar question: how did it happen that the first philosopher to present a well worked out version of direct realism in the whole history of modern philosophy was no other than the American pragmatist, William James?

I expect this question to seem peculiar, because James' pragmatism is often thought of (especially by those who have accepted Richard Rorty as their guide to pragmatist ways of thinking) as a species of *anti*realism. The very fact that James was an ardent defender of a direct realist account of perception will come as a shock to you, if *that* is how you are accustomed to thinking of pragmatism. And even those who are in the end convinced by my reading of William James may still want to challenge my claim that James was the *first* to successfully put forward a direct realist picture. Did not Thomas Reid do just that? And was not James' good friend and friendly (if occasionally scathing) critic, the great founder of pragmatism, Charles Sanders Peirce, also a direct realist years before James was? In addition, some may find the question peculiar. Presumably my title, "Pragmatism and Realism," did not suggest that you were to read a dry discussion of the history of philosophy.

Let me address this last concern. Although the Putnams, Ruth Anna Putnam and myself, are presently writing a book about William James that will provide full textual support for the interpretation I sketch here, my interests are not primarily historical ones. What I understand by the term "direct realism" here is not a particular metaphysical theory, but rather our implicit and everyday conviction that in experience we are immediately aware of such common objects as trees and buildings, not to mention other people. I am interested in James' defense of direct realism (of what he called "natural realism") because I see overcoming the traditional picture of perception—a picture according to which our sensations are as much an impassible barrier between ourselves and the objects we perceive as a mode of access to them—as absolutely necessary if philosophy is ever to stop "spinning its wheels" in a vain attempt to find a resting place in the dispute about metaphysical realism and antirealism.[1] And, although in the end the version of direct realism I would defend is not James', it is nevertheless the case that it was James' defense of direct realism that led me to appreciate the fundamental importance of the issue.

But let me come back to the initial worry, which might also be expressed this way: how can a *pragmatist* also be a *realist?*

James: Pragmatist and Realist

To begin with, let me admit that there are antirealist elements in James' philosophy (even if he would not have regarded them as such). Although James' theory of truth is subtle and complex (so much so that neither James' critics nor his extravagant admirers have really done it justice), I argue elsewhere that it does commit James to a degree of antirealism about the past (and not only about the past) that is quite unacceptable.[2] But, as Bertrand Russell was the first to recognize, it is quite possible to admire James' theory of perception without admiring James' theory of truth.[3]

This observation, however, does not really speak to the concern. Granted that James did have a realist side, how did he reconcile it with a theory of truth that has startlingly antirealist consequences? But that should not really be so great a puzzle either, for two reasons. First, no one seems to have a problem recognizing that Peirce was both a realist and a pragmatist, although (I would argue) Peirce's definition of truth as the opinion to which inquiry would converge if indefinitely pursued has the *same* antirealist consequences about the past, and so on, that James' theory does.[4] Second, neither James nor Peirce admitted that their theories of truth possessed these antirealist consequences. (They were wrong.)[5] If one rejects the facile view that Peirce was a complete realist while James thought anything could be true provided only that it is satisfying to believe, then pragmatism can be seen as a rich source of insights that was not free from errors.

But my concern here is not with the antirealist side of James' thought—which is manifested, to speak much too quickly and inaccurately, in his identification of the true with what will be "verified" in the long run, in his own special sense of "verified"—but with his realism.

James' efforts to work out a satisfactory form of realism began with what can be seen as a turn from psychology to philosophy, were it not misleading to speak of a "turn" in the case of a thinker who had published essays on philosophical topics beginning in the 1870s. Nevertheless, James did not begin to work out a systematic metaphysical view of his own until the 1890s. Indeed, in his monumental *Principles of Psychology* (although he voiced philosophical opinions on a wide range of subjects), his official stance was that he was bound as a psychologist to assume the working philosophy of the experimental psychologist, which he took at that time to be a form of dualism coupled with a belief in psychophysical parallelism. The position of the *Principles of Psychology* as far as metaphysics is concerned is that although this working philosophy is doubtless inadequate, its inadequacy need not trouble the psychologist *qua* psychologist.[6] But in the Epilogue to James' *Psychology: Briefer Course* and also in a lecture to the American Psychological Association in the same period (the early 1890s) James reversed himself,[7] declaring that good psychology requires a more coherent metaphysical stance than we presently possess. In his seminar on "the Feelings," given in 1895–1896, he began to work out the views that he would later present to the world in the form of the articles collected as *Essays in Radical Empiricism.* (By the way, the discovery that James had worked out the essence of his "radical empiricism" as early as 1895–1896 is due to a young scholar at Harvard named David Lamberth, on whose research I am relying in this paragraph.)[8]

The fundamental idea of James' new metaphysics is the radical rejection of the subject-object split. This rejection seems to have been provoked first of all by James' attention to the phenomenology of perception. "Phenomenology" is a word that has been used by different philosophers to stand for very different projects. What those projects have in common is that they all reject the picture of experience in classical and associationist psychology as a false description dictated by a received philosophical view (originally, the view of British empiricism) and imposed willy-nilly on a very complex set of phenomena, and that they all share the aim of replacing this imposed picture with an accurate and philosophically useful description of the actual character of experience. In this sense, one may say that James was already doing "phenomenology" in *The Principles of Psychology,* and indeed we know that Husserl was inspired by that book.[9] Now, the received empiricist psychology, coupled with mind-matter dualism (as in the working philosophy of *The Principles of Psychology*), leads to the following picture of perception. First, in perception we receive "impressions," which are immaterial, totally different—separated by a metaphysical gulf in fact—from all the material objects we normally claim to perceive. And second, from the character of our internal mental impressions we infer how things are in the external physical world. But nothing could be farther from the way perception seems to be, farther from the "phenomenology" of perception. Phenomenologically, we seem to ourselves to be perceiving tables and chairs (or cabbages and kings), not immaterial intermediaries. What we see in James' first attempts to work out his new metaphysics is the conviction that the *phenomenology* of perception is the best guide to a correct *ontology*.[10] In effect, James has entertained the heretical thought: what if all the philosophers are wrong, and the way it seems to be is the way it *is?*

In addition to denying that the immediate objects of our perceptions are immaterial "sensations" or "impressions," James also denies that we are aware of a substantial self (or as he puts it, a substantial "consciousness").[11] In the terminology of James' "Notes for Philosophy 20b: Psychological Seminar—The Feelings," what is given is a "field" of objects that only upon reflection appear to us either as "external" objects that we perceive, or (when we engage in a different mode of reflection) as "sensations," or affectations of our own subjectivity. The datum, the phenomenon, the pure experience, in itself "has no such inner duplicity," James writes.[12] Here too, James regards the phenomenology as the best guide to an ontology. Reality in itself does not consist of two radically different sorts of things, subjects and objects, with a problematic relation. It consists of the data, the phenomena, and it is just that these can be thought about in different ways.

James, as I have been saying, is describing the phenomenology of perception, but he is also doing more than that; he is suggesting that we can take that phenomenology seriously in a way that philosophers have long thought we could not. He is proposing that we return to a standpoint close to what he calls the "natural realism" of the common man.

A Historical Digression

In trying to defend "natural realism" (even if with some philosophical additions and revisions), James was also coming close to an Aristotelian way of thinking about perception, a way that was also the dominant way of thinking in the later Middle Ages. (I doubt that James was aware of this.) Aristotle held that in perception the very form of the object perceived is in the mind. To be sure, there are difficulties with this view.[13] Some of those difficulties are with the essentialism involved in the Aristotelian notion of "form," and those difficulties become serious when we hold that the form of the object is also in the mind when we merely *think* about the object, as well as when we perceive it. It does seem that in conception the form Aristotle speaks of is what he regards as the "essence," and I find serious difficulties with the idea that we can only think about things whose "essence" we know. But Gisela Striker has suggested to me that in the case of perception it is unlikely that Aristotle has so demanding a notion of form in mind. It is plausible that the form that we receive in perception is simply the *sensible form*—the color or the shape or the texture or the sound or whatever.[14] Reading Aristotle in this way, it would seem that what he is saying is simply that in perception we are aware of sensible properties of external things—their shape, their color, and so on.

It may be, of course, that Aristotle also thought that his talk of the same thing (the form) being in two places at once (in the object perceived and in the mind) *explained* how such direct awareness of sensible properties of external things is possible. If so, he was mistaken; the explanation is empty. It is also possible, as indeed the rather strange prose of *De Anima* at this point suggests might be the case, that he is simply using a figure of speech to say that we are directly aware of properties of external things, as we today use the figure of something being "in my mind." But whatever Aristotle may have intended, and whether or not part of what he intended has to be rejected as unhelpful, he *at least* believed that we *do* have an awareness of the sensible properties of "external" things, and that this is not to be cashed out as meaning that we merely have "images" or "representations" of those things before our minds (as the view that has been dominant ever since Descartes holds). And Aquinas followed Aristotle faithfully in all this.

Of course, Aristotle was aware that perception requires many things— the form must somehow be transmitted through the air to the eyes (in the case of sight), and there must be physical modifications in the eyes and (perhaps) in the cognitive organ (which Aristotle took to be the heart and blood stream) before the form can be in our psyche.[15] Perception is supervenient on physical processes. But that is no obstacle to thinking that what *results* from all these transactions between the organism and the environment is the perception of the way something *is*, and not only in the Pickwickian sense of the presence of a "representation" that in some mysterious way refers to the way something is.

By the time of Descartes, however, Scholasticism and Aristotelianism were in ill repute, and the old notion of a "substantial form" smacked of a metaphysics that was no longer acceptable. So, as is usually the case in philosophy, the baby was tossed out with the bathwater, and the representational theory of perception that continues to dominate philosophy and psychology (and, today one can add cognitive science as well) came to seem the only *possible* view; to be a direct realist was to be a "naive realist," and being naive is, of course, *bad.* It is against the background of the centuries-old consensus that "naive realism" had been refuted once and for all that James' amazing philosophical radicalism has to be appreciated.

The Importance of the Issue

Before I describe James' version of direct realism, I want to say a little more about the importance of the issue. One reason I think I have to do this is that, after being at the center of philosophical attention in the first quarter of the twentieth century, the philosophy of perception then receded from view (and almost disappeared from serious attention after the death of J. L. Austin in 1960). Indeed, of the great figures in Anglo-American philosophy only Peter Strawson maintained a steady if intermittent interest in the topic. A second, less sociological, reason is that one aspect of the traditional picture of perception has now been given up, and this may make it appear that the picture is no longer as problematic as it once was.

When I described the traditional picture, I mentioned two elements. First, in perception we receive "impressions" that are immaterial, totally different—separated by a metaphysical gulf in fact—from all the material objects we normally claim to perceive. Second, from the character of our internal mental impressions we infer how things are in the external physical world. Today, however, a majority of our philosophers of mind appear to be hard-core materialists (even if they prefer the more innocuous sounding label "naturalist"), and these philosophers would say that our "impressions" are little more than brain events or processes. These philosophers would say that the representational theory of perception no longer requires us to posit a "metaphysical gulf" between impressions and external objects.

In fact, however, the new view is at least as problematical as the old one. Philosophers who advocate the new view concede that we are not aware of our "sensations" *as* brain processes. We are aware of the blue of the sky as a color extended over an area, not as a cortical process. The claim advanced by Donald Davidson and others that the experience is "identical" with a cortical event trades on a notion of "identity" that seems to me entirely meaningless. (Davidson has admitted, under the pressure of criticism from W. V. Quine, that the criterion he originally offered for what he calls "token identity of events of different types" was fatally flawed.)[16] Moreover, even if we were to grant that our sense impressions are brain processes—that is, even if we suppose that the notion of "identity" can be made sense of in this context (we know-not-how)—the picture remains one in which our cognitive processes extend no further than an "interface" between us and the external objects (an interface consisting now of cortical processes rather than processes in a mental substance). The objects of perception, those cabbages and cabinet ministers, impinge on our mind-brains only causally, not cognitively.

This feature of the current materialist version of the representational theory of perception, the feature that the picture of cognition provided by that picture is in the end a purely causal and not a normative one, has been used by Richard Rorty to argue against the idea that we can think of reference as a relation to objects in the world. "We are connected to the world causally, not semantically," I have heard Rorty say more than once.[17]

In these remarks, Rorty builds on an argument against the "given" used by Wilfrid Sellars. Sellars assumed what I have called the picture of our impressions (our "raw feels," in his terminology) as an "interface" between us and the world (although he does not seem to have been willing to identify them with brain events), and he pointed out that any given impression-report, for example, "I am experiencing E now," must have a multitude of causes, and there is nothing in any one of those causes, *qua* cause, to single it out as "the appropriate" cause of my verbal response or my verbalized thought. Even if my verbal report (or my thought) is caused, in part, by the very quality of the raw feel I am trying to describe, it may still be a misreport; for my report cannot causally depend only on the quality of my "raw feel." If it is to be a report in a language with stable meanings, it must also depend on my prior linguistic conditioning, on attention, on "set," and so on. Like Rorty, Sellars thought that to postulate a semantic relation between linguistic items and nonlinguistic objects that determines when I am successfully "referring" is to postulate a mystery relation.

Rorty generalized Sellars' argument—and, indeed, once one accepts it, it invites immediate generalization—and concluded that if we are connected to the world "causally but not semantically" (a fair summary of Sellars' view), then our words have no determinate real counterparts. Sellars attempted to avoid going as far as Rorty did later by postulating a holistic relation he called "picturing" between our conceptual schemes and reality, postulating further, in Peircean fashion, that with the progress of science our schemes come to "picture" the world more and more accurately, but Rorty rejects Sellarsian "picturing" on the grounds that it is as occult a relation as reference allegedly is.

Now Rorty and Sellars are right in saying that any given event can be traced to a multitude of different causes. As William James wrote in a different context,

> Not a sparrow falls to the ground but some of the remote conditions of his fall are to be found in the milky way, in our federal constitution, or in the early history of Europe. That is to say, alter the milky way, alter the federal constitution, alter the facts of our barbarian ancestry, and the universe would so far be a different universe from what it now is. One fact involved in the difference might be that the particular little street-boy who threw the stone which brought down the sparrow might not find himself opposite the sparrow at that particular moment; or, finding himself there, he might not be in that particular serene and disengaged mood of mind which expressed itself in throwing the stone. But, true as all this is, it would be very foolish for any one who was inquiring the cause of the sparrow's fall to overlook the boy as too personal, proximate, and so to speak anthropomorphic an agent, and to say that the true cause is the federal constitution, the westward migration of the Celtic race, or the structure of the milky way. If we proceeded on that method, we might say with perfect legitimacy that a friend of ours, who slipped on the ice upon his door-step and cracked his skull, some months after dining with thirteen at the table, died because of that ominous feast.[18]

Yet to conclude (from the fact that there is a great difference between asking for the referent of a term and asking for the causes of a particular "tokening" of that term) that we must give up the very idea that there is a relation of reference that holds between some of our terms and objects in the world is to engage in a gesture of repudiation with respect to our whole conception of ourselves as thinkers in a world that is so sweeping as to invite the suspicion that it is simply an empty pose. In this suspicion I am, naturally, joined by metaphysical realists. Metaphysical realists, of course, deplore Rorty's and Sellars' rejection of the very idea of semantical words-world relations. But if (as most of the contemporary ones do) they also wish to endorse a "bald" version of naturalism,[19] they cannot simply *posit* a semantical words-world relation. They must also show that it can be reduced to nonsemantical relations and facts, for to posit irreducible semantic relations is no better from their point of view than to posit immaterial sense data. But all attempts to reduce semantic relations to nonsemantic ones have been utter failures; to the point that we have presently no idea what such a reduction could conceivably look like.[20]

It was in this philosophical climate, I may add, that I advanced my own attempt at a "middle way" between antirealism and metaphysical realism (my so-called "internal realism") in the 1970s and 1980s.[21] Although I still defend some of the ideas involved in those attempts (in particular, the denial that reality dictates one unique description is as central to my thinking as ever), it now seems to me that that attempt too was fatally flawed by its allegiance to the traditional conception of our sensations as an "interface" between us and the world. Thus I can understand from my own experience how, even if we did not very much *discuss* the philosophy of perception in the 1970s and 1980s, we were—and too many of us continue to be—the inheritors of a Cartesian (or Cartesian *cum* materialist) picture of perception. This picture had become all the more coercive for *not* being critically discussed in the way it was when, for example, Russell wrote *The Analysis of Mind,* a book in which Russell, for all his retention of parts of the traditional picture, is extremely aware of the difficulties to which that picture leads, as most of today's philosophers are not.

Another (Shorter) Historical Digression

Even if you are now convinced that it is important to overcome the representational theory of perception, the picture of our sensations as "between" us and those "external objects," there is still the question as to our historical accuracy in giving James and not Thomas Reid the credit for being the first modern philosopher to revive direct realism. It is true that Thomas Reid thoroughly understood the disastrous consequences of the representational theory, and that (both in the *Inquiry* and in the *Intellectual Powers*) he called—indeed, he vigorously polemicized—for a return to a direct realism.[22] Our reason for not counting Reid as, in the end, a successful advocate of the direct realist cause is that he retains the idea that sensations are nonconceptual and internal "signs" (as opposed to *sensings* of what is *there*) as an essential part of his epistemology and ontology. For example, Reid writes "[In perception] there is something which may be called the sign, and something which is signified to us . . . by that sign. . . . Thus when I grasp an ivory ball in my hand, I have a certain sensation of touch. Although this has no similitude to anything material, yet, by the laws of my constitution, it is immediately followed by a conception and belief that there is in my hand a hard smooth body of a spherical character."[23]

This differs from the standard Cartesian account only in adding that, owing to "the laws of my constitution," I am able to form a "conception" of the object itself from this sensation even though it "has no similitude to anything material." But this power necessarily appears to be something *mysterious* in Reid's account, because the mind has "input" something different in *kind* from what it forms conceptions and beliefs about. Similar remarks apply to Peirce's defense of direct realism—indeed, Peirce cites Reid as the one who got it right.[24]

James' Radical Empiricism

James' name for this area of his philosophy is "radical empiricism"; James does not use the term "direct realism," but he does use the much better term "natural realism" a number of times in his *Essays in Radical Empiricism*,[25] and he repeatedly insists that radical empiricism is close to natural realism, or revives it, or shows that it can be maintained. We have already provided an answer to the puzzle as to how a pragmatist came to revive natural realism; it was James' typically pragmatist insistence that we take seriously the way in which we think about—and have to think about—perceptual experience in the course of living our lives that virtually forced natural realism upon him.[26] And James is certainly right that in living our lives we have to think of ourselves as living in what he calls "a common world," that each of us has to think that she is aware of the other's body and not simply a representation of it, and we all have to think that we are aware of many of the same objects. It is true that in elaborating a philosophy that took this idea as correct, James was led to some elaborate metaphysical construction, which I cannot discuss here. For that reason, toward the end of this essay I shall speak to the further question, to what extent can we preserve natural realism *without* accepting all of James' metaphysics of radical empiricism? I shall further suggest that we can find resources for doing this in the writings of J. L. Austin.[27] But even if James' way was not the only way, or even the *best* way, to defend natural realism, the fact remains that it was the *first* way to be proposed after the fateful Cartesian turn in modern philosophy.[28]

James' way involved what others (not James himself, for whom the term "monist" was anathema) have described as a "neutral monist" ontology. In such an ontology, the properties and relations we experience *are* the stuff of the universe; there is no nonexperiental "substratum" (this is an idea of James' with which Russell was in sympathy) and these experienced or experienceable properties and relations (James is unfortunately a little vague at this crucial point) make up both minds and material objects. Moreover, minds and material objects in a sense "overlap"; the very thing I experience as a sensation of red is also, in another context, what I call "a patch of color on the wall." Illusions do not prove that we never "directly experience" external objects; in James' radical empiricist metaphysics, what the phenomena of illusions go to show is that not every bit of pure experience has the status of being a part of a "real" object, not that none do.

Of course, there is the obvious objection that the skeptical epistemological problem has not been "solved." There is, in James' account, no absolutely certain way to *know* when we are subject to an illusion and when we are not. But James would reply that the problem is even worse for the traditional theory. As James puts it, for the Berkleyan school "our lives are a congeries of solipsisms out of which in strict logic only a God could compose a universe even of discourse . . . if the body you actuate is not the very body I see there, but some duplicate body of your own with which that has nothing to do, we belong to different universes, you and I, and for me to speak of you is folly."[29] In short, James argues that several minds, each acquainted only with its own private objects, could not arrive by any process of inference at knowledge or even thought of one another.

The advantage of pragmatism over traditional "foundationalist" epistemology, in James' view, is that the way in which pragmatist philosophers answer skeptical doubts is the way in which doubts are answered in practice, by appealing to tests that in fact work in our lives. If I think that what I see may be an illusion, I can try to touch it, or to look at it from a different position, or ask other people to take a look. There are not, on James' view, two sets of criteria for being "real"—commonsense criteria and philosophical criteria.

With so much, Russell was able to agree in *The Analysis of Mind*. In chapter 8 of that work, the chapter on sensations and images, Russell heartily endorses James' view that "the dualism of mind and matter cannot be allowed as metaphysically valid," writing, "On this subject, we may again quote William James. He points out that when we say we merely 'imagine' things, there are no such effects as would ensue if the things were what we call 'real'. " And at this point Russell quotes James at length and then restates the point in his own terminology: the difference between so-called 'mental' phenomena and 'physical' phenomena is a difference in the causal laws obeyed, not a fundamental dualism.

But there is an important aspect of what James calls "natural realism" with which Russell was unable to agree (although it is not clear that he realized that this was a point of disagreement). For immediately after this, Russell proceeds to give precisely the description of experience that James had already rebelled against in *The Principles of Psychology*: experience consists of color patches, and so on, and we think we see tables and chairs because we make "inferences" of various kinds. Evidently Russell is willing to follow James about color patches—"the sensation that we have when we see a patch of colour simply *is* that patch of color, an actual constituent of the physical world"—but not about tables and chairs.[30]

Here is an example (my own rather than his) of what bothers Russell: although it is true that we normally see tables and chairs *as* tables and chairs, very often we do not see the side away from us; yet seeing something as a chair is seeing it as something that *has* an unseen side, and one of a certain kind. Because that knowledge, the knowledge of the unseen side, cannot be perceptual (this seems evident to Russell) it must be inference.[31] We can only find what is *really* given in sensation by stripping away all "mnemic" (i.e., conceptual) contributions. But James' view is that if there is an original nonconceptual element in perception, we are unable to get back to it (or can get to it only in free reverie—precisely when we are not cognizing). The question, how much of what we perceive is "given" and how much is "added" is, he says in one place, like the question of whether a man essentially walks more on his left leg or his right.[32] Although James was not willing to go as far as Kant and treat perception as a passive exercise of the same conceptual powers that are exercised in judgment,[33] the practical effect of this part of his doctrine is the same. What we perceive, insofar as the perception is available to us as a source of knowledge, is a sort of alloy of sensation and conception *fused*. Given his constant emphasis on the richness and variety of what is given in experience, he could never accept the view that all we really see is color patches. The Russell of *The Analysis of Mind* was strongly influenced by James, but only so far: his direct realism stopped with the color patches. James' natural realism is full-bodied.

James' Excesses

Although I admire this full-bodied natural realism, I indicated earlier that James' "radical empiricism" contains elements that I find excessively metaphysical. One such element is James' restriction of what there is to "pure experience"; however we understand that puzzling notion, this appears to be too restrictive. Although James does at times try to allow not only what is perceptually experienced, but even what is *conceived* as "pure experience," this strain in his thought is never worked out, and is, indeed, in conflict with his own account of conceptual thinking.[34] The world, for James, is the *experienceable* world, and since James has a praiseworthy reluctance to rule out any kind of talk that does real work in our lives, he is forced to reinterpret talk of unobservables in physics, talk of counterfactual connections, mathematical talk, and so on in ways that are unconvincing and ultimately unsuccessful.

In another respect, however, James' ontology is not restrictive *enough*. To explain what I mean, I shall close by bringing in a second figure in the history of the revival of natural realism, and that is the great British philosopher J. L. Austin. I have ventured a hypothesis as to the origin of James' defense of natural realism, but I do not know the etiology of Austin's rejection of the whole idea of sense data as private representations of an external reality, except that that rejection may have come very early in Austin's life;[35] in any case, he is very likely to have been acquainted at least with Russell's account of James' views in *The Analysis of Mind*.

It was, by the way, through reflecting on Austin's *Sense and Sensibilia,* as I did repeatedly starting in the 1970s, that I first began to take direct realism seriously. But although my views today are closer to Austin's than to James', I have to admit that I was not at first convinced by Austin.[36] It was only after I began to teach courses on the philosophy of William James and to focus on his *Radical Empiricism* that I gradually began to see that the endless pattern of recoil we see in modern philosophy, from extravagant versions of realism to equally extravagant versions of antirealism and back again, can never be brought to rest unless we challenge the picture of the mind, and particularly the picture of perception, that makes it seem impossible to take our ordinary talk of perceiving and thinking about objects seriously unless one reinterprets it in terms of a representational theory of the mind—and, when one sees how that theory fails to provide the desired "foundation" for our ordinary talk (since it is just as much a mystery, in the end, how the supposed "mental representations" can refer to objects as it is how our ordinary talk can do so) makes it seem that Rortian nihilism must be the only option remaining (although that too, I would argue, is only the illusion of an option, a *fata morgana* that disappears the moment one tries to embrace it).[37]

The most striking feature of the view put forward in *Sense and Sensibilia,* at least on a first reading, is the rejection of something that the tradition takes as self-evident: namely, that even nonveridical experience must be analyzed on a perceiver-percipient model. If I dream, or am subject to the illusion, or even hallucinate that I see a building I really *do* perceive something, on the traditional view—it is just that what I perceive is not a physical something but a "mental" something. James (and Russell when he was following James) retained just this feature of the traditional view. To be sure, they denied that such mental somethings are made of a different "stuff" from the physical things (this denial was a consequence of their different versions of "neutral monist" metaphysics), but they accepted the perceiver-percipient model. But on Austin's still more radical approach, when, for example, I dream that I see a building, I do not perceive *anything*—I only *seem* to perceive something. With one stroke, Austin banishes the last vestige of the tradition's "sense data." Well, not entirely, you may object; we still feel *pains,* for example, and a pain is not a physical object. That is true, but Austin's point is that the tradition regards *feeling a pain* and *seeing a table* as essentially similar—in both cases I have "sensations"; and it is the use of the notion of a "sensation" in connection with perceptual experiences, be they "veridical" or "nonveridical," that Austin regards as complete nonsense.

Even to sketch Austin's view would require a essay as long as this one. I will only mention one obvious objection to Austin's account (the one that bothered me for a long time). If we give up the idea that there is a mental *object* there in the case of nonveridical experience, how are we to *explain* the similarity between the nonveridical and a corresponding perception? To be sure, Austin's account does not prevent us from saying that how an experience seems to us to be depends on our neural state in such-and-such ways; these causal dependencies are matters of scientific fact. But do we not want to say more than that? Do we not want to say that there is something *identical,* a "common factor," present in the two experiences? Austin's view, which I have come to share, is that one has here only the *illusion of an explanation.*[38]

I will say, however, that Austin's strategy was not available to James, because it was essential to James' whole metaphysical outlook that everything that *seems* to be present in experience is, in some sense, *there*—is, as James sometimes puts it, a "bit" of pure experience. To go from James' bold presentation of his metaphysics of radical empiricism to Austin's *Sense and Sensibilia* is to go from a bold metaphysical construction with deep roots in traditional empiricist metaphysics (roots James repeatedly acknowledged, even as he tried to correct what he saw as the errors of that empiricism), to a bitingly cold attempt to achieve a certain kind of clarity. To some this will seem a loss. But at the end of the day, it is, I believe, a gain; and it even preserves, I believe, the genuine moment of insight in James' ambitious metaphysical project, which was James' realization that our ordinary ways of talking and thinking about our perceptual experiences should be taken seriously in philosophy. In taking so seriously our common sense picture of ourselves as having access to a common world, taking that picture so seriously because it and the actions that are interwoven with it and give it content are essential to our lives together, not just as knowers but as moral agents, William James was, in the best sense, *both* a "pragmatist" and a "realist."

Notes

1 For a discussion of the importance of overcoming this picture, see my "The Dewey Lectures 1994: Sense, Nonsense and the Senses; An Inquiry into the Powers of the Human Mind," *The Journal of Philosophy*, 91(2), September 1994.

2 In "James' Theory of Truth," in *A Companion to William James*, ed. Ruth Anna Putnam (Cambridge: Cambridge University Press, 1997).

3 For Russell's view of James, see the first chapter of my *Pragmatism: An Open Question* (Oxford: Blackwell, 1995).

4 On this, see my "James' Theory of Truth" and "Pragmatism" in *Proceedings of the Aristotelian Society* 95, 1995, pp. 291–306.

5 In Peirce's case, however, the story is more complex because Peirce was willing to make *empirical* assumptions (ones that are not compatible with today's physics) to guarantee that his theory of truth would not be incompatible with his realism. Given his fallibilism, Peirce might even be happy that his theory has been refuted by a scientific discovery. The discovery in question—by Stephen Hawking—is that there is such a thing as the *irretrievable destruction of information*. This refutes Peirce's claim that we are entitled to believe that scientific investigation could discover the answer to *any* factual question if sufficiently long continued, and that claim is necessary to Peirce's defense of the realistic character of his notion of truth.

6 In the preface to the *Principles of Psychology*, James writes, "This book, assuming that thoughts and feelings exist and are vehicles of knowledge, thereupon contends that psychology when she has ascertained the empirical correlation of the various sorts of thought or feeling with definite conditions of the brain, can go no farther—can go no farther, that is, as a natural science. If she goes farther she becomes *metaphysical*" (p. 6).

7 This address, "The Knowing of Things Together," was published in *The Psychological Review* in March 1895, and is reprinted in *Essays in Philosophy* (Cambridge: Harvard University Press, 1978).

8 David C. Lamberth, "James's Varieties Reconsidered: Radical Empiricism, the Extra-Marginal and Conversion," in *The American Journal of Theology and Philosophy*, vol. 15(3), September, 1994. Lamberth's *Metaphysics, Experience and Religion in William James's Thought* (Cambridge: Cambridge University Press, forthcoming) provides a detailed periodization of the development of James' metaphysics.

9 See also Bruce Wilshire's *William James and Phenomenology: A Study of "The Principles of Psychology"* (Bloomington: Indiana University Press, 1968), pp. 4–6.

10 I am referring again to the Epilogue to *Psychology: Briefer Course*, and to James' "Notes for Philosophy 20b: Psychological Seminar—the Feelings," in *The Works of William James: Manuscript Lectures*, edited by Frederick Burkhardt and Fredson Bowers (Cambridge: Harvard University Press, 1988), pp. 212–29.

11 James' denial of a substantial "consciousness" is, of course, not a denial that we are conscious! Although this charge is occasionally brought against James, it seems to depend on the idea that one cannot believe that we are conscious unless there is a *thing*

that is our "consciousness," or at least a substantial self (or at least a transcendental ego, such as Kant's famous "I think"). What James was denying was the need for any of these metaphysical items, not the fact that Jones is conscious of the purring of the cat, or whatever. James' denial that we are *aware* of any such item is, of course, a denial that Kant—who did not think we *experience* the transcendental self—would have agreed with, as, for quite different reasons, would Hume.

12   Pure experience is a term James took from Avenarius, by the way, although he later seems to have quite forgotten this debt, since he spoke in quite scornful tones of that thinker's unreadability! This was pointed out to me by David Lamberth. (The first person to suggest this, to my knowledge, was Ignas K. Skrupskelis in his introduction to *The Works of William James: Manuscript Lectures.*)

   Although the sentence "Experience has no such inner duplicity" comes from "Does 'Consciousness' Exist?", reprinted in *The Works of William James: Essays in Radical Empiricism* (Cambridge: Harvard University Press, 1976), p. 6, the thought is already present in James' "Notes for Philosophy 20b," e.g., point "2," p. 228. "But nothing postulated whose whatness is not of some *nature* given in fields, that is not of field stuff, datum stuff, experience stuff, 'content.' No pure ego, for example, and no material substance. This *is* the hypothesis that we are trying to work out."

13   See "Aristotle after Wittgenstein," reprinted in my *Words and Life* (Cambridge: Harvard University Press, 1994).

14   I did not consider the possibility of this reading in "Aristotle after Wittgenstein," and if I had I would have been more charitable to the Aristotelian view.

15   This has been challenged by Myles Burnyeat. For Burnyeat's paper and a reply defending the interpretation given here see Martha Nussbaum and Amelie Rorty, eds., *Essays on Aristotle's de Anima* (Oxford: Oxford University Press, 1992). Victor Caston has pointed to passages in Aristotle's biological writings in which Aristotle speculates that cognition may involve building of a kind of representation *in the blood stream*. Such representations are not, of course, in our psyche, and are not identical with the perceptual experience. Still the fact that Aristotle himself was willing to speculate in this way shows that an "Aristotelian" view need not be hostile to the idea that subpersonal processes of a model building kind have a role to play in the etiology of perception. (Does this mean Aristotle is the father of cognitive science?)

16   For a fuller discussion of this issue, see H. Putnam, "Sense, Nonsense and the Senses," pp. 477–83.

17   This paragraph and the four that follow are adapted from my "Realism without Absolutes," reprinted in *Words and Life,* see pp. 285–86.

18   William James, "Great Men and Their Environment," in *The Will to Believe and Other Essays in Popular Philosophy* (London: Longmans, Green, 1897), pp. 216–17.

19   I owe the term "bald naturalism" to John McDowell's *Mind and World* (Cambridge: Harvard University Press, 1994).

20   For a critical examination of such attempts see Hilary Putnam, *Renewing Philosophy* (Cambridge: Harvard University Press, 1992).

21   I now find "internal realism" to be an unhappy term, for the reasons given in "Sense, Nonsense and the Senses," pp. 461–63.

22   On this, see John Haldane's "Reid, Scholasticism, and Current Philosophy of Mind," in *The Philosophy of Thomas Reid,* ed. M. Delgarno and E. Mathews (Dordrecht: Kluwer, 1989).

23 Thomas Reid, *The Works of Thomas Reid,* ed. Sir William Hamilton (London: Longmans, Green, 1895), *Intellectual Powers* II, xxi (p. 332), quoted in Haldane, "Reid, Scholasticism."

24 E.g., C. S. Peirce, *Collected Papers* (Cambridge: Harvard University Press, 1960–1966), 5:56, 5:444, 5:539, 6:95.

25 "Natural realism" is a much better term, because as J. L. Austin pointed out in *Sense and Sensibilia* (Oxford and New York: Oxford University Press, 1962), there is a great deal that is problematic with the traditional epistemologist's use of "direct" and "indirect."

26 It is for the same reason that Dewey followed James in this, and that Peirce earlier sought—even if, in my view, unsuccessfully—a return to direct realism.

27 See "Sense, Nonsense and the Senses" for a fuller account.

28 Charles Taylor has objected that I am leaving Hegel out of account here; but even if Hegel can be seen as a kind of direct realist (which is problematic), he seems to have had no influence on James in this respect.

29 James, *Essays in Radical Empiricism,* p. 37.

30 Bertrand Russell, *The Analysis of Mind* (New York: Humanities Press, 1971), pp. 137, 140, 142.

31 In the Notes for the seminar on "the Feelings," James insists that this "pointing" to something more is part of what he calls the "content" of the "datum"; this is the exact opposite of Russell's view.

32 William James, *Pragmatism and the Meaning of Truth* (Cambridge: Harvard University Press, 1978), p. 120.

33 For a recent discussion of the importance of this insight of Kant, see John McDowell's *Mind and World* (Cambridge: Harvard University Press, 1994).

34 I criticize that account in "James' Theory of Truth."

35 In 1936 (Austin was born in 1911), Austin and Isaiah Berlin held a class on C. I. Lewis' *Mind and the World Order,* in which Austin characterized Lewis' doctrine of *qualia*—specific, sensible characteristics—as "complete nonsense." See Isaiah Berlin, *Personal Impressions,* ed. Henry Hardy (New York: Viking, 1981), p. 107. Unfortunately, Berlin does not give Austin's grounds, so one cannot tell whether this means that Austin already held the views that he was to defend in *Sense and Sensibilia.*

36 In "Models and Reality," reprinted in my *Philosophical Papers,* vol. 3, *Realism and Reason* (Cambridge: Cambridge University Press, 1983), I explicitly rejected Austin's views (p. 24). It now seems to me that this rejection led me directly into a cul de sac with respect to the realism and antirealism issue. For an explanation of this remark, see my "Sense, Nonsense and the Senses."

37 For a discussion of Rorty's position, see my *Renewing Philosophy* and chapters 14 and 15 in *Words and Life.*

38 I discuss this question at greater length in "Sense, Nonsense and the Senses," pp. 473–83.

Response to Hilary Putnam's "Pragmatism and Realism"

SIDNEY MORGENBESSER

My first teaching job in philosophy was at the University of Pennsylvania, where I encountered Hilary Putnam as a student. You can believe me, the experience was exciting, unnerving, and instructive. I admired and learned from him then, and I have continued to love, admire, and learn from him. I am honored to try to add a few footnotes to Putnam.

Putnam thinks that many of us have been blind to the richness of the work of the great pragmatists because we had false or misleading views about the interconnection between the work of the pragmatists and pragmatism. Thus, many philosophers do not appreciate the complexity and richness of James' realist view of perception because they tend to think of pragmatism as a species of irrealism. I think, but am not sure, that Putnam means that some philosophers tend to think that if a philosopher is a pragmatist on one issue, he or she ought to be a pragmatist on all other big philosophical issues, that one is or ought to be either a pragmatist or a realist. The truth is that many pragmatists were realist about x and pragmatist about y, and legitimately, because the relevant theses are conceptually independent. One can, perhaps, go further; many of the so-called pragmatic theses that are frequently treated as a unit are conceptually independent of each other. Thus, the famous pragmatic belief-doubt model of inquiry is independent of the pragmatic theory of truth. Again, there are many theses under the rubric of the instrumentalist or pragmatic approach to scientific theories and entities that are conceptually independent of each other. For the record, it should be noted that the great pragmatists did not doubt the reality of scientific theoretical entities; they denied as it were their exclusive reality—the perceived encountered table was as real as the scientific one.

We might also, perhaps, extend Putnam's approach to deal with a topic of concern to this symposium, the cultural role of pragmatism. It might be the case that the great pragmatists, among them Dewey, had a significant impact on this culture because they had two sets of relevant beliefs which influenced people. On the one hand, they defended general philosophical beliefs about truth and knowledge that people found exhilarating and instructive and also defended beliefs about specific social institutions and arrangements. I know, or, perhaps more guardedly, believe, that many who were admirers of Dewey's defense of liberalism and democracy dissented from his pragmatism and they were not incoherent; the relevant theses are independent. There is no essence to pragmatism. I will not comment on the social role currently played by some pragmatists or the current state of liberalism, pragmatic or otherwise. But I will say that many who are labeled irrealists today are critical of objectivity and warranted assertability, but Dewey was not. Gone, too, is the Deweyan optimism about the chances of the realization of our ideals.

Putnam has many interesting things to say about the interconnection between his and James' views on perception and traditional issues of skepticism and foundationalism. He writes: "The advantage of pragmatism over traditional 'foundationalist' epistemology is that the way in which pragmatist philosophers answer skeptical doubts is the way in which doubts are answered in practice, by appealing to tests that in fact work in our lives. If I think that what I see may be an illusion, I can try to touch it, or look at it from a different position, or ask other people to take a look. There are not, in James' view, two sets of criteria for being 'real'—common sense criteria and philosophical criteria." But here I think Hilary is misleading; in these cases skeptical doubt is not involved. Let us say I am sitting in a house and I think I hear noises but I am not sure if it is "a noise in the head" or a real fire engine going by and I hear it, and I go out and look and see the fire engine. I am not having skeptical doubts. I am convinced there is an external world and that I can acquire knowledge of it and it's because I do not have skeptical doubts that I act, go to the window, and see whether I may be under a temporary illusion or not. But perhaps we can try to induce skeptical doubts in everyday life and defend pragmatism on the grounds that it would deal with skeptical doubts in the way that they would be dealt with if they were raised in everyday life. Perhaps, but I am not sure. You go to a guy and say: "Maybe you don't exist." "How do you know I exist?" "How do you know you're not dreaming?" I do not know what he would say; maybe "Go to hell!" In everyday life we frequently dismiss skeptical doubts as pointless, but still may be intrigued by them.

But Putnam's point, revised, may still stand. Pragmatism may be in accord with our cognitive practices—when we think inquiry is called for, when we dismiss requests for justification, and when we seem to feel we are justified without satisfying the quest for certainty. Not quite, for pragmatists often criticize members of their culture for defending a dualism between matters of fact and matters of value, and for not being as open to experimentation about values and commitments as they were, ostensibly, about matters of fact. It would take us too far afield to compare Dewey and James on these issues and to consider the connection between Dewey's commitments to democracy and his commitments to experimentation.

Putnam and many others specify pragmatism as a theory of inquiry, as a method of dealing with doubt—either skeptical or not—without appealing to certainty. He adds that pragmatism can be compatible with realism. Indeed, he must go further: if realism is true, pragmatism, if acceptable, must be compatible with realism especially if pragmatism and realism deal with different questions or issues. The pragmatist wants to tell us how to justify claims about the perceived world if such justification is required without requiring certainty. The realist, who is also Jamesian about perception, wants to tell us about the ontological status of the objects perceived. But this story is not quite complete. There have been some important philosophers such as C. I. Lewis, who were not pragmatists in the sense just specified; they did not subscribe to the pragmatic principles just reviewed—C. I. Lewis appealed to certainty but still was considered a pragmatist. This should not surprise us, since we have seen earlier that someone who is considered a pragmatist is thus considered because he assents to certain doctrines called pragmatic and not necessarily to others. C. I. Lewis had a pragmatic theory of the a priori and that was one of the reasons he was considered a pragmatist; once again someone may subscribe to some pragmatic principles and dissent from others. To return to Putnam, the important point is, as we shall see, that his version of direct perception would rule out, I think, Lewis' theory as acceptable.

Some pragmatists were also naturalists; they tried to develop a naturalistic approach to perception, one that would present us as acting and transacting with nature, thereby becoming reliable perceivers and knowing what we perceive. The pragmatic position just indicated can be developed in a number of ways; I will return later to pragmatism and C. I. Lewis.

Notice that Putnam is not ruling out all cases or, more carefully, all talk of indirect perception.[1] Some philosophers talk of indirectly perceiving x, or, at least, not directly perceiving x by perceiving y, where x is not identical with y. Thus, we do not directly see the car if we see it by seeing its door or, if you wish, its side. And, of course, it is by direct or indirect perception that we get knowledge about the car. It is the public accessibility of these objects that Putnam wants emphasized. What he wants to deny is that in perception we receive impressions that may be considered mental, and from the character of our mental impressions we infer how things are in the external world. And we deny that there are impressions that represent things in the external world and stand in the way of our directly perceiving things in the external world. I shall specify a variant of this position later. In my opinion he correctly gives credit to James for rebutting certain philosophical views about the mental and experience; this supported the approach to perception that Putnam wants abandoned. He adds some intriguing arguments of his own to undercut those who claim that we must be only in causal contact, but not normatively or directly related to things or state of affairs. Putnam develops these views at length in his illuminating Dewey lectures. But as Quine has reminded us, the human condition is the Humean one: by direct perception I see how things are behaving, but will they continue to behave this way, the skeptic asks. I do not know whether Putnam wants to rule this question out as irrelevant. And if things begin to change one way and then another, will we continue to talk about perceiving them?

If we accept Putnam's general approach, some elucidation is required and some problems must be dealt with especially in regard to James' approach to direct perception. It is because of their direct accessibility that we allow ourselves to talk of "the sky," "holes in bagels," "shadows"—not merely "things" such as tables and chairs. Questions can be raised about the ontological status of these objects that cannot be decided by appealing to our ordinary discourse about them. Certain questions can also be raised about the nature of publicly accessible properties, for example, color. According to some, color is a dispositional property; to say that a car is blue is to say that the car has the power to produce experiences or sensations or, as is sometimes said, to produce qualia, where qualia are phenomenal properties of the visual experience. There are many questions about qualia, some of which will be pursued when I return to C. I. Lewis. Notice further that illusions may, in some sense, be public. We may all see the lines as unequal, even though we know that they are equal. Many philosophers seem to hold that even in cases of illusion, we are visually apprehending something, a thesis with which Putnam has little sympathy. He suggests, I think, an intentional reading of perceptual states. If A believes that there are ghosts, it does not follow that there are ghosts; if a phenomenal state presents the lines as crooked, it does not follow that the lines are crooked, or that there are crooked-like private entities to consider. Putnam would, of course, admit that psychologists may offer us interesting explanations of illusions but, I think, add that psychological explanations will by themselves not answer certain metaphysical issues or ontological ones or, if you wish, issues about naturalism and physicalism. Putnam criticizes certain apparently physicalistic positions, for example, those that identify sensations with brain states. His positive position is that perception is supervenient on physical processes, meaning, I suppose, that perceptual states are strongly dependent on physical properties but not identical with them. Putnam would be the first to admit that this is only a sketch, that there are many senses of supervenience now being discussed in the literature. It is only fair to add that many of these discussions are indebted to his contributions to our understanding of the nature of mental states.

Pragmatism has been specified as a method of inquiry, and as being compatible with empiricism, or at least one version of it, but there are some philosophers who think that there is something amiss with empiricism in this version and its account of the role that perceptual experience plays in our cognitive life.[2] This is also the case with pragmatism considered as a species of empiricism. Current empiricists, or some of them, seem to appeal to experience, or perceptual experience, as providing us with a reason for believing, and end up with an account of experience that can only be seen as causing, but not justifying, belief. The reason for these qualifications should be obvious. Empiricism has been applied to a variety of theses and the criticism just referred to would apply to empiricism in some of these senses and not others, which could be subject to criticism on other grounds (notice the allusions by Putnam to the associationist psychology).

A variant of this criticism—that it fails to provide an adequate account of beliefs about immediate and phenomenal experience and their cognitive role—is applied by Putnam, as I understand him, to one version of empiricism to which I alluded before and that I label "complex epistemological empiricism."[3] According to complex epistemological empiricism— a thesis clearly related to Cartesianism and the picture of the mind criticized by Putnam—our beliefs about tables, chairs, rocks, and so on must ultimately be justified by beliefs about our phenomenal states, beliefs that are conceptually and epistemically more basic than beliefs about tables and chairs.[4] These phenomenal states may be caused by physical objects and interactions with them, but they could have occurred even if they were not so caused. By becoming aware of these phenomenal states, we acquire maximally warranted beliefs that can be used to justify beliefs about tables, chairs, rocks, and so on. The relevant beliefs have been specified in a variety of ways: as beliefs about objects of sensory awareness, of sensations, of sense-data of which we are or can become aware,[5] of how things appeared to us, of color expanses. Because there are varied ways of specifying the relevant beliefs, there are diverse versions of complex epistemological empiricism. All of them and limited versions of them are criticized by Putnam for a variety of reasons, some of which have been presented by James and others by Austin.[6] They are conjunctions of mistaken views about perception, of justification; they postulate elusive acts or states of the type just surveyed, for example objects of sensory awareness, of sensation.

Not surprisingly, Putnam is critical of philosophers like C. I. Lewis, who appeal to the apprehension of qualia as a foundation of our empirical beliefs; notice the emphasis on apprehension of qualia. I think, with some hesitation, that Putnam is not required to deny the existence of qualia, but only to claim that it is idle to appeal to them unless such appeal is accompanied by a theory that accounts for our knowledge of qualia, and no such theory is acceptable to him unless such knowledge is seen as derivative of our knowledge of public objects and their properties.[7] But such was not the case, as I understand it, with Lewis' position. I am bypassing issues about the given and the detailed reasons about certainty that play an important role in Lewis' theory.

Many pragmatists have appealed to inquiry to tell us about the nature of the world, and, conversely, to use their knowledge about nature or the world to tell us about perception and the nature of the perceived object. On these issues some pragmatists have been characterized as naturalists. I indicated that they may be interpreted as believing that the perceived table is supervenient upon the physical one. I now add that they may be interpreted as tacitly believing that perception is supervenient on physical processes. Hence, on these issues, Putnam's position, and the position of some of the great pragmatists, may be compatible. I do not know whether the version or versions of pragmatism developed by Dewey and other pragmatists required them to agree with some of Putnam's criticism of some version of naturalism, that is, his criticism of the attempt to reduce semantic facts to nonsemantic ones. The converse is true for pragmatism, and here I am paraphrasing Fodor[8] when it is considered an ally of those who oppose theories that attempt to explain behavior by appeal to mental states that have representational properties or are representations of the world and also play a causal role. I do not know whether Putnam is opposed to such theories in principle or only to certain versions of them, and the same is true for Dewey. The debates between Putnam and the friends of mental representations will, I am sure, continue and when they do, there will be debates about explanation, reduction, and supervenience—debates about issues that have, as we have seen, played important roles in Putnam's work.

Pragmatic naturalists not only concerned themselves with a theory of action, but also presented a theory as to how we can act. They thought that a life lived in accord with naturalist principles can be a rich and meaningful one. They also argued that science, properly used, can enrich our lives and hence they were not post-modern, at least in one sense of the latter phrase. Hilary Putnam has also concerned himself with these issues in his own distinctive way, and with these concerns and others he has enriched our lives. I know he has enriched mine, and I want to thank him for it.

Notes

1 Robert Schwartz in his illuminating article, "Directed Perception" (*Philosophical Psychology* 9[1], 1996, pp. 81–91), critically examines the use of "direct perception" by many psychologists and their explanatory theory or theories of direct perception in their sense.

2 The issues have been discussed in various ways by Rorty, Davidson, McDowell, and Quine.

3 Complex epistemological empiricism is a theory about justification, not an explanatory theory of the sort most notably criticized by Chomsky. Complex epistemological empiricism is primarily a theory about empirical belief. Empiricism about empirical knowledge is compatible with all sorts of nonempiricist theories and other kinds of knowledge, for example, mathematical knowledge.

4 See John W. Yolton, *Perception and Reality: A History from Descartes to Kant* (Ithaca: Cornell University Press, 1996), for a discussion of Descartes, Cartesianism, and many other issues as well.

5 A fuller treatment would distinguish between theories of sense-data, some of which have puzzling ontological commitments and should be distinguished for the approach we are considering.

6 The limited versions would restrict themselves to issues of justification and might end up being reductionist about physical objects. In such versions of empiricism, issues about causation are not introduced at the outset, if at all.

7 I am indebted to Frederick Dretske's article, "Phenomenal Externalism or If Meanings Ain't in the Head, Where are Qualia," in *Perception*, "Philosophical Issues," 7 (Atascadero, CA: Ridgeview Publishing, 1996), pp. 143–58. For an alternative view, see Gilbert Harman's article, "Explaining Color in Terms of Subjective Experience," *Ibid.*, pp. 1–17. See also Roberto Casati and Achille C. Varzi, *Holes and Other Superficialities* (Cambridge: MIT Press, 1994), especially pp. 158–87.

8 See Jerry A. Fodor, *The Elm and the Expert* (Cambridge: MIT Press, 1994), p. 88. He writes, "You might still reasonably wonder what could possibly be the point of having

behavior that's caused by representations of the world. This is, in my view, a perfectly serious question; remember that reflexologists, pragmatists, Direct Realists and Heideggerians (inter alia) have all thought that the success of behavior can be explained without assuming that it's caused by representations." Fodor claims, "For, it's the essence of mental representations that they face two ways at once: They connect with the world by representing it, by and large, veridically; and they connect with behavior by being its typical proximal cause" (83).

The Moral Impulse

RUTH ANNA PUTNAM

Early and late in his philosophical life, William James was concerned to articulate criteria of acceptability for philosophical, in particular metaphysical, positions. The point he made, as a young man and again as an old one, was that we choose our philosophical visions—his terminology in *A Pluralistic Universe*—on passional grounds. We demand that our image of the world be hospitable to our most urgent interests, and James proposed pragmatism as a philosophy that would satisfy this demand.[1] For many philosophers, but by no means for all, this means that an adequate philosophical view must allow room for our moral lives. Kant springs immediately to mind as a philosopher whose life work was dominated by this quest. Of course, I do not intend to suggest that philosophers whose philosophical views do not make sense of their moral lives are immoral. I have known such philosophers; they have been among the most morally admirable human beings I have ever known. I want to suggest merely that such philosophers lead a double life. In everyday life, I contend, all of us act as if we believed that there are other people who share our world, that there are objective moral values, that while much of our behavior is habitual, virtually all our actions are potentially subject to deliberate choice, and that what we do makes a difference in the world. Therefore, philosophers who reject one or more of these beliefs as either false or senseless lead one life in their studies and another outside. Alternatively, one might say that such philosophers are profoundly inconsistent, that the beliefs that would make sense of their conduct contradict some of their philosophical doctrines.

The moral impulse of my title is the passionate desire to find a philosophy that makes room for our moral lives, that would enable us to lead one life, to be as consistent as is humanly possible in all our beliefs. It is, I think, beyond controversy that both James and John Dewey developed their philosophies in response to this impulse.[2] That makes their philosophies not merely attractive to me but leads me to think that pragmatism is important, could play an important role, in the life of this nation and the world. Even if neither James nor Dewey succeeded fully in their attempts, they seem to have pointed us in a fruitful direction, as did the other (other than William James) founder of pragmatism, C. S. Peirce.[3] To say that one has developed one's philosophical position in response to the moral impulse, or in response to any other passionate concern, is not to say that one does not have or has not given intellectually compelling reasons for that position. It is a further and separate point of James', discussed later, that when we lack such reasons, we are nevertheless sometimes entitled to choose a belief on passional grounds.[4]

Of course, I am not wedded to the word "pragmatism." Lately I have come to have considerable sympathy for C. S. Peirce's complaint that the word has come to mean too many different things to too many people; today it is even less clear than it was at the end of the nineteenth century.[5] Nor do I think that, in the limited space at my disposal, I could do justice to the enormously complex ways in which James and Dewey seek to make sense of our moral lives (their ways are not identical). Rather I shall mention certain beliefs that are required if one is to make sense of one's moral life. And I shall gesture at the forms these beliefs and their defense took for James and Dewey. There will emerge a profound difference between them, but it may well be that to other scholars that difference will appear to be superficial. If so, the term "pragmatism" will prove to be less multivocal than it seems to me at present.

The core experiences of our moral lives are these: there are times when life does not proceed smoothly along habitual grooves, yet we do not permit an impulse simply to throw us off course; instead, we deliberate. Again, there are times when we look at what we have wrought, and sometimes are glad and sometimes regret that we chose this path rather than another. It seems to me, but nothing hangs on my being right about this, that moral reflection tends to be prompted by failures more often than by successes. In any case, as James pointed out, regret does not make sense unless the world could have been otherwise, and remorse—a special kind of regret—does not make any sense unless one could have chosen to cause the world to be otherwise.[6] But do we have free will? How is one to deal with this question? Here James and Dewey diverge. For James, the determinism or indeterminism alternative is what he called a genuine option, that is, both alternatives attract us (they are "live" for us, he would say). Nevertheless, we must choose one or the other (we cannot suspend belief), and accepting one of the alternatives or the other will have serious consequences in our lives. Only if one believes in indeterminism, James thought, will one be willing to act morally even at great cost to oneself. Yet James also believed that the question of whether we have free will is one that cannot be settled on intellectual grounds. Consequently, it is the sort of question that one is entitled to answer on passional grounds; James asserts that he has free will.[7] In contrast, Dewey holds that the question of whether we have free will arises out of a radically false worldview—a dualism that regards the moral agent as separate and different from the natural world and takes the world to be deterministic. Dewey takes it that the free-will issue disappears once that radically false worldview is rejected.

Lest I be misunderstood, I want to state quite clearly that James also rejected that dualistic view in all its ramifications. Nevertheless, James took the metaphysical question seriously, while Dewey replaced it by concrete questions concerning the amount of actual freedom, or open alternatives, that the social or political environs of a given agent permit in a world that, as quantum physics teaches, is not deterministic.[8] Neither James nor Dewey understand a morally significant act to be a gratuitous act, both understand that morally significant choices express who we are and shape who we will be, though neither encourages undue preoccupation with the state of one's soul. But this relation between character and conduct leaves room for choice, for moral growth or deterioration, even for dramatic reversals.

As already mentioned, James argued that he could not understand the willingness to act morally, at great cost to oneself, unless one believed that moral values were objective, and that moral values would not be objective if the world were deterministic. But the existence of real possibilities, real contingencies is merely a necessary, not a sufficient condition for objective values and norms. To make sense of our moral lives we must not only believe in free will but we must take it that moral judgments are, indeed, *judgments* subject to intellectual critique and not mere emotional responses.[9]

James is vividly aware of the multifarious sources of our valuations: some are directly or indirectly connected to bodily pains and pleasures, others are immediate deliverances of human sensibility. This, he thought, was the insight of intuitionists, just as the connection with bodily pains and pleasures is an insight of Utilitarians. But in a world with only one thinker, to use his language, values would nevertheless be entirely subjective. Truth requires a standard outside the thinker, a standard provided by the existence of other human beings and the fact that they take an interest in each other. In James's memorable image, two loving people doomed to extinction on a rock would still, as long as they lived, have a full moral life with real goods and real evils.[10] Dewey expressed a similar thought, and a good deal else besides, by saying that morality is social.[11] But morality might be social and yet wholly relative. This is not the place to examine that alternative; neither James nor Dewey were relativists. War is bad, not bad according to this or that set of mores, just bad. How do we know that? Here I can hear someone ask, "what about just wars?" Well, perhaps there are situations in which war is the lesser evil; if so, how do we know that? This question, too, if it is asked as a skeptical question, presupposes a false worldview. In fact, the false worldview presupposed here is intimately related to the false view that, according to Dewey, is presupposed by asking whether we have free will. How we can know that some kind of conduct is right or wrong, some state of affairs good or bad, is mysterious only if we have already accepted the idea that questions of value are radically different from questions of fact, that facts are in and of this world while values, at least moral values, are not.

Traditionally, moral values were held to be transcendent, but in the twentieth century they came to be thought of as nonexistent. When values were thought of as transcendent, it was held that they were known in a unique way: they were intuited. But when positivistic philosophers rejected the very idea of the transcendent, value judgments were thought to be, in the last analysis, not judgments at all but expressions of one or another noncognitive (emotional or volitional) state of mind.[12] Dewey rejected this false worldview, he rejected the so-called fact-value distinction. Dewey pointed out that what we call factual knowledge is shaped by our values: we inquire into matters that matter to us. Dewey noted that factual claims and value claims are so intimately interwoven in our reasoning that one cannot challenge or support a claim of one kind without implicating claims of the other: we evaluate data as relevant or not, as reliable or not, inferences as valid or not, experiments as well designed or nor, and so on.

The web of beliefs includes beliefs concerning facts and beliefs concerning values. It is anchored in experiences that are sense perceptions, those that are enjoyments and sufferings, and those that are doings. Even this formulation suggests too much of a multiplicity. The web of beliefs is anchored in experiences that may be taken as sense perceptions or as enjoyments/sufferings or as doings, and often are taken as any two or all of them.[13] All of this is enormously important, yet all of this might be accepted by a latter day expressionist. All of this might be accepted, and yet one might hold that there are ends or ideals that are not subject to critique and evaluation because they are the ultimate standards.[14] Dewey challenges the very idea of ends that are ultimate in this sense and replaces it by the idea of ends-in-view. Ends-in-view are human responses to problems that human beings face, and they are evaluated as human beings let their conduct be guided by them. Of course, there are values that seem to us beyond challenge—respect for human dignity, for example—and they may indeed survive any possible challenge; I sincerely hope so. But we would be blind to the facts of the real world if we failed to acknowledge that this precious value is challenged again and again wherever prisoners are tortured or women raped. Or, to put this another way, we must steadfastly hold respect for human dignity as an end-in-view precisely because prisoners continue to be tortured and women continue to be raped.

To make sense of our moral lives, our choosings, our praisings and self-congratulations, as well as our blamings and regrettings, I have argued we must believe that we are, indeed, choosing, that our choices make a difference, and that there are standards by which we judge and are judged, standards that are themselves of human making and subject to human critique. Implicit in these beliefs is another, the belief, held by each of us, that one is not alone in the world, that one lives in a peopled world. Just as the fact-value dichotomy, though useful in practical contexts, does not bear any epistemological or ontological weight, so the distinction between ethics and metaphysics or ethics and epistemology bears no philosophical weight, though it is useful in drawing up curricula and assigning responsibilities for teaching and learning. We cannot make sense of our moral lives unless we believe that there are other people and we live in a common world. It makes no sense for me to be careful not to step on your big toe, if the toe I would step on is not identical with the one in which you would feel pain, nor would it make sense for me to be careful not to cause you pain if what I take to be your body is not a minded body, and does not experience pain. To make philosophical sense of our moral lives, our philosophy must underwrite our common sense beliefs in the common sense world. James thought that the common sense world is one that "our ancestors and we, by slow cumulative strokes of choice, have extracted" out of something James in *The Principles of Psychology* called indifferently "the primordial chaos of sensations" and "that black and jointless continuity of space and moving clouds of swarming atoms which science calls the only real world."[15]

Beginning in 1904, in the series of papers later published under the title *Essays in Radical Empiricism,* James returned to the urgent question of how philosophy can escape from the "congeries of solipsisms" into which

Descartes had led her, and "out of which in strict logic only a God could compose a universe even of discourse." He proposed "pure experience" as the "one primal stuff or material . . . out of which everything is composed." Pure experience as such has no essential properties; it is not a kind of substance; it is as varied as our experiences are varied. However, unless we are just born or are just emerging from total anesthesia, we do not have pure experiences. Our experiences are always already conceptualized, already taken to be, say, of a pen, or as being ours, as part of the stream of thought that one calls oneself. So, both you and I can take the same pure experience to be your big toe, and yet take it also severally to be my seeing your big toe and your seeing it. This is not the occasion to discuss the merits and difficulties of James's theory of pure experience, I merely want to mention that it purports to show "how two minds can know one thing." And, James pointed out, "the decisive reason in favor of our minds meeting in *some* common objects at least is that, unless I knew that supposition, I have no motive for assuming that your mind exists at all . . . and for me to speak of you is folly."[16]

In his very sympathetic review of *Essays in Radical Empiricism,* Dewey pointed out that what is truly "radical" in James' empiricism is his insistence that "every kind of thing experienced must somewhere be real." Unlike his sensationalist and associationist predecessors, James took it that relations between things are experienced and thus real. Thus, according to Dewey, he "compelled philosophers to rethink their conclusions upon fundamental matters." Yet for all his enthusiasm, Dewey pointed out that James' premature death "left the new philosophy in too undeveloped a state to win disciples wholesale."[17]

Using for the moment dualistic language, Jamesian pure experiences may be characterized as intersections of a stream of thought and (an interaction between the human organism animated by that stream and) some object. For example, at this moment you are reading these words. That description is itself an illustration of what James means when he says that a pure experience may be taken as part of a physical object or as part of a mind, that a reading is an event that is at once physical and psychical. Whatever the pure experience may be (if we were to describe it, we would already have gone beyond the pure experience), when we call it "reading," we may be understood to refer to a physical or physiological process that ends with your understanding what the words mean.

As mentioned, the normal adult in normal circumstances does not have (is not conscious of having) "pure" experiences; one's conscious interactions with one's environment are always already conceptualized. To be sure, an experience, Dewey held, need not be cognitive, it may be an enjoyment or a suffering, or, again, a doing; it is quite often all of these things. It is precisely because we are not mere spectators of but actors in the world that I need to worry about stepping on your big toe, and it is precisely because I can step on your toe (because we do not merely see but handle objects in the world) that you and I can mean the same thing. The philosopher's problem is not the insoluble problem of inferring or constructing a common and relatively stable world out of private and fleeting sense data; the very notion of a sense datum is the result of a sophisticated analysis of ordinary sense perception guided by knowledge of the very world that is supposed to be called into question.[18] Jamesian pure experiences are, of course, not sense data, not an interface interposed between a questing mind and the world that is its quest; nevertheless, because the normal adult in normal circumstances does not have pure experiences, one cannot help but think that a world of pure experience is too much of a concession to idealism.[19]

Dewey begins with events. Like Jamesian pure experiences, Deweyan events are essentially neither mental nor physical. They are taken as one or the other (or both) after the fact. Experiencing is a taking, an interaction of the organism with its environment, an environment that includes others like it. Of course, one can ask how you and I can succeed to mean the same thing, but we ask it in concrete situations. When you say, "Let's divide this responsibility fairly," do you mean what I mean? How can we find out, how can we avoid a quarrel? When I say, "Let's meet in front of the post office," is that unambiguous? Will we actually meet? But experience also tells us that we often, more often than not, succeed in our efforts to communicate. We do indeed inhabit a common world and share a vast body of beliefs. Only against this background of success do we experience failures to communicate and disagreements in our beliefs concerning how the world is and ought to be, and what is important and what does not matter, etc. etc., and only within this common world can we find answers to these problems.[20]

To summarize: to make sense of our moral lives we need to believe that there are other people with whom we share a common world and that our actions can make a difference to what that world will become. Moral action (good or bad, right or wrong) is action that is chosen for reasons, among which are *moral* judgments, judgments that are as objective, and as fallible, as anything else that human beings believe. Both James and Dewey would have agreed with this. What then is the difference between them? It seems to me that in each case James accepts the received problematique.

No amount of humanly accessible evidence will decide whether we have free will and whether there are real possibilities, in other words, whether we can initiate causal chains. So, James decides the question on passional grounds. Now, I think that having done that, James has pulled the rug from under the original question, but he does not pursue that point. Dewey, in contrast, sees the original question as a diversion, an attempt to distract us from facing a multitude of concrete and vitally important infractions of the liberty of real human beings. Given James' radical empiricism, the view that anything real is experienced and vice versa, values are real if and only if they are experienced.

James believes both that our valuings begin with immediate feelings, that is, experiences, and that values are real—there are objective standards. Moreover, when we consider the complex values called ideals, it is clear that these are to be tested by seeing how attempts to realize them will work out. Once again, Dewey would agree with all this, but it is Dewey and not James to whom we owe the trenchant critique of the fact-value dichotomy. James rejects skepticism out of hand: if we are skeptics, there is no job left for the philosopher; he argues against subjectivism. In a curious sense, although in the end his method for settling moral disputes is empirical, James' problematique assumes a fact-value distinction that is never formally repudiated. Once again, James accepts a traditional philosophical challenge while Dewey denies the very ground upon which that challenge is mounted.

I am inclined to maintain that the same difference manifests itself also in their approaches to the problems of our knowledge of the external world, of the existence of other minds, and of intentionality—three problems that stand and fall together. James takes the problems seriously; he struggles throughout his philosophical career against the idealist solution precisely because that solution fails to make sense of his moral life. His own solution, the neutral monism of his radical empiricism, undermines, to be sure, the very basis of the problem; there can be no "congeries of solipsisms" in a world of pure experience. Dewey's experiences are as neutral as James' pure experiences. The difference, to my mind, is once again that Dewey—I mean, of course, the later Dewey—refuses to play the game, to enter into the philosophical discussion on the terms offered by the tradition.

Both James and Dewey, I have argued, are making sense of our moral lives; they do so in opposition to philosophical views dominant in their times. Part of the difference in their mode of argumentation and in their starting points can be explained by the fact that I have contrasted James with the later Dewey, a James whose opponents are Royce and Bradley with a Dewey whose opponents are Russell and the Logical Positivists. Yet the difference seems to me to be deeper, more significant than that. I am inclined to say that James speaks from inside the philosophical tradition, he takes its problems seriously; his answers, to be sure, lead him beyond the tradition. In contrast, when he wrote his later works, Dewey had already achieved a position outside the tradition, a tradition that reflects and supports social distinctions that he sought passionately to overcome. For Dewey, in the period between the two world wars, philosophy is politics; in spite of the preface to his *Talks to Teachers,*[21] I do not think the connection was ever that intimate for James.

Notes

1 William James, *A Pluralistic Universe* (Cambridge: Harvard University Press, 1977), first published in 1909. James claimed that pragmatism answered our passional demand more satisfactorily than other philosophies popular at the time in the first of a series of lectures delivered in Cambridge, Massachusetts in the winter of 1906–1907 and published as *Pragmatism: A New Name for Some Old Ways of Thinking* in 1907 (Cambridge: Harvard University Press, 1975).

2 It would be inappropriate here to cite Dewey's numerous writings in which the moral impulse of my title is clearly displayed. Some works will be cited later.

3 Although he published numerous articles, Peirce did not publish any books during his lifetime. Many of his writings were published in *Collected Papers of Charles Sanders Peirce*, vols. 1–6, ed. Charles Hartshorne and Paul Weiss; vols. 7–8, ed. A. W. Burks (Cambridge: Harvard University Press, 1931–35 and 1958).

4 Susan Haack drew my attention to this important distinction. An illustration from outside philosophy is this. Medical research is sometimes prompted by a passionate desire to find a cure for a particular illness; yet, if a cure is found, its curative power will have been established by intellectually compelling methods. On the other hand, what keeps an investigator going through months and years of patient research is a belief, *a fortiori* not based on evidence, but chosen on passional grounds.

5 Charles Sanders Peirce, "What Pragmatism Is," in *Collected Papers,* vol. 5, pp. 411–37. In paragraph 414, he writes, "But at present, the word begins to be met with occasionally in the literary journals, where it gets abused in the merciless way that words have to expect when they fall into literary clutches." Henceforth, Peirce continues, he will use the term "pragmaticism" for his view, a term "which is ugly enough to be safe from kidnappers."

6 William James, "The Dilemma of Determinism," in *The Will to Believe and Other Essays in Popular Philosophy* (Cambridge: Harvard University Press, 1979), first published 1897. The essay itself first appeared in 1884.

7 See the title essay in *The Will to Believe* for James' argument that when a genuine option cannot be settled on intellectual grounds we have right to believe either alternative on passional grounds.

8 John Dewey, introduction to *Human Nature and Conduct,* first published in 1922. In *The Middle Works of John Dewey,* ed. Jo Ann Boydston (Carbondale: Southern Illinois University Press, 1988). And John Dewey, *The Quest for Certainty* (New York: G. P. Putnam's Sons, 1960), pp. 248–50, first published 1929.

9 See James, "The Dilemma of Determinism."

10 William James, "The Moral Philosopher and the Moral Life," in *The Will to Believe.*

11 See, for example, Dewey, the concluding chapter of *Human Nature and Conduct.*

12 The former view is found in A. J. Ayer, *Language, Truth and Logic* (London: V. Golancz, 1951). The volitional alternative is presented in Hans Reichenbach, *The Rise of Scientific Philosophy* (Berkeley: University of California Press, 1951).

13 Of Dewey's numerous writings on this subject I shall mention only *Theory of Valuation* (Chicago: University of Chicago Press, 1939), *The Moral Writings of John Dewey: A Selection,* ed. James Gouinlock (New York: Macmillan, 1976). The subject is also discussed in Dewey's *Human Nature and Conduct* and *Quest for Certainty.*

14 For contemporary expressionism, see, for example, Allan Gibbard, *Wise Choice, Apt Feelings* (Cambridge: Harvard University Press, 1990).

15 William James, *The Principles of Psychology* (Cambridge: Harvard University Press, 1981), p. 277.

16 William James, *Essays in Radical Empiricism* (Cambridge: Harvard University Press, 1976), quotes on pp. 37–38, 4, 46, and 38 respectively.

17 John Dewey, Review of *Essays in Radical Empiricism,* in *The Middle Works of John Dewey,* vol. 7, p. 148.

18 That point was made forcefully by Dewey in *Essays in Experimental Logic* (Chicago: University of Chicago Press, 1916).

19 James' colleague at Harvard, Josiah Royce, and F. H. Bradley in England, among others, offered Absolute Idealism as a solution to the problem of how language or thought hooks on to the world, how it is that for me to speak of you is not folly. James found this philosophy profoundly unsatisfactory and offered his radical empiricism as an alternative solution. But I am suggesting that his life-long struggle against Absolute Idealism left its mark on his philosophy. James' relationship to Bradley is the subject of T. L. S. Sprigge, *American Truth and British Reality* (Chicago: Open Court Press, 1993). His relation to Royce is examined by James Conant in his contribution to *The Cambridge Companion to William James,* ed. Ruth Anna Putnam (Cambridge: University of Cambridge Press, 1997).

20 See Dewey, *Human Nature and Conduct, The Quest for Certainty,* and *Essays in Experimental Logic.* Although this essay deals only with James and Dewey, I want to mention in passing that Peirce's philosophy of perception also escapes the "congeries of solipsisms."

21 William James, *Talks to Teachers on Psychology and To Students on Some of Life's Ideals* (Cambridge: Harvard University Press, 1983), first published in 1899. In the preface, James described his philosophy as leading to "the well-known democratic respect for the sacredness of individuality" and used the occasion to express his opposition to the United States' imperialist adventure in the Philippines.

What's the Use of Calling Emerson a Pragmatist?

STANLEY CAVELL

In general I applaud the revival of interest in John Dewey and William James, on various intellectual and political grounds, and seek to learn what is at stake for others in their revival. But I also wish to suspend applause—doubtless more a transcendentalist than a pragmatist gesture on my part—for ideas that seem to be gaining prominence within this movement, expressed by writers and thinkers I admire, according to which Emerson is to be understood as a protopragmatist and Wittgenstein as, let us say, a neopragmatist. Perhaps I will be taken as struggling merely over labels; but sometimes labels should be struggled over.

In the course of working out certain implications of the teachings of the later Wittgenstein and of J. L. Austin, I have, in more recent years, variously recurred to an idea that their sense of the ordinary or everyday in language—as goal and as procedure in philosophy—is well thought of in connection with emphases in Emerson and in Thoreau on what they call the common, the familiar, the low, the near (what Emerson means by "having the day"). As Wittgenstein increasingly was called a pragmatist (or cited for his affinities with pragmatism) I wanted to ask whether John Dewey's reputation as the spokesman, even as the provider of a metaphysics, for the common man might throw some light on the dishearteningly dark matter of the philosophical appeal to the ordinary. Naturally I have felt that the appeal to the ordinary possesses political implications that have barely been touched. Yet I have not heretofore thought that the question of Dewey's relation to that appeal's implied politics of the ordinary—which intuitively seems to mean its pertinence to the democratic ideal—demanded thematizing. In particular, I mean the intuition that the democratic bearing of the philosophical appeal to the ordinary and its methods is at least as strong as, and perhaps in conflict with, its bearing on Dewey's homologous appeal to science and what he calls its method.

To attest my good faith in this struggle over terms such as pragmatism, transcendentalism, and ordinary language philosophy, I acknowledge that if Emerson is the founder of the difference in American thinking, then later American thinkers such as Dewey and James are going to be indebted to Emerson. What I deny is that their thinking, so far as it is recognizable as something distinctly called pragmatism, captures or clarifies or retains all that is rational or moral in the Emersonian event. I quote from my title essay in *Must We Mean What We Say?:* "Wittgenstein's role in combatting the idea of privacy . . . and in emphasizing the *functions* and *contexts* of language, scarcely needs to be mentioned. It might be worth pointing out that these teachings are fundamental to American pragmatism; but then we must keep in mind how different their arguments sound, and admit that in philosophy it is the sound which makes all the difference."[1] The remarks to follow may be taken as a brief gloss on that observation.

One further prefatory remark. It has been said that pragmatists wish their writing, like all good writing, to work—that is, to make a difference. But does writing (or art more generally) work in the ways that logic or technology work; and do any of these work in the way social organization works? Emerson's essay "Experience" may be understood as written to mourn the death of his young son. Freud speaks of mourning as work, something Emerson quite explicitly declares it to be; and Freud speaks in these terms also of an aspect of dreaming.[2] Does the writing of Dewey or James help us understand this idea of work? If it is a viable idea, is it less important than what they understand work to be?

I will formulate in what follows a few differences between Dewey and James, who are uncontentiously pragmatists, and Emerson and Wittgenstein, who are only contentiously so, although I know these differences may be dismissible, roughly on pragmatic grounds. I will then sketch what I consider to be my stake in these matters.

The following sentence from Dewey's *Experience and Education* is, I assume, characteristic of what makes him Dewey: "Scientific method is the only authentic means at our command for getting at the significance of our everyday experiences of the world in which we live."[3] Perhaps Emerson was wrong to identify mourning as a pervasive character of what we know as experience, and perhaps, in any case, philosophy need not regard it as part of "the significance of our everyday experience." Yet Emerson finds a work of what he understands as mourning to be the path to human objectivity with the world, to separating the world from ourselves, from our private interests in it. That understanding offers the possibility of moral relationship. According to Wittgenstein, "Concepts . . . are the expression of our interest, and direct our interest."[4] But interest is to be distinguished from whim, something I have regarded as the task to which Emerson dedicates his writing. Does science have anything different to say about mourning? Is it supposed to? Might one say that science has its own understanding of objectivity, call that intersubjectivity? It is an understanding that neither Emerson nor Wittgenstein can assume to be in effect; the human subject has first to be discovered, as something strange to itself.

Dewey's remark about scientific method as the authentic means for getting at the significance of our everyday experiences in effect insists that the works of men, requiring human intelligence, are part of this everyday. Of some of these works Emerson writes: "In every work of genius we recognize our own rejected thoughts; they come back to us with a certain alienated majesty."[5] Do not be put off by Emerson's liberal use of "genius." For him genius is, as with Plato, something each person has, not something certain people are. Emerson's remark about genius is a kind of definition of the term: If you find the return of your thoughts to be caused by a work in this way, then you are apt, and in a sense justified, to attribute this return to the genius of the work. You might even say that this kind of reading requires what Emerson calls experimenting, something Thoreau calls "trying" people. Does what you might call science, or its philosophy, have an understanding of this use of experimentation, experimentation as provocation? Is this use less important than the understanding science requires? How do the uses get close enough even to seem to conflict—close enough, perhaps, for someone to wish to call Thoreau's use a metaphorical one?

Dewey writes that pragmatism "is the formation of a faith in intelligence, as the one and indispensable belief necessary to moral and social life."[6] Compare this with Emerson: "To believe your own thought, to believe that what is true for you in your private heart is true for all men—that is genius." Emerson expresses what he calls the ground of his hope that man is one, that we are capable of achieving our commonness, by saying that "the deeper [the scholar] dives into his privatest, secretest presentiment, to his wonder he finds, this is the most acceptable, most public, and universally true."[7] Is this route to the universal compatible with what Dewey means by science and its method? This is evidently the most privileged route he envisions to the commonness of the human species, or at least to the reform of certain groupings of them and hence to the possibility of democracy.

I realize I have been shading these comparisons between Emerson and Dewey so as to emphasize a certain air of conflict in philosophy between the appeal to science and the appeal to ordinary language. This is where I came into philosophy. The earliest papers I still use were defenses of Austin's and Wittgenstein's appeals to the ordinary, papers that were attacked as irrational for apparently denying the findings of empirical science (i.e., of Noam Chomsky's new linguistics). Like most issues in philosophy, this one was not exactly settled; rather, each side continued to feel misunderstood, each took what it needed from the exchange, and each went its way. But the issue in various ways still concerns me, perhaps because I still want to understand the source of that philosophical hostility.

The philosophical appeal to the ordinary, to words we are given in common, is inherently taken in opposition to something about my words as they stand. Hence they are in opposition to those (typically philosophers) with whom I had hitherto taken myself to be in a state of intersubjectivity. This appeal presents proposals for what we say, which, requiring something like experimentation, are trials that inherently run the risk of exasperation. The appeal challenges our commonality in favor of a more genuine commonality (surely something that characterizes Dewey's philosophical mission), but in the name of no expertise, no standing adherence to logic or to science, to nothing beyond the genius that fits me for membership in the realm of ends.

William James characteristically philosophizes off of the language of the street, which he respects and wishes to preserve, or to satisfy by clarifying the desire it expresses. This mode of philosophizing seems to me quite uncharacteristic of Dewey. In Dewey's writing, the speech of others, whose ideas Dewey wishes to correct, or rather to replace, especially the speech of children, hardly appears—as though the world into which he is drawn to intervene suffers from a well-defined lack or benightedness. Contrast this with a memorable outburst from Emerson: "Every word they say chagrins us . . . and we know not where to begin to set them right."[8] Before Emerson can say what is repellent in the thoughts or noises of others, he has to discover or rediscover a language in which to say it. This turns out to require an inheritance of philosophy that gives back life to the words it has thought to own—a language in which the traditional vocabulary of philosophy is variously brought to earth, concepts such as "experience," "idea," "impression," "understanding," "reason," "universal," "necessity," or "condition." Emerson retains stretches of the vocabulary of philosophy but divests it of its old claims to mastery. This is why his writing is *difficult* in a way no other American philosopher's (save Thoreau's) has been, certainly not that of James or of Dewey. Are these different responses to language not philosophically fundamental? They seem so to me.

I suggested that I also rather cringe at the idea of thinking of Wittgenstein as a sort of pragmatist, or as having a significant pragmatist dimension to his thought. Hilary Putnam, who is more confident here than I, ends the middle of three lectures entitled *Pragmatism* identifying a central—perhaps, he says, the central—emphasis of pragmatism: its emphasis on the primacy of practice.[9]

I think we must agree that something like this emphasis is definitive for pragmatism. Then look at two passages from Wittgenstein that, I believe, are taken to suggest his affinity with pragmatism. There is, first, the always quoted passage from the *Investigations:* "If I have exhausted the grounds I have reached bedrock, and my spade is turned. Then I am inclined to say: 'This is simply what I do.' "[10] I shall not go over my own grounds for the view of this remark I have urged elsewhere, but merely repeat my conclusion, namely that this passage does not represent a call for the display of a practice at this crossroads. On the contrary, it expresses silence, the recognition that all invocable practices have been canvassed, thus preparing one, providing words, for suffering, awaiting, an inevitable crossroads in the act of teaching. The one who has reached bedrock here describes himself as "inclined to say" something, which at the same time implies that he finds the words that occur to him to be unsayable, empty, their time gone. Saul Kripke is the most prominent of those who understand that passage as equivalent to asserting a practice.

A second passage, or a pair of passages, this time from *On Certainty,*[11] have recently been taken to declare Wittgenstein's pragmatist leanings. At §422: "So I am trying to say something that sounds like pragmatism. Here I am being thwarted by a kind of *Weltanschauung.*" But isn't this to say that sounding like pragmatism is not welcome but burdensome to Wittgenstein? It thwarts his making himself sufficiently clear. (I think I know just how that feels.) The previous section reads: "I am in England.—Everything around me tells me so. . . .—But might I not be shaken if things such as I don't dream of at present were to happen?" This conjunction of sections sounds like a combination expressed at §89: "One would like to say: 'Everything speaks for, and nothing against, the earth's having existed long before.' . . . Yet might I not believe the contrary after all? But the question is: What would the practical effects of this belief be?—Perhaps someone says: 'That's not the point. A belief is what it is whether it has any practical effects or not.' One thinks: It is the same adjustment of the human mind anyway." It is fairly clear that Wittgenstein is dismissing, through interpreting the fantasy of, the one who thinks that practical effects are impertinent to what it is one believes, and indeed to whether one may seriously be said to believe something. At the same time, he is casting suspicion on the introduction of the concept of "believing the contrary."

Questioning the practical effects of a belief does sound like William James, for instance in this passage from "What Pragmatism Means": "The whole function of philosophy ought to be to find out what definite difference it will make to you and me, at definite instants of our life, if this world-formula or that world-formula be the true one."[12] But Wittgenstein's passage had better not be taken to encourage James' evident faith in practicality.

Wittgenstein's case about the earth's existence long before is one in which someone has been led to forget how specialized, even how *weak*, a consideration is in question in saying, in reasonably clear circumstances, "Everything speaks for and nothing speaks against." It is perhaps enough to voice the consideration when the issue is, say, a choice to buy rather than rent a house, under circumstances in which: we already accept that we must do one or the other (that is, the basic decision to move has already been made); the length of stay is not fixed, but the family is committed to at least three years; buying, especially with help available from an institution, will almost certainly save money in the long run; it is not that much more trouble; and so, obviously, on. "Obviously" implies that there is a notable lack of enthusiasm over either prospect. If it were a great house, and an amazing bargain, where the family can at once imagine friends happily visiting, then perhaps it is smitten, and would forget the mild balancing springs of advantages and disadvantages. In other circumstances, to give "everything for and nothing against" as a conclusive reason—say for a couple living together or just going away together for a weekend—would be discouraging. (I take it that *desiring* to be or to go together is not one among other reasons for doing either but is rather the condition for anything counting as a reason, for or against.) And if one is led (for some undetermined reason) to offer so weak and summary a support for so presumably massive a structure as the existence of the earth long before, one places the ensuing, forced invocations of the practical effects of a belief in a perfectly impotent position; they are mere words. (Compare what Wittgenstein writes in the *Philosophical Investigations*: "[A] hundred reasons present themselves, each drowning the voice of the others.")[13]

One moral to draw is that, as my *Claim of Reason* claims, throughout his *Investigations* Wittgenstein is in struggle with the threat of skepticism, as Emerson is (after the big essay on *Nature*). In contrast, neither James nor Dewey seems to take the threat of skepticism seriously. This is hasty. James' treatment of the "sick soul" intersects with something I mean to capture in the concept of skepticism. But on James' account, it does not seem imaginable that *everyone* might be subject to this condition. That is, James perceives the condition as of a particular temperament, not as something coincident with the human as such, as if, as with the skeptical threat that concerns me, it is the necessary consequence of the gift of speech. Or shall we, rather than drawing a moral, lay down definitions that distinguish skeptical pragmatists from nonskeptical pragmatists? To what end? Pragmatism seems designed to refuse to take skepticism seriously, as it refuses—in Dewey's, if not always in James' case—to take metaphysical distinctions seriously.

However, I do not wish either to draw or define lines, but here merely to state differences. I know, as I said, that each of the differences I have mentioned can be rejected or reduced in significance. What is important to me is what I find to be at stake in asserting the differences.

I end by noting, against the idea of pragmatism's attention to practice, Emerson's peroration to "Experience": "I have not found that much was gained by manipular attempts to realize the world of thought. . . . Patience and patience, we shall win at the last."[14] It is hard not to take this plea of Emerson's for suffering and for waiting as pretty flatly the negation of the primacy of practice. Yet things are not so simple. Patience, as in the more obvious case of Thoreau's visible withdrawal or disinvestment from his neighbors, can be exercised aggressively, as an agent of change. Without pursuing the decisive matter of how change is to come, I will let this apparent difference of practice and patience, action and passion we might say, project a difference in the audiences (that is, in the conceptions of audience) at work in the writing of Dewey and of Emerson.

Dewey seeks to address a situation of unintelligence, which I suppose is to say, one that negates whatever predicates of intelligence a philosopher holds dearest, hence a situation that variously manifests superstition, bigotry, gullibility, and incuriousness. In a similar vein Emerson discerns a scene of what he variously calls conformity, timidity, and shame, something he describes as secret melancholy (the condition Thoreau will more famously name quiet desperation), which he perceives to characterize the lives of "the mass of men." The connection between massive unintelligence and general despair is that both are barriers to the future, to the new day whose appearance both Emerson and Dewey, in their ways, would hasten. But the ways are as different as the accompanying ideas of the future; they amount to different ideas of thinking, or reason. I once characterized the difference between Dewey and Emerson by saying that Dewey wanted to get the Enlightenment to happen in America while Emerson was in the later business of addressing the costs of the way it has happened. And again, one may deny that the differences between Enlightenment and post-Enlightenment projects are decisive enough to dislodge the idea of Emerson as a pragmatist, or perhaps take pragmatism as, in James' term, mediating between the two.

To my mind, to understand Emerson as essentially the forerunner of pragmatism is perhaps to consider pragmatism as representing more effectively or rationally what Emerson had undertaken to bring to these shores. This is the latest in the sequence of repressions of Emerson's thought by the culture he helped to found, of what is distinctive in that thought. Such a repression has punctuated Emerson's reputation from the first moment he could be said to have acquired one. So my question becomes: What is lost if Emerson's voice is lost?

In its call for intelligent action, Dewey's writing is self-evidently and famously active. And famous problems with it are, first, that you do not know what in particular he wants you to do, and second, that you do not know whether it is rational to expect the mass of men and women to exercise intelligence in their politics any more than in their religions. You might say that Dewey's writing is a wager on democracy, a wager that is rational not because of the weight of evidence that his writing will prove effective, but because it is worthy of being listened to; because there is some reason to believe that it will be listened to; and because there is no other future worth wagering on and working to achieve.

Emerson's writing, too, is a wager, not exactly of itself as the necessary intellectual preparation for a better future, but rather of itself as a present step into that future, two by two. It cannot be entered alone. ("Two . . . abreast" is the attitude between neighbors that Robert Frost advises in "Mending Wall.") Emerson writes in "Self-Reliance": "But do your work, and I shall know you."[15] Your work now, in reading him, is the reading of his page, and allowing yourself to be changed by it. I have, accordingly, wished to place Emerson's writing in a tradition of perfectionist writing that extends in the West from Plato to Nietzsche, Ibsen, Kierkegaard, Wilde, Shaw, Heidegger, and Wittgenstein. Both Dewey and Emerson are necessary for what each of them thinks of as democracy. To repress Emerson's difference is to deny that America is as transcendentalist as it is pragmatist, that it is in struggle with itself, at a level not articulated by what we understand as the political. But what Dewey calls for, other disciplines can do as well, maybe better, than philosophy. What Emerson calls for is something we do not want to hear, something about the necessity of patience or suffering in allowing ourselves to change. What discipline will call for this if philosophy does not?

Notes

1 This essay, dating from 1957, is the earliest essay of mine that I still use (Stanley Cavell, *Must We Mean What We Say* [New York: Scribner, 1957], p. 36, n. 10).

2 Ralph Waldo Emerson, "Experience," in *Essays and Lectures* (New York: Library of America, 1983), p. 473; Sigmund Freud, "Mourning and Melancholia," *Collected Papers* (New York: Basic Books, 1959), vol. 4, 152–54.

3 John Dewey, *Experience and Education,* in *The Later Works,* ed. Jo Ann Boydston (Carbondale: Southern Illinois University, 1984), vol. 13, p. 59.

4 Ludwig Wittgenstein, *Philosophical Investigations,* trans. G. E. M. Anscombe (New York: Macmillan, 1953), sec. 570.

5 Emerson, "Self Reliance," in *Essays and Lectures,* p. 259.

6 John Dewey, "The Development of American Pragmatism," in *Philosophy and Civilization* (New York: Capricorn Books, 1963), pp. 34–35.

7 Emerson, "The American Scholar," in *Essays and Lectures,* p. 64.

8 Emerson, "Self Reliance," p. 264.

9 Hilary Putnam, *Pragmatism: An Open Question* (Cambridge: Basil Blackwell, 1995).

10 Wittgenstein, *Philosophical Investigations,* sec. 217.

11 Ludwig Wittgenstein, *On Certainty,* ed. G. E. M. Anscombe and G. H. von Wright, trans. Denis Paul and G. E. M. Anscombe (New York: Harper & Row, 1972).

12 William James, "What Pragmatism Means," in *Essays in Pragmatism,* ed. Alburey Castell (New York: Hafner Publishing Company, 1948), p. 141. Earlier, James emphasized the practical rather than definite difference.

13 Wittgenstein, *Philosophical Investigations,* sec. 478.

14 Emerson, "Experience," p. 492.

15 Robert Frost, "Mending Wall," in *The Poetry of Robert Frost,* ed. Edward Connery Lathem (New York: Holt, Rinehart and Winston, 1969), p. 33; Emerson, "Self Reliance," p. 264.

PRAGMATISM
AND THE
REMAKING OF
SOCIAL THOUGHT

Pragmatism: An Old Name for Some New Ways of Thinking?

JAMES T. KLOPPENBERG

William James was stuck. Facing the publication of *Pragmatism* in 1907, he had to decide whether to stress the novelty of his philosophy or its continuity with earlier ideas. James joked that pragmatism would launch "something quite like the protestant reformation" and predicted that it would be "the philosophy of the future." Yet he also believed that he and his fellow pragmatists were building on a foundation laid by philosophers from Socrates to the British empiricists. To soften the blow he was about to deliver, James dedicated *Pragmatism* to the memory of the venerated John Stuart Mill and added the subtitle *A New Name for Some Old Ways of Thinking,* hoping that such a pedigree might restrain those inclined to denounce his progeny. As my inversion of James's subtitle suggests, a historian seeking to analyze and explain the current revival of pragmatism confronts the same question James faced: Have contemporary pragmatists resurrected the ideas of earlier thinkers or rejected everything but the name?[1]

The return of pragmatism is something of a surprise. When David A. Hollinger recounted the career of pragmatism in the *Journal of American History* in 1980, he noted that pragmatism had all but vanished from American historiography during the previous three decades. In 1950, Hollinger recalled, Henry Steele Commager had proclaimed pragmatism "almost the official philosophy of America"; by 1980, in Hollinger's judgment, commentators on American culture had learned to get along just fine without it. "If pragmatism has a future," Hollinger concluded, "it will probably look very different from its past, and the two may not even share a name." Yet pragmatism today is not only alive and well, it is ubiquitous.[2] References to pragmatism occur with dizzying frequency from philosophy to social science, from the study of literature to that of ethnicity, from feminism to legal theory. As Hollinger predicted, much of this pragmatism looks very different from the original version. Some postmodernists are attracted to pragmatism because it offers a devastating critique of all philosophical foundations and justifies a wide-ranging linguistic skepticism against all claims of objectivity, consensus, and truth. So conceived, as a species of postmodernism rather than as an updated version of the quest for truth that James identified with Socrates and Mill, pragmatism has indeed become an old name for new ways of thinking.

In this essay I advance three arguments: First, the early pragmatists emphasized "experience," whereas some contemporary philosophers and critics who have taken "the linguistic turn" are uneasy with that concept. Second, the early pragmatists believed their philosophical ideas had particular ethical and political consequences, whereas some contemporary thinkers who call themselves pragmatists consider it merely a method of analysis. Third, the current controversy about pragmatism matters profoundly to historians. At stake is not merely the historical meaning of early twentieth-century pragmatism, important as that issue is for intellectual history. Looming even larger for historians in contemporary debates about pragmatism are implicit questions about our practice of historical scholarship. Two rival camps are struggling over the legacy of pragmatism. Early twentieth-century pragmatists envisioned a modernist discourse of democratic deliberation in which communities of inquiry tested hypotheses in order to solve problems; such contemporary pragmatists as Richard J. Bernstein and Hilary Putnam sustain that tradition. Other contemporaries such as Richard Rorty and Stanley Fish present pragmatism as a postmodernist discourse of critical commentary that denies that we can escape the conventions and contingencies of language in order to connect with a world of experience outside texts, let alone solve problems in that world. Connecting with experience is precisely what we historians attempt to do. These controversies over pragmatism old and new are thus tied directly to the legitimacy of our practice in studying the past and to the claims of our community of inquiry about the significance of the past for the present.

Experience and Language

The early pragmatists sought to reorient philosophy away from interminable and fruitless debates by insisting that ideas should be tested in practice. As part of their overall commitment to problem solving, their conception of experience linked the philosophies of William James and John Dewey, the pragmatists who most powerfully influenced American culture during the first half of the twentieth century.[3] What did James and

Dewey mean by experience? Both rejected the dualisms—the separation of the mind from the body, and of the subject from the object—that had divided idealists from empiricists since René Descartes and John Locke. They were equally scornful of nineteenth-century idealists' infatuation with introspection and positivists' reduction of all philosophical questions to matter and motion. Instead they preferred other metaphors such as "field" or "stream" or "circuit" to suggest the continuity and meaningfulness of consciousness that had eluded both empiricists and rationalists; their "radical empiricism" rested on their revised concept of consciousness. Immediate experience as James and Dewey conceived of it is always relational (it never exists in the abstract or in isolation from a world containing both other persons and concrete realities, as did Descartes' rationalist *cogito*), creative (it never merely registers sense data passively, as did Locke's empiricist tabula rasa), and imbued with historically specific cultural values (it is never "human" or universal, but always personal and particular). Pragmatists distrusted all forms of foundationalism, all attempts to establish philosophy on unchanging a priori postulates. Rather than grounding values in the bedrock of timeless absolutes, they urged us to evaluate all of our beliefs—philosophical, scientific, religious, ethical, and political—before the test they considered the most demanding of all: our experience as social and historical beings.[4]

The early pragmatists' conception of testing the truth of ideas in experience ignited a fire storm of controversy that continues to rage. Philosophers such as Bertrand Russell, George Santayana, Josiah Royce, and Arthur Lovejoy immediately targeted James. Cultural critics such as Randolphe Bourne, Van Wyck Brooks, and Lewis Mumford and partisans of natural law such as (the erstwhile pragmatist) Walter Lippmann and Mortimer Adler later went after Dewey, as did Marxists such as Theodor Adorno and Max Horkheimer. All these critics charged pragmatists with elevating expedient, novel, narrowly individualistic, instrumental, and technocratic considerations above truth and goodness as revealed by philosophy, art, or theology.[5]

Much as such criticism stung, it sharpened James' and Dewey's formulations of their ideas. Some of their best writing, notably James' *The Meaning of Truth* (1909) and Dewey's *Experience and Nature* (1925), came in response to their critics. Their clarifications reveal why some contemporary postmodernists' enthusiasm and some contemporary traditionalists' scorn are misdirected at James and Dewey. In *Pragmatism* James had tried to head off some misunderstandings in advance. Looking back at his argument, it is difficult to see how anyone could accuse him of identifying truth with whatever it is convenient to believe. He specified "our duty to agree with reality" and expressed exasperation at his critics' "favorite formula for describing" pragmatists—"persons who think that by saying whatever you find it pleasant to say and calling it truth you fulfil every pragmatistic requirement." To the contrary, James protested: "Pent in, as the pragmatist more than anyone else sees himself to be, between the whole body of funded truths squeezed from the past and the coercions of the world of sense about him, who so well as he feels the immense pressure of objective control under which our minds perform their operations?"[6]

When his critics continued to accuse him of counseling his readers to believe any fiction they might find expedient, James responded by writing *The Meaning of Truth*. There he specified the circumstances in which one might invoke the pragmatic test of truth and clarified the conditions necessary for verifying any proposition pragmatically. First, and fundamentally, it must correspond to what is known from experience about the natural world. The following apparently unambiguous sentence has escaped the attention of James's critics—and some of his contemporary champions: "The notion of a reality independent of . . . us, taken from ordinary social experience, lies at the base of the pragmatist definition of truth." Calling himself an "epistemological realist," James explained that he simply took for granted the existence of that independent reality and did not consider its independent existence philosophically interesting or important. Second, to be judged pragmatically true, a proposition must be consistent with the individual's stock of existing beliefs, beliefs that had withstood the severe test of experience. That, James felt sure, would rule out simpleminded wishful thinking. Finally, a statement may be considered pragmatically true *if* it fulfills those two conditions and yields satisfaction. Religious faith represented to James a perfect illustration of the appropriate terrain for testing truth claims pragmatically: in the absence of irrefutable evidence, James judged relevant the consequences of faith for believers.[7] Dewey, whose prodding had helped spur James to refine his position, likewise argued throughout his long career that we should conceive of all our knowledge as hypotheses to be tested in experience.

At the core of James' and Dewey's pragmatism was experience conceived, not as introspection, but as the intersection of the conscious self with the world. They conceived of knowing subjects as embodiments of reason, emotion, and values and they emphasized the inadequacy of philosophers' attempts to freeze, split apart, and compartmentalize the dynamic continuities and multiple dimensions of life as we live it. They conceived of individuals as always enmeshed in social conditions, yet selecting what to attend to from the multiplicity of conscious experience, and making history by making choices. They conceived of experience as intrinsically and irreducibly meaningful, and they insisted that its meanings were not predetermined or deducible from any all-encompassing pattern. They argued that meanings emerge as cultures test their values in practice and that we encounter expressions of those meanings in the historical record.

Language was thus crucial for understanding the experience of others, but for James and Dewey language was only one important part of a richer, broader range that included interpersonal, aesthetic, spiritual, religious, and other prelinguistic or nonlinguistic forms of experience. Moreover, they realized that language not only feeds the imagination but also places constraints on understanding by specifying a particular range of meanings. In *Pragmatism,* James wrote, "All truth thus gets verbally built out, stored up, and made available for everyone. Hence, we must *talk* consistently, just as we must *think* consistently." Although James appreciated what is now characterized as the arbitrariness of signifiers, he drew the following noteworthy conclusion: "Names are arbitrary, but once understood they must be kept to. We mustn't now call Abel 'Cain' or Cain 'Abel.' If we do, we ungear ourselves from the whole book of Genesis, and from all its connexions with the universe of speech and fact down to the present time." We cannot test every proposition ourselves or enter the immediate experience of others. Yet we nevertheless have access to verifiable historical knowledge, even if only indirectly and through language. "*As true as past time itself was,* so true was Julius Caesar, so true were antediluvian monsters, all in their proper dates and settings. That past time itself was, is guaranteed by its coherence with everything that's present. True as the present *is* the past *was* also."[8] When dealing with verifiable data, whether about Caesars or about ceratopsians, we place each datum in the web of evidence we humans have been spinning for centuries. Even when considering unverifiable narratives such as Genesis, we risk losing the coherence that makes communication possible unless we preserve meanings within our web of cultural memory.

Dewey shared that appreciation of the importance of symbols and the indispensability of common understandings. "All discourse, oral or written," he conceded in *Experience and Nature,* "says things that surprise the one that says them." But that makes communication difficult, not impossible. Conversation understood as a quest for mutual understanding, with all its imprecision, provides the appropriate model. In *The Public and Its Problems* (1927) he wrote of "*communication* as a prerequisite" to undertaking social action. Through language "the results of conjoint experience are considered and transmitted. Events cannot be passed from one to another, but meanings may be shared by means of signs"; eventually such sharing converts "a conjoining activity into a community of interest and endeavor." Dewey acknowledged the challenge of such communication: "mutual interest in shared meanings" does not emerge "all at once or completely." Like James, however, Dewey emphasized that such communication can yield provisional understandings of the past, its meanings for the present, and its role in the formulation of shared social aspirations. For Dewey, dialogue between individuals in community, with its "direct give and take," provided the model for such communication: "the winged words of conversation in immediate intercourse have a vital import lacking in the fixed and frozen words of written speech."[9]

Dewey realized that the concept of experience caused difficulties for many analytic philosophers, who defined philosophy as the study of language and logic, but despite their criticism, he clung to it to the end of his life. Dewey toyed with exchanging the word "experience" for "culture" as late as 1951, but in the end he refused: "we need a cautionary and directive word, like experience, to remind us that the world which is lived, suffered and enjoyed as well as logically thought of, has the last word in all human inquiries and surmises."[10] In short, the pragmatic sensibility of James and Dewey was a profoundly historical sensibility.

Listing some of the thinkers who aligned themselves with James and Dewey suggests their enormous impact. Sociologists such as George Herbert Mead, legal theorists such as Oliver Wendell Holmes, Jr., and Louis D. Brandeis, economists such as Richard T. Ely, political theorists such as Herbert Croly, theologians such as Walter Rauschenbusch and Reinhold Niebuhr, founders of the National Association for the Advancement of Colored People such as W. E. B. Du Bois and William English Walling, and feminists such as Jane Addams and Jessie Taft all derived from pragmatism a conception of experience and a way of thinking about abstract and concrete problems that oriented them to historical analysis and away from inherited dogmas. Those who looked to philosophy and social science for solid, permanent principles found pragmatism disappointing and unattractive. But many of those who shared the belief of James and Dewey that the shift from absolutes to the test of experience might encourage independent thinking and democratic decision making endorsed pragmatism because it unsettled traditional ways of thinking without sinking into the morass of subjectivism that swallowed some turn-of-the-century rebels, such as Friedrich Nietzsche. The steadying lifeline of experience prevented pragmatists from sliding into fantasy, cynicism, or self-indulgence.

As the ripples pragmatism sent across American thought extended wider and wider during the early twentieth century, they met—and eventually were submerged by—more powerful waves coming from other directions. Among the most important of these was enthusiasm for the certainty widely attributed to the natural sciences, which stood in sharp contrast to the pragmatists' forthright admission of uncertainty. Behaviorists in psychology, sociology, and political science adopted Dewey's enthusiasm for testing hypotheses but jettisoned his concern with the qualitative dimensions of experience and inquiry in the human sciences.[11]

Philosophers turned increasingly toward the models provided by mathematics and physical science, a trend already underway before European émigrés began arriving in the United States in the 1930s. The émigrés' quest for precision and their impatience with pragmatism combined to transform American philosophy departments by elevating the study of language and logic and marginalizing James' and Dewey's concerns with epistemology, ethics, and political philosophy. A discipline scurrying to master the logical positivism of Rudolf Carnap, which sought to rid philosophy of all questions that could not be answered through scientific verification, had little interest in the early pragmatists' attachment to immediate experience and their democratic reformist sensibilities. Dewey had described the writings that launched the analytic philosophy movement, which sought to reduce philosophy to propositional logic, as "an affront to the common-sense world of action, appreciation, and affection." The work of the British philosophers Bertrand Russell and G. E. Moore, Dewey wrote, threatened to "land philosophy in a formalism like unto scholasticism." James had urged Russell to "say good-bye to mathematical logic if you wish to preserve your relations with concrete realities!" But many midcentury American philosophers preferred Carnap and Russell to "common sense" and "concrete realities"; they shared Russell's longstanding contempt for pragmatism. The new breed of analytic philosophers shunned history, shifted toward technical discourse, and judged meaningless all propositions that could not be verified by scientific procedures. James wrote about religious experience and Dewey about aesthetics, ethics, and politics in the hope of helping philosophy escape such a narrowly restricted role.[12]

Developments within the pragmatist camp also made it increasingly vulnerable to such attacks. In the 1930s and 1940s some champions of pragmatism tried to popularize the ideas of James and Dewey by simplifying them for mass consumption. Whereas James and Dewey had urged their readers to think critically about their own experience and to take responsibility for shaping their culture, such writers as Will Durant, Irwin

Edman, Horace Kallen, Max Otto, Harry Overstreet, John Herman Randall, and Thomas Vernor Smith made available versions of pragmatism that simply endorsed the rough-and-ready democratic sentiments of most middle-class Americans. Such efforts did little to bolster the prestige of pragmatism among professional philosophers or other American intellectuals aspiring to scientific precision rather than democratic deliberation.[13]

After Dewey died in 1952, his ideas faded quickly into the background. Even though one of the most prominent thinkers of the post–World War II period, Reinhold Niebuhr, shared many of Dewey's, and especially James', ideas, his critique of Dewey's optimism helped discredit pragmatism as too sunny minded for serious intellectuals. As Richard Rorty has put it, pragmatism was crushed between "the upper and the nether millstones": a revived interest in theology or existentialism for some, the "hard-edged empiricism" of Carnap for others. For reasons reflecting changes within philosophy and in the broader culture, then, American intellectuals during the 1950s and 1960s either forgot about pragmatism or, as Hollinger put it, learned to get along without it. That is no longer true. Explaining the resurgence of pragmatism requires sketching the complex cultural changes that cleared the ground and made possible its return.[14]

First the claims to objectivity of the natural sciences, which had intimidated humanists while they inspired philosophers and social scientists, were rocked by the historicist analysis of Thomas Kuhn, whose significance in this transformation is difficult to overestimate. Many of the schemes for social engineering hatched by enthusiasts for science led to results that ranged from disappointing (the War on Poverty) to disastrous (the war in Vietnam), as both the findings of researchers and their application to social problems were shown to be grounded in questionable assumptions and, despite the scientists' notion of value neutrality, susceptible to appropriation for ideological purposes.[15] Then social scientists began to admit what pragmatists and such practitioners of the *Geisteswissenschaften* (human sciences) as Wilhelm Dilthey had known since the nineteenth century: Because human experience is meaningful, understanding not only expression but also behavior requires interpreting the complex and shifting systems of symbols through which individuals encounter the world and with which they try to cope with it. Meanings and intentions change over time and across cultures; as that realization spread, hopes of finding a universal logic or a general science of social organization faded. In their place emerged hermeneutics, which relies on methods of interpretation to achieve understanding of historical experience and forgoes efforts to generate rules of transhistorical human behavior.

Marching behind the banner of hermeneutics came an influential band of scholars who challenged the ideal of scientific objectivity in the human sciences: Peter Winch, Clifford Geertz, Charles Taylor, Anthony Giddens, Paul Ricoeur, Michel Foucault, Jacques Derrida, Hans-Georg Gadamer, and Jürgen Habermas—a new litany of saints proclaiming variations on a revolutionary gospel of interpretation. They spoke a different language than did those natural scientists, philosophers, and social scientists who sought to escape the clutter of history. Instead of timeless principles and truth, they referred to revolutionary paradigm shifts, incommensurable forms of life, the complexities of thick description, competing communities of discourse, archaeologies of knowledge, the universal undecidability of texts, the inescapability of prejudices, and the colonization of life worlds by an omnivorous technostructure.[16]

Although among these thinkers only Habermas explicitly placed himself within the pragmatic tradition, Americans familiar with James and Dewey noted the similarities between recent historicist critiques of the sciences and social sciences and those of the early pragmatists. As the work of these thinkers, many of whom were often grouped together (unhelpfully and even misleadingly) under the rubric "postmodernist," became increasingly influential, many scholars began to move away from the model of the natural sciences and toward forms of analysis more congenial to hermeneutics and history, most notably toward pragmatism.[17]

Despite the undeniable importance of those broad changes in American thought, the resurgence of pragmatism is largely due to the remarkable work done by the Trojan horse of analytic philosophy, Richard Rorty. Rorty's historicism has had such explosive force because he attacked the citadel of philosophy from within. Troubling as was his insistence that philosophy could never attain the scientific status analytic philosophers yearned for, even more unnerving was Rorty's equally blunt judgment that the grail of objective knowledge would likewise continue to elude the natural sciences and the social sciences. Rorty first established his credentials with papers discussing standard topics in the analytic tradition. But in his introduction to *The Linguistic Turn* (1967), he suggested that the conflicts within analytic philosophy (between J. L. Austin's ordinary-language philosophy and Carnap's logical positivism, for example) were so fundamental that they could not be resolved, thus subtly challenging the idea of progress in problem solving that analytic philosophers took for granted.[18]

Over the next decade Rorty broadened his focus and sharpened his critique. Echoing arguments made by James and Dewey but presenting them in the discourse of analytic philosophy, he insisted in *Philosophy and* the Mirror of Nature (1979) that problems such as mind-body dualism, the correspondence theory of truth, theories of knowledge and theories of language, and ultimately the entire conception of a systematic philosophy devoted to finding foundations for objective knowledge all rested on misconceptions. He urged his fellow philosophers to move "from epistemology to hermeneutics" and to practice "philosophy without mirrors," embracing interpretation and surrendering the vain hope that their writings might accurately reflect the world as it really is. Systematic philosophers, such as John Locke, Immanuel Kant, and Rudolf Carnap, who sought a science of knowledge that would disclose objective truth, should give way to "edifying philosophers," such as James and Dewey, who would contribute to the "conversation of the West" without promising results philosophy would never be able to deliver. Although others had begun to offer variations on this theme of "historicist undoing," to use Ian Hacking's phrase for it, Rorty's assault seemed especially dramatic because it held out no alternative solutions.[19]

In *Consequences of Pragmatism* (1982), Rorty defended his heretical historicism. We must admit that "there is nothing deep down inside us except what we have put there ourselves"; our most cherished standards and practices are merely conventions. Science, Rorty concluded with the provocative bluntness that has become his trademark, is only "one genre of literature"; all efforts to find solid, unchanging knowledge are futile.[20] Rorty himself realized that there was little in these claims that was completely new. But because enthusiasm for science had overshadowed the historicism of earlier pragmatists, and because Anglo-American philosophers in particular had marched down a road marked "truth" only to find James and Dewey waiting there for them, Rorty's revival of pragmatism seemed revolutionary.

Against critics who assailed him as a relativist, Rorty responded that the notion of relativism itself becomes incoherent when we appreciate the contingent status of all our knowledge. From his perspective, there is nothing for "truth" to be relative to except our tradition, our purposes, and our linguistic conventions. When we have come to that realization, a calm acceptance of our condition becomes possible. While pragmatism cannot offer objectivity, neither does it threaten the survival of civilization. Revolutionary as his message was, Rorty's mood was downright upbeat. He proclaimed pragmatism "the chief glory of our country's intellectual tradition" and noted that James and Dewey, although asking us to surrender "the neurotic Cartesian quest for certainty," nevertheless wrote, as Nietzsche and Heidegger did not, "in a spirit of social hope."[21]

Surprisingly, given the ardent opposition to dualism that Rorty shares with James and Dewey, on the concept of experience he has substituted a new dichotomy for those James and Dewey attacked. Demonstrating the distance between his view and theirs has become considerably easier thanks to the appearance of Rorty's essay "Dewey between Hegel and Darwin" (1994). There Rorty acknowledges the difference between the historical Dewey and his "hypothetical Dewey," a philosopher who would have been "a pragmatist without being a radical empiricist," without, in other words, Dewey's crucial commitment to experience. The central distinction, Rorty now concedes, lies in Dewey's (and James') continuing emphasis on experience, which Rorty finds quaint but unhelpful. He ties it to their purported belief in "panpsychism," a word for the supposed ability of minds to commune with other minds that Rorty has resurrected from the lexicon of James' critics to poke fun at those who consider experience important. According to Rorty, contemporary philosophers "tend to talk about *sentences* a lot but to say very little about ideas or experiences." James' and Dewey's talk about the relation between ideas and experiences, in Rorty's judgment, "runs together sentences with experiences—linguistic entities with introspective entities." They "should have dropped the term *experience* rather than redefined it." "My alternative Dewey," he concludes wistfully, "would have said, we can construe 'thinking' as simply the use of sentences."[22] Seeing the linguistic turn as a step forward rather than a dead end, Rorty dogmatically refuses to accept any philosophy in which something other than language, namely, experience—understood not as introspection but as the intersection between the conscious self and the world—plays an important part. As Rorty now admits, James and Dewey had a very different conception of philosophy, and that difference continues to manifest itself in the contrasting versions of pragmatism in contemporary scholarship. Given historians' strong commitments to referentiality in writing history, to the possibility of connecting the arguments we construct to the lives we write about, and to testing those arguments within our scholarly community, the early pragmatists' emphasis on experience will remain for historians an attractive alternative to Rorty's narrow interest in sentences.

Rorty's move away from James' and Dewey's view of experience and toward a new cultural ideal in which poets and novelists would replace philosophers first became clear in his elegant, widely read *Contingency, Irony, and Solidarity* (1989). His shift has coincided with the new tendency of some literary critics to characterize themselves as pragmatists. Just as dissatisfaction with prevailing orthodoxies has sparked novel approaches in philosophy and the social sciences, so many students of literature have deserted the New Criticism and structuralism and turned toward pragmatism. Reversing the common tendency, stemming from the writings of Randolph Bourne and Van Wyck Brooks and reaching fruition in Lewis Mumford's *The Golden Day* (1925), to contrast the pragmatists' supposedly arid fetish with technique with the transcendentalists' celebration of imagination, some critics now invoke a refashioned pragmatism in their constructions of a rich, home-grown literary heritage. For example, Richard Poirier argues in *Poetry and Pragmatism* (1992) for a continuous tradition of "linguistic skepticism" running from Ralph Waldo Emerson through William James to the modernist poets Robert Frost, Gertrude Stein, Wallace Stevens, and T. S. Eliot. Those poets share, according to Poirier, "a liberating and creative suspicion as to the dependability of words and syntax, especially as it relates to matters of belief."[23]

Poirier enlists James to provide an American alternative to varieties of poststructuralism imported from France and fashionable among contemporary critics. He quotes a phrase from James' *The Principles of Psychology* on "the re-instatement of the vague to its proper place in our mental life"—a phrase consistent with James' portrait of the depth and richness of immediate experience—then draws an etymological line from "vague" to "extravagance" and then to "superfluity." This tenuous link prompts him to assert that for James, as for Emerson, thinking involves punning, so that "gains and losses of meaning are in a continuous and generative interaction." Poirier compares the writings of Emerson and James with those of Frost, Stein, Stevens, and Eliot, whom they resemble in their use of metaphor and their "allusiveness and elusiveness of phrasing." Poirier characterizes James' language as "no less 'superfluous'" than the language of modernist poets, "subject to the same degree of metaphorical proliferation, slippage, and excess." James' language slides "out of bounds, toward the margin, until it becomes loose and vague." Although James conceded the limits imposed on clarity by the ineffable in experience and the unstable in language, as his classic *The Varieties of Religious Experience* makes abundantly clear, in his writings he sought to move beyond the vague, rather than to revel in it.[24]

James sharpened his thinking against the hard edges of the world he encountered in experience, and his own writing reflected his preoccupation with clarity and precision. In a letter to his former student Gertrude Stein, written shortly before his death, James explained why he had not yet finished reading a novel she had sent him: "As a rule reading fiction is as hard for me as trying to hit a target by hurling feathers at it. I need *resistance* to cerebrate!"[25] James' pragmatism also reflects his awareness of the resistance to vagueness offered by the world beyond his own fertile imagination. In the absence of any "resistance" in "external reality," writing can become an exercise in creativity—or an excuse for unrestrained self-indulgence. James also insisted on respecting the conventional meanings of words lest we become "ungeared" from our cultural tradition and unable to communicate with each other. When critics align his pragmatism with a "linguistic skepticism" that encourages creative (mis)readings by "strong poets"—critic Harold Bloom's description of critics who interpret texts unconstrained by conventional understandings—they depart from James' vision.

Two of the most prominent late-twentieth-century pragmatists, Richard J. Bernstein and Hilary Putnam, have challenged versions of pragmatism, including Rorty's and Poirier's, that emphasize language and dismiss the concept of experience. Their work, less known outside philosophy than Rorty's, is of particular interest to historians. For three decades, since the appearance of his first book, *John Dewey* (1966), Bernstein has worked to forge links between recent continental European philosophy and the American tradition of pragmatism. In *Praxis and Action* (1971), he traced the pragmatist philosophy of activity to its roots in Aristotle's philosophy and contrasted the promise of that orientation with the danger that analytic philosophy might sink into scholasticism under the weight of "its own demand for ever-increasing technical mastery." Dewey, by contrast, was alert to "the moral and social consequences" of his ideas, which demanded a community of inquiry devoted to the "shared values of openness and fairness." From the beginning, Bernstein's pragmatism was grounded in a Deweyan conception of experience and its consequences for social organization: "it is only by mutual criticism that we can advance our knowledge and reconstruction of human experience."[26]

The twin pillars of Bernstein's pragmatism have been a community of inquiry and social action. In *The Restructuring of Social and Political Theory* (1976), Bernstein exposed the reductionism of mainstream social science and looked for alternatives in hermeneutics, phenomenology, and Habermas' critical theory. In *Beyond Objectivism and Relativism* (1983), he identified the "Cartesian anxiety" that had dominated and debilitated modern Western thought: "*Either* there is some support for our being, a fixed foundation for our knowledge, *or* we cannot escape the forces of darkness that envelop us with madness, with intellectual and moral chaos." As an alternative Bernstein invoked the ideas of Hans-Georg Gadamer, Hannah Arendt, Habermas, and Rorty, arguing that these thinkers pointed toward "the central themes of dialogue, conversation, undistorted communication, [and] communal judgment" that become possible "when individuals confront each other as equals and participants." Bernstein advanced a characteristically Deweyan conclusion on the consequences of these ideas: we must aim "toward the goal of cultivating the types of dialogical communities" in which practical judgment and practical discourse "become concretely embodied in our everyday practices," whether those practices involve organizing a neighborhood to build a playground or organizing a group of students to investigate a historical controversy and test alternative interpretations against the available evidence. Pragmatism, for Bernstein, originates in reflection on experience and culminates in altered experience.[27]

Putnam established himself by contributing to debates in mathematical logic and philosophy of mind, but like Rorty he has become increasingly disenchanted during the last two decades with much of what passes for professional philosophy in the United States. Without denying the importance of logic, formal studies, or semantics, Putnam has nevertheless described such work as "peripheral" and a reflection of the "scientistic character of logical positivism" that likewise infects much analytic philosophy. "Contemporary analytic metaphysics," he writes acidly, "has no connection with anything but the 'intuitions' of a handful of philosophers." He is equally scornful of the nihilism he sees in Derrida's deconstruction. "Analytic philosophers basically see philosophy as a science, only less developed, vaguer and newer, while Derrida basically sees philosophy as literature, as art. I don't think either is correct." Putnam interprets Rorty's occasional expressions of enthusiasm for Derrida as the lingering effects of Rorty's disappointment with the failure of analytic philosophy to deliver the certainty it promised.[28]

In *Realism with a Human Face* (1990), Putnam sought to clarify his differences from Rorty by listing five principles that he—along with the early pragmatists—endorses, but that he expected Rorty to reject. First, our standards of warranted assertibility are historical; second, they reflect our interests and values; and third, they are always subject to reform, as are all our standards. Rorty accepted those but challenged Putnam's two other principles: first, that "in ordinary circumstances, there is usually a fact of the matter as to whether the statements people make are warranted or not"; and second, "whether a statement is warranted or not is independent of whether the majority of one's cultural peers would *say* it is warranted or unwarranted." From Rorty's perspective, warrant is a sociological question, so we should evade pointless debates about relativism by moving "everything over from epistemology and metaphysics to cultural politics, from claims to knowledge and appeals to self-evidence to suggestions about what we should try." This way of framing the issue illustrates Rorty's characteristic style of argument, which he candidly describes as trying to make his opponent look bad. When Rorty traces this disagreement to Putnam's purported "appeals to self-evidence," he does just that: Putnam's formulation, however, does not depend on self-evidence any more than James' or Dewey's ideas of experience depended on "introspection"; it depends instead on evidence derived from experience.[29]

Their second principal difference, Rorty points out, stems from Putnam's "dislike of, and my enthusiasm for, a picture of human beings as just complicated animals." Putnam has argued that "one of our fundamental self-conceptualizations" as humans "is that we are *thinkers,* and that *as* thinkers we are committed to there being *some* kind of truth." In Putnam's words, "that means that there is no eliminating the normative," and Rorty is correct to emphasize the gulf dividing him from Putnam on this issue. Putnam concedes the historicist point that our ways of using language change, but he insists that even so, "some of our sentences *are* true, and—in spite of Rorty's objections to saying that things 'make' sentences true—the truth of 'I had cereal for breakfast this morning' *does* depend on what happened this morning."[30]

This conclusion, which many historians will find congenial, depends finally on Putnam's Jamesian conception of what it is to be human and his conviction, which he has reiterated again and again during the last fifteen years, that we should characterize the mind as "neither a material nor an immaterial organ but a system of capacities," which returns us to the early pragmatists' theory of voluntary action. In two essays written with Ruth Anna Putnam, Putnam stresses the "continuing interactive nature of experience" as Dewey conceived of it. Thinking involves relating our choices and our actions to their consequences, which requires reflecting not merely on our words but on the experienced effects of our practical activity. "We formulate ends-in-view on the basis of experience," they conclude, "and we appraise these on the basis of additional experience." For a pragmatist, to be engaged in that practice is "to be committed to the existence of truth. Democracy is a social condition of such practice, and therein lies its justification."[31]

For Putnam, as for Bernstein, all inquiry presupposes values such as mutual understanding and cooperation, which in turn require free and open exchanges of ideas among equals who are committed to the value of the practice. All of these are deeply, irreducibly normative notions, and they require a conception of human thinking and agency different from Rorty's view. At the conclusion of *Reason, Truth, and History* (1981), Putnam stated this crucial argument clearly and forcefully: "The notion of truth itself depends for its content on our standards of rational acceptability, and these in turn rest on and presuppose our values."[32]

Rorty's dualisms cannot accommodate the early pragmatists' conception of artistic or religious experience. Rorty shares Dewey's conception of the liberating social value of art, which engages the imagination by destabilizing the established order and suggesting imagined alternatives. But for Dewey, as for James, aesthetic and religious experiences of the sort Dewey characterized as "consummatory" derive their explosive power from qualities that can render them finally inexpressible in language. Rorty admits the importance of such fulfilling experiences—for him they come from art, literature, or the wild orchids that have fascinated him since his childhood—but he denies that such private enjoyments have anything to do with philosophy.[33] James and Dewey disagreed, and the disagreement has important implications.

Dewey's aesthetics differed from the abstract and formal theories of analytic philosophers and New Critics. He emphasized aesthetic *experience* rather than the *objects* of art. He deplored the compartmentalization that cuts art off from the rest of existence, and he denied the authority of elites to define and control what passes for art. As Richard Shusterman argues in *Pragmatist Aesthetics* (1992), Dewey opposed the idea that all artistic experience requires interpretation by trained professionals. Such linguistic universalism, which Shusterman accurately describes as "the deepest dogma of the linguistic turn in both analytic and continental philosophy," he judges "neither self-evident nor immune to challenge." Resurrecting the ideas of James and Dewey, Shusterman insists that pragmatism "more radically recognizes uninterpreted reality, experience, and understandings as already perspectival, prejudiced, and corrigible—in short, as non-foundationally given." He recommends hermeneutics for use only in particular circumstances. Shusterman insists that understanding does not always "require linguistic articulation; a proper reaction, a shudder or a tingle, may be enough to indicate that one has understood. Some of the things we experience and understand"—notably aesthetic and somatic experiences—"are never captured in language."[34]

Rorty, locked inside the tight boundaries of textualism, appreciates such nondiscursive experience but denies it any philosophical significance. Dewey, by contrast, wrote that "a universe of experience is a precondition of a universe of discourse. Without its controlling presence, there is no way to determine the relevancy, weight, or coherence of any designated distinction or relation. The universe of experience surrounds and regulates the universe of discourse but never appears as such within the latter."[35] Linguistic pragmatists such as Rorty and other contemporary thinkers who privilege language and distrust experience not only disagree with Dewey but also thereby dismiss much of what historians value in their efforts to understand the past as it was lived.

In James' introduction to the lectures eventually published as *The Varieties of Religious Experience*, he urged his listeners to think about especially rich, powerful, and sometimes unforgettable experiences that he described as "entirely unparalleled by anything in verbal thought." Giles Gunn, in his fine book *Thinking across the American Grain* (1992), quotes at length a passage that expresses "much of the heritage of pragmatism that Rorty has found problematic." The meaning of such intense experiences, in James' words, "seems to well up from out of their very centre, in a way impossible verbally to describe." On reflection, James observed, our experience of every moment of life seems to expand in the way a revolving disk painted with a spiral pattern appears at once to grow continuously from within itself and yet to remain the same size. Such "self-sustaining in the midst of self-removal, which characterizes all reality and fact, is something absolutely foreign to the nature of language, and even to the nature of logic, commonly so-called," which explains James' aversion to the emerging philosophical obsessions with language and mathematical logic and his stubborn fascination with religious experience.

> Something forever exceeds, escapes from statement, withdraws from definition, must be glimpsed and felt, not told. No one knows this like your genuine professor of philosophy. For what glimmers and twinkles like a bird's wing in the sunshine it is his business to snatch and fix. And every time he fires his volley of new vocables out of his philosophic shot-gun, whatever surface-flush of success he may feel, he secretly kens at the same time the finer hollowness and irrelevance.

Whereas philosophers who have made the linguistic turn might scoff at James' insistence on the inadequacies of language to capture and pin down the magic of experience, historians have good reasons to pay attention.[36]

Indeed, for historians the greater temptation may be to treat experience uncritically, as a court of last appeal, slighting the role of language and communication. Despite the incapacity of language to encompass fully the realms of religious, aesthetic, emotional, and somatic experience, we nevertheless usually have access to the experience of other persons, and communicate our own experience to others, principally through language. Although lived experience may exceed the boundaries of discourse, our expression of it usually, and our discussion of it always, cannot. Moreover, extralinguistic experiences have most often been used to authorize the dogmatic assertions of foundational principles that pragmatists old and new distrust. Traditionally appearing as religious truths proclaimed by believers, more recently such foundational principles have been asserted by those who claim that their race, class, gender, or other characteristic gives them immediate experience and thus insights inaccessible, perhaps even incomprehensible, to those outside the charmed—or maligned—circle.[37] How do we assess and adjudicate such competing claims, grounded in appeals to experience? The early pragmatists' concept of truth is crucial not only because it acknowledges those appeals but because, in its ethical and political dimensions, it offers a method for evaluating such claims. It thus provides a way of attempting to negotiate differences that might otherwise seem irreconcilable. That pragmatic method is democracy.

Ethics and Politics

For both James and Dewey democracy was much more than a form of government or a set of legal arrangements. Dewey urged us to stop "thinking of democracy as something institutional and external" and to see it as "a way of personal life," to realize that "democracy is a moral ideal and so far as it becomes a fact is a moral fact." In James' words, "democracy is a kind of religion," and for pragmatic reasons "we are bound not to admit its failure." Such "faiths and utopias are the noblest exercise of human reason," and we must not surrender them to cynicism.[38]

James and Dewey considered their pragmatism inseparable from their commitment to democracy as an ethical ideal. Both believed that their challenge to inherited philosophical dualisms and absolutes, their conception of truth as fluid and culturally created, and their belief that all experience is meaningful were consistent only with democracy, specifically with the principles of social equality and individual autonomy. The ideals of equality and autonomy appealed to James and Dewey because of their open-endedness and flexibility. They did not entail particular conceptions of the good life for all people at all times, although they did rule out fixed and hierarchical social systems sustained by appeals to allegedly universal truths that all members of the society must embrace.

For appeals to universal truths, James and Dewey substituted a process of inquiry that was both democratic and scientific. Dewey's enthusiasm for science is often misinterpreted as a narrow concern with technique to the exclusion of ethical considerations; to the contrary, Dewey valued the scientific method because it embodied an ethical commitment to open-ended inquiry wherein human values shaped the selection of questions, the formulation of hypotheses, and the evaluation of results. Dewey conceived of the ideal scientific community as a democratically organized, truth-seeking group of independent thinkers who tested their results against pragmatic standards, but those standards always reflected moral, rather than narrowly technical, considerations.

This unifying thread connects all of Dewey's writings. In *The Study of Ethics* (1894), he insisted that knowing cannot be separated from valuing. The qualitative and social dimensions of experience make pure "objectivity" or "neutrality" impossible for human beings. In *The Public and Its Problems* he cautioned that "the glorification of 'pure' science" is but "a rationalization of an escape" because knowledge "is wholly a moral matter." In *Experience and Nature* he stressed the moral and aesthetic dimension of experience, its qualitative as well as cognitive aspect. In *Art as Experience* (1934), Dewey tried once more to clarify the position he defended throughout his career: Although champions as well as critics have interpreted naturalism as "disregard of all values that cannot be reduced to the physical and animal," for Dewey "nature signifies nothing less than the whole complex of the results of the interaction of man, with his memories and hopes, understanding and desire, with that world to which one-sided philosophy confines 'nature.' "[39] Dewey judged the notion of "value-free" inquiry abhorrent as well as incoherent.

An address Dewey wrote for a banquet celebrating his eightieth birthday in 1939 states clearly and concisely the connection between his devotion to democracy and his philosophical conceptions of experience and ethics. Democracy, Dewey proclaimed, is "a way of life" that requires "faith in the capacity of human beings for intelligent judgment and action if proper [that is, democratic] conditions are furnished." To those who judged this faith naïve or utopian, Dewey insisted that it derives neither from metaphysics nor from wishful thinking but from the everyday experience of neighbors and friends gathering "to converse freely with one another. Intolerance, abuse, calling of names because of differences of opinion about religion or politics or business, as well as because of differences of race, color, wealth or degree of culture are treason to the democratic way of life." Anything that blocks communication engenders "antagonistic sects and factions" and undermines democracy. Legal guarantees—the focus of late-twentieth-century efforts to assure the right to free expression—are inadequate when "the give and take of ideas, facts, experiences, is choked by mutual suspicion, by abuse, by fear and hatred." For Dewey democracy required more than securing individual rights. It required faith in the possibility of resolving disputes through uncoerced deliberation, "as cooperative undertakings," instead of having one party suppress the other overtly through violence or more subtly through ridicule or intimidation. If such cooperation is impossible, then deliberative democracy as Dewey conceived of it is impossible.[40]

The emphasis on difference in the contemporary United States does not discredit Dewey's pragmatism, as some writers unfamiliar with his ideas assume; instead it echoes Dewey's own view of diversity. Achieving the cooperation necessary for social life requires "giving differences a chance to show themselves," he insisted. "The expression of difference is not only a right of the other persons but is a means of enriching one's own life-experience." Dewey's conception of democracy involved enriching the range of choices, and expanding the possibilities of finding different kinds of fulfillment, for all persons. Democracy does not impose authority from above but relies instead on "the process of experience as end and as means," as the source of authority and the means of choosing among and testing alternative directions. This process is continuous because its terminus cannot be designated, or even imagined, in advance of democratic social experimentation to create "a freer and more humane experience in which all share and to which all contribute." Dewey harbored no secret desire to bring all diversity to an end under the shelter of a snug but stifling consensus: to the contrary, a democracy without difference was a contradiction in terms, because he believed passionately that all individuals, in their uniqueness, make different contributions to democratic life. The richer the mix, the richer the culture that results from the interaction.[41]

Dewey's commitment to pluralism and diversity, to the recognition and cultivation of difference, and to the potential of communication to engender cooperation and clarify, if not resolve, disputes illustrates how wrongheaded is the familiar charge, which Dewey explicitly and repeatedly denied, that his emphasis on a community of inquiry reveals the latent elitism of pragmatism. Throughout the 1920s, against behaviorists and empirical social scientists who invoked his pragmatism on behalf of their efforts at social engineering, he insisted on expanding the "community of cooperative effort and truth." In *Individualism Old and New* (1929) he elaborated the argument advanced in *The Public and Its Problems* concerning the folly of relying on elites. He admitted that some communities of scientists, "small groups having a somewhat technical ability," did indeed illustrate how the process of inquiry might work, yet he insisted that such groups reveal only "a possibility in the present—one of many possibilities that are a challenge to expansion, and not a ground for retreat and contraction" from democracy. Unfortunately, interpreters of Dewey's ideas sometimes ignore such explicit arguments and assert that there must be something antidemocratic about communities of inquiry, even those that are open, expanding, and democratically constituted.[42]

Although it has long been common to contrast James' individualism to Dewey's commitment to social action, their differences are subtler. They reflect in part the simple fact of James' death in 1910 and Dewey's growing involvement in the distinctive political controversies of the following four decades, rather than any fundamental inconsistency in their political orientations. Both conceived of lived experience as irreducibly social and meaning-laden; both frequently invoked democracy as the social ideal consistent with their pragmatism. James attributed the "unhealthiness" of labor relations, for example, to "the fact that one-half of our fellow-countrymen remain entirely blind to the internal significance of the lives of the other half." Instead of entering imaginatively into their ways of life—to say nothing of entering into constructive, democratic dialogue with them—"everybody remains outside of everybody else's sight." In addition to endorsing deliberative, or discursive, democracy—defined by the creative potential of egalitarian dialogue, not merely democratic institutions or universal rights to participate in political activity—James also championed what would now be designated multiculturalism. His ideal of a democratic culture, grounded on his conception of immediate experience and his commitment to pragmatism, "commands us to tolerate, respect, and indulge" those "harmlessly interested and happy in their own ways, however unintelligible these may be to us." His creed was "Hands off: neither the whole of truth nor the whole of good is revealed to any single observer." The political consequence of James' pragmatism was "the well-known democratic respect for the sacredness of individuality," the "tolerance of whatever is not itself intolerant."[43]

The early pragmatists' arguments for democracy helped inspire generations of social and political activists ranging from Progressive reformers through New Dealers to members of the civil rights movement and the New Left. In the debates that rage among contemporary thinkers concerning the political consequences of pragmatism, the democratic convictions of James and Dewey have slipped out of focus because the political ideas of linguistic pragmatists such as Rorty have attracted so much attention.

Because Rorty's version of liberalism appeals to many Americans disillusioned with politics or cynical about its prospects, it is important to be clear about the similarities and the differences between his ideas and those of the early pragmatists. Rorty has repeatedly characterized the culture and institutions of liberal democracy as a precious achievement and endorsed the social democratic program that has been at the heart of pragmatic political activism since the days of James and Dewey, or Rauschenbusch and Croly. But, unlike James and Dewey, he denies that pragmatism provides any philosophical foundation for such a politics—or that we need one.

Rorty nevertheless characterizes pragmatism as "a philosophy of solidarity rather than despair." He tries to reassure his readers that we need not discard our beliefs about the natural world, or our moral and political values, just because we realize we have made them, rather than found them. Our faith in science, like our other faiths, helps us get things done, and it will continue to help us even after we have stopped trying to "divinize" it—likewise our democratic faith. In the absence of foundations, Rorty recommends that we look instead to history—but from an idiosyncratic, even antihistorical vantage point. We must accept "our inheritance from, and our conversation with, our fellow-humans as our only source of guidance." This is our defense against the nihilism that those who believe in universal principles fear will follow from pragmatism. "Our identification with our community—our society, our political tradition, our intellectual heritage—is heightened when we see this community as *ours* rather than *nature's, shaped* rather than found, one among many which men have made." If we were to surrender our aspirations to certainty, he writes, we "would regard the justification of liberal society simply as a matter of historical comparison with other attempts at social organization." At first glance historians might find Rorty's argument intriguing: He urges us to "try *not* to want something which stands beyond history and institutions" because "a belief can still regulate action" even if we realize it is "caused by nothing deeper than contingent historical circumstances." In Rorty's "liberal utopia," the claim that there is " 'something that stands beyond history' has become unintelligible."[44]

Rorty urges us to discard attempts to provide philosophical props to hold up our humanitarian and democratic values, to face unblinkingly the contingency of our sense of self and our commitments, and to adopt a posture of ironic distance from whatever we now accept as our "final vocabulary." The hero of Rorty's "liberal utopia" can "slough off the Enlightenment vocabulary" of rational foundations underlying universal principles and strive simply to avoid inflicting pain on others, a taboo Rorty simply posits as self-evident to anyone who has inherited our tradition. Having given up his own adolescent attempts to "hold reality and justice in a single vision," Rorty has become convinced that "an intricately-textured collage of private narcissism and public pragmatism" may be our best hope for synthesizing love and justice. We can no longer aim for more than what Alan Ryan calls "welfare-capitalism-with-a-human face," Rorty has written. Terms such as "capitalist economy" and "bourgeois culture" have become meaningless since 1989; in the absence of any contrasting socialist alternatives, "we Western leftists" should "*banalize* our vocabulary of political deliberation." Taking that advice to heart, Rorty claims that our political needs boil down to "security" and "sympathy" or, as he puts it, "mere niceness" to all "featherless bipeds." Such formulations, evidently calculated to infuriate Rorty's earnest critics, no doubt account for much of his notoriety.[45]

Rorty contends that philosophy can no longer offer much guidance to those interested in ethics and politics. For him liberal democratic cultures are simply "a product of time and chance," "an accidental coincidence," or "a fortunate happenstance," and the historical emergence of the United States was "an admirable result" that occurred "just by good luck." Rorty's devil-may-care view of history as caprice and his intentionally banal ethic of "niceness" contrast strikingly with James' stance in such essays as "The Moral Philosopher and the Moral Life" and Dewey's historical analyses of the connections between theories of ethics and political organization, between personal responsibility and social justice. Rorty claims that Dewey's pragmatism "did not tell you what purposes to have; its ethics is situational at best."[46] That could be said generally of James as well. But as Robert Westbrook and I argue, Dewey challenged prevailing systems of ethics and conventional liberal and socialist political theories, but he neither endorsed the judgment of many analytic philosophers that ethics and political philosophy are obsolete nor accepted anything like Rorty's advice that urging sympathy is the best we can do.

James and Dewey both believed that demolishing earlier arguments about ethics and politics cleared the way for critical analysis of personal freedom and responsibility, rather than bringing such discourse to an end. As Dewey put it in 1940, in a statement that indicates the gulf separating him from Rorty, "any theory of activity in social and moral matters, liberal or otherwise, which is not grounded in a comprehensive philosophy, seems to me to be only a projection of arbitrary personal preferences." When Rorty writes that "we do not need philosophy for social criticism"

or contends that "Dewey, like Nietzsche, altered our conception of reason . . . in a way that leaves no room for the idea that democratic ideals can
be supported by invoking ahistorical 'demands of reason,'" he neglects
Dewey's own "comprehensive philosophy." More accurate is Rorty's observation of the difference between his hypothetical Dewey and the historical
Dewey, who cared passionately about demonstrating the connection between experience and the ethical and political ideal of democracy. Historicizing reason, a project many of James' and Dewey's late-twentieth-
century admirers share with them, need not culminate in Rorty's rigid
divisions of language from experience and of the private from the public
sphere, nor in his dismissal of ethics and politics as proper subjects for
philosophers, nor, as I will argue in my conclusion, in his disregard for the
careful and critical study of how and why our tradition has taken its
distinctive shape. Rorty's position is insufficiently pragmatic. Although he
considers himself a partisan of social democratic reforms and criticizes
academic cultural politics, his liberal ironism encourages selfishness, cynicism, and resignation by undercutting efforts to confront the hard facts of
poverty and greed.[47]

Varieties of Contemporary Pragmatism

Numerous contemporary thinkers have invoked pragmatism to bolster a
wide range of political arguments; their contributions to debates about
race, gender, and law make clear how many distinct versions of pragmatism are alive and which versions differ markedly from the ideas of the
early pragmatists. Cornel West has constructed a loose narrative tradition
connecting James and Dewey with Emerson, Du Bois, and such thinkers as
C. Wright Mills, Sidney Hook, and Reinhold Niebuhr. In addition to accurately associating antifoundationalism and democratic sensibility with
American pragmatists, West characterizes them as champions of those
whom the theorist of anticolonialism Frantz Fanon calls "the wretched of
the earth." West distances his position from Rorty's pragmatism, which he
judges too narrowly focused on language and insufficiently attuned to the
pressing need for political activism. "The distinctive appeal of American pragmatism in our postmodern moment," West writes, "is its un-
ashamedly moral emphasis and its unequivocally ameliorative impulse."
Although lack of precision and inattention to detail make West's *The
American Evasion of Philosophy* problematic as a history of philosophy, it is
a spirited and provocative piece of pragmatic cultural criticism.[48]

An ardent admirer of Dewey, West nevertheless argues that Dewey's
pragmatism must be supplemented with the tragic and religious sensibili-

ties of Niebuhr ("the vertical dimension"), the awareness of class of Karl Marx and Antonio Gramsci, and a sharper sensitivity to issues of race and gender (the "horizontal dimension") than the early pragmatists showed.[49] In recent years, as he has attained celebrity status of a sort neither James nor Dewey had to endure, West has become less an academic philosopher than a "jazz freedom fighter" whose "prophetic pragmatism" attempts to translate a philosophical perspective descended from James and Dewey, a religious awareness of evil and finitude, and a radical democratic politics into the idioms of postmodern academic discourse, black spirituality, and hip-hop. Rorty has complained that West's phrase "prophetic pragmatism" sounds as odd as the phrase "charismatic trash pick up."[50] West's cheerleading seems pointless to Rorty since he believes we cannot bridge the gap between the rich possibilities available to us in private life and Dewey's imagined "great community," a now-meaningless utopia we cannot envision on the flattened landscape of welfare capitalism. Between the negative freedoms individuals enjoy in a liberal democracy and the promise of an even richer form of life within a more radically democratic public sphere—the "positive freedom" that Dewey embraced in *Liberalism and Social Action*—falls a chasm. To Rorty, our century illustrates the cruelty that must result from attempts to force community where there is conflict. But to West (and others drawn toward Dewey's ideal), it is essential that pragmatists continue striving for the democratic transformation of everyday experience.

Like West, many feminists endorse pragmatism as an alternative to the sterility of analytic philosophy and the nihilism of post-structuralism and as a lever to dislodge entrenched ways of thinking. Against dueling conceptions of fixed "male" and "female" natures, feminist pragmatists instead call for an open-ended, antiessentialist, experimental approach to gender. In a special issue of the journal *Hypatia* published in 1993, Charlene Haddock Seigfried, who has written extensively on William James, has brought together works by historians, philosophers, and political theorists exploring the potential of pragmatism for feminism.[51] Such early pragmatists as James, Dewey, and George Herbert Mead considered pragmatism a weapon in the campaign against restrictive gender roles for the same reason they considered it a weapon in the campaigns against imperialism and racism and for democracy. They allied with feminist activists and championed feminist scholars such as Jessie Taft because their conception of pragmatism extended beyond language to an awareness of the experience of people who were denied choices, or unnecessarily restricted in their choices, by prevailing assumptions and patterns of social relations.[52]

The pervasiveness of power that many contemporary feminists emphasize has led some, notably Joan Scott, to resist the concept of "experience" because they fear it can lead us away from historicism toward a new foundationalism. But instead of dismissing the concept as Rorty does, Scott recommends examining how experience is said to yield unassailable knowledge, a strategy resembling that of James and Dewey.[53] Similarly, other feminists resist the ideas of a community of inquiry or a deliberative democracy because they fear such ideas valorize white male norms of rationality and are thus inevitably exclusionary. Recent work by pragmatist feminists suggests both how historicizing experience enables us to move beyond language without positing a new foundationalism concerning "women's ways of knowing" or "rational deliberation" and how to acknowledge power relations without positing a new essentialism about "difference" and "power." Pragmatist legal theorists such as Joan Williams and Margaret Jane Radin argue that profound conflicts, for example, those between women who work inside and outside the home and between women who support and who oppose abortion rights, are powerfully shaped by deep but seldom recognized cultural fissures concerning the meanings of freedom and responsibility for men and women. Those divisions can be traced to the nineteenth-century doctrine of separate spheres, unfortunately resurrected as an indirect consequence of early-twentieth-century feminist essentialism. The ironic result was a reinforcing of stereotypes of home and mother that undercut feminists' efforts to loosen gender roles and broaden women's opportunities. Reinscribing a comparable essentialism under the banner of "difference," as some contemporary feminists do, merely resuscitates older versions of separate spheres and notions of privileged knowledge that exclude new categories of outsiders rather than opening doors of understanding that might lead to tolerance or even, potentially, mutual respect. From an explicitly pragmatist perspective, Williams challenges currently fashionable notions of female as well as male identity and the ostensible predispositions of women for "relationships" and "caring" and of men for "justice" and "rights." Radin argues that pragmatist feminists should "reject static, timeless conceptions of reality" in favor of "contextuality, expressed in the commitment of Dewey and James to facts and their meaning in human life, and narrative, expressed in James's unfolding 'epic' universe and Dewey's historicism." Echoing West's challenge to Rorty's narrowing of pragmatism to language, Radin concludes in a Deweyan spirit: "If we are pragmatists, we will recognize the inescapability of perspective and the indissolubility of thought and action," insights that can help feminists avoid rigid and counterproductive dogmas.[54]

Other legal theorists share Williams' and Radin's enthusiasm for pragmatism as a way of resolving the battles pitting those affiliated with the critical legal studies movement on the left or with the law and economics movement on the right against those attempting to keep alive notions of original intent as the standard for interpreting the constitution. From the perspective of such legal pragmatists, much legal reasoning—at both ends of the political spectrum—is blinkered by abstract and absolute principles from seeing how the law has functioned in practice in American culture.[55]

The rise of legal pragmatism may seem surprising. The goal of the legal process is to find truth. Juries are instructed to decide on the basis of the evidence presented; the effects of decisions experienced by defendants and plaintiffs are concrete and determinate. The law might thus seem an especially inhospitable place for a linguistic pragmatism that treats all disputes as ultimately rhetorical contests.

Instead, law offers one of the liveliest arenas of debate about the consequences of pragmatism, and one that should be of particular interest to historians. The jurist Richard Posner, the leading member of the law and economics movement, believes that pragmatists' antiessentialism and consequentialism are compatible with his commitment to "the idea that the law should strive to support competitive markets." He reduces legal pragmatism to the bare minimum: "a rejection of a concept of law as grounded in permanent principles and realized in logical manipulation of those principles, and a determination to use law as an instrument for social ends." For Posner pragmatism is nothing but a method; substantive changes—from attempts to reinstate white supremacy to commitments to securing racial equality—result not from careful reasoning but only from "a sudden deeply emotional switch from one non-rational cluster of beliefs to another that is no more (often less) rational." Holmes at his most cynical could hardly have put the point more bluntly. Posner's pragmatism, like Rorty's, thus appears to consist of nothing more than antifoundationalism.[56]

But the protean critic Stanley Fish, in his recent incarnation as a legal theorist, points out that Posner embraces pragmatism as a fig leaf to conceal economic dogmas concerning market efficiency as absolute as Kant's transcendental aesthetic or Marx's notion of the proletariat. Fish contrasts both Posner's faith in the market and Rorty's faith in strong poets to his own pragmatism, which really does lead nowhere. "Once pragmatism becomes a program"—*any* program, Fish insists—"it turns into the essentialism it challenges."[57]

Fish's linguistic turn carries him even further away from Dewey than does Rorty's. From Fish's perspective, "the law's job" is "to give us ways of re-describing limited partisan programs so that they can be presented as the natural outcomes of abstract interpersonal imperatives." As humans we cannot escape partisanship or perspective; they are inevitable conditions of our existence. For Fish the pursuit of disinterestedness, James' aspiration to tolerance, and Dewey's desire for a deliberative democracy are all chimerical; only the admission that one's own point of view remains partial is consistent with pragmatism. The very pretense of "reasoned exposition"—in judges' opinions or scholarship—is just rhetoric, "impelled by a vision as partisan and contestable as that informing any rhetoric that dares accept that name."[58]

But even Fish slips. He concedes that his antifoundationalism finally has a foundation, the concept of "difference," which, he asserts, "is not a remediable state; it is the bottom line fact of the human condition, the condition of being a finite creature." Although the challenge to the law's generality seems jarring, Fish's proclamation of difference resonates with the pleas of many voices claiming to speak for the marginalized in American discourse today. For James and Dewey, appreciating the inevitability of perspective made pragmatism necessary; it was not—as it is for Fish— the last word. From the realization of difference came the necessity of democracy. This more robust conception of the relation between pragmatism and legal theory is reflected in the writings of those legal theorists, such as Cass Sunstein, who consider the democratic commitments of James and Dewey integral to the pragmatist project.[59]

After surveying the competing versions of pragmatism and postmodernism in legal theory, Sunstein recently concluded that "the valuable postmodern claims tend to be not postmodern at all, but instead part of the philosophical heritage of pragmatism," which unsettled formalism without wallowing in the nihilist resignation that all effort is futile in the face of power. Pragmatism insists that all our categories, legal and otherwise, are constructed. This awareness marks "the beginning of the effort to construct our categories well, by reference to our goals and needs, and not as a reason to abandon the whole enterprise." For Sunstein—as for Dewey and for the legal realists who earlier in the twentieth century embraced pragmatism as the philosophy informing their jurisprudence—deliberative democracy provides the standard for judging the adequacy of our ways of determining those goals and needs.[60]

This crucial argument indicates why democracy is uniquely consistent with pragmatism. As Putnam has accurately pointed out, Dewey offered an "*epistemological justification of democracy.*" Dewey used epistemology to ground democracy, conceived as the testing of hypotheses by free individuals participating in the unfettered pursuit of truth. In our day such a conception of democracy must remain open-ended because we, unlike seventeenth- and eighteenth-century champions of democracy, cannot claim to know what our final ends will be. Since we cannot answer in advance the questions "what are we?" and "how should we live?"—questions earlier democrats thought they could answer through reason or revelation—we must commit ourselves to continuing inquiry. Thus a pragmatist epistemology and ethics in the spirit of James and Dewey culminates necessarily in a democratic politics. In Putnam's words, which echo many similar proclamations in Dewey's work, "democracy is not just a form of social life among other workable forms of social life; it is the precondition for the full application of intelligence to the solution of social problems." It is the form of social life consistent with pragmatism.[61]

Pragmatism and Democracy

This view of the relation between pragmatism and democracy, which intellectual historians have been urging now for a decade, helps explain the resurgence of interest in pragmatism. Now that alternative ideals appear either discredited or impossible, democracy has emerged as a universally attractive norm. But in our multicultural and skeptical age, the case for democracy can no longer be established on the basis of self-evident truths about natural rights or arguments from religious doctrine that no longer command general assent. Is there a philosophical foundation on which democracy can rest at the end of the twentieth century? According to linguistic pragmatists such as Rorty and Fish and postmodernist theorists such as Foucault and Derrida, whose work has influenced much recent American critical theory, there is none. But the great strength of pragmatism as James and Dewey conceived of it, which historians more fully than analytic philosophers and law-seeking social scientists have recognized and demonstrated, lay in its denial of absolutes, its admission of uncertainty, and its resolute commitment to the continuing vitality of the ideal of democracy as a way of life.

Indeed, pragmatism appeals to many American thinkers as a home-grown alternative to postmodernism that escapes the weaknesses of Enlightenment rationalism without surrendering our commitments to the values of autonomy and equality. Textualists such as Rorty and Fish consider pragmatism consistent with the perspective on language most often associated with Derrida. Others see it instead as a way of thinking open to the critical insights of postmodernism but resistant to cynicism and nihilism because of its conception of experience and its commitment to democracy.[62]

In *The New Constellation* (1992), his most recent work, Bernstein faces the postmodernist challenge head on. Foucault and Derrida deny, in radically different ways, the possibility of reaching the democratic understandings that Dewey envisioned. Bernstein successfully undertakes the apparently unpromising task of finding in their writings ethical and political ideas consistent with his own pragmatism.[63] Bernstein shares postmodernists' commitments to antifoundationalism, fallibilism, contingency, and pluralism, but he emphasizes the grounding of pragmatism in the phenomenology of experience. Because experience itself is social, Bernstein believes, our private selves cannot be cordoned off from our ethical responsibilities—even behind the shield of "difference." We must always be prepared to expose our private passions and our personal choices to criticism and to engage in dialogue those who disagree with us, not because we believe that consensus will necessarily result, but because it is only through that process that we learn to understand one another and ourselves.

Bernstein's Deweyan pragmatism pays attention to history, particularly the history of American democracy. Whereas Rorty asserts confidently that Americans who inherit "our tradition" share his own commitments to preserving individual privacy and refusing to inflict pain, Bernstein insists that the "breakdown of moral and political consensus" is "the overwhelming 'fact' of contemporary life." Rorty blithely explains the emergence of American liberal democracy as a product of chance and contingency; his account ignores or trivializes the efforts of historical actors. Behind the values and institutions that Rorty and many postmodernists take for granted lie not only the now-disputed doctrine of natural rights and the notion of God's covenant with a chosen people but also the experiences of countless Americans who have struggled to nudge reality closer to the elusive idea of democracy.[64]

Another important reason for American scholars' renewed interest in pragmatism has been the widespread influence of Jürgen Habermas, arguably the most important philosopher of the late twentieth century, who now describes himself simply "as a good pragmatist." Habermas' affinity with American pragmatism will surprise some historians who know him only by reputation or are acquainted with only parts of his massive work. In his attempt to free Marxism from Marx's scientism and his fetishizing of the proletariat, Habermas has constructed a theory of communicative action centered on what he calls the ideal speech situation. His philosophy depends on ideas of the self constituted through social interaction and of undistorted communication as the paradigm for social democracy that can be traced directly to Mead and Dewey. Although it startles longtime partisans of American pragmatism, interest in these ideas among many younger scholars derives largely from the writings of Habermas.[65]

Habermas too has distanced his understanding of pragmatism from Rorty's. In response to Rorty's jibe that he tends to "go transcendental," Habermas traces his conception of dialogue to "the *already* operative potential for rationality contained in the everyday practices of communication," which depend on our confidence in the validity of propositions, the rightness of norms, and the truthfulness or authenticity of those with whom we communicate. In ordinary experience, Habermas contends, we learn to recognize the (frequently unrealized) potential of dialogue. Dismissing as self-defeating the universal skepticism and resistance of some postmodernists, Habermas opts instead for the perspective of the early pragmatists: "I have for a long time identified myself with that radical democratic mentality which is present in the best American traditions and articulated in American pragmatism. This mentality takes seriously what appears to so-called radical thinkers [such as Foucault and Derrida] as so much reformist naiveté." He endorses Dewey's " 'attempt to make concrete concerns with the daily problems of one's community' [an attempt that] expresses both a practice and an attitude."[66]

These controversies among contemporary pragmatists replay in a different key the familiar contrast between the images of mind as mirror and lamp, between the empiricism of the Enlightenment and the romantics' obsession with the creative potential of the artistic imagination. Their disagreements have helped focus debate and enabled other thinkers, such as Habermas, to clarify their own ideas by sharpening the distinctions between those who embrace linguistic pragmatism and those who see its inadequacies.[67]

Our heightened awareness of the opacity and instability of language has complicated the question of how we should deal with experience, both as scholars and as citizens trying to reach agreement by exchanging views. So too, our heightened awareness of the historicity of our political institutions and our sensitivity to the social and cultural differences that complicate democratic dialogue make it hard for us to see how we can achieve the early pragmatists' political goals. Dewey recognized that he failed to provide clear, detailed political strategies for realizing his ideal of democratic life, and that fuzziness is one of the most troublesome aspects of his legacy.

James' greater sensitivity to the uniqueness of each individual, to the difficulties of communicating the ineffable quality of lived experience, and to the tragic betrayal of some ethical ideal in every choice between irreconcilable conceptions of the good make his variety of pragmatic political thinking perhaps better suited to our own time. For as the experience of community has become ever rarer in the years since Alexis de Tocqueville first announced its endangered status, and as politics is more and more submerged beneath a flood of symbols, finding paths leading toward the creation of democratic communities seems more problematical than ever. History can help, if only we historians have the courage of our conventions.

History and Pragmatic Hermeneutics

Because the community of historians is a paradigmatic example of a pragmatic community of inquiry, distinguishing between pragmatism old and new matters profoundly to us. To "new" textualist pragmatists, history is no more than a linguistic exercise in which professional competitors strive to persuade readers by fashioning arguments that are judged successful according to various contingent and culturally specific criteria. For those "new" textualists, historians are writers of texts who have at their disposal a variety of tools, including but not limited to "evidence," "reason," "logic," and "common sense," all of which require quotation marks to signal their status as merely conventional notions. Canny textualists claim that all such tropes are rhetorical devices deployed (more or less shrewdly and self-consciously) in our discursive tradition to persuade others in our community and to achieve a certain standing within it. It is indeed difficult to see how history written by "new" pragmatists could contribute anything distinctively different from novels or poetry to helping us to understand experience, communicate with each other, or construct a more democratic culture.[68]

To "old" pragmatists and to historians aligned (consciously or not) with James, Dewey, Putnam, and Bernstein, history retains its distinctive significance as the study of "a reality independent of us," to use James' phrase. We understand, as Putnam has argued, that our entire practice as historians—our "form of life," to use Ludwig Wittgenstein's phrase—depends on "our belief that truth and falsity 'reach all the way to' the past and 'do not stop short.'" It is possible to admit, with Putnam, that this belief "*is* part of a picture," but we should acknowledge, with him, that as historians "*the picture is essential to our lives.*" In Putnam's words, "our *lives* show that we believe that there are more and less warranted beliefs about political contingencies, [and] about historical interpretations." Were we to discard that way of looking at the past, we would have to discard our form of life.[69]

Narratives capable of inspiring and justifying the sympathy Rorty prizes in "our tradition" already exist, and not only those of the novelists and poets that Rorty invokes. They include the narratives contained in sacred texts such as the Bible and secular democratic texts such as Judith Sargent Murray's essay "On the Equality of the Sexes," Abraham Lincoln's Second Inaugural, and Martin Luther King Jr.'s speech at the 1963 March on Washington, narratives with powerful ethical and cultural significance transmitted by various traditions and by the community of professional historians. In a society that is ostensibly committed to the ideals of democracy but that falls tragically short in practice, the narratives we historians construct help to perpetuate disturbing and inspiring memories and thus to shape a culture more capable of approximating those ideals. Without historians' commitment to a pragmatic test of truth, which involves subjecting our accounts of the past to rigorous testing by our scholarly community, we are locked into an exercise of textual creation that is arid and pointless.

In *That Noble Dream* (1988), Peter Novick concluded that because the ideal of pure scholarly objectivity has been exposed as chimerical (thanks in part to textualists such as Rorty and Fish), historians have divided into warring camps, unable and unwilling to reach agreement about standards of purpose and critical judgment. Although Novick acknowledged the attempts of Bernstein and Putnam, and of historians such as Thomas Haskell and David Hollinger, to sustain a viable, mediating historical discourse that I have termed pragmatic hermeneutics, he curtly dismissed their effort: "as of the 1980s," he wrote, "hardly anybody was listening."[70] As the spirited debates over pragmatism examined here illustrate, interest in these ideas is now broad and deep. For historians especially, the early pragmatism of James and Dewey presents a sturdy alternative to untenable forms of both objectivism and relativism.

The pragmatic test we should apply to historical scholarship is the same test James and Dewey proposed a century ago: Is it consistent with the evidence we have of others' lived experience, and will it make a difference in our lives? If we historians conceive of our task as the early pragmatists did, we will write not only with an awareness of our rhetorical strategies but also with a desire to document and explain struggles over power in the American past and in the culture that surrounds us and makes our work possible and necessary. Waged by activists inspired by religious and political traditions, these hard-fought battles—and not just the important redescriptions, to use Rorty's preferred term, offered in literary and critical texts—made possible our culture's painfully limited progress toward greater autonomy and equality for all citizens. Historical scholarship understood as pragmatic hermeneutics shows that the outcomes were the result not purely of chance and redescription, as the more cavalier of textualists would have it, but instead of specific struggles fought by people who wielded other weapons besides language.[71]

All of this is not to deny the role interpretation has always played, and will continue to play, in historical writing. Just as people in the past selected parts of their experience to record and preserve in the records they left us, we select parts of the past to examine and we choose how to tell our stories. But to admit that interpretation is important is not to claim that everything is interpretation. It is crucial that we historians be able to distinguish what happened from what did not, and what was written from what was not, and our discursive community must test its propositions in the widest range of public forums. Arguments insisting on the importance of such public verification by appeals to evidence from experience, arguments forcefully made against textualists by Gunn, Shusterman, West, Williams, Putnam, and Bernstein, are also made by historians whose pragmatism derives from James and Dewey. That commitment explains why some of us have worked to establish the difference between pragmatists old and new, between Poirier's extravagant James and the historical James, between Rorty's hypothetical Dewey and the historical Dewey. Pragmatism offers historians something beyond the denial of absolutes, a method for providing reliable, even if provisional, knowledge that can make a difference in how we understand our culture and how we live.[72]

Historians face a choice, then, between newer varieties of linguistic pragmatism that see all truth claims as contingent and older varieties of pragmatism descended more directly from James and Dewey. The latter begin with a nuanced conception of experience as the arena for truth testing and culminate in ethical and democratic activity, the precise content of which cannot be specified in advance or imposed on others because diversity and experimentation are integral to this form of pragmatism. "There can be no final truth in ethics any more than in physics," James wrote, until the last human being "has had his experience and said his say." Or as Dewey put it, "growth itself is the only moral 'end.'"[73]

Notwithstanding those endorsements of indeterminacy, which contemporaries alert to the threat of oppression and exclusion should find attractive, James' and Dewey's pragmatism did not lack substantive values: the ideals of democracy, grounded in their experience as social beings and their commitment to communities of inquiry rigorously testing all truth claims, provided the norms that guided them. Their pragmatism thus extended beyond the boundaries of language in two directions: in its fluid and historicized conception of the social experience that lies behind linguistic expression, and in its dedication to the diverse forms of continuing democratic practice, including the negotiation rather than the elimination of difference. The early pragmatists believed that eliminating the obstacles of outmoded philosophical and political doctrines would free Americans to solve the problems they faced. The tragedies of the twentieth century have made us less sanguine about that prospect; we lack their confidence that pragmatism and democracy by themselves will resolve all our conflicts. Thus some contemporary thinkers, like those romantics disillusioned by the failures of eighteenth-century democratic revolutions, emphasize the instability of meanings, the particularity of personal identities, and the creative genius of individual artists over rational deliberation. The new linguistic pragmatism will no doubt continue to attract attention from many disciplines because it reflects that disappointment and also challenges the persistent impulses to formalism and scientism still powerful in American thought. But a revised version of the pragmatism of James and Dewey, chastened by tragedy to distrust simple democratic cheerleading, can avoid those dangers while offering a method of generating and testing ideas about what happened to Americans in the past and of deliberating on what should happen in the future. For that reason the early pragmatists' ideas will remain valuable for historians committed to explaining why America has taken the shape it has and for citizens committed to solving problems democratically.

The early pragmatists' "old ways of thinking" already incorporated the most valuable insights of the linguistic turn and the postmodern suspicion of power. Those insights did not blind James and Dewey, nor have they blinded the contemporaries who have resurrected the spirit of their pragmatism, to the world of experience that lies beneath and beyond language and to the ties of mutual respect that might bind us together as humans despite our differences. Such clear-sightedness was among the old ways of thinking central to James' and Dewey's pragmatism, and it remains a necessary although not sufficient condition for advancing toward the democratic goals of equality and autonomy. Without it we engage in shadow play, unable to distinguish experience from illusion.

Notes

For stimulating conversation and criticism, I am grateful to Susan Armeny, Thomas Bender, Casey Blake, David Depew, John Diggins, Richard Fox, Giles Gunn, Peter Hansen, David Hollinger, Hans Joas, James Livingston, Timothy Peltason, Amélie Oksenberg Rorty, Dorothy Ross, Charlene Haddock Seigfried, Richard Shusterman, David Thelen, Robert Westbrook, and Joan Williams. I am particularly indebted to Richard J. Bernstein and Richard Rorty for their generosity.

This essay first appeared in the *Journal of American History*, June 1996, and is reprinted here by permission.

1 William James to Henry James, May 4, 1907, in *The Letters of William James*, ed. Henry James (New York: Little, Brown, 1920), vol. 2, p. 279; William James to Theodore Flournoy, January 2, 1907, in Ralph Barton Perry, *The Thought and Character of William James: As Revealed in Unpublished Correspondence and Notes, Together with His Published Writings* (Boston: Little, Brown, 1935), vol. 2, pp. 452–53. James traced pragmatism to its ancient roots in William James, *Pragmatism: A New Name for Some Old Ways of Thinking* (1907: Cambridge: Harvard University Press, 1978), pp. 30–31, 3.

2 David A. Hollinger, "The Problem of Pragmatism in American History," *Journal of American History*, 67 (June 1980): 88, 107. Five years later Hollinger cheerfully admitted that his obituary had been premature. See David A. Hollinger, *In the American Province: Studies in the History and Historiography of Ideas* (Bloomington: Indiana University Press, 1985), pp. 23, 25, 43. A splendid survey is Richard J. Bernstein, "The Resurgence of Pragmatism," *Social Research*, 59 (Winter 1992): 813–40.

3 In this essay I will concentrate on William James and John Dewey instead of Charles Sanders Peirce for two reasons. First, Peirce explained in 1904 that he "invented" pragmatism "to express a certain maxim of logic . . . for the analysis of concepts" rather than "sensation" and grounded it on "an elaborate study of the nature of signs." For the precise reason why Peirce's ideas have influenced analytic philosophers and semioticians, his work is less pertinent here. See H. S. Thayer, *Meaning and Action: A Critical History of Pragmatism* (Indianapolis: Hackett, 1981), pp. 493–94. Second, discussing the recent torrent of work on Peirce is beyond the scope of this essay. For a fine introduction, see James Hoopes, ed., *Peirce on Signs: Writings on Semiotic by Charles Sanders Peirce* (Chapel Hill: University of North Carolina Press, 1991); on Peirce's tortured life see Joseph Brent, *Charles Sanders Peirce: A Life* (Bloomington: Indiana University Press, 1993); and on his philosophy of science, see C. F. Delaney, *Science, Knowledge, and Mind: A Study in the Philosophy of C. S. Peirce* (Notre Dame: University of Notre Dame Press, 1993).

4 On James' concept of immediate experience, see James M. Edie, *William James and Phenomenology* (Bloomington: Indiana University Press, 1987); more comprehensive are Perry, *Thought and Character of William James* (Cambridge: Harvard University Press, 1948); and Gerald E. Myers, *William James: His Life and Thought* (New Haven: Yale University Press, 1986). On Dewey's life and thought, see Robert B. Westbrook, *John Dewey and American Democracy* (Ithaca: Cornell University Press, 1991); on qualitative issues in Dewey's philosophy, see James Gouinlock, *John Dewey's Philosophy of Value* (New York: Humanities Press, 1972).

5 A compilation of these criticisms is in John Patrick Diggins, *The Promise of Pragmatism: Modernism and the Crisis of Knowledge and Authority* (Chicago: University of Chicago Press, 1994). James Hoopes, Robert Westbrook, and I are unpersuaded by Diggins' interpretation of pragmatism. For our explanations and Diggins' response, see James Hoopes, "Peirce's Community of Signs: The Path Untaken in American Social Thought," *Intellectual History Newsletter*, 17 (1995): 3–6; James T. Kloppenberg, "The Authority of Evidence and the Boundaries of Interpretation," *ibid.*, 7–15; Robert West-

brook, "The Authority of Pragmatism," *ibid.*, 16–24; and John Patrick Diggins, "Pragmatism and the Historians," *ibid.*, 25–30. On critics who valued the capacities of creative individuals above pragmatists' concerns with communities of discourse and social justice, see Casey Nelson Blake, *Beloved Community: The Cultural Criticism of Randolph Bourne, Van Wyck Brooks, Waldo Frank, and Lewis Mumford* (Chapel Hill: University of North Carolina Press, 1990). On Walter Lippmann and Mortimer Adler, see Edward A. Purcell Jr., *The Crisis of Democratic Theory: Scientific Naturalism and the Problem of Value* (Lexington: University Press of Kentucky, 1973). On Theodor Adorno and Max Horkheimer, see Martin Jay, *The Dialectical Imagination: A History of the Frankfurt School and the Institute of Social Research, 1923–1950* (Boston: Little, Brown, 1973).

6 James, *Pragmatism*, pp. 111–12.

7 William James, *The Meaning of Truth* (1909; Cambridge: Harvard University Press, 1975), pp. 117, 106, 126–28.

8 James, *Pragmatism*, pp. 102–3.

9 John Dewey, *Experience and Nature*, in John Dewey, *The Later Works, 1925–1953*, ed. Jo Ann Boydston (Carbondale: University of Southern Illinois Press, 1981–1990), vol. 1, p. 152; John Dewey, *The Public and Its Problems, ibid.*, vol. 2, pp. 330–31.

10 Dewey, *Experience and Nature*, appendix 2 (1951), p. 372.

11 On the triumph of scientism in American social science, see Dorothy Ross, *The Origins of American Social Science* (Cambridge: Cambridge University Press, 1991), pp. 390–470.

12 On the relations between scientism and the transformation of philosophy, see Daniel J. Wilson, *Science, Community, and the Transformation of American Philosophy, 1860–1930* (Chicago: University of Chicago Press, 1990); and Laurence C. Smith, *Behaviorism and Logical Positivism: A Reassessment of the Alliance* (Stanford: Stanford University Press, 1986). For Dewey's judgment of Bertrand Russell and G. E. Moore, see John Dewey, *Essays in Experimental Logic*, in John Dewey, *The Middle Works, 1899–1924*, ed. Jo Ann Boydston (Carbondale: University of Southern Illinois Press, 1976–1983), vol. 10, pp. 357–58. William James to Bertrand Russell, Oct. 4, 1908, in James, *Meaning of Truth*, 299–300. Russell's jibe appeared in Bertrand Russell, "Dewey's New Logic," in *The Philosophy of John Dewey*, ed. Paul A. Schilpp (1939; New York: Tudor, 1951), pp. 135–56. On this volume, see Westbrook, *John Dewey and American Democracy*, 496–500.

13 George Cotkin, "Middle-Ground Pragmatists: The Popularization of Philosophy in American Culture," *Journal of the History of Ideas* 55 (April 1994): 283–302. On Will Durant, see Joan Shelley Rubin, *The Making of Middlebrow Culture* (Chapel Hill: University of North Carolina Press, 1992).

14 See Richard Wightman Fox, *Reinhold Niebuhr: A Biography* (New York: Pantheon, 1985); and Daniel F. Rice, *Reinhold Niebuhr and John Dewey: An American Odyssey* (Albany: SUNY Press, 1993). Richard Rorty, "Pragmatism without Method," in Richard Rorty, *Philosophical Papers*, vol. 1, *Objectivity, Relativism, and Truth* (New York: Cambridge University Press, 1991), p. 64. On the shift of American philosophy departments away from pragmatism and toward analytic philosophy and logical positivism, see Hilary Putnam, *Reason, Truth, and History* (New York: Cambridge University Press, 1981), pp. 103–26; Bernstein, "Resurgence of Pragmatism," 815–17; and a fine overview, David Depew, "Philosophy," in *Encyclopedia of the United States in the Twentieth Century*, ed. Stanley Kutler (New York: Charles Scribner's Sons, 1996), vol. 4, pp. 1635–63.

15 Thomas S. Kuhn, *The Structure of Scientific Revolutions* (Chicago: University of Chicago

Press, 1962); Paul Hoyningen-Huene, *Reconstructing Scientific Revolutions: Thomas S. Kuhn's Philosophy of Science*, trans. Alexander T. Levine (Chicago: University of Chicago Press, 1993). On the uses of social science in public policy, see Ellen Herman, *The Romance of American Psychology: Political Culture in the Age of Experts* (Berkeley: University of California Press, 1995).

16 See Richard J. Bernstein, *The Restructuring of Social and Political Theory* (New York: Harcourt Brace Jovanovich, 1976); Fred R. Dallmayr and Thomas A. McCarthy, eds., *Understanding and Social Inquiry* (Notre Dame: University of Notre Dame Press, 1977); and Quentin Skinner, ed., *The Return of Grand Theory in the Human Sciences* (Cambridge: Cambridge University Press, 1985).

17 On these changes in philosophy and political theory, see John Rajchman and Cornel West, eds., *Post-Analytic Philosophy* (New York: Columbia University Press, 1985); and David Held, ed., *Political Theory Today* (Stanford: Stanford University Press, 1991).

18 Richard Rorty, ed., *The Linguistic Turn: Recent Essays in Philosophical Method* (Chicago: University of Chicago Press, 1967).

19 Richard Rorty, *Philosophy and the Mirror of Nature* (Princeton: Princeton University Press, 1979). See Alan Malachowski, ed., *Reading Rorty: Critical Responses to Philosophy and the Mirror of Nature* (Cambridge: B. Blackwell, 1990); and Herman J. Saatkamp, ed., *Rorty and Pragmatism* (Nashville: Vanderbilt University Press, 1995). Ian Hacking, "Two Kinds of 'New Historicism' for Philosophers," in *History and . . . : Histories within the Human Sciences,* ed. Ralph Cohen and Michael S. Roth (Charlottesville: University Press of Virginia, 1995), pp. 296–318. The very useful words "historicism" and "historicist" continue to baffle some historians, probably due to their almost opposite meanings in the work of the philosopher of science Karl Popper and in contemporary critical discourse. Popper used "historicism" to designate (and denigrate) any theory (such as Marxism) that purports to predict the future course of human events according to ostensibly scientific laws. More recent commentators understand historicism as "the theory that social and cultural phenomena are historically determined and that each period in history has its own values that are not directly applicable to other epochs. In philosophy that implies that philosophical issues find their place, importance, and definition in a specific cultural milieu. That is certainly Rorty's opinion." *Ibid.,* 298.

20 Rorty, *Philosophy and the Mirror of Nature,* 392; Richard Rorty, *Consequences of Pragmatism: Essays 1972–1980* (Minneapolis: University of Minnesota Press, 1982), pp. xl, xliii.

21 Rorty, *Consequences of Pragmatism,* pp. xviii, 160, 161.

22 Richard Rorty, "Dewey between Hegel and Darwin," in *Modernist Impulses in the Human Sciences, 1870–1930,* ed. Dorothy Ross (Baltimore: Johns Hopkins University Press, 1994), pp. 46–68. In this essay Rorty acknowledges his debt to intellectual historians for demonstrating the difference between the historical Dewey and his "hypothetical version" but then contends that the ideas of Dewey's generation no longer make sense.

23 Richard Poirier, *Poetry and Pragmatism* (Cambridge: Harvard University Press, 1992), p. 5. On pragmatism as the antithesis of literary theory and a rationale for critics to focus on recovering authors' intentions, see Steven Knapp and Walter Benn Michaels, "Against Theory," *Critical Inquiry,* 8 (Summer 1982): 723–42. For the claim that we must supplement pragmatism with other value orientations (such as Marxism) because the pragmatic method "cannot help us do the social work of transformation,"

see Frank Lentricchia, *Criticism and Social Change* (Chicago: University of Chicago Press, 1983), p. 4. Stanley Fish argues that we create the meaning of texts when we interpret them; trying to catch what Fish means by pragmatism is thus like trying to catch a fly with a fish net. See, for example, Stanley Fish, *Doing What Comes Naturally* (Durham: Duke University Press, 1989). On one version of Fish's pragmatism, see the examination of legal theory later in this chapter.

24 Poirier, *Poetry and Pragmatism*, pp. 44, 46, 92, 131. Compare James' own cautionary words about language, which might seem to confirm Poirier's view: "Good and evil reconciled in a laugh! Don't you see the difference, don't you see the identity?" James asked. "By George, nothing but *othing*! That sounds like nonsense, but it is pure *onsense*!" James published these epigrams, however, to show how words that struck him as brilliant when he wrote them—under the influence of nitrous oxide–dissolved into meaninglessness when the nitrous oxide wore off. In such extravagant language, James said, "reason and silliness united." See William James, *The Will to Believe and Other Essays in Popular Philosophy* (1897; Cambridge: Harvard University Press, 1979), pp. 219–20; see also William James, *The Principles of Psychology* (1890; Cambridge: Harvard University Press, 1981), vol. 1, pp. 254–55. For an interpretation that stresses the instability of James' writings but emphasizes what James hoped to accomplish thereby, see William Joseph Gavin, *William James and the Reinstatement of the Vague* (Philadelphia: Temple University Press, 1992).

25 William James to Gertrude Stein, May 25, 1910, William James Papers, Houghton Library, Harvard University, Cambridge. On William James' letters to his brother Henry that contrast the writing of fiction with his own struggles against the "resistance" of "facts" and the ideas of "other philosophers," see R. W. B. Lewis, *The Jameses: A Family Narrative* (New York: Farrar, Straus, Giroux, 1991), 409–10. Poirier, *Poetry and Pragmatism*, pp. 166–67. For an alternative view, see David Bromwich, "Recent Work in Literary Criticism," *Social Research*, 53 (Autumn 1986): 447. Too often, Bromwich writes (with Fredric Jameson and Terry Eagleton in mind), critics who indulge their own impulses as readers obliterate the past, minimizing "the differentness of the past," a consciousness of which "performs a critical function." Historical materials "are not altogether tractable: they will not do everything we want them to." When recounting changes in literary criticism, Poirier underscores Bromwich's point by shifting from the "linguistic skepticism" he endorses in theory to a commonsense reliance on shared meanings of words. See Poirier, *Poetry and Pragmatism*, 171–93.

26 Richard J. Bernstein, *John Dewey* (New York: Washington Square Press, 1966); Richard J. Bernstein, *Praxis and Action: Contemporary Philosophies of Human Activity* (Philadelphia: University of Pennsylvania Press, 1971), pp. 319, 314.

27 Bernstein, *Restructuring of Social and Political Theory*; Richard J. Bernstein, *Beyond Objectivism and Relativism: Science, Hermeneutics, and Praxis* (Philadelphia: University of Pennsylvania Press, 1983), pp. 18, 223.

28 Putnam, *Reason, Truth, and History*, p. 126; Hilary Putnam, *Renewing Philosophy* (Cambridge: Harvard University Press, 1992), p. 197; interview with Putnam in Giovanna Borradori, *The American Philosopher*, trans. Rosanna Crocitto (Chicago: University of Chicago Press, 1994), pp. 60–61, 66.

29 Hilary Putnam, *Realism with a Human Face* (Cambridge: Harvard University Press, 1990), p. 21; Richard Rorty, "Putnam and the Relativist Menace," *Journal of Philosophy* 90 (Sept. 1993): 449, 457.

30 Rorty, "Putnam and the Relativist Menace," p. 458; Hilary Putnam, "Why Reason Can't Be Naturalized," in Hilary Putnam, *Philosophical Papers*, vol. 3, *Realism and Reason* (New York: Cambridge University Press, 1983), pp. 229–47. See also Richard Rorty, "Putnam on Truth," *Philosophy and Phenomenological Research*, 52 (June 1992): 415–18; and Hilary Putnam, "Truth, Activation Vectors, and Possessive Conditions for Concepts," *ibid.*, 431–47. Hilary Putnam, "The Question of Realism," in Hilary Putnam, *Words and Life*. ed. James Conant (Cambridge: Harvard University Press, 1994), pp. 299–302.

31 Putnam, "Question of Realism," pp. 305, 292n6. On the early pragmatists' theory of voluntary action and its relation to their conception of truth, see James T. Kloppenberg, *Uncertain Victory: Social Democracy and Progressivism in European and American Thought, 1870–1920* (New York: Oxford University Press, 1986), pp. 79–94. Hilary Putnam and Ruth Anna Putnam, "Education for Democracy," in Putnam, *Words and Life*, p. 227; and Hilary Putnam and Ruth Anna Putnam, "Dewey's *Logic:* Epistemology as Hypothesis," *ibid.*, p. 218.

32 Putnam, *Reason, Truth, and History*, 215. For a recent restatement of this argument, see Putnam, "Pragmatism and Moral Objectivity," in Putnam, *Words and Life*, pp. 151–81.

33 See Richard Rorty, "Trotsky and the Wild Orchids," *Common Knowledge* 1 (Winter 1992): 140–53.

34 Richard Shusterman, *Pragmatist Aesthetics: Living Beauty, Rethinking Art* (Oxford: B. Blackwell, 1992), pp. 22, 32, 62, 76, 120–34. See also David R. Hiley, James F. Bohman, and Richard Shusterman, eds., *The Interpretive Turn: Philosophy, Science, Culture* (Ithaca: Cornell University Press, 1991). On the difference between nineteenth- and twentieth-century hermeneutics, and the reasons why historians should recover the former, see Michael Ermarth, "The Transformation of Hermeneutics: 19th-Century Ancients and 20th-Century Moderns," *Monist* 64 (April 1981): 176–94.

35 John Dewey, *Logic: The Theory of Inquiry* (1938) in Dewey, *Later Works*, vol. 12, p. 74. See also the thoughtful discussion in Richard Shusterman, "Dewey on Experience: Foundations or Reconstruction?," *Philosophical Forum* 26 (Winter 1994): 127–48.

36 Giles Gunn, *Thinking Across the American Grain: Ideology, Intellect, and the New Pragmatism* (Chicago: University of Chicago Press, 1992), pp. 112–13. For James' draft of the opening of his Clifford lectures in Edinburgh, the basis for *The Varieties of Religious Experience*, see Perry, *Thought and Character of William James*, vol. 2, pp. 328–29.

37 For an incisive discussion from an implicitly pragmatist perspective, see David A. Hollinger, *Postethnic America: Beyond Multiculturalism* (New York: Basic Books, 1995).

38 John Dewey, "Creative Democracy—The Task Before Us," in Dewey, *Later Works*, vol. 14, p. 228; William James, "The Social Value of the College Bred," in William James, *Writings, 1902–1910*, ed. Bruce Kuklick (New York: Library of America, 1987), p. 1245.

39 John Dewey, *The Study of Ethics: A Syllabus*, in John Dewey, *The Early Works, 1882–1898*, ed. Jo Ann Boydston (Carbondale: University of Southern Illinois Press, 1967–1972), vol. 4, p. 339; Dewey, *Public and Its Problems*, 344–45; Dewey, *Experience and Nature*, 74–76; and Dewey, *Art as Experience*, in Dewey, *Later Works*, vol. 10, p. 156.

40 Dewey, "Creative Democracy," pp. 224–30, esp. 226–28.

41 *Ibid.*, 228–30. On this dimension of Dewey's pragmatism, see also Hilary Putnam, "A Reconsideration of Deweyan Democracy," in *Pragmatism in Law and Society*, ed. Michael Brint and William Weaver (Boulder: Westview, 1991), pp. 217–43. On the importance of pluralism to pragmatism, see also Putnam, *Words and Life*, pp. 194–95.

42 John Dewey, *Individualism Old and New*, in Dewey, *Later Works*, vol. 5, p. 115. The

assumption that knowledge inevitably masks and imposes power often underlies such charges of elitism. From a Deweyan perspective one might concede the point and ask what alternative is preferable to stipulating that democratic principles should shape the process of inquiry and the formation of those communities that evaluate knowledge claims. Particularly for scholars, the refusal to admit that there are better and worse— more and less democratic—ways to generate knowledge is self-defeating. See the judicious review essay: Thomas Bender, "Social Science, Objectivity and Pragmatism" *Annals of Scholarship*, 9 (Winter–Spring 1992): 183–97.

43 William James, *Talks to Teachers on Psychology; and to Students on Some of Life's Ideals* (1899; New York: Holt, 1958), pp. 188–89, 169, 19–20. On James' tragic sensibility and Dewey's indomitable democratic faith, see Kloppenberg, *Uncertain Victory*, pp. 115–95, 340–415. On James' politics, compare the contrasting emphases of Deborah J. Coon, " 'One Moment in the World's Salvation': Anarchism and the Radicalization of William James," *Journal of American History*, 83 (June 1996): 70–99; and George Cotkin, *William James: Public Philosopher* (Baltimore: Johns Hopkins University Press, 1990). On Dewey's democratic ideas, see Westbrook, *John Dewey and American Democracy*; and Alan Ryan, *John Dewey and the High Tide of American Liberalism* (New York: W. W. Norton, 1995). For the long-standard view of the differences between James' and Dewey's outlooks, see James Campbell, *The Community Reconstructs: The Meaning of Pragmatic Social Thought* (Urbana: University of Illinois Press, 1992). For criticism of Dewey, George Herbert Mead, and James Tufts for trying to moderate class conflict and to translate their Protestantism and republicanism into a reformism supposedly ill suited to the industrial era, see Andrew Feffer, *The Chicago Pragmatists and American Progressivism* (Ithaca: Cornell University Press, 1993). An imaginative analysis that credits Dewey and especially James with realizing that corporate capitalism ushered in possibilities for a "postmodern subjectivity" is James Livingston, *Pragmatism and the Political Economy of Cultural Revolution, 1850–1940* (Chapel Hill: University of North Carolina Press, 1994).

44 Richard Rorty, "Solidarity or Objectivity," in *Post-Analytic Philosophy*, ed. John Rajchman and Cornel West (New York: Columbia University Press, 1985), pp. 15–16; Rorty, *Consequences of Pragmatism*, p. 166; Richard Rorty, *Contingency, Irony, and Solidarity* (New York: Cambridge University Press, 1989), pp. xvi, 53, 189–90.

45 Rorty, *Contingency, Irony, and Solidarity*, p. 53; Rorty, "Trotsky and the Wild Orchids," pp. 140–53; Rorty, *Philosophical Papers*, vol. 1, p. 210; Richard Rorty, "The Intellectuals at the End of Socialism," *Yale Review*, 80 (April 1992): 1–16; Richard Rorty, "Human Rights, Rationality and Sentimentality," *ibid.*, 81 (October 1993): 1–20.

46 Rorty, *Contingency, Irony, and Solidarity*, pp. 22, 37, 68; Rorty, "Dewey Between Hegel and Darwin," pp. 65, 64.

47 John Dewey, "Nature in Experience," in Dewey, *Later Works*, vol. 14, p. 150; Borradori, *American Philosopher*, trans. Crocitto, p. 117; Rorty, "Dewey Between Hegel and Darwin," p. 68. On the contrast between Rorty's ideas about history, religion, ethics, and politics and those of other pragmatists, see James T. Kloppenberg, "Democracy and Disenchantment: From Weber and Dewey to Habermas and Rorty," in *Modernist Impulses in the Human Sciences*, pp. 69–90; and James T. Kloppenberg, "Knowledge and Belief in American Public Life," in *Knowledge and Belief: Enlightenment Traditions and Modern Religious Thought*, ed. William M. Shea and Peter A. Huff (New York: Cambridge University Press, 1995), pp. 27–51. On the connection between Dewey's ideas

about ethics and his commitment to democracy, see Westbrook, *John Dewey and American Democracy*. See also Richard Rorty, "Intellectuals in Politics," *Dissent*, 38 (Fall 1991): 483–90.

48 Cornel West, *The American Evasion of Philosophy: A Genealogy of Pragmatism* (Madison: University of Wisconsin Press, 1989), p. 4.

49 Cornel West, "Politics of American Neo-Pragmatism," in *Post-Analytic Philosophy*, pp. 259–72. On West's account of American pragmatism and his "prophetic pragmatism," see Kloppenberg, "Knowledge and Belief in American Public Life." Fine studies of philosophy, religion, and ethics from pragmatist perspectives are Henry Samuel Levinson, *The Religious Investigations of William James* (Chapel Hill: University of North Carolina Press, 1981), and Steven C. Rockefeller, *John Dewey: Religious Faith and Democratic Humanism* (New York: Columbia University Press, 1991). For a "modest pragmatism" that does not rely explicitly on Dewey but echoes many of his ideas, see Jeffrey Stout, *Ethics after Babel: The Languages of Morals and Their Discontents* (Boston: Beacon, 1988).

50 Cornel West, *Race Matters* (1993; New York: Vintage Press, 1994), pp. 150–51. For Henry Louis Gates Jr.'s description of West as "the preeminent African-American intellectual of our time," see Jack E. White, "Philosopher with a Mission," *Time* (June 7, 1993): 60–62; for another generous assessment of West, see Robert Boynton, "The New Intellectuals," *Atlantic Monthly* 275 (March 1995): 53–70. Compare the pyrotechnic display of *ressentiment* by Leon Wieseltier, "All and Nothing at All," *New Republic* (March 6, 1995): 31–36. For responses from readers (including Rorty), see "Decline of Cornel West," *New Republic* (April 3, 1995): 6–7. Richard Rorty, review of *The American Evasion of Philosophy* by Cornel West, *Transition* 52 (1991): 75–77.

51 Charlene Haddock Seigfried, *Chaos and Context: A Study in William James* (Athens, Ohio: Ohio University Press, 1978); Charlene Haddock Seigfried, *William James's Radical Reconstruction of Philosophy* (Albany: SUNY Press, 1990). Seigfried brought together a group of essays with her introduction, Charlene Haddock Seigfried, "The Missing Perspective: Feminist Pragmatism," *Transactions of the Charles S. Peirce Society* 27 (Fall 1991): 405–74. And see the special issue "Feminism and Pragmatism," ed. Charlene Haddock Seigfried, *Hypatia* 8 (Spring 1993). There are no specifically pragmatist or feminist doctrines about philosophical or political issues, according to Richard Rorty, "Feminism, Ideology, and Deconstruction: A Pragmatist View," *ibid.*, 96–103.

52 The special issue "Feminism and Pragmatism" contains essays on the importance of experience for early feminist pragmatists and responses to contemporary linguistic pragmatists. See especially Jane Upin, "Charlotte Perkins Gilman: Instrumentalism Beyond Dewey," *Hypatia*, 8 (Spring 1993): 38–63; M. Regina Leffers, "Pragmatists Jane Addams and John Dewey Inform the Ethic of Care," *ibid.*, pp. 64–77; Gregory Fernando Pappas, "Dewey and Feminism: The Affective and Relationships in Dewey's Ethics," *ibid.*, pp. 78–95; Timothy V. Kaufman-Osborn, "Teasing Feminist Sense from Experience," *ibid.*, pp. 124–44; Mitchell Aboulafia, "Was George Herbert Mead a Feminist?," *ibid.*, pp. 145–58; Jane Duran, "The Intersection of Feminism and Pragmatism," *ibid.*, pp. 159–71; and Lynn Hankinson Nelson, "A Question of Evidence," *ibid.*, pp. 172–89. For documents illuminating Jessie Taft's pragmatist feminism and demonstrating James's commitment to feminism in practice, see "Archive," *ibid.*, pp. 215–33.

53 For a persuasive case for historicizing the concept of experience and examining critically all appeals to experience that resembles the perspective I call pragmatic herme-

neutics, see Joan Scott, "The Evidence of Experience," *Critical Inquiry* 17 (Summer 1991): 773–97. Cf. James T. Kloppenberg, "Objectivity and Historicism: A Century of American Historical Writing," *American Historical Review* 94 (October 1989): 1011–30. For a feminist perspective on the uses of the concept of experience, see Lorraine Code, "Who Cares? The Poverty of Objectivism for a Moral Epistemology," *Annals of Scholarship* 9 (Winter–Spring 1992): 1–18.

54 Joan Williams, "Gender Wars: Selfless Women in the Republic of Choice," *New York University Law Review* 66 (Dec. 1991): 1559–1634. See also Joan Williams, "Deconstructing Gender," *Michigan Law Review* 87 (February 1989): 797–845; and Joan Williams, "Virtue and Oppression," *Nomos: Yearbook of the American Society of Political and Legal Philosophy*, ed. John W. Chapman and William A. Galston (New York: New York University Press, 1992), pp. 309–37. Margaret Jane Radin, "The Pragmatist and the Feminist," in *Pragmatism in Law and Society*, pp. 127–53.

55 See Joan Williams, "Critical Legal Studies: The Death of Transcendence and the Rise of the New Langdells," *New York University Law Review* 62 (June 1987): 429–96.

56 Richard Posner, "What Has Pragmatism to Offer Law?," in *Pragmatism in Law and Society*, pp. 42, 44. See also Richard Posner, *The Problems of Jurisprudence* (Cambridge: Harvard University Press, 1990), p. 150.

57 Stanley Fish, "Almost Pragmatism: The Jurisprudence of Richard Posner, Richard Rorty, and Ronald Dworkin," in *Pragmatism in Law and Society*, p. 63.

58 *Ibid.*, pp. 71, 56. At an interdisciplinary conference on pragmatism held in November 1995 at the City University of New York, Fish was chosen to provide the closing remarks, which allowed him to offer as the last word on the subject his version of pragmatism— which might fairly be summarized as "anything goes." Although Bernstein, Putnam, and Westbrook participated in the conference, discussion centered on the ideas of thinkers such as Rorty and Fish. That focus reflects the current academic debate; this essay attempts to demonstrate the differences between linguistic pragmatism and the ideas of earlier pragmatists and to show what has been lost in the transformation. [*Editor's Note*: This is the conference from which this book originated. Every effort was made to include the widest range of views of neopragmatism, as well as criticism of those views. Professor Kloppenberg himself was invited to participate, and when a scheduling conflict prevented him from attending, was urged to submit a paper for this volume.]

59 *Ibid.*, p. 72. For versions of pragmatist legal theory more Deweyan than Rortyan (or Fishy), see especially: Thomas C. Grey, "What Good is Legal Pragmatism?," in *Pragmatism in Law and Society*, pp. 9–27; Cornel West, "The Limits of Neopragmatism," *ibid.*, pp. 121–26; Radin, "Pragmatist and the Feminist," *ibid.*, pp. 127–53; Joan C. Williams, "Rorty, Radicalism, Romanticism: The Politics of the Gaze," *ibid.*, pp. 155–80; Jean Bethke Elshtain, "Civic Identity and the State," *ibid.*, pp. 181–96; Martha Minow and Elizabeth V. Spelman, "In Context," *ibid.*, pp. 247–73; Catharine Wells, "Situated Decisionmaking," *ibid.*, pp. 275–93; and especially Putnam, "Reconsideration of Deweyan Democracy," *ibid.*, pp. 217–43.

60 Cass Sunstein, *The Partial Constitution* (Cambridge: Harvard University Press, 1993), p. 127. For criticism of Sunstein's program as reinstating the power of educated white male elites, see Robin West, "The Constitution of Reasons," *Michigan Law Review* 92 (May 1994): 1409–37. Cf. James T. Kloppenberg, "Deliberative Democracy and Judicial Supremacy," *Law and History Review* 13 (Fall 1995): 393–411. On the relation between

pragmatism and legal realism, see Morton J. Horwitz, *The Transformation of American Law, 1870–1960: The Crisis of Legal Orthodoxy* (New York: Oxford University Press, 1992); and James T. Kloppenberg, "The Theory and Practice of Legal History," *Harvard Law Review* 106 (April 1993): 1332–51.

61 Putnam, "Reconsideration of Deweyan Democracy," p. 217. On the link between this "modern view of truth" and democracy, see also Putnam and Putnam, "Dewey's *Logic,*" pp. 198, 215–17; and Hilary Putnam in Borradori, *American Philosopher,* pp. 61–62.

62 I am grateful to Richard Fox, Robert Westbrook, and Joan Williams for conversations that helped sharpen my understanding of the issues discussed in this paragraph.

63 Richard J. Bernstein, *The New Constellation: The Ethical-Political Horizons of Modernity/Postmodernity* (Cambridge: MIT Press, 1992).

64 Bernstein, *New Constellation,* pp. 326–39; for Bernstein's extended discussion of Rorty, see *ibid.,* pp. 233–92. See also Richard J. Bernstein, *Philosophical Profiles: Essays in a Pragmatic Mode* (Philadelphia: University of Pennsylvania Press, 1986), pp. 260–72.

65 Jürgen Habermas, "Questions and Counterquestions," in *Habermas and Modernity,* ed. Richard J. Bernstein (Cambridge: MIT Press, 1995), p. 198. On the strange career of pragmatism in Europe, see Hans Joas, *Pragmatism and Social Theory,* trans. Jeremy Gaines, Raymond Meyer, and Steven Minner (Chicago: University of Chicago Press, 1993). Joas has also written the best study of George Herbert Mead: Hans Joas, *G. H. Mead: A Contemporary Re-examination of His Thought* (Cambridge: MIT Press, 1985). See the significant restatement of pragmatism in Hans Joas, *The Creativity of Action,* translated by Jeremy Gaines and Paul Keast (Chicago: University of Chicago Press, 1996).

66 Habermas, "Questions and Counterquestions," 196–98. Habermas traces refinements in his major works to insights derived from Mead's symbolic interactionism. See the new concluding chapter written for the English edition of Jürgen Habermas, *Moral Consciousness and Communicative Action,* trans. Christian Lenhardt and Shierry Weber Nicholsen (1983; Cambridge: MIT Press, 1990), pp. 195–202.

67 See Bernstein, "Resurgence of Pragmatism," and Richard J. Bernstein, "American Pragmatism: The Conflict of Narratives," in *Rorty and Pragmatism,* ed. Saatkamp, 54–67. Those contemporaries I have linked together as Deweyan critics of linguistic pragmatism do not necessarily share my perception of their similarities. See, for example, Robert Westbrook, "A New Pragmatism," *American Quarterly* 45 (Sept. 1993): 438–44; and the spirited exchange: Giles Gunn, "Response to Robert Westbrook," *ibid.,* 46 (June 1994): 297–303; and Robert Westbrook, "Response to Giles Gunn," *ibid.,* 304–7.

68 By their qualifications and caveats, two recent endorsements of textualism illustrate the lure of a more Deweyan pragmatism. On the necessity of giving some determinate shape to the past even if one abandons grand narratives, see Dorothy Ross, "Grand Narrative in American Historical Writing: From Romance to Uncertainty," *American Historical Review* 100 (June 1995): 675–77. For an argument that "strong misreading"— of the sort Rorty recommends and Derrida practices—"is altogether misplaced as historical reading and critique" because "history does not emulate creative writing and is constrained by different norms of inquiry," see Dominick LaCapra, "History, Language, and Reading: Waiting for Crillon," *American Historical Review* 100 (June 1995): 814, 816.

69 James, *Pragmatism,* 111–12, 102–3; Putnam, *Words and Life,* 276–77; Hilary Putnam, *The Many Faces of Realism* (La Salle: Open Court, 1987), pp. 70–71.

70 Peter Novick, *That Noble Dream: The "Objectivity Question" and the American Historical Profession* (New York: Cambridge University Press, 1988), p. 629. For readings of American historians' practice that discern widespread if implicit commitment to something resembling pragmatic hermeneutics, see Kloppenberg, "Objectivity and Historicism"; Thomas Haskell, "Objectivity Is Not Neutrality: Rhetoric vs. Practice in Peter Novick's *That Noble Dream*," *History and Theory*, 29, no. 2 (1990): 129–57; and David A. Hollinger, "Postmodernist Theory and Wissenschaftliche Practice," *American Historical Review* 96 (June 1991): 688–92.

71 On the relation between religious faith, social reform, and pragmatism, see Kloppenberg, "Knowledge and Belief in American Public Life."

72 On the inevitability of selection and interpretation in historical writing, see Putnam, *Words and Life*, 206–7. For a recent endorsement of pragmatism as an alternative to postmodern skepticism about historical truth, which recommends combining it with "practical realism" because pragmatism is otherwise rudderless due to its "deference to practice over principle," see Joyce Appleby, Lynn Hunt, and Margaret Jacob, *Telling the Truth About History* (New York: W. W. Norton, 1994), pp. 283–91. This familiar but historically inaccurate characterization of pragmatism as nothing more than antifoundationalism underestimates its resources for historians' practice.

73 William James, "The Moral Philosopher and the Moral Life," in James, *Will to Believe*, 141; John Dewey, *Reconstruction in Philosophy*, in Dewey, *Middle Works*, vol. 12, p. 173.

Pragmatism and Democracy: Reconstructing the Logic of John Dewey's Faith

ROBERT B. WESTBROOK

Contemporary American pragmatism—or "neopragmatism," as it is usually called—is not of one mind; indeed, one might well say, with John Diggins, that it has a "split personality." Few would deny that the revival among American intellectuals of interest in pragmatism—and in the work of John Dewey, in particular—has turned on the influence of Richard Rorty, who declared in 1979 that Dewey is, along with Heidegger and Wittgenstein, one of the "three most important philosophers of our century," and then proceeded to tie Dewey to the controversial arguments that have made Rorty one of the most important philosophers of this century's waning hour. Yet Rorty has attracted sharp criticism from philosophers such as Richard Bernstein, Hilary Putnam, and Richard Shusterman, who think of themselves as pragmatists no less than he.[1]

American intellectual historians have also been among Rorty's severest critics, and I would include myself in that number. Having labored hard to figure out what Dewey had to say, we strenuously object when Rorty tries to get him to say things he did not say and that we cannot imagine him saying. Like Rorty's neopragmatist critics among philosophers, we historians have targeted much of our criticism on his effort to fashion pragmatism into a kind of home-grown poststructuralism, his "Dewey is Nietzsche and Foucault with a big serving of social hope and confidence in the promise of American life" argument. Thus, over the last several years historians such as James Kloppenberg and I have found ourselves participating regularly with Rorty in conferences and symposia in which our role is to say to him, often repeatedly, "Gee, that argument that you say that you and Dewey make is very provocative, but Dewey never made it and I do not believe he ever would make it since it is at odds with arguments he did make." Rorty then shrugs his shoulders and acknowledges genially that the Dewey he is talking about is one of his "imaginary playmates," a "hypothetical Dewey" who says the sort of things Dewey would have said had he made the "linguistic turn" and stops saying the things he in fact did say because he had not made that turn. We then grant Rorty every right to play with whomever he wishes, asking only that he stop saying things such as "Those who share Dewey's pragmatism will say that although [democracy] may need philosophical articulation, it does not need philosophical backup."[2]

But what of Rorty's neopragmatist critics? Are they any less guilty of fashioning a hypothetical Dewey to serve their purposes? Rather than repeat an exercise in what has come to be called "Rorty-bashing," I would like here to examine the Dewey of one of Rorty's most discerning neopragmatist critics, Hilary Putnam. In particular, I want to scrutinize Putnam's recent contention that he has found an "*epistemological justification of democracy*" in Dewey's philosophy. Not only is this contention important in its own right, but it points up a significant difference in the approach of Rorty and Putnam to their pragmatist predecessors. Whereas Rorty has lamented those efforts Dewey made to provide some "philosophical backup" for democracy, Putnam has sought to improve upon those efforts. Whereas Rorty regards pragmatism as a form of antifoundationalist "trash disposal" that can serve even opposing political "prophecies," Putnam sees pragmatism as a theory of knowledge, meaning, and truth with a special affinity for radical democracy.[3]

On the face of it, Putnam's contention that he finds an epistemological argument for democracy in Dewey's philosophy is jarring for intellectual historians. We may be sure, I think, that Dewey never offered anything that he *called* "an epistemological justification of democracy," for "epistemology" was a dirty word in Dewey's vocabulary. He blamed what he termed the "epistemology industry" of modern philosophy since Descartes for creating all the unsolvable problems that he wanted philosophers to stop trying to solve and simply get over. But, on inspection, what Putnam is offering is an argument that he ties principally to Dewey's theory of inquiry, that is, his logic. His central claim, which he also attributes to Dewey, is that "Democracy is not just one form of social life among other workable forms of social life; it is the precondition for the full application of intelligence to the solution of social problems." Putnam says that for him (and Dewey) democracy is a "cognitive value" insofar as it is "a requirement for experimental inquiry in any area. To reject democracy is to reject the idea of being experimental."[4]

If Dewey did indeed offer this argument he probably would have called it a "logical argument for democracy," insofar as logic was where he lodged his constructive efforts to write about knowledge, meaning, and truth after he himself got over the problems of epistemology. Nonetheless, as far as I know, for all his efforts to link democracy and experimental science Dewey never referred to a "logical argument for democracy." Putnam never directs us to Dewey's use of anything like such a phrase. Of course, the fact that Dewey never made an argument that he called a "logical argument for democracy" does not mean he did not make the argument Putnam describes. But it does leave one wondering at the outset whether we are again being invited to entertain an imaginary playmate.

Putnam's notion that Dewey had a logical argument for democracy intrigues me because I believe that in my own efforts to discern, as I put it elsewhere, "the implications for democracy of every aspect of [Dewey's] thinking," I have given his logic short shrift.[5] To be sure, there are historians who have done a better job of tying Dewey's logic to his democratic faith. Kloppenberg, for example, has said that Dewey was taking on the challenge of "constructing a democratic political culture on the quicksand of instrumentalist logic." He met this challenge, Kloppenberg suggests, by deflecting the view of Max Weber who contended that "the logic of instrumental rationality contradicts the logic of democracy" and by arguing instead that "democracy is uniquely suited to the twentieth century" precisely "because the democratic community replicates the community of broadly conceived scientific enquiry that serves as the prototype of instrumental reasoning." As Kloppenberg put it, "Free and creative individuals, in democratic as in scientific communities, collectively test hypotheses to find out what works best. These communities set their own goals, determine their own tests, and evaluate their results in a spirit of constructive cooperation."[6] I think Kloppenberg is absolutely right to say that Dewey asserted this analogy between democratic community and scientific communities of inquiry guided by instrumental logic. But the analogy is not self-evident (as Weber would say), and we need to know more about the *argument* Dewey offered for it. My own view is that, strictly speaking, Dewey never offered such an argument, though he often seemed to promise one.

So when Putnam says "one can find" an "epistemological argument for democracy" in Dewey's work, what he must mean is that one can reconstruct or piece together such an argument, an argument for which Dewey provided the elements but which he never put together himself. Putnam is thus not making an argument, like many of Rorty's, which he knows Dewey would not have made, but he is making an argument that Dewey did not make. Yet Putnam is in effect saying that Dewey could have made this argument, and I think he is correct.[7]

I

Putnam's account of Dewey's logical argument has three elements, each of which builds on that preceding it in the course of the argument. First, Dewey, following Peirce, held that the best way human beings had found to fix beliefs—or, as Dewey preferred to call them, "warranted assertions"—was by means of the methods, practices, and values of a community of competent inquirers, the best exemplification of which was the community of modern science. Such communities began their investigations under the stimulus of particular doubts within the context of a body of warranted assertions that they had no good reason to doubt. And they settled such particular doubts with warranted assertions that, like all warranted assertions, were not certain but fallible and subject to revision should fresh doubts about their warrant arise. Putnam says that the recognition "one can be both fallibilistic *and* antiskeptical is perhaps *the* unique insight of American pragmatism."[8] Dewey's logic was an inquiry into inquiry, an examination of the methods, practices, and values of communities of inquiry that had best served to generate warranted assertions.

Second, Dewey extended the range of inquiry to include judgments of practice and moral judgments. This move is of particular significance for the argument, because it is the application of inquiry to value-laden "problematic situations" that makes inquiry available for the sort of issues that are most likely to confront social and political communities. As Putnam says, Dewey believed that "we have learned something about how to conduct inquiry in general, and that what applies to intelligently conducted inquiry in general applies to ethical inquiry in particular."[9]

Finally, Dewey argued that a community of inquiry should be democratic, not (in this case) on ethical grounds, but on what Putnam terms "cognitive" grounds. That is, the quality of inquiry is affected by the degree to which that community is inclusive or exclusive of all the potential, competent participants in that inquiry and by the democratic or undemocratic character of the norms that guide its practice. Here, Putnam draws on Dewey's argument in *The Public and Its Problems* (1927) against resting content with elite inquiry into social problems and for including the wider public in the making of public policy. Dewey argued that without the participation of the public in the formulation of such policy, it could not reflect the common needs and interests of the society because these needs and interests were known only to the public. And these needs and interests could not be made known without democratic "consultation and discussion which uncover social needs and troubles." Hence, Dewey said, "A class of experts is inevitably so removed from common interests as to become a class with private interests and private knowledge, which in social matters is not knowledge at all."[10] Elite rule was thus cognitively debilitating.

Effective inquiry required that the community of inquiry not only be inclusive but that its practices be democratic. For Dewey, Putnam says, "the need for fundamental democratic institutions as freedom of thought and speech follows . . . from requirements of scientific procedure in general: the unimpeded flow of information and the freedom to offer and to criticize hypotheses."[11] Successful inquiry in all fields, including science, rested in part on a democratic "discourse ethics" that shaped the cooperation of the community of inquirers. As Putnam puts it:

> Where there is no opportunity to challenge accepted hypotheses by criticizing the evidence upon which their acceptance was based, or by criticizing the application of the norms of scientific inquiry to that evidence, or by offering rival hypotheses, and where questions and suggestions are systematically ignored, the scientific enterprise always suffers. When relations among scientists become relations of hierarchy and dependence, or when scientists instrumentalize other scientists, again the scientific enterprise suffers.[12]

Dewey well recognized that the democratic values embedded in inquiry were a "regulative ideal" and he was not blind to the corruptions that afflicted inquiry, even in science. But without such democratic norms, inquiry was doomed.

II

I think Putnam has indeed "found" a logical argument for democracy in Dewey's work, and structured it in a fashion that I can well imagine Dewey emulating. It should be said, however, that not all of the elements of this argument were well-developed by Dewey. The most elaborated aspect of the argument was the second, the claim that one could, as he put it in the title of an early and damnably obscure article, identify the "logical conditions of a scientific treatment of morality." This is one of Dewey's best known, and most notorious, claims, and he worked it out in many of his logical writings over the course of his career. It is also the part of the argument to which Putnam devotes most of his attention, not only by way of sympathetically considering Dewey's efforts to develop a logic for moral inquiry but also by contributing arguments of his own to the cause.

Putnam's attentiveness to the second stage in his reconstruction of Dewey's logical argument for democracy is not surprising, for it is here that we begin to feel underfoot what Kloppenberg nicely terms "the quicksand of instrumentalist logic." As Putnam says, Dewey made two claims that leave many readers unsure that he is on solid ground. First, he complained (repeatedly) that many of the ills of modern society derive from a failure to bring scientific reasoning to bear on ethical problems. Although we are perfectly willing to allow such reasoning to enter into our consideration of the means to our valued ends, we refuse to apply it to an evaluation of those ends themselves. Dewey tells us, Putnam observes, that we have "to see every problem as an invitation to inquiry, to understand all inquiry as of one pattern, and to abandon the demands for ends that are beyond all evaluation." But having told us that scientific inquiry can do something that many do not believe it can do, Dewey then goes on to ratify our conception of scientific rationality as "an affair of the relations of means and consequences."[13] In other words, having got our hopes up that science could do something we did not think it could do, which we presumed meant that Dewey was going to offer us a new conception of scientific reasoning, he confirms our view of scientific reasoning and seems simply to be saying that we have decidedly underestimated what it—that is, instrumental reasoning—can do. Not surprisingly, many have remained skeptical of this claim.

As Putnam says, Dewey's argument essentially took the form of showing how moral judgments, like all judgments, are made in the context of particular problematic situations. In these situations our ends are transformed into what Dewey called ends-in-view. As such, they take shape as means to the resolution of the particular problem at hand. And as such, they are subject to inquiry, for we are now asking the question "Will this end-in-view solve this problem?" Dewey is trying to show us, as Putnam says, that "ends are neither laid up in a Platonic heaven nor the whims of individuals; they are, rather, ends-in-view, they guide conduct; in that capacity they are themselves means to solving a problem and as such rationality is competent to pronounce judgment on them."[14]

If one is willing to go this far with Dewey, a nagging question remains; that is, what *criteria* do we use to evaluate the success of our ends-in-view? When do we know that an evaluative problem has been successfully resolved? Here Putnam says several things that he claims Dewey says, but I believe Dewey did not say such things as clearly as Putnam does—and he often left them all too implicit. First, in the spirit of Peirce's critique of wholesale doubt, Putnam observes that communities of moral inquiry do not start from the position of doubting all of their values and prior evaluations. As he says, "As long as discussion is still possible, as long as one is not facing coercion or violence or total refusal to discuss, the participants in an actual discussion always share a large number of both factual assumptions and value assumptions that are not in question in the specific dispute. Very often, parties to a disagreement can agree that the disagreement has, in fact, been resolved, not by appeal to a universal set of 'criteria' but by appeal to values which are not in question in *that* dispute."[15]

Putnam acknowledges that a persistent critic might still claim that "there is no reason to think that people who follow Dewey's method will come to agreement on values, even if each person separately leads what we might regard as a rational life." Dewey, Putnam says, responds that he is not in the business of making a priori claims one way or the other. As an antiskeptical fallibilist, he claims only that we should not presume that no such agreement is possible in advance of inquiry. There is no good reason to believe that moral inquiry "must lead to *unresolvable* problems, even if there is no a priori guarantee that the problems it leads to are resolvable."[16]

Putnam's Dewey would also have us be aware that the resolution of a moral problem need not be agreement on values:

> If you and I disagree in our 'values' a resolution need not take the form of a universalistic principle that you and I and all other persons can accept as valid. If the value disagreement concerns only our separate lives, then the apparent disagreement may be resolvable by simply relativizing the judgments in question; it may be the case that it is well for you to live your life in one way and for me to live mine in another. . . . The idea of ethical objectivity is not the same as and does not presuppose the idea of *a universal way of life.* Dewey supports the former and consistently opposes the latter. Not only individuals but also communities and nations may have different but satisfactory ways of life.[17]

Finally, Putnam says Dewey would readily admit that there are problems that moral inquiry cannot solve. "Believing that ethical objectivity is possible is not the same thing as believing that there are no undecidable cases or no problems which, alas, cannot be solved."[18] This possibility of unresolvable problems does not distinguish moral inquiry from other inquiry: "not all problems in physics or mathematics or geology or history can be settled either, but that does not support the idea that warranted assertibility and truth exist in one domain but not in another."[19]

When it comes to the resolution of moral problems through inquiry,

Putnam admits that "Dewey can sound unreasonably optimistic if one does not keep in mind the range of different things that can count as the resolution of a problem."[20] My own view is that it is less Dewey than Putnam who brings this "range of resolution" to light.

One reason I think Putnam's version of Dewey's conception of moral inquiry is more satisfying than Dewey's own is that Putnam is more attentive to its intersubjective context than Dewey. Perhaps surprisingly, Dewey had much less to say about the communitarian context of inquiry generally—the first stage of the logical argument for democracy—than one might think. Although Dewey endorses Peirce's conception of the community of inquiry in the *Logic*, it was not until the 1930s that he really made much use of Peirce. And in his earlier work, he treats inquiry largely from the point of view of the individual, and does not really say much about what difference the communitarian context of scientific investigation makes to its practices.[21] This neglect of the social context of inquiry points, I think, to a curious feature of Dewey's philosophy generally, which I am hard-pressed to explain. Although he was always insisting on the primacy of the social, Dewey really did not have a whole lot to say that could in any strict sense be termed social theory. For example, although he claimed that psychology had to be a social psychology, he did not give us much social psychology, even in *Human Nature and Conduct* (1922), which was subtitled *An Introduction to Social Psychology*. For a well-developed, pragmatist social psychology, one has to turn to his friend, George Herbert Mead.

As I say, I think the neglect of social context in moral inquiry is a particularly noteworthy (and troubling) feature of Dewey's logical argument for democracy. Putnam is much too generous when he says that Dewey dealt capably with the problem of "moral disagreement."[22] As Kloppenberg and I have both observed, Dewey had too little to say even about intractable moral conflicts within individuals. Although he acknowledged that often the most an agent could do in any moral conflict was to "make the best adjustment he can among forces which are genuinely disparate," he was forever implying that such forces could be "unified" without ever, as William James put it, "butchering the ideal."[23] About moral disagreements between individuals, Dewey had even less to say. Dewey argued that in the final analysis moral decisions were shaped by character, by the sort of person one was or desired to be. But significant moral disagreements within a community of inquiry might well involve conflicts between individuals with quite different conceptions of the good life. Putnam to the contrary, Dewey does not seem to me to have ever addressed this problem head on. Putnam is giving Dewey too much credit when he says, in a Rawlsian or Habermasian vein, that Dewey

> anticipated an idea that has become a commonplace in contemporary moral philosophy, the idea that disagreement in individual conceptions of the good need not make it impossible to approximate (even if we never finally arrive at) agreement on just procedures and even agreement on such abstract and formal values as respect for one another's autonomy, non-instrumentalization of other persons, and such regulative ideas as the idea that in all our institutions we should strive to replace relations of hierarchy and dependence by relations of "symmetric reciprocity."[24]

Or, to put it another way, it is very difficult to discern a "theory of justice" in Dewey's logic of moral inquiry.

By far the sketchiest part of the logical argument for democracy in Dewey's work is its contention that communities of inquiry must be democratic if inquiry was to be effective. But Putnam's recapitulation of the argument is so brief as to leave out an important consideration that Dewey did address forthrightly in contending that the community of inquiry engaged in the making of public policy should be inclusively democratic. That is, one might contend that because participation in communities of inquiry is limited to the *competent,* and because most members of the public are not competent, there is no need to include them and, indeed, including them would damage rather than enhance the relevant inquiries.

Dewey did not dispute the provision that inquiry should be left in the hands of the competent; it was an essential provision of the regulative ideal of inquiry that he shared with Peirce. But he contested the claim that most members of the public were not capable of competent participation in the inquiry necessary for the making of public policy. Most of the inquiries tributary to making public policy were, he agreed, best left to experts. One did not want a garage mechanic making economic predictions, any more than one wanted an economist working on one's car. But when it came to judging "the bearing of the knowledge supplied by others upon common concerns" he believed that most people possessed this capacity, and he charged that advocates of the rule of experts greatly exaggerated the intelligence and ability it took to render these kinds of judgments.[25] This is not to say that Dewey did not believe that the quality of public opinion could be improved. Indeed, for this purpose, he advocated a kind of public education that would reconstruct a common schooling for American children that would provide them with the skills and knowledge necessary to effective citizenship. He envisioned schools that would "cultivate the habit of suspended judgment, of skepticism, of desire for evidence, of appeal to observation rather than sentiment, discussion rather than bias, inquiry rather than conventional idealizations."[26] Dewey also called for the revitalization of local "publics" in which adults could also learn by doing. The education that participating in such local, face-to-face publics provided would, he predicted, "render nugatory the indictment of democracy drawn on the basis of the ignorance, bias, and levity of the masses."[27] In sum, as Putnam concludes, Dewey's logical argument for democracy was a logical argument for a radical democracy, one "which develops the capacities of all its men and women to think for themselves, to participate in the design and testing of social policies, and to judge results."[28]

Of course, a logical argument for democracy is not necessarily a convincing logical argument for democracy, and Putnam's Deweyan argument is vulnerable to criticism at every step in its progression. Even pragmatists cannot be presumed to consent to it. Rorty, who wants a "pragmatism without method" and has done his best to read Peirce out of the pragmatist canon, gets off the boat before it sets sail.[29] Peirce himself did not think inquiry could be extended to matters of moral judgment, and hence departs at the second stop. And Walter Lippmann, who thought in the 1920s that public policy could and should be submitted to a community of inquiry, called for excluding the public from that inquiry on the grounds of its incompetence. And even Dewey felt compelled to buttress his logic with an appeal to faith. Democracy, he said on his eightieth birthday, "is a way of personal life controlled not merely by faith in human nature in general but by faith in the capacity of human beings for intelligent judgment and action if proper conditions are furnished." This faith "is so deeply embedded in the methods which are intrinsic to democracy that when a professed democrat denies the faith he convicts himself of treachery to his profession."[30]

III

As this last remark of Dewey's suggests, Putnam's logical argument for democracy is not the only argument for democracy that one can find in his work. Dewey himself made ethical, aesthetic, and even metaphysical arguments for democracy. Perhaps, the best way to fit the logical argument within the larger context of Dewey's democratic thought is to see it as elements of an argument for *procedural* democracy. Dewey, of course, was impatient with procedural arguments for democracy, believing that too often they *reduced* democracy to its procedures and slighted its wider meaning as a "way of life." But democracy is, among other things, a set of procedures, and in the pieces of the logical argument Putnam pieces together, Dewey was, I think, reaching for a normative ideal for procedural democracy rooted in an expansive conception of the community of inquiry.

Seen in this light, I think we might say that Dewey was anticipating an ideal that contemporary democratic theorists have dubbed "deliberative democracy." Indeed, I wish this term was in the air when I was writing *John Dewey and American Democracy*, for I think it captures Dewey's procedural ideals better than the term I used, "participatory democracy," since it suggests something of the character of the participation involved in democratic associations.[31] One can well imagine democratic associations, such as nineteenth-century American political parties, that were highly participatory but were far from cooperative communities of inquiry.

The flavor of what deliberative democracy means can be conveyed by its features as stipulated by political theorist Joshua Cohen. A deliberative democracy, Cohen says, is an ongoing, independent association whose members share "a commitment to co-ordinating their activities within institutions that make deliberation possible and according to norms that they arrive at through their deliberation." It is a pluralistic association in which members "have diverse preferences, convictions and ideals concerning the conduct of their own lives." The members also "recognize one another as having deliberative capacities, i.e., the capacities required for entering into a public exchange of reasons and for acting on the result of such public reasoning." In a deliberative democracy, deliberation will ideally be free and reasoned and will take place among parties who are formally and substantively equal. Deliberation aims, Cohen says, at a "rationally motivated *consensus*"—though there is no guarantee that such a consensus will emerge.[32]

The family resemblances between Dewey's conception of democracy as a community of inquiry and this conception of deliberative democracy are no doubt obvious. To use Dewey's language, one might say that a deliberative democracy is an association in which individual members seek by means of deliberation to transform their individual "desires" into a collective consensus about what is "desirable." Thus, though Dewey does not have as fully elaborated a logical argument for democracy as one might hope, his logic might still prove of interest to theorists of deliberative democracy as they work out a conception of what "deliberation" amounts to.

Of course, deliberative democracy forecasts—as it did in Dewey's day— a substantial redistribution of power, even in those modern states that proclaim themselves democratic. A good argument for deliberative democracy is a purely academic exercise without a politics designed to push reality closer to its regulative ideals. And, as Dewey was often painfully aware, creating such a politics requires much more than sound logic.

Notes

1   John Patrick Diggins, *The Promise of Pragmatism: Modernism and the Crisis of Knowledge and Authority* (Chicago: University of Chicago Press, 1994), p. 455; Richard Rorty, *Philosophy and the Mirror of Nature* (Princeton: Princeton University Press, 1979), p. 5.
2   Richard Rorty, "Philosophy of the Oddball," *New Republic* (19 June 1989): 38; "Dewey between Hegel and Darwin" in *Modernist Impulses in the Human Sciences, 1870–1930,* ed. Dorothy Ross (Baltimore: Johns Hopkins University Press, 1994), p. 56; "The Priority of Democracy to Philosophy" in *Objectivity, Relativism, and Truth;* Vol. 1, *Philosophical Papers* (Cambridge: Cambridge University Press, 1991), p. 178. For a good example of an intellectual historian saying to Rorty the sort of things I describe, see James T. Kloppenberg, "Democracy and Disenchantment: From Weber and Dewey to Habermas and Rorty" in *Modernist Impulses,* ed. Ross, pp. 188–90. See also my *John Dewey and American Democracy* (Ithaca: Cornell University Press, 1991), pp. 539–42.
3   Richard Rorty, "The Professor and the Prophet," *Transition* 52 (1991): 75. For a sampling of debates between Rorty and Putnam see Putnam, *Realism with a Human Face* (Cambridge: Harvard University Press, 1990), pp. ix, 18–26; Rorty, "Putnam and the Relativist Menace," *Journal of Philosophy* 90 (1993): 443–61.
4   Hilary Putnam, "A Reconsideration of Deweyan Democracy" in Putnam, *Renewing Philosophy* (Cambridge: Harvard University Press, 1992), p. 180; and "Between the New Left and Judaism," in *The American Philosopher,* ed. Giovanna Borradori (Chicago: University of Chicago Press, 1994), p. 64.
5   Westbrook, *John Dewey and American Democracy,* pp. x–xi.
6   Kloppenberg, "Democracy and Disenchantment," pp. 71, 79.
7   I think this poses an important yet neglected issue for intellectual historians. Too often in summarizing the work of our subjects we fail to distinguish between arguments they did in fact make and arguments they could conceivably have made, which we have cobbled together from disparate sources.
8   Hilary Putnam, "Pragmatism and Moral Objectivity" in *Words and Life,* ed. Hilary Putnam (Cambridge: Harvard University Press, 1994), p. 152.
9   Putnam, "Reconsideration of Deweyan Democracy," p. 186.
10 *Ibid.,* pp. 188–89.
11 *Ibid.,* p. 188.
12 Putnam, "Pragmatism and Moral Objectivity," p. 172.
13 Hilary Putnam, with Ruth Anna Putnam, "Dewey's *Logic:* Epistemology as Hypothesis," *Words and Life,* pp. 199–200.
14 Putnam, "Dewey's *Logic,*" p. 200.
15 Putnam, "Pragmatism and Moral Objectivity," pp. 175–76.
16 Putnam, "Dewey's *Logic,*" p. 214.
17 *Ibid.,* pp. 214–15.

18 Putnam, "Pragmatism and Moral Objectivity," p. 176.

19 Putnam, "Dewey's *Logic*," p. 215.

20 *Ibid.*, p. 214.

21 The most notable exception, I would say, is a long, illuminating, and relatively neglected essay on "The Problem of Truth," *Middle Works of John Dewey*, ed. Jo Ann Boydston (Carbondale: Southern Illinois University Press, 1978), vol. 6, pp. 12–79.

22 Putnam, "Pragmatism and Moral Objectivity," p. 155.

23 John Dewey, "Three Independent Factors in Morals" (1930), *Later Works of John Dewey*, ed. Jo Ann Boydston (Carbondale: Southern Illinois University Press, 1984), vol. 5, p. 288. See James T. Kloppenberg, *Uncertain Victory: Social Democracy and Progressivism in European and American Thought, 1870–1920* (New York: Oxford, 1986), pp. 132–44; and Westbrook, *John Dewey and American Democracy*, pp. 163, 416–17. Putnam is himself alert to this weakness of Dewey's ethics. See the comparison with James in "Reconsideration of Deweyan Democracy," pp. 190–99.

24 Putnam, "Pragmatism and Moral Objectivity," p. 155.

25 John Dewey, *The Public and Its Problems* (1927), in *Later Works of John Dewey*, vol. 2, p. 364.

26 John Dewey, "Education as Politics" (1922), *Middle Works of John Dewey*, vol. 13, p. 334.

27 Dewey, *The Public and Its Problems*, 371.

28 Putnam, "Reconsideration of Deweyan Democracy," p. 199.

29 Richard Rorty, "Pragmatism without Method," in Rorty, *Objectivity, Relativism, and Truth*, pp. 63–77.

30 John Dewey, "Creative Democracy—The Task Before Us" (1939), in *Later Works of John Dewey*, vol. 14, p. 227.

31 The term "deliberative democracy" also does not risk the confusion with "direct democracy," which is a liability of "participatory democracy." Some of the critics of my *John Dewey and American Democracy* have taken the rendering there of Dewey's philosophy as a defense of "participatory democracy" to be a defense of strictly "direct" democracy, despite my efforts to avoid this confusion. Advocates of deliberative democracy differ on the degree of direct democracy necessary to deliberative democracy but most seem to take a position close to Dewey's (and my own) that deliberative democracy is best served by a combination of directly and representatively democratic institutions—all of which in their internal procedures are deliberative.

32 Joshua Cohen, "Deliberation and Democratic Legitimacy" *The Good Polity: Normative Analysis of the State*, ed. Alan Hamlin and Philip Pettit (London: Blackwell, 1989), pp. 21–23.

Community in the Pragmatic Tradition

RICHARD J. BERNSTEIN

Regarded as an idea, democracy is not an alternative to other principles of associated life. It is the idea of community life itself.—John Dewey, *The Public and Its Problems*

Hans Joas, the perceptive German social theorist who has a nuanced understanding of American philosophy, begins a recent paper by citing this famous claim made by John Dewey. Joas tells us:

> This sentence of John Dewey taken from his 1927 book, "The Public and Its Problems," sounds very strange to German ears. The semantics of the term "community" in America are very different from the cultural traditions in Germany, and this difference is certainly bigger than in the case of the term "democracy." In Germany, every positive use of the term "community" today will meet with the skepticism of those who suspect therein antidemocratic effects. "Whoever calls for more community in this country will immediately come under the suspicion to be an old-fashion fool or a sinister ideologist."[1]

Joas is not only pointing out cultural differences between the United States and Germany, and reminding us of the ugly resonances of the appeal to "*Volksgemeinschaft*" in Nazi propaganda; he is also calling attention to a deep ambiguity that clings to the idea of community. Frequently, as with John Dewey, the idea of community is intended to call our attention to the democratic virtues of active citizenship that are required to ameliorate the ills of the rampant individualism of modern bourgeois life, and sometimes it has much more conservative and even sinister overtones. Whenever we speak of or appeal to community life, the crucial issue is always, what do we mean by "community," and what type of community are we advocating.

Nevertheless, Joas' observations remind us just how central and persistent the notion of community has been in American philosophy—long before the recent debates about communitarianism, and how the idea of community has been positively valorized. What I want to do here is to review some of the key moments in this ongoing discussion in order to focus on what aspects of community life have been emphasized in our philosophic tradition. My primary purpose is to describe and evaluate the strengths and weaknesses of this tradition—especially when we look upon it as a resource confronting our contemporary problems of community life. Specifically, I want to focus on the contributions of four thinkers: Peirce, Royce, Dewey, and Mead.

We tend to forget just how radical Peirce was in his reflections about community. Peirce, perhaps more emphatically than any previous thinker, highlighted the *metaphysical* significance of the very idea of community. I remind you that it was Peirce who declared: "The real, then, is that which, sooner or later, information and reasoning would finally result in, and which is therefore independent of the vagaries of me and you, Thus, the very origin of the conception of reality shows that this conception essentially involves the notion of a COMMUNITY, without definite limits, and capable of a definite increase of knowledge" (5.311).[2]

Although Peirce modified this claim in order to underscore its regulative import, he never abandoned it. Not only does Peirce elevate the notion of community to a fundamental metaphysical principle, he is a key figure in initiating the paradigm shift *from* the philosophy of subjectivity and consciousness that had dominated so much of modern philosophy *to* what Habermas and Apel have called the paradigm of communicative rationality. For it is in the 1868 articles that Peirce sharply criticized Cartesianism, foundationalism, and what Wilfrid Sellars later dubbed "the myth of the given."[3] There is a direct continuity from the notion of the community of inquirers that Peirce adumbrates in these papers and Wilfrid Sellars' claim made almost a century later that "empirical knowledge, like its sophisticated extension science, is rational, not because it has a foundation, but because it is a self-correcting enterprise which can put any claim in jeopardy, though not *all* at once."[4]

We can also view this principle from the perspective of Peirce's contribution to an understanding of human finitude. Why is this notion of community so important? It is because each of us is conditioned by the prejudgments and the prejudices that have shaped us—prejudices that are at once enabling, but which can also prevent us from knowing what is real; prejudices responsible for the "vagaries of you and me." Individually, we cannot hope to escape from these vagaries, but in a critical community it is possible to transcend our individual biases. Peirce's reflections on the community of inquirers also highlight what is so important for him—the need to develop and cultivate the *critical* habits required for such a community. This is one of the reasons why Peirce gives such prominence to the ongoing development of self correcting critical habits—a point that has also been emphasized in different ways by Wilfrid Sellars and Karl Popper.

All "reasoning as deliberate is essentially critical" (5.108) and requires self-control. Furthermore, "a rational person . . . not merely has habits, but also can exert a measure of self-control over his future actions" (5.418). There are degrees of self-control. Peirce makes this point in a passage that anticipates his understanding of the hierarchy of normative disciplines:

> There are inhibitions and coordinations that entirely escape consciousness. There are, in the next place, modes of self-control which seem quite instinctive. Next there is a kind of self-control which results from training. Next, a man can be his own training-master and thus control his self-control. When this point is reached much or all the training may be conducted in imagination. When a man trains himself, thus controlling control, he must have some moral rule in view, however special and irrational it may be. But next he may undertake to improve this rule; that is, to exercise a control over his control of control. To do this he must have in view something higher than an irrational rule. He must have some sort of moral principle. This, in turn, may be controlled by reference to an esthetic ideal of what is fine. There are certainly more grades than I have enumerated. Perhaps their number is indefinite. The brutes are certainly capable of more than one grade of control; but it seems to me that our superiority to them is due to our greater number of grades of self-control than it is to our versatility. (5.533)

There is something like a hermeneutical circle in the reciprocal relation between developing self-control and the critical community of inquirers. For such a community requires the development of the habits of reflective self-control, and these very habits strengthen the existence of critical communities.

Peirce, as we know, opposed all forms of nominalism. Sometimes he seems to find traces of nominalism in every modern philosopher (including Hegel). But Peirce's critique of nominalism was not exclusively motivated by technical philosophic considerations. He felt that it was the source of the pathologies of modern life. He believed that in practice nominalism leads to the doctrine of individualistic greed. Peirce was motivated by an ideal that he discovered in the Duns Scotus and Gothic architecture.

> Nothing is more striking in either of the great intellectual products of that age, than the complete absence of self-conceit on the part of the artist or philosopher. . . . His work is not designed to embody his ideas, but the universal truth. . . . The individual feels his own worthlessness in comparison with his task, and does not dare to introduce his vanity into the doing of it. . . . Finally, there is nothing in which the scholastic philosophy and the Gothic architecture resemble one another more than in the gradually increasing sense of immensity which impresses the mind of the student as he learns to appreciate the real dimension and cost of each. (8.11)

This passage that Peirce wrote in 1871 anticipates his own self-conscious formulation of the intrinsically "admirable ideal," which he took to be the summum bonum. The development of Reason in and through the community of inquirers is always in a state of incipiency; it is always on the way. The development of Reason—concrete reasonableness—requires embodiment and manifestation. There is (and can be) no finality to this dynamic creation. Peirce tells us:

> I do not see how one can have a more satisfying ideal of the admirable than the development of Reason so understood. The one thing whose admirableness is not due to an ulterior reason is Reason itself comprehended in its fullness, so far as we can comprehend it. Under this conception, the ideal of conduct will be to exercise our little function in the operation of the creation by giving a hand toward rendering the world more reasonable whenever, as the slang is, it is "up to us" to do so. (1.615)

Peirce was not a thinker who was primarily concerned with the social and political problems of his time. I can even imagine Peirce wincing at Dewey's claim that democracy "is the idea of community life itself." Whatever consequences we may draw from Peirce's understanding of the community of inquirers, such a community is not necessarily a democratic community, but one whose members have the skills, talents, and education to be scientific investigators. Yet, as we shall see, the Peircian notion of community does have important consequences for democratic theory. Dewey and Mead were especially sensitive to these implications. But before passing on to their reflections on community life, I want to consider the contributions of Josiah Royce.

Despite the noble efforts of some outstanding Roycean scholars, Royce's legacy has never had a deep and pervasive influence on American philosophy. Yet, Royce—more than any other American thinker—appropriated the Peircian notion of community and extended Peirce's analysis in novel ways. Royce himself called attention to the centrality of the idea of community in his own philosophy when he said: "I strongly feel that my deepest motives and problems have centered about the idea of the Community, although this idea has only come gradually to my clear consciousness."[5] J. Lowenberg, Royce's student, perceptively states in his introduction to Royce's *Fugitive Essays* that:

> In the idea of the Community, as he understood it, modern thought has received one of its richest philosophic conceptions. With its aid Royce sought to interpret the deepest issues of metaphysics, the profoundest problems of knowledge, the ultimate questions of religion. And so focal is it in his ethics that, from his point of view, the whole moral task of humanity finds in terms of the community articulate expression.[6]

I want to emphasize two aspects of Royce's development of the idea of community. The first concerns the way in which Royce appropriates Peirce's semiotics—especially Peirce's understanding of the triadic character of signification and the role of the interpretant; and the second concerns the semantical significance of Royce's shift from Peirce's "community of inquirers" to "the community of interpretation."

Peirce's most original contribution to semiotics is that signification is essentially a triadic process in which every sign necessarily calls forth another sign—its interpretant. Peirce tells us "A sign is only a sign *in actu* by virtue of its receiving an interpretation, that is by virtue of its determining another sign of the same object" (5.570). Signification involves a sign-vehicle, an object that is signified, and an interpretant. But every interpretation (or rather every interpretant) is itself a sign that calls forth another (potential) interpretant. Royce saw clearly (although it is implicit in Peirce's understanding of signification) that this analysis of signification entails the idea of an infinite community—a social infinite. There can be no absolute finality to the process of interpretation. Interpretation is essentially open to the future and the process of interpretation requires a community of interpreters. John E. Smith succinctly sums up this Roycean appropriation of Peirce:

> The fact that every interpretation is addressed to the future and also that it is itself a sign necessitates that the process of interpretation is infinite in character, that is, there is no proposed interpretation not

a sign, and hence no interpretation fails to stand under the condition of requiring further interpretation. Interpretation, according to Royce, always needs three terms and the result is a sign which calls for the process to be repeated, unless we possess an interpretation which is final, which would be the same as absolute truth. Since no finality is possible in any domain, interpretation never ceases. Royce says, "and so,—at least in ideal,—*the social process involved is endless.*" This is precisely the form in which the infinite is actual, namely, as universal community of interpretation which is without end.[7]

I also think that it is significant that Royce does not merely speak about inquiry but about *interpretation.* Peirce's model of the community of inquirers represents an "idealization" of the community of laboratory scientists. What Royce rightly underscores is that the heart of Peirce's understanding of the idea of community is based on his semiotics—his analysis of signification. If we follow out the implications of Peirce's semiotic analysis, then we can grasp what Peirce means when he declares that man is a sign. Reformulated in Roycean terms, this means that our being-in-the-world is to be a being who is "always already" an interpreting being— to be a member of a potentially infinite community of interpretation.

I have already suggested that there is a significant overlap between Peirce's reflections on the idea of community and the understanding of communicative rationality in Habermas and Apel. But there is also an affinity between Royce's understanding of the community of interpretation and Gadamer's ontological hermeneutics. Although Gadamer draws his inspiration from Heidegger, and Royce from Peirce, there is also a common source in the way in which Royce and Gadamer are influenced by the tradition of German idealism. Gadamer, too, develops an understanding of interpretation in which there is necessarily a process of infinite interpretation, and where all interpretation is open to further interpretation. Royce would certainly agree with Gadamer's understanding of hermeneutics as ontological—that our being-in-the-world is to be essentially interpreters.

For all the insight of Peirce and Royce in linking community, reality, truth, inquiry, signification, and interpretation, we may (especially in light of the opening citation from John Dewey) feel that there is something missing—something that at least has not yet been brought into the foreground of discussion. For it is not yet clear what precisely is the relevance of these reflections to what most concerned Dewey—the linkage of democracy and community.

There are, of course, features of the Peircian and Roycean understandings of community that are clearly relevant for a normative understanding of democracy. An adequate theory of democracy should incorporate the principle of fallibility, the openness of all inquiry and interpretation, the need for the cultivation of critical habits of deliberation that Peirce and Royce emphasize. But I do not think we can move *directly* from Peirce's "community of inquirers" or Royce's "community of interpreters" to the idea of a democratic community. After all, there are many features of democracy that are not reflected in Peirce's understanding of a community of inquirers or Royce's infinite community of interpretation. We must also frankly recognize that there are aspects of Peirce's conception of a community of inquirers that are alien to democracy. There are stringent conditions on who is a member of such a community. One needs special talents, training, and education. Peirce himself was rather scornful of those who failed to appreciate the striking difference between scientific communities and other sorts of communities.

Dewey did seek to appropriate what he learned from Peirce to the idea of a democratic community, but he was worried about a very different sort of problem. For most of his intellectual career, Dewey was concerned with the fate of democracy. He felt that the laissez faire tendencies that he discerned in social and political life in the United States—and in much of modern life—were at once betraying and undermining what he took so essential for genuine democracy—a creative democracy in which "all share and all participate." Dewey stressed the idea of a democratic community as a moral or ethical ideal—as a way of life. Robert Westbrook gives a succinct and eloquent description of Dewey's radical vision when he writes:

> Among liberal intellectuals of the twentieth century, Dewey was the most important advocate of participatory democracy, that is of the belief that democracy as an ethical ideal calls upon men and women to build communities in which the necessary opportunities and resources are available for every individual to realize fully his or her particular capacities and powers through participation in political, social, and cultural life. This ideal rested on a "faith in the capacity of human beings for intelligent judgment and action if proper conditions are furnished."[8]

Many of Dewey's fellow liberals lost this faith in the "common man"—or thought that it was utopian to believe that in mass democracies with the powerful influence of the media, one could expect that it was even viable to believe there can be a genuinely informed citizenry capable of intelligent deliberation and decisions. Dewey was not naively utopian, but he was stubbornly persistent in believing that the cure for the ills of democracy was more democracy. The basic issue for him was to "retrieve" a viable idea of community and public life. I say "retrieve" because, even though Dewey strongly identified himself with the Jeffersonian tradition of "small republics" or wards in which citizens would actively participate, he did not think that the transformation of the United States from an agricultural to an industrial democracy necessarily entailed the decline of democratic community life. There has been an "eclipse of the public," and there is a need to encourage the type of face-to-face open communication where communal life as an ethical ideal is emotionally, intellectually, and consciously sustained. Like Hannah Arendt, Dewey argued for the need to create public spaces in which human beings can encounter each other as equals.

In *The Public and Its Problems,* Dewey spoke of the transformation of the Great Society into the Great Community, but he did not think of the Great Community as single homogeneous community. It is the ideal of a community of democratic communities. From the standpoint of the individual, the democratic idea

> consists in having a responsible share according to capacity in forming and directing the activities of the groups to which one belongs and in participating according to need in the values which the groups sustain. From the standpoint of the groups, it demands liberation of the potentialities of members of a group in harmony with the interests and goods that are common. . . . There is free give-and-take: fullness of integrated personality is therefore possible of achievement, since the pulls and responses of different groups reinforce one another and their values accord.[9]

Dewey's notion of community is essentially pluralistic. And in *The Public and Its Problems,* he stressed the need to develop local publics and communities. "Unless local communal life can be restored, the public cannot adequately resolve its most urgent problem: to find and identify itself."[10]

Dewey, like Horace Kallen, was extremely skeptical of the melting pot metaphor. Dewey declared that "the theory of the melting pot always gave me rather a pang."[11] He stressed the need for cultural pluralism in the United States and internationally. What Dewey wrote in 1917 is just as relevant—perhaps even more relevant—in 1998.

> No matter how loudly any one proclaims his Americanism, if he assumes that any one racial strain, any one component culture, no matter how early settled it was in our territory, or how effective it has

proved in its own land, is to furnish a pattern to which all other strains and cultures are to conform, he is a traitor to an American nationalism. Our unity cannot be a homogenous thing like that of the separate states of Europe from which our population is drawn; it must be a unity created by drawing out and composing into a harmonious whole the best, the most characteristic which each contributing race and people has to offer.[12]

If Dewey is to be faulted, it is because, at times in his reliance on metaphors of harmony and organic unity, Dewey underestimates the conflict, dissonance, and asymmetrical power relationships that disrupt "the harmonious whole." I do think that, at times, Dewey is excessively optimistic about the real social and political possibilities of resolving serious social conflicts by open communication. Although this is a weakness in Dewey's thinking, we can read him in a different way. For we can interpret Dewey as telling us that it is precisely because conflicts between different groups run so deep, that it becomes all the more urgent to develop those habits and virtues by which we can intelligently seek to negotiate and reconcile differences. Dewey was as harsh in his criticism of those tendencies that promoted a "standardization favorable to mediocrity" as he was of the centrifugal social and cultural tendencies that isolated and segregated different groups from each other.[13] Though Dewey was committed to the belief that all human beings can develop their "creative intelligence" and practical judgment, he did not think that rational discussion itself is sufficient to bring about genuine social reform. It is not accidental that Dewey rarely speaks of "reason." He always stresses the ongoing creative task of nurturing the habits of intelligence—habits that can only be sustained in critical, open, tolerant communities.

There is a strand in Dewey's thinking that suggests that democracy itself is little more than the application of the experimental scientific method to the practices of everyday life. But here, too, there is a more generous way of reading Dewey. He was deeply skeptical about the role of so-called experts in democratic communities—as if there is a group of individuals by virtue of their "scientific" expertise better able to make the type of judgments and decisions required in our everyday lives. "A class of experts is inevitably so removed from common interests as to become a class with private interests and private knowledge."[14] The virtues of openness, fallibility, experimentation, ongoing criticism, and imagination are what Dewey took to be characteristic virtues of the community of inquirers. These are the virtues that he sought to appropriate for the idea of a democratic community.

Although Dewey was not utopian, he was, as Alan Ryan says in the concluding remarks of *John Dewey and the High Tide of American Liberalism,* a visionary—"a curious visionary, because he did not speak of a distant goal of a city not built with hands."

> He was a visionary about the here and now, about the potentiality of the modern world, modern society, modern man, and thus, as it happened, America and Americans in the twentieth century. It was his ability to infuse the here and now with a kind of transcendent glow that overcame the denseness and awkwardness of his prose and the vagueness of his message and secured such widespread conviction . . . he will remain for the foreseeable future a rich source of intellectual nourishment for anyone not absolutely locked within the anxieties of his or her own heart and not absolutely despondent about the prospects of the modern world.[15]

George Herbert Mead has too often stood in the shadow of John Dewey. But in the past few decades, many thinkers have begun to appreciate the originality of Mead, especially concerning his analysis of community. Mead shared many of Dewey's commitments to radical democratic communities. But Mead, more systematically than any other American thinkers, sought to address the issue of how communities are generated, how selves are formed in a community, and how the type of individuality that is achieved in a community is itself dependent on the type of community generated. Mead moves from the language of animal gestures, to vocal gestures, to role playing, to learning to internalize the attitude of the other, to the achievement of unity of the self that results from the incorporation of the "generalized other" into one's own dialogue with oneself. As we follow Mead's genealogical account of the dialogical self and democratic communities, we see how it is Mead who enables us to understand Dewey's striking claim that democracy "is the idea of community life itself." Like Dewey, Mead was, of course, aware that there are nondemocratic communities. But if we follow the logic of the development of the idea of community, if we realize that selfhood depends upon the capacity of the individual to assume the attitudes and the role of others, then we can detect an inner dynamic in the development of community life. This is a tendency, which may, of course, be frustrated and distorted, but it is a dynamic toward the achievement of *mutual recognition.* Implicit in the very idea of community is the regulative ideal of a universal democratic community.

Even if it is acknowledged that there is a rich and varied pragmatic tradition of reflection on the ideal and institutionalization of a democratic community, the question may still be asked: Is that tradition really relevant for illuminating and confronting our contemporary problems and conflicts? My fundamental thesis is that there are the resources in this tradition that enable us to think creatively about these problems. One of the primary reasons why there has been a resurgence of interest in pragmatism is precisely because it helps us to move beyond some of the false antitheses and entrenched extremes that mark recent debates. Let me briefly illustrate this with reference to two recent, interrelated controversies. The first concerns the tangled controversies between liberals and communitarians; and the second concerns the polemical debates that have swirled around multiculturalism.

When John Rawls published his now famous book, *A Theory of Justice,* he was sharply criticized by Michael Sandel (and others) for basing his theory of justice on a thin, eviscerated, ahistorical conception of the self. Rawls' communitarian critics argued that not only his version of liberalism but all forms of liberalism failed to do justice to the ways in which our political, social, and cultural lives are situated and embodied in concrete historical traditions and communities. Liberalism, allegedly, neglected the significance of communal bonds. For a community is not just an aggregate of individuals who share values and common concerns. There is a "strong" sense of community in which our very *identity* as individuals is constituted by the communities to which we belong. Liberals, on the other hand, have criticized their communitarian opponents for failing to acknowledge that homogeneous face-to-face communities are frequently based upon stringent tacit rules of exclusion. A "strong" sense of community presupposes "insiders" and "outsiders." Even the republican tradition that emphasizes the role of active citizen participation has tended to favor political elites. Furthermore, liberals argue that republican communitarianism is a totally inadequate model for dealing with "really existing" twentieth-century complex democratic societies—democratic societies that comprise heterogeneous cultural, ethnic, and religious populations.

Both liberals and communitarians have a tendency to caricature their opponents. Some communitarians argue that all forms of liberalism are based on a doctrine of "possessive individualism." And militant liberals sometimes argue as if all communitarians are leading us down the path to tyranny and totalitarianism. Liberals and communitarians both have valid and important positive insights—and each "side" has detected the weaknesses of their opponents. Liberals have always stressed individual liberty and the need for the protection of individual rights. Communitarians—especially those who draw their inspiration from the republican tradition—have been especially alert to the importance for active citizen communal participation in order to foster a genuine democratic ethos.

As these debates have played themselves out during the past few decades, it has become increasingly evident that the two "extremes" are moving closer and closer together. Liberals are now much more sensitive to the central role of communal life in democratic societies. Communities need not be considered antiliberal and anti-individualist. Communitarians recognize the need to protect communities from becoming parochial and ethnocentric. There is always an imperative to safeguard individual rights, including the rights of those who do not belong to one's community. It is no longer oxymoronic to speak of a liberal communitarianism or a communitarian liberalism. There are still differences, but these are differences of *emphasis* rather than hard-and-fast cleavages.

There are specific historical contexts in which the most pressing concern is to defend the liberal values of individual liberty and the protection of rights. For example, the appeal to liberal values played a crucial role in the dissident cultures of Eastern Europe before the collapse of communism. In such a context, the appeal to "community" was anathema because "community" was a code term for the Communist party. And as Hans Joas has noted, the appeal to "community" in a German context has most frequently had a conservative or sinister connotation. But the danger that Dewey detected in the United States—and it is still a danger—is the eclipse of the public, the disintegration of a democratic communal life, and a failure of active citizen participation. I do not want to underestimate the extent to which there are consequential political disputes about whether liberal or communitarian values ought to prevail. But that is just the point—the differences are those of political judgment, requiring a sensitivity to context. They are not differences that can be theoretically resolved when abstracted from specific political contexts. This contesting of priorities is itself essential for a vital democratic polity. The strength of the pragmatists is the recognition that both individual liberty and active communal life are essential for a democratic polity.

The pragmatists argued that the very quality of our individuality is itself dependent on the types of communities in which we live. As Alan Ryan tells us, Dewey (and his fellow pragmatists) knew that what is needed is "a society that does justice both to our individuality and to our need for social connection. This is the great modern need and nowhere more so than in the United States. . . . Individuals need communities, and liberal communities consist of associated individuals. Modern individuals need flexible, forward-looking, tolerant communities to live in, and such communities can be sustained only by modern individuals who are looking for a meaningful existence in association with similarly autonomous people."[16] In short, we might say that from a pragmatic perspective, the opposition between liberalism and communitarianism is a false antithesis. They are codependent, and it requires practical judgment to balance the demands of individual liberty and communal active citizenship.

I have already anticipated some of the ways in which a pragmatic orientation can help to illuminate recent controversies concerning "multiculturalism." Unfortunately, the very expression "multiculturalism" is a misleading term because historically most societies (especially modern ones) have been constituted by different cultural groups. It is a dangerous myth to think that there are any modern societies that have been completely homogeneous—or have homogeneous origins. Furthermore, the expression "multiculturalism" has become emotionally overloaded. It is typically used as a polemic weapon in the so-called "culture wars." Some extreme advocates of multiculturalism argue as if the "new" politics of identity and difference requires the abandonment of all "Enlightenment ideals," all appeals to "universal norms," and all appeals to "reasonableness" or "rationality." These are taken as signifiers that only mask ugly brute power and domination. And there are those who seem to think that multiculturalism—when unmasked—is nothing but an ideological weapon used to attack the foundations of Western civilization and American democracy.

Once again, appealing to the pragmatic tradition can bring some sanity to what has become a polemical and even a vicious controversy. No one can accuse the pragmatists of neglecting the importance of universality, and a commitment to "concrete reasonableness." These are central to the Peircian idea of a community of inquirers and the Roycean idea of a community of interpreters. We should not forget that it is the pragmatists who made "pluralism" into a respectable and central philosophic epithet. It was William James who labeled his philosophy "pluralism." And it was James' student, Horace Kallen, who "invented" the term "cultural pluralism." In the vision that he and John Dewey sought to articulate for a democratic society, the vitality of democratic life itself depends on recognizing the integrity and contribution of different cultural and ethnic groups. There is no incompatibility in being a "hyphenated" American—Jewish-American, German-American, Irish-American, and so on. Both of them would have been appalled by the strident rhetoric of those who claim that cultural identity must be "centrist" and exclusive, as well as those who claim that the recognition of cultural and ethnic differences "entails" a threat to the basic "values" of Western civilization.

As I indicated earlier, Dewey does not always appreciate the depth of cultural conflicts and the anger of those who experience the pain and humiliation of being excluded. But we should not forget that for Dewey, philosophic reflection itself is provoked by the social conflicts we experience in our everyday lives. In a democratic society the search for a resolution of these conflicts can best be achieved by intelligent deliberation and reasonable debate. The pragmatists never subscribed to the belief that there can be a "final" reconciliation or resolution to all social conflicts. The agonistic quality of democratic politics is intrinsic to creative democracy.

There is another important lesson to be learned from the pragmatists. Many commentators have noted that what characterizes current controversies is not so much serious debate and reasonable discussion, but a "clash of absolutes," emotivist shouting matches, media manipulation, and negative advertising. Even when so-called public debates are staged, what becomes most manifest is not the debate, but the "staging." The pragmatists have always been relentless in their criticism of all varieties of absolutism, foundationalism, and fundamentalism. But they have also rejected relativism and extreme skepticism. They have advanced an ideal of "concrete reasonableness." We can distinguish better and worse options, and we should try to support our convictions with the best available evidence and reasons. Even what we consider to be evidence and good reasons can be intelligently contested. The pragmatists believed that we can learn to think and act without relying on rigid banisters. Much of the pathos of what is called "postmodernism" results from the claim that there are no firm fixed foundations for any of our beliefs.

But despite the rhetoric of postmodern thinkers questioning binary oppositions, there has been a tendency to fall into the "classic" binary opposition between absolutism and relativism. If there are no firm foundations, then presumably there is no escape from an "anything goes" relativism. Long ago the pragmatists argued that we never escape from contingency, uncertainty, and ambiguity. But the pragmatists also passionately argued that the response to contingency and uncertainty should not be despair, wild relativism, or the flight to new absolutes. Our task—and it is a difficult never-ending task—is to learn to live with this contingency, to respond as intelligently as we can to the new conflicts and crises that arise in our everyday lives.

In conclusion, I want to reflect upon this concern with the idea of community that has been so fundamental in the pragmatic tradition. In all the thinkers that I have discussed, fallibility, openness, criticism, mutual respect, and recognition are essential dimensions of their understanding of community. These are the regulative ideals that ought to govern our thinking about the development of democratic communities. These thinkers are aware of the fragility of the existence of such communities. They only come into existence to the extent that those reflective habits required for critical communities are cultivated. This nurturing is an ongoing task. It is a primary reason why Dewey so emphasized the role of education in a democratic polity. In social and political terms, the issue is never one of even thinking of the individual and the community in opposition to each other. Individuality is not a given but an *achievement*—and the type of individuality we can achieve is itself dependent on the type of communities we develop. There is a recognition of the plurality of different types of overlapping communities—and the fertility of conflict and dissonance among these communities. Cultural pluralism is not simply to be tolerated but encouraged in a modern democratic polity. At a time when we seem to be threatened by opposing extremes—bland homogenization and standardization or a politics of separatist identity and difference—it is worthwhile to recall what is best in our own tradition—a recognition of plurality and unity, of difference and commonness, of agonistic conflict combined with more universal solidarity with our fellow human beings.

Finally, I would like to cite the entire passage from which my opening remarks from John Dewey were taken, for we can now more fully appreciate what he means.

> Regarded as an idea, democracy is not an alternative to other principles of associated life. It is the idea of community life itself. It is an ideal in the only intelligible sense of an ideal: namely, the tendency and movement of some thing which exists carried to its final limit, viewed as completed, perfected. Since things do not attain such fulfillment but are in actuality distracted and interfered with, democracy in this sense is not a fact and never will be. But neither in this sense is there or has there ever been anything which is a community in its full measure, a community unalloyed by alien elements. The idea or ideal of a community presents, however, actual phases of associated life as they are freed from restrictive and disturbing elements, and are contemplated as having attained their limit of development. Wherever there is conjoint activity whose consequences are appreciated as good by all singular persons who take part in it, and where the realization of the good is such as to effect an energetic desire and effort to sustain it in being just because it is a good shed by all, there is in so far a community. The clear consciousness of a communal life, in all its implications, constitutes the idea of democracy.[17]

Notes

1 Hans Joas, "Communitarianism: A German Perspective," *Distinguished Lecturer Series* 6 (Bloomington: Indiana University Press, 1995), p. 1.

2 All references to Peirce are to the *Collected Papers of Charles Sanders Peirce*, ed. Charles Hartshorne and Paul Weiss (Cambridge: Harvard University Press, 1931–35).

3 The three papers that Peirce published in the *Journal of Speculative Philosophy* series of 1868 are: "Questions Concerning Certain Faculties Claimed for Man"; "Some Consequences of Four Incapacities"; and "Grounds of Validity of the Laws of Logic: Further Consequences of Four Incapacities."

4 Wilfrid Sellars, "Empiricism and the Philosophy of Mind," in *Minnesota Studies in the Philosophy of Science*, ed. Herbert Feigl and Michael Scriven (Minneapolis: University of Minnesota Press, 1956), vol. 1, p. 300.

5 Cited in John E. Smith, *Royce's Social Infinite* (New York: Liberal Arts Press, 1950), p. 3.

6 J. Lowenberg, "Editor's Introduction" to Josiah Royce, *Fugitive Essays* (Cambridge: Harvard University Press, 1920), p. 37.

7 Smith, *Royce's Social Infinite*, p. 85.

8 Robert Westbrook, *John Dewey and American Democracy* (Ithaca: Cornell University Press, 1991), p. xv.

9 John Dewey, *The Public and Its Problems* (New York: Henry Holt, 1927), pp. 147–48.

10 *Ibid.*, p. 216.

11 Cited in Westbrook, *John Dewey and American Democracy*, p. 213. See Westbrook's discussion of Dewey's and Kallen's understanding of cultural pluralism, pp. 212–14.

12 John Dewey, "The Principle of Nationality," in *The Middle Works of John Dewey*, ed. Jo Ann Boydston (Carbondale: Southern Illinois University Press, 1976–1983), vol. 10, pp. 288–89.

13 Dewey, *The Public and Its Problems*, p. 115.

14 *Ibid.*, p. 207.

15 Alan Ryan, *John Dewey and the High Tide of American Liberalism* (New York: W. W. Norton, 1995), p. 369.

16 *Ibid.*, p. 359.

17 Dewey, *The Public and Its Problems*, pp. 148–49.

Another Pragmatism: Alain Locke, Critical "Race" Theory, and the Politics of Culture

NANCY FRASER

In *The American Evasion of Philosophy,* Cornel West offers an unusually broad view of the pragmatist tradition. Far from restricting himself to the usual trinity of Peirce, James, and Dewey, West includes the life and thought of W. E. B. Du Bois.[1] In thus expanding the pragmatist canon to encompass a major body of critical reflection on "race" and racism in the United States, West also poses a challenge to anyone contemplating a revival of pragmatism today. We are challenged to cast a net wide enough to catch not only the concerns of Stanley Fish, Hilary Putnam, and Richard Rorty, but also what Du Bois famously called "the problem of the color line," a problem certain to outlast the twentieth century and a crucial test for the pragmatist enterprise of using social intelligence to guide social practice.

In this essay, I intend to take up Cornel West's challenge. I am going to discuss a recently rediscovered work by another African-American theorist of "race" and racism who was trained in Philosophy at Harvard under Josiah Royce and William James early in this century and who also deserves a place in the pragmatist pantheon. Alain Locke is remembered today primarily as an aesthetician. To be sure, he was the leading theorist of the Harlem Renaissance; the creator of "the New Negro"; the editor of the 1925 volume of that name that anthologized Langston Hughes, Zora Neale Hurston, and Countee Cullen; and a prominent early exponent of the idea of a distinctive, syncretistic African-American culture. But the work I shall discuss reveals a forgotten side of Locke. This Alain Locke is not only a theorist of culture and a proponent of black cultural nationalism. He is also a critical theorist of society, specifically of the history and political economy of racism. Even more important, he is a thinker who is grappling precisely with the tangled relations between culture, political economy, and "race" in ways that remain highly relevant today.

To introduce this relatively unknown Locke, I shall propose a reading of

157

his 1916 lectures on "Race Contacts and Interracial Relations." Focusing on his account of the concept of "race" in this early, youthful work, I seek to illuminate four overlapping sets of concerns. The first is the interpretation and assessment of Locke's mature cultural nationalism. Much writing on the Harlem Renaissance assumes that he was naive in emphasizing black cultural production as opposed to economic interests and political struggle.[2] Yet the 1916 lectures reveal that his cultural politics rested on a social-theoretical substructure in which power and political economy were central. Seen in this light, I shall argue, Locke was no simpleminded cultural nationalist, but a sophisticated pragmatist and "strategic essentialist."[3]

My second concern is Locke's place in the broader field of critical theorizing about "race." The key debates in this field have often turned on the relative weight of political economy and culture in the construction of "race." The economistic side, best exemplified by the West Indian–American Marxist sociologist Oliver Cromwell Cox, holds that "race" is a mystification of class, a superstructural ideological effect of the capitalist-imperialist organization of exploitation.[4] The culturalist side, exemplified in its essentialist form by the early W. E. B. Du Bois, and in its more recent anti-essentialist form by Kwame Anthony Appiah, holds that "race" is a cultural classification, corresponding for Du Bois to actual historical forms of human differentiation, corresponding for Appiah to nothing at all.[5] What is chiefly at stake in these debates is the remedy for racism: for the economistic side, the key to overcoming racism is economic transformation or redistribution; for the culturalist side, in contrast, it is cultural recognition or, more recently, deconstruction.[6] Yet Locke's 1916 lectures cast the issue in a different light. Proposing a novel, three-tiered analysis of the concept of "race," he was seeking to encompass both political economy and culture. The result should have been to expose the economism-culturalism opposition as a false antithesis and to show that overcoming racism requires redistribution, recognition, *and* deconstruction. In fact, however, as we shall see, Locke did not himself draw that conclusion. Rather, he effectively endorsed Booker T. Washington's postponement of politics by proposing a "culture first" strategy. I hope to show, nevertheless, that Locke's early three-tiered account of the category of "race" constitutes an important contribution to critical "race" theorizing, one whose implications have still not been appreciated.

My third concern is the assessment of pragmatist social thought. Many commentators have noted the overly integrative and idealist character of the social thought of the classical pragmatists. Their many important insights notwithstanding, John Dewey, George Herbert Mead, Jane Addams, and W. I. Thomas are widely seen as having failed to give adequate weight to the "hard facts" of power and domination in social life.[7] Assuming the inevitable unfolding of an increasingly integrated world civilization, and emphasizing culture at the expense of political economy, they tended at times to posit imaginary, holistic "solutions" to difficult, sometimes irreconcilable, social conflicts. Yet Locke's 1916 lectures provide a glimpse of another pragmatism. Because he was theorizing about "race" and racism, he linked cultural issues directly to the problem of inequality; and he stressed the centrality of power to the regulation of group differences in the United States. Thus, in contrast to the mainstream pragmatists of the World War I period, Locke pioneered an approach to social theory that took domination seriously. He himself, however, did not consistently hew to this approach; he sometimes overestimated the integrative tendencies of modern societies, especially when assessing the prospects for Negro "assimilation" in the United States. I shall suggest, nevertheless, that his 1916 lectures contain the seeds of a version of pragmatist social thought that can escape the charge of idealism.

The fourth and final context for my reading of Locke is today's debate about multiculturalism. The debate tends at times to recapitulate the weaknesses of mainstream pragmatist discussions of "cultural pluralism" in the 1920s. Divorcing the question of cultural differences from questions of power and political economy, influential multiculturalists such as Charles Taylor implicitly treat ethnicity as the privileged model of social differentiation, as if group differences were simply cultural variations.[8] They tend accordingly to hypostatize culture, to neglect domination and group interaction, and to decouple the politics of recognition from the politics of redistribution.[9] Locke's 1916 lectures, in contrast, suggest the possibility of another approach. Grounding his understanding of group differences in an account of the history of domination and of international political economy, he developed a nonessentializing, syncretistic conception of culture that foregrounded group interaction. Implicit in Locke's approach, moreover, although by no means fully developed, is the prospect of an alternative multiculturalism that would integrate a nonessentialist cultural politics with an egalitarian social politics. Or so I shall suggest in what follows.

The Background of the 1916 Lectures

"Race Contacts and Interracial Relations" began as a series of five lectures that Locke delivered at Howard University in March and April of 1916. The lectures remained unpublished and were presumed lost until the transcriptions were discovered in the Howard archives in 1982. Edited and introduced by Jeffrey C. Stewart, the text of the lectures was published in 1992 by Howard University Press.[10]

At the time of the lectures Locke was thirty years old. He had not yet begun his Harvard Ph.D. work, but he had already completed his B.A. there in Philosophy and English. He had also studied at Oxford, where he was the first African-American Rhodes scholar (and the last until the 1960s), and at the University of Berlin. As a Harvard undergraduate, Locke worked mainly with George Herbert Palmer and Josiah Royce. His exposure to William James, in contrast, was at this stage only indirect, via Horace Kallen, then a graduate student and Locke's Teaching Assistant in Greek philosophy. Locke and Kallen formed a close intellectual friendship, which continued when both men went to Oxford. According to Kallen, it was discussions with Locke in 1907–1908 about the significance of "racial differences" that gave rise to the expression "cultural pluralism," an expression Kallen is credited with originating. It was at Oxford, meanwhile, that Locke first encountered fierce, visceral racism and an internationalist framework for interpreting it. Constrained by racist practices of exclusion to fraternize primarily with colonial students of color, he was exposed to anticolonialist and socialist critiques of imperialism. Later, at Berlin, he studied the social-interactionist sociology of Georg Simmel and the historical economics of Gustav Schmoller. Back in London for the Universal Race Congress of 1911, he appears to have heard Franz Boas lecture on "The Instability of Race Types." Refuting reigning anthropological views of fixed racial natures, Boas argued that civilizations progressed via cultural exchanges. Locke's 1916 lectures drew on these views and drew out their implications for the American Negro's struggle against racism. Before returning to the United States, however, he traveled in Eastern Europe, observing ethnic antagonisms and the emergence of new nationalities. These he would treat in his lectures as products not of Volkisch essences but of social interaction, historical economics, and cultural and political activism.[11]

Here, then, was the remarkable combination of intellectual influences that Locke brought back to the United States: a Roycean tendency to cast what appeared as differences in kind as differences in degree; a Jamesian view of an open pluriverse of human possibilities; a conception of cultural pluralism that served primarily to contest the "Americanization" of U.S. immigrants but that could be extended to the struggle against racism; a Boasian critique of racial essentialism; a nonessentialist understanding of nationalism; and a critical perspective on international imperialism. It was from these materials that Locke forged a distinctive synthesis in his Howard University lectures.

The immediate context provided two powerful impetuses to his thinking. The first was the steeply declining situation of African Americans since the 1890s. Disfranchisement, lynchings, debt peonage, and the imposition of Jim Crow in the South and in the federal government mocked the hopes raised by Reconstruction. To justify segregation, meanwhile, a surge of racialist thinking pervaded intellectual life, including the universities. Locke's aim in the lectures was to rebut such thinking in hopes of reopening some space for "racial progress." The second critical impetus was World War I. An early and militant opponent of the war, Locke analyzed it as "an imperialist race war" in which the European powers fought over the spoils of colonialism, that is, for title to exploit peoples of color. But in his eyes the war served to demystify imperialism's principal rationale. Showing themselves to be the true barbarians, the European belligerents could no longer credibly claim to be the bearers of a civilizing mission; their racialist ideology could now be delegitimated. "Race war" abroad and rampant racialism at home thus spurred Locke to rethink the question of "race."

Rethinking Race: A Three-Tiered Analysis

The aim of "Race Contacts and Interracial Relations" is at once simple and highly ambitious: to interrogate the concept of race from the ground up.[12] Noting that the term "race" has not one meaning but many, Locke proposes to clarify the subject by distinguishing three principal levels of meaning and proceeding systematically to analyze them. Beginning with what he calls "the theoretical and scientific conceptions of race," he goes on to examine "the practical and political conceptions of race," and finally "the social conception of race." The point of the exercise is evaluative. Locke seeks through "scientific scrutiny of the various meanings . . . to discriminate among them and to perpetuate [only] those meanings—those concepts—which are promising and really sound" (1).

The result is an original analysis of race as a concept with three distinct tiers. The first, "theoretical" tier comprises biological and physical interpretations of race. The second, "practical" tier comprehends a political-economic interpretation of race as a construct of imperialist domination. The third, "social" tier encompasses modern forms of solidarity that could in principle be decoupled from domination. After distinguishing these tiers analytically, Locke subjects each of them to a distinctive mode of analysis: the theoretical conception is demystified, the practical conception is genealogized, and the social conception is reconstructed. Each conception, too, he evaluates for its promise and soundness, distinguishing those that can be "redeemed" and should be revised from those that cannot and must be dropped. Finally, the three levels of Locke's analysis are connected in an overarching argument. When the first, biological tier is shown to be beyond redemption, he is led to the second, political-economic tier in order to explain whence the first tier originates and why it has enjoyed credibility. Likewise, when his political-economic critique establishes the practical basis of the concept of race in domination, Locke is led in turn to the third, social tier in order to determine whether and how a new understanding of race could serve the Negro's struggle *against* domination, without, however, resurrecting the retrogressive racialism he has just so painstakingly demystified, and without jeopardizing the larger solidarities he deems appropriate to a modern civilization. Although each tier of Locke's analysis is impressive taken singly, the three taken together are a tour de force.

In what follows I want to explicate Locke's argument in some detail. Along the way, I shall pay special attention to what I take to be the key critical strands of his thought: his pragmatism and "strategic essentialism," his attempt to encompass both culture and political economy in the analysis of "race," his insistence on facing up to "the fact of domination," and his effort to envision a critical multiculturalism.

"Theoretical Race": A Demystification

Locke's first lecture, titled "The Theoretical and Scientific Conceptions of Race," undertakes to explicate and evaluate the physical and biological meanings of the term. It is chiefly an exercise in demystification. Sketching a conceptual history of racialist theorizing from Gobineau to Boas, Locke exposes the epistemological deficiencies of pseudoscience. In the process, he anticipates virtually every argument recently made by the critics of *The Bell Curve*.[13]

Racialist thought conflates the descriptive enterprise of classifying human groups with the normative project of distinguishing "superior" from "inferior" groups. Casting racial inequalities as effects of prior racial differences, it inverts the proper order of causation and assumes what it claims to prove. More generally, these "theoretical conceptions of race" mistake what are actually sociocultural factors for biological and anthropological factors; they neglect the great variation within human groups, while exaggerating variation among them. In addition, these theories maintain a false "fetish" of group purity. In fact, says Locke, *soi-disant* racial groups "have neither purity of blood nor purity of type. They are the products of countless interminglings [and] infinite crossings of types" (10). Finally, and most important, racialist theory neglects history. Appealing to static, fixed racial types, it misses the dynamic development of human culture and even human biology, a curious anachronism in the age of Darwin. Marshaling Boasian arguments, then, Locke concludes that "there are no static factors of race at all. Even the anthropological factors are variable. . . . [R]ace inequalities must have an historical explanation" (10). "Any true history of race must be . . . sociological" (11).

Mingled with these Boasian arguments are some distinctively pragmatist strands. Although biological race is "an ethnic fiction," Locke insists that it is not as a result simply nonexistent, but has practical uses and effects. Overall the effects have been pernicious. Nevertheless, some advantages must accrue to a group that "considers itself an ethnic unit." Thus, Locke clearly distinguishes the plausible pragmatist claim that a group may need in some circumstances and for some purposes to consider itself "an ethnic unit" from the untenable pseudoscientific view that the group is in fact such a unit. Considered in this light, the question whether African Americans should "conserve the Negro race" takes on a different valence than it had in Du Bois' influential 1896 essay, "The Conservation of Races."

It is in the spirit of pragmatism, too, that Locke asks whether a genuinely scientific biological theory of race is possible or desirable. On both counts, his answer is no. Racialist theories, like all theories, develop in relation to "men's practical ideas about human society." When these practical ideas change, so too must the idea of race. Racialist theory emerged in a period of initial, relatively sparse "contacts" between widely divergent groups. In that context, it served the practical needs of dominant groups, providing a "brief for the prevailing civilization." But this context is now giving way. The present tendency is toward a "world civilization" in which all "social cultures" will be bound up with one another and none will be insulated from the rest. In this new context of vastly increased "race contacts," there will not necessarily emerge a "single type of social culture"; and practical needs for human classification may well persist. But the kind of classification needed will change. Static, purity-obsessed, biological conceptions will have to give way to dynamic, interactive, sociological ones. Only insofar as it is transformed in this manner will the concept of race survive.

Locke's first lecture, then, elaborated a Boasian critique of "the theoretical and scientific conceptions of race," inflected with a pragmatist spin. The crucial point was not simply that "race relations" are not physically determined, but also that they are not definitively fixed. Essentially historical and dynamic, the product of social interaction, race relations can be changed by deliberate human action. "Variability," he states in a later lecture, "provides a margin of social control, and establishes . . . the moral responsibility of society in these matters" (54).

"Practical Race": A Political-Economic Genealogy

Having disposed in his first lecture of "physical race," Locke turns in his second to "the political and practical conception of race." The move is quintessentially pragmatist. Descending from the biological theory of racialism to the social practice that underlies it, Locke shifts the analysis from the "modern race creed" to the "modern race practice." That practice he designates as "imperialism." "Imperialism," he says, is "the practical aspect of what one might call 'race practice' as distinguished from race theory" (24). Or, as we might say today: racialism is the theory; imperialism is the practice.

The approach in this lecture is genealogical. Locke argues that the idea of race is a creature of the practices of power. Following the pragmatist heuristic that ideas have roots in social practice, he inverts the prevailing racialist view that a preexisting condition of white superiority is the basis for white supremacy. On the contrary, he claims, political supremacy spawns the idea of superiority.

> The conception of "inferior" races or "backward" races and of "advanced" races or "superior" races largely comes from the political fortunes and political capacities of peoples. [T]he people who have not been successful in acquiring dominance . . . will be called the inferior people. . . . The ruling people not only dominate the group practically but control the . . . class distinctions . . . justifying their success in terms of . . . innate forms. . . . It behooves us then to keep our distinctions in their proper places and . . . to assume humbly that such notions as "superiority" refer only to the political fortunes of a group and not to any intrinsic or inherent qualities with respect to social culture. (22–23)

Racial categorization, then, is the offspring of domination.

The domination in question is imperialism, moreover, which Locke defines as "the practices of dominant or ruling groups." This is, of course, a broad definition, which encompasses both ancient and modern, non-racialist and racialist, systems of domination. For a genealogy of race, however, Locke must specify the narrower historical conditions that gave rise to a distinctively modern, racialist form of imperialism. The crucial factor, he claims, is an international economic system of competitive commerce. In this system, which has included both slavery and colonialism, European nation-states vie with one another for domination over non-western peoples. Seeking markets for their manufactures, imperial powers aim to implant their mode of life in the colonies and to uproot indigenous cultural forms. They rationalize these commercial imperatives, with the aid of Christian missionaries, by proclaiming their own civilization to be the only true civilization and by deprecating the cultural capacities of colonized peoples. Thus, commercial imperialism spawns racialist theory and a "practical culture" of alleged Anglo-Saxon superiority. Locke invokes his own painful experiences at the "Imperial Training School," that is, Oxford University, to illustrate the character of that culture.

By late twentieth-century standards, of course, Locke's account of modern imperialism is rudimentary. Elaborated chiefly in terms of competition for Third World markets, it says little about the extraction of primary resources or the exploitation of labor power. Nevertheless, he clearly distinguishes the nonracialist and at times relatively tolerant character of ancient tribute-collecting empires from modern color-based commercial imperialism, which depreciates and even destroys indigenous cultures. More important than its content, moreover, is the role Locke's account of imperialism plays in his overall argument. Introducing an international dimension to the practical genealogy of race, imperialism supplies the "broader" context he insists is needed to understand racial practice in the United States (35).

Having established his international frame, Locke turns in his third and fourth lectures to U.S. intranational "race relations." His account begins implausibly with the denial that the United States is an imperial power—a curious lapse of critical judgment in 1916. Nevertheless, he goes on to argue, imperialist culture pervades the society and inflects its internal racial order. Institutionalized in Jim Crow, the practical feeling of Anglo-Saxon superiority imperils the social standing not only of colonized peoples but also of freed people of color living as minorities in predominantly Anglo-Saxon countries.

To explain the specific racial dynamics of the United States, Locke constructs a synthetic account that combines economics, historical sociology, and social psychology. A democratic (white settler) society, the country has no fixed caste hierarchy (among whites) and relatively fluid class lines.

Social mobility and economic uncertainty generate status anxiety, hence a longing for fixed divisions and boundaries, a longing that Jim Crow arrangements seem to satisfy. Elites exploit these anxieties, which are rooted not only in economics, but also in social conditions and social psychology. Racial antagonism waxes and wanes with shifts in economic conditions, status anxiety, and the deliberate fomenting of racism by elites.

His gaffe about U.S. imperialism notwithstanding, then, Locke's account of intranational racial antagonisms is sophisticated. Anticipating recent conceptions of "Herrenvolk democracy," it avoids the twin reductions of economism and culturalism. Thus, it points beyond the standard oppositions in critical "race" theory to a pragmatic conception of race that can encompass both culture and political economy.

All told, then, the second tier of Locke's analysis roots the idea of race in the practices of white supremacist domination: both international imperialism and intranational Jim Crow. Race in this "political" sense is a practical reality, to be sure, but Locke maintains that its existence is historically contingent. Speculating that racial domination may no longer be functional for modern economic life, he considers the future of political race to be "doubtful." His goal, in any case, is to put an end to race in the practical sense of domination. It follows from the logic of his argument, moreover, that this requires dismantling modern imperialism, although Locke himself fails to draw that conclusion.[14]

"Social Race": A Reconstruction

Having demystified biological race and delegitimated political race, Locke arrives at the question, what remains of the idea of race? What, if anything, is left after we have refuted the "theoretical conception" intellectually and dismantled the "political conception" practically, presumably by abolishing imperialism? Today, perhaps, the most plausible answer is "nothing." But that reply is rejected by Locke. He contends that something potentially useful and pragmatically defensible remains: namely, "the social conception of race."

The social conception of race constitutes the third tier of Locke's analysis and the subject of his fifth and final lecture, titled "Racial Progress and Race Adjustment." Here he argues, on pragmatic grounds, that the idea of race ought not to be eradicated. Instead, it should be "revised" and "redeemed." A properly reformulated "social conception of race" could serve a salutary function, helping to resolve racial antagonisms and to advance the progress of civilization.

How can this be? How can a category that has produced such baleful effects in the past now be expected to have positive uses? To make his case, Locke retrieves a "very old" aspect of the idea of race, namely, the sense of group belonging and solidarity. This he maintains will never entirely disappear, as it is necessary to human society. He wagers, however, that this sense of race can now be dissociated from both the false biological sense and the unjust political sense. Thus, he claims to have discovered the kernel of a pragmatically defensible—"social"—conception of race that should be reconstructed and preserved.

So far, however, the social conception of race remains abstract. Fleshing it out involves elaborating a modern sense of group belonging and solidarity, one that does not feed imperial domination, segregation, or "reactionary nationalism." What sort of modern solidarity can "redeem" the social conception of race?

Locke's response is formulated at two levels. One pertains to the general developmental tendencies of modern societies, while the other concerns the specific situation of subordinated groups within them, especially American Negroes.

Social Race as Modern "Civilization Type"

On the first level, the key question for Locke is, what is the appropriate unit of solidarity in a modern society? His answer hinges on the general tendency of such societies to produce a single "standard of living," not in the sense of economic equality but in the sense of shared practices and modes of life consistent with participation in a competitive economy and other common core institutions. (In this modern societies differ from feudal societies and ancient imperial systems, which encompassed several distinct "standards of living.") Consequently, modern societies also tend to produce a single "civilization type," an ideal-typical sort of person, which members come roughly to approximate by virtue of participating in a common social structure and institutional framework. "Civilization type," according to Locke, is the proper overarching unit of solidarity in modern societies. Those who conform to "type" must be admitted as full citizens and partners. What precisely this entails Locke unfortunately does not say, although he explicitly denies that conformity to civilization type requires either homogeneity of customs and belief or religious and artistic conformity. These latter sorts of homogeneity and conformity he associates with a very different idea, mentioned earlier, which he refers to as "social culture."

Locke's effort to "redeem" the idea of race as a defensible form of modern social solidarity turns largely on the contrast between civilization type and social culture. The distinction, alas, is not directly explained in "Race Contacts and Interracial Relations." But its essence can be read between the lines. More restricted than a "civilization type," a "social culture" in Locke's usage comprehends a substantive nexus of concrete life forms, including ethical horizons and interpretive traditions. Civilization type, in contrast, comprehends the more abstract, formal structures that subtend such life forms in a modern pluralist society. Thus, a single modern civilization type can encompass a plurality of social cultures. To invoke a language not available to Locke, members of different ethnicities, subcultures, "communities of value," and religious confessions can all participate in the same civilization type. Or, as theorists of multiculturalism might put it today, whereas a social culture is an ethnos with an ethical or cultural identity, a civilization type is a demos with a political identity.

Conformity to civilization type, then, does not require the homogenization of social cultures. For Locke, moreover, the essential point is this: A civilization type has nothing whatever to do with blood. Unlike an ethnic type, it encompasses those qualities required for integration into the principal institutions of a modern society. Hence, the former Berlin student uses the term 'civilization,' as opposed to 'culture' or 'Volk.'

With the idea of "civilization type," Locke claims to have found an adequate basis for modern sociability and thus a "redeemed" "social conception" of race. "The only kind of race that is left to believe in and to be applied to modern problems is what we call the idea of social race, [defined] as a conception of civilization type. This seems to be the only thoroughly rational meaning of race. . . . [T]his is to be the race concept of the future" (88).

Where does this leave the American Negro? According to Locke, conformity to civilization type is both a necessary and sufficient condition for full membership in a modern nation-state. It is necessary in that modern forms of economic and social integration require it. It is sufficient in that a nation has no right to require more. Thus, for their part, Negroes must conform to the emerging American civilization type. But then for *their* part, white Americans must accept Negroes as full members. In general, then, Locke's notion of civilization type functions in part to argue that American nationality cannot be based on race or ethnicity. "If a nation should be expanded and incorporate other . . . elements, the same kind of [social] race type would be shared by people who . . . biologically have no connection, proving that a rational cult of a nation will never make the mistake of basing national type and civilization type upon a [biological] racial division" (86).

It is in the looming shadow of Jim Crow that Locke insists on the necessarily "assimilative" tendencies of modern societies. There is no way to prevent Negro assimilation, he claims, however much segregationists try. Assimilation is the inevitable outcome of interaction, and segregation cannot eliminate interaction. Thus, dominant groups do not control assimilation. But assimilation is not a one way street. The "civilization type" that emerges under modern social conditions cannot be identified with traits specific to any single constituent subgroup. On the contrary, it is in part a composite result of interaction among subgroups. It incorporates traits previously associated with various groups and in so doing transforms all the parties. Thus, the Negro has contributed, and will continue to contribute, to the making of the American civilization type, hence to the evolving social culture of Anglo-America.

Historically, of course, Locke was wildly over-optimistic, greatly underestimating the capacity of segregation to marginalize Black America and prevent its "assimilation," while also failing to contemplate the possibility that such assimilation as did occur might spawn a vacuous, lowest-common-denominator mass culture. We should note, however, that he was not only making (bad) historical predictions, but also elaborating an ideal. To this point, Locke's ideal resonates with Israel Zangwill's vision of America as a "melting pot," to which he refers with approval. Because he is theorizing with a view to the situation of the Negro under Jim Crow, and hence with a view to the question of power, Locke appreciates the emancipatory dimension of this ideal. Unlike Randolph Bourne and Horace Kallen, for example, he does not conflate it with "Americanization" in the sense of the forced Anglosaxonization of European immigrants.[15]

One may question whether Locke can consistently endorse both the melting pot vision and the view of a modern civilization type as comprehending a plurality of social cultures. To find the answer, one must recall that he does not end his discussion of social race here. Rather, he goes on to propose a second redemptive conception tailored specifically to the situation of American Negroes.

"Secondary Race Consciousness"

This second conception of social race Locke calls "secondary race consciousness." He commends it to American Negroes on pragmatic grounds. Anticipating the spirit of Hannah Arendt's dictum that "when one is attacked as a Jew, one must defend oneself as a Jew," Locke argues that "while social assimilation is in progress there seems to be necessary some . . . counter-doctrine [of] racial solidarity and culture. The stimulation of a secondary race-consciousness within a [dominated] group . . . is necessary for . . . practical reasons. The group needs . . . to get a right conception of itself, and it can only do that through stimulation of pride in itself" (96–97). "Race pride or secondary race consciousness [is] the social equivalent to self-respect in the individual moral life" (97).

Secondary race consciousness for the Negro is thus a matter of self-defense and self-respect. In addition, it will serve to stimulate the sort of "collective activity" that will hasten Negro "assimilation" to the emerging "civilization type" and therefore admission to full membership in American society. Thus, Locke claims that secondary race pride and "loyalty to the joint or common civilization type" are not mutually antithetical. On the contrary, the first serves as a means for realizing the second. In what only appears to be a paradox, then, "we will find it necessary to recreate the race type . . . only for the purpose ultimately to merge it with the general civilization type" (97).

Thus, Locke proposes Negro "race pride" as a pragmatic transitional strategy for realizing the long-term goal of "assimilation." Inflecting Du Bois' term "conservation" with an antiracialist, antiessentialist, pragmatic spirit, he suggests a program of Negro "*social* conservation," which does not rely on a "doctrine of race integrity" (98, my emphasis). Whereas Du Bois' argument for "conserving the Negro race" was premised on an essentialist racialist ontology, Locke's argument turns on a political pragmatics. He was, in Gayatri Spivak's terms, a "strategic essentialist" *avant la lettre*.[16]

How, then, is secondary race consciousness created? The chief avenue, according to Locke, is via cultural production. Negroes should cultivate a self-conscious relation to their distinctive "social culture," which is a syncretistic blend of African and Anglo-American elements. This requires recovering what is valuable in African traditions, from which Negroes have been cut off as a result of slavery. It also involves giving expression to African-American traditions in public cultural forms, such as literature, music, and painting, where they can be recognized by the larger society. Locke recommends that American Negroes follow the example of the Poles and the Irish in Europe and pursue an intranational variant of cultural nationalism. In those cases, he says, a "racial sense" has inspired great movements in arts and letters, which have "redeemed" the false meanings of race. Negroes should therefore pursue "culture-citizenship" both to forge solidarity among themselves and to win respect from Anglo-America. By making their own distinctive contribution to the emerging joint civilization, as opposed to merely imitating the dominant culture, they will eventually win full citizenship.

Here, at last, we begin to recognize the future Alain Locke of the Harlem Renaissance. But that Alain Locke now looks somewhat different. The New Negro project appears a bid for "culture-citizenship" as a step on the way to political and economic citizenship. Locke's mature cultural nationalism thus appears as a strategy aimed at overcoming a form of racial domination that he understood as ultimately economic and political. Its roots lie in a sophisticated pragmatist understanding of race conjoined with an anti-imperialist political analysis.

The strategy is, of course, paradoxical. In these lectures, as we have seen, Locke traced the roots of race and of racism to imperialism, to political domination based in historical economics. Why, then, does he propose to "redeem" the idea of race and overcome racism through the creation of Negro literature and art? Why propose a cultural remedy for a political-economic harm? Why cultural production instead of political struggle?

The answer surely lies in part in the bleakness of 1916. At that moment the prospects were dim indeed for Negro civil and political rights, not to mention the social and economic rights that the mass of sharecroppers would have needed to make civil and political rights meaningful. In addition, Locke's squeamishness about political struggle betrays some remnants of the influence of Booker T. Washington, from whose patronage he had earlier benefited. He ends the Howard lectures by acknowledging that his culture-citizenship strategy appears to "fall in line" with the dominant segregationist agenda, even as he maintains, nevertheless, that it is the necessary "forerunner . . . of that kind of recognition [we] are ultimately striving for, namely, recognition of an economic, civic, and social sort" (99–100).

Here, of course, history again proved Locke wrong. The extraordinary flowering of Black cultural production he envisioned and promoted did not serve to win civil and political rights. Only mass political struggle, directly confronting the racist state, could do that. Notwithstanding the theoretical sophistication of Locke's pragmatist antiessentialism, then, it was not he, but the Hegelian racialist-essentialist Du Bois, who understood this.

Locke concluded his 1916 lectures by returning to his first conception of social race, defined as "civilization type." This, he proclaims, is the goal of "race progress and race adjustment": the creation of a novel, composite "civilization type." This finally redeems the idea of race. "Whatever theory or practice moves toward [this end] is sound," the pragmatist adds; "whatever opposes and retards it false" (100).

Another Pragmatism

Pragmatism undoubtedly lay at the core of Locke's 1916 vision. It was central to the overall plan and argument of his Howard University lectures and is at the root of several of his best insights. It was through pragmatism that Locke first came to reject racialist essentialism and to embrace Franz Boas' alternative. Yet it was also as a result of his pragmatism that he was not content to stop there but went on to seek out the roots of racialist theory in racist-imperialist social practice. Likewise, it was as a pragmatist that Locke contemplated the future of the concept of race and the uses of a successor concept. Seeking a form of social integration appropriate to a modern civilization, he envisioned a "social conception of race" as "civilization type" utterly divorced from ethnicity and blood. Yet it was also as a pragmatist, finally, that Locke found mere civilization type insufficient. He realized that a dominated group such as American Negroes required a "secondary race consciousness" in order to struggle for liberation and inclusion. Pragmatism, in short, was the key to his "strategic essentialism."

If many of Locke's insights derive from his pragmatism, his lectures present a strand of pragmatist thought that differs importantly from the mainstream of the movement. Like Kallen, Bourne, and Dewey, Locke was concerned with the regulation of group difference in twentieth-century America. Unlike them, however, he did not understand the problem as one of harmoniously orchestrating the cultural differences of immigrant groups, a view largely irrelevant to Negroes and to the struggle against racism. Rather, Locke understood difference in the light of power, domination, and political economy. Thus, unlike the pragmatist mainstream, he grasped that a dominated group might need to forge a cultural identity as a weapon of struggle against oppression. Locke represents, in sum, another pragmatism.

Locke's pragmatism also has an ironic side, however, one that those seeking to revive pragmatism today would do well to contemplate. The theoretically sophisticated antiessentialist, antiracialist Locke was considerably less pragmatically grounded with respect to politics than the Hegelian racialist-essentialist (and soon-to-be-Marxist) Du Bois. Locke's philosophical pragmatism was apparently no guarantee of political astuteness.

Locke's 1916 lectures did not influence his mainstream pragmatist contemporaries—at least not so far as we know. Nevertheless, they might still prove instructive for us today. They provide a point of contrast that highlights some of the limits of the mainstream tradition of classical pragmatist social thought: its neglect of power, its emphasis on culture at the expense of political economy, and its tendency to posit imaginary holistic "solutions" to difficult, sometimes irreconcilable, conflicts. These limits were perhaps less clear in 1916 because pragmatism was then part of a broad-based movement for democratization in social, economic, and political life, as well as in intellectual spheres. Today, however, the situation is more ambiguous. Some revivals of pragmatism seem actually to celebrate the decline of the democratizing movements of our day, while others apparently hope that appeals to the spirit of Dewey can help rekindle such movements, even as the Progressive-era legacy is being dismantled before our eyes. In this context it is salutary to read the youthful Alain Locke. His 1916 lectures give us a sense of those aspects of pragmatism that are genuinely worth reviving.

At the same time, Locke's lectures also supply some more specific critical insights into contemporary conflicts over cultural identity and multiculturalism. His distinction between civilization type and social culture, although by no means adequately developed, anticipates promising recent efforts to distinguish political solidarity and citizenship, on the one hand, from ethical solidarity and ethnicity, on the other.[17] Equally important, Locke's conception of secondary race consciousness introduces the hard fact of domination squarely into discussions that too often rely on the euphemistic idioms of "difference" and "pluralism." He thereby exposes the false symmetry of approaches that assume that all groups and individuals stand in essentially the same relation to the problem of recognition of difference. Locke reminds us, rather, that systematically dominated social groups have pragmatic political needs for solidarity that differ from the needs of others. In the case of African Americans, such domination continues to encompass both cultural misrecognition and political-economic maldistribution. Thus, Locke's attempt to connect the struggle for recognition with a struggle for redistribution remains relevant to this day.

What, finally, can we learn from this "other pragmatism" of the unknown Alain Locke? The most important lesson for those proposing to revive pragmatism today is this: There is not one, but several different pragmatisms. We had better know which of them we want to revive.

Notes

1   Cornel West, *The American Evasion of Philosophy* (Madison: University of Wisconsin Press, 1989).

2   See, for example, Nathan Irvin Huggins, *Harlem Renaissance* (New York: Oxford University Press, 1971).

3   I borrow this expression from Gayatri Spivak. See Gayatri Spivak with Ellen Rooney, "In a Word," *differences* 1 (Summer 1989): 2.

4   Oliver Cromwell Cox, *Caste, Class, and Race* (New York: Monthly Review Press, 1970). For a recent version of this position, see Barbara Fields, "Ideology and Race in American History," in *Region, Race, and Reconstruction: Essays in Honor of C. Vann Woodward,* ed. J. M. Kousser and J. M. McPherson (Oxford: Oxford University Press, 1982).

5   W. E. B. Du Bois, "The Conservation of Races," *American Negro Academy Occasional Papers,* no. 2, 1897. Reprinted in *W. E. B. Du Bois Speaks: Speeches and Addresses 1890–1919,* ed. Philip S. Foner (New York: Pathfinder Press, 1970). Kwame Anthony Appiah, *In My Father's House: Africa in the Philosophy of Culture* (Oxford: Oxford University Press, 1992).

6   For a fuller account of these various tendencies, see Nancy Fraser, "From Redistribution to Recognition? Dilemmas of Justice in a 'Postsocialist' Age," *New Left Review* 212 (July/August 1995): 68–93, reprinted in Nancy Fraser, *Justice Interruptus: Critical Reflections on the 'Postsocialist' Condition* (New York: Routledge, 1997).

7   For an interesting reflection on this question, see Robert Westbrook's discussion of Dewey's early socialism in his *John Dewey and American Democracy* (Ithaca: Cornell University Press, 1991).

8   Charles Taylor, *Multiculturalism: Examining the Politics of Recognition,* ed. Amy Gutmann (Princeton: Princeton University Press, 1994). Another writer who privileges the ethnic model of differentiation, even while seeking to deal with power and political economy, is Iris Marion Young, *Justice and the Politics of Difference* (Princeton: Princeton University Press, 1990). For a critique of Taylor's implicit privileging of the ethnic model, see Linda Nicholson, "To Be or Not To Be: Charles Taylor on The Politics of Recognition," *Constellations* 3 (April 1996): 1. For a critique of the parallel move in Young, see Nancy Fraser, "Redistribution or Recognition? A Critical Reading of Iris Young's *Justice and the Politics of Difference,*" *Journal of Political Philosophy* 3; 2 (June 1995): 166–80; a revised version is reprinted under the title "Culture, Political Economy, and Difference," in Fraser, *Justice Interruptus.*

9   See Fraser, "From Redistribution to Recognition?"

10 Alain Locke, *Race Contacts and Interracial Relations,* edited and introduced by Jeffrey C. Stewart (Washington, D.C.: Howard University Press, 1992). All references are to this edition; page numbers are cited in parentheses in the body of this essay.

11 Jeffrey C. Stewart, "Introduction," *ibid.*

12 Heretofore I placed the term 'race' in scare quotes in accord with current critical "race" theory usage and my own philosophical-political commitments. It is unlikely, however, that Locke would have used scare quotes, given the conventions in force in 1916. Accordingly, I shall follow Jeffrey Stewart's practice of omitting scare quotes when explicating the argument of Locke's lectures. Following standard practice in contemporary philosophical writing, I shall use single quotes when the word 'race' is mentioned, as opposed to used. For a discussion of the use of scare quotes, see Henry Louis Gates Jr. ed., *"Race," Writing, and Difference* (Chicago: University of Chicago Press, 1986).

13 Richard J. Herrnstein and Charles Murray, *The Bell Curve: Intelligence and Class Structure in American Life* (New York: Free Press, 1994).

14 This is another point at which Locke shrinks from drawing out the full implications of

his argument. Instead of calling for the dismantling of imperialism, he seems at points to assume it is destined to persist.

15 See Horace M. Kallen, "Democracy and the Melting Pot," in *Culture and Democracy in the United States: Studies in the Group Psychology of the American Peoples,* ed. Horace M. Kallen (New York: Boni and Liveright, 1924); and Randolph S. Bourne, "Trans-National America," in *The Radical Will: Randolph Bourne—Selected Writings, 1911–1918,* ed. Olaf Hansen (New York: Urizen, 1977). For a thoughtful discussion, see Werner Sollors, *Beyond Ethnicity: Consent and Descent in American Culture* (New York: Oxford University Press, 1986).

16 Gayatri Spivak with Ellen Rooney, "In a Word."

17 See, for example, Jürgen Habermas, "Struggles for Recognition in the Democratic Constitutional State," in Taylor, *Multiculturalism.*

Going Astray, Going Forward: Du Boisian Pragmatism and Its Lineage

ROSS POSNOCK

Philosophy can always go astray, which is the sole reason why it can go forward. This has been recognized in pragmatism, most recently in Dewey's wholly humane version.—Adorno, *Negative Dialectics*

Mention pragmatism in black intellectual history and the name likeliest to come to mind is Booker T. Washington's. The self-made "wizard," with his genius for accommodation and compromise, has long been regarded as a consummate pragmatist. As head of the white-funded "Tuskegee Machine," Washington not only spread the gospel of industrial training but maintained an iron grip over black media and political patronage. Incensed at Washington's repression of all dissent, W. E. B. Du Bois and his "talented tenth" cohort rebelled. The rest is history, or, rather, that familiar historical set piece Washington versus Du Bois, which is usually painted in dramatic polarities: the steely pragmatist schooled in slavery pitted against a Harvard and Berlin educated Hegelian idealist who scorned Washington's mammonism, his counsels of submission, and philistine intolerance of book education.

This scenario requires at least two qualifications and both hinge on the still insufficiently recognized disjunction between the colloquial and philosophical senses of pragmatism. A masterful organizer and disciplinarian, Washington was a pragmatist in the colloquial sense but the virtual antithesis of a philosophical pragmatist. Du Bois inverts these distinctions; as a political strategist he seldom acted with pragmatic efficiency but often with chronic "incongruity" (as Harold Cruse says) that usually left him "either too far ahead or too far behind, but out of step with mass thinking."[1] But Du Bois' missteps are the very imprint of his philosophic pragmatism, which he learned directly from William James.

Not for Du Bois the "singleness of vision and thorough oneness with his age" that he noted in Washington's career and disdained as provincialism.[2]

Instead, Du Bois cultivates what in *The Souls of Black Folk* he calls "double consciousness" and "unreconciled strivings," tensions that become the very structure of his vision (*W*, pp. 364–65). Sociologist, historian, novelist, editor, essayist and poet, romantic racialist as well as universalist, Du Bois spent nearly a century strategically adapting, revising, and resisting a panoply of stances—nationalist, assimilationist, integrationist, segregationist, pan-Africanist, Marxist socialist, and communist. What anchors Du Bois' career of course is unwavering activism on behalf of equality for black Americans. But this anchorage functioned as the pivot from which, as he says, "I flew round and round with the Zeitgeist, waving my pen . . . to see, forsee and prophesy" (*W*, p. 555).

"The turning was due to William James." Thus Du Bois recalls James encouraging him to move from studying philosophy to history and social problems, but he also neatly distills the philosopher's catalytic impact (*W*, p. 582). To be fermentative, a favorite Jamesian word, was precisely the point of pragmatism.[3]

Du Bois' career is one of turnings, of transition, of going astray. To claim that pragmatism orients this career would seem to reduce it to the tidy dimensions that any single label imposes. Yet because pragmatism makes the classifying impulse itself a prime object of critique, it is a label that functions not to arrest but to lead (in James' word). What it leads to is heightened understanding not only of Du Bois' commitment to simultaneous and multiple forms of inquiry but to the freedom this affords him.[4] In turbulent acts of turning, he achieves the "strenuous life" that the Jamesian pluralist embraces. "Without assurances or guarantees," the pluralist's "world is always vulnerable, for some part may go astray," notes James.[5] And that risk is what Du Bois embraces as freedom. He grasps pragmatism in precisely the spirit James intended, as an "attitude of orientation" that "stands for no particular results" since it is "less a solution than a program for more work" (*WJ*, pp. 509–10). A method for conducting a career, for creating a literary style, for living "the strenuous life," Du Boisian pragmatism is creative revisionary practice. Thus, in good pragmatist fashion, he interrogated the limits of James' thought, pressing beyond his mentor's attenuated historical understanding and naive faith in "the New England ethic of life" (*W*, p. 1315). The instilling of a temperament, a mode of conduct, "is what the pragmatic method means," says James. Du Bois internalized the pragmatist temper that is skeptical of "principles, categories, supposed necessities" (*WJ*, p. 510), preferring instead to risk improvising under the pressure of changing historical experience: "I faced situations that called—shrieked—for action."

Du Bois here recalls, in a remarkable but seldom-quoted retrospective essay of 1944, the change in perspective he underwent after joining the NAACP in 1910 and assuming editorship of the *Crisis*. Finding himself immersed in "continuous, kaleidoscopic change of conditions," Du Bois breaks with his "previous purely scientific program," for he realizes that "the social scientist could not sit apart and study *in vacuo*." No longer will he conduct a positivist sociology dedicated to tabulating immutable "scientific law," but instead will now "measure the element of Chance," a pursuit whose source, he says, is "Jamesian pragmatism, applied not simply to ethics, but to all human action." Then, in a decidedly Jamesian phrase, Du Bois draws out the consequences of his paradigm shift: "My work assumed from now on a certain tingling challenge of risk."[6] Abandoning the insulation of a spectator theory of knowledge (to borrow John Dewey's famous phrase), Du Bois was "willing to live on possibilities that are not certainties" (*WJ*, p. 941).[7]

The fruits of Du Bois' pragmatism are found in later figures such as Alain Locke, Zora Neale Hurston, and Ralph Ellison. In the thought of each pragmatism flowers in diverse ways, yet their own exfoliations could be said to have grown from soil first tilled by Du Bois—skepticism of "identity logic," rationalism's prime instrument of knowledge. According to William James, the logic of identity (or "intellectualism") construes definition as the naming of a thing's essence and reduces experience to knowledge of these essences. We shall see that the "attitude of orientation" shared by the aforementioned writers exemplifies the pragmatist "spirit" that John Dewey once described as a revolt against "that habit of mind which disposes of anything by tucking it away in the pigeon holes of a filing cabinet."[8]

To understand why pragmatism was so compelling to Du Bois requires a brief look at the anomalous position of the black intellectual around 1900. To Booker T. Washington and his white northern patrons, the phrase "black intellectual" was a repugnant oxymoron that referred to deracinated northerners determined to live by their wits. For Tuskegee had normalized blackness to mean rural southerner, one "humble, simple, and of service to the community."[9] A black intellectual must define himself as a race man—an ascetic exemplar seamlessly fused with the group. To act otherwise smacked of the decadence of a dandified urban fop, a warning Washington sought to convey in his ridicule of the "educated Negro, with a high hat . . . and showy walking stick."[10] The dapper, goateed Du Bois in fact carried a walking stick, loved aesthetic contemplation, and declared as his stated goal, the end of his striving, "to be a co-worker in the kingdom of culture," a phrase that deftly defines the vocation of the literary intellectual and is silent about race work (*W*, p. 365). Du Bois conceives the kingdom as a deracialized realm "above the Veil" where men will be judged "by their souls and not by their skins" (*W*, p. 544).

But within the Veil how would Du Bois negotiate the tension between service and a life of free intellectual inquiry? He wrestled with that question in his Berlin rooms on his twenty-fifth birthday. "I am striving to make my life all that life may be," he grandly declares in his journal, even as he is "firmly convinced" that his "own best development is not one and the same with the best development of the world." The world's best development would be "the rise of the Negro people," and as he dedicates himself to the role of race-man he twice describes his decision as a "sacrifice"—"to the world's good" (*A*, p. 171). Half a century later, in *Dusk of Dawn*, he would speak of this sacrifice again, this time less personally, when he describes the " 'race' man" as a "prisoner" of the "group," an imprisonment that makes him "provincial" (*W*, p. 651). Compounding this stifling pressure, Du Bois lived daily with an acute sense of being "kept within bounds" by a white world "settled and determined upon the fact that I was and must be a thing apart" (*W*, p. 653). Sacrificing himself to group identity, viscerally enduring Jim Crow's mania for frozen classification, Du Bois' lifelong challenge becomes to find a margin of freedom, a way to mitigate, if not evade, the twin sacrifice demanded by the repressions of coerced identity—as race man and as "a colored man in a white world" (*W*, p. 653).

Little wonder that Du Bois found inspiring pragmatism's esteem for the unclassified and insouciance toward "supposed necessities." Along with Franz Boas' anthropology (which by 1911 helped Du Bois begin to revise his romantic racialism), pragmatism was a tool that, virtually alone among turn-of-the-century behavioral and social sciences, could oppose the theory and practice of white supremacy. William James' anti-imperialist defense of the dark-skinned alien reflects his pragmatism's refusal of absolutist systems and purified essences, the modes of thought often employed to defend racialist assumptions and racism. Thus Hegel was one of James' inevitable antagonists, as was American Hegelianism, which enjoyed a great vogue in the post–Civil War United States. Hegel's vision of America as "the land of the future" where "the Burden of the World's History shall reveal itself" in effect invited an orgy of exceptionalism.[11] American Hegelians used the philosopher to legitimate American nationalism and racism within an optimistic Christian teleology of manifest destiny.

The received wisdom is that Du Bois was an Hegelian. But this sim-plification ignores how Jamesian pragmatism shapes Du Bois' relation to Hegel. The matter is complicated but I have space here only to sketch an alternative view. In the 1880s an old Walt Whitman and a young John Dewey were among those swept up in affirming the harmonious unity of a progressive, rational state.[12] Half a century later, Dewey saluted Hegel for having permanently liberated him from the shackles of Cartesian dual-isms. But Dewey noted that he had drifted away from the philosopher's "mechanical dialectical" form, a "schematism" of system that eventually came to seem "artificial to the last degree," as artificial as Absolute Idealism would become for Dewey.[13] William James also rejected Hegel's system, yet preserved what he, like Dewey, found vital in Hegel—his dialectical vision, his stress on the concrete and on becoming. But unheeded by James the staunch individualist was the lesson of Hegel's dialectical logic for man and society. Two pragmatists of the next generation, Dewey and Du Bois, embraced Hegel's insistence on the primacy of mediation, of social bonds, of the contextual. Thus the Hegelian deposit in both men's thought in-flected their pragmatism with a critical historicism.

From a pragmatist's point of view, the trouble with Absolute Idealism, as George Herbert Mead once said, is that it denies that "our life is an adventure. There can be nothing novel in the Absolute. . . . All that is to take place has already taken place in an Absolute."[14] Du Bois' particular challenge became how to dispense with Hegel's synthetic system, which denied a place both for the "tingling challenge of risk" he valued and for the negative particularity of African-American enslavement, while retain-ing Hegel's redemptive historicist teleology for black Americans.[15] In an influential discussion of "how Du Bois became a Hegelian," the historian Joel Williamson persuasively shows that Hegel's model of World Spirit presides over the opening pages of *The Souls of Black Folk,* where Du Bois extends the six world historical peoples that Hegel posits to include the Negro as "a sort of seventh son" with its own message for the world. But Williamson overstates Hegel's impact when he says: "Hegel gave Du Bois a philosophy and a purpose in life, both of which he very much needed" and also gave him a separatist "formula" for psychic survival (409).[16] In sum, Williamson would have us believe that Du Bois seized Hegel's blueprint as truth and the rest, as they say, is history.

Implied in Williamson's reading is that because Du Bois studied at the University of Berlin in the midst of a Hegelian revival, his earlier training in James' evolving pragmatism was washed away when Hegel swept him off his feet. But when Du Bois encountered Hegel he had already assimilated James' critique of the philosopher, which was part of the process of how James worked toward pragmatism. "My quarrel" with Hegel, James remarked, "is entirely apropos of the problem of identity. I think all his other faults derivative from that."[17] He conducts this quarrel in "On Some Hegelisms" (1882). James regrets that in Hegel's logic, contradiction—the identification of opposites—functions as a "universal solvent; or, rather, there is no longer any need of a solvent," because all things have been dissolved into each other. James finds Hegelism a virtual frenzy of "reconciliation" (reconciliation, quips James, "characterizes the 'maudlin' stage of alcoholic drunkenness"), an intoxicating emotion but one whose inevitable outcome is "*indifferentism,*"—blindness to particularity and to "irreducible . . . real conflicts." Hegel's "all-devouring" system abstracts all individuality, leaving "no residuum."[18] Identity is the enemy of the residuum that James champions as the emblem of what escapes classification and closed systems.

James' esteem for risk, particularity, and residuum informed Du Bois' own encounter with Hegel's closed system, which he felt compelled to revise not least because it failed to account for his own embodied residuum—mixed racial ancestry. Hegel accorded mulattoes no reality for he regarded cultural hybridity as impossible. Given his own mixed blood and his training in philosophic pragmatism, Du Bois had ample reason to be sensitized to the repressions of fixed identity and the need to defend the precarious residuum. Thus he injected "adventure" into Hegel's teleology by refusing synthesis or closure: "unreconciled strivings," he wrote in *The Souls,* animate African-American psyches and history.[19]

In short, rather than choosing between pragmatism and Hegelianism, as some of his commentators seem compelled to do, Du Bois instead let them mutually revise each other. With its emphasis on mobility and turning, pragmatist method inclines the practitioner toward an adaptive eclecticism, and that mode seems to have been particularly congenial to the intellectually voracious Du Bois. His passionate feasting at the remarkable intellectual banquet that was his international education was the source of the energy and creativity of his pragmatist makings and remakings. To adapt and refashion became Du Bois' reflex response to the many theories and systems of thought to which he was exposed. Dewey's summary of his own similar disposition is resonant here: "I seem to be unstable, chameleon-like, yielding one after another to many diverse and even incompatible influences; struggling to assimilate something from each."[20]

The intellectual lability of Dewey and Du Bois made them wary of "identity logic" and receptive to James' pragmatist pluralism which made "'ever not quite'" its "heraldic device." This motto, says James, honors "residual resistance to verbalization, formulation, and discursification" (*WJ*, p. 1313). In the famous opening pages of *The Souls of Black Folk*, Du Bois distilled this resistance into the word "problem," as he ponders how "being a problem is a strange experience" (*W*, p. 363). Rather than resolve "being a problem," Du Bois himself embodied it throughout his career, as an act of fidelity to the reality of unsettlement: as he said in 1924, "Negro America is travelling" a "curious path . . . [that] turns and twists so frequently that one cannot see just where one is going."[21] Du Bois' willingness to turn and "grope," to risk the vulnerability of revising and improvising amid uncertainty, reflects his pragmatist historicism that believes that "no idea is perfect and forever valid. Always to be living and apposite and timely, it must be modified and adapted to changing facts" (*W*, p. 776).

He not only theorized this historicism but acted upon it. Indeed Du Bois made the preceding statement to explain one of the most controversial decisions of his career—his 1934 effort to revise the raison d'etre of the organization he helped create in 1910: the sacred commitment to racial integration and opposition to segregation. Interrogating this goal in light of the NAACP's first twenty-four years of existence, Du Bois found that the net result of the campaign against segregation "has been a little less than nothing" (*W*, p. 1241). To reinsert himself in the moving present, that "zone of insecurity in human affairs," as James called it, Du Bois was willing to expose himself to predictable (and ahistoricist) charges of betraying the struggle for equality. The NAACP ousted him after he attempted to unsettle its identity from within by urging voluntary economic segregation. Although fully aware that he was "touching an old and bleeding sore in Negro thought," Du Bois hoped to turn segregation from a traditional "badge of servitude" into one of self-respect (*W*, p. 777).

One consequence of his mobility, combined with a temperamental aloofness, was a certain isolation: "He could find no clear role for himself in the ranks of the Left" and "frustrated many potential allies with his complex positions" runs a representative capsule assessment.[22] Such was the cost of making the "strenuous life" a model of political practice; one is without "assurances or guarantees" of clear political alliances and fixed social affiliations (*WJ*, p. 941). So profound was Du Bois' investment in James' strenuous ideal that he rendered the 1944 retrospective narrative of his career in its heroic colors. "I was continually the surgeon probing blindly, yet with what knowledge and skill I could muster, for unknown ill" is how Du Bois sums up his embattled stance (*E*, p. 57). This is a metaphor of crisis, of authority stripped of authority and flirting with chaos as it confronts the hazards of unmastered experience in a "tramp and vagrant world, adrift in space" (*WJ*, p. 601). A surgeon blindly probing, Du Bois is willing to risk the pain of reopening wounds, ripping off scabs of habit grown indurate, of boundaries and identities grown sclerotic, all in an effort to reinstate the rawness of experience pregnant with possibility and potential. In taking upon himself the "tingling challenge of risk," Du Bois turned James' legacy into a way of being free in a world determined to cage him.

Like Du Bois, such later pragmatists as Locke, Hurston, and Ellison are particularly alert to the threat to freedom embodied in what James calls "vicious intellectualism" and Dewey the "fallacy of definition"—the use of concepts to erect rigid classifications that devour "transitional and connecting links."[23] The effort to preserve such links will shape the responses of the later black pragmatists to what, by the 1920s, was a national preoccupation: the question of what constitutes American identity. According to the received wisdom, pragmatism's answer is cultural pluralism, promulgated in 1915 by Horace Kallen, a former student of James'. Defying nativist demands for "one hundred per cent Americanism," cultural pluralism honors the multiethnic reality of the United States by celebrating the immigrant who resists assimilation and preserves his origins to become a hyphenated American. But cultural pluralism was silent about black Americans, ignoring that they had, in Du Bois' words, "actively . . . woven" themselves "in the very warp and woof of this nation" (*W*, p. 545). Blindness (or indifference) to such hybridity is symptomatic of Kallen's other problem—that his pluralism was actually unpragmatist in its essentialist affirmation of identity as immutable ethnic difference. As Dewey told Kallen in 1915, he disliked the "implication of segregation" in the latter's conception of a pluralist democracy as an orchestra comprised of atomized, static group identities.[24] The hyphen must connect, not separate, warned Dewey. In a similar cosmopolitan spirit, Du Bois, just prior to World War I, sought, he said, to build an "Internation" founded on an "interracial culture, broader and more catholic than" any currently existing here (*E*, p. 58). But the war derailed his dream of establishing a "human unity."

As an alternative to Kallen's essentialism and his neglect of black Americans, we can trace an underappreciated countertradition, a pragmatist cultural pluralism visible with varying degrees of explicitness in Du Bois, Dewey, Locke, Hurston, and Ellison. It aims to restore the connectives eliminated by the deadening effects of segregation, both racial and philo-sophical, by reinstating, in Dewey's phrase, "what is left over . . . excluded by definition from full reality," what goes astray by eluding or disrupting the reign of system.[25] Pragmatist pluralism is, to borrow Hurston's words, "disturbing to the pigeon-hole way of life" for it disinters what all forms of absolutism—including identity claims grounded in biology, ethnicity, foundational philosophy, doctrinaire Marxism, or white supremacy—seek to keep buried: tangled and muddy overlap, "motley mixtures" (Ellison).[26] Belief in "blood magic and blood thinking," notes Ellison in 1978, allows one to flee the discomfiting reality of America's interracial "wholeness," a "vortex" of discordancy in "cacaphonic motion," as Ellison describes the "fluid, pluralistic turbulence of the democratic process."[27] Pragmatism, as mediated by Locke's avid admiration for William James' pluralistic uni-verse of anarchic interplay, helped shape Ellison's view. The novelist ac-knowledged this debt when he said that Locke understood above all that modern American culture was "the experience of human beings living in a world of turbulent transition," an emphasis derived from "his studies with James and Royce."[28]

Locke, who helped Kallen devise cultural pluralism, but who only adopted it provisionally, described racial and ethnic identity as "fictions" upholding "the fetish of biological purity" to conceal the fact of "countless interminglings" and "infinite crossings" of type.[29] Locke proposed a si-multaneous dual strategy of assimilation and provisional "race solidarity" or "race pride" for achieving "culture-citizenship."[30] In her autobiography *Dust Tracks On a Road,* Hurston, who knew Locke at Howard University, would express disdain of the "forced grouping" implicit in "race con-sciousness": "There is no possible classification so catholic that it will cover us all": "There is no *The Negro* here." And she would be scathing in her estimate of "Race Men," including Du Bois and Locke, whom she believed dealt in "easy generalization."[31]

Du Bois might well have agreed with her. In *Dusk of Dawn: An Essay Toward an Autobiography of a Race Concept,* published in 1940, two years before Hurston's memoir, Du Bois does not blink the fact that race lead-ers necessarily traffic in the monolithic abstractions of group identity. Though less acidly than Hurston and from an immanent position, Du Bois confesses frustrations with the inherent confinements of representing the race, for his sensibility is shaped by an abiding tension between a conviction that human action is most creative when most imbued with a "certain tingling challenge of risk" and the knowledge that the sober re-sponsibilities of the race man confine him to "unending loyalty" which "balks at almost no sacrifice" (*W,* p. 651). Such self-abnegation necessarily "congeals" into bitter resentment toward white people. Du Bois speaks frankly of race leadership as a symptom of the pathologies of segregation, which he images as being entombed in a "dark cave" of a mountainside, helpless behind transparent thick plate glass (*W*, p. 650–51).

Du Bois notes the burden of "group imprisonment" in the penultimate paragraph of the book's central chapter "The Concept of Race." The concluding paragraph begins: "This was the race concept which has dominated my life, and the history of which I have attempted to make the leading theme of this book. It had as I have tried to show all sorts of illogical trends and irreconcilable tendencies. Perhaps it is wrong to speak of it at all as a 'concept' rather than as a group of contradictory forces, facts, and tendencies. At any rate, I hope I have made its meaning to me clear" (*W*, p. 651). Here at the center of his autobiography, Du Bois turns against his own subtitle for its factitious tidiness and dissolves "race concept" into the "whirlpool of social entanglement and inner psychological paradox" which expresses his "life and action" (*W*, p. 555). Given that concepts, says James, "cut out and fix, and exclude," Du Bois' revisionary move crystallizes what one might call the pragmatist aesthetic moment in the Du Boisian text, the dispersal of the concept into "irreconcilable" and "contradictory" indeterminacy (*WJ*, p. 746). Thus he eludes an epistemology of segregation founded on the coercions of identity logic.

Resistance to segregation suffuses the impassioned opening two chapters of Dewey's *Experience and Nature*, which renews for the 1920s the radical empiricism that James articulated in *A Pluralistic Universe* (1909).[32] Dewey redescribes philosophy as a "critique of prejudices," particularly of those prejudices embedded in the "classificatory device[s]" used by the classic and "genteel tradition" to elevate "unity" and "permanence" to supreme Being while relegating "unreconciled diversity," "the recalcitrant particular . . . the ambiguousness and ambivalence of reality," to a "metaphysically inferior" order of existence (*EN*, pp. 41–42). This invidious segregation makes "the uncertain and unfinished" unreal by minimizing the hazards of change and chance that saturate primary experience. Here "the obscure and vague," "dark and twilight abound," and "there are always potentialities which are not explicit" (*EN*, pp. 20–21). By immersing us in noncognitive "primary experience, in all its fulness and heterogeneity," Dewey's naturalism reanimates what initiates philosophy: the tension of "reciprocal resistances" that draw their energy from the fact that stability and uncertainty are inextricably mixed. Stability and uncertainty, according to Dewey, may be recognized "separately but we cannot divide them, for . . . they grow from the same root."[33]

Critiquing prejudices, recovering mixture, dissolving segregation, redeeming what is classified as inferior: Dewey's stance in 1925 amounts to a war on philosophy's Jim Crow regime, a war that complements his political practice and thinking. As a board member of the NAACP upon its founding, Dewey worked with Du Bois, who later (in 1929) was his colleague in the short-lived socialist League of Independent Political Action. *Experience and Nature* philosophically evokes Dewey's activism on behalf of democratic equality, for here Dewey describes the texture of a world at last unshackled from the "metaphysics of feudalism." Upheld by prevailing philosophies and even emancipatory social theories, this metaphysics is grounded on "a notion that inherently some realities are superior to others" and that the world is defined by a "fixed order of species, grades or degrees."[34] In contrast, democratic equality flourishes in a world still in the making, a "vision of a new mode of life" that William James first enunciated. In *A Pluralistic Universe* and "A World of Pure Experience" (1904) we glimpse experience untethered to prefabricated categories, where "life is in the transitions as much as in the terms connected." Experience "grows by its edges," with one moment "proliferating into the next by transitions," in a "mosaic" of "overlap"—"all shades and no boundaries" (*WJ*, pp. 1181, 761). Like *Experience and Nature*, James' radical empiricism can be read as an eloquent philosophical allegory of what a world beyond the Veil of the color line would be like to live in, a world not deformed by what every foundationalist philosophy requires—a principle of a "single, final, and unalterable authority."[35]

That it was read as allegory is apparent. Consider, for instance, the opening lines of Locke's "The New Negro": "in the last decade something beyond the watch and guard of statistics has happened in the life of the American Negro and the three norns who have traditionally presided over the Negro problem have a changeling in their laps. The sociologist, the Philanthropist, the Race-Leader are not unaware of the New Negro, but they are at a loss to account for him. He simply cannot be swathed in their formulae."[36] With his love of the "unclassified residuum," James would have cherished the existence of this elusive changeling defiant of categories, including separatism, who affirms his Africanity as part of America's pluralist democracy. Ellison salutes this changeling and devises one of his own in his figure of the "little man" behind the stove at Chehaw station. He becomes a metaphor for the dissonant, incalculable possibilities bred by democratic turbulence, "a whirlpool of odds and ends," to quote a bit of Ellison's strikingly Jamesian imagery that suffuses his evocations of American cacophonic "wholeness." The little man, in turn, echoes the Invisible Man's epiphany about those unaccountable "men of transition" who wander "outside of historical time," like "birds of passage who were too obscure for learned classification . . . of natures too ambiguous for the most ambiguous words."[37] These straying remnants, the Invisible Man realizes, mock the Brotherhood's pretensions to control history as one would a force in a laboratory experiment. For Du Boisian pluralists, pragmatism and radical empiricism embody a liberating skepticism fertile with metaphors for poetry.

Notes

1 Harold Cruse, *The Crisis of the Negro Intellectual* (New York: Morrow, 1967), p. 176.

2 W. E. B. Du Bois, *Writings* (New York: Library of America, 1986), p. 393, hereafter cited in text as *W*.

3 "God be praised" that I "landed squarely in the arms of William James of Harvard," Du Bois recalled in *Dusk of Dawn* (*W*, p. 578). "I became a devoted follower of James at the time [1888] he was developing his pragmatic philosophy" (*The Autobiography of W. E. B. Du Bois*, New York: International, 1968, p. 133), hereafter cited in text as *A*. In claiming that the impact of Du Bois' beloved professor was not merely local and contained but internalized, I depart from scholarly work on Du Bois' relation to James. This work has largely been confined to the latter's influence on Du Bois' famous notion of "double consciousness." For useful assessments of Du Bois' use of Jamesian psychology see Eric Sundquist, *To Wake the Nations* (Cambridge: Harvard University Press, 1993) and David Levering Lewis, *W. E. B. Du Bois: Biography of a Race* (New York: Holt, 1993). In *The American Evasion of Philosophy* (Madison: University of Wisconsin Press, 1989) Cornel West discusses Du Bois as a "Jamesian organic intellectual," but he does not examine the nearly oxymoronic status of this phrase, given that the cosmopolitanism of James and Du Bois qualifies and complicates their "organic" stance.

4 Du Bois' autobiographical writings represent his life "not so much as a linear trajectory but as a palimpsest in visible and continuous process" as Shamoon Zamir remarks in *Dark Voices* (Chicago: University of Chicago Press, 1995), p. 205.

5 William James, *Writings 1902–1910* (New York: Library of America, 1987), p. 940, hereafter cited in text as *WJ*.

6 W. E. B. Du Bois, "My Evolving Program For Negro Freedom," in *What the Negro Wants*, ed. Rayford Logan (Chapel Hill: University of North Carolina Press, 1944), pp. 57–58. Hereafter cited in text as *E*.

7 Currently we are in the midst of a Du Bois revival but, predictably, his intellectual identity still remains elusive, creating little agreement among critics. David Levering Lewis and George Hutchinson acknowledge James' profound impact, but conclude that "in the end Du Bois hung on to a tenuous idealism, strongly inflected by Hegel and Royce," to quote Hutchinson's summary of his and Lewis' views (George Hutchinson, *The Harlem Renaissance in Black and White*, Cambridge: Harvard University Press, 1995, p. 456). Shamoon Zamir rejects the notion of Du Bois as pragmatist: "neopragmatist readings of James, of Du Bois, and of their relationship present, at best, a highly distorted picture" (46). He contests Cornel West's inclusion of Du Bois in a "genealogy of pragmatism" because there is too much in James that is conservative, not only his "ahistorical and apolitical accounts of the self," but, most pernicious, his bias against reflective thought as a hindrance to action (pp. 116, 36–38). For more on Zamir see note 19.

8   Dewey, quoted in Timothy Kaufman-Osborn, *Politics/Sense/Experience* (Ithaca: Cornell University Press, 1991), p. 12.

9   Quoted by Kevin Gaines, *Uplifting the Race* (Chapel Hill: University of North Carolina Press, 1996), p. 264. Washington had little patience for blacks who relied on brain rather than brawn; he dubbed such opponents as Du Bois and Monroe Trotter "intellectuals": if only "these men could have gone into the South" and made contact "with people and things," declares Washington, they would have seen "actual progress" and relented in their criticism (*My Larger Education*, 1911; Miami: Mnemosyne, 1969, pp. 113, 120). In merciful and stark contrast stood serene Tuskegee, rooted, Washington implied, "upon the solid and never deceptive foundation of Mother Nature, where all nations and races that have ever succeeded have gotten their start" (*Up From Slavery*, in *Three Negro Classics*, ed. John Hope Franklin, New York: Avon 1965, p. 77).

10 Washington, *Up From Slavery*, p. 92. At Tuskegee students were discouraged from even being seen carrying books because, as Franklin Frazier personally remembered, "white people passed through the campus and would get the impression that Tuskegee was training the Negro's intellect rather than his heart and hand" (Franklin Frazier, *Black Bourgeoisie*, New York: Collier, 1962, p. 203). It should be noted that Robert Park, Washington's publicist and ghostwriter (and in later years a pioneering sociologist of black American life) called Washington's educational creed of "learn by doing" a great enactment of John Dewey's educational philosophy. Yet Park ignored that Dewey's emphasis on doing was in the service not of obedience but of nurturing creative, active, experimental habits of mind.

11 Georg Wilhelm Friedrich Hegel, *Lectures on the Philosophy of History*, quoted in *The American Hegelians*, ed. William Goetzmann (New York: Knopf, 1973), p. 20.

12 See Zamir, *Dark Voices*, pp. 121–25.

13 John Dewey, "From Absolutism to Experimentalism," in *The Philosophy of John Dewey*, ed. John J. McDermott (Chicago: University of Chicago Press, 1981), p. 8.

14 G. H. Mead, *Movements of Thought* (Chicago: University of Chicago Press, 1936), p. 508.

15 See Zamir, *Dark Voices*, p. 126.

16 Joel Williamson, *The Crucible of Race* (New York: Oxford University Press, 1984), p. 409.

17 William James, quoted in Ralph Barton Berry, *The Thought and Character of William James*, vol. 1. (Boston: Little, Brown, 1935), p. 765.

18 William James, "On Some Hegelisms," *The Will To Believe* (1897; Cambridge: Harvard University Press, 1979), pp. 205, 217–21, 214. Twenty-six years later, James would give a more sympathetic and less defensive assessment of Hegel, one that virtually inverts his earlier critique. James credits him with a "revolutionary" understanding of concepts. For, like James, Hegel conceived them not as the "static self-contained things that previous logicians had supposed." Hegel's "dialectic logic" superseded " 'the logic of identity' in which, since Aristotle, all Europe had been brought up." Like all good philosophy, Hegel in his *Logic* shows us that "we must never view identity as abstract identity, to the exclusion of all difference." Hegel's error, in James' view, is his rationalism, expressed in his dogmatic insistence on possessing "*the* truth," single, "incontrovertible," "binding on everyone" (50) (William James, "Hegel and his Method," *A Pluralistic Universe*, 1909; Cambridge: Harvard University Press, 1977, 46–47).

19 Zamir describes Du Bois as primarily a Hegelian, but one who does not "*adopt* Hegel" (as Williamson argued in *The Crucible of Race*) but rather "*adapts* him to his own ends" (p. 114; his emphases). Those ends differ from the "upbeat" uses of the nineteenth-

century American Hegelians (p. 120). Rather, Du Bois' adaptation, says Zamir, recovers the negativity of Hegelian "unhappy consciousness" (rewriting it as "double consciousness") as a critical historicist psychology that places Du Bois in the company of Marx, Sartre, and Kojeve. This thesis is founded on Zamir's important point that in 1889–1890 Du Bois read the *Phenomenology of Mind* with his Harvard tutor Santayana and thus developed a more profound understanding of Hegel than James (who never read the *Phenomenology*) ever did. This is a provocative reading of Du Bois, to which Zamir brings considerable intensity. But it is unclear why the maximizing of Hegel requires, for Zamir, the minimizing of pragmatism, especially since it is not a philosophy replete with doctrine but a method. And it is a method that encourages precisely the distinction that Zamir makes so much of—the practice of creative adaptation rather than passive adoption.

20 Dewey, "From Absolutism," p. 9.

21 W. E. B. Du Bois, "The Dilemma of the Negro," *American Mercury* (Oct. 1924): 179–85, quote at p. 180. I discuss the content and context of Du Bois' remark in "The Distinction of Du Bois: Aesthetics, Pragmatism, Politics," *American Literary History* (Fall, 1995).

22 John Patrick Diggins, *The Rise and Fall of the American Left* (New York: Norton, 1992), p. 134.

23 John Dewey, *Art as Experience* (1934; New York: Capricorn, 1958), pp. 216–17.

24 Quoted in Robert Westbrook, *John Dewey and American Democracy* (Ithaca: Cornell University Press, 1991), p. 214.

25 John Dewey, *Experience and Nature*, 2nd ed. (La Salle, Ill.: Open Court, 1929), p. 48. Hereafter cited in text as *EN*.

26 Zora Neale Hurston, *Dust Tracks On a Road* (1942; New York: Harper, 1991), p. 25.

27 Ralph Ellison, *Going to the Territory* (1986; New York: Vintage, 1987), pp. 20, 15–16.

28 Ralph Ellison, *The Collected Essays of Ralph Ellison,* ed. John F. Callahan (New York: Random House, 1995), p. 444.

29 Alain Locke, *Race Contacts and Interracial Relations,* ed. Jeffrey C. Stewart (Washington, D.C.: Howard University Press, 1992), pp. 10–11.

30 *Ibid.,* pp. 97, 99.

31 Hurston, *Dust Tracks,* pp. 215, 240, 172, 238.

32 The relation of pragmatism to radical empiricism remains a subject of debate. Richard Rorty, for one, is impatient with the radical empiricist turn in James and Dewey because it violates the pragmatist taboo on epistemology and metaphysics. Instead of dropping the term experience, as Rorty wishes he had, Dewey (like the James of *A Pluralistic Universe*) posited a kind of vitalism in the form of a prelinguistic immediacy of flux. But Rorty acknowledges that the Dewey he prefers is a "hypothetical" construct, "a pragmatist without being a radical empiricist" (Richard Rorty, "Dewey Between Hegel and Darwin," in *Modernist Impulses in the Human Sciences,* ed. Dorothy Ross, Baltimore: Johns Hopkins University Press, 1994, p. 56).

33 Dewey, *Art as Experience,* p. 161; *EN,* p. 41, 43.

34 John Dewey, "Philosophy and Democracy" (1917), *Political Writings,* ed. Debra Morris and Ian Shapiro (Indianapolis: Bobbs-Merrill, 1993), pp. 45–46.

35 *Ibid.,* p. 46.

36 In *The New Negro,* ed. Alain Locke (1925; New York: Atheneum, 1992), p. 3.

37 Ralph Ellison, *Invisible Man* (1952; New York: Vintage, 1989), pp. 439–40.

The Inspiration of Pragmatism:
Some Personal Remarks

HANS JOAS

More than twenty years ago, when I was still a student, I suddenly fell in love with American pragmatism. At first it was only one of its main thinkers, perhaps the most obscure of the classical quartet, who attracted my attention: namely George Herbert Mead. But soon my feelings of love expanded and extended to the other three (Peirce, James, and Dewey) and their company since then has remained a source of continual inspiration and deep satisfaction for me. What were the reasons for this development?

To fall in love and to remain in love: these processes are difficult to explain. In a certain sense all explanatory attempts leave a feeling of futility. These processes presuppose deep-seated characteristics of the lover and the beloved; an important role is played by the context of their first encounter and the conditions of their later relationship. In my own case, one could easily argue that my love fell on a rather exotic object of desire. Pragmatism is—and nobody has serious doubts about this—deeply American, deeply philosophical, deeply influenced by its Protestant background. Now, I am not American, but German. I am not a trained philosopher, but a sociologist and social theorist. And I am not Protestant, but Catholic. I think I have never tended to ignore these characteristics nor to mistake them for being only superficial accessories. And I have never tried to go too far in my identification and behave as if I were an American Protestant philosopher. How then could this relationship prove to be so stable?

It would, of course, be completely inappropriate and utterly immodest if I bothered the reader here with too much autobiographical detail. But as the task assigned to me is to contribute a European perspective to the debate about a current revival of pragmatism, some contextualization of a German's interest might be in place.

First, if I were to describe the intellectual situation in Germany in which I came across pragmatism I would mention three traditions as powerful:

(1) the persistent influence of the German tradition of hermeneutics and historicism including Nietzschean *Lebensphilosophie* and so-called philosophical anthropology, traditions powerful not only in philosophy, but in all the social sciences and humanities in Germany; (2) a sudden rediscovery of an intellectually attractive Marxism, superseding dogmatic Soviet Marxism by reexamining the rich leftist debates of the 1920s and catching up with emigrants' writings, the older Frankfurt School's "Critical Theory," and new work in Western Marxism; and (3) the professionalization of the social sciences by importing modern methods of empirical research, Parsonian sociological theory, and analytical philosophy of science. At the time I felt attracted by all three of them—and simultaneously repelled. This way of putting it is, of course, an understatement of the tensions built into such a situation. I did admire some works and thinkers of the German tradition, but I could not ignore how many of its proponents had played a role for the antidemocratic, nationalist, and chauvinist radicalization of German thought and its criminal consequences.

I put some hope in Marxism as a truly egalitarian philosophy focusing on the problems of social inequality and as a powerful means to analyze the mechanisms of a capitalist economy. But if earlier concerns had not been sufficient, for me at least the Soviet intervention in Czechoslovakia in 1968, just when I finished school, definitively destroyed the possibility of believing in a Marxism that could not develop a theory of democracy. And I felt that modern social science, theoretically and empirically, should not fall behind or below the standards set mostly by the American social sciences in the post–World War II era. But I also realized that professionalization alone can make the social sciences mute in public discourse.

Pragmatism immediately enabled me to accept what was reasonable in the three traditions I have mentioned without accepting their dangerous implications. Pragmatism develops the insights of the hermeneutical tradition and German *Lebensphilosophie* ("philosophy of life") without falling into their irrationalist and partly chauvinistic tendencies. That made it so important for me to understand, for example, what Mead had learned from his teacher Dilthey, what Dewey had taken from Hegel and Neo-Hegelianism, how Georg Simmel followed William James, and why the German, French, and Italian reception of pragmatism is a concatenation of misunderstandings. Pragmatism, I thought, could also serve as a corrective for Marxism insofar as an economic theory of capitalism without a theory of democracy should be integrated with a philosophy for the framework of which democracy was absolutely crucial. The more I learned from pragmatism, however, the more I gave up this idea and the more critical I became of Marxism in general. It was not a question of contingent gaps in an otherwise admirable framework, but of a deeply undemocratic way of thinking that revealed itself in all versions of Marxism, including the extremely elitist Critical Theory of Horkheimer and Adorno. This insight made it even more necessary to develop an alternative full-blown social theory out of pragmatist motives. And lastly, pragmatism appeared to me to be a school of thinking and research that developed its public importance not by ignoring professional standards and satisfying the public with popularized extracts from the real world of science, but by drawing out the logical implications of the scientific methods themselves for a logic of reasonable argumentation and an ethics of discussion. Pragmatism in all three respects thus could appear as the solution to otherwise unsolvable problems, as a salvation from the aporiae of German thought.

Second, pragmatism is certainly not a philosophy for philosophers only. Historically, pragmatism was a powerful form of public philosophy. Its influence in several social-scientific disciplines in the United States can be called formative. But this fact makes it all the more surprising that the pragmatist voice remained conspicuously absent in the more recent theoretical debates of the social sciences. The school of "symbolic interactionism," for example, produced marvelous empirical work, but never turned itself into a serious competitor for Parsonian or Marxian theorists. Instead of analyzing the more historical aspects of these theoretical developments here, I would like to explore the extent to which contemporary sociological and social theory pays attention to the rediscovery of pragmatism.

In many of the most ambitious synthetic treatises of sociological theory, Mead and the other pragmatists are not to be found. Jeffrey Alexander, for example, in his *Theoretical Logic in Sociology,* dealt extensively with Durkheim, Marx, Max Weber, and Parsons, but had nothing to say about Mead or pragmatism.[1] This changed a bit in his later work, but in his book on sociological theory after 1945 he had serious difficulties fitting pragmatism (and phenomenology) into his narrative. Neither of these schools should be considered a mere particularistic deviation from Parsons' synthetic achievements nor were they variants of Alexander's metatheoretical scheme. James Coleman, in his *Foundations of Social Theory,* mentions Mead once and the other pragmatists not at all, and the only passing reference to Mead is a somewhat awkward presentation of his concept of the self.[2]

Randall Collins, today's main proponent of a conflict approach in sociology, has attempted a synthesis of Mead's theory of mind with his own theory of interaction ritual chains. To put it less benevolently, he has attempted to establish his own theory as a "neo-Meadian" sociology of mind. He combined this attempt with an explanatory approach to Mead's intellectual development, explanatory in a strict nomological, not hermeneutical sense. Mead himself thus becomes a case for the application of Collins' sociology of mind. The responses Collins received for this effort were certainly not encouraging.[3] Anthony Giddens comes very close to Mead in some aspects of his "theory of structuration," but he does not spend much time on an interpretation of Mead's work or the writings of the other pragmatists. This is quite surprising, since he wrote long interpretations of other sociological classics and a book-long comment on interpretative schools of sociological research. The major exception among sociological theorists in this respect is Jürgen Habermas. In his *Theory of Communicative Action* Mead is treated like Weber, Marx, and Durkheim as one of the classics worthy of extensive interpretation. Even beyond Weber and Marx he is considered, alongside Wittgenstein and the later Durkheim, as the source of inspiration for the fundamental paradigm shift Habermas himself proposes: "from purposive to communicative action."[4] This emphasis on Mead in Habermas' magnum opus has helped Mead's reception in Germany enormously; and perhaps even in the United States it could be considered a parallel to the importance of Richard Rorty's praise of Dewey. But one should not forget the fact that Mead is not really treated like the other classics in the chapter dedicated to him. Habermas did not really give as lively a portrait of Mead's theory in its development and its ramifications as he did, for example, of Max Weber's theories. What he presents is a highly selective conceptual reconstruction of some parts of Mead's theory by means of analytical philosophy.

If we extend the range of our interest from sociological theory to social theory in general, some of the same observations apply. Most communitarians, for example, develop arguments very similar to Dewey's and Mead's without mentioning them. This statement includes Michael Sandel and Amitai Etzioni; the major exception here is Philip Selznick, whose *The Moral Commonwealth* is clearly based on Dewey *and* Mead.[5] Charles Taylor, who is, according to Alan Ryan, "for the most part a Deweyan without knowing it," refers to Dewey and Mead only very superficially and sometimes misleadingly in his masterpiece, *Sources of the Self.*[6] For him "Mead is too close to behaviorism and not aware of the constitutive role of language in the definition of self and relations."[7] But wasn't this the reason that Mead is considered the inaugurator of the symbolic-interactionist tradition?

Thus the strange history of the reception of pragmatism in general, and Mead in particular, infects even today's most advanced attempts in social and sociological theory. I do not claim that Mead and Dewey (or James and Peirce) had the correct answer to everything and that all problems of contemporary theorizing could be solved if their writings were taken seriously. On the contrary, I am convinced that the level of political and sociological analysis that lies between the abstract universality of statements about the origins of human communication and the overly concrete comment on social conflicts of the day was relatively neglected by the major pragmatists. What I do claim, however, is that their ideas about human action and experience can be a serious competitor for the other synthetic approaches in social theory today. In my book, *The Creativity of Action*, I have tried to develop in a systematic way what a pragmatist action theory for today would look like, how it is to be distinguished from other sociological approaches, and what it prejudges or precludes in terms of macrosociological theory.[8] This is the way I think pragmatism as a theory of the creative character of human action could prove to be superior to the two dominating approaches that focus either on rational action or on normatively oriented action. And though it may be true—as many critics say—that pragmatism is in need of a theory of power, this is too easy an objection, especially if the critics do not clarify which theory of power they themselves propose and with which model of action such a theory should be compatible.

Third, as I said in the beginning, the Protestant background of the pragmatists is quite obvious. But several of them, like Dewey and Mead, clearly turned away from their religious origins. I am deeply opposed to any reductionism here, as if "in the last instance" the achievements of American pragmatist philosophy and, for example, the Chicago school of sociology that developed under its influence, could be criticized as Puritanism in disguise. Nor does it seem possible to me to speak meaningfully of a merely secularized form of Christianity, given the extremely anti-Puritanical motives of many of the school's members.

But we also should not forget that Peirce and James remained firmly religious. In James' case one of his central ambitions was certainly the defense of a sphere of personal religious belief against the pressures of a modern scientific worldview. This defense of our "will to believe" or our "right to believe" inspired his empirical study of the varieties of religious experience, a book that gave a completely new and modernist turn to the scientific study of religion. His personal attitude toward religion certainly cannot be characterized as "hopeful atheism" or "romantic polytheism." It could be more correctly described as a theism without belief in the omnipotence of God. Instead of debating the theological viability of his ideas elaborated in his 1909 book *A Pluralistic Universe,* I prefer to draw your attention to John Dewey's relationship to religion. This is in response to Richard Rorty's interpretation, because I think that Dewey's book on religion is more than a plea for tolerance between atheists and religionists.

One has to remember the biographical point at which Dewey wrote his book on religion. As a young man he had been, like all his American contemporaries, profoundly influenced by Christian religion. The biographical literature contains allusions to an early mystical experience, and there can be no doubt that Dewey knew what he was speaking about when he talked about the freedom from worry and the sense of oneness with nature that come with faith. The longing for a non-Puritan form of religiosity was one of the motives that drove Dewey to Hegelianism and to early forms of a sacralization of democracy and intelligence. But after 1894 and before 1930 there are only few traces of a direct and explicit discussion of religion. Tendencies toward secularization were interpreted in a very optimistic fashion as symptoms not of moral and cultural decay but of a transformation of religious motives—their release from dogmatic forms of teaching and from narrow types of institutionalization. If particular churches were to pass out of existence in a process of the universalization of Christian impulses, this would be considered not as a loss but as progress. This combination of optimism with a decreasing interest in religious phenomena did not last, however. After the First World War and particularly after the stock market crash of 1929 with its devastating consequences Dewey became, as Steven Rockefeller writes, "increasingly convinced that the minds and hearts of the American people would not be unified around a constructive philosophy such as he proposed unless their religious emotions and commitments were engaged. Only a fresh act of religious faith in widely shared ideals would bring unity and purpose to the life of the individual and inspire the necessary cooperative action on behalf of reform."[9]

In the introduction to his book on religion, Dewey describes the intellectual situation as a conflict between atheism and religion in which both sides identify the religious with a belief in supernatural beings. It is this identification that he tries to break up. If it were possible to separate "the religious phase of experience . . . from the supernatural and the things that have grown up about it," Dewey hopes, endless conflicts between science and democracy on the one hand and the cognitive and moral prescriptions of religions on the other hand could be superseded. As a consequence, "what is genuinely religious will undergo an emancipation"; for the first time in human history, "the religious aspect of experience will be free to develop freely on its own account," and people who are "repelled from what exists as a religion by its intellectual and moral implications" will become "aware of attitudes in themselves that if they come to fruition would be genuinely religious." This view constitutes a radicalization of Dewey's earlier attitude, not so much with respect to the idea that there is a sacred core in people's value orientations, but because of the anti-institutional tendency that Dewey professes here. Institutional forms of religion and fixed practices or teachings are repeatedly called mere "historical encumbrances," "adventitious" additions and irrelevant fixations. Dewey portrays institutionalized religion as cognitively and morally restrictive; hence, the deinstitutionalization of religion will not weaken but release the force of human religiosity. In such a new form of religion, the word "God" would no longer mean a particular Being having prior existence but would denote instead "the unity of all ideal ends arousing us for desire and actions." In such a sense, Dewey the atheist would even be willing to accept the conception of "God."[10]

But could anybody believe in such a God? Is it really true that institutionalized religion has always been restrictive for intellectual and moral progress? Can we, sixty years later, still share the optimism that the de-institutionalization of religion will emancipate and release what is genuinely religious? I think the answer to all three questions can only be negative. To imagine that a philosopher's decision to use the term God for an intellectual abstraction could move anybody and develop any transforming power is almost ridiculous. Religion has often been not an impediment but a driving impulse for intellectual and moral advances. Dewey did not care enough about the history and sociology of religion to make such encompassing claims. Let me just mention Max Weber's sophisticated studies of the activist and passivist, this-worldly or other-worldly orientation of major world religions, in order to show that more is needed for a fair balance of the cultural consequences of institutionalized religion. And, finally, I think that John Herman Randall, Jr., was right when he wrote in the Festschrift celebrating Dewey's eightieth birthday that Dewey made an "effort to disentangle religious feeling and sentiment from any particular kind of institutionalized behavior . . . [and] in thus seeking the universal through cutting loose from the historical relativities of any particular religious tradition, he has bound himself all the more closely to the relativities of his own culture. He has sought the religious function in general; and he emerges as the spokesman of the habits of mind of the liberal American Protestant Christian of our generation.

Could any other possibly have found the essence of religion to be a personal attitude?"[11] I am not so sure that Dewey should be seen as the spokesman for liberal American Protestantism, but he surely reminds today's reader of what is called "Sheila-ism" in Robert Bellah's study *Habits of the Heart,* a purely personal form of religion named after the person who defends it, completely cut off from the richness of thousands of years of tradition and the wisdom of religious professionals.[12]

But if we turn away from these "post-Enlightenment banalities"—as Charles Taylor would put it—to the more productive aspects of Dewey's endeavor, we can interpret his work on religion as a contribution to the analysis of those types of human experience in which our commitment to values arises. We need a phenomenology of the experiences of self-transcendence and a theory of the genesis of values, a theory that is independent of the religious attitudes of its proponents. Such a theory can fill the gap, I think, between the heritage of American pragmatism and the vision of new value-oriented social movements as they are represented today, for example, in the debates about communitarianism.[13]

Notes

1 Jeffrey Alexander, *Theoretical Logic in Sociology,* 4 vols. (Berkeley: University of California Press, 1982–1983); *Twenty Lectures: Sociological Theory after 1945* (Berkeley: University of California Press, 1987).

2 James S. Coleman, *Foundations of Social Theory* (Cambridge: Harvard University Press, 1990), quotation on p. 507.

3 Randall Collins, "Toward a Neo-Meadian Sociology of Mind," in *Symbolic Interaction* 12 (1989): 1–32. The same issue contains comments on Collins by a large number of Mead scholars and symbolic interactionists and a response by Collins. See also my own response, "How to Explain What Collins Thinks," *ibid.,* p. 63, 64.

4 Jürgen Habermas, *The Theory of Communicative Action,* vol. 2 (Boston: Beacon Press, 1987). See my remarks on Habermas' interpretation of Mead in *Pragmatism and Social Theory* (Chicago: University of Chicago Press, 1993), pp. 137, 138.

5 Philip Selznick, *The Moral Commonwealth: Social Theory and the Promise of Community* (Berkeley: University of California Press, 1992).

6 Alan Ryan, *John Dewey and the High Tide of American Liberalism* (New York: W. W. Norton, 1995); quotation on Taylor is on p. 361.

7 Charles Taylor, *Sources of the Self* (Cambridge: Harvard University Press, 1989), p. 525 fn. 12.

8 Hans Joas, *The Creativity of Action* (Chicago: University of Chicago Press, 1996).

9 Steven Rockefeller, *John Dewey: Religious Faith and Democratic Humanism* (New York: Columbia University Press, 1991), p. 446.

10 John Dewey, *A Common Faith* (New York: 1934), pp. 2, 9, 42.

11 John Herman Randall Jr., "The Religion of Shared Experience," in *The Philosopher of*

the Common Man: Essays in Honor of John Dewey to Celebrate His Eightieth Birthday, ed. Sidney Ratner (New York: 1940), pp. 106–145, quote on pp. 37–38.

12   Robert Bellah, et al., *Habits of the Heart, Individualism and Commitment in American Life* (Berkeley: University of California Press, 1985).

13   On this gap see, e.g., Hans Joas, "Economic Action, Social Action, and the Genesis of Values: An Essay on Amitai Etzioni's Contribution to Social Theory," in David Sciulli, *Macro Socio-Economics: From Theory to Activism,* ed. David Sciulli (Armonk, N.Y.: M. E. Sharpe, 1996), pp. 35–50; also see Hans Joas, *Die Enstehung der Werte* (Frankfurt/ Main: Suhrkamp, 1997).

The Missing Pragmatic Revival in American Social Science

ALAN WOLFE

The revival of pragmatism can itself be explained on pragmatic grounds. If ever there were a case of experience shaping thought, it would be the ways in which the events of the 1960s and after influenced those who now find in pragmatism a way of thinking about democracy, race, and gender. Dewey-like warnings about the quest for certainty were inevitable after the failures of the best and the brightest. If pragmatism did not exist, our current intellectual mood of dissatisfaction and uncertainty would have invented it.

Pragmatism's revival has had mixed effects, generating not only a war of words about what pragmatism "really" is, but also raising as many questions about being, knowledge, method, morality, art, and politics as it answers. At its worst, pragmatism is (perhaps) the last gasp of a left that has run out of historical agents on which to pin its hopes. If we cannot be Marxists, proponents of this view seem to be saying, let's be pragmatists; the important things are to dislike this world and to find a way of imagining another. At its best, pragmatism is not a politics but a sensibility, a reminder of the impossibility of thinking about human beings without putting humans at the center of the inquiry. Somehow it fits a pragmatic moment that there should be no certainty, not only about what pragmatism is, but also what its consequences are.

Even at its best, the pragmatic revival remains uneven. Whatever the disputes among those claiming the mantle, the reception of pragmatism varies significantly across the intellectual and academic landscape. Although Dewey, James, and Peirce made scientific inquiry the focus of much of their writings, modern science continues to function as if pragmatism never happened. Biologists and chemists are blithely unaware of the differences between pragmatism, postmodernism, ethnomethodology, and science studies; for them, all efforts to render natural reality tentative are equally absurd.[1] In literature departments, by contrast, pragmatism has been received most warmly, and not merely because at least some pragmatists (William James) wrote literature. The pragmatic revival allows for indeterminacy, but, unlike European versions of deconstruction and postmodernism, it also allows for authors. No wonder that the most compelling and original papers presented at the conference out of which this book grew were presented by literary scholars.

In this essay I want to talk about pragmatism's reception, or lack of one, in the social sciences—those way stations between science and literature.[2] It is, I think, worth pointing out that with the exception of historians and a German (Hans Joas), there are no practicing social scientists among the contributors to this volume.[3] At one level this is because of the tilt toward the natural sciences among social scientists. Academic economists, to take one example, conduct their business with formal models and technical precision in ways that are the envy of the more scientific side of all the social sciences. Yet this cannot be the only explanation for the relative lack of interest in pragmatism among social scientists, for the more humanistic among them have read Richard Bernstein's wonderful books and have been introduced to Dilthey, Habermas, and various hermeneutic offshoots.[4]

Much qualitative research in sociology has been influenced by theorists close to pragmatism such as George Herbert Mead and Herbert Blumer (one of those who took the notes on Mead's lectures, which were turned into *Mind, Self, and Society*).[5] But there are few serious reflections on social science method from a pragmatic viewpoint where one would most expect to find them—that is, among people engaged in actual social research about real people living in real world situations.[6] Even C. Wright Mills, who influenced so many social scientists rebelling against "abstract empiricism," is remembered for his semipopular accounts of American institutions, not his intellectual debt to pragmatism—the subject of his doctoral dissertation.[7]

What explains the missing pragmatic reception in social science? If, in Judith Shklar's formulation, the first duty of a liberal is to avoid cruelty, then the first duty of a social scientist is to get social reality right. Social science, dealing with human beings, has a humanistic dimension and thus ought to be influenced by pragmatism. But social science, because it is obligated to take cognizance of the real world, finds itself with a pragmatism problem. Of the many strengths of pragmatism, realism is not one. That is why John Diggins is right to contrast pragmatism unfavorably with the quite different worldview of Max Weber, the preeminent realistic social scientist of the modern period.[8] Especially in the writings of the pragmatist most closely identified with social themes, John Dewey, an idealistic inclination to imagine a world better than this one assumes far more pride of place than a realistic commitment to understanding the world we have. What makes pragmatism attractive as a mode of social reform makes it far less workable as a way of doing social science.

The current fascination with pragmatism among philosophers and social theorists (as opposed to empirically oriented social scientists) illustrates the conflict between reality as it is and reality as pragmatists would like it to be. As Richard Bernstein points out, the attraction of pragmatism lies in its appeal to the possibility of undistorted communication among equals.[9] No one takes these ideals as a description of an actual social reality; pragmatism, at least in its Habermasian form, draws its strength from positing an "ideal speech situation" meant to be contrasted with reality. But that simply means that the conditions that deny the ideal—distorted communication and inequality—themselves have a tenacity that deserves sociological respect. The point is not to apologize for them or to explain them away. The point is to understand why they exist, which I take to mean suspending one's judgment that they are necessarily bad until one has understood more about them.

Ambiguities, misdirections, dishonesty, and ill intentions—all those aspects of communication that seem to lead, not to cooperation, but to conflict—serve a sociological purpose insufficiently appreciated by those who would transform them. Human beings who engage in undistorted communication would not be human beings as we have known them. Indeed, in an ironic way not fully appreciated by Habermasians, removing the distortions from communication also removes the hermeneutic; interpretation is richer and more interesting when distortion is maximized. Sociological richness is dependent upon human imperfections. Erving Goffman, whose training and interests can be traced back to Herbert Blumer and through him to George Herbert Mead, ought to have become a pragmatist. Instead he became a sociological realist, documenting for us the ways in which people strategize to avoid saying what they mean or doing what they say.[10] In contrast to Habermas' rational public world, Goffman never lets us forget an irrational private one.[11] He is not even a Rortyian liberal ironist; although there is much irony in his oeuvre, there is precious little that is liberal (or conservative) in Goffman's presentation of ourselves to ourselves. Goffman, anything but a positivist and formalist, could nonetheless never become a pragmatist because existing social reality was his turf.

If undistorted communication is not necessarily an objective to which human beings ought to aspire, neither, depending on how it is defined, is equality. Surely the reformist element in pragmatism is correct to point out that people who are unequal can never work together to establish their common goals. Democracy, in that Deweyan sense, cannot work without substantially more equality than presently exists. But without engaging in the controversial question about whether human beings, even in democratic societies, have a pronounced taste for inequality, it is sufficient to argue that, whatever the fate of equality, there will always—and there always ought to—exist significant differences among people.

Under the influence of the pragmatic revival, a proper concern with inequality too often leads to an improper suspicion of difference. Discussing William James' influence on W. E. B. Du Bois, Ross Posnock writes that "Pragmatism makes the classifying impulse itself a prime object of critique."[12] A suspicion of demarcations is part of pragmatism's appeal, especially to those persuaded that the more powerful the boundary, the more likely its arbitrary construction and ultimate unjustifiability. As James Kloppenberg points out, feminists find in pragmatism grounds for questioning the boundary between male and female.[13] In a similar vein, Cornel West relies on pragmatism to avoid "any policing of borders and boundaries of 'blackness,' 'maleness,' 'femaleness,' or 'whiteness.' "[14] Yet boundaries, which to reformers are suspect, are essential to social scientists.[15] Sociology could not exist without sharp distinctions among groups, surely a reason why, from Durkheim to Mary Douglas, "the classifying impulse" has had pride of place.[16] The subjects of sociology—ethnicity, religion, nationality—are the stuff of difference. Indeed if a single term were needed to encompass the focus of modern sociology it would be "culture," a phenomenon that requires borders, particularisms, and distinctions. If reality consists of differences among people, pragmatists, suspicious of difference, have little to offer to those who take such differences not as an invidious invitation to inequality but as an introduction to human richness. A world in which all people had the same identity would be as sociologically impoverished as a world in which people's communication was never distorted.

The great fear of pragmatists is that recognition of reality will lead to an accommodation with reality. Realism—not the philosophical kind, but the version that lies closer to *realpolitik*—is seen as a conservative temptation; to understand the world as it is is the first step toward accepting that it can be no other way. If this were true, there would exist an unreconcilable tension between pragmatism as a movement of social reform and pragmatism as a way of doing social science. We would then have all we needed to know about the missing pragmatic revival in social science; it would be missing because more social scientists would rather understand the world than change it. But this is not, I believe, the proper conclusion. Realism is, in fact, compatible with a wide variety of political dispositions: in many ways, Marx was a realist, describing the contours of capitalism with something close to loving detail, while romanticism and nostalgia have often been closely identified with conservatism. A desire for social reform cannot serve as a rationale for not taking the existing world seriously; in some ways, it demands that reality comes first.

For this reason, it might be helpful briefly to compare the pragmatists to a group of thinkers who took realism even more literally than Max Weber. If John Dewey, as Robert Westbrook argues, anticipated many of the themes of the New Left,[17] the New Right was strongly influenced by the Italian realists Gaetano Mosca, Roberto Michels, and Vilfredo Pareto.[18] The careers of the Italian writers and the careers of many of America's leading pragmatists overlapped. Given his longevity, almost no one could be Dewey's contemporary, but Mosca came close: he was born in 1858 (Dewey in 1859) and died in 1941 (Dewey in 1952). Like the American pragmatists, the Italian realists were responding to World War I, the advent of socialism, and the future of liberal democracy. But there all similarity ends. The Italian writers eventually became sympathetic to fascism, and while they did have a certain influence in the United States, that lay more with the Progressives around whom pragmatists like Dewey were always a bit uncomfortable.[19] On the surface of the matter, these divergent trajectories would seem to underscore a pragmatic suspicion of realism: what, after all, could be more conservative than sympathy for the most antidemocratic right-wing movements of the twentieth century?

Yet the story does not end there. For one thing, the Italian antidemocrats had a significant impact on the left as well as the right; Antonio Gramsci wrote within the same tradition of respect for Machiavelli that they did.[20] But even more importantly, the commitment to realism on the part of the Italians provided contributions to an understanding of the modern world that far outlasted their political commitments. Pareto, whose writings were studied carefully by sociologists led by Talcott Parsons to see if they could find a credible alternative to Marx, has had a significant impact on the contemporary American academy.[21] Pareto optimality is a term of choice among economists and moral philosophers interested in distributive justice. But an even more appropriate example comes from Michels, whose empirically oriented study of the German Social Democratic Party prompted his "iron law of oligarchy": any form of organization will persist indefinitely, even those that proclaim organization itself the enemy.[22] Michels intended his book as an exposure of the hypocrisy of socialists who preach one way and act another, but it would be just as appropriate to conclude that social democrats could not be trusted with socialism, hardly a conservative message. The realism of Michels' social science has long outlived the realism of his conservatism.

Much the opposite is true of the pragmatists, who have bequeathed more of a mood than a method. We read Dewey today not to learn about how social institutions actually worked but to see how they ought to work to further human potential. The kind of rigorous empirical description of an actual institution that remains in the reader's mind long after he has dismissed Michels' politics does not exist with Dewey. His "understanding of how religious life would operate in the absence of what we currently call churches," Alan Ryan writes, "was much like his understanding of how education would proceed in the absence of what we now call schools."[23] That may well be why the Deweyan contribution to reality has been so mixed. It is indeed unfair to blame some of the failed experiments in public education on Dewey's pedagogical writing, but it is not totally unfair.[24] Surely someone who would urge reform upon the schools ought to take into account what actually happens when teachers interact with students under conditions of fiscal and pedagogical limits. When we read Dewey on social institutions, we come away with a different feeling from when we read Michels. We remember his politics, his good intentions, and his exhortations, but there is precious little about actual institutions in his writings to remember at all.

For an approach to knowledge premised on the notion that classifications are suspect, pragmatists, at least insofar as they concerned themselves with social institutions, took far too seriously the distinction between social science and social criticism. There was no necessary reason to avoid too close an identification with existing social reality for fear that it would compromise imagination and vision. If anything, social science can inform social criticism and vice versa.[25] Just as a scientist who hates disease may be led to research its origins and epidemiology, a social critic who hates poverty can, and probably must, approach his subject dispassionately—for how can the effects of poverty be reduced unless the phenomenon itself is first understood? The problem of reconciling scientific detachment with social engagement—a problem that faces all social scientists, not just radicals and visionaries—can only be resolved, as Weber rightly emphasized, by the calling of the social scientist. The pragmatic temperament has manifested half of that calling: the one dealing with engagement. It has yet to demonstrate in sufficient measure the one dealing with detachment.

It is, therefore, not necessarily a bad thing that the revival of pragmatism has been so half-hearted in the social sciences. As one who has never been comfortable with the number-crunching, technique-worshipping formalism of so much American social science—perhaps because one of my graduate school professors assigned Dewey's *Quest for Certainty*—I would welcome a revival of pragmatism for its insistence on the importance of human beings, its emphasis on indeterminacy, language, and skepticism. But as someone who believes that the first task of social science is to get reality right, the same pragmatic revival looks less positive. Indeed, were social scientists to take up pragmatism in an effort to substitute longings for a better world for the need to understand this one first—as they have done with Marxism, the Frankfurt School, and whatever variety of European theory is au courant—a revival of pragmatism in the social sciences could prove counterproductive. Our most pragmatic response ought to be to welcome the revival of pragmatism, and then go back to our business, appreciating its qualities, but refusing to turn it into a panacea for the dilemmas that are at the heart of social science inquiry.

Notes

1 The most prominent recent critique of the critics of science is Paul R. Gross and Norman Levitt, *Higher Superstition: The Academic Left and Its Quarrels with Science* (Baltimore: Johns Hopkins University Press, 1994). It was a reading of this book that led the NYU physicist Alan Sokal to submit a preposterously argued essay to *Social Text.*

2 Wolf Lepenies, *Between Literature and Science: The Rise of Sociology,* trans. R. J. Hollingdale (Cambridge: Cambridge University Press, 1988).

3 I do consider myself a "practicing social scientist."

4 Especially Richard Bernstein, *The Restructuring of Social and Political Theory* (New York: Harcourt, Brace, Jovanovich, 1976). See also "Community in the Pragmatic Tradition," Bernstein's contribution to this volume.

5 Herbert Blumer, *Symbolic Interactionism: Perspective and Method* (Englewood Cliffs, N.J.: Prentice Hall, 1969) is the inspiration for a good deal of ethnographic sociological observation.

6 A prominent exception is Donald McCloskey, *The Rhetoric of Economics* (Madison: University of Wisconsin Press, 1985), which relies on many traditions, including pragmatism, to demonstrate its point that, even at its most formalistic, social science nonetheless possesses a narrative dimension.

7 C. Wright Mills, *Sociology and Pragmatism: The Higher Learning in America* (New York: Paine-Whitman, 1964).

8 John Patrick Diggins, *The Promise of Pragmatism: Modernism and the Crisis of Knowledge and Authority* (Chicago: University of Chicago Press, 1994).

9 Richard Bernstein, *Beyond Objectivism and Relativism: Science, Hermeneutics, and Praxis* (Philadelphia: University of Pennsylvania Press, 1983).

10 See especially Erving Goffman, *The Presentation of Self in Everyday Life* (Garden City, N.Y.: Doubleday, 1959).

11 I contrast Goffman and Habermas at greater length in "Public and Private in Theory and Practice: Some Implications of an Uncertain Boundary," in *Public and Private in Thought and Practice: Perspectives on a Grand Dichotomy*, ed. Jeff Weintraub and Krishnan Kumar (Chicago: University of Chicago Press, 1996).

12 Ross Posnock, "Going Astray, Going Forward: Du Boisian Pragmatism and Its Lineage," this volume.

13 James Kloppenberg, "Pragmatism: An Old Name for Some New Ways of Thinking?" this volume.

14 Cornel West, *Race Matters* (Boston: Beacon Press, 1993), pp. 150–51, cited in Kloppenberg, this volume.

15 The discussion in the rest of this paragraph summarizes my essay "Democracy Versus Sociology: Boundaries and Their Political Consequences," in *Cultivating Differences: Symbolic Boundaries and the Making of Inequality*, ed. Michele Lamont and Marcel Fournier (Chicago: University of Chicago Press, 1992), 309–25.

16 Emile Durkheim and Marcel Mauss, *Primitive Classification*, trans. Rodney Needham (Chicago: University of Chicago Press, 1963); Mary Douglas, *Natural Symbols: Explorations in Cosmology* (New York: Pantheon, 1970).

17 See Robert Westbrook, *John Dewey and American Democracy* (Ithaca: Cornell University Press, 1991), as well as "Pragmatism and Democracy: Reconstructing the Logic of John Dewey's Faith," his contribution to this volume.

18 James Burnham, a former Trotskyite who would become a prominent writer for *The National Review*, was one of the first Americans to call attention to these writers in *The Machiavellians: Defenders of Freedom* (New York: John Day, 1943).

19 John P. Diggins, *Mussolini and Fascism: The View from America* (Princeton: Princeton University Press, 1972). Diggins (pp. 474–75) notes in passing the failure of pragmatism to anticipate fascism in Europe.

20 Antonio Gramsci, *Selections from The Prison Notebooks*, trans. Quintin Hoare and Geoffrey Nowell Smith (New York: International Publishers, 1971), pp. 123–205.

21 Alvin Gouldner, *The Coming Crisis of Western Sociology* (New York: Basic Books, 1970), pp. 148–51.

22 Roberto Michels, *Political Parties: A Sociological Study of the Oligarchic Tendencies of Modern Democracy*, trans. Eden Paul and Cedar Paul (Glencoe: Free Press, 1950).

23 Alan Ryan, *John Dewey and the High Tide of American Liberalism* (New York: Norton, 1995), p. 271.

24 This is the theme of Arthur Zilversmit, *Changing Schools: Progressive Education Theory and Practice 1930–1960* (Chicago: University of Chicago Press, 1993).

25 I elaborate this theme at greater length in *Marginalized in the Middle* (Chicago: University of Chicago Press, 1996).

Pragmatism and Its Limits

JOHN PATRICK DIGGINS

The Fallacy of "More Democracy"

Can democracy have a foundation in a philosophy that is itself antifoundational? Robert Westbrook examines whether Hilary Putnam was right to claim that he had found "an epistemological justification of democracy" in John Dewey's philosophy. Richard Rorty, Westbrook points out, sees pragmatism as offering no philosophical support to democracy, whereas Putnam believes that pragmatism continues to provide "a theory of knowledge, meaning, and truth with a special affinity for radical democracy." While the philosopher Putnam offers a "logical argument for democracy," the historian James T. Kloppenberg argues that Dewey found justification for democracy by likening it to the processes of scientific inquiry involving experimenting with tests and evaluating the outcomes in the "spirit of constructive cooperation."

One wonders whether a case for democracy can be derived from the thinking of Dewey. When in American history did democracy so conduct itself? What does it mean for democracy to have a logic or a binding mode of inquiry?

Logic, if I am not mistaken, is an inherent feature of thought that tells us that something is valid when it follows as a conclusion that is itself a consequence of its own premises. Democracy presupposes that the conditions of life can be freely willed and chosen, either by means of participation or by representation. These may be the premises of democracy, but what follows as a consequence? A glance at Tocqueville's *Democracy in America* should indicate that democracy is too full of tensions and contradictions to be subsumed under logical formulas. Start with the premise of freedom and autonomy and the democrat ends up with fear and conformity, the very submissive creature against whom Emerson and Thoreau inveighed. The constructions of logic, based on ideal axioms, would be embarrassed by the realities of democracy as it moved through the course of American history. Whether or not Dewey developed a logic of democracy, he for certain dared not ponder Tocqueville's classic text for much the same reason that the Catholic Church dared not look into Galileo's telescope and risk loss of faith. For if there is a logic to democracy, it is the logic of contradiction in which the relations among ideas entail their opposite as liberal and authoritarian impulses grow in American history like leaves of grass.

The idea that democracy can be likened to science in that both enterprises allegedly involve inquiry is a belief so accepted that the time has come to question it. How can one talk about democracy without addressing the more difficult issue of politics? Dewey assumes that democracy and science are so compatible that they can only reinforce one another. When Max Weber delivered his now-famous addresses at the end of the First World War, he made no effort to link "Politics as a Vocation" to "Science as a Vocation." Weber understood what escaped Dewey. To equate democracy with science meant that politics could only issue in specialization, routinization, and bureaucratization. Science cannot address issues of justice, meaning, and value, and politics cannot escape the world of power, control, and domination. What does it mean, Weber asked students in Munich in 1919, to have "an inward calling" for politics? What is decisive are "passion, responsibility, devotion to a cause, and a sense of proportion," qualities Weber hoped to find in the few rather than the many, leaders rather than followers. Dewey abhorred the idea of leadership as authoritarian.[1]

Except for educational reform and a brief involvement with the pacifist movement in the United States, and also his courageous intervention in the Trotsky countertrial, Dewey rarely became caught up in American politics at the local or national level. Unlike Walter Lippmann and Henry Adams, he never wrote about democratic politics and representative government as actual, day-to-day realities. Unlike Weber and Tocqueville, he never wrote on the necessity of reconstituting representative political institutions or held any public office that required coping with the wheeling and dealing of electoral politics. Thus Dewey, like our contemporary neopragmatists, was reluctant to admit that many problems facing the country derived directly from democracy itself. Contrary to the view of the pragmatist, it is not the lack of participation and involvement on the part of the citizen that has led the United States to the crisis of liberalism that Adams, Lippmann, and Weber saw coming almost a century ago.

In *The Public And Its Problems* and elsewhere, Dewey declared that the answer to the problems of democracy is "more democracy." Nowhere in his writings did he seem to understand that more democracy means more politics, and with more political participation the American people end up with more institutions and agencies, more structures and systems, even, and especially, those that have become alienated from the very people who consented to their creation. Bureaucracy springs forth from an environment of mass democracy. The leveling of social differences, the demands for equality before the law, the constitutional guarantee of procedural rights all result in more regulation, while popular demands made upon the state result in greater expenditures from the public treasury together with the proliferation of agencies to administer government programs and supervise budget allocations. Democratization and bureaucratization may go hand in hand as each professes to be objective and to be treating people alike. But in a rights-based culture, derived from America's liberal tradition, government is pressured to serve particular constituencies. It is not enough to claim that interest politics represents a betrayal of democracy, for it occurs whenever people have the chance to express their desires. Whether in 1776 or 1996, whether democracy is breaking the bonds of domination or enjoying the fruits of liberation, no government dare ask the American people to pay for the services and protections they enjoy.

What is democracy? "There is no word about which a denser mist of vague language, and a larger heap of loose metaphors, has collected," observed Henry Maine in *Popular Government* (1885). "Although Democracy does signify something indeterminate, there is nothing vague about it. It is simply and solely a form of government."[2] Oliver Wendell Holmes, Jr., a contemporary of Maine and a tough-minded pragmatist, would agree with Maine, and with Weber, that democracy is nothing more than a form of representative government capable of enforcing its laws and thereby ruling as an expression of domination, however vaguely felt. But today we have tender-minded neopragmatists who take us back to the "denser mist" of the past in their efforts to describe democracy in soothing terms.

Longing for Community

Richard Bernstein quotes Dewey telling us that democracy "is the idea of community life itself." When one thinks of the fate of communities in American life, one cannot help but think of Eliot's women speaking of Michelangelo—they come and go. Tocqueville was not the only observer to note that communal voluntary associations break up and disappear more quickly than they had formed, leaving neither a thought nor a trace.

As historians have noted, the only experiments in community life that succeeded in enduring for some reasonable time in the United States were communities with strong systems of authority, either religious or personal and charismatic.[3] But rather than rest on authority, community rests, according to Bernstein, on the disparate thoughts of Charles S. Peirce, Josiah Royce, John Dewey, and George Herbert Mead.

Peirce certainly did theorize about community, but I am not sure Bernstein is correct in insisting that the philosopher was "radical" in his reflections about the subject. In the passage Bernstein quotes, Peirce is demonstrating how the "real" can be known to the extent that inquiry continues unobstructed and thought continues over time until the mind, working in cooperation with other minds, approximates and comes closer to converging upon its object. To be sure, we cannot escape our personal vagaries, as Bernstein notes, and only in a "critical community" is it "possible to transcend our individual biases" by the "ongoing development of self-correcting habits." Bernstein then quotes a paragraph by Peirce in which the expression "control," "controlled," and "controlling" is mentioned ten times. Next we are told that Peirce suspected that nominalism led to the practice of "individualistic greed," after which we have a moving account of Peirce finding a certain transcendence in contemplating medieval architecture. It seems that Peirce may have been "the last Puritan," one who strove toward perfection through the imperatives of self-control so that he may add to the perfectibility of the community as a whole. But the challenge is to show how science alone enables us to overcome the self-centered ego and give ourselves over to the community.

As to Royce, his own preoccupation with community may have derived from his experiences in California as a youth, when he saw potential communities in mining towns ravaged by hooliganism and gold-driven lust. Royce shared Peirce's semiotical conviction that all knowledge is an endless system of interpretation that can only refer to the future, which suggests that community has a stretched temporal meaning, a stance involving deference to what lies ahead as opposed to an ethic requiring an immediate decision or a public philosophy involving the common good. Dewey is praised, despite his weakness for "metaphors of harmony and unity," as a theorist of community precisely because he sensed so much conflict and discord, one who called for, in Bernstein's words, the "virtues of openness, fallibility, experimentation, [and] ongoing criticism." And Mead's contribution to democratic community lies in his ideas about gesture, role playing, and the self as a socially interactive construction.

Putnam, Westbrook, and Bernstein, as well as Kloppenberg and just about everyone writing about democracy as a pragmatist, rest their thoughts on two assumptions that presuppose what has yet to be proven: that the values they like as part of the pragmatic temperament can be found in democracy and, even more audaciously, that democracy itself is radical. Both assumptions ache with desperation.

For a country that has never reconsidered its basic political institutions and values for more than two centuries, a country that had to go to war to settle a moral issue like slavery, a country that takes up arms for either the purpose of territorial expansion or national security, it is hard to see in what ways democracy practices "openness, fallibility, experimentation, [and] ongoing criticism." Rather than rendering America open and experimental, American democracy became, in the observations of writers like Tocqueville, Emerson, Thoreau, and James Fenimore Cooper, more unquestioning, servile, and susceptible to demagogy and to "the courtier spirit" than even monarchist Europe. Rather than offering Peirce's critique of "individualistic greed," American democracy and its politics turned into a form of what Weber called *Betrieb*, an affair of business management and capital investment. "Intellect," wrote Oswald Spengler, "reaches the throne only when money puts it there. Democracy is the completed equating of money with political power."[4]

It should be recalled that many who today regard themselves as neopragmatists hail from the sixties generation. And it was that generation that called for democratizing American politics by means of increased participation, which required that the old caucus system for electing candidates be reduced, if not eliminated, and the two-party system rendered more opened and accessible to the new and the young. No one seemed to anticipate that Dewey's ideal of "more democracy" meant more politics, which translates as more time and effort and energy, more campaigning and media blitzing, more hiring of experts and spin artists. Today, in democratic America, more money circulates through politics than centuries ago in the regal epochs of opulent aristocracies and unabashed court corruptions. However the pragmatist longs for a democracy of community, we are, in the sad but true words of the historian Richard Hofstadter, a "democracy of cupidity."[5]

The Deweyite pragmatist assumes not only that democracy is itself adequate to any task it confronts but that it is also "radical," a term Dewey rarely used but one bandied about by today's neopragmatists. The neopragmatist response to critics who point out the deficiencies of democracy is somewhat the same as the response devout Christians give to the critics of Christianity—as a way of life its religious doctrines have yet to be lived up to. The reasoning is similar to Dewey's, except that when he concedes the limits of democracy as we know it, he adds that democracy cannot fulfill itself until the idea of community is fully realized and that community can only be possible when "actual phases of associated life as they are freed from restrictive and disturbing elements" reach a level of development "whose consequences are appreciated as good by all singular persons who take part in it." Which comes first, democracy or community?

> Only when we start from a community as a fact, grasp the fact in thought so as to clarify and enhance its constituent elements, can we reach an idea of democracy which is not utopian. The conceptions and shibboleths which are traditionally associated with the idea of democracy take on a veridical and directive meaning only when they are construed as marks and traits of an association which realizes the defining characteristics of community. Fraternity, liberty, and equality isolated from communal life are hopeless abstractions. Their separate assertion leads to mushy sentimentalism or else to extravagant and fanatical violence which in the end defeats its own aims.[6]

Pragmatism rests all knowledge on "experience"; yet Dewey cannot point to any episode in history when community flourished along with liberty, fraternity, and equality. The high point of community in American history was the seventeenth-century New England Puritans. John Winthrop preached to his followers why it was necessary to live within the close ties of association and brotherly love, and to walk toward one another in the spirit of "love and mercy."[7] But he also emphasized that God had deliberately created humankind unequal so that each of us would have "need" of one another. Curiously, when the spirit of equality does take hold in American history, as it did with the Declaration of Independence, its author Thomas Jefferson insisted that people had no need of one another, and hence liberty and equality rose at the expense of community and fraternity. As to fraternity, Henry David Thoreau regarded it as a "miracle," a rare experience of brotherly friendship that by no means can be universally repeated with all others. Rather than "hopeless abstractions," as Dewey put it, fraternity and equality are hopeless conjunctions.

The problem of community has always been the problem of individual autonomy and diversity. But since Dewey denies dualism, he sees little distinction between the community and the individual. He is also unwilling to see that liberty, equality, and fraternity are value preferences and, as such, are incompatible with one another. Abraham Lincoln believed in the "family of man," but he was also aware that the North and South had different understandings of liberty, and that democracy, more than any form of government, had to face differences and conflicting value systems. Lincoln saw democracy as tragic in that one of its ideals could be fulfilled only by frustrating the other. Nowhere were the tensions within democracy more dramatic than in the debate over the Kansas-Nebraska Act and the doctrine of "popular sovereignty" advocated to admit the territories as slave states. Democracy is no guarantee that people will restrain themselves from oppressing fellow human beings.

Dewey's going back and forth between the inadequacies of actual democracy and the promises of ideal community leaves unsolved the problem of how to move from democracy to community by an act of intelligent choice alone. It may very well be the case that the values of community must be present and deeply felt prior to people choosing community as a way of life. For all his organic metaphors about "growth," Dewey rarely dealt with the question of human motivation. Motives imply desires. When in American history can it be shown that people desired to live within the confines of a community? Even Dewey himself left small-town Vermont and had no desire to return and settle down there.

The Myth of "Radical Democracy"

Dewey's warnings about the danger of "fanatical violence," made in 1927 with both communism and fascism in mind, should suggest that he was more moderate than radical as a political thinker. Today it is fashionable to associate Dewey with the radical Left, but in his own time radicalism meant the revolutionary Left, and Dewey had no wish to identify, as did many members of the Greenwich Village "Lyrical Left," with Lenin and the Bolshevik Revolution, or, as did many of the Old Left, with Stalin and the Popular Front.[8]

Technically the term radical means "to go to the root," and in the Marxist tradition this meant assaulting property so that the conditions of production can be appropriated from private hands. Even if Dewey's vague invoking of "community" and "associative living" represented a genteel way of calling for some measure of socialism in America, some way of bringing banks, railroads, and other enterprises under public control, this stance would still not make democracy radical. The very term "democratic socialism" is misleading; it came into existence as a result of socialists desiring to distinguish their position from that of totalitarian communists, but it remains a label of identity rather than a theoretical possibility. The notion that democracy itself is radical, or even potentially radical, is an assumption that is not only historically undemonstrable but conceptually incoherent.

Poststructuralists have recognized only recently what the *Federalist* authors knew two centuries ago: that all governments rest on nothing but "opinion," not on rational first principles but on what James Madison called the "cloudy" medium of language and its representations. It is unclear whether Dewey ever read the *Federalist,* but if he had he would have found no support in his conviction about community reinforcing democracy. The authors of that document did not see what Dewey believed was the curse of America's political culture: the "isolated individual" standing over and against the wholesomeness of community and the common good. People acted not as separate individuals but in concert with one another in "factions," and the divisiveness of factions could not be eliminated but only controlled. Had people behaved as individuals, government could appeal to their conscience, sense of reputation, and devotion to the rule of law. But acting collectively, people are moved by "passions and interest" and hence remain unresponsive to reason and virtue and instead are in the grip of opinion and impression.[9]

By the time of the Jacksonian era, when mass democracy broke free of the Federalist party and its elite leadership, and when "popular factions" broke free of the Constitution and its countervailing controls, the United States fell under what Tocqueville called the "tyranny of the majority" governed by nothing more than "public opinion." To him this new phenomenon carried the potential of "democratic despotism" on the part of an American people desirous of change and fearful of revolution; they became "venturous conservatives."[10] Actually, democracy became exactly what some neopragmatists want it to be today, a system of government without philosophical foundations whose legitimacy consists in belief alone, with no appeal to anything essential or transcendent, with no truth or reality outside popular opinion. If people are sovereign in that all candidates and elected officials must presently cater to their opinions and values, if polls determined politics, why does American democracy remain conservative rather than becoming radical?

It is curious that poststructuralists and neopragmatists insist that we see ourselves as "social constructions," for it is that possibility that precludes democracy from being radically transformative. As Ernest Gellner has written, democracy depends upon our consent; that approval cannot readily be given independently of the social order that we have neither consciously consented to nor made by our own conscious actions. "What one consents to depends on what one *is,* and what one is, in the end, springs from the society which has formed one. Could a vote have been taken, in the late Middle Ages, on whether mankind was to move onwards to a secular and industrial world? The question would have been unintelligible. Those who were capable of thought at all endorsed the world they knew. They knew it to be right and proper, and they knew radical changes to be accursed."[11]

The loss of the conscious subject, which poststructuralists and some neopragmatists hail as radically liberating, actually leads to the opposite result, rendering democracy cowering when we are told that it can be daring, submissive rather than subversive. If postmodernism is true, if there is no self but only structures, no actors but only actions, democracy cannot do what Dewey promised it could do. How can we see ourselves as the products of the forces of change, as Dewey insisted, and still be equipped to strive to bring about radical change? Again Gellner:

> *Fundamental changes transform identities.* Yet without a single, persisting and somehow authoritative identity, there is no one available to give his full consent to a radical transformation. No one is available to confer the democratic sacrament, blessing and vindication on it. Small changes, within a preserved identity, can of course be endorsed, or repudiated, by consent. The notion of democracy, of government validated by consent, does have a meaning, and is possible, within an overall cultural situation which is more or less stable and taken for granted, and which confers identities on its members. But when applied to the making or validating of fundamental and radical choices, the idea of consent quite literally has no meaning.
>
> Critics of actual democratic systems like to say that they only work where their basic organizational assumptions are not challenged. The charge can be strengthened: it is only then that the idea of democracy has any meaning. When truly radical options are faced, there simply is no one available to give that overall consent. You cannot consent to a change of identity. There is no "you." The very notion of a change of identity precludes it. The pre-metamorphosis self is no longer, and the post-metamorphosis self is not yet.[12]

Westbrook cites Joshua Cohen as advocating democracy as a "rationally motivated *consensus*," without seeming to be aware that consensus without identity is precisely what makes democracy conservative and that, as James would put it, one must desire to be rational before one can reason as such. It is curious that Westbrook takes Rorty to task for allegedly misusing Dewey. Convinced that language shapes our beliefs, Rorty advises that things can be made to look good by appropriate description or, when bad, by redescription. The point of post-philosophy is not to prove but to persuade. Is not Westbrook doing just this? In his paper he shifts discussion from "participatory democracy" to "procedural democracy" to "deliberative democracy," all along assuming he can solve the theoretical incongruences of democracy by simply changing the terms of discourse. He may be a Rortyean *malgré lui.*

The Fetish of Experience

Yet Westbrook sees things differently. In his valuable narrative biography of John Dewey, Westbrook claims, against Rorty and others, that Dewey sought not to "deconstruct" but to "reconstruct" philosophy, and the latter expression did indeed constitute the title of one of Dewey's books.[13] But if Dewey's genius was in showing what philosophy could not do, his failure was in assuming what it could do once reconstructed as a scientific proposition. Ever since David Hume, and perhaps earlier, it was understood that the empirical world could teach nothing of the moral world; and with Weber's brooding presence in the modern world, it was understood that science meant routinization and regimentation. Listen to Dewey in *Individualism Old and New* (1930). "Take science (including its application to the machine) for what it is, and we shall begin to envisage it as a potential creator of new values and ends. We shall have an intimation, on a wide and generous scale, of the release, the increased initiative, independence and inventiveness, which science now brings in its own specialized fields to the individual scientist. It will be seen as a means of originality and variation."[14]

Twenty years later, in one of his last essays, written a few years before his death in 1952, Dewey came upon Weber's "Science as a Vocation" and informed Americans that "one of the most distinguished sociologists of the last century" made us aware that science cannot answer the basic human need for "meaning," and that science stands silent before Tolstoy's questions that had haunted Weber: "What shall we do and how shall we live?" Dewey acknowledged that optimism about science had turned to pessimism "but," he added, "the fact that the remarks about science come from those who had no interest in attacking science from a theological point of view renders it the more impressive." Dewey went on to reaffirm his faith in science but the earlier confidence that led him to hail it as "the potential creator of new values and ends" had turned to hesitations almost touching on self-doubt.[15]

Aside from science, what of the other promises of pragmatism? In his comprehensive paper Kloppenberg tells us that Dewey and James successfully made "experience" the basis of philosophy's reorientation, and they meant by experience the overcoming of dualisms such as mind and body, the distrust of formal a priori knowledge as isolated and apart from the "stream" of things, and the evaluation of our beliefs in terms of "our experience as social and historical beings."

It is commonly understood that for a Deweyan pragmatist there can be no knowledge outside or beyond experience. Very well, but can there be knowledge within or inside experience? One reason I regard the term as cognitively empty is that I did what a good pragmatist is supposed to do—I tested it to see if the concept of experience actually worked to provide genuine knowledge. I tested the criterion of experience by bringing the study of historical experience to bear, and particularly by bringing into the discourse a historian, Henry Adams. Adams pondered the issue again and again after writing volumes of books trying to figure out the meaning of historical events, after observing politics first-hand, after interviewing statesmen like Garibaldi and sensing that the significance of history eluded even leaders who thought they were controlling it. After engaging in all such quests for knowledge of the meaning of history, Adams concluded that "experience ceases to educate."[16]

For Dewey, it should be noted, the idea of experience had nothing to do with the past; nor did he equate it with knowledge itself or even suggest in what way we might learn from experience. How could he if he viewed reality as in flux and events contingent and in transition? Without indicating what lessons we are to learn from the past, Dewey simply exhorted us to turn our faces to the future, and to do so by treating "life experiences" as "potential disclosures of meaning and values that are to be used as a means to a fuller and more significant experience."[17] It is precisely because the past cannot be an object of experience that Dewey declared that an "American philosophy of history must perforce be a philosophy for the future."[18]

How did such a reorientation of philosophy help Dewey orient himself to politics and historical developments? It didn't. Herewith the dilemma: the historian Adams demonstrated, after writing nine volumes of history, that we cannot know for sure what is experienced after people have historically experienced it, that the War of 1812 remained beyond the grasp of those who presumed to be controlling it. The philosopher Dewey advised that we cannot know anything until we experience it and then we do not really know for sure because events are contingent and experience unrepeatable in a world of change and transition.

Surely this is the greatest failure of pragmatism, and for historians not to acknowledge it is puzzling. Dewey felt confident that philosophy could turn to history to learn from action what could not be learned from contemplation. Although philosophy cannot get to the bottom of metaphysical truths, it can at least enable us to cope with events. But Dewey himself could barely cope with historical developments, could scarcely function as a pragmatist, especially when confronting episodes like the First and Second World Wars, and thus pragmatism failed to provide the means of knowing the world around us and explaining it to ourselves. No wonder Dewey spent his last years trying to clarify what he meant by "experience."[19] Thus in 1944 he agreed with Joseph Ratner that the very term should be dropped.

The concept of experience is not only cognitively dubious, it is politically mischievous. Some neopragmatists assume that the taking up of experience as philosophy's new outlook is part of what makes pragmatism a "radical" turning point in the history of modern thought. Here Rorty seems to be the only neopragmatist aware that pragmatism has no political significance since its implications can lead to numerous ideological directions, as indeed they did in the 1920s when both communism and fascism were regarded as "experiments."[20] But the concept of experience should be even more troubling to those who seek to push pragmatism toward the Left. Historically, it was precisely experience that was invoked against the Left by conservatives who charged their opponents with being unrealistic and utopian. From Edmund Burke to Irving Babbitt, whether attacking Paine or Rousseau, the conservative charged the radical with being out of touch with the facts of life as actually experienced.

The framers of the Constitution, not exactly Dewey's exemplars, announced that they would be guided not by "reason" but by "experience," particularly the historical experience of failure. They saw all republican regimes based on "civic virtue" as having failed to endure, as leaving the masses of people in a state of misery. In American history when an institution or movement (such as the American Federation of Labor, as opposed to the Socialist Workers Party) was said to have succeeded, it was described as exercising a pragmatic realism in contrast to the unrealizable ideals of its rivals. During the Cold War "pragmatism" was juxtaposed to "ideology" to claim the superior political wisdom of a prudent United States over a zealous Soviet Union. Today a student can study pragmatism and poststructuralism and go on to a job on Wall Street without missing a beat. What is marketing and selling but experimentation and representation?

The political implications of Dewey's philosophy are all the more awkward to the extent he could not bring himself to face the realities of

American history. Anyone who thinks the idea of community will redeem America should stay clear of Dewey's idol Thomas Jefferson, who extolled the clash of differences and insisted that interdependency would beget servility. More than any other founder, Jefferson bequeathed the United States its rights-based political culture, a debilitating spectacle of *incivisme* that has turned out to be so divisive that Dewey would no longer be able to confidently believe the old individualism will give way to the new. The idea that American history had at one time a "beloved community" that can be reinvigorated would be credible if some historian could show us where it can be found in the past. Pragmatism is supposed to make democracy compatible with science because both involve "inquiry." Yet no one has successfully searched into the American past of ordinary people, as opposed to the present scene of intellectuals, to establish what Dewey so cherished, and thus the philosopher looks to Jefferson, a Lockean individualist, to inspire America to overcome liberal individualism.

If the idea of community is to be found in American history as an answer to unenlightened individualism, one might better look not to Jeffersonianism but to Hamiltonianism. Although an elitist skeptical of democracy, Alexander Hamilton was the one founder who tried to articulate a concept of the communal public good. As Judith Shklar noted, Hamilton was the pioneer of "parliamentary social science," and to understand the activity of organized power is to know why his legacy "reemerges in the Age of Progressivism and especially with the New Deal and after." Hamilton believed in a broadly based suffrage with the interests of its members considered as part of the common commitment to national development. Hamilton can teach about power and government because he believed in using both, whereas Jefferson believed in neither, and thus his *Notes on the State of Virginia*, as Shklar observes, oscillates between anthropological speculation about racial types and the natural topography of the continent. The difference between Jefferson and Hamilton is the difference between a race-struck naturalist and a race-free political scientist.[21]

"Reaching Forward into the Unknown": Dewey as "Futurist"

Can one be a pragmatist and still be convinced in the possibility of truthful knowledge and reliable beliefs? Some thinkers, namely Rorty, Nietzsche, and our own (as historians) Henry Adams, concluded it wiser to forget about truth lest we confuse our own predilections for real possibilities. Kloppenberg and Putnam, however, continue to believe in truth and both are drawn toward James' *The Meaning of Truth*. What gives us at least a "warranted assertibility" about truth, according to Putnam, is that its context is historical, its meaning affects our interests, and its status is revisable. Kloppenberg is fond of quoting James, who shortly before he died, and in response to his many critics, called himself an "epistemological realist" and professed to believe in the existence of "a reality independent of us." For something to be true in a Jamesian sense, according to Kloppenberg, it must be consistent with "prior beliefs that had withstood the severe test of experience," results in "satisfaction," and, "in the absence of irrefutable evidence," renders useful "the consequences of faith for believers." Why should truth be at the service of our interests, yield satisfaction rather than frustration, pleasure rather than pain? James may have deferred to the notion of "a reality independent of us," but there is no question that he himself could not believe that knowledge would incline itself to anything other than the fulfillment of individual interest and satisfaction. "Leave out that whole notion of *satisfactory working or leading* (which is the essence of my pragmatist account) and call truth a static logical relation, independent even of possible leadings or satisfactions, and it seems to me you cut all ground from under you. . . . There is, in short, no *room* for any grade or sort of truth outside of the framework or the pragmatic system."[22]

The philosopher Peirce was aghast at the thought that one would regard truth as a function of the interest that wills it. But James did so, and Dewey himself merely collectivized James' individualistic, satisfaction basis of truth by insisting that democracy could never be conceived as standing in the way of people's growth and development. A free-market capitalist could not agree more with both pragmatists, which raises the problem of how to proceed from pragmatism as a theory of knowledge to pragmatism as a theory of politics, social philosophy, and intellectual inquiry.

Take the question of political philosophy. Dewey wrote on democracy. But in political thought the idea of the public had connotations of classical republicanism that had juxtaposed "virtue" to "interest" and called upon citizens to subordinate their private satisfactions to the common welfare. Today there has been much talk of returning to "civic republicanism," and some even speak of pragmatism and republicanism in the same breath. Not only is republicanism a myth when it is believed to have existed in the past, or at least the American past, its connection with pragmatism reads like a study of immiscibility. Dewey would deny that public virtue is in conflict with the pursuit of interest, and he would also choke on the thought that classical politics calls for a *ricorso,* a return to the republic's first principles.

Those historians who seek to salvage Dewey from his misplaced hopes are in contention with those who, like Rorty, seek to show that Dewey left us in an impasse politically as well as epistemologically. "Rorty's position," Kloppenberg tells us, "is insufficiently pragmatic" because he continues to see tensions and immiscibilities where Kloppenberg only sees wholeness and harmonies. And such a position of "liberal ironism encourages self-ishness, cynicism, and resignation" in the face of public issues. In his present paper and in other writings, Kloppenberg has argued that Rorty has rendered American pragmatism almost unrecognizable by giving it a poststructuralist face-lift. Drawing on the "French Nietzcheans" (as Jürgen Habermas has dubbed Jacques Derrida and Michel Foucault), Rorty concluded that because philosophy cannot prove anything about truth and reality, it should become a self-conscious language activity, a way of writing and not solely a way of knowing. Kloppenberg believes this "linguistic turn" results in relativism and a defeatist skepticism about knowledge, particularly historical knowledge. Referring to Peter Novick's *That Noble Dream* (1988), which left historiography in an epistemological impasse, Kloppenberg claims to show a way out with his idea of "pragmatic hermeneutics" that would render relevant the old pragmatism to the study of the past and keep the newer version at bay. In the *American Historical Review*, Kloppenberg confidently announced:

> As James understood and Dewey reaffirmed, there is in pragmatic theory a fruitful alternative to relativism. Hypothesis—such as historical interpretation—can be checked against all the available evidence and subjected to the most rigorous critical tests the community of historians can devise. If they are verified provisionally, they stand. If they are disproved, new interpretations must be advanced and subjected to similar testing. The process is imperfect but not random; the results are always tentative but not worthless. It is this strand of pragmatic hermeneutics . . . which has been present in best work of American historians since the first decade of the twentieth century.[23]

The historian wants us to believe in pragmatism, which tells us that truth cannot be established in the past but a "new truth" may be made to happen in the future; in history, which, as the study of change, tells us that truth cannot be sustained over time; and in hermeneutics, which tells us that it cannot be found but only interpreted through signs and representations.

Why cannot the pragmatic idea of experience be applied to the study of historical experience? Because, as Dewey made clear in his critique of empiricism, "what has taken place . . . is conceived of as tied up to what has been, or is 'given.' But experience in its vital form is experimental, an effort to change the given; it is characterized by a projection, by reaching forward into the unknown; connection with a future is its salient point." To Kloppenberg's claim that pragmatism offers a way out of the problem of relativism, listen to what Dewey has to say: "No doctrine about knowledge can hinder the belief . . . that what we know as past may be something which has *irretrievably* undergone just the difference which knowledge makes." Not only does knowing alter the thing known, the only thing that can be known is what is undergoing change, that is "itself in transition," and inquirers can know it by acting upon it as experimenters and observing the results.[24]

A pragmatic sensibility toward knowledge is useless to the historian, for how can history attain cognitive certainty by "reaching forward into the unknown"? The pragmatist verification theory is closer to literature than to history and it remains consistent with science. Whether through experimentation or imagination, the scientist or artist brings into existence something new that need not be consonant with any antecedent truth or reality. Whatever the future of science and literature, history is dead and, as Dewey once put it, perhaps whimsically, "let the dead bury the dead," a quip he made when suggesting that history be supplanted with the study of sociology.[25]

In 1950, Dewey, age ninety-one with a little more than a year to live, responded to a letter from the intellectual historian Merle Curti, who had raised some questions based on an article by another historian accusing pragmatism of leading to relativism. Dewey held that the question of whether history could be known unconditioned by the processes of knowing was futile to raise. But he was "flabbergasted" by the "caricature" of him made by the historian who accused him of endorsing an "unqualified" and "exclusive presentism." Dewey replied that it would have been closer to the mark to accuse him of "futurism" rather than "presentism."[26] Here and elsewhere Dewey emphasized a point that renders pragmatism irrelevant to the study of history. Inquiry can deal with the future, and not a past that has left no traces or effects, for all genuine inquiry involves the transformation of its object, and science is the study of the observable effects of experimentation and change.

Interpretive Communities and Pragmatic Hermeneutics

Contemporary neopragmatism is characterized by a split personality. On one side are Rorty and the linguistic fixated poststructuralists, skeptics, and atheists convinced that what we seek is not there and what we find is little more than our own projected interpretations imposed on a world without philosophical foundations. On the other side are the reconstructionists, scholars like Jürgen Habermas and Stanley Fish who believe that we can be saved from the abyss of nihilism by forming communities of inquiry that will succeed in overcoming doubt and relativism by reaching common agreement through practicing rule-governed procedures of communication and discourse. One reason for Kloppenberg's upbeat, optimistic paper is that he partakes of the reconstructionist perspective. As a historian concerned with the past, Kloppenberg has great confidence in "pragmatic hermeneutics," the method of regarding an interpretation as simply a "hypothesis" that can be objectively "checked against all the available evidence and subjected to the most rigorous critical tests the community of historians can devise."

Kloppenberg's paper originally appeared in the *Journal of American History*, and no doubt the editors and outside reviewers all agreed with its import. But what does such consensus of agreement signify in the end?

In the original article are photos of the pantheon of American pragmatists: James, Dewey, Rorty, and Bernstein. Curiously, one of the most influential pragmatists in American history is excluded from the pantheon. This scrappy and courageous philosopher, Sidney Hook, had risen (almost) from his deathbed to take on Allan Bloom and to make a distinction between cultural relativism and cognitive relationism, thereby truly carrying on in the spirit of Dewey. Hook is also remembered for being a thinker who left his impact on politics and diplomacy; the first philosopher to render pragmatism cosmopolitan by relating it to European currents of thought involving Hegel, Heidegger, and Marx; a social thinker who debated the nature of the economy and became an antagonist to Friedrich Von Hayek; and a citizen who spoke out against racism and in support of desegregation (about which James and Dewey remained silent). Why was Hook excluded?

The pragmatic reconstructionist believes "more in the Deweyan spirit of Bernstein than in the increasingly Derridean spirit of Rorty," and he seeks to make the point that we need not worry about relativism since "our convictions can be rooted in conventions rather than Truth and still have important consequences."[27] Apparently it was the conviction of the neopragmatists and those who think the way they think to rely upon their own "conventions" when writing about pragmatism, and thus we have an interpretation that can hardly be said to have been put "to the most rigorous critical tests the community of historians can devise." Although the neopragmatist agrees with Bernstein that in community inquiry we "transcend our individual biases" by the "ongoing development of self-correcting habits," there is little evidence of such virtues in his interpretation of pragmatism. The method of "pragmatic hermeneutics" may only lead to a consensus-contrived interpretation that reflects little more than a specific generation's subjective dispositions.

It would hardly be difficult to document the reasons for Hook's disappearance from the history of pragmatism. The 1960s generation of historians announced their manifesto in *Towards A New Past: Dissenting Essays in American History,* published in that tumultuous year, 1968. There and in other writings Christopher Lasch assaulted Hook for his stance on the Cold War, claiming the philosopher read into the Soviet Union a dangerous "utopianism or messianism" that had more to do with his own Marxist background than with historical reality, and he even claimed that the pragmatist critique of communism "tended to merge with fascism."[28]

In recent years younger neopragmatists made every effort to rescue Dewey and James from Lasch's misunderstandings about pragmatism without saying a word about Hook, no doubt because the 1960s generation also takes a view of the Cold War different from his. Ironically, the view the 1960s generation takes toward the Cold War is in some ways similar to the view that the late nineteenth-century generation took toward the Civil War, the view W. E. B. Du Bois had to face.

Just as the Cold War was blamed on the misplaced zeal of the intellectual class, for whom "pragmatism became something of a religion" (Lasch), so too was the outbreak of the Civil War attributed to the abolitionists, Transcendentalists, and other reformist intellectuals bent on driving evil from the face of the earth. The conviction that the Civil War could have been prevented had it not been for "the blundering generation" of statesmen in the 1850s had its echo in the "quagmire" thesis about the Vietnam War in the 1960s. Moreover, the conviction that people living under "proletarian regimes" were content with communism had an earlier sentiment in the conviction that African Americans living under plantation systems were content with slavery. Whether it was Staughton Lynd writing about "Who Started The Cold War?" or Lasch about "The Cultural Cold War," neither had any doubt that the United States had been mistaken in its course of action. They and other historians of the 1960s agreed to agree, and continue to agree, that they remain right in their views, just as J. G. Randall never changed his mind that the Civil War could have been avoided had it not been for "fanaticism."[29]

These parallels may be overdrawn, but they may also serve the purpose of suggesting the false promises of "pragmatic hermeneutics" in guaranteeing a historical narrative free of subjectivity and relativism. The idea that "our convictions" based on nothing more than "our conventions" can be a reliable guide to the past amounts to hubris. No doubt historians of the last century were certain of their convictions, and they could be judged even less critically since they were unaware of the crisis of knowledge that awaited the twentieth century. In that confident age, historians were certain they could recapture the past in its pristine actuality, and they did not, as do some of our neopragmatists, believe that an intersubjective consensus among a community of inquirers can make up for lack of an objective access to reality. But those few of us, at least in the academic world of history, who take a view different from the 1960s generation about interpreting recent events, find ourselves in the same predicament as Du Bois in coming up against a consensus resistant to challenge from without and self-doubt from within. "Nearly all recent books on Reconstruction agree with each other," wrote Du Bois, describing the conventional consensus of historical interpretation of his era. Du Bois lamented the degeneration of history into "lies agreed upon."[30] "Pragmatic hermeneutics" tells us that truth is arrived at through agreement.

Pragmatism, Feminism, and the Black Intellectual

In the academic world the subject of pragmatism has become so popular a trend that to raise questions about its validity is to risk obloquy. In certain subjects such as law and sociology pragmatism has had a long and rich legacy. But in new fields such as feminism and black studies, today's academic pragmatism seems to have come out of nowhere, since the expression was seldom used in the past with respect to either the women's movement or the situation of African Americans.

Charlene Haddock Seigfried's *Pragmatism and Feminism: Reweaving the Social Fabric* argues that Dewey's philosophy helped women liberate themselves by showing that truth was a fixation of the dominant class, that there could be no neutral take on reality, and that "experience is to be understood as," quoting Dewey, " 'an affair of the intercourse of a living being with its physical and social environment.' " The idea that feminism begins when traditional philosophy ends is certainly a dictum of our times. "Feminist pragmatism rejects the a priori cookie-cutter model of knowledge and theory. Although anyone who wields a tool can judge its efficacy, theory for feminist pragmatists is modeled as inquiry directed toward changing situations, preeminently social situations, which always include human participants."[31]

A current impression sees pragmatism as freeing up the cause of whatever one wants to champion, and all other modes of thinking are doctrinaire and hierarchical. Yet Dewey himself said little about the women's movement, while writers who were critical of pragmatism, such as Walter Lippmann and Reinhold Niebuhr, wrote sympathetically about it. The idea that feminism can now join forces with Deweyan pragmatism stumbles on the proposition of democracy, even participatory democracy. At every step of the way in American history the cause of women enjoyed little support from popular democracy, and even when they won the right to vote, the status of women changed little. It would be more accurate to say that the very ideas that Dewey rejected did more for women than those he espoused. It was not science and the experimental method but the antique doctrine of natural rights, the Lockean idea—which was antipatriarchal as well as antimonarchical, that in the state of nature no one is authorized to dominate others—that did more to liberate women in our time. The Constitution's principle of the equal protection of laws and the Supreme Court's mandated civil rights moved women into professional positions in ways democracy failed them in the past. Professor Seigfried may well believe in popular experimentation from the bottom up, but the key to power lies in affirmative action from the top down.

The recent adoption of pragmatism as a philosophical deliverance for blacks is as dubious as it is for women. In the provocatively titled essay in this volume, "Going Astray, Going Forward: Du Boisian Pragmatism and Its Lineage," Ross Posnock makes the case that the country's greatest scholar on African-American history must be reappraised as a pragmatist. Posnock cites the familiar "double consciousness" remark of Du Bois that has a Jamesian ring, and he seeks to show that other scholars are wrong in insisting that Du Bois retained a Hegelian outlook from his years of study in Berlin. Posnock describes pragmatism as endowing Du Bois with a sense of engagement rather than detachment, a distrust of "supposed necessities" in events and of fixed, changeless categories, and a desire to be part of ongoing struggle and a willingness to face risks and adopt new stances. As Posnock puts it, "Du Bois' willingness to turn and 'grope,' to risk the vulnerability of revising and improvising amid uncertainty, reflects his pragmatist historicism which believes that 'no idea is perfect and forever valid. Always to be living and apposite and timely, it must be modified and adapted to changing facts.'"

Such descriptions of a mind and temperament may make Du Bois into something of a pragmatist. But could he sustain such an outlook and render insightful judgments on American history? On the issue of democracy, for example, Du Bois sounds more Tocquevillian than Deweyan. More specifically, he invokes a Rousseauian idea as a critique of the abuses of democracy when it is conceived as the individual opportunity of some to the exclusion of others. "Democracy does not and cannot mean freedom. On the contrary it means coercion. It means submission of the individual will to the general will and it is justified in this compulsion only if the will is general and not the will of special privilege."[32] Du Bois' belief in the possibility of a dominant general will is at odds with pragmatic pluralism and the idea of "submission" could cause James and Dewey to wince. It should also be recalled that Du Bois had a Prussian respect for authority at the top. "Bismarck was my hero. He had made a nation out of a mass of bickering peoples. . . . This foreshadowed in my mind the kind of thing that American Negroes must do, marching forth with strength and determination under trained leadership."[33] For all Posnock's descriptions of Du Bois' Jamesian "tingling challenge of risk," he was not about to regard education as a trial and error affair, and he took culture and the classics more seriously than did Dewey with his emphasis on vocational training.

The description of Du Bois' penchant for adaptation, improvisation, and the valuing of change cannot be said to characterize the tone of his masterful dissertation, "Suppression of the Slave Trade." As Du Bois studied the various regions of the United States from the period of the Revolution to the Civil War, he noted that "changing economic conditions" compelled the reopening of the slave trade, that it was impossible to sustain a "firm moral sense" against "a fatal spirit of temporizing," and that what became uppermost was "expediency," "compromise," and "interest," in the end too powerful for even the "Puritan conscience." In a section entitled "The Lessons for Americans," Du Bois, noting that Americans prefer avoiding being "harassed with great social questions," observed: "Consequently we often congratulate ourselves more on getting rid of a problem than on solving it."[34] Dewey thought that Darwinism showed philosophy why it is possible to accept the "abandonment" of a problem. "We do not solve them: we get over them. Old questions are solved by disappearing."[35] Would Du Bois agree?

It is too bad Du Bois, Alain Locke, and other black intellectuals who went through a Marxist phase are not alive today. If Locke were alive, and he had somewhat the same pragmatic temperament that Du Bois enjoyed, at least according to Posnock, would he still hold the views today at the end of the Cold War that he held during the years of the First World War? Nancy Fraser would have to answer yes, and she thinks that Locke's analysis of the origins of racism remains valid. The analysis had many subscribers in the West in the years of the Bolshevik Revolution, many who believed that racism derives from imperialism, imperialism from capitalism, capitalism from the profit system, and the profit system from the institution of private property. When Lenin announced, in 1918, "We must organize everything!" he proceeded to abolish private property; supposedly all the sins based on it would soon disappear. In the 1930s a black intellectual like Paul Robeson thought he saw a race-free society in Stalin's Russia, and some fellow travelers thought they saw in China the disappearance of sexism as well as racism.

Curiously, there are only two entities in the world that have eliminated racism: Castro's Cuba and the U.S. armed forces. Both are authoritarian, militaristic, and anti-gay. Democracy and socialism have had sufficient opportunity to overcome racism. The record is not very encouraging.

There is a tendency recently to bring almost all of black intellectual life under the rubric of pragmatism. "The fruits of Du Bois's pragmatism," Posnock claims, "are found in the later figures such as Alain Locke, Zora Neale Hurston, and Ralph Ellison." Fraser scarcely demonstrated that Locke partook of the pragmatic idiom, and although I cannot address the subject of Hurston, I can say that Ellison, like his friend Robert Penn Warren, had many doubts about pragmatism as an outlook toward life and politics.

It did not trouble Ellison that "democracy is always pregnant with its contradictions," and although he did believe that the future of black America was tied up with America itself and that both must take their guidance from the "American experience," which involved the ideals of the Declaration of Independence and the mechanisms of the Constitution, he saw the country in need of a sense of irony, tragedy, sin, and evil, qualities found more in Niebuhr, Dewey's antagonist, than in pragmatism. Ellison did see in jazz an impulse for unrestrained experimentation and in popular culture "an American compulsion to improvise upon the given," and he wanted to see blacks take control of their own fate and begin undertaking redeeming narratives. But pragmatism could also put the human mind too much at one with the world, forsaking the very dualisms within which value resides as a creation of the human imagination. In his essay on "Twentieth Century Fiction and the Black Mask of Reality," Ellison observes of the aftermath of *Huckleberry Finn* that "it is not accidental that the disappearance of the Negro from our fiction coincides with the disappearance of deep-probing doubt and a sense of evil." As did Du Bois, Ellison saw Americans as avoiding moral problems instead of facing them, and the shift from Mark Twain to Ernest Hemingway indicated a naturalistic turn in thought that substituted technical perfection for tragic insight: "The writer puts down nothing but what he pragmatically 'knows,'" and "seldom was he able to transcend the limitations of pragmatic reality." Like Van Wyck Brooks years earlier, Ellison saw pragmatism as relying too much on intelligence to the neglect of imagination, too much on the practical how of things than on the more challenging metaphysical why. "This particular naturalism explored everything except the nature of man," observed Ellison of a "hard-boiled school" of literature too disillusioned to take seriously questions involving the human condition.[36]

"Old questions," Dewey advised, "are solved by disappearing." What about new questions like truth and power, questions vital to gender and race? Does pragmatism have an answer to questions that refuse to disappear?

Notes

1 Max Weber, "Politics as a Vocation," and "Science as a Vocation," in *From Max Weber: Essays in Sociology,* ed. H. H. Gerth and C. Wright Mills (New York: Oxford University Press, 1948), pp. 77–156.

2 Henry Maine, *Popular Government* (1885; Indianapolis: Liberty Classics, 1976), pp. 79–80.

3 Laurence Veysey, *The Communal Experience: Anarchist and Mystical Communities in Twentieth-Century America* (Chicago: University of Chicago Press, 1978).

4 Oswald Spengler, *The Decline of the West: Perspectives of World History,* trans. Charles Francis Atkinson (New York: Alfred Knopf, 1928), vol. 2, p. 485.

5 Richard Hofstadter, *The American Political Tradition and the Men Who Made It* (New York: Knopf, 1948), p. viii.

6 John Dewey, *The Public and Its Problems* (1927; Denver: Swallow, 1954), p. 149.

7 Perry Miller, *The New England Mind* (1939; Boston: Beacon, 1961), pp. 3–110.

8 Both Max Eastman and Sidney Hook tried to get Dewey interested in revolutionary Russia in particular and in Marxism in general. See my *Up From Communism: Conservative Odysseys in American Intellectual History* (New York: Harper, 1975).

9 Among the most insightful analyses of the thoughts of the framers of the Constitution is Arthur O. Lovejoy, *Reflections on Human Nature* (Baltimore: Johns Hopkins University Press, 1961).

10 Alexis de Tocqueville, *Democracy in America,* ed. J. P. Mayer, trans. George Lawrence (Garden City, N.Y.: Doubleday Anchor, 1969), pp. 503–705.

11 Ernest Gellner, *Plough, Sword, and Book: The Structure of Human History* (Chicago: University of Chicago Press, 1989), pp. 193–94.

12 *Ibid.,* 194.

13 Robert B. Westbrook, *John Dewey and American Democracy* (Ithaca: Cornell University Press, 1991), pp. 539–42.

14 John Dewey, *Individualism Old and New* (1930; New York: Capricorn, 1962), 160–61.

15 John Dewey, "Philosophy's Future in Our Scientific Age," in *John Dewey: The Later Works,* vol. 16, 1949–1952, edited by Jo Ann Boydston (Carbondale: Southern Illinois University Press, 1989), pp. 372–73.

16 Henry Adams, *The Education of Henry Adams* (1918; New York: Modern Library, 1931), p. 294.

17 John Dewey, "What I Believe," *Forum*, 83 (1930): 176–82.

18 *German Philosophy and Politics* (New York: Holt, 1915), p. 132.

19 Apparently Dewey asked a younger philosopher to look up the various meanings of "experience" as used throughout the history of philosophy. Joseph Ratner to John Dewey, "Notes on Experience," Dewey Mss. 102 75/1, n.d. May 12, 1944, Dewey manuscripts, Morris Library, Southern Illinois University, Carbondale; see also *Dewey: Later Works*, pp. 552–54.

20 During both the period of the Greenwich Village Lyrical Left and the time of the Old Left of the 1930s, American intellectuals attempted to relate pragmatism to Marxism. See John Patrick Diggins, *The Rise and Fall of the American Left* (New York: Norton, 1992). As to fascism, during the 1920s the Harvard political philosopher William Y. Elliot created a stir with his *The Pragmatic Revolt in Politics*, which related pragmatism to Italian Fascism. Georges Sorel, who had considerable influence on syndicalist-turned fascists, wrote on pragmatism as a theory of direct action. As for Mussolini, he liked to call himself a "pragmatist," but when Herbert Schneider interviewed him in 1927, he came away convinced that Il Duce only knew the title of a book by James but little about the substance of pragmatism as a philosophical position. See John Patrick Diggins, *Mussolini and Fascism: The View from America* (Princeton: Princeton University Press, 1972).

21 Judith K. Shklar, "Alexander Hamilton and the Language of Political Science," in *The Language of Political Theory in Early Modern Europe*, ed. Anthony Pagden (Cambridge: Cambridge University Press, 1987), pp. 339–55.

22 William James, *The Meaning of Truth* (1909; Cambridge: Harvard University Press, 1975), p. 89.

23 James T. Kloppenberg, "Objectivity and Historicism: A Century of American Historical Writing," *American Historical Review* 94 (1989): 1011–30.

24 John Dewey et al., *Creative Intelligence: Essays in the Pragmatic Attitude* (1917; New York: Rhinehart, 1945), p. 7; *Philosophy and Civilization* (New York: Milton Balch, 1931), pp. 39–40.

25 John Dewey, *Moral Principles in Education* (Boston: Houghton Mifflin, 1909), p. 36; "History for the Educator," *Progressive Journal of Education* 1 (1909): 1–4.

26 John Dewey to Merle Curti, June 10, 12, 23; July 11, 1950, Dewey manuscripts, Morris Library, Southern Illinois University, Carbondale.

27 Kloppenberg, "Objectivity and Historicism," p. 1027.

28 Christopher Lasch, "The Cultural Cold War," in *Towards a New Past: Dissenting Essays in American History*, ed. Barton J. Bernstein (New York: Pantheon, 1968), pp. 322–59; *The New Radicalism in America, 1889–1963: The Intellectual as a Social Type* (New York: Vintage, 1967), pp. 306–7, 332–33.

29 Randall is quoted in *Slavery as a Cause of the Civil War*, edited by Edwin C. Rozwenc (Boston: Heath, 1949), p. x.

30 W. E. B. Du Bois, "The Propaganda of History," in W. E. B. Du Bois, *Writings*, ed. Nathan Huggins (New York: Library of America, 1986), pp. 1027–47.

31 Charlene Haddock Seigfried, *Pragmatism and Feminism: Reweaving the Social Fabric* (Chicago: University of Chicago Press, 1996), p. 263.

32 W. E. B. Du Bois, "The Revelation of Saint Orgne," in *Writings*, p. 1065.

33 W. E. B. Du Bois, "Dusk of Dawn," in *ibid.*, p. 577.

34 W. E. B. Du Bois, "Suppression of the Slave Trade," *ibid.*, pp. 193–97.

35 John Dewey, "The Influence of Darwinism on Philosophy," in *American Thought: Civil War to World War I*, ed. Perry Miller (New York: Rhinehart, 1954), pp. 214–25.

36 Ralph Ellison, "Twentieth-Century Fiction and the Black Mask of Humanity," "The Little Man at Chehaw Station," "Going To The Territory," "Society, Morality, and the Novel," in *The Collected Essays of Ralph Ellison*, ed. John F. Callahan (New York: Modern Library, 1995), pp. 81–99, 489–519, 599–612, 694–725.

PRAGMATISM
AND LAW

Pragmatic Adjudication

RICHARD A. POSNER

Pragmatism is at one level a philosophical position, just as scientific realism, transcendental idealism, existentialism, utilitarianism, and logical positivism are. It is the level well-illustrated by a recently published book in which Richard Rorty and his critics go at each other hammer and tongs over such questions as whether language reflects reality, whether free will is compatible with a scientific outlook, and whether such questions are even meaningful.[1] My concern is at a different level, with an issue in "applied" pragmatism, although after listening to Professor Grey's paper at the conference about the independence of legal from philosophical pragmatism I realize that this term may be inapt.[2] I shall take up that issue at the end of this essay. The "applied" issue that is my subject till then is whether adjudication, particularly appellate adjudication, can or should be pragmatic.

The issue is at once spongy and, for me at least, urgent. It is spongy because "pragmatism" is such a vague term. Among the Supreme Court Justices who have been called "pragmatists" are Oliver Wendell Holmes, Louis Brandeis, Felix Frankfurter, Robert Jackson, William O. Douglas, William Brennan, Lewis Powell, John Paul Stevens, Edward White, and now Stephen Breyer; others could easily be added to the list.[3] Among theorists of adjudication, the label has been applied not only to those who call themselves pragmatists, of whom there are now quite a number, but also to Ronald Dworkin, who calls pragmatism, at least Rorty's conception of pragmatism, an intellectual meal fit only for a dog (and I take it he does not much like dogs).[4] Some might think the inclusion of Frankfurter in my list even more peculiar than the inclusion of Dworkin. But it is justified by Frankfurter's rejection of First Amendment absolutism, notably in the flag-salute cases, and to his espousal of a "shocks the conscience" test for substantive due process. This is a refined version of Holmes' "puke" test—a statute or other act of government violates the Constitution if and only if it makes you want to throw up.[5] Can it be an accident that Frankfurter announced his test in a case about pumping the stomach of a suspect for evidence?[6]

The "puke" test is shorthand for Holmes' more considered formulation, in his dissent in *Lochner:* a statute does not work a deprivation of "liberty" without due process of law within the meaning of the due process clauses of the Fifth and Fourteenth Amendments "unless it can be said that a rational and fair man necessarily would admit that the statute proposed [opposed?] would infringe fundamental principles as they have been understood by the traditions of our people and our law."[7] By "fundamental principles" Holmes meant principles of morality so deeply rooted in the judge's being that the judge would find their rejection incomprehensible. The qualification "the traditions of our people and our law" is significant, however, as I shall explain later.

What makes the issue of whether adjudication is or should be pragmatic an urgent one for me is that my critics do not consider my theory of adjudication pragmatic at all. They think it is in the spirit of logical positivism, from which pragmatists try to distance themselves. The logical positivists believed that moral assertions, because they are neither tautological nor verifiable empirically, have no truth value at all—are matters purely of taste or of unreasoned emotion.[8] Jeffrey Rosen, for example, argues that my book *Overcoming Law* endorses a visceral, personalized, ruleless, free-wheeling, unstructured conception of judging.[9] And well before I thought of myself as a pragmatist, I was criticized for being "a captive of a thin and unsatisfactory epistemology," which is just the sort of criticism that a purely emotive theory of judging would invite.[10] Am I, then, backsliding? I had better try to make clear what I think pragmatic adjudication is.

I

An initial difficulty is that pragmatic adjudication cannot be derived from pragmatism as a philosophical stance. For it would be entirely consistent with pragmatism the philosophy *not* to want judges to be pragmatists, just as it would be entirely consistent with utilitarianism not to want judges to conceive their role as being to maximize utility. One might believe for example that overall utility would be maximized if judges confined themselves to the application of rules, because discretionary justice, with all the uncertainty it would create, might be thought on balance to reduce rather than to increase utility. Similarly, a pragmatist committed to judging a legal system by the results the system produced might think that the best results would be produced if the judges did not make pragmatic judgments but simply applied rules. He might, by analogy to rule utilitarians, be a "rule pragmatist."

So pragmatic adjudication will have to be defended—pragmatically— on its own terms rather than as a corollary of philosophical pragmatism. (This would be necessary anyway, because of the vagueness of the philosophical concept.) But what exactly is to be defended? I do not accept Dworkin's definition: "the pragmatist thinks judges should always do the best they can for the future, in the circumstances, unchecked by any need to respect or secure consistency in principle with what other officials have done or will do."[11] That is Dworkin the polemicist speaking. But if his definition is rewritten as follows—"a pragmatist judge always tries to do the best he can do for the present and the future, unchecked by any felt *duty* to secure consistency in principle with what other officials have done in the past"—then I can accept it as a working definition of the concept of pragmatic adjudication. On this construal the difference between, say, a judge who is a legal positivist in the strong sense of believing that the law is a system of rules laid down by legislatures and merely applied by judges, and a pragmatic judge, is that the former is centrally concerned with securing consistency with past enactments, and the latter is concerned with securing consistency with the past only to the extent that decisions in accordance with precedent may happen to conduce to producing the best results for the future.

II

What does the pragmatic approach to judging entail? What are the pros and cons (pragmatically evaluated, of course)? And is it, on balance, the right approach for judges to take?

Consider to begin with the differences in the way the judicial positivist and the judicial pragmatist might weigh or order the materials bearing on the decision of a case. By "judicial positivist" I mean a judge who believes not only that the positivist account of law is descriptively accurate—that the meaning of law is exhausted in positive law—but also that the positivist account should guide judicial decision-making in the strong sense that no right should be recognized or duty imposed that does not have its source in positive law. (A weaker sense will be considered later.) The judicial positivist would begin and usually end with a consideration of cases, statutes, administrative regulations, and constitutional provisions—all these and only these being "authorities" to which the judge must defer in accordance with the principle that a judge who is not a pragmatist has a duty to secure consistency in principle with what other officials have done in the past. If the authorities all line up in one direction, the decision of the present case is likely to be foreordained, because to go against the authorities would, unless there are compelling reasons to do so, violate the duty to the past. The most compelling reason would be that some other line of cases had adopted a principle inconsistent with the authorities directly relevant to the present case. It would be the judges' duty, by comparing the two lines and bringing to bear other principles manifest or latent in case law, statute, and constitutional provision, to find the result in the present case that would promote or cohere with the best interpretation of the legal background as a whole.

The pragmatist judge has different priorities. That judge wants to come up with the best decision having in mind present and future needs, and so does not regard the maintenance of consistency with past decisions as an end in itself, but only as a means for bringing about the best results in the present case. He is not uninterested in past decisions, in statutes, and so forth. Far from it. For one thing, these are repositories of knowledge, even, sometimes, of wisdom, and so it would be folly to ignore them even if they had no authoritative significance. For another, a decision that destabilized the law by departing too abruptly from precedent might, on balance, have bad results. There is often a tradeoff between rendering substantive justice in the case under consideration and maintaining the law's certainty and predictability. This tradeoff, which is perhaps clearest in cases in which a defense of statute of limitations is raised, will sometimes justify sacrificing substantive justice in the individual case to consistency with previous cases or with statutes or, in short, with well-founded expectations necessary to the orderly management of society's business. Another reason not to ignore the past is that often it is difficult to determine the purpose and scope of a rule without tracing the rule to its origins.

The pragmatist judge thus regards precedent, statutes, and constitutions both as sources of potentially valuable information about the likely best result in the present case and as signposts that he must be careful not to obliterate or obscure gratuitously, because people may be relying upon them. But because the pragmatist judge sees these "authorities" merely as sources of information and as limited constraints on his freedom of decision, he does not depend upon them to supply the rule of decision for the truly novel case. For that he looks also or instead to sources that bear directly on the wisdom of the rule that he is being asked to adopt or modify.

Some years ago the Supreme Court held that if there are two possible grounds for dismissing a suit filed in federal court, one being that it is not within the court's jurisdiction and the other being that the suit has no merit, and if the jurisdictional ground is unclear but the lack of merit is clear, the court can dismiss the suit on the merits without deciding whether there is jurisdiction.[12] This approach is "illogical." Jurisdiction is the power to decide the merits of a claim; so a decision on the merits presupposes jurisdiction. The pragmatic justification for occasionally putting the merits cart before the jurisdictional horse begins by asking why federal courts have a limited jurisdiction and have made rather a fetish of keeping within its bounds. The answer I think is that these are extraordinarily powerful courts and the concept of limited jurisdiction enables them both to limit the occasions for the exercise of power and to demonstrate self-restraint.[13] But if the lack of merits of a case is clear, a decision so holding will not enlarge federal judicial power but will merely exercise it well within its outer bounds. If, therefore, the question of jurisdiction is unclear in a case whose lack of merit is clear, the prudent and economical course may be to skip over the jurisdictional question and dismiss the case on the merits.

Here is another example of the difference between positivistic and pragmatic adjudication. When oil and gas first became commercially valuable, the question arose whether they should be treated like other "mobile" resources, such as wild animals, where the rule of the common law was (and is) that you have no property right until you take possession of the animal, or, instead, like land and other "stable" property, title to which can be obtained by recording a deed in a public registry or by some other paper record without the owner's having to take physical possession of the good.[14] A judicial positivist who was asked whether only possessory rights should be recognized in oil and gas would be likely to start with the cases on property rights in wild animals and consider whether oil and gas are enough "like" them to justify subsuming these minerals under the legal concept of *ferae naturae,* which would mean enforcing only property rights obtained by possession. (So no one could own oil until it was pumped to the surface.) The pragmatic judge would be more inclined to start with the teachings of natural-resources economists and oil and gas engineers, to use the advice of these experts to decide which regime of property rights (possessory or title) would produce the better results when applied to oil and gas, and only then to examine the wild-animal cases and other authorities to see whether they might block the decision that would be best for the exploitation of oil and gas.

I am aware that the pragmatic judge may fall on his face. He may not be able to understand what the petroleum engineers and the economists are trying to tell him or to translate it into a workable legal rule. The plodding positivist, his steps wholly predictable, will at least promote stability in law, a genuine public good, and the legislature can always step in and prescribe an economically sound scheme of property rights. That is pretty much the history of property rights in oil and gas. Perhaps nothing better could realistically be expected. But American legislatures, in contrast to European parliaments, are so sluggish when it comes to correcting judicial mistakes that a heavy burden of legal creativity falls inescapably on the shoulders of the judges. I do not think that the judges can bear the burden unless they are pragmatists. But I admit that they will not be able to bear it comfortably until changes in legal education and practice make law a more richly theoretical and empirical, and less formal and casuistic, field.

My third example is a current focus of controversy, the issue of the enforceability of contracts of surrogate motherhood. In holding that they are unenforceable the Supreme Court of New Jersey in the *Baby M* case engaged in a labored and rather windy tour of legal sources and concepts, overlooking the two issues, both factual in the broad sense, that would matter most to a pragmatist.[15] The first is whether women who agree to be surrogate mothers typically or at least frequently experience intense regret when the moment comes to surrender the newborn baby to the father and his wife. The second is whether contracts of surrogate motherhood are typically or frequently exploitive in the sense that the surrogate mother is a poor woman who enters into the contract out of desperation. If the answers to both questions are "no," then, given the benefits of the contracts to the signatories, the pragmatist judge would probably enforce such contracts.[16]

These examples should help us see that although both the positivist and the pragmatist are interested in the authorities *and* the facts (broadly construed—I am not talking only or even mainly about the facts developed at a trial through testimony, exhibits, and cross-examination), the positivist starts with and gives more weight to the authorities, while the pragmatist starts with and gives more weight to the facts. This is the most succinct description of pragmatic adjudication that I can come up with. It helps, incidentally, to explain two features of Holmes' judicial philosophy that seem at first glance antipathetic to pragmatic adjudication: his lack of interest, of which Brandeis complained, in economic and other data, and his reluctance to overrule previous decisions. A pragmatic judge believes that the future should not be the slave of the past, but he need not have faith in any particular bodies of data as guides to making the decision that will best serve the future. If like Holmes you lacked confidence that you or anyone else had any very clear idea of what the best decision on some particular issue would be, the pragmatic posture would be one of reluctance to overrule past decisions, since the effect of overruling would be to sacrifice certainty and stability for a merely conjectural gain.

I have said nothing about the pragmatic judge's exercising a "legislative" function, although the kind of facts that he would need in order to decide the oil and gas case in pragmatic fashion would be the kind that students of administrative law call "legislative" to distinguish them from the sort of facts ("adjudicative") that judge and jury, cabined by the rules of evidence, are called upon to find. Holmes said that judges were "interstitial" legislators whenever they were called upon to decide a case the outcome of which was not dictated by unquestioned authorities. This is a misleading usage because of the many differences in procedures, training, experience, outlook, knowledge, tools, timing, constraints, and incentives between judges and legislators. Scope is not the only difference, as Holmes' formulation suggests. What he should have said was that judges are rulemakers as well as rule appliers. A judge is a different kind of rulemaker from a legislator. An appellate judge has to decide in particular cases whether to apply an old rule unmodified, modify and apply the old rule, or create and apply a new rule. If he is a pragmatist he will be guided in this decision-making process by the goal of making the choice that will produce the best results. To make that choice he will have to do more than consult cases, statutes, regulations, constitutions, conventional legal treatises, and other orthodox legal materials.

III

I want to examine a little more systematically the objections to the pragmatic approach to judging. One objection to inviting the judge, as I just did, to stray beyond the boundaries of the orthodox legal materials of decision is that he is not trained to analyze and absorb the theories and data of social science. The example of Brandeis is not reassuring. Although Brandeis was a brilliant man of wide intellectual interests, his forays into social science whether as advocate or as judge were far from an unqualified success. Indeed, most social scientists today would probably agree that Brandeis' indefatigable industry in marshaling economic data and viewing them through the lens of economic theory was largely misguided. It led him to support (and to try to make a part of the law) such since-discredited policies as limiting women's employment rights, fostering small business at the expense of large, and encouraging public utility and common carrier regulation. Holmes, as I have said, had reservations about the reliability of social scientific theories, but his unshakable faith in the eugenics movement, an early twentieth-century product of social and biological theory, undergirds his most criticized opinion (incidentally one joined by Brandeis)—*Buck v. Bell*.[17] One of the deformities of the majority opinion in *Roe v. Wade* is that the opinion makes it seem that the issue of abortion rights is a medical one and that the reason for invalidating state laws forbidding abortion is simply that they interfere with the autonomy of the medical profession—a "practical" angle reflecting Justice Blackmun's long association with the Mayo Clinic.[18] The effects of abortion laws on women, children, and the family, which are the effects that are important to evaluating the laws, are not considered.

A second and related objection to the use of nonlegal materials to decide cases is that it is bound often to degenerate into "gut reaction" judging. I think that this appraisal is basically correct, provided the phrase "gut reaction" is taken figuratively rather than literally, but that the word "degenerate" is too strong. Cases do not wait upon the accumulation of some critical mass of social scientific knowledge that will enable the properly advised judge to arrive at the decision that will have the best results. The decisions of the Supreme Court in the area of sexual and reproductive autonomy, for example, came in advance of reliable, comprehensive, and accessible scholarship on sexuality, the family, and the status of women. The court had to decide whether capital punishment is cruel and unusual punishment at a time when the scientific study of the deterrent effects of capital punishment was just beginning. When the court decided to redistrict the nation according to the "one man, one vote" principle it cannot have had a clear idea about the effects, which political scientists still do not agree upon more than thirty years later. The examples are not limited to the Supreme Court or to constitutional law. Common law judges had to resolve such issues as whether to extend the domain of strict liability, substitute comparative negligence for contributory negligence, simplify the rules of occupiers' liability, excuse breach of contract because of impossibility of performance, limit consequential damages, enforce waivers of liability, and so forth long before economists and economically minded lawyers got around to studying the economic consequences of these choices. When judges try to make the decision that will produce the "best results," without having any body of organized knowledge to turn to for help in making that decision, it seems that they must rely on their intuitions.

The fancy term for the body of bedrock beliefs that guide decision is natural law. Does this mean that the pragmatic approach to adjudication is just another version of the natural-law approach? I think not. The pragmatist does not look to God or other transcendental sources of moral principle to validate his departures from statute or precedent or other conventional "sources" of law. He has not the confidence of secure foundations and this should make him a little more tentative, cautious, and piecemeal in imposing his vision of the Good on society in the name of legal justice. If Holmes really thought he was applying a "puke" test to statutes challenged as unconstitutional rather than evaluating those statutes for conformity with transcendental criteria, this would help explain his restrained approach to constitutional adjudication. On the other hand, a pragmatic justice such as Robert Jackson, who unlike Holmes had a rich background of involvement in high-level political questions, was not bashful in drawing upon his extrajudicial experience for guidance to the content of constitutional doctrine.[19] The pragmatic judge is not always a modest judge.

The reason that using the "puke" test or one's "gut reactions" or even one's pre-judicial high-governmental experiences to make judicial decisions sounds scandalous[20] is that the legal profession, and particularly its academic and judicial branches, want the added legitimacy that accrues to the decisions of people whose opinions are grounded in expert knowledge. The expert knowledge of another discipline is not what is wanted, although it is better than no expert knowledge at all. Both the law professor and the judge feel naked before society when the positions they take on novel cases, however carefully those positions are dressed up in legal jargon, are seen to reflect unstructured intuition based on personal and professional (but nonjudicial) experiences, and on character and temperament, rather than on disciplined, rigorous, and articulate inquiry.

Things are not quite so bad as that. It is not as if American judges were chosen at random and made political decisions in a vacuum. Judges of the higher American courts are generally picked from the upper tail of the population distribution in terms of age, education, intelligence, disinterest, and sobriety. They are not tops in all these departments but they are well above average, at least in the federal courts because of the elaborate preappointment screening of candidates for federal judgeships. Judges are schooled in a profession that sets a high value on listening to both sides of an issue before making up one's mind, on sifting truth from falsehood, and on exercising a detached judgment. Their decisions are anchored in the facts of concrete disputes between real people. Members of the legal profession have played a central role in the political history of the United States, and the profession's institutions and usages are reflectors of the fundamental political values that have emerged from that history. Appellate judges in nonroutine cases are expected to express as best they can the reasons for their decision in signed, public documents (the published decisions of these courts) and this practice creates accountability and fosters a certain reflectiveness and self-discipline. None of these things guarantees wisdom, especially since the reasons given for a decision are not always the real reasons behind it. But at their best American appellate courts are councils of wise elders and it is not completely insane to entrust them with responsibility for deciding cases in a way that will produce the best results in the circumstances rather than just deciding cases in accordance with rules created by other organs of government or in accordance with their own previous decisions, although that is what they will be doing most of the time.

Nor do I flinch from another implication of conceiving American appellate courts in the way that I have suggested. It is that these courts will tend to treat the Constitution and the common law, and to a lesser extent bodies of statute law, as a kind of putty that can be used to fill embarrassing holes in the legal framework. In the case of property rights in oil and gas, a court could take the position that it had no power to create new rules and must therefore subsume these newly valuable resources under the closest existing rule, the rule governing wild animals. It might even take the position that it had no power to enlarge the boundaries of existing rules, and in that event no property rights in oil and gas would be recognized until the legislature created a system of property rights for these resources. Under this approach, if Connecticut has a crazy law (as it did until *Griswold v. Connecticut* struck it down) forbidding married couples to use contraceptives, but no provision of the Constitution limits state regulation of the family, then the crazy law will stand until it is repealed or the Constitution amended to invalidate it.[21] Or if the Eighth Amendment's prohibition against cruel and unusual punishments has reference only to the *method* of punishment or to the propriety of punishing *at all* in particular circumstances (for example, for simply being poor, or an addict), then a state can with constitutional impunity sentence a sixteen-year-old to life imprisonment without possibility of parole for the sale of one marijuana cigarette, which in fact seems to be the Supreme Court's current view, one that I find very difficult to stomach.[22] I do not think a pragmatic Justice of the Supreme Court *would* stomach it, although he would give due weight to the implications for judicial caseloads of bringing the length of prison sentences under judicial scrutiny, and to the difficulty of working out defensible norms of proportionality. The pragmatic judge does not think that he should throw up his hands and say "sorry, no law to apply" when he is confronted with outrageous conduct that the framers of the Constitution neglected to foresee and make specific provision for.

Oddly, this basic principle of pragmatic judging has received at least limited recognition by even the most orthodox judges, with respect to statutes. It is accepted that if reading a statute the way it is written produces absurd results, the judges may rewrite it.[23] Most judges do not put it quite this way—they say that statutory interpretation is a search for meaning and Congress can't have meant the absurd result—but it comes to the same thing. And, at least in this country, common law judges reserve the right to "rewrite" the common law as they go along. I am merely suggesting that a similar approach, prudently employed, is the pragmatic approach to constitutional adjudication as well.

I do not belittle the dangers of the approach. People can feel very strongly about a subject and be quite wrong. Certitude is not the test of certainty. A wise person realizes that even his unshakable convictions may be wrong—but not all of us are wise. In a pluralistic society, moreover, which the United States seems to be more and more every year, a judge's unshakable convictions may not be shared by enough other people that he can base a decision on those convictions and be reasonably confident that it will be accepted. So the wise judge will try to check his convictions against those of some broader community of opinion, as suggested by Holmes in his dissent in *Lochner*. It was not irrelevant, from a pragmatic standpoint, to the outcome of *Brown v. Board of Education* that official racial segregation had been abolished outside the South and that it bore a disturbing resemblance to Nazi racial laws.[24] It was not irrelevant to the outcome of *Griswold v. Connecticut* that, as the court neglected to mention, only one other state (Massachusetts) had a similar law. If I were writing an opinion invalidating the life sentence in my hypothetical marijuana case I would look at the punishments for this conduct in other states and in the foreign countries, such as England and France, that we consider in some sense our peers. For if a law could be said to be contrary to world public opinion I would consider this a reason, not compelling but not negligible either, for regarding a state law as unconstitutional even if the Constitution's text had to be stretched a bit to cover it. The study of other laws, or of world public opinion as crystallized in foreign law and practices, is a more profitable inquiry than trying to find some bit of eighteenth-century evidence for thinking that maybe the framers of the Constitution wanted courts to make sure that punishments prescribed by statute were proportional to the gravity, or difficulty of apprehension, or profitability, or some other relevant characteristic of the crime. If I found such evidence I would think it a valuable bone to toss to a positivist or formalist colleague but I would not be embarrassed by its absence because I would not think myself duty-bound to maintain consistency with past decisions.

I would even think it pertinent to the pragmatic response to my hypothetical marijuana case to investigate or perhaps even just to speculate (if factual investigation proved fruitless) about the psychological and social meaning of imprisoning a young person for his entire life for the commission of a minor crime. What happens to a person in such a situation? Does he adjust? Deteriorate? What is the likely impact on his family, and on the larger society? How should one feel as a judge if one allows such a punishment to be imposed? And are these sentences for real, or are preposterously severe sentences soon commuted? Could it be that the deterrent effect of so harsh a sentence will be so great that the total number of years of imprisonment for violation of the drug laws will be reduced, making the sacrifice of this young person a utility-maximizing venture after all? Is utility the right criterion here? Is the sale of marijuana perhaps far more destructive than some ivory-tower judge or professor thinks? Do judges become callous if a large proportion of the criminal cases that they review involve very long sentences? If a defendant appealed who received "only" a five-year sentence, would the appellate judge's reaction be, "Why are you complaining about such a trivial punishment?"[25]

The response to the hypothetical case of the young man sentenced to life for selling marijuana is bound in the end to be an emotional rather than a closely reasoned one, because so many imponderables enter into that response, as my questions were intended to indicate. But emotion is not pure glandular secretion. It is influenced by experience, information, and imagination, and can thus be disciplined by fact.[26] Indignation or disgust founded on a responsible appreciation of a situation need not be thought a disreputable motive for action, even for a judge; it is indeed the absence of any emotion in such a situation that would be discreditable. It would be nice, though, if judges and law professors were more knowledgeable practitioners or at least consumers of social science (broadly defined to include history and philosophy), so that their "emotional" judgments were better informed.

My earlier reference to the ages of judges suggests another objection to pragmatic adjudication. Aristotle said, and I agree, that young people tend to be forward-looking. Their life lies ahead of them and they have only a limited stock of experience to draw upon in coping with the future, while old people tend to be backward-looking because they face an opposite balance between past and future.[27] If, therefore, a pragmatic judge is forward-looking, does that mean that we should invert the age profile of judges? Should Holmes have been made a judge at thirty and put out to pasture at fifty? Or, on the contrary, is it not the case that judges perform an important "balance wheel" function, one that requires them to be backward-looking, one that is peculiarly apt, therefore, for the aged? Have I not argued this myself, and also pointed out that, contrary to the conventional view, the great failing of the German judges in the Nazi period was not their positivism but their insistence on interpreting and applying the laws of the New Order to further the aims, the spirit, of those laws?[28]

These criticisms pivot on an ambiguity in the term "forward-looking." If it is meant to carry overtones of disdain for history, origins, and traditions, then the criticisms I have mentioned are entirely just. But I do not myself understand "forward-looking" in that sense. I understand it to mean that the past is valued not in itself but only in relation to the present and the future. That relation may be a very important one. It may be that the best the judge can do for the present and the future is to insist that breaks with the past be duly considered. That would be entirely consistent with pragmatism; it would be positivism-as-pragmatism. All that would be missing would be a sense of reverence for the past, a felt "duty" of continuity with the past. That reverence, that sense of duty, would be inconsistent with the forward-looking stance, and hence with pragmatism.

I think, likewise, that pragmatism is wholly neutral with regard to the question of whether the law should be dominated by rules or by standards. The pragmatist rejects the idea that law is not law unless it consists of rules, because that kind of conceptual analysis is not pragmatic. But he is open to any pragmatic argument in favor of rules, for example, that judges cannot be trusted to make intelligent decisions unless they are guided by rules or that decisions based on standards produce uncertainty disproportionate to any gain in flexibility. A pragmatic judge thus need not be recognizable by a distinctive style of judging. What would be distinctive would be that the style of thinking (which might be encapsulated as positivist or formalist rhetoric) owed nothing to ideas about the nature of law or the moral duty to abide by past decisions or some other nonpragmatic grounding of judicial attitudes. I likewise leave open just what are the criteria for the "best results" for which the pragmatic judge is striving. They are not what is best for the particular case without consideration of the implications for other cases. Pragmatism will not tell us what is best but, provided there is a fair degree of value consensus among the judges, as I think there is, it can help judges seek the best results unhampered by philosophical doubts.

The greatest danger of judicial pragmatism is intellectual laziness. It is a lot simpler to react to a case than to analyze it. The pragmatic judge must bear in mind at all times that he is a judge and that this means that he must consider all the legal materials and arguments that are or can be brought to bear upon the case. If legal reasoning is modestly defined as reasoning with reference to distinctive legal materials such as statutes and legal doctrines and to the law's traditional preoccupations, for example, with stability and the right to be heard and the other "rule of law" virtues, then it ought to be an ingredient of every legal decision, though not necessarily the be-all and end-all of the decision.[29] Just as some people think that an artist must prove that he is a competent draftsman before he should be taken seriously as an abstract artist, so I believe that a judge must prove—anew in every case—that he is a competent legal reasoner before he should be taken seriously as a pragmatic judge.

To put this point differently, the pragmatic judge must never forget that he is a judge and that the role of a judge is constraining as well as empowering. Several years ago the Chicago public schools were unable to open at the beginning of the school year because the state refused to approve the school district's budget. An injunction was sought to compel the schools to open, on the ground that their closure violated a judicial decree forbidding de facto racial segregation in the city's public schools. The basis on which the injunction was sought was not that the state's refusal to approve the budget had been motivated by any racial animus—there was no suggestion of that—but that the ultimate goal of the judicial decree, which was to improve the education and life prospects of black children in Chicago, would be thwarted if the schools were not open to educate them. The trial judge granted the request for an injunction, and did so on an avowedly pragmatic ground: the cost to Chicago's school-children, of whatever race, of being denied an education. My court reversed.[30] We could not find any basis in federal law for the injunction.

The desegregation decree had not commanded the city to open the public schools on some particular date, or for that matter to open them at all, or even to *have* public schools, let alone to flout a state law requiring financial responsibility in the administration of the public school system. It seemed to us that what the judge had done was not so much pragmatic as lawless. Even if one rejects the view, as do I, that pragmatism requires judges to eschew pragmatic adjudication, they must not ignore the good of compliance with settled rules of law. If a federal judge is free to issue an injunction that has no basis in federal law, merely because he thinks the injunction will have good results, then we do not have pragmatic adjudication; we have judicial tyranny, which few Americans consider acceptable even if they are persuaded that the tyrant can be counted on to be generally benign.

The judge in the Chicago school case was guilty of what might be called myopic pragmatism, which may be Dworkin's conception of pragmatism. The only consequence that the judge took into consideration in deciding whether to issue the injunction was that children enrolled in the public schools would be deprived of schooling until the schools opened. The consequence that he ignored was the consequence for the political and governmental systems of granting federal judges an uncanalized discretion to intervene in political disputes. Had the power that the judge claimed been upheld, you can be sure that henceforth the financing of Chicago's public schools would be determined by a federal judge rather than by elected officials. The judge thought that unless he ordered the schools to open, the contending parties would never agree on a budget. The reverse was true. Only the fact that the schools were closed exerted pressure on the parties to settle their dispute. And indeed, as soon as we lifted the injunction, the parties came to terms and the schools opened. The consequence that the judge ignored was a consequence for the schoolchildren as well as for other members of society, so that it is possible that even the narrowest group affected by the decree would, in the long run, have been hurt had the decree been allowed to stand.

If intellectual laziness is a danger of pragmatic adjudication, and I think it is, it is also a danger of not being pragmatic. The conventional judge is apt not to question his premises. If he thinks that "hate speech" is deeply harmful, or that banning hate speech would endanger political liberty, he is not likely to take the next step, which is to recognize that he may be wrong and to seek through investigation to determine whether he is wrong.[31] The deeper the belief—the closer it lies to our core values—the less likely we are to be willing to question it. Our disposition will be not to question but to defend. As Peirce and Dewey emphasized, doubt rather than belief is the spur to inquiry; and doubt is a disposition that pragmatism encourages, precisely in order to spur inquiry. One reason that attitudes toward hate speech are held generally as dogmas rather than hypotheses—one reason that so little is known about the actual consequences of hate speech—is that a pragmatic approach has not been taken to the subject.

IV

I have been trying to explain my conception of pragmatic adjudication and to defend it against the critics of pragmatic adjudication. But I would not like to leave the impression that I think pragmatic adjudication is *the* right way for all courts to go. Philosophical pragmatism, although one can find echoes or anticipations of it in German philosophy and elsewhere (Hume, Nietzsche, and Wittgenstein, for example), is basically an American philosophy, and it may not travel well to other countries. The same may be true for pragmatic adjudication. Concretely, the case for such adjudication is weaker in a parliamentary democracy than in a U.S.-style checks and balances federalist democracy. Many parliamentary systems (notably the English, which is the one I know best) are effectively unicameral and, what is more, the parliament is controlled by the executive. The legislative branch of so highly centralized a system can pass new laws pretty easily and rapidly and word them clearly. If the courts identify a gap in existing law, they can have reasonable confidence that it will be quickly filled by Parliament, so that only a temporary injustice will be done if the judges refrain from filling the gap themselves. English judges thus can afford to be stodgier, more rule-bound, less pragmatic than our judges; the cost in substantive injustice is lower.

Some parliamentary systems have a federal structure, some have constitutional review, and some have both. Some, the English for example, have neither. The ones that have neither have much clearer law, whereas to determine someone's legal obligation in the United States will often require consideration of state law (and perhaps the laws of several states), federal statutory law (and sometimes federal common law), and state and federal constitutional law. Our government is one of the most decentralized in the world. We have effectively a tricameral federal legislature, since the president through his veto power and his role in one of the major political parties is a full participant in the legislative process. This tricameral structure makes it extremely difficult to pass laws, let alone clearly worded laws (unclear wording in a contract or a statute facilitates agreement on the contract or statute as a whole by deferring resolution of the most contentious points). Moreover, the tricameral federal structure is layered on top of similarly three-headed state legislatures. American courts cannot, if they want "the best results," leave all rulemaking to legislatures, for that would result in legal gaps and perversities galore. The lateral-entry character of the American judiciary, the absence of uniform criteria for appointment, the moral, intellectual, and political diversity of the nation (and hence, given the previous two points, of the judges), the individualistic and antiauthoritarian character of the population, and the extraordinary complexity and dynamism of the society are further obstacles to American judges confining themselves to the application of rules laid down by legislatures, regulators, or the framers of the Constitution.

I am exaggerating the differences between the systems. But it *is* more natural for an English, Austrian, or Danish judge to think of himself or herself as mainly just a rule applier than it is for an American judge to do so, and since there are good pragmatic arguments in favor of judicial modesty, it is far from clear that English, Austrian, or Danish judges would be right on pragmatic grounds to become pragmatic adjudicators. I do not think that U.S. appellate judges have a choice.

V

I said I would come back to the question of whether it is accurate to describe this as a paper in "applied" pragmatism. I conjecture two relations between philosophical and legal pragmatism. First, the tendency of most philosophical speculation—and what makes it a proper staple of college education—is to shake up a person's presuppositions, so that if he happens to be a judge or lawyer reading philosophy he is likely to feel the presuppositions that define his professional culture shift beneath him. Philosophy, especially the philosophy of pragmatism, incites doubt, and doubt incites inquiry, making the judge less of a dogmatic, more of a pragmatic, adjudicator.

Second, philosophy, theology, and law have, to a significant extent, parallel conceptual structures. This is not surprising, because Christian theology was so heavily influenced by Greek and Roman philosophy, and Western law by Christianity. The orthodox versions of the three systems of thought have rather similar views on matters such as scientific and moral realism, free will, and mind-body dualism. A challenge to any of the systems, therefore, is a challenge to all three. Pragmatism in its role (which it shares with logical positivism, and here it should be pointed out that to the nonspecialist the similarities among the characteristic modern schools of philosophy are more conspicuous than the differences)[32] as skeptical challenger to orthodox philosophy encourages a skeptical view of the foundations of orthodox law with its many parallels to orthodox philosophy. That is why Rorty, who rarely discusses legal issues, is cited so frequently in law reviews.

Philosophical pragmatism does not dictate legal pragmatism or any other jurisprudential stance. But it may play a paternal and enabling role in relation to pragmatic theories of law, including the theory of pragmatic adjudication that I have tried to sketch in this paper.

Notes

This paper is the revised text of a talk given on November 3, 1995, at a conference on "The Revival of Pragmatism" sponsored by the Center for the Humanities of the City University of New York. I thank Scott Brewer, William Eskridge, Lawrence Lessig, Martha Nussbaum, Eric Posner, and Cass Sunstein, along with the commenters and other participants at the conference, for very helpful comments on an earlier draft.

1 Herman J. Saatkamp, ed., *Rorty & Pragmatism: The Philosopher Responds to His Critics* (Nashville: Vanderbilt University Press, 1995). Professor Hilary Putnam's talk at the conference was very much of this character.

2 See also Matthew H. Kramer, "The Philosopher-Judge: Some Friendly Criticisms of Richard Posner's Jurisprudence," *Modern Law Review* 59 (1996): 465, 475–78, where he states that "Metaphysical or philosophical pragmatism is a relativist position which denies that knowledge can be grounded on absolute foundations. Methodological or intellectual pragmatism is a position that attaches great importance to lively debate and open-mindedness and flexibility in the sciences, the humanities and the arts. Political pragmatism is a position that attaches great importance to civil liberties and to tolerance and to flexible experimentation in the discussions and institutions that shape the arrangements of human intercourse. . . . [T]hese three modes of pragmatism do not entail one another."

3 See, for example, Daniel A. Farber, "Reinventing Brandeis: Legal Pragmatism for the Twenty-First Century," *University of Illinois Law Review* (1995): 163.

4 For a list of pragmatists, see Richard A. Posner, *Overcoming Law* (Cambridge: Harvard University Press, 1995): 388–89. See also Richard Rorty, "The Banality of Pragmatism and the Poetry of Justice," in *Pragmatism in Law and Society,* edited by Michael Brint and William Weaver (1991), p. 89, and Ronald Dworkin, "Pragmatism, Right Answers, and True Banality," in *ibid.,* pp. 359, 360.

5 See Posner, *Overcoming Law,* p. 192.

6 *Rochin v. California,* 342 U.S. 165 (1952).

7 *Lochner v. New York,* 198 U.S. 45, 76 (1905) (Holmes' dissenting opinion).

8 Some are; for example, "murder is bad," since badness is built into the definition of "murder" (as distinct from "killing"), at least the popular as distinct from the legal definition. The distinction is important, because some forms of murder in the legal sense, such as a cuckold's killing the adulterer in flagrante delicto, are not considered morally wrong by a significant part of the community.

9 Rosen, "Overcoming Posner," *Yale Law Journal* 105 (1995): 581, 584–96.

10 Paul M. Bator, "The Judicial Universe of Judge Richard Posner," *University of Chicago Law Review* 52 (1985): 1146, 1161.

11 Ronald Dworkin, *Law's Empire* (Cambridge: Belknap Press, 1986), p. 161.

12 *Norton v. Mathews,* 427 U.S. 524, 532 (1976).

13 To quote Isabel in *Measure for Measure,* Act II, sc. 2, ll. 108–10: "Oh, it is excellent to have a giant's strength: but it is tyrannous to use it like a giant."

14 A chair, for example: it moves only when someone moves it, whereas gravity or air pressure will cause oil and gas to flow into an empty space even if no (other) force is applied. I think that when the animal rules were first applied to oil and gas, these resources were erroneously thought to have an internal principle of notion, to "move on their own," like animals. I set to one side property that is not physical at all, i.e., intellectual property.

15 Re *Baby M,* 537 A.2d 1227 (N.J. 1988).

16 See generally Richard A. Posner, *Sex and Reason* (Cambridge: Harvard University Press, 1992), pp. 420–28.

17 *Buck v. Bell,* 274 U.S. 200, 207 (1927) ("Three generations of imbeciles are enough").

18 *Roe v. Wade,* 410 U.S. 113 (1973).

19 Quite the contrary. As he said in his famous concurrence in the steel-seizure case, "That comprehensive and undefined presidential powers hold both practical advantages and grave dangers for the country will impress anyone who has served as legal adviser to a President in time of transition and public anxiety. While an interval of detached reflection may temper teachings of that experience, they probably are a more realistic influence on my views than the conventional materials of judicial decision which seem unduly to accentuate doctrine and legal fiction." *Youngstown Sheet & Tube Co. v. Sawyer,* 343 U.S. 579, 634 (1952) (Jackson, J., concurring).

20 Making the statement by Justice Jackson that I quoted in the preceding footnote remarkable for its candor; but am I mistaken in sensing a faintly apologetic tone?

21 See *Griswold v. Connecticut,* 381 U.S. 479 (1965).

22 See *Harmelin v. Michigan,* 501 U.S. 957 (1991).

23 See, for example, *Burns v. United States,* 501 U.S. 129, 137, (1991); *Green v. Bock Laundry Machine Co.,* 490 U.S. 504, 527 (1989) (Scalia, J., concurring).

24 Which for these purposes however included the District of Columbia! See *Bolling v. Sharpe,* 347 U.S. 497 (1954).

25 I believe in fact that this is increasingly the reaction of federal appellate judges, as federal sentences become ever longer and the number of criminal appeals even greater.

26 I refer the reader once again to the striking quotation from Justice Jackson, in *Harmelin v. Michigan.* This is the theme of Martha C. Nussbaum's 1993 Gifford Lectures (to be published by Cambridge University Press), *Upheavals of Thought: A Theory of the Emotions.* One would not expect, for example, a person who had become genuinely, disinterestedly convinced that the Holocaust had never occurred to feel the same concern about anti-Semitism that people who believed it had occurred would tend to have.

27 I elaborate upon Aristotle's view in Chapter 5 of my book *Aging and Old Age* (1995).

28 As I argue in *ibid.,* Chapter 8. Posner, *Overcoming Law,* p. 155, discusses the issue of law in Nazi Germany. I would not be inclined to swing to the other extreme and blame Nazi jurisprudence on pragmatism. National Socialism was not a pragmatic faith.

29 As in Joseph Raz, "On the Autonomy of Legal Reasoning," in Raz, *Ethics in the Public Domain: Essays in the Morality of Law and Politics* 310 (1994).

30 *United States v. Board of Education,* 11 F.3d 668 (7th Cir. 1993).

31 My discussion of this subject was stimulated by a very interesting paper by Michel Rosenfeld, "Pragmatism, Pluralism and Legal Interpretation: Posner's and Rorty's Justice without Metaphysics Meets Hate Speech," in this volume.

32 Hilary Putnam's brand of pragmatism, for example, as is plain from his paper in this volume, is a position within, rather than against, analytic philosophy.

Freestanding Legal Pragmatism

THOMAS C. GREY

John Rawls recently presented liberalism as a political philosophy that can stand free of the comprehensive moral and metaphysical views with which it has been associated. You do not have to be a neo-Kantian like Rawls, so he argues, to accept his Kantian-sounding theory of justice. Millian utilitarians, Aristotelian perfectionists, and Thomistic theists can also commit to the basic liberal rights: democratic government, freedom of speech and religion, equal opportunity, the rule of law, private property, and a welfare safety net. Rawls believes there is no need for citizens to resolve their deepest philosophical disagreements in order to be able to agree on principles of justice.[1]

In a similar spirit, I want to suggest that pragmatism in legal theory can stand free of *philosophical* pragmatism, whether old (William James, John Dewey) or new (Richard Rorty, Hilary Putnam). Epistemological foundationalists, metaphysical realists, Kantian moralists, and even theologically conservative Christians may find that they are jurisprudential pragmatists. So may lawyers who, though reflective about their profession, are not much interested in most of the questions debated by philosophers.

The analogy is by no means perfect. Rawlsian liberalism is contractual and limited in scope, a set of terms proposed as a basis for political cooperation by people of different views. As such it is a theory that naturally invites treatment as a freestanding module. Pragmatism, by contrast, presents itself as an encompassing orientation toward inquiry—one that stresses the agent's perspective; the interaction of impulse, habit, and reflection; and a holistic approach to justification. We are only political part of the time (at least so liberals believe), but we are always inquirers. Becoming a pragmatist, which changes the way one understands inquiry, feels more like a conversion than like being persuaded that a proposed deal is reasonable. For these reasons it may seem paradoxical to speak of a *partial* pragmatism, a pragmatism for jurisprudential purposes only—can anyone really switch so encompassing a philosophy on and off like the lights to the law library?

Another reason to doubt that pragmatism in legal theory can be independent of pragmatism in philosophy is that they are closely related conceptually and genealogically. It is no accident that the same term is used for these two ways of thinking. Legal pragmatists naturally describe their jurisprudence as simply the application within law of a generally pragmatist approach to inquiry.[2]

Let me first sketch my understanding of pragmatism in philosophy and in legal theory, emphasizing their common elements and mutual influences. Then I will argue that despite all that seems to hold them together, the jurisprudence can and should stand free of the philosophy, at least as the latter is now understood.

What they have in common is an account of inquiry that is at the same time contextualist and instrumentalist. The pragmatist revival in philosophy began with Richard Rorty's imaginative incorporation of Heidegger and the later Wittgenstein into the pragmatist canon, grouped with Dewey in a new twentieth-century pragmatist trinity.[3] As Rorty told the story, the advantage of the pragmatists over later analytical philosophers was the contextual, historically oriented side of their account of inquiry—their emphasis on the fact that human thought is constituted out of a background of *practices,* cultural and individual, as well as being *practical* in the sense of purposively directed to action. Dewey's explicit attention to the centrality of language, culture, and history was paralleled by Heidegger's focus on the inescapable place of background presuppositions or "prejudices" in human thought, and by the primacy the later Wittgenstein's gave to the concepts of a language game and a form of life. Rorty also linked these contextualist themes to the antifoundationalism movement in late twentieth-century analytical philosophy, and to the influential reinterpretation of natural science as a path-dependent cultural practice. Finally, Rorty argued that some technical developments in post-positivist analytical philosophy of language, most notably Donald Davidson's critique of the idea of representation, could be understood as promoting pragmatic contextualism.[4]

Rorty also continued the instrumentalist side of the pragmatic tradition by criticizing philosophers for "frivolously neglecting the duty to offer [cultural criticism] by getting hung up on 'the external world.' "[5] And other pragmatists both old and new have condemned traditional philosophers for escapist retreating from the problems of life into an imagined realm populated by eternal questions: How and what can we Know? What is Being? What is Truth? Are there Essences? Is there a World outside the mind? To pragmatists, philosophical energy spent attempting to answer these questions (or to prove them unanswerable) means philosophical time wasted. Thus as Peirce disparaged merely imaginary Cartesian doubt, James insisted that "the trail of the human serpent is over all," and Dewey attacked the quest for certainty, other recent pragmatists have joined Rorty in continuing the attack on philosophical escapism. Thus Hilary Putnam has enthusiastically adopted James and his human serpent, and Cornel West has celebrated "the American evasion" of first philosophy in favor of social criticism.[6]

Similarly, pragmatist jurisprudence has from the beginning conceived of legal thought as an enterprise that is practical in the two related senses suggested by Justice Holmes' dictum that "all thought is social, is on its way to action."[7] Thus juristic thinking is contextual, arising as it does in the course of familiar collective activities: the practice of law, the administration of justice, the adjudication of disputes. At the same time it is instrumental, aiming to make these activities serve human purposes. Legal thought issues as commentary, heuristic and critical reflection upon practice and administration, and upon prior commentary. This kind of practical interpretation and criticism is not something that comes into the juristic enterprise from outside or from above; it is one of the activities that constitute the enterprise. And legal theorizing is just the more general and abstract kind of commentary, neither supreme over nor epiphenomenal to but rather coordinate with the other practices that make up the law.

The contextualist and the instrumentalist strands of legal thought were independently well-established, generally in opposition to each other, long before pragmatism came on the scene. The official jurisprudence of the common law tradition from Coke and Blackstone to the present has always been explicitly contextualist, with common lawyers stressing the centrality of custom and practice, and preaching the virtues of tradition and experience and the dangers of top-down rationalism. By contrast, instrumentalist jurisprudence from Hobbes through Bentham up to modern legal-economic policy science has emphasized that law is a conscious human product created to realize social ends. The common lawyers and the utilitarian codifiers saw themselves and were seen by others as rival schools of legal theory presenting alternative and mutually inconsistent conceptions of law. The contribution of the American legal pragmatists, from Holmes through Roscoe Pound, Benjamin Cardozo, Karl Llewellyn, and Lon Fuller to Richard Posner, has been to argue instead that historical and instrumental jurisprudence present two compatible and equally necessary perspectives on the complex reality of law. To quote Holmes again, in law "continuity with the past is no duty" (contra Coke and Blackstone) "but only a necessity" (contra Hobbes and Bentham).[8]

Pragmatist jurisprudence thus seems to follow from the jointly contextual and instrumental account of inquiry characteristic of American philosophical pragmatism. And indeed of the legal pragmatists, at least Pound, Cardozo, Fuller, and Posner have clearly shown the influence of James and Dewey. Even Holmes, who criticized James' pragmatism, expressed great admiration for Dewey's philosophy, formed like his own out of the apparently incompatible Romantic and scientific positivist currents of nineteenth-century thought.[9] And Dewey later stated his own jurisprudential pragmatism in just the terms I have used: as a synthesis of the historical jurists' descriptive emphasis on law as custom and practice with the analytical utilitarians' instrumentalist approach to legal criticism and reform.[10]

Following on the revival of philosophical pragmatism, recent pragmatist legal thought has renewed this tradition of eclectic mediation between instrumental and contextual theories of law. The jurisprudence of the last two decades has seen a proliferation of theoretical approaches drawing on intellectual movements outside law, each of which has tended to present itself in traditional theoretical fashion as the one true path to understanding the legal system. The most pervasive and influential of these has been economic analysis, which treats law as a mechanism of wealth maximization, and serves as the latest and most sophisticated manifestation of the Benthamite instrumentalist tradition in legal theory.[11] Writers taking various hermeneutic approaches have portrayed law as a relatively coherent and stable activity involving the authoritative interpretation of socially binding practices and texts; their work gives a new interdisciplinary slant to the contextualist tradition long familiar in legal thought.[12] A variety of Critical legal theories, all presupposing oppositional political stances, have portrayed law as an unstable mixture of inherited forms with apologetic and utopian discursive practices invoked to justify the organized use of force.[13] Finally, a number of theorists have carried on the natural law tradition, in various ways treating law as a vehicle for the implementation of fundamental moral truths in human affairs.[14]

Each of these "law and" approaches challenges the others as defective, and partly as a result they tend to cancel each other out in practice, leaving the effective triumph to the ever-present professional default option: law is law, an autonomous activity with its own self-justifying standards of internal reflection and deliberation—"thinking like a lawyer." Unlike the other recent jurisprudential approaches, legal pragmatism is inclusive, treating the current theories as perspectives, each of which can add to the understanding of law. This is because pragmatists conceive of law as a cluster of activities too complex to be captured and subdued by any theory—the element of truth in antitheoretical professionalism.

Pragmatists see law as both policy and principle, both wealth maximization and interpretation, both detached scientific tool sharpening and engaged cultural immersion. As contextualists, they take legal actors' pretheoretical patterns of problem-solving activity as the starting point for theorizing, and as a result they doubt that wholesale abandonment of existing practices is an option. On the other hand (unlike legal traditionalists) they give no strong normative authority to unreflective practice. When law is viewed instrumentally, some of what is normally done could be done better, some of it may no longer serve any useful purpose, and some altogether new things might be tried. Those with perspectives not previously represented within professional ranks are likely to point out neglected opportunities and injustices and hypocrisies that have been complacently accepted, though new voices are not guaranteed to speak virtuously or wisely. Finally, pragmatic contextualism does not exclude belief in human rights; pragmatists can support enforceable universal prohibitions against practices like slavery and torture, and so become practical proponents of natural law.[15]

In its self-conscious eclecticism, legal pragmatism thus seems to pick up the antifoundational contextualist strand in recent philosophical pragmatism. On the instrumental side, however, there is no apparent legal analogue to the pragmatist critique of traditional philosophy for its alleged escapism. No one writing on law is heard insisting that "the trail of the human serpent is over all," because it has not occurred to any recent legal theorist to say or assume otherwise.

The instrumentalist side of pragmatist legal theory rather takes the form of a critique of jurisprudential formalism, the family of approaches that forbid or discount the consideration of practical consequences in justifying legal judgments. Langdell provided a classical example of such a jurisprudence when he dismissed as legally "irrelevant" the objection that a doctrine mandated by his highly conceptual theory of contract law was both inefficient and unjust.[16] Ernest Weinrib provides a clear contemporary example when he argues that "the purpose of private law is simply to be private law," and Ronald Dworkin supplies a more subtle and debatable case with his promotion of "integrity" as an intrinsic and distinctively legal value that should constrain the law's pursuit of justice and the common good.[17] But from the point of view of the philosophical critique of escapism, formalist theories are as practical as pragmatist ones; like all legal theories, they bear on how actual legal questions should be decided.

My proposal that pragmatist legal theory should be conceived as standing free of philosophical pragmatism begins with this point, that legal and philosophical pragmatists do not mean the same thing by instrumentalism. Less obviously, they do not mean the same thing by contextualism either. Legal pragmatism does not depend on and indeed can make no use of the pragmatist philosophers' critiques of metaphysics and epistemological foundationalism.

I missed this point myself in an earlier discussion of legal pragmatism, but I have been helped to see where I went astray by David Luban's eloquent and challenging essay "Doubts About the New Pragmatism."[18] Luban does me the honor of taking my summary of philosophical pragmatism as representative. He then assumes that pragmatism in legal theory depends on the philosophical view summarized, the critique of traditional speculative metaphysics and epistemology that is roughly common to James, Dewey, and Rorty, so that a defense of speculative philosophy against that critique undermines legal pragmatism. This now seems to me a mistake.

Luban follows Plato and Aristotle in portraying philosophy as an activity that "begins in wonder and ends in the rapt, silent, yet active contemplation of truths—regardless of whether they pay." As he says, it was against this picture of thought that William James launched the pragmatist polemic, centered around metaphors ("cash value," what "pays") suggesting that thought is worthless unless it issues in action.[19] Dewey, following James on this point, argued that the history of western thought had been distorted by the Greeks' privileging of contemplative over practical thought, and diagnosed this as the characteristic judgment of aristocrats who valued leisure and looked down on work. Philosophical democrats, he argued, should abandon this hierarchy.[20] And Rorty now carries on this tradition when he urges that philosophy should replace the (escapist) contemplation of eternal questions with criticisms of contemporary culture in the service of liberal and democratic political ideals.[21]

Luban rejects this whole pragmatist attack on thought for thought's sake as philistine.[22] Recalling the episode of Wittgenstein's unhappy stint as a schoolteacher in the Austrian village of Trattenbach, where the local peasants refused to pay him to teach their children more arithmetic than they needed to keep books and make change, he says that pragmatist philosophers are "good Trattenbachers," and that the confrontation between them and traditional philosophy starkly poses the choice "Athens or Trattenbach: there is no third way."[23]

This is a choice most clearly posed in contemporary philosophy, Luban suggests, by the question of what attitude to take toward philosophical skepticism. Should teachers of philosophy run their students through Descartes, Berkeley, and Hume and end up asking how any of us can know that we are not brains floating in vats tended by neuroscientists? Yes, say the analytical philosophers who have in recent years revived the skeptical tradition; they argue that when we rationally generalize our reflections on everyday difficulties with justification, we are driven to face the challenge of full-fledged skepticism.[24]

The pragmatist response to skepticism has always been that once the agent's point of view is seen as primary, the question of Descartes' Evil Deceiver or the modern skeptic's neuroscientist tending a brain in a vat is shown to be an unreal one. What might anyone do differently (taking "do" in the broadest possible sense) upon becoming convinced that he might be only a brain in a vat? It seems apparent the answer is "nothing." As Hume said, "the first and most trivial event in life will put to flight all [the skeptic's] doubts and scruples, and leave him the same, in every point of action and speculation, with the philosophers of every other sect, or with those who never concerned themselves with any philosophical researches."[25] If this is so, then contemplating the possibility is a waste of time, and for a philosopher to cultivate the *frisson* such a fantasy may stimulate is sentimental self-indulgence.

As Hilary Putnam says, "from the earliest of Peirce's Pragmatist writings, Pragmatism has been characterized by *antiscepticism*. . . . That one can be both fallibilistic *and* antisceptical is perhaps *the* basic insight of American Pragmatism."[26] Fallibilism follows from the pragmatist disbelief that knowledge has foundations; it means that any given belief might be wrong. As such, it gives genuine counsel—keep an open mind, be ready to revise any belief, because new contexts or purposes may require it. Philosophical skepticism by contrast proposes that *all* beliefs might be wrong, a view that can give no counsel at all, and hence (from the agent perspective) drops out.[27]

The pragmatist project in philosophy thus requires resisting the apparently natural move from "any of our beliefs might be wrong" to "all of our beliefs might be wrong." This is what leads contemporary pragmatists' rejection of metaphysical realism. In Rorty, this rejection takes particularly dramatic form; he wants us (when we talk as philosophers) to abandon the whole notion of representation, to stop thinking and talking of true beliefs or true statements as accurately representing reality. When we say "that's the way it is," or deny it, we are being philosophically ungrammatical. Putnam is not so radical in his revisionist ambitions; as an "internal realist" he only wants us to recognize that our judgments of "how it is" are true or false only from inside a given conceptual scheme; there is no way it *really* is apart from any such scheme. (Rorty, by contrast, follows Davidson in dismissing "the very idea of a conceptual scheme.")[28]

Pragmatists reject full-fledged or external realism about the world because they think that to accept it is to let in the skepticism that the pragmatic agent perspective compels us to reject. If there exists a way the world is, independent of our words and thoughts, and if (as many contemporary analytical philosophers agree) there are available no *foundations* for knowledge, no reliable methods for establishing certainly true beliefs about the world, then we must admit that we might after all be brains in vats. Or as Thomas Nagel puts a more poignant version of the same possibility, we may be no more able to understand what the universe is really like than a nine-year old is able to understand quantum mechanics.[29]

To recapitulate: following their instrumentalist creed, philosophical pragmatists object to escapism, evasion of real human problems in favor of questions whose answers could have no bearing on life. They take the most prominent example of such a question in contemporary analytical philosophy to be "could I be a brain in a vat?" But this question arises naturally if we think there is a world external to us that is independent of our concepts and beliefs, a world that those beliefs (or statements of them) can more or less accurately represent. If they can succeed, they can fail, and if they can fail they can fail completely. Therefore, says the antiskeptical pragmatist, there is not a world external to us.

Now speaking as a simple country lawyer, I have trouble seeing how *this* view—Rorty's metaphysical antirealism (or alternatively Putnam's "internal realism")—is supposed to help deal with those "real human problems" which the pragmatists say philosophers should work on. As Thomas Nagel has said of metaphysical realism "the problem is to explain [it] in a nontrivial way that cannot easily be admitted by everyone."[30] It takes someone intimately familiar with the structures of argumentation developed within philosophy to make anything of the debate between realists and antirealists. The disputants are not arguing over whether there is a "fact of the matter" about, say, whether O.J. Simpson killed Nicole Brown. Rorty, Putnam, Goodman, Davidson, and the rest of the antirealists all agree that there is such a fact of the matter. Contrary to misunderstandings made popular in the current culture wars, none of them believes that thinking or saying it to be so (or not so) has any tendency to make it so (or not so) with respect to whether O.J. did it. On this they have no disagreement with Nagel, Bernard Williams, Searle, and the realists.

It seems, then, that in answering the traditional philosophers' impractical epistemological skepticism, the pragmatists have been driven to an equally impractical and purely contemplative philosophical position: metaphysical antirealism. In terms of Luban's distinction, actual philosophical pragmatists turn out to be Athenians rather than Trattenbachers; they are as impractical, in the Trattenbachian sense, as their opponents. This makes their antirealism (or internal realism) entirely irrelevant to disputes between pragmatists and their opponents within legal theory, where all sides agree that theory should be practical in the mundane sense that it should bear on outcomes reached by the legal system.

One conclusion from this might be that contemporary philosophical pragmatists are falsely appropriating the label they inherit from James and Dewey, because they have abandoned the pragmatic agent's perspective to go off on a purely speculative philosophical frolic. Before I say more about how I think legal pragmatism stands free of the debates about pragmatism in philosophy, let me say why this seems wrong—why contemporary pragmatist philosophers seem to me to have stayed within their tradition, even as they argue against metaphysical realism.

One of Dewey's best ideas was what he called "the continuum of ends-means."[31] We find it useful to distinguish between means and ends in practical deliberation, he said, and this tempts us to suppose that we can readily sort entities in the world into the one category or the other. But this is not so. Very few valued activities are done solely for their own sake, with no hope of future reward; or conversely solely for the sake of something else, with no intrinsic satisfaction. Activities that come close to the purely consummatory (cocaine snorting?) or purely instrumental (boring work for money?) are likely to be pathological, not prototypical, cases. Good work is satisfying as well as remunerative; good play is instructive as well as fun. To take Dewey's own favorite example, art is not pursued purely for art's sake, but rather aesthetic experience works to expand the horizons and capacities of the artist or audience as well as giving immediate satisfaction; and the better the art, the more its lasting effects outweigh its momentary ones.[32] The economist's categories of consumption and production do not classify actual human activities, but rather distinguish the consummatory and instrumental aspects that are blended in different proportions in most such activities. And one aspect of the human capacity for language and culture is that activities undertaken at first mainly as means to immediate ends can become valued in themselves, and then can be transformed by their practitioners in pursuit of the new satisfactions they open up. Mathematics begins as practical counting and measuring, and becomes (*pace* the parents of Trattenbach) a wondrous body of abstractions elaborated mainly for their own sake, whose further practical applications come as unintended consequences.

The ends-means continuum was Dewey's answer, and remains the best answer, to the common charge that pragmatism is philistine. Human beings develop activities as they pursue satisfactions in an experimental and culturally inventive spirit, and pursue these activities in turn as they prove fruitful of satisfactions both immediate and remote. Art, pure mathematics, music, gardening, sport, exploration, all justify themselves in this way. These are forms of activity that are not necessary to the survival of the species or of any given society, but which give moderate satisfaction to many people, and each of which is supremely meaningful and absorbing to a few.

Why cannot the same be said of contemplative philosophy, including the speculation surrounding the brain-in-a-vat question and the externality of the world? The legal pragmatist and lifelong philosophical amateur Holmes accounted for philosophy in terms just like these when writing to his friend, the professional philosopher Morris Cohen: "Man is like a strawberry plant, the shoots that he throws out take root and become independent centres. And one illustration of the tendency is the transformation of means into ends. . . . Until now it never occurred to me I think that the same is true of philosophy . . . Philosophy as a fellow once said to me is only thinking. Thinking is an instrument of adjustment to the conditions of life—but it becomes an end in itself."[33] But most full-time philosophers are not able to see their work in this spirit. They continue to write as if they were debating foundational issues, even when they have explicitly conceded that human inquiry can and does go ahead quite independently of philosophers' debates over whether knowledge is possible or not.

Thus Luban writes that "[t]he main problems of philosophy connect so intimately with our other intellectual concerns that they await us on every path we might take. They can be ignored only by closing our eyes as we flee."[34] This turns the pragmatist charge of escapism against itself, implying that we can escape the problems of knowledge, of other minds, and of the external world only by a kind of willful blindness or intellectual cowardice. But it is surely not the case that every thoughtful and courageous person must wrestle with the riddle of the brain in the vat, or with how external the world is. Philosophy is not compulsory, in the way that religion is in the eyes of a true believer. People need not be ashamed if they have no taste for metaphysics and epistemology, and instead put their energy into development economics, low-temperature physics, Chinese poetry, or antitrust law, to mention only some intellectual pursuits.

A related fallacy is what might be called cultural foundationalism, the argument that valuable social practices are undermined when speculative philosophy goes astray. After noting that "the antirealist takes his car to a mechanic to get it fixed and brushes his teeth, just as if he believed they were objects in an external world," John Searle goes on to say that antirealism in metaphysics "is an essential component of the attacks on epistemic objectivity, rationality, truth, and intelligence in contemporary intellectual life," and that establishing the truth of metaphysical realism is "[t]he first step in combating irrationalism" in western culture.[35] But his own remark about fixing cars and brushing teeth suggests why this is bad sociology of knowledge. Only a tiny fraction of people come close to understanding what is at stake in the debates between realists and antirealists in metaphysics, and if there is a dangerous upsurge of irrationalism in our culture—as indeed there seems to be—these people are no part of it.[36] It is the people who stop (doing the equivalent of) brushing their teeth and getting their car serviced who are the problem.

On the pragmatist side, one finds similarly overheated statements of what is at stake in the epistemological and metaphysical debates. Rorty has spoken of the "shame" of philosophy professors who "infect the freshmen" by treating the brain-in-a-vat question as a live one.[37] But when professors agitate freshmen by introducing them to Romantic poetry or Mayan archaeology or Cantorian set theory, does anyone send for the doctor? As a freshman myself, I was drawn to philosophy by Descartes, Berkeley, and Hume on the external world. I did not experience my fascination as diseased then, and reflecting back on it, after reading Rorty and Putnam on the one hand and Nagel and Cavell on the other, all with pleasure and profit, I still do not. Nor do I see how our culture is diminished if university philosophy departments continue to teach these problems as central to their subject.[38]

Rorty writes with large cultural projects in mind: he wants to continue the Enlightenment critique of supernatural religion, while raising the cultural prestige of the humanities vis-à-vis the natural sciences, and hanging onto (indeed spreading) liberal political values and institutions. But as someone with roughly similar cultural politics, I cannot see that these projects have any significant contact with whether the brain-in-a-vat problem is taught in Philosophy 101, any more than with whether metered or free verse dominates the poetry magazines, or whether formalists or Platonists are in charge of the courses on metamathematics.

Still speaking from my outsider's perspective, I like the way Robert Nozick describes the pursuit of first philosophy.[39] Philosophical questions ask for explanations of how something can be possible, given something else; for instance, given that any of our beliefs might be false, how can we know anything? No result we reached in such an investigation would purport to undermine the working standards by which we assess claims based on evidence and argument, *pace* Searle. Nor is the pursuit of philosophical explanations compulsory on pain of having one's character impugned, *pace* Luban.

In describing philosophy this way, Nozick does not trivialize it. He says that the problems of first philosophy make him "tremble," and he treats the philosophical understanding as "intrinsically valuable." But he "would not try to bludgeon anyone into needing or wanting it."[40] He offers us a contemporary version of Hume's freedom of movement between the world of common life, where the question of generalized skepticism could not arise, and his study, where it was all-absorbing.

So philosophical pragmatism involves some of its practitioners in first philosophy, and is none the worse for that. Its relationship to the agent perspective and the instrumental or evolutionary account of inquiry is genealogical—and it is nonetheless pragmatist for that. Pragmatists ask, in assessing theories, what good they are for anything. But an answer to this question must, pragmatically, take context into account. In the philosophical context, it is enough that a question should provoke wonder or curiosity, and should lead on to interesting arguments, explanations, or speculations. As an outsider, a philosophical amateur, I am inclined to wish that pragmatist philosophers would drop the charge of escapism from their arsenal. I do not see how the agent perspective that is central to pragmatism condemns metaphysics or epistemology across the board, any more than it condemns number theory or ancient history.[41]

Now let me come back to law, and say some more about why I think legal pragmatism can stand free of pragmatism in philosophy. One part of the answer is implicit in what I have just said; legal theory is necessarily practical in a way philosophy is not. Law may suggest genuine philosophical problems worth pursuing for their own sake, but when it does, the ensuing discussions hive off from legal theory and join speculative philosophy.[42] And if we look at the concerns of pragmatist legal theorists, we can see that these are quite different from those of pragmatist philosophers.

Recall what legal pragmatists are up to these days. As against the jurisprudential grand theorists—the proponents of law-and-economics, hermeneutics, committed critique, and updated natural law—pragmatists remind lawyers that their activities are complex and multifarious, and unlikely to be completely accounted for by any single theory, however compelling its application in any particular context. As against the much more numerous antitheoretical lawyers, pragmatists argue that the grand theories, understood as partial perspectives, do not cancel each other out but rather can all contribute to the understanding of law. The proof of the pudding is in the eating, but if the practical lawyer won't try the pudding on the ground that meat and potatoes are good enough, the test can't be run.

Stated in general terms, pragmatist jurisprudence is a theoretical middle way between grand theorizing and anti-intellectual business as usual. The latter is usually the prevailing jurisprudence of those with the most influence on the working legal system, but the best response to neglect of theory is not a pragmatist jurisprudential sermon, but a concrete demonstration of how theoretical approaches can help solve practical problems. It is against those who claim to have found the one true theoretical way that it makes sense to counterpose pragmatist theory in general terms, and in the last generation legal academia has seen quite a lot of theoretical grandiosity.

Countering this tendency, though, does not depend in the slightest degree on accepting any of the arguments against metaphysical realism, or for that matter epistemological foundationalism.[43] That point has two other implications. First, a lawyer may be completely uninterested in the issues these philosophers debate with their opponents, and yet find legal pragmatism as I have described it a congenial account of the place of theory in law. Second, another lawyer may be very interested in the relevant philosophical debates, and be completely opposed to everything Rorty and Putnam (or James, or Dewey) stand for philosophically, and yet may be a pragmatist in legal theory.

Let me illustrate this latter point by imagining a dialogue with a friend who is a real absolutist, a theologically conservative Protestant with a serious interest in philosophy.[44] This person is as far removed as he could be from philosophical pragmatism as it is now understood. He is an external realist in metaphysics, believing that the ultimate reality is an infinite transcendent God, and that God's creation forms an immediate reality entirely independent of human thought and language. An epistemological foundationalist, he takes Descartes' thought experiment in the original Cartesian spirit, believing that we might indeed be entirely deceived about the external world if we were in the hands of an Evil Deceiver, but that the beneficent as well as omnipotent God who created us would not have made our senses and reason incorrigibly deceptive. As a finite and temporal being, my friend believes that God, who is infinite and eternal, must remain in certain respects mysterious to mortal capacities. But he thinks much can be known with certainty by human natural reason, while the faithful can know still more when reason is aided by revelation.

By contrast, I am an atheistic pragmatist whose favorite philosopher is Dewey; and I believe that human beings are just biological organisms endowed by natural selection with large brains and a capacity for language. But though there is no hope that my friend and I can agree about these matters, that is not the end of our talk. My friend is sure he is right, and yet he also realizes that he sees everything through the lens of his faith. He does hope that I (and indeed everyone) will come to share his Christian faith, but he expects this to come about, if at all, through Divine grace, not through proof or rational argument. He thinks that many things are beyond rational demonstration, including the very existence of God, as well as many of the details of his faith; and indeed some aspects of his creed (the mysteries) he recognizes as rationally inexplicable. I am sure enough for practical purposes that I am right, too, but at the same time I think that people's deepest beliefs are strongly conditioned by background, experience, and temperament, and therefore disagreement among reasonable people on fundamentals is to be expected.

Making our respective allowances for each other, we agree to disagree about first philosophy, and then turn to law, where we start to find common ground. My friend talks about original sin and rendering unto Caesar where I use a different vocabulary, but we agree that law is a temporal enterprise largely devoted to finding less disagreeable ways of dealing with disagreements. We both think that the rule of law is an important aspect of a good society, and that it is the political ideal of most direct concern to lawyers in their work. That means trying to find rules and procedures for settling disputes that can win wider agreement than does the subject matter of the underlying disputes themselves, and finding ways to guard against the abuse of the power needed to enforce rules and settle disputes. Rules of conduct made according to established procedures, administered by responsible officials, with factual and interpretive disputes subject to resolution by independent judges, are the main devices that our tradition has come up with along these lines, and we agree that these work better than any readily available arrangements that have any prospect of winning broad acceptance.

This makes us liberal constitutionalists, but not quite yet legal pragmatists. Before getting to that, we stop to note a further disagreement between us, which has to do with our liberalism. My friend is a *political* liberal, in Rawls' sense; he thinks the basic liberal rights are important to the maintenance of a reasonably just society. But unlike me, he is not an ethical liberal or pluralist. I value the autonomy of each person in forming individual conceptions of the good life, and think of the diversity of conceptions that result from this as a positive good. He accepts the absolute sovereignty of God, and believes that the single overriding goal of human life is salvation; in his view, the greatest human good would be for all persons to see this truth and live accordingly. But given the actual diversity of conceptions of the good that exist in the world, he also values freedom from coercive imposition of an official conception of the good, and is prepared to respect that freedom even if he and his coreligionists become politically dominant. When asked if this is not a mere political compromise (what Rawls calls a modus vivendi), he says that it is indeed part of a way of living together, but one that is rooted in facts that are likely to persist, facts like the fall of humankind and the legacy of original sin.

As we come back to the subject of law, my friend and I agree that this difference in our philosophical conception of liberalism does not affect the main features of our view of what law is about or what it can do. We now start to talk about some things we have in common on which we disagree with other lawyers of our acquaintance, both religious and secular. We both like abstract thought and theory, and are mindful of the emotional and aesthetic power ideas can have for people like ourselves. We agree that many lawyers are drawn to the profession by a mixture of intellectuality and worldliness, a fondness for ideas combined with the ambition to exercise power. We agree that people with this combination of qualities have a dangerous tendency to be attracted to a theory by its elegance, conclude that it is true, and move to implement it, without recognizing how much of what drew them to the theory was its esthetic component. People of this kind think of us as wishy-washy or lukewarm; we think of them as scary simplifiers.

We believe that any working system of law is a complex social practice made up mostly of habits, tacit beliefs, and implicit patterns of interaction, and that any explicit theory is likely to miss much of this tacit dimension. Imposing legal theory on practice from the top down is likely to have unforeseen consequences. Theory meant to guide practice should take existing practice as the starting point and try to move it in the direction the theory suggests, stopping frequently to check whether the intended improvements are indeed occurring, and also checking for other unexpected side-effects good or bad.

My friend says that the creed of his faith is, among other things, a set of truths and precepts designed to guide practice. He accepts its authority as absolute where it speaks, but thinks there are many matters on which it does not speak with a clear voice. He finds that many of his coreligionists hear their faith speaking with a clearer voice on a wider range of issues than he does—especially issues that involve the regulation of conduct and the resolution of disputes among people who are in serious (and, for the moment at least, intractable) disagreement of the kind he and I have just been discussing.

Similarly, I note my respect for natural science. I think its internal logic is to seek an objective account of reality, aiming to make precise generalizations that hold good independent of context and observer, and I also think that much of its success stems from this effort to view the world "from nowhere." But I also find many of my fellow secularists dogmatically scientistic, tending to extend the claims and methods of science to matters on which it does not speak clearly—especially the complex and confounded human and social phenomena with which law is mainly concerned.

At this point (or perhaps after more discussion along the same lines) my friend and I find that we can agree on the general approach to law that I have called pragmatist, the jurisprudence common to the main line of American legal theorists in this century. Law is contextual: it is rooted in practice and custom, and takes its substance from existing patterns of human conduct and interaction. To an equal degree, law is instrumental, meant to advance the human good of those it serves, hence subject to alteration to achieve this end. Law so conceived is a set of practical measures for cooperative social life, using signals and sanctions to guide and channel conduct. More precise and determinate general theories of the nature and function of law should be viewed with suspicion, at least when put forward to control practice. Finally, we agree that law itself imposes no absolute moral claims, though the rule of law is a political ideal worthy of respect and thus to be weighed in any individual's deliberations about what he or she finally should do.[45]

This jurisprudential view descends historically from philosophical pragmatism, which at least in its most prominent current manifestation (Rorty's version) has pervasively secular and naturalistic presuppositions that many religious believers cannot accept.[46] It has been developed by legal thinkers in whose jurisprudence religious conceptions play no substantial role. But nothing in it is incompatible with belief in a transcendent

God who rules over a creation in which human beings, though fallen, may know absolute truths. My friend thus turns out to be a pragmatist for legal purposes, though not a pragmatist all the way down. As such he dramatizes the claim that legal pragmatism can and should stand free from the philosophical commitments that are generally understood to define pragmatism today, and from philosophical comprehensive views more generally.

Notes

1 John Rawls, *Political Liberalism* (New York: Columbia University Press, 1993). Since the first publication of the book, Rawls has made clear that his primary purpose has been to argue for the compatibility of liberalism with devout religious faith of the kind that rejects secular humanism: "Thus the question should be more sharply put this way: How is it possible for those affirming a religious doctrine that is based on religious authority, for example the Church or the Bible, also to hold a reasonable political conception that supports a just democratic regime?" Introduction to the paperback edition of *Political Liberalism* (forthcoming), 2.

2 I described it that way myself in Thomas C. Grey, "Holmes and Legal Pragmatism," *Stanford Law Review* 41 (1989): 787–870, at 788.

3 Richard Rorty, *Philosophy and the Mirror of Nature* (Princeton, N.J.: Princeton University Press, 1979).

4 Richard Rorty, *Philosophical Papers*, vol. 1, *Objectivity, Relativism, and Truth* (New York: Cambridge University Press, 1991), pt. 2, pp. 113–72; for Davidson's response, see "A Coherence Theory of Truth and Knowledge," in Alan Malachowski, ed., *Reading Rorty*, ed. Alan Malachowski (Cambridge: Basil Blackwell, 1990), pp. 134–37.

5 Richard Rorty, "Cavell on Skepticism," in *Consequences of Pragmatism: Essays, 1972–1980* (Minneapolis: University of Minnesota Press, 1982), p. 179. For the latest of Rorty's many programmatic statements to the same effect, see "Philosophy and the Future," in *Rorty and Pragmatism: The Philosopher Responds to His Critics*, ed. Herman J. Saatkamp (Nashville: Vanderbilt University Press, 1995), pp. 197–205; see also Rorty, "The Priority of Democracy to Philosophy" in Rorty, *Objectivity, Relativism, and Truth*, 175–96; and Rorty, *Philosophy and the Mirror of Nature*, 389–94.

6 See Cornel West, *The American Evasion of Philosophy* (Madison: University of Wisconsin Press, 1989), p. 5 ("evasion of epistemology-centered philosophy" in favor of "a continuous cultural commentary or set of interpretations that attempt to explain America to itself at a particular historical moment"); Hilary Putnam, "The Permanence of William James," in *Pragmatism: An Open Question* (Cambridge, Mass.: Blackwell, 1995), pp. 5–26, esp. 22–23.

7 Oliver Wendell Holmes, "John Marshall," in *The Collected Works of Justice Holmes: Complete Public Writings and Selected Judicial Opinions of Oliver Wendell Holmes*, ed. Sheldon M. Novick (Chicago: University of Chicago Press, 1995), vol. 3, p. 502.

8 Oliver Wendell Holmes, "Law in Science and Science in Law," in *Collected Works of Justice Holmes*, ed. Novick, vol. 3, p. 406.

9 See Grey, "Holmes and Legal Pragmatism," pp. 805–15; on Holmes' relation to Peirce, James, and Dewey, see *ibid.*, pp. 864–70.

10   John Dewey, in *My Philosophy of Law: Credos of Sixteen American Scholars,* Julius Rosenthal Foundation (Boston: Boston Law Book, 1941), pp. 71–85.

11   See generally Richard A. Posner, *Economic Analysis of Law,* 4th ed. (Boston: Little, Brown, 1992).

12   For some of the many varieties of contemporary hermeneutic approaches to law, see Ronald M. Dworkin, *Law's Empire* (Cambridge: Harvard University Press, 1986); James Boyd White, *Justice as Translation* (Chicago: University of Chicago Press, 1990); Ronald R. Garet, "Comparative Normative Hermeneutics: Scripture, Literature, Constitution," *Southern California Law Review* 58 (1985): 35–134; Anthony T. Kronman, *The Lost Lawyer: Failing Ideals of the Legal Profession* (Cambridge: Harvard University Press, 1993).

13   The recent Critical schools of jurisprudence, including Critical Legal Studies, Feminist Jurisprudence, and Critical Race Theory, have taken theoretical inspiration from a variety of sources, including Frankfurt School neo-Marxism, Foucauldian genealogical critique, deconstruction, American Legal Realism and its closely related American radical debunking tradition (Veblen, Galbraith), feminist theory, "anticolonial" cultural studies (Bourdieu), and race-based radical theory (Du Bois, Fanon).

14   John Finnis, *Natural Law and Natural Rights* (Oxford, England: Clarendon Press, 1979); Michael Moore, "Moral Reality," *Wisconsin Law Review* 1982: 1061–115; Ernest J. Weinrib, *The Idea of Private Law* (Cambridge: Harvard University Press, 1995). See also the recent revival of an explicitly theistic jurisprudential perspective: Stephen L. Carter, *The Culture of Disbelief: How American Law and Politics Trivialize Religious Devotion* (New York: Basic Books, 1993); Anthony E. Cook, "The Death of God in American Pragmatism and Realism: Resurrecting the Value of Love in Contemporary Jurisprudence," *Georgetown Law Journal* 82 (1994): 1431–1517; Kent Greenawalt, *Private Consciences and Public Reasons* (New York: Oxford University Press, 1995).

15   On this score, I have had trouble understanding Richard Rorty's objections to what he calls "universalism"; a pragmatist would not rule out a priori the possibility of enforceable practical measures against agreed forms of cruelty and oppression. Indeed Rorty's own utopia includes a picture of "a planet-wide democracy in which torture, or the closing down of a university or a newspaper, on the other side of the world is as much a cause for outrage as when it happens at home." "Philosophy and the Future," 203. But sometimes he writes as though he would support such measures only if all the parties to the convention would stipulate that nothing they had read in a philosophy book had influenced them to sign on. See, e.g., *Contingency, Irony, and Solidarity* (New York: Cambridge University Press, 1989), pp. 189–98; "Cosmopolitanism without Emancipation: A Response to Jean-François Lyotard" in *Objectivity, Relativism, and Truth,* 211–22. Other times he simply seems to think that universalist rhetoric, like calling cruelty and oppression "inhumanity," gets in the way of the practical attainment of universal measures; see his "Justice as a Larger Loyalty" (forthcoming). I tend to disagree with the practical judgment—and to suspect that Rorty's oversensitive nose for remnants of theology has led him astray in making it.

16   C. C. Langdell, *A Summary of the Law of Contracts,* 2d ed. (Boston: Little, Brown, 1880), p. 21.

17   Weinrib, *Idea of Private Law,* p. 21. An important difference from Langdell is that Weinrib would not say that the justice of outcomes is irrelevant to their legality; indeed the legality of private law outcomes *is* their justice for Weinrib, but justice of a pecu-

liarly private-lawish kind—corrective justice. Weinrib also has acute discussions of Aristotle's and Kant's notions of corrective justice, which Langdell would have seen as disqualifying his work as juristic science, and converting its genre to philosophy. See also Dworkin, *Law's Empire*, pp. 176–224. The case is complex because Dworkin does link legal integrity to a political value, fraternity, or community. A pragmatist interpretation of the legal virtue that lawyers invoke when they criticize "unprincipled" decisions would relate it to extrajudicial conceptions of justice as consistency (treating like cases alike), and to the heuristic value of system in law.

18 See "Holmes and Legal Pragmatism," pp. 793–815, where I first describe pragmatic instrumentalism and contextualism as developed by philosophers (Dewey, supplemented by Rorty), and then (p. 805) purport to "apply" these "tenets" to law and emerge with the pragmatist jurisprudence of Holmes. For Luban's essay, see his *Legal Modernism* (Ann Arbor: University of Michigan Press, 1994), pp. 125–78. This is the place to thank David Luban for all he has done to enlighten me on this subject, both in the essay in question and in private correspondence; he is the model of a good philosophical interlocutor.

19 *Ibid.,* 126.

20 John Dewey, *The Quest for Certainty: A Study of the Relation of Knowledge and Action* (1929; reprint, New York: G. P. Putnam's Sons, 1960). But, significantly, Dewey nowhere proposed the abandonment of speculation for its own sake.

21 Rorty, "Priority of Democracy to Philosophy"; Rorty, "Philosophy and the Future."

22 Cf. Bertrand Russell, "Pragmatism," in *Philosophical Essays* (New York: Simon & Schuster, 1966), pp. 110–11: "Pragmatism appeals to the temper of mind which finds on the surface of this planet the whole of its imaginative material," but "for those . . . who do not find Man an adequate object of their worship, the pragmatist's world will seem narrow and petty." See also his reference to Dewey's philosophy as representing "cosmic impiety," (Bertrand Russell, *A History of Western Philosophy,* New York: Simon & Schuster, 1972, 828), which is echoed in Thomas Nagel's criticism of philosophical contextualism (which he identifies with idealism) as showing "a lack of humility" and "an attempt to cut the universe down to size" (Thomas Nagel, *The View from Nowhere,* New York: Oxford University Press, 1986), p. 109.

23 Luban, *Legal Modernism*, pp. 125, 129.

24 Bernard Williams, *Descartes: The Project of Pure Enquiry* (Atlantic Highlands, N.J.: Humanities Press, 1978) and *Ethics and the Limits of Philosophy* (Cambridge: Harvard University Press, 1985), chap. 8 (on "the absolute conception"); Stanley Cavell, *The Claim of Reason: Wittgenstein, Skepticism, Morality, and Tragedy* (New York: Oxford University Press, 1979); Barry Stroud, *The Significance of Philosophical Scepticism* (New York: Oxford University Press, 1984); Robert Nozick, *Philosophical Explanations* (Cambridge: Harvard University Press, 1981); Nagel, *View from Nowhere;* Michael Williams, *Unnatural Doubts: Epistemological Realism and the Basis of Skepticism* (Cambridge, Mass.: Basil Blackwell, 1991); John R. Searle, *The Construction of Social Reality* (New York: Free Press, 1995). David Luban argues to this same effect in his critical essay on legal pragmatism, "Doubts about the New Pragmatism." Of the writers listed, at least Michael Williams and Searle think they have effective responses to the skeptic, but consider the skeptical challenge important to confront.

25 David Hume, *Enquiries Concerning Human Understanding and Concerning the Principles of Morals,* edited by L. A. Selby-Bigge, 3d ed. (London: Oxford University Press, 1975), sec. 12, pt. 2, p. 160.

26 Putnam, *Pragmatism,* pp. 20–21.
27 And again: "The heart of pragmatism ... is the supremacy of the agent point of view. If we find we must ... use a certain 'conceptual system,' when we are engaged in practical activity, in the widest sense of 'practical activity,' then we must not simultaneously advance the claim that it is not really 'the way things are in themselves.'" Hilary Putnam, *The Many Faces of Realism* (LaSalle, Ill.: Open Court Press, 1987), p. 70.
28 See Hilary Putnam, *Realism With a Human Face,* ed. James Conant (Cambridge: Harvard University Press, 1990), pp. 3–29; Rorty, *Objectivity, Relativism, and Truth,* pp. 126–50. Rorty and Putnam also differ in their analysis of truth, which Putnam treats (or sometimes has treated) as idealized warranted assertibility, while Rorty treats it simply as the unanalyzable ultimate compliment that we pay to approved statements. I will stay away from debates over pragmatist and other theories of truth in what follows, on the ground that these debates quite clearly have nothing to do with jurisprudential questions.
29 Nagel, *View from Nowhere,* pp. 95–98. He says: "The realism I am defending says the world may be inconceivable to *our* minds, and the idealism [or pragmatism] I am opposing says it could not be." Justice Holmes, whom I have called a pragmatist, wrote "the universe has more in it than we understand ... the private soldiers have not been told the plan of campaign, or even that there is one, rather than some vaster unthinkable to which every predicate is an impertinence." (Oliver Wendell Holmes, "Natural Law," in *Collected Works of Justice Holmes,* ed. Novick, vol. 3, p. 448.
30 Nagel, *View From Nowhere,* p. 90.
31 John Dewey, *Theory of Valuation* (Chicago: University of Chicago Press, 1939), pp. 40–50.
32 John Dewey, *Art as Experience* (New York: Minton, Balch & Co., 1934); John Dewey, *Experience and Nature,* 2d ed. (LaSalle, Ill.: Open Court Press, 1965).
33 Leonora Rosenfield, ed., *Portrait of a Philosopher: Morris R. Cohen in Life and Letters* (New York: Harcourt, Brace & World, 1962), p. 321.
34 Luban, *Legal Modernism,* 169. Wittgenstein said: "The real discovery is the one that makes me capable of stopping philosophy when I want to" (Ludwig Wittgenstein, *Philosophical Investigations,* 2d ed., Oxford: Basil Blackwell, 1958, pt. I, para. 133). The skeptical philosophical questions certainly arise "naturally" in the sense that they arise within the order of nature, but they do not arise for most people, and do not prove pressing even to most people for whom they do arise.
35 Searle, *Construction of Social Reality,* p. 197.
36 It is true that some badly confused legal and literary writers cite Rorty in their footnotes, generally in support of incoherent relativist positions that he has warned against. Similar writers used to cite Kuhn, and before that Heisenberg or Einstein.
37 Rorty, "Cavell on Skepticism," pp. 175, 179.
38 Putnam speaks of "the human metaphysical urge," but argues that "the time has come for a moratorium on Ontology and a moratorium on Epistemology." But he is unable to comply with his own edict: "Or rather, the time has come for a moratorium on the kind of ontological speculation that seeks to describe the Furniture of the Universe and what is Really There and what is Only a Human Projection, and for a moratorium on the kind of epistemological speculation that seeks to tell us the One Method by which all our beliefs can be appraised" (Putnam, *Realism With A Human Face,* pp. 105, 118).
39 Nozick, *Philosophical Explanations,* 1–24.
40 *Ibid.,* 10.

41 Dewey's *Experience and Nature,* 2d ed. (New York: Dover Publications, 1958), for example, seems to me a masterpiece of pragmatist metaphysics, as does Heidegger's *Being
and Time,* translated by John Macquarrie and Edward Robinson (New York: Harper,
1962). Quite consistently, Rorty thinks these books represent the less valuable side of
their authors' work; see Rorty, "Overcoming the Tradition: Heidegger and Dewey," and
"Dewey's Metaphysics," in *Consequences of Pragmatism,* 37–59, 72–89.

42 The clearest example is the philosophical discussion of free will, which may proceed
unconstrained by any need to end up with workable proposals for dealing with issues of
civil or criminal responsibility. These discussions may help legal theorists insofar as
they suggest solutions to the practical legal issue, but may also lead to speculative
conclusions that give no useful guidance to legal reform.

43 The point is ironically brought home by Putnam's essay "Are Moral and Legal Values
Made or Discovered?" *Legal Theory* 1 (1995): 5–19. Despite the word "legal" in the title,
the essay is not about law, or the theory of adjudication at all, but about the ontology of
value. Putnam writes that "the question of 'hard cases' [theory of adjudication] is really
outside my expertise"; he is willing to suppose (relying on Dworkin) that moral questions play a role in legal reasoning, but "what weight they have, and what role they
legitimately may play in the final decision, is a question to be settled by legal reasoning
rather than by moral reasoning." It left unclear what bearing realism versus antirealism
in meta-ethics has on any legal question.

44 Secular humanists who find this conjunction oxymoronic, or at least implausible,
should re-examine their prejudices. I run my thought experiment with a Protestant
Christian; it would sound somewhat different, but I suspect a comparable exercise
would be possible, with a Catholic, Orthodox Jew, or Muslim.

45 Within the pragmatist consensus we have reached, we would have to discuss further
whether in a society divided among secularists and varied kinds of religious believers,
the faithful should agree to eschew any attempt to support legal conclusions by religious arguments in official legal forums. See the discussion of "public reason" in
Rawls, *Political Liberalism,* pp. 212–54, as modified in his introduction to the paperback
edition (forthcoming), Rawls' argument for "bracketing out" at least revelation-based
religious claims from public discourse on constitutional questions has not been widely
accepted by religious writers; but see Leslie Griffin, "Good Catholics Should Be Rawlsian Liberals," *Southern California Interdisciplinary Law Journal* 5 (1997): 297–373.

46 James and Peirce were, however, religious believers, as is Cornel West among contemporary pragmatists. For West's account of the relation of religion and pragmatism, see
American Evasion of Philosophy, pp. 150–64 (on Reinhold Niebuhr's "Christian pragmatism"), and 233. West's and Niebuhr's religious (and associated philosophical) views are
compatible with philosophical pragmatism in a way my more theologically conservative friend's views are not.

What's Pragmatic about Legal Pragmatism?

DAVID LUBAN

Does legal pragmatism have anything at all to do with pragmatism? Both Thomas Grey and Richard Posner suggest that in important respects the answer is no. Grey tells us that even a devout antipragmatist in matters ontological can endorse legal pragmatism, while Posner adds the converse, that pragmatic philosophy may at times impel a judge to decide cases like a formalist. These conclusions suggest that talk of legal pragmatism may simply be a pun on what philosophers take pragmatism to be. Lest this appear a far-fetched suggestion, remember that in philosophy the word "realism" often refers to the belief that abstract entities such as laws *really* exist, while in law "realism" refers to the opposite, to the belief that abstract entities such as laws do not exist. I am not suggesting that legal pragmatism is the opposite of philosophical pragmatism, as legal realism is the opposite of philosophical realism; but if Grey is right, legal and philosophical pragmatism need have nothing whatever to do with each other.

I

Grey and Posner agree to a considerable extent on what legal pragmatism is. It is, first of all, *eclecticism.* The pragmatist mistrusts the pretensions of totalizing Big Think theories to capture all that is important in law. The pragmatist is willing to give every theory a hearing, however, and to appropriate insights from any source if they seem useful.

Second, legal pragmatism is *result oriented* or *instrumental.* Its focus is the well-being of the community, not the purity or integrity of legal doctrine. Pragmatists nevertheless recognize that conforming to inherited legal doctrine and attending to history may be good for the community, so doctrinal integrity remains instrumentally important. Pursuing the good of *this* community requires us to know and respect its unique history. Thus a pragmatist is *historically minded* though, oddly enough, this is for entirely future-directed reasons. Finally, and this is the fourth feature of legal pragmatism as Grey and Posner describe it, formalism is always the enemy of pragmatism. By formalism, I mean cabining legal analysis to logical and analogical manipulation of pre-existing doctrine. In sum, for both Grey and Posner, a legal pragmatist is an eclectic, result-oriented, historically minded antiformalist.

I want to stress that, in their present papers at least, that is *all* a legal pragmatist is. If so, it is unsurprising that legal pragmatism doesn't have much to do with philosophical pragmatism, because you can reach these same four very general features from a wide variety of philosophical perspectives. Take eclecticism. All that you need to reject Totalizing Legal Theory is a recognition that "law" is not a single, well-defined object of study, any more than art, or science, or history are single, well-defined objects of study. To hold that a single theory explains everything legal is to have an objectionably narrow concept of the legal. You do not have to be a philosophical pragmatist to see that.

Likewise, virtually everyone agrees that legal decision-making cannot simply disregard history or pre-existing doctrine. Indeed, that is legal pragmatism's bow to formalism; or, in Posner's canine imagery, it is the "bone" he is willing to toss to his formalist and positivist colleagues. (Posner evidently thinks that formalism is a dog's dinner.)

Being result-oriented is a bit more controversial, but here too legal pragmatists are far from unique. They are joined by utilitarians, even when the utilitarians are metaethical antipragmatists who believe that the principle of utility represents objective moral truth. Actually, legal pragmatists are also joined in their instrumentalism by Thomistic natural lawyers who argue that law is directed to the common good. Even Kant connected laws with the well-being of the community. When all is said, very few people think that lawyers should be indifferent to the outcomes of legal decisions. *Fiat lex, pereat mundi!* is a maxim that could be accepted only by the most dyed-in-the-wool formalist.

Indeed, the only feature of legal pragmatism that cannot be reached from most philosophical positions is antiformalism. Yet formalists acknowledge that courts possess formidable equity powers, and that statutes and regulations frequently vest result-oriented discretion in officials. And we have already seen that legal pragmatists sometimes bow in the direction of formalism. They cannot help it. Formalism means accepting the logical consequences of rules and doctrines that you accept. Pragmatists differ from formalists because they see no inherent virtue in logical consistency if it leads to unacceptable outcomes; what pragmatists seek in legal reasoning is not logical neatness but persuasion in the service of reasonable outcomes. (It is unsurprising, then, that in a recent book Posner takes sides with the ancient sophists against the dialecticians.)[1] However, a legal argument—a judicial opinion, for example, or a rules committee report—will never be persuasive if it commits flagrant logical fouls. Hypocrisy, Rochefoucauld remarked, is the homage that vice pays to virtue; it turns out that hypocrisy is also the homage that sophistry pays to dialectic, because the legal pragmatist persuades best by masquerading as a formalist. In the end, then, the practical difference between legal pragmatism and legal formalism turns out to be one of motivation rather than legal reasoning, and *philosophical* formalists might reject a completely inflexible legal formalism.

The point is that if legal pragmatism is *only* eclectic, result-oriented, historically minded antiformalism, it turns out to be a remarkably uncontroversial doctrine. It stands free of philosophical controversy only because it stands free of *all* controversy, and it avoids controversy by saying very little. This in fact is Grey's conclusion: "Stated in that very general way, legal pragmatist theory is quite banal."

The waters become muddy because as theorists elaborate it, legal pragmatism is far more than eclectic, result-oriented, historically minded antiformalism. Legal pragmatists take stands on a number of vastly more controversial topics. To take one distinguished example, Posner's book on jurisprudence defends a behaviorist treatment of mental states, a soft determinism about free will, a moderate skepticism in epistemology, and an economic conception of rationality. More generally, legal pragmatists seem to favor tough-minded over tender-minded legal theories. They view with suspicion appeals to "soft" concepts such as the Kantian insistence that human beings possess an inherent dignity that is not a price.

At this point, legal pragmatist theory has stopped being banal, and started being controversially philosophical. And at this point, Grey and Posner part company. In the present paper, Posner describes his enterprise as "an issue in 'applied' pragmatism," which clearly suggests that pragmatic philosophy—"pure" pragmatism, if that is not an oxymoron—underwrites Posner's version of legal pragmatism. Grey, on the other hand, argues that legal pragmatism is freestanding, relying on no philosophy in particular, including pragmatic philosophy. Grey's point is a subtle one and a nice one. Nowadays pragmatism is often identified as a philosophical position that rejects the claim that practical activities require philosophical foundations. Grey goes further, arguing that legal pragmatism requires no philosophical foundations *including foundations in the philosophy that says that legal pragmatism requires no philosophical foundations.*

To see more clearly the divide between Grey and Posner, it will help to distinguish two versions of pragmatic philosophy. One, which I will call *philosophical pragmatism,* advances recognizably philosophical theses, supported by recognizably philosophical arguments, and fits comfortably within the ambit of academic philosophy. For example, one canonical version of philosophical pragmatism backs antirealism against realism, defines truth as the ideal end of inquiry rather than correspondence or coherence, defines knowledge in terms of warranted assertibility rather than truth, rejects mind-body dualism, asserts the theory-ladenness of observation statements, denies the analytic-synthetic distinction, argues for epistemological holism against foundationalism, takes a compatibilist view of the free will problem, and naturalizes ethics. Though I do not know whether Posner endorses these positions, his own jurisprudence seems of a piece with philosophical pragmatism—and his legal pragmatism *does* have philosophical foundations, in the sense that it is "applied" philosophical pragmatism. Philosophical pragmatism represents one version of what used to be called "first philosophy," the subjects of metaphysics and epistemology, which nowadays includes philosophical logic, metaethics, and the philosophies of mind, of language, and of science.[2]

More prominent on the present intellectual scene is what I shall call *postphilosophical pragmatism,* of which Richard Rorty is the most distinguished exemplar. Postphilosophical pragmatists are antiphilosophers, who think that all the standard "isms" represent a holdover, or perhaps a hangover, from a worldview that has outlived its usefulness. To the postphilosophical pragmatist, adjudicating among theories of truth is about as useful as adjudicating between the Athanasian and Monophysite doctrines of Christ's Body. And if a philosopher, with long gray beard and glittering eye, wishes to discuss his favorite albatross with you, the pragmatically correct reply is Timothy Leary's contribution to the war on drugs: "Just say 'no thanks.' "

The operational distinction between philosophical and postphilosophical pragmatism is very simple. The philosophical pragmatist defends, let us say, some version of antirealism. The postphilosophical pragmatist rejects the whole question of realism versus antirealism with a polite but firm "no thanks!"

Postphilosophical pragmatists combine classical pragmatic themes with Wittgenstein's understanding of philosophical problems as candidates for therapy rather than solution—wrongly, I think, because as I read him

Wittgenstein was our century's greatest *anti*-pragmatic philosopher. After all, it was Wittgenstein who mocked pragmatism with these questions: "Does man think, then, because he has found that thinking pays?—Because he thinks it advantageous to think? (Does he bring up his children because he has found it pays?)"[3] And it was Wittgenstein who once wrote, "So I am trying to say something that sounds like pragmatism," but then added bitterly, "Here I am being thwarted by a kind of *Weltanschauung*."[4] But Wittgenstein's relationship to pragmatism belongs in another story, and it is time to return to Grey's and Posner's.[5]

II

In our earlier exchange to which Grey kindly alludes, I objected to the postphilosophical pragmatists' efforts to end first philosophy by what seemed to me fiat. Grey, who defended the postphilosophical outlook in "Holmes and Legal Pragmatism," has now come to agree with this objection. As a result, if I understand him correctly, he has come to reject postphilosophical pragmatism, though he retains his admiration for philosophical pragmatism, the metaphysics of Dewey's *Experience and Nature,* for example. His main point, however, is that when it comes to law, it doesn't much matter what position you hold on issues of first philosophy. Here he seems to differ from Posner.

Grey illustrates the irrelevance of first philosophy to law with the example of radical epistemological skepticism, the kind of skepticism founded on Cartesian Deceiver or brain-in-a-vat stories. Grey admits what many pragmatists deny, that radical skepticism is a proper philosophical issue, but then quite properly asks what difference it could possibly make to law.

I find his question an important one, if only because skepticism was my own example of an issue that pragmatists have dismissed on inadequate grounds. Oddly enough, I *do* think it has at least indirect bearing on legal theory. Historically, Learned Hand and Oliver Wendell Holmes defended theories of judicial restraint on grounds of philosophical skepticism. They thought it improper for a judge to override a democratic decision because doing so requires knowledge that no one can have.[6] Now I don't think their arguments are sound, and in that sense at any rate skepticism rightly understood remains irrelevant to law. But it takes some philosophical analysis to show why their arguments fail, and that *is* first philosophy.

There is a more important reason that skepticism bears on legal theory. Skepticism is not an isolated issue. Ultimately, the problem of skepticism derives from the egocentric predicament, what Nietzsche called our inability to look around our own corner.[7] Inevitably, efforts to address skepticism entail all the other philosophical problems that arise from the egocentric predicament—problems of the objectivity of ethics, of the distinction between theories and observation, of free will and determinism, of personal identity. So Grey's question must be broadened: is it possible to "do" law in a way that stands free of all of these issues of first philosophy?

In the end, I will argue that legal pragmatism cannot be freestanding, at least if "legal pragmatism" means anything more ambitious than eclectic, result-oriented, historically minded antiformalism. As a practical matter, however, Grey has to be right. Surely no issue of legal significance can or should turn on the validity of the analytic-synthetic distinction, or even on whether you are an ethical noncognitivist. And if you find judges boning up on Davidson or Derrida or Dummett to decide cases, it is probably time to update your passport and pack your satchel. Shortly, I will take up the question why in greater detail, but for the moment I content myself with the observation that the relationship between pragmatic and nonpragmatic first philosophy, on the one hand, and legal pragmatism in theory and practice, on the other, is remarkably elusive. It is this relationship that I propose to explore.

III

I do not think that Grey's question admits of a simple or straightforward answer, because it runs up against a fundamental question about what the philosophical enterprise is and should be—what hopes philosophy can harbor for itself, what the aims of philosophy are. I myself am deeply ambivalent, and probably deeply confused, about this question. My problem is that the nature of the philosophical enterprise is itself one of the most basic issues in philosophy, and the history of philosophy includes many different answers to the question. Broadly speaking, I think that three of these answers, or families of answers, are particularly influential; at different times, I find them all compelling even though at least the latter two are inconsistent with each other.

The first is uncontroversial, and is the most congenial to contemporary analytic philosophy. On this view, philosophy should not be defined as the study of certain traditional problems, though it includes that study. Rather, philosophy consists in the careful examination of arguments, aiming to clarify concepts, expose fallacies, and eliminate confusions. Since many of these confusions are deeply entrenched in the discourse of the arts, the sciences, and law, philosophical thinking has an important role to play. It is, however, a reactive, housecleaning role. As Posner has put it, "[l]ike most philosophy, all that jurisprudence can do is to arm one against philosophical arguments"—in this case, against the bad philosophical arguments that jurists build into their work.[8]

If philosophy is nothing more than intellectual hygiene, however, the discipline of philosophy would have no connection to law provided jurists refrain from undisciplined philosophizing. If nothing of any worth to a jurist is sacrificed by abjuring philosophy, Grey would then be right that legal pragmatism is freestanding; more generally, that law is freestanding.

On the other hand, philosophy has always harbored ambitions larger than tidying up other people's messy arguments, and if those ambitions are more than sheer vainglory, something of worth *is* sacrificed by abjuring philosophy. When Grey argues that legal pragmatism can stand free of philosophy, I believe that he has the more ambitious conception of philosophy in mind. He does not mean only that if jurists avoid philosophical fallacies then the services of philosophers will not be required; rather, he means that reflection on the traditional main problems of philosophy is unnecessary for a pragmatic approach to law. To think with Grey about this issue, we must consider views of philosophy that make it something more than just another name for clear thinking. I suggest that there are two other pictures of philosophy.

On the first, philosophy is the effort to solve problems. Some of these are extremely difficult, and resonate with profound aspects of human experience: Do we have free will? Are mind and body distinct kinds of entities? Is radical skepticism true? Are values objective? Other problems are more like brain teasers (Newcomb's Problem, or the Paradox of the Unexpected Hanging, are good examples); still others are scholastic attempts to iron out wrinkles in theories. Though problems of these latter kinds may seem uninteresting and unimportant, even brain teasers and theory-debugging often turn out to implicate the main problems of philosophy.

The crucial point about philosophy as problem solving is that its practitioners believe, and perhaps must believe, that their problems have solutions. It seems at least thinkable that someday we will get these problems right, and thus that there is such a thing as progress in philosophy. I think it is fair to say that a great deal of analytic philosophy presumes that something like this picture of philosophy is correct. For that matter, so does a good deal of nonanalytic philosophy. Edmund Husserl, to take a notable example, believed that by inventing phenomenology he had invented a new and rigorous science, a *strenge Wissenschaft* on a par with the natural sciences, with a research program that was fully capable of making discoveries and stockpiling results.

The problem-solving picture of philosophy prevails in analytic jurisprudence as well as analytic first philosophy. Textbooks on analytic jurisprudence address questions such as these: Is positivism true? Does the law contain gaps? Are corporations legal fictions? What is the correct theory of impossible attempts? Who wins the canonical debates—the Hart-Fuller debate on interpretation, the Hart-Devlin debate on legal moralism, the Coleman-Weinrib debate on the foundations of tort liability, the MacKinnon-Ronald Dworkin debate on pornography? Theorists who engage with these questions do so, or at least so it seems, in the expectation that, given sufficient ingenuity and hard work, the questions can be laid to rest once and for all.

Now, if this overall picture of philosophy is correct, then in principle philosophical questions have right and wrong answers, and legal decisions that presuppose philosophical positions can be criticized for getting them wrong. On this line of thinking, we find a straightforward and relatively uncontroversial way in which legal pragmatism cannot be said to be freestanding. Legal decisions will turn on right answers to philosophical questions in the same way that they turn on right answers to factual questions. And a judge who tries to "do" law while ignoring the relevant questions of first philosophy can be accused of intellectual and professional irresponsibility.

There is something undeniably attractive about the picture of philosophy as *strenge Wissenschaft* aimed at formulating, analyzing, and once and for all settling questions, in the sense of discovering the right answers to them. As I mentioned earlier, when one is actually engaged in philosophical inquiry, the picture is virtually inescapable. It would be hard to philosophize if we did not believe that the problems we were working on might yield to our efforts; if nothing else, belief in the problem-solving picture is what Holmes once called "the trick by which nature keeps us at our job."[9]

IV

Nevertheless, there is another picture of the philosophical endeavor, radically different from the picture of philosophy as *strenge Wissenschaft,* that is equally venerable and at least as plausible. This is the view that philosophy doesn't aim to solve problems and doesn't seek to make progress. After all, the history of philosophy hardly looks like a history of cumulative achievement, or even of successful problem-solving within a succession of Kuhnian paradigms. Instead, arguments that at first blush seem novel and decisive turn out on closer inspection to be versions of traditional or even ancient views. Out-of-fashion philosophies undergo periodic refurbishings and resurrections. The most fashionable view in contemporary ethical theory is Aristotle's; Heidegger devoted decades of his career to the study of the presocratic philosophers, who he was convinced hold the key to long-forgotten truth. Or, to take a very different and striking example, two sophisticated recent contributions to analytic epistemology revive arguments attributed to Agrippa, a long-forgotten Hellenistic skeptic.[10] One is tempted to say that the history of philosophy teaches only one enduring lesson: that the day after tomorrow, we will discover that today's breakthrough is a disguised version of yesterday's dead end.

All this suggests that philosophy is not *and never was* problem-solving. Perhaps, as Hannah Arendt thought, it is a kind of Penelope's web, in which what is achieved by day is unwoven by night.[11] In a letter to Mary McCarthy, Arendt explained her conception of philosophy thus:

> [T]hinking is always result-less. That is the difference between "philosophy" and science: Science has results, philosophy never. Thinking starts after an experience of truth has struck home, so to speak. . . . This notion that truth is the result of thought is very old and goes back to ancient classical philosophy, possibly to Socrates himself. If I am right and it is a fallacy, then it probably is the oldest fallacy of Western philosophy.[12]

Arendt is not the only one to believe that the aim of philosophy is not an increase in knowledge, but an attempt to understand the *meaning* of whatever it is that the philosopher is thinking about. Philosophy, Wilfrid Sellars wrote, is the attempt to say "how things in the broadest possible sense of the term hang together in the broadest possible sense of the term."[13] Though Sellars, who is very much a problem-solving philosopher, would most likely disagree, I find implicit in his often-quoted characterization the idea that philosophy does not aim at results, but rather attempts to place the various aspects of our experience in a satisfying system. Sellars is broadly Kantian in his outlook, and thus it is perhaps no coincidence that such systematic ordering is what Kant thought the aim of reason is.

Indeed, it was Kant who first cautioned that although philosophical inquiry may feel like problem solving, the deep fact of the matter is that this feeling represents a kind of illusion. To quote the familiar first sentence of the *Critique of Pure Reason,* "Human reason has this peculiar fate that in one species of its knowledge it is burdened by questions which, as prescribed by the very nature of reason itself, it is not able to ignore, but which, as transcending all its powers, it is also not able to answer."[14] These questions generate endless and in principle undecidable controversies, and Kant explains that "[t]he battle-field of these endless controversies is called metaphysics."[15] Kant's view that philosophical inquiry is at once necessary and doomed to defeat was echoed by Oliver Wendell Holmes, the ancestor of legal pragmatism, in a joke that I think he intended seriously: "I always say the chief end of man is to form general propositions—adding that no general proposition is worth a damn."[16]

Kant believed that the undecidability of philosophical questions is intrinsic to the nature of human reason. There are other explanations as well, however, not nearly so threatening to the picture of philosophy as *strenge Wissenschaft*. Perhaps the problems are solvable, but not by us, because the state of our art is too primitive.[17] A Babylonian astronomer might have wondered what makes the Sun burn, but the state of science would not be in a position to answer the question for 2500 years; that does not make the Babylonian's question in principle undecidable. Perhaps philosophy is like that, and in 2500 years we will know whether determinism is true. In a similar but more pessimistic vein, Colin McGinn has argued that although philosophical problems may be solvable in principle, our mental abilities evolved for purposes very different from metaphysical speculation, and simply are not up to the task, any more than a dog's mental abilities are up to doing long division.[18] Still another explanation is that philosophical problems are solvable *and have been solved*. The catch is that once a philosophical problem gets solved, we no longer call it philosophy. Zeno's paradoxes began as philosophical puzzles and ended as exercises in university mathematics texts. If philosophy is, by definition, the residue of as-yet-unsolved problems about how things hang together, it is small wonder that what we now, and still, call metaphysics is fated by reason to resemble a battlefield of endless controversies.[19]

Suppose, though, that Kant is right that philosophy contains some genuinely intractable problems; suppose further that Arendt is right that philosophy aims at exploring what these problems mean rather than solving them. What, under that assumption, shall we say about whether it is possible to "do" law in a way that stands free of all the issues of first philosophy?

The answer seems to be that we *must* do law in a way that stands free of the issues of first philosophy, and thus in one way I am certain that Grey is right. If philosophy is an eternal round of inconclusive arguments, while legislators, rule-makers, and judges must reach conclusions in real time, then the jurists will be compelled to step clear of the round of philosophical arguments. Furthermore, I believe that in a great many cases they will reach the same conclusions they would if they adhered to pragmatic first philosophy.

Why the last? The reason has to do with how philosophical problems originate. In typical cases, they begin with a distinction that we use in everyday life, for example the distinction between voluntary and involuntary action, or between justified and unjustified belief. A philosophical problem arises because it turns out that natural arguments show that the distinction is specious or inexplicable. Determinists argue that because nature is a causal order, all actions are in the end involuntary; voluntarists counter that the will is indeed free, but cannot find an explanation of how free will and causality interact. Likewise, skeptics argue that since there is no way to rule out Cartesian possibilities, no beliefs are in the end justifiable; antiskeptics counter that ordinary knowledge-claims are justified, but cannot explain how to rule out the possibility of global error.

If we admit that these standoffs are in some sense intractable, then we must also admit that our everyday distinctions between voluntary and involuntary actions, or justified and unjustified beliefs, are arbitrary, not in the sense that we can classify actions or beliefs any which way, but in the sense that we have no principle for our classification. We use the everyday distinctions nevertheless, because we have no idea how to do without them. And that means we behave in practice as though we are pragmatists in theory.

Consider, for example, the well-known 1973 case *United States v. Moore,* in which a drug addict claimed that his addicted status implied that crimes he committed to get heroin were not genuinely voluntary and should not be punished.[20] The judges on the D.C. Circuit panel wrote a remarkably thoughtful series of opinions debating where to draw the line between voluntary and involuntary actions. (Similar issues arise in contemporary debates about the validity of "abuse excuses.") The philosophical problem, of course, is that once you admit one deterministic excuse, it becomes hard to exclude others, and one of the judges, David Bazelon, seemed willing to exculpate accused criminals for reasons including drug addiction and even bad social upbringing.

But no judge, including Bazelon, has ever argued that because all behavior is caused no one should ever be convicted of a crime; likewise, even the most rigid devotees of free will in the law never argue that all bad acts are equally voluntary and blameworthy. Instead, the legal system draws philosophically arbitrary lines that reflect little more than legislative and judicial hunches about who is responsible and who is not. This strategy corresponds with a recognizably pragmatic position in first philosophy: it combines compatibilism (the view that determinism is compatible with responsibility) with conventionalism (the view that there is no such thing as responsibility apart from social conventions for ascribing it). If I am right, legal officials must act as though they are philosophical pragmatists even if, in their heart of hearts, they are determinists. (Holmes, who often avowed determinism in his letters and private papers, never doubted that we must distinguish in law between voluntary and involuntary actions.) If so, Grey is right that legal pragmatism is indeed freestanding—and not just legal pragmatism in the minimal sense of eclectic, instrumental, historically minded antiformalism, but legal pragmatism in the more ambitious sense favored by Posner.

I am not satisfied that this is the end of the story. For one thing, it seems clear that views about first philosophy affect where we draw our pragmatically necessary lines. In the *Moore* case, it seems likely that Judge Bazelon's determinist and incompatibilist sympathies moved him to accept the heroin addict's claim that his crimes were involuntary, where the more voluntarist views of the panel's majority moved them to deny the claim. Differences in first philosophy may well explain why jurists so seldom agree on laws and cases, and the study of philosophy helps clarify what is at stake in legal debates. A philosophical pragmatist is likely to locate the distinctions-of-convenience that pragmatism recommends at a different point than would someone of different philosophical bent.

More important, however, is a point that arises when we acknowledge that the aim of philosophy is not to settle questions but to show what they mean. If so, then the question of whether it is possible to "do" law in a way that stands free of philosophy must be reformulated along the following lines. Is it possible to "do" law without being moved to speculate about what it means, for example, to hold a heroin addict responsible without speculating about the relationship between subjective compulsion and responsibility? And, if it is not, can two lawyers, or two judges, "do" law in exactly the same way despite their fundamental differences in first philosophy?

V

Let us consider the first of these questions by considering parallel questions about mathematics and the sciences. At various times, mathematical and scientific investigations raise what seem to be thorny philosophical difficulties. Newton's theories involved him in philosophical controversies over the nature of space and the vacuum and the possibility of action at a distance. The calculus raised equally difficult problems about the existence of infinitesimals. The early twentieth-century attempt to introduce rigor into mathematics by grounding it in set theory and logic produced paradoxes. The work of Gödel and Cohen showed that seemingly well-formed mathematical propositions such as the axiom of choice and the continuum hypothesis can neither be proven nor disproven. The collapse of the wave function when quantum-mechanical systems are measured creates an extraordinary form of idealist paradoxes, inasmuch as a human perceiver is a measuring device. The two most successful physical theories in history, quantum mechanics and general relativity, are inconsistent with each other. Each of these conundrums has generated ingenious and complex efforts to show how things in the broadest possible sense of the term hang together in the broadest possible sense of the term.

The fact of the matter is, however, that very few mathematicians and scientists care about the seeming disarray in the foundations of their disciplines. The "disarray," moreover, has neither halted nor even slowed inquiry within the sciences. According to pragmatists, this is how it ought to be. Moreover, when scientists have tried to set their foundations in order, the result has often been either embarrassing pataphysical pronouncements or abstruse technical work within the disciplines. Wittgenstein acutely remarks that "what a mathematician is inclined to say about the objectivity and reality of mathematical facts, is not a philosophy of mathematics, but something for philosophical *treatment,*" by which Wittgenstein means something akin to therapy, and anyone who reads the metaphysical lucubrations of scientists about their disciplines will surely agree. Likewise, Wittgenstein observed that "[a] 'leading problem of mathematical logic' is for us a problem of mathematics like any other," and here, too, to peruse mathematicians' *technical* responses to philosophical problems in mathematics is to see straightaway that he is correct.[21]

Wittgenstein's explanation of these phenomena is simple and drastic. In his view, the philosophical questions that arise in connection with mathematics and physical science only *seem* like the "foundations" of disciplines that in actuality require no foundation. "The *mathematical* problems of what is called foundations are no more the foundation of mathematics for us than the painted rock is the support of a painted tower."[22] The image is a brilliant one. Paint out the rock and the tower will not budge on the canvas; discover a paradox in the foundations of quantum mechanics, and physicists will continue to investigate quantum phenomena unfazed. Wittgenstein's moral is that the activity is its own foundation—in *On Certainty*, he adopts Goethe's formula "In the beginning was the act"—and a philosophical pragmatist is likely to agree. Nevertheless, without the rock the picture will look surreal (Magritte once painted an enormous boulder suspended in mid-air over a mountain range) and in the same way the reflective mathematician or physicist will find the state of her discipline disconcerting.[23] For Wittgenstein as for Dewey, this sense of wonderment, which Plato (*Theaetetus* 155D) identified as the source of philosophy, is in reality merely "something for philosophical treatment."

The question is whether the same considerations hold in law. In one way, the answer seems plainly to be yes. The same three points that lead Wittgensteinians to doubt the foundational picture of mathematics and the sciences are true in law as well: Very few judges and legislators care about the seeming disarray at the foundations of, for example, the theories of criminal responsibility or tort liability. The "disarray" certainly does not slow the pace of legislation or adjudication. And when jurists begin to philosophize, the results are often as embarrassing as the metaphysical vapors of physicists and brain biologists.

I think there is a difference. Although legal questions are occasionally technical, at bottom we answer them by ordinary arguments, employing ordinary concepts, using ordinary language. For this reason, when a philosophical question arises in connection with a legal issue, it is *continuous* with legal argument in a way that, for example, a question about the nature of mathematical truth is not continuous with the inquiries of a research mathematician.

A simple example will illustrate what I have in mind. In the case *Jones v. Barnes*,[24] a convicted robber asked Melinger, his assigned counsel, to brief several issues on appeal in addition to those Melinger had chosen to focus on. Melinger refused to do so, even though Barnes's issues were non-frivolous. When Barnes' appeal failed, he filed for habeas relief, arguing that he had received ineffective assistance of counsel from Melinger.

The Supreme Court ruled against Barnes. Chief Justice Burger's majority opinion offered a frankly paternalistic argument: Good advocates know that raising too many issues on appeal is likely to backfire by diverting the court's attention from the strongest issues. Questions of tactics are properly left to lawyers, not clients, because lawyers know better than clients what is in the clients' best interest; to hold otherwise "would disserve the very goal of vigorous and effective advocacy." The dissenters, Justices Brennan and Marshall, replied with a straightforwardly Millian and Kantian argument against paternalism: "[T]oday's ruling denigrates the values of individual autonomy and dignity. . . . The role of the defense lawyer should be above all to function as the instrument and defender of the client's autonomy and dignity."[25] This requires briefing the issues that matter to the client, even if the lawyer thinks they are sure losers, provided that they are nonfrivolous.

It seems clear that the issue between the majority and the dissent turns entirely on a familiar philosophical debate over the justification of paternalism and the importance of autonomy and dignity. It didn't have to. The majority could have focused on the likelihood (probably quite high) that Barnes wanted losing issues raised only because he had received bad advice from a jailhouse lawyer, not because the issues mattered to him. The dissenters could have focused on the likelihood (also probably high) that Melinger simply did not want to invest any more time in researching and writing Barnes' brief. Yet to argue in this way would evade the issue of principle that the Court *rightly* addressed, and that issue of principle is a philosophical issue that invites philosophical questions about the nature of autonomy and dignity. If these philosophical questions are no more than a painted rock supporting a painted tower, then the entire opinion in *Jones v. Barnes* is a painted rock supporting a painted tower; if the dissenters' remarks about autonomy and dignity are "not a philosophy, but something for philosophical treatment," then the treatment would extirpate the only issue of principle the case raises.

One possible response to this or similar examples is that what Justice Brennan is doing only *sounds* like philosophy, whereas in reality he is not using *philosophical* concepts when he speaks of dignity and autonomy. In "The Path of the Law," Holmes argued that moral terms in the law should be bathed in cynical acid to strip them of their moral connotations, which simply confuse legal issues that can better be understood without moralism. In effect, Holmes was arguing that moral terms appearing in the law are little more than homonyms of their ordinary-language counterparts: "The law is full of phraseology drawn from morals, and by the mere force of language continually invites us to pass from one domain to the other without perceiving it, as we are sure to do unless we have the boundary constantly before our minds."[26] Within the law, moral words become terms of art. One might generalize Holmes' argument and suggest that in law terms like "autonomy" are merely misleading homonyms of their philosophical counterparts.

The homonym theory is very implausible, however. For one thing, it would be odd if the law transformed only philosophical words and phrases into terms of art, because that would suggest that legislators, lawyers, and judges have a post-Wittgensteinian philosopher's keenly-honed intuitions about where philosophy leaves off and ordinary life begins. As this is plainly not so, the homonym theory would make sense only as a special case of a more general view: that the language of law turns *all* words and phrases, philosophical or not, into terms of art that are mere homonyms of their ordinary counterparts. There is simply no evidence on behalf of this theory, however, and plenty of evidence against it. For example, it is the everyday practice of courts to resort to the dictionary in order to settle questions of the meanings of terms contested in litigation, and this practice would make no sense at all if legal terms were merely homonyms of their ordinary language counterparts.[27]

Admittedly, it *would* be bizarre and improper if Justice Brennan had tried to cinch his argument by grounding human dignity in a theory of the noumenal self, and worse yet had he liberally larded his argument with citations to contemporary Kant scholarship. Does this not show that his raising of a philosophical issue is very different from arguing philosophically about it?

In one way, the answer is of course "yes," but the reason for this answer has little to do with philosophy, and everything to do with the institutional competence and institutional function of judges. It would be bizarre and improper for a judge to try to cinch *any* argument, empirical as well as philosophical, by taking sides in a complex and contested academic debate. To take a pointed example, even if the judge is a respected economist, such as Posner or Guido Calabresi, and even if the academic debate concerns economics, it would be outrageous to make an issue of law turn on the judge's assessment about who has the better side of a running debate in the *American Economic Review.* The judge may be competent on such questions, but the court is not, and the court, not the judge, issues the opinion.

This is not to say that courts can rely on specialist findings only when the specialists are unanimous. It *is* to say that courts should not pretend to participate in specialist debates.[28] The function of a court is to offer the public and the litigants legitimating reasons for the court's decision, and claiming to resolve nonlegal issues that life-long students of the subject are still contesting would make the court's decision less legitimate, not more.[29]

Then why should Justice Brennan raise the issue of autonomy at all? Here I am inclined to agree with Arendt, who insisted that the purpose of thinking, including philosophical thinking, is to grapple with the meaning of issues, not to generate knowledge about them. This is worth doing even if one's own position rests in the end on faith—in *Barnes,* faith that some account of human dignity can maintain itself before the tribunal of reason. Raising the philosophical question is meant to inspire us to think once again about something that has already been thought. If *Barnes* incites us to reflect on whether we really do believe in autonomy and dignity, then it connects us to a tradition of thought that is no less important because it is inconclusive. Cases like *Barnes* show us what is at stake philosophically in legal problems. They are contributions, incitements, to philosophical thinking, and the relationship is perhaps that we should ask not what philosophy can do for law but what law can do for philosophy.

In short, one might say that *of course* it is possible to "do" law without being moved to philosophical musings about it. Although doing so is not intellectually irresponsible, as it would be if philosophy were *strenge Wissenschaft,* it does signal a kind of shallowness. Oddly enough, Holmes, who Grey has rightly identified as the founder of legal pragmatism, made this point in eloquent and famous words: "The remoter and more general aspects of the law are those which give it universal interest. It is through them that you not only become a great master in your calling but connect your subject with the universe and catch an echo of the infinite, a glimpse of its unfathomable process, a hint of the universal law."[30]

VI

Paternalism is not the only legal issue turning on the philosophical concept of human dignity, with its related concepts of personhood and autonomy. I said earlier that legal pragmatists typically prefer to avoid such squishy and, dare I say it, Kantian concepts. Yet without appealing to human dignity or some facsimile thereof, it is hard to make sense of such legal ideas as due process of law, the wrongfulness of executing the insane, or even retributive punishment. Deterrent punishment is instrumental and forward-looking—it is thoroughly pragmatic—but retribution, which looks backward at the character of the wrongdoer's conduct rather than forward at the consequences of punishing it, is entwined with the philosophical concepts of human dignity and personhood in two distinct ways. First, the root idea of retribution is that wrongdoers *deserve* their punishment, and the most plausible account of what makes them appropriate objects of desert rather than merely of social control is their human dignity.[31] Second, the most plausible justification of retributive punishment is that it reaffirms the dignity of those who were victimized by wrongdoing.[32] The justification of punishment is an issue in which philosophical stance makes an immense practical difference, and not only in criminal law. Pragmatists argue on economic grounds that optimal deterrence can be obtained by scaling punitive damages to actual damages.[33] Retributivists such as Marc Galanter and myself reply that actual damages don't measure the wrongfulness of the tortious act, and for that reason we oppose formulaic caps on punitive damages, which are intended to rectify indignities by "expressively defeating" wrongdoers.[34]

In a wholly different legal arena, it turns out to be extremely difficult to justify the right against self-incrimination on pragmatic rather than dignitary grounds. Famously, Jeremy Bentham proposed abolishing testimonial privileges because they diminish social utility by obstructing justice.[35] Why forbid law enforcement officials from obtaining inculpatory information from a guilty criminal, who may be the sole reliable source? Concern about torture and the third degree is no explanation: torture and the third degree can be outlawed, and if they persist in the back rooms of police stations nothing will prevent the authorities from torturing a suspect to compel him to waive his right against self-incrimination. The best explanation of the right against self-incrimination is that forcing criminals to confess in the name of social utility affronts deep-seated intuitions about human dignity: it is all too reminiscent of Arthur Koestler's Rubashov, the fictionalized version of Bukharin who confesses to crimes against Stalin's state because his own ideology teaches him that the state is everything and the self is merely a "grammatical fiction," "a multitude of one million divided by one million."[36]

Such intuitions about human dignity and personality run deep. In 1964, the Supreme Court argued that without the right against self-incrimination criminals would confront a "cruel trilemma of self-accusation, perjury, or contempt" (if they refuse to testify), a trilemma that offends against "our respect for the inviolability of the human personality."[37] But this "cruel trilemma" argument unknowingly echoed a similar argument made in a 1698 papal study criticizing the Inquisition's practice of compelling suspected heretics to profess their faith under oath. Compelling the oath was, according to the study's author, "a form of torture more cruel than physical torture because it tormented one's soul by tempting a man to save himself from punishment by perjuring himself."[38] The Supreme Court's "inviolability of the human personality" may best be understood as a secular counterpart of the immortal soul that concerned the Inquisition. It is a philosophical concept, and it is hard to see how the legal argument can stand free of the philosophical arguments that support the conclusion that human personality is inviolable.

Most importantly, however, human dignity and the related concepts of fairness and equality figure prominently in what I believe to be the only persuasive account of our moral obligation to obey the law, the fair-play argument of Hart and Rawls. This takes us back to the very first problem in the philosophy of law, Socrates' conundrum in the *Crito* about whether he must accept his unjust death sentence without trying to escape. Without an answer to Socrates' question, law cannot hope to be more than a regime of force imposed on a domain of cynicism.[39]

Now a philosophical pragmatist such as Posner might be willing to forego legal doctrines grounded in a metaphysical conception of personality and human dignity, regarding them as the fruits of a poisoned tree, fruits unfit even for a dog's dinner. If so, I think he is wrong on the merits. But if I have interpreted my examples correctly, Posner's instinct to ground legal pragmatism in its philosophical counterpart is right, and his task will be to find a suitable pragmatic reconstruction of the metaphysical concepts he rejects. Eclectic, result-oriented, historically minded antiformalism is indeed freestanding—but legal pragmatism disconnected from the philosophical impulse purchases its independence at the cost of condemning itself to meaninglessness.

VII

In the preceding section, I suggested that arguments central to the law presuppose philosophical positions. I illustrated this suggestion with arguments connecting antipaternalism, retributive punishment, the right against self-incrimination, and legal obligation to the notions of human dignity, autonomy, and personality. At this point I would like to consider another illustration, the metaphysically fascinating question of whether corporations have personality. I do so partly in order to dispel the suspicion that the examples I offered were exceptional, but also because Dewey discussed the subject of my illustration in terms very close to Grey's.

The issue was of considerable interest to jurists at the turn of the century. In 1886, the U.S. Supreme Court held that business corporations are "persons" in the sense of the Fourteenth Amendment, and are therefore entitled to the rights of persons, and other countries developed analogous doctrines of corporate personality.[40] The best-known legal theorists of the day debated the claim that corporations possess real personalities. In response, Dewey in 1926 published an article in the *Yale Law Journal* that aimed to deflate the metaphysical question.[41] Dewey defended the following propositions:

(1) In law, the word "person" denotes nothing more than the bearer of rights and responsibilities, and thus stating that something is a person "would convey no implications, except that the unit has those rights and duties which the courts find it to have." (p. 656)

(2) Theorists err, therefore, when they draw inferences about legal personality—in particular, about corporate personality—derived from pre-legal or extra-legal ideas about what a person is. In particular, philosophical theories ascribing will or moral personhood or subjectivity to corporations have nothing to offer law except confusion. Indeed, Dewey rejects any theory other than "legal agnosticism, holding that even if there be such an ulterior subject *per se*, it is no concern to law, since courts can do their work without respect to its nature, much less having to settle it." (p. 660)

Dewey considers the objection "that such an attitude does not become jurisprudence, that some theory is *implied* in the procedure of courts, and that the business of the theory of law is to make explicit what is implied, particularly as false theories have done practical harm" (p. 660). To this he replies that at a "deeper level . . . there are two radically different types of definitions. . . . [One] proceeds in terms of an essential and universal inhering nature[, while the other] proceeds in terms of *consequences*. In brief, for the latter a thing is—is defined as—what it does, 'what—it—does' being stated in terms of specific effects *extrinsically* wrought in other things" (pp. 660–61). Borrowing a term from Whitehead, Dewey labels the latter method "extensive abstraction," and argues for the following:

(3) In law, the term "person" should be defined by extensive abstraction, that is, by examining whether attributing rights and duties to different sorts of things makes any consequential difference. If so, the thing is a person; if not, not.

(4) Corporations, unlike molecules or trees, do behave differently if given rights and duties. That is why corporations are persons, not because they have the essential nature of personality.

(5) The method of extensive abstraction is "the pragmatistic rule," but it "has no inherent dependence upon pragmatism as a philosophy" (p. 661). In Grey's terms, Dewey is here asserting that his analysis in propositions (1) through (4) exemplifies freestanding legal pragmatism.

(6) Unfortunately, for centuries legal discussions of corporate personhood have been muddied by "the introduction of irrelevant conceptions, imported into legal discussion (and often into legal prac-

tice) from uncritical popular beliefs, from psychology, and from a metaphysics ultimately derived from theology" (pp. 663–64). Invariably, these importations are confusions that engender further confusion. They have been extremely influential in the development of law, but that does nothing to make them confusions any the less.

The remainder of Dewey's paper is a magnificent tour de force—an overview of the various political uses to which theories of corporate personality have been put from the thirteenth century to the twentieth, designed to show that "[e]ach theory has been used to serve the same ends, and each has been used to serve opposing ends" (p. 669). Sometimes writers have defended corporate personality in order to shield individual corporate members from the state; sometimes they defended corporate personality in order to make it easier to penalize collectivities.[42] These, Dewey says, "are political rather than legal considerations, but they have affected law" (p. 669). The result, he concludes, is a muddle that can be avoided only by hewing to the truths embodied in propositions (1) through (3).

My principal interest in Dewey's argument lies in the contrast he draws between defining terms by their consequences ("extensive abstraction," which is "the pragmatistic rule") and defining them by examining their underlying nature, for the former represents freestanding legal pragmatism, while the latter represents the procedure of legal philosophy. Dewey believes that extensive abstraction is the dominant method in the natural sciences, and in this he is probably right. Consider Isaac Newton's famous response, in the second edition of the *Principia*, to Leibniz's objection "that gravity will be a scholastic occult quality or else the effect of a miracle":[43] "Hitherto we have explained the phenomena of the heavens and of our sea by the power of gravity, but have not yet assigned the cause of this power. . . . [H]itherto I have not been able to discover the cause of those properties of gravity from phenomena, and I frame no hypotheses [*hypotheses non fingo*]; for whatever is not deduced from the phenomena is to be called an hypothesis; and hypotheses, whether metaphysical or physical, whether of occult qualities or mechanical, have no place in experimental philosophy."[44] *Hypotheses non fingo*, transferred from physics to law, is simply a more elegant expression of the legal agnosticism Dewey recommends in proposition (2), and it expresses as well Grey's idea that legal pragmatism is freestanding. Ultimately, I think, Newton's stricture explains why in physics the painted tower of inquiry can stand without the support of the painted rock: so long as inquiry concerns itself with effects rather than causes, and treats causes only in their relation to effects rather than in themselves, it can proceed without intellectually satisfying hypotheses about what early modern writers referred to as "true causes."

The same cannot be said of law, however, and this is Dewey's error. Consider proposition (1), which asserts that to describe a person as "a right-and-duty-bearing unit . . . would be truistic, tautological. Hence it would convey no implications, except that the unit has those rights and duties which the courts find it to have."[45] This proposition is closely related to the realists' predictive theory of law, according to which law is simply "prophecies of what the courts will do in fact."[46] The predictive theory doubtless attracted Dewey because it defines law itself pragmatically, by looking to "specific effects *extrinsically* wrought in other things," these effects being the decisions of judges.

It is, however, a familiar objection to the predictive theory that it is perfectly useless to a judge, who obviously cannot answer the question "what is the law of this case?" by predicting what she herself is about to say in answer to this very question.[47] For the same reason, Dewey's analysis of corporate personality—that it "has those rights and duties which the courts find it to have"—will prove wholly useless to courts trying to determine the rights and duties corporate persons should have.

Dewey was misled, I think, by one of the idées fixés of U.S. legal thought in the late nineteenth and early twentieth centuries, namely that law should be reconstructed on a scientific basis, generating its principles by inductions from data. This was an idea held in common by Langellian formalists, who regarded cases as the data, and their realist opponents, who regarded "what the courts will do in fact" as the data. The ideal of legal science explains Dewey's argument that extensive abstraction is the best method of definition to use in law because it is the best method of definition to use in natural science and mathematics.

The crucial difference is that the data of science are measured physical quantities, not the holdings of other scientists. If the data of science were the holdings of scientists, natural science would face the same problem of circularity that faces the realist judge: scientists would have to answer a question by predicting how scientists, including themselves, would answer that very question.[48] The threat of circularity explains why courts must look beyond the perimeter of their own findings about corporate persons in order to develop the law. Dewey to the contrary, courts must look to popular beliefs, psychology, and metaphysics to develop the metaphor of corporate personhood. In law, the appropriate response to *hypotheses non fingo* is *necesse est hypotheses fingere*—I necessarily frame hypotheses.

Four years after the Supreme Court held that corporations are persons for purposes of Fourteenth Amendment rights, Congress explicitly applied the criminal as well as the civil prohibitions of the Sherman Act to corporations as well as natural persons. This was a large step: in all but a few exceptional cases, criminal liability traditionally requires a mental element of culpability, which makes sense in the case of natural persons but is plainly shaky in the case of corporate persons. In 1909 the Supreme Court nevertheless upheld the idea that corporations can commit crimes.[49]

At that point, the fun began, as courts developed corporate analogues to criminal law doctrines that originated with natural persons in mind. Consider a few examples drawn from cases decided since 1980. Courts have held that a corporation can conspire with its own employee, even though the corporation is criminally liable only because the employee's wrongdoing is ascribed to it.[50] To determine whether a corporation "knowingly" committed an offense, the First Circuit Court of Appeals has proclaimed that an organization's "knowledge is the totality of what all of the employees know," whether or not they communicate with each other—a definition of collective knowledge as bizarre as announcing that four fiddlers playing in separate rooms make a string quartet.[51] Courts have held that a corporation can be sentenced to a prison term.[52]

One response to these decisions is that they are metaphysical absurdities. Take the idea that a corporation can be imprisoned. Judge Doumar explained that when he was thinking about sentencing the Allegheny Bottling Company to imprisonment, "the United States Marshal for the Eastern District of Virginia, Roger Ray, was contacted. When asked if he could imprison Allegheny Pepsi, he stated that he could,"[53] by chaining up the plant and restricting employees' access. Judge Doumar sentenced the company to three years' imprisonment, but then suspended the sentence. The court of appeals later voided the sentence as a nullity—legalese for "metaphysical absurdity"—and no wonder. Judge Doumar had confused the corporation with its property: after all, a company can sell its plant and nevertheless remain the same company. Federal Marshall Ray could no more imprison Allegheny Pepsi by chaining up the plant than he could imprison its CEO by locking up his shoes. It is noteworthy that even authors who don't regard themselves as metaphysicians have assumed that corporate imprisonment is a conceptual impossibility; Posner, for example, once wrote that an imprisoned offender "is *necessarily* an individual: a corporation or other 'artificial' person cannot, of course, be punished by imprisonment."[54]

When I describe such arguments as "metaphysical," I mean that they proceed by asking what the defining characteristics of a person are, and then examining corporations to find analogues to these characteristics.[55] Dewey, however, could not diagnose the problem with *Allegheny Bottling* as a metaphysical error, because he is committed to legal agnosticism about the metaphysics of corporate persons (proposition (2)). He would regard the argument that Judge Doumar had confused the corporation with its property as a formalist quibble: There is no logical contradiction if courts identify a factory with the corporate person for some legal purposes (such as imprisonment) and with the corporate person's property for others, because in law the word " 'person' . . . would convey no implications, except that the unit has those rights and duties which the courts find it to have."[56]

For Dewey, evidently, the field of implication, and hence the semantics, of legal terms is wholly under the control of judges and other officials, wholly artificial, and wholly discrete from the semantics of the same term in nonlegal contexts. Dewey's argument, in other words, rests in the end on our old friend the homonym theory of legal language. And we have seen that the homonym theory is unacceptable.

Let me connect this objection with points previously made. On Dewey's diagnosis in proposition (6), Judge Doumar, like the courts analyzing corporate conspiracy and collective knowledge, are guilty of importing extralegal ideas about personality into a purely legal discussion. As we have seen from our discussion of the predictive theory's shortcomings, however, jurists have no alternative to reaching beyond the law whenever their task is to extend its concepts beyond their settled applications. Law is too continuous with non-law for legal officials simply to stipulate the philosophical implications of its terminology out of existence. In that case, however, it is hard to see how legal pragmatism can be freestanding.

VIII

Let me return to Grey's argument. In his closing pages, Grey aims to demonstrate that legal pragmatism stands free of philosophical pragmatism by showing how even an evangelical Christian can come to agree with Grey that law should be approached pragmatically and not dogmatically. I am not persuaded by this demonstration. True, Grey and his evangelical friend are able to agree on the fundamentals of the liberal *Rechtsstaat,* but that is because the liberal *Rechtsstaat* was designed specifically to allow adherents to a wide variety of fighting faiths to lay down their arms in peaceable coexistence. Can Grey come to similar agreement with his friend about legal questions more contentious than the legitimacy of the *Rechtsstaat,* for example the permissibility of abortion, or euthanasia, or gay marriage? I am inclined to doubt it, and that is because these issues turn on differences in first philosophy, and philosophical differences show us what is at stake in our legal disagreements.

Take the example of legalizing gay marriage, which evangelical Christians oppose and many liberals support. Opponents of gay marriage often offer secular arguments against it, typically the argument that permitting gay marriage would undermine the monogamous family. These arguments are always disingenuous, however, since nobody has an honest story to tell about how it would harm monogamous families to permit otherwise-single people to form them. "Practical" arguments that permitting gay marriage would harm states' economies because of Christian tourists' boycotts are even feebler: they are morally unprincipled, and in any event evidence suggests that gay "buycotts" are economically more weighty than evangelical boycotts.[57]

It is perfectly clear that these feeble arguments are rationalizations, and that hostility to gay marriage reflects nothing more than distaste for gays (not in itself a reason for legalized discrimination) or—in the case of the religious right—reliance on *Leviticus* 18:22, "You shall not lie with a male as with a woman. It is an abomination." Let us focus on the biblical source of opposition to gay marriage. The biblical argument depends entirely on a handful of beliefs that are straightforwardly philosophical: the metaphysical belief that God exists, the metaethical belief that God's commandments morally bind us, and the epistemological belief that the Bible, literally interpreted, infallibly states God's commandments and is inherently more credible than any evidence or argument to the contrary, or for that matter any evidence or argument that the Bible is human in origin.

Let me suppose that Grey and his evangelical friend disagree about whether gay marriage should be legalized; let me suppose as well that Grey's evangelical friend honestly acknowledges that his opposition to gay marriage derives entirely from *Leviticus* 18:22 and related biblical texts. Their dispute is a legal one: they disagree about what laws should be enacted, and probably about how constitutional guarantees of due process and equal protection should be read in the context of gay rights. It is also a philosophical one: if Grey's friend abandoned his fundamentalist metaphysics, metaethics, or epistemology, then his honesty would lead him to abandon his opposition to gay marriage as well. Or if Grey came to believe that *Leviticus* 18:22 is an infallible expression of morally binding divine will, then he would oppose gay marriage. How could it be otherwise? And in that case, how can legal pragmatism stand free of first philosophy, of metaphysics, metaethics, and epistemology?

Notes

I have been greatly assisted in thinking through this paper by Tom Grey, Deborah Hellman, Peter Levine, and Judy Lichtenberg.

1 Richard A. Posner, *Overcoming Law* (Cambridge: Harvard University Press, 1995), chapter 24.

2 I discuss Posner's views in more detail in David Luban, "The Posner Variations (Twenty-Seven Variations on a Theme By Holmes)," *Stanford Law Review* 48 (April 1996): 1001–1036. There I argue that in *Overcoming Law* Posner represents a third strand of pragmatism—pragmatism understood in its everyday sense of not being much interested in pursuing philosophical arguments that have no practical use.

3 Ludwig Wittgenstein, *Philosophical Investigations,* 3d ed., translated by G. E. M. Anscombe (New York: Macmillan, 1958), §467, at 134e.

4 Ludwig Wittgenstein, *On Certainty,* edited by G. E. M. Anscombe and G. H. von Wright, translated by Denis Paul and G. E. M. Anscombe (New York: Macmillan, 1969), §422.

5 I discuss the connection between Wittgenstein and pragmatism, or rather the lack thereof, in David Luban, "Doubts About the New Pragmatism," in *Legal Modernism* (Ann Arbor: University of Michigan Press, 1994), pp. 158–64. See also Cavell's essay in the present volume.

6 E.g., Gerald Gunther, *Learned Hand: The Man and the Judge* (New York: Knopf, 1994), pp. xvii, 655; Ronald Dworkin, "Mr. Liberty," *New York Review of Books,* Aug. 11, 1994: 17; David Luban, "Justice Holmes and the Metaphysics of Judicial Restraint," *Duke Law Journal* 44 (1994): 511–13.

7 Friedrich Nietzsche, *The Gay Science,* edited and translated by Walter Kaufmann (New York: Vintage, 1974), §374.

8 Posner, *Overcoming Law,* p. 80.

9 I take this phrase from a letter from Oliver Wendell Holmes, Jr., to John Wu, May 5, 1926, in *Justice Holmes to Doctor Wu: An Intimate Correspondence, 1921–1932* (n.p., n.d.), p. 36.

10 Robert Fogelin, *Pyrrhonian Reflections on Knowledge and Justification* (New York: Oxford University Press, 1994); Michael Williams, *Unnatural Doubts: Epistemological Realism and the Basis of Scepticism* (Oxford: Blackwell, 1991).

11 Hannah Arendt, *The Life of the Mind,* vol. 1, *Thinking* (New York: Harcourt Brace, 1978), p. 88.

12 Letter of Aug. 20, 1954, in Carol Brightman, ed., *Between Friends: The Correspondence of Hannah Arendt and Mary McCarthy 1949–1975* (New York: Harcourt Brace, 1995), pp. 24–25.

13 I take this characterization from Wilfrid Sellars, "Philosophy and the Scientific Image of Man," in *Science, Perception and Reality* (London: Routledge & Kegan Paul, 1963), p. 1.

14 Immanuel Kant, *Critique of Pure Reason,* translated by Norman Kemp Smith (New York: St. Martin's Press, 1929), p. 7, Avii.

15 *Ibid.,* Aviii.

16 Letter from Holmes to Sir Frederick Pollock, May 26, 1919, in Mark DeWolfe Howe, ed., *Holmes-Pollock Letters: The Correspondence of Mr. Justice Holmes and Sir Frederick Pollock 1874–1932*, vol. 2 (Cambridge: Harvard University Press, 1941), p. 13.

17 Thomas Nagel has intimated something like this idea in *The View From Nowhere* (New York: Oxford University Press, 1986), p. 10.

18 Colin McGinn, *Problems in Philosophy: The Limits of Inquiry* (Oxford: Blackwell, 1993). For a summary of McGinn's argument, see his paper "The Problems of Philosophy," *Philosophical Studies* 76 (1994): 133–56.

19 I owe this argument to Judith Lichtenberg.

20 *United States v. Moore*, 486 F.2d 1139 (D.C. Cir.) (en banc), cert. denied, 414 U.S. 980 1973). The discussion that follows was inspired in part by Richard Boldt, "The Construction of Responsibility in the Criminal Law," *University of Pennsylvania Law Review* 140 (1992): 2245–2332.

21 Wittgenstein, *Philosophical Investigations*, §254, 124. Well-known examples of the mathematician's technical responses include the Zermelo-Frankel and von Neumann-Bernays-Gödel axiomatizations of set theory; Abraham Robinson's development of mathematical analysis using real infinitesimals in *Non-Standard Analysis* (New York: American Elsevier, 1974); and the development of intuitionistic mathematics in Errett Bishop, *Foundations of Constructive Analysis* (New York: McGraw-Hill, 1967). These are all major achievements, but they are philosophically inspired achievements *within* mathematics, rather than mathematical resolutions of philosophical problems.

22 Ludwig Wittgenstein, *Remarks on the Foundations of Mathematics,* ed. G. H. von Wright, R. Rhees, and G. E. M. Anscombe, translated by G. E. M. Anscombe (Cambridge, Mass.: MIT Press, 1976), p. 171e.

23 *La clef de verre* (1959), in the D. and J. de Menil Collection, Houston, reproduced in David Sylvester, *Rene Magritte* (New York: Praeger, 1959), p. 103.

24 *Jones v. Barnes*, 463 U.S. 745 (1983).

25 *Ibid.*, pp. 754, 763.

26 Oliver Wendell Holmes Jr., "The Path of the Law," in *Collected Legal Papers* (New York: Peter Smith, 1923), pp. 169–79, quote at p. 171.

27 The Supreme Court has had increasing recourse to the dictionary in statutory interpretation in recent terms. See "Note: Looking It Up: Dictionaries and Statutory Interpretation," *Harvard Law Review* 107 (1994): 1439–40.

28 Interestingly, the Supreme Court suggested as much in *Daubert v. Merrell Dow Pharmaceuticals, Inc.,* 509 U.S. 579 (1993), when it included general acceptance by the relevant research community as one important factor in determining whether scientific evidence is admissible in trials. This criterion suggests that when a specialist question has no generally acceptable answer, it does not belong in court. Ironically, in reaching its conclusion the Supreme Court relied on writings of Carl Hempel and Karl Popper, two philosophers whose theories are not themselves generally accepted by philosophers of science, and which would probably be inadmissible under the *Daubert* test. If anything, *Daubert* offers a cautionary study of the perils of philosophizing in the midst of judicial opinions. For a sophisticated discussion of the philosophy of science issues in *Daubert,* see Heidi Li Feldman, "Science and Uncertainty in Mass Exposure Litigation," *Texas Law Review* 74 (1995): 1–48.

29 One counterexample to this point that will occur to many readers is Chief Justice Warren's opinion in *Brown v. Board of Education.* In order to prove that separate black schools can never provide their students an equal education, Warren relied on contro-

versial psychological experiments by Kenneth Clark showing that segregation causes black children to believe in their own inferiority. I do not regard this as a counterexample to the proposition that when courts take sides in specialist controversies they undermine the legitimacy of their decisions. For Clark's experiments were merely confirming something that, as Posner rightly observes, "was obvious and had been so from the inception of the practice" of segregation. Posner, *Overcoming Law*, p. 61.

30 Holmes, "The Path of the Law," p. 202.

31 This *locus classicus* of this argument is Herbert Morris, "Persons and Punishment," chapter 2 in *On Guilt and Innocence* (Berkeley: University of California Press, 1976).

32 My views on retributive punishment derive from the work of Jean Hampton: her essays in Jeffrie R. Murphy and Jean Hampton, *Forgiveness and Mercy* (Cambridge: Cambridge University Press, 1988), pp. 35–87, 111–61, and "Correcting Harms Versus Righting Wrongs: The Goal of Retribution," *UCLA Law Review* 39 (1992): 1659–702.

33 See Robert D. Cooter, "Economic Analysis of Punitive Damages," *Southern California Law Review* 56 (1982): 79–101. The size of the cap varies depending on whether the tort is negligence or strict liability.

34 Marc Galanter and David Luban, "Poetic Justice: Punitive Damages and Legal Pluralism," *American University Law Review* 42 (1993): 1393–463.

35 Jeremy Bentham, *Rationale of Judicial Evidence, Specially Applied to English Practice* (New York: Garland Publishing, 1978 reprint of 1827 edition), vol. 5, pp. 207–83. An excellent contemporary critique of the right against self-incrimination, largely on utilitarian grounds, is David Dolinko, "Is There a Rationale for the Privilege Against Self-Incrimination?" *UCLA Law Review* 33 (1986): 1063–148.

36 Arthur Koestler, *Darkness at Noon* (New York: Bantam Books, 1941), p. 208; the phrase "grammatical fiction" appears on p. 125. I have argued for this analysis of the right against self-incrimination in David Luban, *Lawyers and Justice: An Ethical Study* (Princeton: Princeton University Press, 1988), pp. 194–95. See Louis M. Seidman, "Rubashov's Question: Self-Incrimination and the Problem of Coerced Preferences," *Yale Journal of Law and the Humanities* 2 (1990): 149–80.

37 *Murphy v. Waterfront Commission*, 378 U.S. 52, 55 (1964). For a skeptical view of *Murphy*'s "cruel trilemma" analysis, see Akhil Reed Amar and Renee B. Lettow, "Fifth Amendment First Principles: The Self-Incrimination Clause," *Michigan Law Review* 93 (1995): 890.

38 On the papal study, see Leonard Levy, *The Origins of the Fifth Amendment* (New York: Oxford University Press, 1968), p. 24.

39 For a similar argument, see Jules Coleman, "Legal Theory and Practice," *Georgetown Law Journal* 83 (1995): 2579–617, especially 2587–89, 2606–7.

40 *Santa Clara Co. v. Southern Pacific R.R.*, 118 U.S. 394, 396 (1886).

41 John Dewey, "The Historic Background of Corporate Legal Personality," *Yale Law Journal* 35 (1926), pp. 655–73.

42 For example, "Corporate groups less than the state have had real personality ascribed to them, both in order to make them more amenable to liability, as in the case of trade-unions, and to exalt their dignity and vital power, as against external control. Their personality has been denied for like reasons; they have been pulverized into mere aggregates of separate persons in order to protect other laborers from them, to make more difficult their unified action in trade disputes, as in collective bargaining, and to enable union property to escape liability, the associated individuals in their severalty having no property to levy upon" (*ibid.*, pp. 669–70).

43 Letter to Conti, Nov. or Dec. 1715, quoted in H. G. Alexander, ed., *The Leibniz-Clarke Correspondence* (Manchester, U.K.: Manchester University Press, 1956), p. 184.

44 Isaac Newton, *Newton's Principia,* vol. 2, ed. Florian Cajori, translated by Andrew Motte (Berkeley: University of California Press, 1966), pp. 546–47.

45 Dewey, "The Historic Background of Corporate Personality," p. 656.

46 Holmes, "The Path of the Law," p. 173. See also Felix Cohen, "The Problems of a Functional Jurisprudence," *Modern Law Review* 1 (1937): 16.

47 I have developed this argument in *Lawyers and Justice,* pp. 20–24; but it is an objection to the predictive theory that dates back at least to the 1930s.

48 Grey himself has offered a penetrating analysis of the problem of circularity in legal science: Thomas Grey, "Langdell's Orthodoxy," *University of Pittsburgh Law Review* 45 (1983): 20–24.

49 *New York Central & Hudson River R.R. v. United States,* 212 U.S. 481 (1909).

50 *United States v. Hughes Aircraft Co.,* 20 F. 3d 974 (9th Cir. 1994).

51 *United States v. Bank of New England, N.A.,* 821 F.2d 844 (1st Cir.), cert. denied, 484 U.S. 943 (1987). This theory has subsequently been dubbed the "collective knowledge doctrine." The collective knowledge doctrine is an attempt to deal with the problem that "corporations cannot in and of themselves possess a mental state," *United States v. Investment Enterprises, Inc.,* 10 F.3d 263, 266 (5th Cir. 1993).

52 *United States v. Allegheny Bottling Co.,* 695 F. Supp. 856 (E.D. Va. 1988), aff'd, 870 F.2d 655 (4th Cir. 1989)(sentencing a corporation to three years' imprisonment). See also *State v. Shepherd Construction Co.,* 281 S.E.2d (Ga. 1981), cert. denied, 454 U.S. 1055 (1981)(holding that a corporation can be convicted under a criminal statute that carries only a penalty of imprisonment).

53 *Allegheny Bottling Co.,* 695 F. Supp. at 861.

54 Richard Posner, "Optimal Sentences For White Collar Criminals," *American Criminal Law Review* 17 (1980): 411 (emphasis added). Nowadays, the received Chicago-school metaphysic maintains that a corporation is not a person but a nexus of contracts. See Frank H. Easterbrook and Daniel R. Fischel, *The Economic Structure of Corporate Law* (Cambridge: Harvard University Press, 1991), pp. 8–12. You cannot chain up a nexus of contracts.

   A pragmatist might argue that there is a good instrumental reason, unrelated to metaphysics, for voiding the sentence in *Allegheny Bottling.* Otherwise, individual defendants could cite *Allegheny Bottling* as precedent establishing that imprisonment doesn't require incarceration. But this is really no argument at all, absent some showing that imprisonment does require incarceration. This is easier said than done. Writing in a formalistic vein, Judge Doumar appealed to the dictionary and the law of torts to argue that "imprisonment simply means restraint" rather than incarceration; in a pragmatic vein, it seems likely that alternative, non-incarcerative, forms of imprisonment would be socially beneficial. Neither the formalist nor the instrumental argument for non-incarcerative imprisonments will be easy to overcome.

55 For an example of such an argument, see Peter French, *Collective and Corporate Responsibility* (New York: Columbia University Press, 1984).

56 Dewey, "The Historic Background of Corporate Personality," p. 656.

57 For a calculation of the relative economic effects, see Jennifer Gerarda Brown, "Competitive Federalism and the Legislative Incentives to Recognize Same-Sex Marriage," *Southern California Law Review* 68 (1995): 753–814.

Pragmatism and Law: A Response
to David Luban

RICHARD RORTY

Judge Posner's "Pragmatic Adjudication" is enormously refreshing. It cuts through an immense amount of tiresome and pointless talk about "the nature of law" and "the relation of law to politics" and gets down to the question: how should the appellate court judges in a particular country at a particular time do their work? It not only argues lucidly for a particular answer to that question, but gives you a good sense of what it must be like to be in Posner's shoes. Posner helps you understand what sorts of things judges have to worry about, and what sorts of self-doubt they experience. His frankness about the need (given certain specifically American conditions) for judicial rule-making is as cheering as it is infrequent. So is his claim that judges would be blameworthy if they failed to have emotional reactions to certain statutes, and his reminder that, in the end, every society has to trust its wise elders.

If, having read Posner, you wish there were more judges like him, you might nevertheless agree (as I do) with Thomas Grey that these desirable judges need never have considered, and can forever remain in blithe ignorance of, "the pragmatist philosopher's critiques of metaphysics and epistemological foundationalism." Though Posner himself has read lots of pragmatist and nonpragmatist philosophers, another judge, one who would endorse everything in Posner's paper, might well have read so little philosophy as to have no views whatever on such questions as:

1. Should true beliefs be thought of (a) as accurate representations of reality, or (b) as useful rules of action?

2. Does reality (a) have an intrinsic nature that we must try to discover, or (b) are all possible descriptions of it equally relational and extrinsic, in the sense of having been chosen in order to gratify various human needs and interests?

3. Are the traditional problems of metaphysics and epistemology (a) inevitably encountered by any reflective mind, or (b) do they arise only in

certain sociocultural situations? Should we try (a) to solve them or (b) by altering our own sociocultural situation, to dissolve them?

4. Do we think (a) because we take pleasure (as David Luban puts it) "in the rapt, silent, yet active contemplation of truths, regardless of whether they pay" or (b) in order to solve problems?

I think Grey is right to suggest that this philosophical ignoramus could, *ceteris paribus,* be just as good a judge as Posner. We want our judges to have read widely—to be cultivated men and women—but if one judge cannot read novels, another cannot read economics, and still another cannot read metaphysics and epistemology, that is no great matter. Somebody can be cultivated even if he or she has a few blind spots. Lots of useful political thinkers and agents seem to have found metaphysics and epistemology pretty silly. Thomas Jefferson professed himself unable to read Plato, despite repeated attempts. He showed no interest whatever in the epistemological works of Hume and Locke, though he sopped up their political writings. Some people just cannot hack metaphysics and epistemology (or even metaethics) but that does not prevent them fulfilling their sociopolitical functions very well indeed.

What about the judge who does enjoy reading philosophy, but has bad philosophical taste? This judge answers "a" to each of the preceding questions. Would her commitment to these wrong answers make her less ready to accept Posner's description of how she should do her job? I cannot see why it should. Such a judge might be thoroughly sympathetic to Posner's account of what our country needs from its appellate courts, even though she is also thoroughly sympathetic to John Searle's warnings against the baneful influence of Kuhn, Derrida, and Rorty. If Posner had used some buzzword like "holist" to contrast with "positivist," instead of using "pragmatist," his colleague might never have suspected that Posner would (or so I fondly imagine) answer "b" to those same questions.

Suppose she finds out that she disagrees with Posner on all matters epistemological, metaphysical, metaethical, and metaphilosophical. Once she recovers from the initial shock, I suspect this would matter as little to their collaboration on the bench as her discovery that Posner is an atheist (while she is a cradle Catholic who has never had any serious doubts about the faith, even though she regards the present pope as an old fuddy-duddy). Few of Jefferson's contemporaries could have imagined that one day you would see atheistical and devout jurists sitting around the same table, arguing out, peaceably and fruitfully, the constitutionality of legal barriers to gay marriage. But one of the nice things about contemporary

America is that such arguments take place all the time. The concluding section of Grey's paper helps one see how this is possible.

Like Grey, I "have trouble seeing how . . . Rorty's metaphysical antirealism (or alternatively Putnam's 'internal realism')—is supposed to help deal with those 'real human problems,' which the pragmatists say philosophers should work on."[1] But, as Grey goes on to say, not all pragmatist philosophy professors should spend all their time on real human problems. Some of us are detailed to work part-time on, for example, Searle.[2] We carry out this assignment by refining still further the ever more complex and technical arguments for "b" and against "a." Searle is to us as Cardinal Ratzinger is to Hans Küng and his allies. Küng hopes that his church will spend less time on theology and more on real human problems, and that the future will hold ever fewer Ratzingers. But, trained as a theologian, he serves a useful function by doing his little reactive thing—even while foreseeing that thing's eventual obsolescence.

David Luban and I disagree on this question of obsolescence. He is inclined to answer "a" to question (3), above, though doubtless he would add some qualifications. Luban sees something like a natural order of argument stretching from jurisprudence to philosophy. He sees metaphysical and epistemological disputes not as optional, but as inevitable once one presses, Socratically, for justification of morally significant decisions. He says, for example:

> The Supreme Court's "inviolability of the human personality" [a phrase the court used in deciding a case about the right to self-incrimination] may best be interpreted as a secular counterpart of the immortal soul that concerned the Inquisition. It is a philosophical concept, and it is hard to see how the legal argument can stand free of the philosophical arguments that support the conclusion that human personality is inviolable.

I agree that this phrase refers to a secular counterpart of the immortal soul, but I am not sure I know what philosophical arguments Luban has in mind. I think of Kant, for example, as having used this inviolability as a premise rather than as deduced it as a conclusion. More generally, I think of Enlightenment thinkers as having said: the immortality of the human soul needs argument, but the dignity of human beings does not. We can peel off our moral intuitions from the theological premises from which they were once deduced—intuitions that, had we lacked a religious upbringing, we might not have had. We can hold these intuitive truths to be self-evident.

Suppose the court, when asked why it thought that the human personality is inviolable, replied that this principle is embedded in the beliefs of most Americans, that it is central to our moral and legal tradition, and that the court is not about to look behind it for premises from which it might be inferred. This would be a move like the one Rawls makes when he says that his conception of justice is "political, not metaphysical," and when he responds to Habermas that

> Justice as fairness is substantive . . . in the sense that it springs from and belongs to the tradition of liberal thought and the larger community of political culture of democratic societies. It fails then to be properly formal and truly universal, and thus to be part of the quasi-transcendental presuppositions (as Habermas sometimes says) established by the theory of communicative action.[3]

Or suppose that the court, in response to a request for philosophical backup, simply cited this passage, and similar passages, in Rawls. Suppose it just said: we don't have a philosophical argument, we just have an appeal to American common sense. Would this be to make the American legal system what Luban calls "a regime of force imposed on a domain of cynicism"? Would it no longer be such a regime if the court quoted, and convinced people by quoting, the parts of Rawls that offer what Luban calls "the fair-play argument of Hart and Rawls?"[4] Is the difference between the indirect appeal to intuition made by the premises of a fair-play argument and the direct appeal to common sense and tradition really that big a deal? Does the difference between the latter appeal and an appeal to the quasi-transcendental, the difference between Rawls and Habermas (whose theory of communicative action is a sort of surrogate for metaphysics and epistemology), matter all that much?

My sense is that it does not, but Luban clearly differs, and I am not sure how to argue the point. For I take Grey to have already answered, in the concluding section of his paper, the rhetorical question with which Luban ends his: "how can legal pragmatism stand free of first philosophy, of metaphysics, metaethics, and epistemology?" Grey's account of the common ground that he and his evangelical friend manage to find, common ground that would enable them to work together as Posner-style judges, seems to me perfectly plausible.

All I can add to what Grey has already done is to remark that the kind of religious believer Luban and Grey have in mind—the kind whose appeal to Scripture is backed up with what Luban calls "a handful of beliefs that are straightforwardly philosophical"—is pretty rare. Even Thomists do not try to give an argument from unaided natural reason for including *Leviticus* in the scriptural canon, much less for coming down hard on 18:22 while weaseling out of obedience to all those other divine commandments (the dress code, for example). Kierkegaardians and Tillichians, and most listeners to the televangelists, would not dream of trying to give such arguments, even for belief in the existence of God. They have *faith*, and do not think they need to answer Socratic questions (nor that Euthyphro needed to). The Grey-Luban philosophy buff who is also a fundamentalist is a helpful fantasy, but I have never run into anybody much like him.

Let me conclude with some more general remarks on the relation between philosophy and the rest of culture. Luban offers three conceptions of philosophy to choose from: intellectual hygiene, "*strenge Wissenschaft* aimed at formulating, analyzing, and once and for all settling questions," and Arendt's Heidegger-like view that "philosophy doesn't aim to solve problems and doesn't seek to make progress." Luban assimilates this third view to Wilfrid Sellars' definition of philosophy as "how things in the broadest possible sense of the term hang together in the broadest sense of the term."

I favor a fourth conception, one that also incorporates Sellars' definition. My conception entails neither that philosophy does not seek to make progress, nor Arendt's suggestion that "the aim of philosophy is not an increase in knowledge, but an attempt to understand the *meaning* of whatever it is that the philosopher is thinking about."

That latter suggestion goes hand-in-hand with the view—currently held by Stanley Cavell, Thomas Nagel, and Barry Stroud, among others—that the deepest and most important philosophical problems come naturally to the human mind, and arise independently of that mind's socio-historical circumstances.[5] It also goes along with Luban's claim that "Philosophical problems . . . begin with a distinction that we use in everyday life, for example the distinction between voluntary and involuntary action, or between justified and unjustified belief. A philosophical problem arises because it turns out that natural arguments show that the distinction is specious or inexplicable." Contrast this view, which tempts people to answer "a" to question (3), above, with Dewey's view that "When it is acknowledged that under disguise of dealing with ultimate reality philosophy has been occupied with the precious values embodied in social traditions, that it has sprung from a clash of social ends and from a conflict of inherited institutions with incompatible contemporary tendencies, it will be seen that the task of future philosophy is to clarify men's ideas as to the social and moral strifes of their own day."[6]

This sort of clarification of ideas is not the same sort of thing as Arendt's "attempt to understand the *meaning* of whatever it is that the philosopher is thinking about." Arendt thought that she and Socrates were both thinking about a lot of the same things: justice, for example. For Dewey, we and Socrates cannot really think about many of the same things, because the problems we are trying to solve are so different. We live in different times, believe a lot of different things, and have different senses of what is relevant to what. There are some abstract similarities between justice then and justice now, but these similarities neither help formulate the current problems, nor provide much help in solving them. (Analogously, there are some abstract similarities between Democritus' atoms and Bohr's, but there is an obvious sense in which these two scientists were not talking about the same things.)

I think that Dewey's description of philosophy can be synthesized with Sellars' by saying that the "things" the philosopher wants to make hang together keep changing. Philosophy has and will make progress, at least if one agrees with Dewey that we have been making a lot of moral, political, and social progress in recent centuries. For philosophical progress piggybacks on this latter sort of progress. We philosophers do not have a *strenge Wissenschaft* nowadays, but the things we are trying to make hang together are bigger and better than the things Socrates talked about.

They are bigger in the sense that they are much more complicated. They are better in that we live in a better age of the world: one in which the idea of finding an authority to which to subject ourselves is gradually getting replaced by the idea of coming to an agreement among ourselves. Socrates, or at any rate the Socrates of Plato's *Republic,* wanted an unwobbling pivot, something that would stay fixed forever and serve as a guiding star. So did St. Thomas and Luther, and so did the thinkers of the Enlightenment who made much of the notions of "Reason" and "Science" and "Nature."

We are better off than these intellectual ancestors because we have a lot of historical knowledge about how and why such stars first blazed, and then faded out—knowledge that has made us wonder whether we might not be able to get along without any such stars. The switch in modern philosophy from what Habermas calls "subject-centered reason" to what he calls "communicative reason"—a change Dewey embodies best—is a recognition of the historical contingency of philosophical problems, and of sociopolitical vocabularies and institutions. That switch is the most recent version of the revolt against authority that found expression first in the Reformation, and then in the Enlightenment.

For Deweyans, the whole idea of "authority" is suspect. We can still say, if we like, that the American legal system possesses a legitimate authority, and that we have an obligation to obey our country's laws. But we should not press either point. Dewey preferred to skip talk of "authority," "legitimacy," and "obligation" and to talk instead about "applied intelligence" and "democracy." He hoped we would stop using the juridical vocabulary Kant made fashionable among philosophers, and start using metaphors drawn from town meetings rather than from tribunals. He wanted the first question of both politics and philosophy to be not "What is legitimate?" or "What is authoritative?" but "What can we get together and agree on?" This is the strand in Dewey's thought that Rawls, especially in his later writings, picked up and extended.

Posner's vision of the function of American judges—his vision of their ability to range back and forth between the present and the future and try to fashion a moral unity out of our national history—fits nicely into Dewey's way of thinking. Nor is Posner's vision very different, I suspect, from that of most Americans who take an interest in what the courts, and especially the Supreme Court, are up to—at least those who are grateful for the court's decision in *Brown v. Board of Education*. If one thinks that the Civil Rights Movement, the movement that *Brown* initiated, was an enormous boost to our national self-respect, and a reassuring instance of our continuing capacity for moral progress, the thought that the courts do not just apply rules, but make them, is no longer frightening. Nor is the Deweyan suggestion that it is a waste of effort to try to figure out just where, in *Brown* and similar decisions, finding and applying old law stops and making new law begins.

Luban is nostalgic for unwobbling pivots, for the kind of authority that is supposed to be possessed by those raptly and silently contemplated truths of which he speaks. Luban uses the same language as Kant, who thought that only the fixed and eternal could fill the mind with awe (e.g., "the starry heavens above, and the moral law within"). He fears that without respect for the authority of the fixed and eternal, we shall become Trattenbachers: "Take away Plato and you take away Euclid. Take away Euclid and you find yourself in Trattenbach. Athens or Trattenbach: there is no third way."[7]

This seems to me just wrong. We have been inventing alternatives to both Athens and Trattenbach for a long time. Of these, contemporary America, warts and all, is the best so far discovered. The wise elders whom Posner describes, doing their best to keep the United States intact by keeping our political responses to surprising developments in harmony with our moral intuitions and our national traditions, are, and deserve to be, revered. As our presidents, political parties, and legislators become ever more corrupt and frivolous, we turn to the judiciary as the only political institution for which we can still feel something like awe. This awe is not reverence for the Euclid-like immutability of Law. It is respect for the ability of decent men and women to sit down around tables, argue things out, and arrive at a reasonable consensus.

Notes

1 I prefer Luban's description of me as a "postphilosophical pragmatist" to Grey's suggestion that I still hold a metaphysical view. But I see what Grey means.

2 See John Searle, "Realism and Relativism: What Difference Does it Make?" *Daedelus* 122, no. 4 (Fall 1992): 55–84, and my reply: "Does Academic Freedom Have Philosophical Presuppositions?" *Academe* 80, no. 6 (November/December 1994): 52–63. The latter piece is reprinted in *The Future of Academic Freedom,* edited by Louis Menand (Chicago: University of Chicago Press, 1996), pp. 21–42.

3 John Rawls, "Reply to Habermas," *The Journal of Philosophy* 92 (March 1995): 179.

4 I am not quite sure what argument Luban has in mind here, but I think that it would be hard to find in Hart or Rawls an attempt to ground anything in "a metaphysical conception of personality and human dignity."

5 Luban cites Nagel's metaphilosophical views with approval in his long, complex, and valuable article "Doubts about the New Pragmatism," reprinted in his *Legal Modernism* (Ann Arbor: University of Michigan Press, 1994), p. 132. He also argues in that article that "the neopragmatists have drastically misunderstood Wittgenstein" (p. 131) by treating him as one of themselves. Luban has a point. Wittgenstein did, indeed, recoil in distaste from the realization that what he was saying sounded like pragmatism. So did Nietzsche. The question is whether it is these men's pragmatist-like views, or their last-minute fears of turning into Trattenbachers, that most deserve our attention.

6 John Dewey, *Reconstruction in Philosophy: The Middle Works of John Dewey, 1899–1924,* ed. Jo Ann Boydston et al. (Carbondale: Southern Illinois University Press, 1976–1983), vol. 12, p. 94. I have enlarged on this definition of Dewey's, and offered some examples of the strifes he was talking about, in "Philosophy and the Future" in *Rorty and Pragmatism,* ed. Herman Saatkamp, Jr. (Nashville, Tenn.: Vanderbilt University Press, 1995), pp. 197–205.

7 Luban, *Legal Modernism,* p. 129.

It's a Positivist, It's a Pragmatist, It's a Codifier!
Reflections on Nietzsche and Stendhal

RICHARD H. WEISBERG

Argument. The modern movement called "Pragmatism" either is trivially associated with an absurdly wide range of adherents (including Richard Posner and Thomas Grey) or is dangerous in its implications for original, unmediated, and creative thinking. Lawyers instead would benefit from the approach of the *codifier*, who seeks to link a private creative vision to a public political program. The models for the *codifier* come from philosophy and literature and help to challenge Richard Rorty's view that the public and private realms are inevitably disjoined.

Richard Rorty writes that "Nowadays, Allan Bloom and Michael Moore seem to be the only people who still think pragmatism is dangerous to the moral health of the people."[1] Given the source, I would not contest the generalization. Nor would I seek to correct the adjective about pragmatism used more than once by Professors Rorty and Grey: "banal."[2] Indeed, the popularity of pragmatism may reflect its banality. Its amorphous nature has produced strange alliances. For example, the same Stanley Fish who once declared Richard Posner's humanistic forays to be "execrable" now joins Posner's pragmatic program almost without qualification.[3] If Pragmatism's tent is big enough to cover such disparate personalities, its grounding is unlikely to be distinctive or even identifiable. On the other hand, when we consider that pretenders to pragmatist status have included the disparate Holmes, Cardozo, Brandeis, Pound, Llewellyn, Fuller, Frankfurter, Douglas, Brennan, and Powell, we must ask who was or would be rash enough, imprudent enough, to wish to be excluded?

There is no conceivable way that an amateur in pragmatism like myself could summarize the pragmatist program for law better than do the papers of Professor Grey or Judge Posner. Judge Posner has characteristically raised the adjectival stakes by calling pragmatism "vague" (which is in some ways worse than banal), and calling the very issue he has explored in these pages "spongy."[4] But I *can* add my name to the tiny list of dissenters. I think that pragmatism is, on the terms offered by its proponents, harmful to contemporary legal thought and practice.

The sources for my brief antipragmatist argument are a pair of nineteenth-century writers, one of whom has never been described as a pragmatist, and the other would roll over in his grave in hearing himself so labeled. The latter is Friedrich Nietzsche, the former a novelist whose nonpragmatic art Nietzsche admired greatly: Stendhal.[5] These writers may help us today to distinguish a kind of legal and judicial temperament that is fundamentally different from that of the pragmatist's and—in my view— far more appropriate to the challenges we face as a culture of law in the late twentieth century.

To situate my sense of pragmatism's untimeliness, I shall note that Professor Grey has elsewhere cited William James to the effect that "in this matter of belief we are all extreme conservatives," so that—now in Grey's own words—"Only when habit and practice become problematic is there occasion for inquiry."[6] Such a pragmatic method has appeal and looks like the way most people proceed who think or do law and justice. For me, though, such a method has *itself* become intensely "problematic," for—as I shall discuss briefly towards the end of this response—the events of our century have called into radical question the appropriateness of conservative belief structures, or of only incrementalist growth, for law. The habit and practice of law have, in recent decades, "become problematic."

To situate my argument further, I will concede the distinction made in Judge Posner's paper between pragmatism and positivism; Professor Grey has elsewhere cogently separated pragmatism from formalism and other rationalistic systems (including traditional positivism).[7] If pragmatism and any formalism were indeed similar, few antiformalist contemporary legal thinkers would have become its fellow travelers. Instead, as I mentioned earlier, most of them are card carrying members. But I will also return (and also briefly) to the question of positivism.

The pragmatist-formalist opposition conceded, I want instead to articulate a dichotomy between the pragmatist and another jurisprudential type, the one I argue we need today. Because no school has been built— at least recently—around this type of lawyer, I shall give her the name *codifier.*[8] The distinction between the pragmatist and the codifier has the merit of being tangible rather than spongy, and it may also bring with it the possibility of setting apart the two preceding papers. So, whereas there is no reason to question Grey's sincerity in couching his allegiance to pragmatism in the oxymoronic terms of a "conversion" or at least a "partial conversion" to that banal condition, I argue that Posner is an apostate to pragmatism. He is, rather, a *codifier.*

A codifier is that actor who deliberately seeks to embody into law a revolutionary program already situated prelegislatively on the brink of social acceptance by the actor's—or group of actors'—political, military, or verbal achievements. The actor is sometimes utterly but always mostly uninterested in the pragmatic likelihood of her program's implementation or acceptability. There is instead a kind of "prophetic" commitment to the program, in the spirit and often in the manner of unpopular idealists whose ambitions went against the grain of the already imbedded popular agenda. Examples of codifiers are Moses, Jeremiah, Socrates, the Icelandic saga writers, the French and American Revolutionary generations, Napoleon, and Friedrich Nietzsche. All paid a price for their beliefs, but all succeeded in part because pragmatic "incrementalism" played no part in their enterprise or belief system.

The codifier, from the perspective of pragmatist theory, does not exist. She could not, because the positing of any abstract ideal toward which one works independently of the infinite flexibility of a pragmatic collectivity is, of course, anathema to the pragmatist. Because the codifier creates through act and word the ideal that she then wishes to transform into text—*and especially because the codifier is a solo player, inclined to lead and not to follow the masses*—she cannot and would never wish to be a pragmatist.

But she is alluded to as an *absence* to pragmatists, or perhaps as a shadow in the space recently discovered and emphasized by Richard Rorty in his extraordinary book, *Contingency, Irony, and Solidarity.* There Rorty lucidly identifies what he sees as an unbridgeable gap between the private person striving for individuality and the public person engaged in social improvement. For Rorty, Nietzsche exemplifies—with Baudelaire and Proust—the quest for the self-created life, a life striving for "private perfection." On the other hand, thinkers like Marx, Dewey, Habermas, and Rawls contribute to a "shared, social effort—the effort to make our institutions and practices more just and less cruel." In the space between them, Rorty situates the pragmatic "liberal ironist," a figure resigned to the unalterable difference between the two types, a difference Rorty couches in the strongest terms:

> We shall only think of these two kinds of writers as *opposed* if we think that a more comprehensive philosophical outlook would let us

hold self-creation and justice, private perfection and human solidarity, in a single vision.

There is no way in which philosophy, or any other theoretical discipline, will ever let us do that.[9]

The *codifier* disproves this uncharacteristically universal statement. And she does so as a construct of the two realms used by Rorty to *absent* her: philosophy and literature. Now first it must be noticed that Rorty's move to stories may well be the beginning of his own trajectory toward the codifier. Rorty's book directs us to literary sources as guidelines to the sensitivity of the liberal ironist. (Both Posner and Grey have analogously asked the not always receptive world of lawyers to think about poets, novelists, and other storytellers, although a strain in the legal world that might be classified as "pragmatist" tends to resist this literary suggestion, and Posner conspicuously cites history and philosophy but *not* literature as appropriate reading for appellate judges.) Rorty's move to stories may join with our burgeoning Law and Literature movement to enhance the lawyer's professional options.

Yet, on his own terms, Rorty disjoins definitively the act of the creative self-fulfilling individual from the act of the communally minded person. For Rorty, and for most pragmatists, the private and public realms will not be merged. Our pragmatic social actor might be kinder and gentler because he is well read, or he may develop a keen sense of irony that leaves him free to do what he will, but the ironist is never the codifier.[10]

Suppose, as I deeply believe, that the gap between the self-created life and the public world of law *can be breached!* Suppose that a set of readings, which like that proposed by Rorty focuses on Nietzsche, shows us how the most creative private program leads to a socially useful text?

Stendhal, as well as Nietzsche, provides us with our antipragmatic program. Nietzsche admired Stendhal, as he admired few other nineteenth-century novelists, precisely because of Stendhal's unpragmatic heroes. These characters, like their creator, refused to be constrained by an insipid notion of collective and conformist behavior. But neither does the thrust of their actions derive purely from an unmediated personal vision. Instead, Stendhal is everywhere concerned in his stories with the notion of *devoir,* or duty. His characters' drive to act well is not, on this model of *devoir,* purely *self*-generated. Often contrasted with mere pragmatism or prudence, *devoir* imposes on the protagonist an externally-inspired set of affirmative and negative constraints. Heroic action, both in the private and public spheres, is defined in Stendhal's world as both self-willed and socially constructed by external models, particularly by the model of Napoleon as at once conqueror and codifier.

Julien Sorel, the youthful hero of *Le Rouge et le Noir*, conceives of himself this way. He imposes on himself a series of outlets for his ambition, but (as René Girard stresses) these outlets reflect a model of heroism derived from an outside source, in Julien's case, Napoleon.[11] Thus Julien associates heroism on a smaller scale with each act of duty—each *devoir*—that he imposes on himself in the domains of romance, politics, and thought.[12] Although Stendhal treats his protagonists with irony on occasion, there can be little doubt that he, like his Julien, found the *source* of heroic duty in Napoleon. A man of action in his early life, Stendhal proceeded to imitate the Napoleonic model—a striking merger of action and writing. Napoleon's conquests gave birth to his majestic codes of law, sections of which Stendhal used to read nightly to guide him in creating his own masterpieces.[13] Julien's image of Napoleon equally marries heroic action to legislative text. The narrative associates Napoleon with Julien's self-willed accomplishments more than twenty times; equally to my point, Julien does Napoleon the seemingly unheroic compliment of memorizing the Napoleonic Codes. When Julien is arrested for the attempt on Mme. de Renal's life, which he at first believes to have succeeded, he announces to the examining magistrate, "I caused death with premeditation. . . . I bought the pistols from —— the gunsmith, and had him load them. Article 1342 of the Penal Code is explicit. I deserve death, and I am ready for it."[14] Julien is probably the only transgressing hero in literature who knows in advance of his crime (and by heart) the code section under which he will be tried. His continuing reverence for the code and its codifier is obvious in that he seeks immediate punishment under its terms.

Creator and character join in an admiration for Napoleon as both heroic actor and legislator. In a theme picked up more subtly by Melville in the descriptions of Admiral Nelson from *Billy Budd, Sailor*,[15] Stendhal moves us towards the bridging of the gap that only irony seems to bring about in the late twentieth century. For, in an age of *great codifiers*, individuals are able to think unironically about external standards for their actions, not as a limiting factor only (the law says I can't do this or that) but as a positive inducement to action (the law sets standards that encourage me to act a certain way, say as the codifier might have acted).

The creative individual striving for Rorty's "private perfection" is not, on this view, inevitably disjoined from the public world, even the seemingly banal public world of legislation. But to understand the codifier, we will need to see this process described genealogically, at its origin in the acts and in the thoughts of the codifier herself. We will need Nietzsche.

Nietzsche takes the admiration for Napoleon that he shared with Stendhal one step further.[16] Instead of disjoining a public program from the personal, creative will to power (Rorty's reading), Nietzsche consistently binds the public to the private.[17] Rorty in fact allows, correctly, that Nietzsche is a pluralist (or perspectivalist) only in a fraction of what he writes, thus privileging Nietzsche's more typically hierarchical scheme of moral valuation. But Rorty then errs by seeing the will to power as a merely *private* actor. In fact, the Nietzschean will to power becomes publicly expressed *through law*, that very *locus* denied by Rorty's basic claim that these two worlds can never meet.

The great legislator is himself (or herself) conceived of as one whose act of social codification begins with a private program of creative self-fulfillment. Nietzsche goes so far as to *describe* the process by which the creative personal striving at its most positive becomes socialized through a legislative text. Let us listen to this central text from *On the Genealogy of Morals;* in the eleventh aphorism of the second essay, Nietzsche first disposes of the link between justice and kneejerk revenge or *ressentiment,* and then offers us this account of justice on earth:

> To what sphere is the basic management of law, indeed the entire drive towards law, most connected? In the sphere of reactive people? Absolutely not. Much more so in the realm of the active, strong, spontaneous, aggressive. Historically understood, the place of justice on earth . . . is situated as a battle *against* the reactive emotions, a war waged by means of that active and aggressive power that here uses a part of its strength to quiet the ceaseless rumblings of *ressentiment* and to enforce a settlement.
>
> The most decisive move, however, made by the higher power against the predomination of grudge and spite, is the establishment of *the law,* the imperial elucidation of what counts in [the codifier's] eyes as permitted, as just, and what counts as forbidden and unjust. . . . From then on, the eye will seek an increasingly *impersonal* evaluation of the deed, even the eye of the victim itself, although this will be the last to do so.[18]

This is a remarkable passage because it at first seems so different from what post-modernists have made of Nietzsche. He is linking to social justice the most controversial and value-laden aspect of his personal moral agenda: the ranking of nobility above *ressentiment,* of action above reaction, of the heroic Old Testament code above the rococo, privatized spiritualization of the Gospels.[19] The will to power emerges from the realm of self-perfection into the world of socialized humanity. The individual striver—think of Moses, the Revolutionary generation, or some recent feminists—devotes some of her time to codewriting! And, from the time of codification on, as the rest of this aphorism tells us, people's actions are gauged coolly and impersonally along the lines of their *duty,* as prescribed by the codifier.

Happy is the generation whose best private actors are regulated by such a code, and whose mass of people share the same reverence for its codifier! But, as Stendhal shows us through Julien's scorn of the prudent French generation around him, people are quickly overcome by *ressentiment.* They lose sight of the greatness of the code, or they live in times where there simply is no great code. Or, worse still, they live in totalitarian times, where the values of *ressentiment,* of limitless violence, have been codified and are followed by millions of people.

I believe that the lesson of the awful codes of twentieth-century Germany and other European states has largely brought on Professor Rorty's liberal ironist, with her programmatic disjunction of the private and the public realms. She reflects the absence of reverence in our times for the constraints of a code. Put more literarily, who among us would emulate Stendhal and voluntarily crack the spine of any legal code written under western skies, much less delve into it for creative guidance? The modern rift between law and letters seems most striking in the difference, say, between the Internal Revenue Code and our favorite novel.[20]

But this does not eliminate the *normative* possibility of the arrival of a new codifier. And for those like Judge Posner and myself sensitive to the shadow of European history, ours is a period that might demand, rather than ironize, the linkage of private and public that the codifier brings. Certain periods mandate codification over pragmatics. Our is such a generation. As Judge Posner observes, evoking a debate he had with me about legal rhetoric during the period of Vichy France, ours is a period in which the example of law in Nazi Europe imposes comparisons at every moment to some of our own techniques and practices.[21] As I have suggested, particularly when a system so similar to ours in its basic story—the system under which French lawyers were trained—behaves in the pragmatic manner typical of Vichy law—accommodating incrementally to an evil inversion of the traditional egalitarian story—we must reassess the premises of analogous movements seeking prominence in our jurisprudence. If positivism were the villain, the stakes would still be high; but note that Posner dissociates Nazi judges from positivism—and I believe he is correct, surely so if the referent is also Vichy France—and places them implicitly within the dilemma for pragmatism. Recall that Posner the pragmatist earlier defines the pragmatic judge—and in part his own approach—as follows: "A pragmatist judge always tries to do the best he can do for the present and the future, unchecked by any felt *duty* to secure consistency in principle with what other officials have done in the past."

Well, if this be pragmatism, and if the pragmatic judge in fact has no Sorel- (or Dworkin-) like *devoir* to any worthy codifier, what keeps us from replicating the model of European law during World War II? What prevents us from going with the flow of the latest accepted and fashionable movement, however grotesquely out of line with our country's previously long held traditions? Posner's answer is not reassuring, neither here nor in his earlier writings; in his paper here, he advises that Nazi judges might have resisted more if they had been "backward looking" instead of advancing a radical Third Reich program foreign to their traditions. But this suggestion, which is in the service of Posner's "council of wise elders" approach, only helps if the wise elders have unpragmatically assimilated the egalitarian code as a certain guideline for decision-making. This, however, did not happen in Vichy; and Posner's earlier consistently pragmatic suggestions about what lawyers should have done in that situation involve such lower-level questions as how does one get published during times of oppression if one does not at least partially accommodate; how does one manage both to write and to hide one's true feelings; and why should one be expected to "step forward" to resist directly when "heroes are rare."[22]

It is probably not entirely fair to conclude from what I have read so far about pragmatism that it does not help us (at least no more so than other contemporary patterns of legal thought) with the issue I have identified and Judge Posner has reflected upon. But Posner's definition of what it means to be a judge seems to me so far from the common understanding of pragmatism that it offers a step in the direction of an answer. For it seems to me that Posner, here and perhaps in his practice as a judge, is more the codifier than the pragmatist. He believes that judges, wise or foolish, old or young, should act on a body of "organized knowledge" of a "disciplined, rigorous and articulate," rather than an unstructured intuition—surely not on the basis of anterior constraint.

Unanchored from precedent, the codifying judge may seek occasion to instantiate his own sense of social utility. A microeconomic generalization, first impressed upon lawyers by Posner's extrajudicial writings, is now raised to the level of appellate rule.[23]

One need not be a judge to be a codifier. One can also be a law professor and consultant to municipal governments; here I believe that the example of Catherine MacKinnon is helpful. Like Posner, she has moved from a base of powerful theoretical writing to articulate her private academic beliefs into a socially viable code, in her case *literally* a code.[24]

Unlike pragmatism and some other more recent jurisprudential approaches, the move toward codification has the merit of baring the values of the otherwise private thinker or actor to full social scrutiny. Whatever drove Napoleon to conquer Europe, his lasting contribution in the domain of the written codes elucidates the social component of his private ambitions. When we look to the codes there is no avoiding the value system of the codifier. Perceiving Posner or MacKinnon as codifiers, more than as pragmatic or feminist theorists, engages our social-policy instincts most forcefully. The stakes are always high when legislation is promulgated. It was on this legislative plane that Holmes consistently expressed a dislike for Napoleon—and maybe that is why Holmes might accept contentedly the label "pragmatist" imposed on him by the preceding authors and would resist the label "codifier," much evidence about his legal method to the contrary notwithstanding.[25]

But it will be up to us, under the codifier model, not merely to criticize or to rationalize the codes of others that we may not like. The challenge for us is to develop and perfect our own private beliefs and, if they are good enough, to make them public. From then on, we will be treated by *skeptical* others as wrongheaded and ephemeral but at least as "entitled to our beliefs" or as "off the wall" but still within the operations of "the system."[26] *Admiring* others will have a chance to say we are correct and inspired. If we attract a sufficiently large group of admirers, we may ironically produce a form of positivism that Nietzsche of all people seems to endorse in the unlikely scenario of the reappearance of a codifier worthy of the name.

Notes

1 Richard Rorty, "The Banality of Pragmatism and the Poetry of Justice," in *Pragmatism in Law and Society,* ed. Michael Brint and William Weaver (Boulder: Westview Press, 1991), pp. 90–91.

2 Rorty, *ibid.,* at 89 and again at 90; Thomas Grey, "Holmes and Legal Pragmatism," 41 *Stanford L. Rev* 787 (1989): 814; and "Freestanding Legal Pragmatism," this volume.

3 Fish finds little to disagree with in Posner's approach to legal reasoning, which he calls "Almost Pragmatism," in *Pragmatism in Law,* p. 55. Fish's harsh assessment of Posner's earlier attempts in the humanities related to Posner's *Law and Literature: A Misunderstood Relation* (Cambridge: Harvard University Press, 1988); Fish's critique is found, for example, in Winkler, "Controversial Judge and Legal Theorist Jumps Into the Debate on Law and Literature," *The Chronicle of Higher Education* (December 7, 1988): A10.

4 "Perverse," "hectoring," and "peripheral" are some nonpragmatic adjectives Judge Posner has used in writing about my treatment of a topic to which he returns late in his

paper in this volume—judgment under totalitarian regimes. See Posner, *Law and Literature*, pp. 171, 174, 175. There are those who think he later came to accept my primary position on adjudication in these regimes—and he surely used my primary evidence—in a later piece. See his review of Ingo Müller's *Hitler's Justice,* in *The New Republic* (17 June, 1991): 36.

5 On Nietzsche's admiration for Stendhal, see *The Twilight of the Idols,* section 45.

6 Grey, "Holmes," pp. 799–800.

7 *Ibid.,* pp. 789–91. Grey allows that the "instrumental aspects" of pragmatism are harder to distinguish from some means-ends qualities of the positivist program (*ibid.,* at 852–54).

8 In his response to my remarks at the conference, Judge Posner noted that my pronomial choice degendered him even as I was paying him the compliment of calling him a codifier. But the real pronomial choice relating to his work on legal economics is in my *title,* which is partly meant to convey the abysmal and depersonalizing effect upon the law of Posner's brand of economic reasoning.

9 Richard Rorty, *Contingency, Irony, and Solidarity* (Cambridge: Cambridge University Press, 1989), p. xiv.

10 Note that the well-read Newt Gingrich has been loudly proclaimed a pragmatist in a *New York Times* headline, "Gingrich, Long Seen as a Purist, Shows His Worth as a Pragmatist" (October 27, 1995: A1). Gingrich is proving to be a Rortian ironist more than he is a successful codifier, as attests the Republican Party's recent deletion of references to its "Contract with America."

11 See Girard, *Mensonge romantique et vérité romanesque* (translated as *Deceit, Desire and the Novel*). To simplify for my present purposes: Girard approaches the characters in Stendhal, and other writers, in terms of "triangular desire": the structuring of the character's self-imposed goals through *another,* through a model whom the character emulates. For Julien, the goal of seducing Mme. de Renal or of achieving certain political ends, is a triangulated reflection of Napoleon's own achievements.

12 I use the English edition here, with a translation by Catherine Slater, *The Red and the Black* (New York: Oxford University Press, 1991). *Le Rouge et le Noir* was first published in 1830 by Stendhal (aka Henri Beyle), and I am using the *Livre de Poche* version of the original (Paris: Librairie générale française, 1958). The word *devoir* ("duty") is employed narratively to characterize Julien's various self-imposed public and private challenges: the *duty* to embrace Mme. de Renal, pp. 57, 86 (see especially: "*He had done his duty, his heroic duty,*" p. 59); the duty to fulfill M. de la Mole's restorationist scheme, see chapter 21, *passim,* and p. 411. For the *devoir* of cooling Mathilde de la Mole's passion for him, see p. 444; for the *devoir* of growing personally through self-criticism, see p. 343.

13 See, for example, Stendhal's letter to Balzac of October 28–29, 1840, in which he reveals that he needed a nightly dose of at least three pages of the Code Civil while writing *La Chartreuse de Parme* in order to attain the proper tone in his own novels. H. Martineau, ed., *Stendhal, Correspondence* (Paris: Gallimard, 1968), p. 401.

14 Slater translation, p. 470.

15 See my *The Failure of the Word: The Protagonist as Lawyer in Modern Fiction* (New Haven: Yale University Press, 1984), chapters 8 and 9.

16 See, e.g., *Zur Genealogie der Moral,* I, 16, in Nietzsche, *Sämtliche Werke* (Stuttgart: Kröner Verlag, 1964), vol. 76, p. 281. "Like a last signpost to the *other* path, Napoleon appeared, the most isolated and late-born man there has even been, and in him the

problem of the *noble ideal as such* made flesh—one might well ponder *what* kind of problem it is: Napoleon, this synthesis of the *inhuman* and *superhuman*" (*Basic Writings of Nietzsche,* trans. Walter Kaufmann (New York: Modern Library, 1968), p. 490).

17 Rorty, *Contingency, Irony, and Solidarity,* p. 106.

18 *Genealogie,* II, 11, vol. 76, pp. 306–7 (my translation). The original language reads as follows: [I]n welcher Sphäre ist denn bisher überhaupt die ganze Handhabung des Rechts, auch das eigentliche Bedürfnis nach Recht auf Erden heimisch gewesen? Etwa in der Sphäre reaktiven Menschen? Ganz und gar nicht: vielmehr in der der Aktiven, Starken, Spontanen, Aggressiven. Historisch betrachtet, stellt das Recht auf Erden . . . den Kampf gerade *wieder* die reaktiven Gefühle vor, den Krieg mit denselben seitens aktiver und aggressiver Mächte, welche, ihre Stärke zum Teil dazu verwendten, der Ausschweifung des reaktiven Pathos Halt und Mass zu gebieten und einen Vergleich zu erzwingen.

Das Entscheidenste aber, was die oberste Gewalt gegen die Übermacht der Gegen- und Nachgefühle tut und durchsetzt—sie tut es immer, sobald sie irgendwie stark genug dazu ist—, ist die Aufrichtung des *Gesetzes,* die imperativische Erklärung darüber, was überhaupt unter ihren Augen als erlaubt, als recht, was als verboten, als unrecht zu gelten habe; . . . von nun an wird das Auge für eine immer *unpersönlichere* Abschätzung der Tat eingeübt, sogar das Auge des Geschädigten selbst (obschon dies am allerlefzten).

19 See, e.g., *Beyond Good and Evil,* aphorisms 52, 251.

20 See, e.g., Robert Ferguson, *Law and Letters in American Culture* (Cambridge: Harvard University Press, 1984).

21 Compare Posner, *Law and Literature,* pp. 171–75 with Weisberg, *The Failure of the Word,* introduction and appendix on French lawyer, Joseph Haennig, and Weisberg, *Poethics, And Other Strategies of Law and Literature* (New York: Columbia University Press, 1992), chapter 5 and essay 15. See also Posner, "Pragmatic Adjudication," this volume.

22 Posner, *Law and Literature,* pp. 173, 174.

23 See, e.g., Landes and Posner, *The Economic Structure of Tort Law* (Cambridge: Harvard University Press, 1987), as well as the recent *Edwards* decision on proximate cause, limiting corporate liability even where the plaintiff is foreseeable at the time of the negligent act. See *Edwards v. Honeywell, Inc.* 50 F.3d 484 (7th Cir. 1995).

24 See, e.g., "Pornography, Civil Rights, and Speech," 20 *Harvard Civil Rights-Civil Liber. L. Rev* 1 (1985). See also MacKinnon and Andrea Dworkin's Indianapolis antipornography statute. But see *American Booksellers Ass'n v. Hudnut,* 771 F.2d 323 (7th Cir. 1985), *aff'd* without opinion, 475 US 1001 (1986). Some Canadian jurisdictions have adopted MacKinnon's code.

25 A scan of the many mentions of Napoleon by Holmes in his correspondence reveals his distaste for the French hero-codifier. See, e.g., *Holmes-Laski Letters,* ed. Mark DeWolf Howe (abridged by Alger Hiss; New York: Atheneum, 1963), letters of April 30, 1921 (where he does express an interest in Melville); September 26, 1921; October 9, 1921 ("Kant after more than a century counted for more than Napoleon"). It was his admirer Cardozo who, in *Pokora v. Wabash Ry Co.,* 54 S. Ct. 580 (1934), reluctantly had to correct the bald, unpragmatic assertiveness of Holmes' "stop and get out of his vehicle" railway crossing absolute rule in *Baltimore B & O R. Co. v. Goodman,* 48 S. Ct. 24 (1927). For that matter, on the level of style, Cardozo certainly painted Holmes in the terms of the codifier, with his epigrammatic, monarchical "type magisterial." See Cardozo, "Law

and Literature," in M. E. Hall, *Selected Writings of Benjamin N. Cardozo* (Albany: Matthew Bender, 1947, 1975), pp. 347–48. For Cardozo, Holmes might have been a kind of Nietzschean "last signpost" to the times of judges who—on their sole authority—could write boldly and without further justification in pragmatics or (even) experience. On this view, Holmes, although not in the Napoleonic mode, was more a codifier than a pragmatist.

26 Stanley Fish, *Is There A Text in This Class?* (Cambridge: Harvard University Press, 1980), p. 357.

Pragmatism, Pluralism and Legal Interpretation: Posner's and Rorty's Justice without Metaphysics Meets Hate Speech

MICHEL ROSENFELD

Pluralist societies with widely diverging conceptions of the good foster sharp disagreements over interpretation of legal texts—and in particular of those that deal with broadly encompassing fundamental rights such as liberty, equality, or privacy. Without widely shared religious, ethical, and political values, legal interpretations are unlikely to reconcile justice according to law with justice beyond law.[1] This makes pragmatism particularly attractive, because of its rejection of the need for foundations, its orientation towards the future, and its "down to earth" approach, which purports to offer practical solutions to concrete problems. Indeed, pragmatism raises the possibility of settling questions of justice according to law without any need to appeal to justice beyond the law or to take sides in the contest among competing conceptions of the good.

Notwithstanding its great promise, pragmatism, in large measure owing to its great success, has meant so many different things to such a large number of people as to raise as many questions as it answers. It is not clear, for instance, whether pragmatism revolves around a common core of tenets; whether there is any link between pragmatism in philosophy and in law; or whether pragmatism can solve the vexing problems surrounding legal interpretation. This essay tackles these issues by contrasting two very different versions of pragmatism—namely the traditional scientific pragmatism of Richard Posner and the neopragmatism of Richard Rorty—and by inquiring how they fare with respect to the difficult and highly divisive interpretive conflicts raised by hate speech.

I

Pragmatism radiates far afield over the philosophical and the legal landscape. In philosophy pragmatism regroups such diverse figures as Charles Sanders Peirce, William James, John Dewey, and Richard Rorty; and, in contemporary American legal theory, it arguably encompasses everyone but the most rigid of formalists.[2] Consistent with this broad sweep, pragmatism shifts the focus from foundations to actual consequences, and prompts people to leave aside normative disputes to engage in the common pursuit of practical results. Thus, under pragmatism, justice according to law is measured by the practical consequences to which it leads.

There is however, a nagging question. Assuming that different interpretations of the same law would lead to different practical consequences, can recourse to pragmatism determine which of the available alternatives ought to be pursued? In short, is pragmatism self-sufficient or is it merely *parasitic* on certain contestable conceptions of the good? This last question is crucial, for if pragmatism proved merely parasitic, its attractiveness would be very limited. It could help avoid normative disputes with no demonstrable practical consequences, but would otherwise do little to overcome clashes between conceptions of the good.

Pragmatists encompass a wide span of political ideologies and there is a great divergence between old pragmatist and new pragmatist conceptions of "what works." For old pragmatists, like Peirce and Dewey, "what works" was understood in terms of scientifically grounded experience.[3] For neopragmatists like Rorty, on the other hand, "what works" is conceived in terms of a "linguistic redescription" susceptible of gaining widespread acceptance primarily on account of its aesthetic appeal.[4] Given these differences, a pragmatism completely freed from the grip of contestable conceptions of the good is highly unrealistic whereas a pragmatism parasitic on such conceptions is largely uninteresting. This leaves the possibility of a pragmatism that falls between these two extremes. The latter—"intermediate pragmatism"—is worth investigating because unlike parasitic pragmatism, which is reducible to a pragmatism of means, it purports to be a pragmatism of means and *some* ends (or at the very least, a special pragmatism of means allowing for a different perspective on ends).

The search for intermediate pragmatism is complicated by the fact that pragmatists tend to treat the relationship between means and ends with a remarkable lack of concern.[5] To sharpen the contrast between means and ends, I shall explore intermediate pragmatism through a comparison between Richard Posner's brand of old pragmatism and Richard Rorty's neopragmatism. Moreover, what makes a comparison between Posner, who is on the right of the American political spectrum, and Rorty, who is on its left, particularly apt is that they seem flexible and broad minded regarding ends and both agree that pragmatism justifies extensive freedom of expression rights.[6]

II

Before further discussion of pragmatism's potential for legal interpretation, an important preliminary question must be addressed: What links, if any, can be established between pragmatism in philosophy and pragmatism in law?

Significantly, neither Rorty nor Posner sees any intimate relationship between philosophical pragmatism and pragmatism in law. As Rorty states "judges will probably not find pragmatist philosophers—either old or new—useful."[7] This is not to say, however, that Posner and Rorty see *no* relationship between pragmatism in philosophy and in law. According to them, pragmatist philosophy performs a useful task that facilitates the practice of legal pragmatism, but that task involves the removal of obstacles—or, in Posner's words, "clear[ing] the underbrush"—rather than building a philosophical framework affording backing to legal practice.[8] According to this view, pragmatist philosophy's antifoundationalism has a liberating effect on law, by freeing the legal theorist from having to justify practical solutions to legal problems under any comprehensive theory. In the words of Thomas Grey, "pragmatism is freedom from theory—guilt."[9]

The apparent liberation afforded to law by pragmatist philosophy may have at least three different meanings. First, it may mean that pragmatist philosophy frees law from the need to have any ties to philosophy. Second, it may mean that pragmatist philosophy enables law to pick and choose whatever it may find useful among all available philosophies, without regard for comprehensiveness. Or, third, it may mean that, while law need not derive something positive from pragmatist philosophy, legal pragmatism depends on pragmatic philosophy for purposes of keeping at bay any encroachments from foundationalism or comprehensive theory. In the first case, philosophical pragmatism would make the case that legal pragmatism has altogether no use for philosophy. In the second case, legal pragmatism would emerge as a parasitic pragmatism that could be engrafted on any philosophy of one's choosing without concern for consistency or comprehensiveness. Finally, in the third case, philosophical pragmatism and legal pragmatism would have a mutual connection allowing them to combine together into some version of intermediate pragmatism.

A complete emancipation of law from philosophy seems highly unlikely. In any complex advanced legal system, law must determine at least some ends. Such determinations, moreover, cannot always be achieved by mere reference to law. For example, the question of whether a broadly articulated constitutional equality right should be construed to prohibit discrimination against homosexuals, or whether a generally phrased constitutional privacy right requires protecting a woman's right to an abortion, is unlikely to be cogently addressed without any reference to ethical norms or other broader philosophical concerns. Thus, focus on consequences alone cannot supply a principled answer to the relevant question confronting the constitutional judge. For example, protecting homosexual lifestyles is likely to have *certain* practical consequences, and refusal to do so *certain other* practical consequences. Because of this, a judge cannot cogently resolve the constitutional issue at hand on the basis of a legal pragmatism completely severed from ethics or philosophy.

The second case stems from an understanding of the liberating effect of pragmatist philosophy on law that, in effect, reverses the respective positions of philosophy and law. In a conventional foundationalist setting, philosophy can be viewed as preceding, and standing above, law. In the antifoundationalist setting carved out by pragmatist philosophy, in contrast, practical solutions to actual legal problems would become paramount and philosophical justifications would play a subsidiary role. Thus, the principal objective would be to find an acceptable and workable practical solution to an actual legal problem, and then resort to philosophy only to allay fears that the adopted solution is arbitrary or unethical.

Subordinating philosophy to law may promote greater flexibility, but only proves attractive when set against a background of widespread consensus on relevant values or when a particular practical legal solution to a problem happens to be consistent with several otherwise inconsistent philosophical positions. In any event, philosophy's low profile and subordinate position are not likely to last once background consensus dissolves in the face of a sharply divisive issue, such as abortion. Indeed, when dealing with an issue like abortion, the luxury of relegating theoretical concerns to a secondary plane quickly vanishes, as conflict between proponents of different practical ends is bound to erupt, and the advocates of each contending position are called upon to justify their preferences. Moreover, as the debate sharpens, it becomes increasingly necessary to develop a more consistent and more comprehensive position to counter the attacks of adversaries bent on exploiting every possible inconsistency or weakness. In sum, when dealing with genuinely divisive issues susceptible to competing practical solutions, legal pragmatism cannot completely avoid philosophic considerations or remain merely parasitic upon them.

That leaves the third case according to which legal and philosophical pragmatism combine to yield some kind of intermediate pragmatism. In this last case, pragmatic philosophy's liberation of legal pragmatism from the constraints of comprehensive theory does not mean liberation from all philosophy or freedom to pick and choose among all philosophies. It means, instead, freedom from all philosophies other than pragmatism on the condition of submitting to the constraints dictated by pragmatist philosophy. And if these constraints are often hard to discern, it is because they seem to be primarily negative ones. To test this out, let us take a closer look at Posner and Rorty.

III

Richard Posner purports to blend his philosophical pragmatism with his commitment to the economic approach to law and to liberal individualism. Moreover, Posner's pragmatism seems a good candidate for an intermediate pragmatism, as he denies that law is autonomous, and asserts that it is pragmatism that justifies the economic approach to law and adherence to liberal individualism. Furthermore, since Posner maintains that neither the economic approach to law nor individualistic liberalism is comprehensive, his pragmatism calls for some but, by no means all ends.[10]

Posner's brand of pragmatism is scientific in the tradition of Peirce and Dewey. It is antifoundationalist and anti-Cartesian, experimental and culturally relativistic, and open to a seemingly unlimited array of ultimate value preferences and conceptions of the good. Posner insists, moreover, that his pragmatism is antidogmatic and moderately skeptical.

While Posner's pragmatism remains open-ended regarding ultimate ends, it turns out, upon more exacting scrutiny, to be quite rigid when it comes to means. Specifically, Posner seems agnostic concerning ultimate ends, but he insists that the economic approach to law and liberal individualism afford the best means toward maximizing the opportunities for everyone to pursue his or her conception of the good. To be sure, if all plausible ends call for the same means, then a singular set of means is consistent with a plurality of ends. But rigidity concerning means may also result from dogmatism concealed through an apparent inversion of means and ends. In the latter case, what appears to be intermediate pragmatism turns out to be parasitic pragmatism in disguise.

To assess fairly whether Posner's pragmatism ultimately rests on a reversal of means and ends, I shall first explore to what extent his combination of agnosticism regarding ends, advocacy of the economic approach to law, and embrace of liberal individualism can be cogently construed as yielding intermediate pragmatism. To this end, I should first point out that agnosticism regarding ends need not mean that all ends are literally equivalent. Indeed, consistent with pragmatism's antifoundationalism, agnosticism regarding ends can be linked to the belief that no conception of the good could ever be definitively established as superior to all of its rivals. Based on that belief, moreover, the pragmatist can justify putting one end on a different plane than all the others, namely the end of maximizing equal freedom to pursue other ends. This special end thus becomes a second-order end while all other ends remain on the same plane as first-order ends. Under pragmatic skepticism, therefore, agnosticism regarding ends should be understood as being limited to first-order ends.

The second-order end may be but a means toward first-order ends, but because the pragmatic skeptic can give no definitive endorsement to any first-order end, he or she must rely on the second-order end as the only constant objective against which the practicality of all available means must be eventually tested. Therefore, in as much as Posner's agnosticism implies commitment to the second-order end, this raises the question of whether his economic approach to law can be successfully defended as the best possible practical means toward the achievement of that second-order end.

It is not necessary to delve in any detail into Posner's well-known views of law and economics to realize the implausibility of the claim that wealth maximization is *universally* justifiable as *the* pragmatic means to all conceivable ends attainable through law. At the very least, in a world in which wealth-maximization is perceived as a precondition to the achievement of a plurality of ends, there is a serious danger that attention to wealth-maximizing means would overshadow the pursuit of moral ends. Accordingly, although in theory wealth-maximization would only serve as means, in practice it would force all other ends to be continuously postponed or relegated to a lesser plane. Moreover, whereas it would be absurd to pretend that economics has nothing to contribute to just interpretations, in some areas of law, economics and wealth maximization seem largely irrelevant. For example, as Posner himself acknowledges, law and economics cannot establish whether a right to abortion would be wealth-maximizing, let alone determine whether constitutional liberty, equality, or privacy should be interpreted as justifying a woman's right to an abortion.[11]

To his credit, and true to his commitment to pragmatism, Posner has acknowledged the limits of law and economics in his more recent works.[12] But once wealth maximization is no longer conceived as a potentially all pervasive means, then the question of pragmatic means becomes highly unsettling. Under those circumstances, pragmatically justified means would vary according to the particular ends sought, which would in turn depend on adhesion to one among many competing conceptions of the good. Accordingly, far from sustaining intermediate pragmatism, Posner's law and economics appears at best compatible with parasitic pragmatism.

In the last analysis, Posner's pragmatism is perhaps best understood as an adjunct to his commitment to the principle of wealth maximization rather than the other way around. From this latter perspective, wealth maximization is not a neutral engine designed to optimize choices for everyone, but the product of a conception of the good that competes with several others. What is deceiving about wealth maximization is that it does not foreclose the pursuit of certain other first-order ends, and is thus easily confused as being part and parcel of a second-order end. For example, wealth maximization privileges individualism and competition over communitarianism and solidarity and is accordingly much more amenable to conceptions of the good predicated on the former than on those dependent on the latter. It does not follow, however, that wealth maximization completely precludes the pursuit of preferences based on solidarity or that it must necessarily take sides among competing conceptions of the good rooted in individualism. Nevertheless, the essential points remain that wealth maximization is not neutral and that the fate of other conceptions of the good are subordinated to it rather than the other way around.

Once wealth maximization is posited as the predominant pursuit, agnosticism regarding other conceptions of the good can be mobilized to parry the thrust of attacks launched from ideological standpoints inimical to the law and economics ethos. Consistent with this, pragmatism can be invoked to deflect the sting of revelations concerning wealth maximization's limitations and contradictions. Accordingly, not only would Posner's pragmatism prove to be merely parasitic rather than intermediate, but its principal usefulness would derive from its ability to deflect attention from the dogmatic idealization of wealth maximization. Nevertheless, this still does not preclude Posner from joining the ranks of intermediate pragmatism through his defense of freedom of speech. Before tackling that issue, however, I turn to Richard Rorty's rather different brand of pragmatism, which seems potentially superior to Posner's in as much as it appears to pave the way for a smoother and more flexible reconciliation of means and ends.

IV

Richard Rorty is the preeminent proponent of neopragmatism, a postmodern reformulation of the pragmatist project by means of shift in focus from experience to language. Rorty's pragmatism is shaped by his radical reinterpretation of the meaning and implications of the rejection of foundationalism. For Rorty, antifoundationalism requires that we refrain from according science and "the scientific method" any special deference and that we abandon viewing language as a medium of representation referring to, or corresponding to, a reality beyond it. Rather, language is most profitably conceived in Wittgensteinian terms, as a game making possible the use of alternative vocabularies relating to one another more "like alternative tools than like bits of a jigsaw puzzle." Rorty invites us to turn away from the interpretive subject and its elusive objects, and to accept that the human self makes its mark by choosing among alternative vocabularies evaluated in terms of their practical consequences—of whether they are likely to lead to a greater and more fruitful consensus among members of the polity.[13]

Consistent with the place of language games in Rorty's vision, language figures as means and end as well as the bridge between them. Moreover, within this framework, justice is more likely to emerge out of the poet's imagination than out of the philosopher's search for normative coherence, and, as Rorty emphasizes, there is a prophetic side to justice.[14] This, however, squarely raises the vexing question of whether the prophetic quality of justice has anything to do with pragmatism other than that pragmatism's removal of foundations may do away with cumbersome constraints on the uses of imagination and prophecy.

Arguably, there is no intrinsic connection between Rorty's prophetic strand and his pragmatism.[15] Furthermore, in that case, the poetry of justice would belie any nexus between justice according to law and justice beyond law, and would confine the former to the realm of aesthetics. Legal interpretations could only be meaningfully evaluated in terms of their appeal, and judges would have to rely on their imaginations with the hope that their opinions will be able to kindle a favorable and uplifting response. In this scenario, justice would be entirely liberated from philosophy, and the legitimacy of legal interpretations could only be measured by the lasting power of their aesthetic appeal.

Another plausible reading of the link between pragmatism and prophecy, however, allows bringing Rorty's contribution closer to intermediate pragmatism. Under this alternative reading, antifoundationalist philosophy and the turn to language do not merely play a negative role, but also bestow legitimacy on certain particular positive undertakings. In other words, in this alternative, pragmatism not only clears away obstacles that stand in the way of prophecy, but also furnishes positive backing for certain crucial elements in the prophetic vision such as the quest for social justice. With this in mind, let us now focus on the potential of Rorty's pragmatism for forging plausible links between the critical work stemming from antifoundationalism and the constructive task of the prophetic poet.

Rorty's antifoundationalism is closely connected to an inevitable existential confrontation with contingency. Indeed, those willing to accept contingency can replace the Kantian tradition of viewing truth as a vertical relationship between representation and what is represented with a conception of truth as a horizontal process consisting in the "reinterpretation of our predecessors' reinterpretation of their predecessors' reinterpretation."[16] Moreover, the point of such reinterpretation is not discovery or realization of any transcendent or immanent truth, but redescription in the hope of finding better-suited ways to handle our contingency upon the realization that it is fruitless to attempt to escape from it.

The justification for choosing redescription over appeal to vertical truth is pragmatic. The search for vertical truth is unproductive much in the same way as it is not helpful to become bogged down with questions about the existence or the nature of God. Just as the secularist maintains that we should not dwell upon questions beyond our capacities to resolve, so, too, the pragmatist insists that we should not waste our time worrying about the truth, since we are not in a position to ascertain its existence or precise nature.[17]

The critical side of Rorty's antifoundationalism leads thus to the same conclusion as does Posner's: no one can prove that his or her conception of the good—or in Rorty's characterization, his or her "final vocabulary"—is superior to any other.[18] Furthermore, agnosticism concerning final vocabularies calls for a split between first-order ends and the second-order end of maximizing freedom to develop, and choosing among, final vocabularies. Accordingly, Rorty's prophetic vision seems a good candidate to complement critical antifoundationalism and furnish the requisite positive component needed to elaborate a coherent practical approach for dealing with the contingency, diversity, and volatility of first-order ends. It remains to be seen, however, whether Rorty's prophetic vision can be integrated into a workable conception of intermediate pragmatism.

What drives Rorty's positive contribution is the redescription of the liberal project consistent with the practical implications of his critical analysis. The protagonist of Rorty's prophetic journey is the "liberal ironist." To be "liberal," in Rorty's redescription, is to think that "cruelty is the worst thing we do"; to be an "ironist" is to recognize the contingency of one's innermost beliefs and desires. Thus, the liberal ironist seems bound to be committed to the pursuit of two distinct ends: eradicating cruelty and combatting the forceful imposition of any final vocabulary. The first of these calls for solidarity and is a collective end; the second, which relies on self-creation, amounts to an individualistic aim.[19] Both these ends appear consistent with the concept of intermediate pragmatism in that they can be plausibly integrated into a project to secure a second-order end to allow for maximization of equal opportunities to pursue first-order ends.

For those who reject Rorty's utopian vision, however, the two objectives of making more room for individual idiosyncrasy and of fomenting greater solidarity may well seem to be at loggerheads. Arguably, following the threads of one's idiosyncratic imagination is a rather solipsistic endeavor, whereas developing sufficient empathy towards other human beings to perceive them as fellow sufferers, on the contrary, requires a certain measure of self-abnegation and an altruistic gesture of openness towards the other. Accordingly, the tension between the individualist and the collective objective raises serious questions concerning whether Rorty's positive prophetic conception can be ultimately reconciled with intermediate pragmatism. This question is best postponed until after completion of our examination of the promise of Rorty's prophetic vision. For the moment, suffice it to note that the difficulties in the case of Rorty concern the suitability of means rather than inversion between means and ends as was the case with Posner.

From within Rorty's own perspective, what binds individualism and solidarity closer together is not logic, but the consequences of contingency. Because of the precariousness and vulnerability of the individual who cannot ground any final vocabulary on a solid foundation, everyone is relegated to projecting into the future a plausible hope of redemption that will make up for the painful limitations inherent in his or her present predicament. Consistent with this, moreover, self-creation does not become any less individualistic, but the individual remains open to solidarity for fear of being trivialized and humiliated in the desire to give free rein to his or her own idiosyncratic imagination in order to overcome present insufficiencies.[20]

The political means Rorty considers suitable to achieve this redemption, entailing individualistic self-creation and solidarity in the struggle against cruelty, are startlingly simple and familiar. He embraces John Stuart Mill's suggestion that government strike a balance between staying out of the private sphere and preventing suffering. Consistent with this, in Rorty's ideal liberal society, change stems from persuasion rather than force, reform rather than revolution. Moreover, since the key to coming closer to that ideal depends on fostering useful redescriptions, Rorty values discussion for its own sake and preaches uninhibited freedom of expression as the best hope for peaceful progress instead of the use of force.[21]

The paramountcy of freedom of expression is doubly justified in Rorty's prophetic vision. On the one hand, it enlarges the horizon for redescription; on the other, it serves to channel conflicts toward resolution by means of discussion as opposed to force. It is Rorty's hope that in a liberal society committed to freedom of expression the poet and the innovator will prevail. And if that makes life harder for others, Rorty reassures us that we need not worry, for it will be harder "only by words, and not deeds."[22]

Rorty's critical analysis and his prophetic vision can be plausibly combined to yield a seemingly coherent version of intermediate pragmatism. Moreover, because Rorty's philosophy is driven by at least one constant objective, namely the hope for more useful redescription, the intermediate pragmatism to which it apparently leads would qualify as a pragmatism of ends, at least with respect to one end. That (second-order) end is the maximization of opportunities for imaginative redescriptions, and it calls for at least one legal norm, namely affording the greatest possible protection to freedom of expression.

In spite of their otherwise significant differences, Posner and Rorty both concur that pragmatist philosophy lends support to freedom of expression. It is now time to take a closer critical look at this common conclusion, by inquiring whether the pragmatist defense of freedom of expression can overcome the daunting challenge posed by extremist and hate speech. Also, this inquiry should put us in a better position to determine whether Rorty's prophetic vision is ultimately unpragmatic.

V

There is a strong affinity between the pragmatist justification of freedom of speech and the utilitarian one elaborated by John Stuart Mill. In both cases, the justification for freedom of expression is predicated on the impossibility of complete or immutable truth.

Mill's strong defense of freedom of expression is far reaching as it extends protection even to expressions that are directly harmful to others, provided they do not amount to *incitements* to violence.[23] Moreover, underlying Mill's opposition to regulating harmful speech is his firm belief that free discussion is indispensable to the discovery of incremental truth and to social progress.[24] Thus, stripped to its utilitarian essentials, Mill's broad justification of freedom of expression, which was imported into the constitutional jurisprudence of the United States as the "marketplace of ideas" justification of speech, boils down to the following: the long term benefits (in relation to truth and social progress) of uninhibited discussion are bound to outweigh the sum of harms attributable to (non-inciting) expression.[25]

Constitutional provisions affording protection to speech tend to be uniformly sweeping and indeterminate.[26] Moreover, they lead to contradictory results in the context of extremist and hate speech. For example, U.S. jurisprudence on the issue stands in sharp contrast to that of many other Western democracies.[27]

Extremist and hate speech give rise to what Karl Popper has called the "paradox of tolerance."[28] Briefly, the paradox arises as a consequence of tolerating the intolerant. In a tolerant society, the intolerant can take advantage of the broad protection of speech to spread extremist views. And if these views prove persuasive to a large enough audience, the intolerant may well be in a position to ascend to power and to eradicate tolerance.[29] Hence the quandary: to remain tolerant, must a society be consistently tolerant towards all? Or must it, to protect itself, be intolerant of the intolerant?

At first, recourse to pragmatism apparently affords the best means to deal with the paradox under consideration. Indeed, no systematic solution looms as wholly satisfactory as it cannot solve numerous theoretical and practical problems posed by hate speech. For example, a complete ban would sweep much too broadly, equate the hatred of the oppressor with that of the oppressed, blur the distinction between endorsement of, and satirical reference to, reprehensible views, and generate difficult line-drawing problems.[30] The complete absence of any ban, on the other hand, would facilitate the imposition of oppression and its perpetuation, would encourage violence in certain circumstances, and would stand in the way of implementing a policy of equal dignity and equal respect for every member of society.[31] In contrast, a pragmatic approach focusing on likely actual consequences might seem best suited to avoid undesirable extremes without sacrificing worthwhile goals to satisfy the impractical demands of theoretical coherence.[32] Thus, for example, American legal commentators have argued that tolerance of extremist speech is justified in the United States although it may not be in Germany, because the respective historical experiences of both countries make the United States much less vulnerable than Germany to the perils of Nazism.[33]

Upon further reflection, however, the pragmatist approach to hate speech proves to be seriously deficient, if not largely circular. Because of the complexities inherent in the dialectic between tolerance and intolerance, the practical consequences of different approaches to hate speech are likely to be varied and nuanced rather than clear-cut.[34] Accordingly, the focus on practical consequences would at best prove inconclusive, thus triggering the need to choose among different sets of similarly plausible practical consequences. To a significant degree, moreover, the practical consequences of tolerance or intolerance toward certain views may simply be unpredictable. It does not follow from this that choosing between tolerance and intolerance should no longer be considered a matter of concern. But it may well follow that the choice in question, while normatively important, does not depend, by and large, on practical consequences.

That no single pragmatic course of action emerges in the context of hate speech is well illustrated by the contrast between the respective constitutional jurisprudence of Canada and the United States. Although neither Canada nor the United States afford unqualified protection to speech, the constitutional jurisprudence of the United States has displayed much greater tolerance toward hate speech than that of Canada.[35] Indeed, although the issue is divisive on both sides of the border, in more recent times, U.S. courts have come down on the side of toleration of hate speech, and Canadian courts on the opposite side.[36] The dominant position in the United States, consistent with a marketplace of ideas approach, is that content-based regulations of speech pose a serious threat to the ideal of an "uninhibited, robust and wide open" debate on public issues, which lies at the core of the U.S. commitment to free speech.[37] Accordingly, hate speech that falls short of "fighting words" or of triggering an incitement to violence ought to be tolerated, and fought with more speech rather than with censorship. In contrast, the position adopted by a majority on the Supreme Court in Canada is that some sacrifice in the scope of public debate is warranted in order to deal with the serious harm threatened by hate speech. Stressing Canada's commitment to equality and to multiculturalism, the Supreme Court upheld the ban on hate speech because of its serious potential for humiliating and degrading those whom it targets, and for gradually prejudicing the remainder of society against members of the targeted group.[38]

Once one realizes that the United States and Canada have certain different priorities, it becomes obvious that nothing inherent in either approach makes it more pragmatic than the other. If one is concerned with the gradual yet potentially devastating effect of hate speech on self-esteem and on respect for others, then the Canadian approach looms as more pragmatic than that of the United States. Indeed, by allowing restrictions on speech only if it poses a "clear and present danger" to society or if it amounts to an incitement to violence U.S. constitutional jurisprudence is poorly adapted, from a practical standpoint, to deal with speech that produces humiliation instead of provoking violence, and gradually undermines the very fabric of social cohesion instead of immediately threatening to tear it to shreds.[39] Conversely, of course, if the object is to foster the greatest dissemination of available views, limited only by avoidance of imminent danger and violence, then the U.S. approach clearly seems more pragmatically suited than its Canadian counterpart.

There is probably no reliable way to predict the practical consequences of tolerating hate speech, as the number and complexity of relevant factors and as the full gamut of contextual variations far exceed our grasp. Accordingly, pragmatism would be of little help in selecting a constitutional approach to hate speech. That would by no means obviate the need for one, but the choice would have to depend on conceptions of the good and value-preferences rather than on practical considerations. Consistent with this, the Canadian approach would be better suited for those with a more egalitarian and multicultural outlook, while the U.S. approach would seem preferable for those with a libertarian bent.

The preceding observations suggest that the pragmatists' trust in the Millian ideal is misplaced. In line with the analysis of the Supreme Court of Canada, uninhibited discussion is insufficient to ward off the great evils threatened by hate speech, and a marketplace of ideas open to hate speech would most likely lead to more harm than good.[40] Moreover, rejection of the Millian ideal seems particularly damaging to Rorty's prophetic vision of a society devoted to persuasion and redescription. To be sure, Rorty, unlike Mill, is not concerned with advancing the cause of truth. Nevertheless, very much in the tradition of Mill, Rorty assumes that harms perpetrated by words are less serious than those perpetrated by deeds. To the extent that hate speech belies that assumption, however, persuasion and redescription may inflict harms that are comparable to those flowing from evil deeds. Pragmatism can offer no assurance that Rorty's prophetic utopian dream of solidarity among poets will not turn into a harrowing nightmare of hate propaganda and humiliation. In short, even if Rorty's objective of marking room for more useful redescription can be fully justified under pragmatism, the Millian marketplace of ideas fails the pragmatist test for qualifying as a suitable means toward that end.

Posner, on the other hand, generally endorses the Millian marketplace of ideas, but has more recently retreated to a more nuanced position. Significantly, Posner's recent retreat seems consistent with the conclusion reached here, namely, that neither pragmatist ends nor pragmatist means necessarily justify unlimited protection for all speech that does not immediately incite to violence. Indeed, as Posner now emphasizes, the harms of hate speech impose costs that must be empirically ascertained. And it is only on the basis of those costs, and of other relevant costs and benefits, that a legitimate decision can be made on whether hate speech should be tolerated or prohibited.[41] Moreover, the only cogent and consistent ways to determine and weigh the "costs" and "benefits" in question seem to be in terms of a wealth maximization criterion or some other substantive normative criterion such as libertarianism or egalitarianism. In short, consistent with Posner's own recent remarks, pragmatism itself can offer no justification for or against tolerating hate speech.

VI

The analysis concerning hate speech also extends to freedom of speech in general. Indeed, whether we tackle freedom of speech at its core or at the margins, any cogent justification for it ultimately depends on linkage to ends that are not reducible to pragmatism. Furthermore, the failure of the pragmatic justification of freedom of expression calls into question whether the very notion of intermediate pragmatism is devoid of any practical consequences. To resolve this question, it is necessary to focus briefly on the distinction between critical and constructive pragmatism. As will be remembered, critical pragmatism refers to antifoundationalism, skepticism, and contingency, whereas constructive pragmatism designates whatever positive aims or programs may derive their justification from pragmatism. Assuming for the moment that critical pragmatism is generally unproblematic, the question boils down to whether anything remains to constructive pragmatism after the conclusion that there is no cogent purely pragmatic justification for freedom of expression.

Arguably, the only constructive prescription to which critical pragmatism leads is the necessity of embracing as a second-order end the maximization of equal freedom to pursue first-order ends. At first, it appeared that the promotion of freedom of speech could be subsumed under this second-order end, but that did not prove to be the case. Moreover, although critical pragmatism *does not foreclose* pursuing the above-mentioned second-order end, it by no means requires it. After accepting the conclusion that no conception of the good can be convincingly established as superior to others, the pragmatist must confront the need to determine the best practical course to follow under the circumstances. Suppose now that embracing the conception of the good shared by a majority would lead to greater peace and stability whereas adopting the second-order end would lead to greater freedom and sense of fairness. In that case, is either of the two options preferable to the other from a pragmatist standpoint? The answer is clearly no, as the first option offers the best practical means towards the (nonpragmatic) end of stability whereas the same is true for the second option with respect to the non-pragmatic objective of greater freedom. At least when it comes to constructive pragmatism, therefore, the concept of intermediate pragmatism ultimately proves empty.

What about critical pragmatism? Do antifoundationalism, contingency, or moderate skepticism have anything peculiarly pragmatic about them? Here again, the answer seems to be clearly in the negative. Antifoundationalism is typical of the postmetaphysical era, and counts many advocates, like the deconstructionists, who are not necessarily pragmatists.[42] The same is true of contingency, which has been invoked by existentialists, among others.[43] Finally, skepticism is hardly an invention of pragmatists, and "moderate skepticism," to the extent that it is a feature of pragmatism, seems far from coherent.[44] Specifically, once the hope of constructive pragmatism is cast aside, what is there to constrain skepticism? If the answer is "what we cannot help but believe in," it is purely circular. In that case, "moderate skepticism" either dissolves into a mere tautology: "I believe in what I believe in and I doubt what I cannot believe"; or it ends up amounting to an arbitrary refusal to ride skepticism to its logical conclusion.

Critical pragmatism thus seems as parasitic as constructive pragmatism, but its orientation toward practical concerns may still make a positive though limited contribution to legal interpretation. At the legislative level, it can help to weed out unworkable or obviously counterproductive legislation. Similarly, at the judicial level, critical pragmatism may help judges recognize and reject legal interpretations that lead to patently impractical consequences. But in the great many cases in which different judicial interpretations would lead to different practical results, critical pragmatism could at best but play a minor role.

In the last analysis, critical pragmatism's orientation toward the future is linked to its antifoundationalism and to its concern with practical consequences. Stated in conventional terms, pragmatism is designed to allow us to rid ourselves of cumbersome historical baggage and to concentrate on what works as measured by actual future consequences. On the level of common sense, this certainly sounds like a useful and practical, even if very banal, approach. From a more critical theoretical perspective, however, combining pragmatism's antifoundationalism with its future orientation leads to a vexing contradiction. Viewed closely, it is pragmatism's orientation toward the future that shapes and sustains its antifoundationalism. This is most obvious with respect to metaphysics as in the postmetaphysical age, most people believe that, and behave as if, science rather than metaphysics helps to solve the practical problems that arise in the course of shaping one's future. But from the standpoint of pragmatism, the proof of any theory or hypothesis lies in its consequences, and since the future cannot ever be known ex ante, strictly speaking no action could ever be pragmatically justified before, or at the time of, its occurrence without recourse to some foundation. Consequently, the old pragmatists were foundationalists who relied on science and experience to justify their future oriented actions. Neopragmatists like Rorty, on the other hand, reject empirical science as incompatible with pragmatism's antifoundationalism, but replace it with arbitrary foundations of their own. Thus, to the extent that Rorty goes beyond claiming that use of language and redescription are inevitable facts of our past and present lives, and prophesies about future self-creation and solidarity, he falls into the foundationalist trap. Indeed, without any foundations, there is no reason to believe that any particular future consequence, as opposed to any other, would follow from any present use of language, or from any past or present effort at redescription. In sum, if pragmatism's antifoundationalism and its orientation toward the future are taken together and taken seriously they logically lead to only one outcome, namely complete paralysis. Therefore, not only does pragmatism's failure to deal with ends condemn it to a purely parasitic existence, but also, when logically interpreted, its antifoundationalism combined with its future orientation deprive it of any legitimate basis for dealing with means.

Based on the preceding analysis, pragmatism offers no viable solution to the crisis concerning legal interpretation in a pluralist society. Because of the failure of the promise of pragmatism, it seems impossible to overcome the split between justice according to law and justice beyond law through a mere rejection of foundations or through exclusive focus on means to the exclusion of contestable ends. Therefore, the challenge posed by the intellectual journey of pragmatism is to discover foundations consistent with contingency and a plurality of conceptions of the good. That is obviously a rather formidable challenge, but one that seems unavoidable.

Notes

1 As I have elsewhere written: "Justice according to law is achieved when each person is treated in conformity with his or her legal entitlement. Justice [beyond] law, on the other hand, is the justice that makes it plausible to claim that a law is unjust (even if it is scrupulously applied in strict compliance with the entitlements which the law establishes)" (Michel Rosenfeld, "Autopoeisis and Justice," *Cardozo Law Review* 13 (1992): 1681.

2 See Richard Rorty, "The Banality of Pragmatism and the Poetry of Justice," in *Pragmatism in Law and Society*, ed. Michael Brint and William Weaver (Boulder: Westview Press, 1991), pp. 89–91.

3 See, for example, Charles S. Pierce, "The Fixation of Belief," in *The Philosophy of Peirce: Selected Writings*, ed. Justus Buchler (New York: AMS Press, 1956); John Dewey, *Logic: The Theory of Inquiry* (New York: Henry Holt, 1938); and John Patrick Diggins, *The Promise of Pragmatism* (Chicago: University of Chicago Press, 1994).

4 See Richard Rorty, *Contingency, Irony, and Solidarity* (Cambridge: Cambridge University Press, 1989), pp. 7–22.

5 Thus, for instance, "Dewey saw no troubling dualism between means and ends because he regarded ends as given" (Diggins, *The Promise of Pragmatism*, p. 242).

6 See Richard A. Posner, "What Has Pragmatism to Offer Law?" in *Pragmatism in Law & Society*, ed. Michael Brint and William Weaver (Boulder: Westview Press, 1991), pp. 36–37; Rorty, *Contingency, Irony, and Solidarity*, p. 60; and Richard Rorty, *Consequences of Pragmatism* (Minneapolis: Minnesota University Press, 1982), pp. 69–70.

7 See Rorty, "The Banality of Pragmatism," p. 92.

8 Posner, "What Has Pragmatism to Offer Law," p. 44.

9 Thomas Grey, "What Good is Legal Pragmatism?" in *Pragmatism in Law & Society*, ed. Michael Brint and William Weaver (Boulder: Westview Press, 1991), p. 10.

10 See Richard A. Posner, *Overcoming Law* (Cambridge: Harvard University Press, 1995), pp. 15–29; Richard A. Posner, *The Problems of Jurisprudence* (Cambridge: Harvard University Press, 1990), pp. 428–53.

11 Posner, *Overcoming Law*, p. 22.

12 Compare Richard A. Posner, *Economic Analysis of Law*, 2d ed. (Boston: Little Brown, 1977) with Posner, *The Problems of Jurisprudence* and *Overcoming Law*.

13 See Rorty, *Contingency, Irony, and Solidarity*, pp. 7, 9–11, 52, quote on p. 11.

14 See Rorty, "The Banality of Pragmatism," pp. 92–93.

15 See Lynn A. Baker, "Just Do It: Pragmatism and Progressive Social Change," in *Pragmatism in Law and Society*, ed. Michael Brint and William Weaver (Boulder: Westview Press, 1991), pp. 99–119 (arguing that Rorty's utopianism and call for social change bears no intrinsic connection to his pragmatism).

16 See Rorty, *Consequences of Pragmatism*, p. 166, 92, quote at p. 92.

17 *Ibid.*, p. xiv.

18 See Rorty, *Contingency, Irony, and Solidarity*, p. 73: "All human beings carry about a set of words which they employ to justify their actions, their beliefs, and their lives. . . . I shall call these words a person's final vocabulary."

19 *Ibid.*, p. xv.

20 Ibid., pp. 86, 92.

21 *Ibid.*, pp. 52, 60, 63.

22 *Ibid.,* p. 61.

23 *Ibid.,* p. 53. Cf. *Brandenburg v. Ohio,* 395 U.S. 444 (1969) (speech that "incites" to violence rather than merely "advocating" violence is not constitutionally protected).

24 See John Stuart Mill, *On Liberty,* ed. Elizabeth Rapaport (Indianapolis: Hackett Publishing, 1959), pp. 50–52. Suppressing expression that incites to violence is consistent with Mill's view that the broadest possible uninhibited discussion offers the best means toward truth and progress. Indeed, inciting speech is by its very nature more likely to lead to violence than to more speech. See Martin H. Redish, *Freedom of Expression: A Critical Analysis* (Charlottesville, VA: Michie, 1984), p. 191.

25 See *Abrams v. United States,* 250 U.S. 616, 630 (1919) (Holmes, J., dissenting).

26 See Frederick Schauer, "Free Speech and the Cultural Contingency of Constitutional Categories," in *Constitutionalism, Identity, Difference, and Legitimacy: Theoretical Perspectives,* ed. Michel Rosenfeld (Durham: Duke University Press, 1994), pp. 356–57.

27 See, for example, 3R.S.C. c.46, § 319 (1985) (Canada); Public Order Act, 1986, Ch. 64 §§ 17–29 (United Kingdom); and Convention on the Elimination of All forms of Racial Discrimination (1965), U.N.G.A. Res. 2106 Axx, 600 U.N.T.S. 195 (1969).

28 See Karl Popper, *The Open Society and Its Enemies,* 5th ed. (Princeton: Princeton University Press, 1966), p. 265n4. Popper (p. 266n4) suggests resolving the paradox by limiting tolerance to the tolerant. For a more extended analysis of the constitutional implication of this paradox, see Michel Rosenfeld, "Extremist Speech and the Paradox of Tolerance," book rev., *Harvard Law Review* 100 (1987): 1457.

29 Analogously, if hate propaganda succeeds in vilifying its target group by fomenting contempt among nonvictims, coupled with self-doubt and withdrawal among victims, the marketplace of ideas is in grave danger of becoming thoroughly corrupted and extremism fostered.

30 See, for example, Anthony Skillen, "Freedom of Speech," in *Contemporary Political Philosophy,* ed. Keith Graham (Cambridge: Cambridge University Press, 1982), p. 142 (noting the irony of the fact that the first person to be convicted under the British 1965 Race Relations Act for uttering a racially derogatory expression was a black). In the late 1960s, *All in the Family,* an American fictional television series was a satire meant to ridicule Archie Bunker, an unenlightened racial bigot. Significantly, however, public surveys indicated that a (sizeable) portion of the viewers identified with, not against, Archie Bunker. See Wilson Key, *Subliminal Seduction* (New York: Signet Books, 1973), p. 159. Finally, should the ban encompass advocacy but not a sympathetic depiction of an extremist position in the course of a classroom discussion? Should the ban extend to a true statement exploited for purposes of propagating racial hatred? Cf. Sec. 319 (3) of the Canadian Criminal Code (Truth is a defense to criminal charges for propagating hatred against an identifiable group pursuable to Sec. 319 (2)).

31 See *Regina v. Keegstra* 3 S.C.R. 697 (1990) (Majority opinion of Supreme Court of Canada upholding constitutionality of statute criminalizing hate propaganda).

32 See, for example, Grey, "What Good is Legal Pragmatism?" pp. 22–26 (advocating a pragmatic solution to the problem of hate speech on university campuses by borrowing from different theories that respectively buttress constitutional liberty and constitutional equality without attempting to reconcile the two).

33 See Lee Bollinger, *The Tolerant Society* (New York: Oxford University Press, 1986), pp. 198–99; and Schauer, "Free Speech," pp. 365–57.

34 For a more extended examination of this dialectic, see Rosenfeld, "Extremist Speech," pp. 1460–66.

35 In the case of Canada, for example, *Regina v. Keegstra,* above, note 31 (criminalization of hate speech held constitutional); in that of the United States, see, for example, *Chaplinsky v. New Hampshire,* 315 U.S. 568 (1942) ("Fighting words" are not protected speech).

36 For example, the Supreme Court of Canada decided the *Keegstra* case, *supra* by a four to three majority. Meanwhile the refusal of U.S. courts to exclude hate speech from constitutional protection has been surrounded by an often strident and bitter polemic. See, for example, Bollinger, *The Tolerant Society,* pp. 14–15 (discussing upheaval and dissent within the American Civil Liberties Union [ACLU] pursuant to its decision to represent Neo-Nazis bent on marching in full uniform including swastika in a suburban area heavily populated by Jewish survivors of Nazi concentration camps); Mari Matsuda, "Public Response to Racist Speech: Considering the Victim's Story," *Michigan Law Review* 87 (1989): 2320 (arguing that severe impact of hate speech on its victims justifies criminalization). See also *Brandenburg v. Ohio,* 395 U.S. 444 (1969) (Ku Klux Klan "advocacy" of [as opposed to "incitement" to] violence against Jews and Blacks is constitutionally protected); *Collin v. Smith,* 578 F.2d 1197 (7th Cir. 1978), *cert. den.* 439 U.S. 916 (1978) (Neo-Nazi March in Jewish neighborhood is constitutionally protected); and *R.A.V. v. City of St. Paul, Minnesota,* 505 U.S. 377 (1992) (statute criminalizing hate speech held unconstitutional as applied to Ku Klux Klan style cross burning). Compare with *Regina v. Keegstra,* above (upholding constitutionality of criminalization of antisemitic hate propaganda).

37 *New York Times Co. v. Sullivan,* 376 U.S. 254, 270 (1964).

38 See *Regina v. Keegstra,* above, note 31, pp. 746–748, 795.

39 See *Schenck v. United States,* 249 U.S. 47 (1919); *Brandenburg v. Ohio, supra.*

40 *Regina v. Keegstra,* above, note 31, p. 744.

41 See Posner, *Overcoming Law,* p. 396.

42 See Michel Rosenfeld, "Deconstruction and Legal Interpretation: Conflict, Indeterminacy, and the Temptations of the New Legal Formalism," in *Deconstruction and the Possibility of Justice,* ed. Drucilla Cornell, Michel Rosenfeld, and David Gray Carlson (New York: Routledge, 1992).

43 See, for example, Jean-Paul Sartre, *Being and Nothingness* (New York: Philosophical Library, 1956).

44 Skeptical thinking has historical roots going as far back as the pre-Socratic philosophers (see Richard H. Popkin, "Skepticism," in *Encyclopedia of Philosophy,* ed. Paul Edwards, New York: Collier-Macmillan, 1967, vol. 7). Also, among twentieth-century skeptics must be included such diverse philosophers as Albert Camus and George Santayana (*Ibid.*, p. 458).

PRAGMATISM,

CULTURE,

AND ART

Why Do Pragmatists Want to Be Like Poets?

RICHARD POIRIER

The only people who take serious poetry seriously these days, or so it seems to me, are some poets, a few philosophers, and a diminishing handful of critics. In the category of serious poetry I of course include prose, any kind of writing in which the words speak to one another, sometimes across great textual expanses or among several texts; they clarify, inflect, argue among themselves; they merge into metaphoric or tonal concentrations, then self-divide and branch out toward other concentrations and developments. In this sense Sir Thomas Browne or Dickens or Darwin wrote poetry as much as Emily Dickinson or Yeats, and need to be read with the same degree of effort and expectation. So when I say that only a few can take such writing seriously, I mean that the reading, hard enough even for the few, is prohibitively so for most people, and it should be remembered there aren't many people who read poetry to begin with. There are admittedly a good number of academics who assume that when they look into writing they are reading it as it seriously intends to be read. But their assumptions about reading are not mine. Academic departments of literature are now heavily populated with persons who imagine that poetry, as I have defined it, really doesn't exist; they assume that its language has already *been* interpreted by the cultural-historical discourses that presumably surround and penetrate it at every point.

In addition to these factors, there seem to me good reasons to wonder if and by how much poetry *can* be culturally available even under the best and most remote of circumstances—circumstances, that is, in which it might be imagined that great numbers of people *do* know how to take it seriously. In using the phrase "culturally available" I am taking a clue, as I have in the past, from a comment by Stanley Cavell, when he writes about two of his great loves, Emerson and Thoreau: "Working within an aspiration of philosophy that feeds, and is fed by, a desire to inherit Emerson and Thoreau as thinkers," he says, "I take it for granted that their thinking is unknown to the culture whose thinking they worked to found"—and then the essential clarification—"(I mean culturally unpossessed, unassumable among those who care for books, however possessed by shifting bands of individuals), in a way it would not be thinkable for Kant and Schiller and Goethe to be unknown to the culture of Germany, or Descartes and Rousseau to France, or Locke and Hume and John Stuart Mill to England."[1]

I can think of no reason to quarrel with Cavell's essential point. I want to add, however, that the comparisons between, on the one hand, the American receptivity to these two resident geniuses and, on the other, the greater receptivity in Germany, France, and England to comparable figures of their own, ought to be understood in the light of traditions of seriousness, when it comes to literatures and philosophies, which each of these countries is able and ready to bring to its own writers, as contrasted to the lack of such traditions in the United States and to a corresponding desire in the writing of both Emerson and Thoreau, not to mention William James, Dewey, or Rorty, to cater to a relatively general if educated audience. For that reason, it strikes me that Emerson is frequently asking not to be taken as seriously as he meanwhile hopes to be taken, which may be why the entries devoted to his aphorisms in Bartlett far outnumber those given to the other writers Cavell mentions.

In this, Emerson is more like Shakespeare than like Descartes or Mill, all the more because there is a question as to just how seriously Shakespeare himself was taken by the "culture whose thinking he worked to found." Shakespeare waited much longer than Emerson to find an interpreter like Cavell or even those "shifting bands of individuals" to which he alludes. The essay by Cavell from which I have quoted was published in 1988, a little over a hundred years after Emerson's death in 1882. Some corresponding dates for Shakespeare reveal how *un*seriously even he was read, and for a longer time. He died in 1616, and for close to 150 years, following Nahum Tate's adaptation of *King Lear* in 1681, productions of the play continued to adhere to Tate's wretched version. This was a rewritten version in which the ending of the play allows Cordelia to emerge victorious. Tate's textual barbarism received the blessing of even Dr. Johnson in his Preface to Shakespeare of 1765. "In the present case the public has decided. Cordelia, from the time of Tate, has always retired with victory and felicity. And, if my sensations could add anything to the general suffrage, I might relate, that I was many years ago so shocked by Cordelia's death, that I know not whether I ever endured to read again the last scenes of the play till I undertook to revise them as an editor."[2]

"The public has decided." Decided *what*? It was a "public" not much concerned with language, which is all that the play is made of; it was concerned with characters and plots and the appropriateness of these not to the language of the play but to life, that is, to "the general suffrage" as to what life is supposed to be like. To have changed the end to suit "the public," was not, however, merely, to change the plot, as Johnson seemed to suggest. It was to cut into the immensely intricate arteries and veins that connect the words at the end of the play to words all the way back to the first scene. It was a hacking amputation from which the play was left to bleed. It may be, as nearly everyone noddingly agrees, that Johnson was the greatest of English critics, but he could also display a markedly deficient sense of metaphorical language and of how it works.

I briefly mention Johnson's reputation as a critic and the textual history of *King Lear* only as part of the larger question of, again, whether or by now how much *any* of the writings of any strong poet can be culturally available or even widely understood within a culture he or she supposedly helped to found, especially if it is, like ours, a democratic culture. The phrase "strong poets" is one of Harold Bloom's formulations, much indebted, as is the anxiety of influence, to Emerson, and it is enthusiastically adapted by Rorty to elucidate his own version of pragmatism. With reference to the "strong poet" or to "strong poetry," Bloom wrote in 1976 that "Pragmatically, a trope's revenge is against an earlier trope. . . . We can define a strong poet," he goes on, "as one who will not tolerate words that intervene between him and the Word, or precursors standing between him and the Muse."[3] Ten years later, citing "Bloom's notion of the strong poet," Rorty goes on to make two stipulations crucial to his own adaptations of it. First, that "a sense of human history as the history of successive metaphors would let us see the poet, in the generic sense of the maker of new words, the shaper of new languages, as the vanguard of the species." And, second, that "central to what I have been saying [is] that the world does not provide us with any criterion of choice between alternative metaphors, that we can only compare languages and metaphors with one another, not with something beyond language called 'fact.' "[4]

I want in passing to intervene here on Rorty's behalf so that his references to "new words" and "new language," will not be misunderstood. Even Gertrude Stein admitted that no such things can exist, and Rorty is only being overenthusiastic.[5] In the next chapter of *Contingency, Irony, and Solidarity,* he concedes, as William James had done in "Pragmatism and Humanism," that in fact "metaphors are unfamiliar uses of old words, but such uses are possible only against the background of other old words being used in old familiar ways."[6] I take this to be an admission, which

Rorty readily makes elsewhere, that even the strongest poet has to find ways to be understood by nonpoets, by ordinary people who feel at home in the old metaphors, though they might be willing to take a chance that the old metaphors are to be displaced.

At such points Rorty sufficiently exonerates himself, insofar as he chooses to, from complaints by some of his critics that he is too much the ironic elitist, too easily satisfied with a sharp division between private visions and public arrangements. His concession to old words is no greater, however, than the concession made even by the strongest poets, like Emily Dickinson or Gertrude Stein, concessions to life as it exists *outside* the life of linguistic struggle. I mean the struggle that marks those intimate, often covert relations between words, the love affairs, and divorcements that get acted out among strong poets and within their poems. Rorty—and Bloom in *Kabbalah and Criticism*—want to distinguish themselves from Nietzsche's divination of the strong poet, and one way of doing this is to point to that poet's dependence on, as well as resistance to, other poets and readers. As Nietzsche put it, although truth is "a mobile army of metaphors," it is an army whose mobility depends upon service and supply operations outside as well as within the ranks of poetry.[7] The language of strong poets must be "available" to those not directly involved in the making of it. But the attendant kind of participation ideally expected of readers strikes me as extremely hard to secure, harder to maintain, and demanding to an often exhausting degree. Bloom's bland reference, in a passage quoted by Rorty, to the "good will of the reader" scarcely takes care of it, and Rorty's language sounds just a little too easygoing and sanguine when he writes: "For even if we agree that languages are not media of representation or expression, they will remain media of communication, tools for social interaction, ways of tying oneself up with other human beings."[8]

Rorty's ingratiating style attests to his own willingness to tie himself to other human beings; he likes to say what he thinks in quite ordinary English, free of jargon; he is not afraid to be understood, even at the risk of being understood too simply. And yet it is this same forthrightness that allows us clear access to some apparent divides in his thinking and feeling. In the case at hand, for example, he is admitting (in "The Contingency of Selfhood") that language can and must, if it is to remain a medium of communication, pay due respect to already constituted versions of reality even as it sets out to dislodge them; it accommodates itself to "previous truths" and to the "heirlooms" of language, as James calls them. But to be told that languages should remain "tools for social interaction," is to be reminded that in the previous chapter, "The Contingency of Language," he has just expressed strong reservations about Wittgenstein's analogy between "tools and vocabularies." Tools, Rorty argues at that earlier point, are not for the likes of Galileo, Yeats, or Hegel, "strong poets" all, writers who want to " 'make things new' . . . to make something that has never been dreamed of before," to make a "new, third, vocabulary." Old words are good enough for "craftsmen," because craftsmen, unlike strong poets, are content to discover only "how old vocabularies fit together." Having said this, he only then feels free to use the word "tool" to describe the language of the "strong poet," but the word does not by that point sound at all like a "tool for social interaction"; rather it is said to be, "a tool for doing something which could not have been envisaged prior to the development of a particular set of descriptions, those which it itself helps to provide."[9]

Conflict may be too strong a word to describe this interaction of Rorty's sentences, so let us say that there is at least some considerable variance in his writing between the view, on the one hand, that the language of strong poet-pragmatists must be destructive of existing usages and, on the other, the view that this language must at the same time prove compliant enough with those same usages so as to further the strong poet-pragmatists social and cultural purposes. What's the good of being self-reliant if, for fear of losing that self-reliance, you cannot even talk about it to anyone else? What happens when you do? To recall Emerson, "As soon as [the self-reliant person] has once acted or spoken with éclat he is a committed person"—one who has thereby devised only another prison for himself—"watched by the sympathy or the hatred of hundreds, whose affections must now enter into his account. There is no Lethe for this."[10]

It was the desire of the strong poet-pragmatist to be conversant with ordinary folk while being at the same time the redeemer (not an easy task even for the parable-speaking Jesus). From this flowed the determination to write, as Gertrude Stein puts it, "for god or mammon,"[11] when obviously one is required, as she concedes, to write for both at once. This is so divided a purpose that Stein herself, as she was writing her most designedly popular, money-making work, *Autobiography of Alice B. Toklas,* was also writing (to salve her conscience) *Stanzas in Meditation,* among her most inaccessible. (She was, as is well known, one of James' favored students while she was at Radcliffe.) A similar incentive informs the curious blends of aphorism with evasiveness or density in the writings of Emerson, and later in Frost and Stevens, who were also at Harvard while James was the leading figure in its philosophy department. Writing for such as these may pretend to be a representation of life as it is; however, it is more surely the representation of writing itself as an activity, of thinking rather than of thought, a dramatization of *how* life may be created out of words.

Writing in these circumstances is not an avocation, to resort to a familiar distinction of Frost's, and it is not a vocation either; it is a way of being in life, of being alive, there on the spot, on the page or in the sentence. At central moments, it is imagined by Emerson and Stevens, for instance, that new metaphors emerge *not* from already fertilized grounds at all, but from what Stevens calls "the rock" in his great poem of that title. A century earlier, in "Experience," Emerson had already had recourse to "these bleak rocks," and he says that "the God [is] the native" of them. He does not mean God a divinity summoned from on high; he means "the God" of the moment. And this God emerges, we are told, out of a "poverty" that is "scandalous," meaning that you are apt in such circumstances to stumble. Such destitution becomes so intolerable that it creates the God out of nothingness, just as it is claimed in Stevens' poem, that "nothingness" contains a "métier"—a profession or poetic calling. It is this "nothingness" that produces in his poem the illusion that "green leaves" and "lilacs" came to "cover the rock."

Visions of this kind, however eloquent and sublime, are also terrifying, especially to anyone who isn't interested in trying his or her luck on the rocks; it takes a strong poet to discover thereon any sort of creative incentive or occasion. The claims made under such circumstances for the power of poetry—for renewal not simply of but through the power of words—is altogether incredible. Let me read the whole passage from Emerson about these "bleak rocks," since I once nominated them as the Plymouth Rock of American pragmatism:

> And yet is the God the native of these bleak rocks. That need makes in morals the capital virtue of self-trust. We must hold hard to this poverty, however scandalous, and by more vigorous self-recoveries, after the sallies of action, possess our axis more firmly. The life of truth is cold, and so far mournful; but it is not the slave of tears, contritions, and perturbations. It does not attempt another's work, nor adopt another's facts. It is a main lesson of wisdom to know your own from another's. I have learned that I cannot dispose of other people's facts; but I possess such a key to my own, as persuades me against all their denials, that they also have a key to theirs. A sympathetic person is placed in the dilemma of a swimmer among drown-

ing men, who all catch at him, and if he give so much as a leg or a finger, they will drown him. They wish to be saved from the mischiefs of their vices, but not from their vices.[12]

What is this passage recommending that we do? And, if we do it, what then is promised us in return? What's in it for *me?* This is always Emerson's question, so let it be ours. The answers are not at all easy to locate in the visionary, blurred figurations of the writing. It appears that we are enjoined to take several different actions, none very appealing; as for the promised rewards—which, as I make them out, are "the God" and "the life of truth"—you are assured that at least the latter of these is "cold" and "mournful." And what is required of you to qualify even for these? To begin with, you must recover or discover a "self-trust" totally shorn of self-pity. And as proof of self-trust you must not seek the company of others who are as impoverished as you are. If they seek *you* out, it is only because they are deficient in self-trust. Accordingly, you must spurn them, lest their dependency drag you down. (I am reminded of Emerson's witty disdain, in "New England Reformers," at the expense of people who turn to others for support: "I have failed, and you have failed, but perhaps together we shall not fail.")[13] Indeed not only human contact but all outward show—as in the phrase "sallies of action"—are to be foresworn. Why? So that you may concentrate entirely on what is called "our axis" the axis, as I understand it, of self. And what is that? It appears to be some imaginary straight line about which you might then revolve or turn or otherwise effect change in your self alone, in your self-descriptions to yourself of yourself.

In the pragmatist vocabulary of Emerson and, even more, of James, disinheritance and impoverishment are of necessity self-inflicted. One's inheritances are already so abundant that it takes an act of will to *shed* them; Ahab complains in a relevant passage in *Moby-Dick,* that cultural accumulation "heaps me."[14]

Furthermore—and this is a vital part of the always murky idea of pragmatist "action"—the act of divestiture must then become a continuing process. If we must not settle for what philosophical tradition has bequeathed us, we must not then settle, as Rorty says we shouldn't, for what any particular poetry or poet has bequeathed us or even for what we ourselves invent. Poetry must not be thought of as a mere storehouse of wisdom, a treasure-trove. It is, rather, an exemplary act or instrumentality for the continuous creation of truth, an act that must be personal and private and never ending. "To begin to begin again," is Stein's way of putting it.[15] Rorty might be paraphrasing the passage from Emerson's "Experience" when he admits that "My 'poeticized' culture is one which has given up the attempt to unite one's private ways of dealing with one's finitude and one's sense of obligation to other human beings."[16] Maybe so, but has one also "given up" this attempt when the other human beings are people for whom you are writing? I recently heard Rorty refer approvingly to James' distinction in *Varieties of Religious Experience* between beliefs created "on our own time" and beliefs created in cooperation with others.[17] But I wonder what the phrase "on our own time" can mean when that time is spent in writing or reading, where in effect you must cooperate with others in using a common language? It is Emerson, remember, who confesses: "I am not solitary whilst I read and write, though nobody is with me."[18]

I move on now to the idea of "work." "Work" is a key word in pragmatist writing from Emerson to James to Dewey, and when Emerson uses it in the passage I have quoted, it is to say that he has learned that if he is to live the life of truth, then he cannot at the same time "attempt another's work, nor adopt another's facts." Another's "work" or another's "facts" are perforce references to already familiar and knowable forms of life, and it is the central task of the pragmatist-poet to "turn" away from these. At the same time, the more "firmly" you "possess" your "axis," the more you are then able also to turn away even from your *own* creations, your *own* "facts," for fear that these, too, will become fixed and fixing. As Emerson says in "The Poet," quoting his own essay "Intellect": "Every thought is also a prison; every heaven is also a prison. Therefore we love the poet, the inventor, who in any form, whether in an ode, or in an action, or in looks and behavior, has yielded us a new thought."[19]

Emerson here looks forward to James' "What Pragmatism Means." There James, as if picking up on Emerson's figure of the "axis," makes repeated use of the word "turn": "A pragmatist turns his back resolutely and once for all upon a lot of inveterate habits dear to professional philosophers. He turns away from abstraction and insufficiency, from verbal solutions, from bad a priori reasons, from fixed principles, closed systems, and pretended absolutes and origins. He turns towards concreteness and adequacy, towards facts, towards action, and towards power."[20]

What can this "turning" or "action" or "power" be referring to except the activity of the strong pragmatist poet, an activity confined to his or her own writing, to his or her own *mind?* With the exception of Dewey, who effectively avoids the problem I am describing, pragmatist philosophers and poets like to promote the illusion that all of us readers are, in one way or another, also strong poets. But that is obviously not true. It is obvious that strong poet-philosophers do *their* work exclusively in and with words, while the rest of us are making do with all kinds of lesser things. That is the only place—in words—where these strong poets *can* create and effect changes. "Do your work," says Emerson, "& I shall know you." "Do your thing," he had written in the journals.[21] We can all tag along with that, I assume. And share, too, in his Deweyan claim that "the poet" can come in *any* form—in "an action, or in looks and behavior."[22] But, alas, one doesn't *publish* "an action" or publish "looks and behavior." So we need to be told what kind of work might make us known to the strong poet, as he makes himself known to us by writing? Any kind of work? The daily, routine work of a bread winner? How are most kinds of work, even cultural work, metaphorically equivalent to the writing of strong poets, when "strong" is itself a metaphor for a cultural *übermensch,* someone who can effect cultural change?

This seems to be something of a problem, to put it mildly. And very much *their* problem, the problem of pragmatist-poet–philosophers proposing to write for a democratic audience. Rorty is admirably direct, as I have been suggesting, in owning up to the problem. But of course one reason we can identify the problem at all is that it is at least inferable from the prose of Emerson and James. It becomes especially inferable if you read, as I do, with a high degree of skepticism about the social and cultural power claimed by and for poets and philosophers. Thus it is that the "Emerson" who is said to have had such enormous influence on American life and American thinking is the aphoristic Emerson, which is not Emerson at all as I am able to understand him, or, as, say, Cavell and George Kateb account for him. Similarly, James' sporting efforts to buddy up to the reader only mean that what he is more importantly saying sometimes gets lost in the, for me, consequent social embarrassments. Thus, in the best known sentences from the paragraphs I've been discussing, he says, notoriously, that pragmatists are in pursuit of "practical cash value." This is a metaphor for which he has an unfortunate enthusiasm throughout *Pragmatism,* where, for instance, he later says that "truth lives, in fact, for the most part on a credit system," and goes on to compare "truth" to the passing of "banknotes."[23]

I particularly object to these metaphors because they have given an undue license to those who scrounge around for evidence that James' (and Emerson's) rhetoric, and the rhetoric of pragmatism generally, has been thoroughly corrupted by the discursive modes of American corporate capitalism. For me, all James is doing at such moments is what pragmatists often tend to do. He is trying to sound like the readers he meantime wants to convert; to sound as if he's closer to the average guy than to the strong poet or the professional philosopher. At the same time, what he is actually, essentially talking about are activities that average people cannot engage in at all and can only rarely appreciate. While all of us hope to change bank notes, how many of us, like strong poets, can hope to change the order of things? The term "cash-value" in James' metaphor is an icon *meant* to be subservient to the subject, which is poetry—the effort to effect and also perpetuate newness in the language—but the icon in this case usurps the place of the subject. "If you follow the pragmatic method," he writes, "you cannot look on any such [power bringing] word as closing your quest. You must bring out of each word its practical cash-value, set it at work within the stream of your experience. It appears less as a solution, then, than as a program for more work, and more particularly as an indication of the ways in which existing realities may be *changed*."[24]

This description of how words are put to work could pass as a description of how a given metaphor works in a strong poem, alert to the constraints of its own doubleness, combining and contending with other elements in the poem in an ongoing process of inflection and change. The fact is, however, that nowhere in James does he talk seriously in this way about the language of a poem. He likes poetry for its sentiments, its attitudes toward life, its capacities to offer consolation or to "lead" us in certain directions of which he approves. So that, on the one hand, there are indications that he is favorably disposed to Rorty's sense that philosophy might be a form of strong poetry, while on the other he never wants to say so with anything like Rorty's forthrightness. Instead, he chooses, in the interest of social persuasion and social self-projection, to hint at strengths *other* than those of a strong poet or an appreciative reader of strong poetry. Indeed, he was always deeply suspicious of too intense or prolonged an indulgence in the reading of novels and poems. The effect, he believed, could be a weakening of character and, especially, of the will to *act*. He would rather imagine an audience not of writers or readers merely but of men active in the world, captains of finance, explorers, warriors, and the like.

I am describing a problem that is evident in a good deal of pragmatist writing, especially when it wants to satisfy the contradictory desire to be popular and, at the same time, to display a severe self-reliance, in the manner of Emerson and Frost. These are writers who, like James, make an effort to reach beyond any particular literary or professional or coterie readership; they want readers in the thousands so as to promote Rorty's "poeticized culture." In trying to achieve this, they frequently put themselves in the position of being seriously misunderstood, as Emerson and Frost still are, of sending messages that get warped or diluted in transmission. Thus, in the passage from James we have just looked at, the already sketchy image it projects of the strong poet is submerged further by that of a white-collar entrepreneur, as in the rhetorical figure of "practical cash value," which everyone remembers if they remember nothing else from *Pragmatism*. No phrase in all of pragmatist writing has exerted more, or more damaging, power over the popular idea of what pragmatism means. In another passage, in the 1898 essay "Philosophical Conceptions and Practical Results," he comes much closer to openly endorsing the pragmatist philosopher as the strong poet. But once again he combines him with a figure from the world of more he-man and heroic mold, this time a version of Natty Bumpo. "Philosophers," he there admits, "are after all like poets," and then immediately adds, "They are pathfinders"; they are "so many spots, or blazes,—blazes made by the axe of human intellect on the trees of the otherwise trackless forest of human experience."[25]

Rorty intends to get round the problem I am describing when, in a sentence we have already looked at, he argues that the public philosopher can find a way to accommodate both "the ironist's *private* sense of identity" and his or her felt ties to community, without the risk of confusing one with the other. He would hope for accommodation well short of identity of purpose. My 'poeticized' culture," we recall, "is one which has given up the attempt to *unite* [italics added] one's private ways of dealing with one's finitude and one's sense of obligation to other human beings."[26] This is a purely Emersonian sentiment commendably free of hedging. And yet it seems obvious to me that however much one wants to endorse such a hope, the reality is that the distinction it rests upon—between private and communal—can rarely be achieved in writing and is always being blurred by readers, including scholarly ones, who refuse to abide by it. Misreading is never entirely the fault of readers, and it is of great cultural importance that many readers persist in the belief that metaphors, like "cash value" or Emerson's comparison of the loss of his son to the loss of an estate, are evidence of how culturally weak both of these writers can be in the very act of trying to give evidence of strength. Having compared his poet-philosopher to an axe-wielding pathfinder, James ends the passage by referring to the marks they leave behind. They are indications, he says, of "the thin and spotty and half-casual character of their operations."[27] Fair enough—if he means to suggest that no one's signs or metaphors ever do end the need to produce new ones. But why "half-casual"? Does he mean that the operations are themselves unsure of purpose? Can a strong poet ever be a half-casual one?

There's nothing necessarily the matter with James' efforts to sound, as a public philosopher, like a regular guy, which is also how Rorty can sometimes sound, or even with his having a limited notion of what "regular" might mean. What does matter is that these sounds and notions as they take shape in his prose can substantially run counter, as they do not in Rorty, to what he means to say. One of Dewey's very rare criticisms of James in his private correspondence is pertinent in this regard, and with specific reference to the most popular and best selling of James' works, the 1906 essay-pamphlet "The Moral Equivalent of War." In 1915, five years after James' death, Dewey writes to a friend, Scudder Klyce, that the essay

> seemed to me to show that even his sympathies were limited by his experience; the idea that most people need any substitute for fighting for life, or that they have to have life made artificially hard for them in order to keep up their battling nerve, could come only from a man who was brought up an aristocrat and who had lived a sheltered existence. I think he had no real intimation that the 'labor problem' has always been for the great mass of people a much harder fight than any war; in fact one reason people are so ready to fight is the fact that that is so much easier than their ordinary existence.[28]

I infer from Dewey's letter what I have already been inferring from James' style: that such elitism as can be found in him has far less to do with the elitism natural to the strong poet and more to do with an elitism of class. And his hope to disguise, by companionable idioms, the trivial elitism of the one sort only undermines his strength as a poet.

The "labor problem," to recall a Dewey phrase, is a further clue to the literary-cultural issue I am exploring. It casts a critical light on the repeated efforts by a number of pragmatist poet-philosophers to create and maintain some metaphoric relation between literary work—the active, daily struggle with language—and the daily manual labor of ordinary persons. We have already noticed James' loose but rather obsessional references to "work," to which might be added some sentences from "What Makes a Life Significant" (1899). Having there allied himself with Carlyle by discovering "great fields of heroism lying round about . . . in the daily life of the laboring classes," he later turns toward Tolstoy, and dismissively away from people like his colleagues at Harvard: "your college professor, with a starched shirt and spectacles, would, if a stock of ideals were all alone by itself enough to render a life significant, be the most absolutely and deeply significant of men. Tolstoi would be completely blind in despising him for a prig, a pedant and a parody; and all our new insight into the divinity of muscular labor would be altogether off the track of truth."[29]

This is a rather shallow if charming echo of what Emerson, whose references to work are to be found everywhere in his writing, says in "The American Scholar." Emerson there looks forward, as does James, to Frost's poems of work. But much more evidently than James, Emerson is talking about how strong poetry *is* in itself work. Strong poetry, poetry that "destroys the old to build the new," is not, that is, simply *like* other work; it is *the* essential form of cultural labor. "Not out of those, on whom systems of education have exhausted their culture, comes the helpful giant," he writes. (I would suggest, parenthetically, that this figure of the giant anticipates the giant in Stevens' "A Primitive Like an Orb," "And the giant ever changing, living in change," the giant who, as Bloom says, becomes language itself.)[30] Emerson's "helpful giant," arrives "to destroy the old and to build the new"; it comes "out of unhandselled savage nature, out of terrible Druids and Beserkirs." And from these, he says, "came at last Alfred and Shakespeare." It is only then that Emerson gets a bit wobbly and literal about work: "I hear therefore with joy whatever is beginning to be said of the dignity and necessity of labor to every citizen. There is virtue yet in the hoe and the spade, for learned as well as unlearned hands."[31]

Dewey was not given to confusions of this sort as between actual physical labor and the writing of strong poetry. But one must therefore admire Dewey, or not, in light of the evidence that he pays no regard whatever to strong poetry, that is, to poetry as primarily work *in* and *against* language. Louis Menand has read far more widely in the massive writings of Dewey than I have, and will know if I'm on the right track in saying that while there are many passages in Dewey, notably in *Art and Experience* (e.g., "The Common Substance of the Arts") where he talks about language and poetry, and in *Democracy and Education,* where he has interesting things to say about work in conjunction with poetry, he does not ever talk about the writing of poetry as a struggle with words, a difficult, potentially revolutionary effort to change language on the way toward possible changes in cultural concepts of reality. It is true that, like Emerson before him, he insists that the word "work" designates a process in writing and reading and not simply a product of them, and it is the process of creation, and not its products, that he wants to endow with special privilege. But while thinking of this kind is similar to thinking that goes on in strong poets, what Dewey has in mind is what he calls " 'the labor problem', " a deep and growing problem of social alienation in industrial society. It is in that spirit that he asks "why the idea is so current that work involves subordination of an activity to an ulterior material result."[32] Superficially, this sounds like Thoreau working in his bean field and assuring us that his "labor yielded an instant and immeasurable crop. It was no longer beans that I hoed nor I that hoed beans." And yet the difference becomes almost immediately apparent when, later in the same paragraph, Thoreau proudly asserts that his work in the fields was "for the sake of tropes and expression, to serve a parable-maker one day."[33]

Robert Frost's poems of work, which include some of his greatest, like "Mowing" or "The Tuft of Flowers" or "Mending Wall" or "After Apple-Picking," are nuanced in exactly this fashion, only with much greater subtlety than one finds in Thoreau. They become poems about the veritable work of writing poems, work that persuades the poet and the reader that, indeed, "The face is the sweetest dream that labor knows."[34] Frost, a student and teacher of the writings of William James, is not, however, always so successful in other of his poems, as David Bromwich shows in a most persuasive criticism of that famous "work" poem "Two Tramps in Mud Time." The speaker, you may recall, is Frost both as wood chopper and poet, having a silent face-off with two tramps who emerge out of the "mud," that is from the undifferentiated mass, and who want to take over the work so as to earn a living wage. No way. (The poem can be dated in 1934, the depth of the Depression and the beginnings of the New Deal.) It is one of those occasions when Frost, like James, resorts to rhetorical bluster about how the needs of self-reliance require a willed abridgement of charity, of human sympathy and social conscience. We find him, as Bromwich puts it, exhibiting "an outsize respect for the rhetorical leverage afforded by the style of the ordinary man," to the point where he also exhibits "a distrust of being seen to be a poet." He sounds reluctant "to come to grips with both vocations," to the point where one may wonder if perhaps poetry, rather than wood cutting, is his "avocation."[35] Here we have yet another instance of the problem I'm concerned with: how does the strong poet-pragmatist find a language that is simultaneously appropriate to his lonely task and to his audience, those other human beings with whom he seeks a life in common?

Notes

1 Stanley Cavell, *In Quest of the Ordinary* (Chicago: University of Chicago Press, 1988), p. 27.
2 Samuel Johnson, "The Preface and Notes to Shakespeare," in *The Tragedy of King Lear,* ed. Russell Fraser (New York: Signet, 1963), p. 224.

3   Harold Bloom, *Poetry and Repression* (New Haven: Yale University Press, 1976), p. 10.

4   Richard Rorty, *Contingency, Irony, and Solidarity* (New York: Cambridge University Press, 1989), p. 20.

5   See Gertrude Stein, "Poetry and Grammar," in *Lectures In America* (New York: Random House, 1935), pp. 237–38: "Of course you might say why not invent new names new languages but that cannot be done. It takes a tremendous amount of inner necessity to invent even one word."

6   Rorty, *Contingency*, p. 41.

7   Friedrich Nietzsche, "On Truth and Lie in an Extra-Moral Sense," in *The Portable Nietzsche*, ed. Walter Kaufmann (New York: Viking, 1954), pp. 46–47.

8   Rorty, *Contingency*, p. 41.

9   *Ibid.*, pp. 12–13.

10 Ralph Waldo Emerson, "Self-Reliance," in *Essays and Lectures* (New York: Library of America, 1983), p. 261.

11 Gertrude Stein, "What is English Literature," in *Lectures in America*, p. 54.

12 Emerson, "Experience," in *Essays and Lectures*, p. 490.

13 Emerson, "New England Reformers," in *Essays and Lectures*, p. 598.

14 Herman Melville, *Moby-Dick*, ed. Harrison Haywood and Herschel Parker (New York: Norton, 1967), p. 144.

15 A phrase used frequently by Stein, as in her *Lectures in America* and in *The Making of Americans*.

16 Rorty, *Contingency*, p. 68.

17 See Rorty, "Pragmatism as Romantic Polytheism," in this volume.

18 Emerson, *Nature* in *Essays and Lectures*, p. 9.

19 Emerson, "The Poet," in *Essays and Lectures*, p. 463.

20 William James, *Pragmatism* (Cambridge: Harvard University Press, 1975), p. 31.

21 See *Journals*, July 7, 1839, in Joel Porte, ed. *Emerson in his Journals* (Cambridge: Harvard University Press, 1982), p. 221.

22 Emerson, "The Poet," in *Essays and Lectures*, p. 463.

23 James, *Pragmatism*, p. 100; see also pp. 32, 41, 46–48, 62.

24 *Ibid.*, pp. 31–32.

25 James, "Philosophical Conceptions and Practical Results," in *The Writings of William James*, ed. John J. McDermott (New York: Random House, 1967), p. 347.

26 Rorty, *Contingency*, p. 68.

27 James, "Philosophical Conceptions," p. 347.

28 Dewey's letter to Klyce is quoted in Gerald Meyers, *William James: His Life and Thought* (New Haven: Yale University Press, 1986), p. 602.

29 James, "What Makes a Life Significant," in *The Writings of William James*, p. 657.

30 Harold Bloom, *Wallace Stevens: The Poems of Our Climate* (Ithaca: Cornell University Press, 1976), p. 293.

31 Emerson, in "The American Scholar," *Essays and Lectures*, pp. 62–63.

32 John Dewey, *Democracy and Education* (New York: Free Press, 1966), p. 204.

33 Henry David Thoreau, *Walden* (New York: Library of America, 1985), p. 449.

34 Robert Frost, "Mowing."

35 David Bromwich, *A Choice of Inheritance* (Cambridge: Harvard University Press, 1989), pp. 225–26.

Pragmatists and Poets: A Response
to Richard Poirier

LOUIS MENAND

I

The two people whose work in what we are calling "The Pragmatist Revival" have meant the most to me are Richard Poirier and Richard Rorty. So when, at a certain point in my first reading of Richard Poirier's paper, I realized that he was criticizing something written by Richard Rorty, I was a little distressed, since I saw that I had gotten myself into a position in which I might be expected to choose sides. The only way around this dilemma was the popular coward's course of trying to show that Poirier and Rorty are not really in disagreement at all; and that is the course I have chosen in what follows.

As I understand him, Poirier is making the following argument. Serious poetry is defined by a profound awareness that the power of written language is also a trap. Each time it is used in a new sentence, each time it appears in the company of different other words, a word strikes out in a new semantic direction, but it also pushes off, so to speak, from the accumulated history of previous uses generated by its presence in the company of previous different words. This quality of words constitutes a kind of energy, which the poet, with effort and vigilance, can harness, or channel, by making a composition of words that is alive to all the ways in which bits of language can hitch up to other bits of language, and also to the ways in which the hitching and the unhitching alters the directions and the energies of all the bits involved.

That's the up side. The trap is the belief that by harnessing words in this sense you can get something out of them; or rather, that you can get out of them something you intended to get or wanted to get out of them, when in fact the more tightly you harness, the more it is the case that the words are getting something out of you instead. The danger, in short, is that you will invest, in the *form*, rather than in the process, of your writing, your sense of your self. There is a point at which you will be tempted to step back

362

from the canvas, and in that moment of self-satisfaction, you will mistake as final and determinate what can only be indeterminate and forever vulnerable to future hitchings and unhitchings. And as with words, so with selves. Words have this duplicity because they cannot come to rest on some point of referential relation, on a relation to something that is not another word. And because no word is exempt from this condition, because there can be no word to serve as the anchor for other words, linguistic relations are irremediably unstable. You can see how it is that this way of thinking about poetry can be called pragmatist.

Poirier thinks that serious poetry is written by people who understand that writing, like being, is therefore basically a matter of treading water—a matter of knowing that the only way to stay where you are is to move around a lot. The *reading* of serious poetry, he believes, is demanding in the same way. It requires attention to all the work of knowing that words do with their positively charged ions, so to speak, and, at the same time, a keen awareness of all the work of unknowing that they do with their negatively charged ions.

Poirier believes that most people are not up to this kind of reading because most people want to get something out of what they read, and they therefore assume that the writer must have put something comparably determinate into it. Often the writer *has* put something comparably determinate into it—Poirier calls these kinds of meaning "aphorisms"— but this is a sort of Potemkin village effect, since there is always something else going on behind the ostensive show of exportable significance, and it is there that the seriousness is to be found. This is actually not the most accurate metaphor, since it implies that texts have a surface and a depth, and one of the points Poirier is making is that depth is just one of the illusions surface makes.

When Poirier asks, "Why do pragmatists want to be like poets?," he is posing a challenge to an argument put forward by Richard Rorty in *Contingency, Irony and Solidarity*. Rorty proposes there that the strong poet might be regarded as what he calls "the vanguard of the species"—what used to be called a culture hero—in the sort of liberal society he is describing in that book. Rorty is driven to this suggestion by his effort to redefine the nature of progress by making it synonymous with adaptation. On this view, we make progress as a society by retrofitting our stock of metaphors to enable us to cope with new conditions. There is nothing teleological about this kind of progress any more than there is anything teleological about evolution. There is just the mundane business of making our way as best we can in a world shot through with contingency. Because the strong poet, on the definition that Rorty and Poirier both borrow from Harold Bloom, is the maker of new metaphors, or the troper of old tropes, he or she becomes, for Rorty, the representative figure for how this business of adaptation works.

Poirier is suggesting that this sounds a lot like the bad idea that poetry is the kind of thing you can get something useful out of. Poirier concedes that Rorty seems, elsewhere in *Contingency, Irony and Solidarity*, to have a more complicated view of poetry than this. But his point is that even on the complicated view of poetry, Rorty seems to assume either that serious poetry is something everybody does, or that serious poetry is something enough people in a liberal society know how to read that the strong poet's tropings and redescriptions can be put to work in the business of general social adaptation. Poirier doubts both of these assumptions, and therefore concludes by asking, quoting from Rorty, how one does "unite one's private ways of dealing with one's finitude and one's sense of obligation to other human beings."[1]

I can see how the problem arises, but I think it is a confusion of terms rather than a difference of belief. Rorty gets into this business about the strong poet, and thereby finds Poirier on his tail, because language, for reasons easily located in twentieth-century intellectual history, figures much more centrally in his pragmatism than it does in the pragmatisms of James and Dewey. The simple response to the question Poirier raises is that Rorty does *not* want to find a way to "unite one's private ways of dealing with one's finitude and one's sense of obligation to other human beings," and therefore the question of how it is that the poet's private struggles with language can issue in prescriptions good for social change does not arise. The point of Rorty's book is that there *is* no philosophical metarationale for those two enterprises. The effort to make them commensurable, to guide conduct in each by reference to a single worldview, only leads to trouble. All that Rorty requires the two enterprises to have in common is the acknowledgment of contingency. I take this acknowledgment to be the contribution pragmatism makes.

So that the serious poet, as Poirier defines the type, is engaged in exactly that activity of redescription—the activity Poirier himself refers to elsewhere as "writing off the self"—which Rorty prescribes for the private sphere. The job of the pragmatist is not to imitate the poet; it is only to show how the activity of redescription in which the poet is engaged might be a paradigm of self-realization in a liberal regime in which private activities are pursued in the interest of one kind of fulfillment and public activities are pursued in interests of a different kind of fulfillment.

Still, this business of private self-redescription is plainly not the same as the business of social adaptation I mentioned earlier—the business of coming up with fresh metaphors to help us as a species cope with the world—and this is where the confusion arises. The confusion is the consequence of running together several different things under the term "language." Two of these are speech and writing. We get these phenomena mixed up when we talk, for example, about literature or philosophy as a conversation. Speech is somatic; it is not restricted to utterance, and it is pretty plainly constitutive of being human. Writing is a technology, and it is no more constitutive of being human than knowing how to drive is.

A third thing for which the term language now gets used a lot is "culture," and this is the relevant confusion. Culture and language are today often treated as synonymous, as though cultures were essentially systems of metaphors. I think that there are a lot of conceptual problems with this conflation, but my point here is that I suspect that what happened in *Contingency, Irony and Solidarity* is that the notion of the poet as a writer in the private redescription sense got carried over into the notion of social adaptation as a matter of cultural redescription. This is how Galileo and Yeats ended up in the same sentence as examples of strong poets. If what Poirier is saying is that it is a good idea to keep these two notions of redescription separate—the notion entailed in the activity of writing poetry on the one hand and the notion entailed in the activity of coming up with a better vocabulary for doing things with gravity, or whatever, on the other—he is probably right, and I would imagine that Rorty would agree with him. If this is so, they do not disagree after all.

II

William James used to complain that the reason people who dislike pragmatism tend to give is "It's not true, and furthermore, we already knew this stuff." When the movement of thought loosely known as poststructuralism emerged in the American academy in the 1970s, a lot of people reacted by saying "It's not true," but there were a few people who said, "We already knew this stuff," and Richard Poirier and Richard Rorty were two of those people. In Poirier's case, what we already knew we knew from reading Emerson and Frost; in Rorty's case, we knew it from reading James and Dewey.

Poirier and Rorty saw poststructuralism not as a set of fresh theoretical instruments, which is how most people were seeing it in the 1970s, but as simply the undoing of formalism, the debunking, among other things, of the notion that fresh theoretical instruments are the main things we need to understand texts. They also realized that the undoing of formalisms is the central impulse in the most important traditions of American thought. They believed that this impulse has always been in danger of being suppressed by academicism—that academicism had written it out of American intellectual life in the past, and that the new academicism of the American interpreters of Derrida and Foucault was threatening to write it out again. Poirier and Rorty understood this at a time when very few other people did. They persisted in treating what everyone else was treating as a fancy Gallic import as just another version of an American idea, and the more they persisted, the more they convinced other people to think that way, too. This volume is a tribute to their success.

In patching up the disagreement between Poirier and Rorty, I have avoided the really radical, and, it seems to me, very brilliant and profound, challenge that Poirier's paper presents. This challenge relates to a problem central to several of the chapters in this volume, notably those on legal pragmatism. It is the problem of where, on a pragmatist conception, judgment comes from, which is just a version of the general problem of how change occurs.

The problem arises because pragmatists have a tendency to talk in a contradictory way about human beings. On the one hand, they talk about people as culturally constituted all the way down; on the other hand, they talk about all these language games out there that we can somehow move around in order to get what we want. But given that we are culturally constituted, who is the *we* that gets to do all this intelligent moving around? I take Richard Posner and Thomas Grey, for example, in their essays in this volume, to be saying that the pragmatic judge takes a bit of this and a bit of that to get to what he or she has in effect already decided is the best outcome. So where does the decision that this is the best outcome come from? The lazy answer is that it comes out of the language, or out of the culture. Poirier's point is that this cannot possibly be the right answer, and that this is what Emerson is trying to show us. I agree with Poirier's point completely, but I have a slightly different way of getting there.

I know that it is way too late in the day to do anything about it, but I have never understood the attraction of the term "strong poet." It's not just that it replaces the old, influence-hunting school of literary genealogy, in which literary history got figured as a kind of correspondence chess, with a new school of literary genealogy in which it gets figured as a kind of correspondence thumb-wrestling. I can understand that the advantage of "strong" is that it's a term of relation, and therefore a way of measuring poems by other poems. But even in this sense, I am often puzzled by the way it is used.

I don't want to seem to be holding a brief for him, but it seems to me that on most senses of the term strong, the strongest poet in English in this century has been T. S. Eliot. Eliot has, if this matters, a much firmer claim to the pragmatist philosophical tradition than Frost or Stein or Stevens ever did. He wrote a doctoral dissertation in the Harvard department that William James created, and if he had not met Ezra Pound and married Vivien Haigh-Wood when he went to London in 1914, he would very likely have become a member of the department himself. For years, Eliot's dissertation was ludicrously misread, when it was not being ludicrously unread, by the Eliot scholarly establishment, but as Walter Michaels has shown, and as Eliot himself virtually admitted, it is a pragmatist dissertation.[2]

If we are looking for sheer muscle tone, it has always seemed to me that the strongest line in twentieth-century poetry is "April is the cruellest month," a line that turns the entire tradition of Romantic nature poetry back in the direction of the Christian mythology from which it sprang. And I don't see how an account of poetry as words that speak back and forth to each other across a single poem or many poems cannot see that this is one of the obvious accomplishments of Eliot's poetry. Eliot invented a lot of catch-phrases, like "mythic method" and "objective correlative," but it ought to be obvious that they have nothing to do with his practice as a poet. He's a weird, reactionary, deeply suspicious writer, who suffered from his academic enshrinement in almost exactly the same degree that Frost, during the same years, suffered from his academic neglect.

But Eliot is almost entirely absent from the literary genealogies of people who talk about strong poets. If you ask them why he doesn't count in the way that Frost or Stevens does, they tend to say something like, "Well, you know, he suppressed his debt to Emerson." So *that's* it. I had somehow thought suppressing your debts was exactly the sort of thing strong poets were supposed to do. Or else they say something like, "His struggle with Whitman was ultimately unsuccessful, you see." But until the theory of strong poetry came along, it had never occurred to anyone that the way to read Eliot was to see him as trying to trope Walt Whitman.

My point is not that Eliot is a strong poet, or that he is an unjustly neglected poet, or that he is a poet we might profitably give more attention to. My point is that people write poetry for all kinds of reasons and people read poetry for all kinds of reasons, and isolating some one aspect of this business of writing and reading in order to say, "This is strong poetry" or "This is serious poetry" is a way of reinstantiating exactly the sort of formalism pragmatism is meant to undo. Surely the case is that we read

Frost because he is writing about things we're interested in, like work and sex and charity, and we don't read Eliot any more because we're not interested in the things he is writing about, like the death throes of Christian faith and the failed transcendences of nineteenth-century European symbolism. The character of the writing qua writing has nothing to do with this interest, because we would not know how to think about writing qua writing. We can only think of it as writing *about* something.

Since I think this, I obviously also think that it is a mistake to carry over this notion of strong poetry into the discussion of how social change occurs—to figure social change as a matter of coming up with better metaphors. The consequence of this current way of talking is that there are now ten thousand professors out there trying to come up with new twists on old metaphors as the necessary prolegomenon to moving the world.

Somehow I don't think that this is the way it actually works. Poirier is right when he says that the number of people who can really read poetry is very small. I have had many students whose capacity for, as we say, doing things with texts was much greater than mine. My advantage was the advantage every professor has, which is that for them it was the first time around the block and for me it was the ninety-ninth time, so I could lay a few booby-traps to trip them up and make them think I was naturally better at the game than they were. But this kind of capacity for doing things with texts is largely just a function of brain power. You can acquire it by learning how to imitate the ways in which the business is done. It usually has very little to do with a genuine intuitive understanding of literature. That kind of understanding is something very few people have. It is precisely not imitable, because it arises from a sensibility and not from a paradigm. It isn't really learned, and it doesn't correlate in any predictable way with things like brain power or cultural background. It is simply a gift for talking about what it is like to read something. Some people can do it, just as some people can throw a football farther than other people, some people can do mathematical calculations in their heads, and some people have a personal beauty that knocks down all of life's doors.

There is nothing undemocratic about this, since the whole point is that such gifts are randomly distributed. You never know who will have them, or what conditions will allow them their proper scope, though we know in a rough way through experience that some sets of conditions are more favorable than others. At a time when it has become common to say that changing our world begins with changing our culture, and when many people are eager to tell other people what sort of culture is right for them and what sort is wrong for them, it might be suggested that the real source of human change lies not in the culture or in the theoretical descriptions we propose for it, but in the mysteries of personality, which are a scandal to theory. I don't think I know what culture is. It has become a term like the term "ether" in nineteenth-century science; it is the necessary medium for explaining why everything else does what it does. But whatever culture is, I do not think it is synonymous with human agency.

The first sentence of the first article Oliver Wendell Holmes ever wrote, in 1870, before Peirce articulated his doctrine of pragmatism, is this: "It is the merit of the common law that it decides the case first and determines the principle afterwards."[3] This is the sentence echoed thirty-five years later in the famous Lochner dissent: "General propositions do not decide concrete cases."[4] And it is the sentence echoed here by those latter day Holmesians Richard Posner and Thomas Grey. Holmes spent much of his life trying to figure out where, if it wasn't general principles, the judge's decisions did come from. In the end, he thought that this was a question it was impossible to answer, because in the end, we do not know, in any determinate way, where our judgments come from. All we can say is that we seem to have, as naturally associated beings, a powerful social incentive to rationalize and justify the choices we make.

It is sometimes complained that pragmatism is a bootstrap theory—that it cannot tell us where we should want to go or how we can get there. The answer to this is that theory can never tell us where to go; only we can tell us where to go. Theories are just one of the ways we make sense of our choices. We wake up one morning and find ourselves in a new place, and then we build a ladder to explain how we got there. As Charles Darwin and a thousand pop performers since Darwin have recommended, change happens because you go out and mix your unique set of genes with another person's unique set of genes. That is what makes the human world spin. Try it tonight.

Notes

1 Richard Rorty, *Contingency, Irony and Solidarity* (New York: Cambridge University Press, 1989), p. 68.

2 See T. S. Eliot to Norbert Wiener, January 6, 1915, *The Letters of T. S. Eliot: Volume 1, 1898–1922,* ed. Valerie Eliot (San Diego: Harcourt Brace Jovanovich, 1988), pp. 79–81; Walter Benn Michaels, "Philosophy in Kinkanja: Eliot's Pragmatism," *Glyph* 8 (1981): 170–202.

3 Oliver Wendell Holmes, "Codes, and the Arrangement of the Law" (1870), *The Collected Works of Justice Holmes: Complete Public Writings and Selected Judicial Opinions of Oliver Wendell Holmes,* ed. Sheldon M. Novick (Chicago: University of Chicago Press, 1995), vol. 1, p. 212.

4 *Lochner v. New York,* 198 U.S. 45 (1905), 76.

The Novelist of Everyday Life

DAVID BROMWICH

Richard Poirier gives a sympathetic survey of the alliance between pragmatists and poets, but a survey with a warning in it. A democratic impulse was at work in the pragmatic widening of the field as well as the definition of imagination, and the romance of pragmatism, as Poirier reminds us, included a hope that just as poetry was only an extension of "the real language of men in a state of vivid sensation," so philosophy might become a generalization of the ad hoc inventiveness of ordinary life. In this sense, the first statement of pragmatist doctrine is Emerson's "American Scholar," which says that everything we need for thinking is already ours. William James and Frost likewise tell their audiences (with growing degrees of popular investment as we go forward in the tradition): "This way of looking at things, which models itself on poetry, which is perhaps poetry, comes from your life and belongs to you." There may exist in all non-Platonic thought an impulse to regard thinking itself as a usual product of social exchange, but the reception of poetry and philosophy in the pragmatist line suggests that it is an unusual product. By the democratic constituents who are meant to be its beneficiaries, the liberating gift is not so much spurned as not seen to have been given.

Poetry informed by the Emersonian and Jamesian hope, a kind of poetry written not only by Frost but by Moore, Stevens, Wheelwright, and others, has appealed mainly to an elite of letters, the very people whose distinctiveness pragmatism sought to scour from the thinking world. The elite for their part mostly accept pragmatism as they would accept any secular idealism free of the misanthropic taint. This looks like an indifferent consensus, without many inroads to conduct. What happens to the picture, though, if we shift the genre of comparison from poetry to fiction? Does the novel offer more plausible grounds for the alliance between pragmatism and ordinary life? One reason I feel sure this is a legitimate question is the number of philosophers who, without ever asking it, imply that they have already arrived at an answer. The aspect of pragmatism concerned with the social self, they seem to say, has an interest in the coming to light of self-knowledge and a knowledge of other people, and that is the sort of process that we can see unfold in a novel. I offer in evidence four brief passages with a common intuition about the relationship between the reading and writing of novels and the human capacity for thinking without stereotype about one's own experience of life.

In an essay published in 1976 called "Professionalized Philosophy and Transcendentalist Culture," Richard Rorty observed that "Novels and poems are now the principal means by which a bright youth gains a self-image. Criticism of novels is the principal form in which the acquisition of a moral character is made articulate."[1] I don't know whether Rorty knew, or was involuntarily echoing, a sentence published half a century earlier by George Herbert Mead: "It is fair to say that the modern western world has lately done much of its thinking in the form of the novel."[2] Mead's claim is the more sweeping of the two, yet his tone is matter-of-fact. He was writing just a few years after Henry James went on his lecture tour to the United States to read "The Lesson of Balzac," where, with a montage of personal sketches of the temperamental variety of novelists, James defended his presumption in thus appearing to invite his readers into the workshop: "It will strike you perhaps that I speak as if we all, as if you all, without exception were novelists, haunting the back shop, the laboratory, or, more nobly expressed, the inner shrine of the temple; but such assumptions, in this age of print—if I may not say this age of poetry—are perhaps never too wide of the mark."[3] Now "The Lesson of Balzac" is in some ways a popular performance, but its credo on the task of the novelist is as scrupulous as anything James ever wrote, and there is a remarkably similar passage in the essay on Flaubert he published in 1902 as an introduction to *Madame Bovary*. James here considers the wager by which a masterpiece at last becomes what individual readers have backed it to be. Passing in review the posthumous growth of a work of art that accompanies the discernment of its audience, he notes that while "the significance comes by a process slow and small," something does follow from "the fact only that one perceptive private reader after another discovers at his convenience that the book is rare." These readers, says James, "accumulate and count. They count by their quality and continuity of attention; so they have gathered for *Madame Bovary,* and so they are held. . . . Such is my reason, definitely, for speaking of Flaubert as the novelist's novelist. Are we not moreover—and let it pass this time as a happy hope!— pretty well all novelists now?"[4]

I think Henry James was in earnest when he spoke with wonder, in a letter to William, of "the extent to which all my life I have (like M. Jourdain) unconsciously pragmatised."[5] The four passages I have just quoted all support the sincerity of his confession. The novelist's novelist—if we are pretty well all novelists now—becomes, by virtue of that fact, the experiencer's experiencer, a man or woman who has been accorded the distinction of representative interpreter by a process akin not to scientific discovery but rather like the choosing of a lawgiver, if we could imagine it happening over time. James takes for granted that all of us, given sufficient means and sufficient imagination, could give the law to ourselves, and in this sense all of us are candidates for becoming the heroes of our own lives.

Emerson wrote in "The American Scholar": "What deafness, what stone-blind custom, what overgrown error you behold is there only by sufferance—by your sufferance. See it to be a lie and you have already dealt it its mortal blow."[6] The same, according to James, holds true for the classic of art, which by displacing a previous representation of life assists in the change of human nature. A book like *Madame Bovary* comes to be, it exists and it survives, only by the positive suffrage of many readers. The difference between the novelist and the experiencer lies not in the process but in the result—the novelist producing a work of fiction, the rest of us a continuous and maybe recordless work of self-examination and inquisitive concern with life. Interpretation as James understands it, and as Mead and Rorty understand it also, is in most contexts an activity that involves a fair amount of characterizing. We find ourselves imposing a certain coherence of outline, a complexion, a face and a profile, on persons or events that we have an interest in regarding as if they did hang together. Of course, to speak at all of character or characteristic qualities is to engage in anthropomorphism, and a critic like Paul de Man, who despised every humanism, was canny in seeing that truly to rid ourselves of the illusion of moral agency and historical time with its cause and consequence, it was necessary to go to the root of the trope-bearing two-legged machine and weed out *all* our anthropomorphisms.

This choice of therapy may have been utopian or the reverse. It was certainly antipragmatic, and what both William and Henry James are saying, if I have them right, is that we will go on following our habits of characterization and personification so long as we continue to desire certain ends. Human beings do not come to us whole, they need to be humanized and made to hang together, and that is what novelists do. It is what the rest of us do, as novelists of everyday life. Critics, too, with the confidence of novelists, may do it when they have a decided opinion.

There is a hint of that tone in Poirier when he demands of Dr. Johnson whether the public has really settled anything: he concludes that the eighteenth-century *Lear* with Nahum Tate's happy ending, which spared the audience so much blood on the stage, actually bled the play to death. It is a curious way of talking about an inanimate thing, a text; but I doubt that he intended an impartial homage to the First Folio text or any hard-heartedness toward the characters Tate had saved. This way of talking was a gesture of loyalty to a work of art, and loyalty carried him away.

Pragmatism is never as dandyish as the version of skepticism Emerson canvassed in "Experience": "Let us treat the men and women well; treat them as if they were real; perhaps they are."[7] It treats the work of art as if it *were* real. This seems to me what critics are always doing with the works they care for, and there is no point disguising it, any more than there would be in showing off our habits of personification as if they were a badge of conspicuous merit. These acts of characterizing, whether in criticism or common life, are not a virtue but, to repeat, a habit, a mark of the intensity of awe and affection that drives the activity itself. A poem, a play, or a novel is the plausible and provisional end of something having been worked through or thought through. The process will continue in the minds of readers. To the extent that we model our knowledge of works of art on our knowledge of people, the author matters as a creation the work projects, and not as a previous known quantity that the work secretes. There are poems that are more like a person than the poet who produced them. And, as Yeats remarked when he wrote about the "antithetical self," the projection may be false to the facts. There is a late Victorian fantasy in which, in a sequence of caricatures, Browning is observed to grow easy, hearty, even-keeled, square-heeled, the image of a bourgeois banker as his poems turn cross-grained and grotesque beyond fathoming, while Tennyson, as his verse is polished to the last gleam of a conciliating propriety, becomes himself in appearance every year more wasted, distraught, and prophetic. Artists do not know their works more deeply than we can know them, and, on the pragmatic view, we would have to say the same of self-knowledge and the knowledge of other people.

These sorts of knowledge are not composed of distinct materials, and although it may be flattering to think we know something either isolated or continuous about ourselves that is denied to others, it is equally true that they know something about us that is denied to ourselves. We may cut a figure in the story we make of our lives, and a different figure in the story they make of us, and whether we like it or not their figure may be more vivid than ours. I say vivid rather than true, because anything anyone believes of someone on good circumstantial evidence is likely to be part of a probable truth.[8] It is the probability rather than the truth that matters to the novelist, and to the novelist of everyday life. When we characterize a work of art, or a person or a situation, we bring into being an allegory more memorable than the accidents that compose it.

For illustration, consider an unforgettable scene of *The Portrait of a Lady,* the "vigil" of the heroine Isabel Archer, in which she tries to construe or decode an impression that disturbs her from the attitude in which she has come upon Gilbert Osmond and Madame Merle together. Their conduct and almost their posture suggest a prior relation between them, and there is a sense, deeply interesting to James, in which Isabel's discovery about them is a discovery about herself. The chapter soon after, in which she reflects on what her marriage has become, was the part of the book in which James took the keenest pride, "a representation simply of her motionlessly *seeing,*" as he put it in his preface. And yet there may be a danger in prizing the work of consciousness at such moments, lest it turn us into aesthetes regarding our own lives and regarding the moral claims of others. Osmond, inert as he is, turns out to be this sort of aesthete, a skillful practitioner of the arts of watching and waiting; and the hero of *The Beast in the Jungle,* though he is not an aesthete, exhibits a similar want of belief and absence of will. It is, as that story suggests, another name for a failure of life. I take all these characters to be a warning delivered by Henry James on the possible sickliness of an idealism he stood for nevertheless, an idealism about the way belief leads on to action, and both belief and action take their start from an absorbed watching and waiting.

William James, as much as his brother, wanted to believe that seeing and knowing and acting were not opposed but leagued in human life, that they could be strung along a single continuum. Yet a worry very like Henry's, about the way "motionlessly *seeing*" may be an impediment to action, seems to have been a motive for his digression in *The Principles of Psychology* on the habits of spectatorship. Poirier has alluded to this passage in his remark about William's dismay at the effects of works of art—that the emotions they induce should so often merely demoralize and sap our nerve power—but the whole observation is so peculiar and so true it deserves to be quoted at length:

> A tendency to act only becomes effectively ingrained in us in proportion to the uninterrupted frequency with which the actions actually occur, and the brain "grows" to their use. Every time a resolve or a fine glow of feeling evaporates without bearing practical fruit is

worse than a chance lost; it works so as positively to hinder future resolutions and emotions from taking the normal path of discharge. There is no more contemptible type of human character than that of the nerveless sentimentalist and dreamer, who spends his life in a weltering sea of sensibility and emotion, but who never does a manly concrete deed. . . . The habit of excessive novel-reading and theatre-going will produce true monsters in this line. The weeping of a Russian lady over the fictitious personages in the play, while her coachman is freezing to death on his seat outside, is the sort of thing that everywhere happens on a less glaring scale. Even the habit of excessive indulgence in music, for those who are neither performers themselves nor musically gifted enough to take it in a purely intellectual way, has probably a relaxing effect upon the character. . . . The remedy would be, never to suffer one's self to have an emotion at a concert, without expressing it afterward in *some* active way. Let the expression be the least thing in the world—speaking genially to one's aunt, or giving up one's seat in a horse-car, if nothing more heroic offers—but let it not fail to take place.[9]

James' warning is an extension of the words of doubt he occasionally utters in the *Psychology* and elsewhere about the effects of imagination. So long as we think of philosophers and novelists as people who look on the scene from a place outside it, we will admire their works for the authority of their stage effects, and our position will be that of spectators, well equipped to praise those superior spectators, the writers and sages. William and Henry James despised this view of philosophy and of art. A novelist's stories, they say, and the more abstract stories philosophers tell, interest us not mainly because we like to suppose we share the inventions of genius but because, in our intervals of characteristic thought, we feel ourselves to be what the novelists have long said we were, namely readers of our own experience.

Notes

1 Richard Rorty, "Professionalized Philosophy and Transcendentalist Culture," *Georgia Review* 30 (1976), reprinted in *Consequences of Pragmatism* (Minneapolis: University of Minnesota Press, 1982), p. 66.
2 George Herbert Mead, "The Social Self," *Journal of Philosophy* 10 (1913): 378. For an expanded version of the argument, see Mead's lectures of 1914 on social psychology, in *The Individual and the Social Self*, ed. David L. Miller (Chicago: University of Chicago Press, 1982), pp. 100–5. Novels assist thinking by a counter-action against the habitual

process by which "the person [states] others to himself in terms of a single positive abstract relation. This is overcome through increase of content in the relation" (p. 100). It follows that the reading and writing of novels—for Mead, realistic novels above all—are among the acts of thoughtful citizenship in a democracy.

3   Henry James, "The Lesson of Balzac," in *Literary Criticism: European Writers and the Prefaces* (New York: Library of America, 1984), p. 138.

4   *Ibid.*, pp. 345–46.

5   Quoted in F. O. Matthiessen, *The James Family* (New York: Knopf, 1947), p. 343.

6   *Selections from Ralph Waldo Emerson*, ed. Stephen Whicher (Boston: Houghton Mifflin, 1957), p. 75.

7   *Ibid.*, p. 262.

8   On circumstantial evidence and its relation to the modern idea of character, see Alexander Welsh, *Strong Representations* (Baltimore: Johns Hopkins University Press, 1992).

9   William James, *The Principles of Psychology*, 2 vols. (New York: Holt, 1890), vol. 1, pp. 125–26.

When Mind Is a Verb: Thomas Eakins and the Work of Doing

RAY CARNEY

All to form the Hand of the mind;—to instruct us that "good thoughts are no better than good dreams, unless they be executed!"—Ralph Waldo Emerson, *Nature*

Mind is primarily a verb.—John Dewey, *Art as Experience*

I want to proceed somewhat differently from most of the other contributors to this volume. The pieces gathered here generally focus on the twentieth-century cultural situation, bringing pragmatism up-to-date as it were, but I want to return to the nineteenth century, not only to reestablish contact with the historical moment out of which pragmatism emerged, but also to explore whether cultural phenomena ordinarily not associated with pragmatism might be connected with it. My assumption is that our new understanding of Emerson, James, and Dewey can change our understanding of earlier American culture, throwing light on areas dimmed by the over-familiarity of conventional wisdom. The present is not the only thing that changes when we make new discoveries; the past keeps changing too. Such is the case, I would argue, when it comes to pragmatism and nineteenth-century American painting. In the light of what the pragmatists are teaching us, even a standard art historical concept like "American realism" is due for revision.

As my mention of painting should suggest, another difference is that my focus will not be on general cultural practices and structures of knowledge, but particular works of art. Robert Frost once asserted that his poems had criticism in them, and in a similar vein, I would argue that works of art can have a lot of philosophy in them. To the extent that we subscribe to the importance of philosophy, we certainly do not want to confine it to philosophical texts. My working premise is that art can make assertions about reality and the nature of truth that are as philosophically complex as anything in the writing of professional philosophers. Specifically, I want to use the paintings of Thomas Eakins to explore the extent to which works of art can figure philosophical stances. What might it mean to treat Eakins as the philosophical peer of James or Dewey?[1]

I should also note that insofar as I shall be using works of art as my source material, it will be necessary for my argument to be far more grounded in specific, observed details than the other sort of argument. While social, legal, and cultural analysis may be conducted at a fairly abstract level, if a work of art is to be taken seriously as a way of knowing, it can only be by coming to grips with its particulars. Art is a classic instance of what Clifford Geertz calls "local knowledge"—knowledge that, to some extent, *resists* generalization. It is not knowledge of anything, anywhere, anytime, but knowledge anchored in a specific sequence of experiences, inflected by a uniquely personal point of view.

Artistic knowledge further differs from social, legal, and cultural knowledge in that it is sensorily embodied. It is not merely mental or intellectual in nature. It is a form of knowledge that is inextricably intertwined in temporal, spatial, and experiential particularities. It lives in the world and plays itself out along the senses; it is brought into existence in the form of bodies, gestures, movements, tones, and feelings.[2]

The qualities I have just described make artistic forms of knowledge uniquely suited to expressing pragmatic understandings of experience. In the first place, pragmatism is quintessentially the philosophy of particulars. James summed it up in *The Meaning of Truth* when he wrote that, "The whole originality of pragmatism, the whole point of it, is its concrete way of seeing. It begins with concreteness, and returns and ends with it."[3] In the second place, one of the most important contributions of pragmatism to the history of philosophy is its determination to force philosophical knowledge to take account of the look and feel of sensory experience.

The need for a sensorily informed mode of knowledge is a theme that runs throughout James' work—from his warnings about the dangers of "vicious abstractionism" to his exhortations to his reader to "dive back into the flux [and] turn your face toward sensation, that fleshbound thing which rationalism has always loaded with abuse."[4] James repeatedly argued that in order to "fathom" what he called the "thickness" of experience we must engage ourselves with it in a temporally aware and spatially responsive way. As he wrote in *A Pluralistic Universe* (with a possible allusion to Satan's negotiation of Chaos in *Paradise Lost*): "Sensible reality is too concrete to be entirely manageable [abstractly]. . . . To get from one point in it to another, we have to plough or wade through the whole intolerable interval. No detail is spared us, it is as bad as the barbed-wire complications at Port Arthur, and we grow old and die in the process."[5]

In a sense, James is telling us how we should approach works of art as well. Applied to the activity of artistic interpretation, James' point is that *not* to "wade though the whole intolerable interval," *not* to negotiate the "barbed-wire complications"—merely to summarize the work, floating somewhere above it, disengaged from the specific spaces, times, and bodies that bring it to us—is to betray the very forms of understanding art provides. One might adapt James' metaphor and say that the pragmatist shows us not only that we must creep and crawl through the work, but, even more importantly, that such prickly intricacies of involvement are the supreme value of the artistic experience.

Because, in the pragmatic view, the only way to experience something truly is to experience it in all of its "thickness" and "fullness," the closeness and sensory content of my readings of these paintings might be said to be an attempt to be faithful to the pragmatic method itself. Precisely because the works I shall be examining embrace pragmatic forms of understanding, they require the closest of close readings. (As James' crawling-through-barbed-wire metaphor suggests, the degree of closeness may even be uncomfortable.) Sensorily concrete and experientially detailed methods of analysis are the only way to deal with works that are so deeply committed to sensorily concrete and experientially detailed conceptions of truth.

Painting and pragmatism may seem an odd conjunction, but it is a truism to observe that intellectual revolutions are no respecters of boundaries. It is clear to me that, however it came about, Eakins deserves to be regarded as a pragmatist. At the same time, it is necessary to resist the impulse to understand any parallels we may find between the work of James and Eakins as examples of "influence." If influence ever explains anything (and it seldom does), it clearly does not apply here. Though James and Eakins were almost exact contemporaries (Eakins two years younger than James, and outliving him by six years), there is no evidence that either of them ever heard of the other, let alone knew anything of the other's work. Eakins' paintings did not reach a significant national audience until after his death, and most of the ones I am going to be discussing were painted *before* James had published his major philosophical work, so similarities will have to be attributed to the cultural milieu that nurtured both (a milieu shaped, at least in part, by Emerson, who hovers over all of subsequent American culture as a ghostly protopragmatic presence).

But however we may account for the resemblance, I would argue that James' (and later Dewey's) conception of replacing the philosophy of "being" with a philosophy of "doing" finds a striking anticipation in Eakins' work. To adapt the phrases in my epigraph, Emerson, Eakins,

James, and Dewey can all be understood to be exploring the ramifications of "forming the hand of the mind" or "transforming mind into a verb." All four ask us to translate mental processes into practical activities. All four ask us, as James might have phrased it, to reestablish the connection between "conceptions" and "perceptions." Eakins' paintings, as I understand them, dramatize Emerson's, James', and Dewey's vision of the possible merging our mental and our manual "grasp."

"Forming the hand of the mind" is an ideal in Emerson, a set of philosophical insights and procedures in James, and a literal depiction in dozens of Eakins' paintings. Few artists have more deeply explored the relation of idea and execution. For a quick introduction one need only glance at two of Eakins' best known works: *The Gross Clinic* and *The Agnew Clinic*. They clearly take the relation of hand and mind as their subject. (I reproduce Eakins' preferred version of the former.)

Mind is vividly represented in both. Gross and Agnew are portrayed at moments of deep thoughtfulness. At the moment Eakins chooses to imagine, each professor of surgery has briefly paused in his operation (and his lecture) to ponder something. A variety of effects emphasize their thoughtfulness. In the first place, there is the presentation of the head. Each is placed against a darker background and lighted so as prominently to display his high-domed forehead, furrowed brows, and deep-set eyes. (Gross is more theatrically presented than Agnew, illuminated as he is by a single source of light which leaves half of his face dramatically shadowed and creates a semi-spiritualized aureole out of his light gray hair). As he does in many other works, Eakins heightens the expressive effect of both heads by highly modeling them and placing them against backgrounds that are much "flatter" than they are (both in the sense of being less three-dimensionally rendered and being painted with less oily, more thinned-down pigments).

The placement of the surgeons with respect to the operating tables contributes to our sense that, at the moment Eakins has chosen to represent, each of the men has momentarily taken a meditative step off to one side of the heaving sea of activity around him. Each is marginalized by a spatial caesura (smaller for Gross and larger for Agnew), and pivoted slightly away from both the students he addresses and the operation he conducts. As both doctors are turned away from their assistants, and their eyes are averted from contact with anyone around them, it is impossible to read the figures of Gross and Agnew as interacting socially or physically with anyone at the moment we glimpse them. We are meant to read them as "thinking." Their visual positioning figures their imaginative position: a

Thomas Eakins, *The Gross Clinic*, 1875–76 (India ink and watercolor on cardboard), The Metropolitan Museum of Art, Rogers Fund, 1923 (23.94).

state of contemplative withdrawal or meditative separation from the welter of events.[6]

But it is critical to observe their states of withdrawal are only partial; both doctors are still immersed in and engaged with a series of practical events. After all, Eakins chooses to depict Gross and Agnew not in their studies as thinkers, but very much at work as doers. As surgeons and teachers in the midst of an operation, surrounded by hordes of others with various claims on their attention, they are in the middle of the most complex course of actions imaginable. This is a world in which action counts as much as thought—or, to put it more accurately, a world in which action cannot be separated from thought.

I would argue that the point of both paintings is precisely the ways Gross and Agnew bridge the realms of thinking and doing. Eakins brings the point home to us through a series of contrasts in which the meaningful connection of the two realms—of being with doing, of mental impulses to manual expressions—is flawed or absent in various ways. There are dozens of arms and hands visible (and invisible) in both paintings, and their sheer number and prominence draw our attention to them, but one of the things we slowly realize is that there are only a few in which hand and mind are linked in a disciplined, productive relationship—one in which mind informs hand and hand informs mind with the same degree of subtlety that Eakins' own hand and mind obviously worked in concert when he painted his work. Consider the most important groups of hands and arms in the two works:

—First, there are the students' hands and arms, almost all of which are slack and lacking any executive function, if they are not simply absent (most blatantly in the centrally positioned student in the Agnew painting, who cannot bother to remove his hands from his pockets to take notes).[7]

—Then there are the hands and arms of the figures in the entranceways to each operating theater. One man in the Gross portrait uses his arm to lean against the wall; another lounges against the opposite wall with his arms down at his sides. The figure in the Agnew portrait uses his hand to shield his whisper. None of the three might be said to put his limbs to productive use.

—Next, there are the partially or totally obscured hands and arms of both patients, which represent a third form of slackness or inattentiveness, cut off from mental control and usefulness by the haze of anesthesia.

—Then there are the arms and hands of the patient's mother (if that is what she is) writhing in pain in *The Gross Clinic*. (Several sketches survive documenting the care Eakins put into her depiction.) Her arms and hands contrast with those of both the students and the patients without being any more usefully employed. Her gestures are highly expressive, but completely undisciplined and uncontrolled.

—At the other expressive extreme, there are the arms and hands of the recording secretary in the Gross portrait, and the arms and hands of the various surgical assistants in both paintings. They figure a different, but equally limited, relationship of hand and mind. One might say that

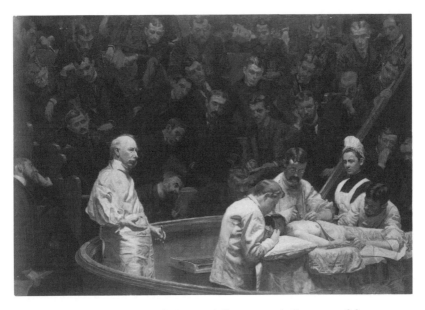

Thomas Eakins, *The Agnew Clinic,* 1899 (oil on canvas), Courtesy of the
University of Pennsylvania Art Collection, Philadelphia, Pennsylvania.

they are examples of being *all hand.* They are instances of masterful manual dexterity (the ability to restrain, to anesthetize, to cut, and to record),
but they lack the capacity to make creative decisions. They merely follow
Gross' and Agnew's instructions.

In this whirl of compared and contrasted limbs and gestures, illustrat-
ing various forms and degrees of mental and manual disconnection or
infacility, only Agnew and Gross truly combine mindfulness and handiness. They erase the distinction between manual and mental dexterity,
insofar as their scalpel-wielding hands are clearly energized and mobilized
by their thoughts as much as their thoughts are disciplined and instructed
by their practical performances.

The particular positions and gestures of both doctors express the blend-
ing of the realms. The verticality of their presentation tells us that the
doctors rise above the merely executive functions of the horizontally displayed elements of the operating tables beside them—yet without losing
touch with that realm of activity. As they step aside to think or make a
point in their lectures, both doctors significantly hold scalpels poised for
imminent action; they are not just lecturing about surgery, but practicing
surgeons still at work. (No other figure is given a scalpel in either paint-

ing.) Gross is placed in an especially complex double position: even as he takes a half-step back and turns halfway to the side, he is shown continuing to lean on the operating table, with his left arm and his hand touching it (or the patient), maintaining intimate practical contact with the work at hand. Turns out of experience energize returns to experience.

The same point is made less conceptually and more perceptually by the presentation of the group engaged in the operation in the Gross portrait. Eakins organizes the visual space so that, of all the medical figures in the work, only Gross presents a coherent, clearly legible visual identity. In their merely manual functionality, the other figures around the operating table are all on the verge of dissolving into visual incoherence. The impression is all the more vivid when the painting is viewed not in a page-size reproduction but in life. In Eakins' looming, larger-than-life canvas, it becomes extremely hard to decipher the sprawl of the figures on and around the operating table (especially given the dark monochrome of the color scheme). Even in reduced-size reproduction, there is such a confusing overlap of bodies and limbs (with the patient crisscrossed by a network of assistants' hands and arms) that it becomes difficult to tell what limb belongs to what person, or where one body ends and the next begins (an effect heightened through the use of severe foreshortening). Gross alone presents a unitary bodily and mental presence, being granted a clear and separate visual identity. That is to say, as a blotch of paint, Gross organizes the visual spaces of his painting similar to the way, as a doctor, he organizes the surgical space. His visual composure and organization is a kind of metaphor for his psychological and functional composure and organization.[8]

That is to say, the paintings are not only theatrical in their amphitheater settings and lighting effects, but subscribe to what might be called a fundamentally theatrical conception of personal identity. Figures express themselves not merely (as in traditional portrait painting) through their clothing, posture, gestures, and facial expressions, but by means of practical forms of action and interaction with others. They are defined not simply in terms of states of *being* (which might be said to be the expressive mode of most other portraits), but in their practical mastery of forms of *doing*. In Eakins' definition of who and what we are, consciousness is not a merely personal, private, internal state, but is required to externalize itself in a concrete course of action. The shift from the one definition of identity to the other might be called the pragmatic turn. We *are*, at least in large part, what we *do*. We are our hands as much as our minds. The union of the realms is crucial to the meaning of both paintings. For Eakins and all pragmatists, mental activity is not a time out from practical performance. Thought is not an alternative to action or action an alternative to thought (as in Platonic philosophy), but each is a continuation of the other. Gross' and Agnew's unique achievement is to bridge the realms of thinking and doing. They masterfully inject mind into the world.

When in "What Pragmatism Means" James called for a philosophy that "turns towards concreteness and adequacy, towards facts, towards action and towards power,"[9] he might have been describing not only the philosophical predilections of the sitters Eakins was interested in painting (many of whom are men known for their practical accomplishments), but Eakins' own fact-imbued forms of depiction. With his use of photography, his studies of perspective (and frequent use of perspective grids in his sketches), his motion studies, and his interest in science and engineering, Eakins was so devoted to concreteness and factuality that he laid himself open to frequent criticisms of what was said to be his overly "scientific," "factual," or "literal" treatment of his subjects. As Frank Stella once wittily remarked, works of art are always at least to some extent "lifted off the ground, up in the air," but Eakins' goal, like that of James, is to reestablish contact between ideals and practical realities.

It is not at all uncommon for artists to choose men of action and practical achievement as their subjects, but what distinguishes Eakins' work from that of most other nineteenth-century artists is his democratic and egalitarian definition of what constitutes achievement. As Elizabeth Johns has pointed out, heroism in Eakins' paintings (as in Whitman's poetry) is not confined to grand figures—clergymen, statesmen, and generals—but is a quality that almost anyone, anywhere can display: surgeons, scientists, and inventors—even rowers, boxers, baseball players, and hunters.[10]

Eakins' work is, as Johns understands, about a new kind of heroism, but I would argue that what is most distinctive and important about Eakins' conception of heroism is *not* the fact that it includes the common man, but rather the mutually supportive relationship it imagines to exist between consciousness and performance. As both the Gross and the Agnew portraits demonstrate, the essence of this distinctively American conception of heroism is its stunning equation of mental and practical power, as if there were no inherent obstacle in converting the one into the other. That daring leap of faith from mind to matter is the heart and soul of the pragmatic position and the deepest connection between Eakins' work and pragmatic philosophy. Seeing, being, and doing merge.

"American heroism," for Eakins as for James and Emerson, is precisely the ability of the individual to express his consciousness in worldly actions and events. To describe that transaction between inner and outer realms, Emerson invented the concept of "the heroic mind"—a term that signifies a state of blended thought and action in which the "thinking" and the "doing" are one (a concept James borrowed verbatim from Emerson).[11] It would not be too much to say that this belief that the individual can perform his imagination in the world *was* the American dream: It was the vision that certain Romantic ideals of originality, creativity, and freedom (which English Romantics and German Idealists were willing to let remain states of consciousness) could be expressed in the ordinary doings of everyday life. To put it most baldly: The American dream consisted of the belief that to have a free imagination is actually to be able to make oneself free in society. As Emerson tantalizingly put it at several points in his writing, the mind was endowed with the capacity to "realize" itself.

But even Emerson seems slightly more cautious about the relation of the imagination to worldly expression than Eakins. When Emerson concludes "Experience" with the stirring peroration that "the true romance which the world exists to realize, will be the transformation of genius into practical power," he at least has the prudence to call the ideal a "romance" and to locate it somewhere in the indefinite future (the place Emerson typically locates all of his ideals). Eakins puts the "realization of genius" in the here and now. The subject of almost all of his work is the intimate connection between ideas and acts, impulses and executions.

Over and over again, his portraits are about the "realization" of thought (whether at the level of genius or less). If Doctors Gross and Agnew translate from the mind to the world via their scalpels, Eakins' athletes, hunters, outdoorsmen, and other figures express their "heroic minds" with even more mundane implements—with oars, poles, guns, sailboats, baseball bats, boxing gloves, chess pieces, writing implements, and even a child's building blocks (in *Baby at Play*). The critical point is the inseparability of thought and action. The linkage of the two realms is what matters. Eakins' subject, like James' and Dewey's, is the *performance* of the heroic mind. His figures *enact* their imaginative identities in a challenging course of action and interaction—never more complexly than in the feats of physical dexterity illustrated by the sports paintings.

Pushing for Rail and *Will Schuster and Blackman Going Shooting* feature complex acts of coordination and balance in which one or more boats is held in place and steadied by one man while another loads his rifle, aims, or fires at a moving target. Given the incredible instability of a flat-bottomed boat with two men standing upright in it, with the stern man up on the gunwale a foot or more above the water line (not to mention the destabilizing kick of the gun being fired), either work is the visual equivalent of painting the Flying Wallendas executing a pyramid on the high wire. The challenging relation of intention to execution in these situations is precisely what attracted Eakins to them.

Just as he did in the Gross and Agnew works, Eakins presents a double text that emphasizes both the figures' mental focus and their manual mastery—and in fact suggests the inseparability of the two realms. The figures' faces and eyes register intense states of concentration as they aim, fire, and hold the boats steady; at the same time, the care Eakins lavishes on detailing the placement of the pole-pushers' feet, bodies, arms, and hands emphasizes the physical prowess of their performances. (The flickering of the reflected light from the water onto the hull of the boat in the Will Schuster painting in particular reminds us of the precariousness of the men's act of balance. They are not only walking on water, but the water is clearly in motion.)[12]

The paintings imagine performances of balletic balance and agility. Eakins' decision in both paintings to contrast stolid, short, firmly planted, red-shirted hunters with one or more taller, thinner, lighter-shirted, and more delicate looking pole-bearers visually suggests both the strength and the grace necessary in the performances. As the viewer's eye skims across the crystalline surface of *Pushing for Rail* in particular, the visual play of contrasted body positions and pole placements sets up eddies of suspended motion that capture the dynamic poise of these acts of mutually interdependent balance and timing. The figures are abstracted into a delicate visual interplay of half-rhyming positions. The impression is further heightened by the Dutch-like-sheen and attention to detail of Eakins' diminutive treatment of the subject. The tininess of the figures makes them seem almost weightless; the unnaturally sharp focus of the details makes the acts of balance seem slightly uncanny.

The rowing paintings depict similar manual and mental transactions, communicating the degree to which rowing depends on an intricate interaction of body and spirit. It is not too much to argue that in these works the mind acts and the hand thinks, to the point that thought becomes indistinguishable from action. To focus only on *The Biglin Brothers Turning the Stake,* the mindfulness of the two rowers in the foreground is communicated not only by the concentration of their facial expressions, but, as in the clinic paintings, by the slight inclination of their heads, their positioning against a neutral background, and the use of a single source of light (in this case, the sun) to heighten their three-dimensionality (which

Thomas Eakins, *The Biglin Brothers Turning the Stake*, 1873 (oil on canvas), © The Cleveland Museum of Art, 1997, The Hinman B. Hurlbut Collection, 1984.27.

contrasts with the flatness of the water's surface behind them). Eakins employs cool blues (in the kerchiefs, the trim on the brothers' shirts, the stake flag, and the water around the Biglins' boat) that contrast with the hotter colors and visual agitation in the painting's background (the red flag and kerchiefs of the opposing team, the whiter water, and the visual busyness of the shoreline) to emphasize their meditativeness. The Biglins may be in the heat of action, but the tones emphasize their intellectual and emotional coolness.[13] They are in the middle of a race, at one of its most crucial junctures, but their minds are as calmly composed as those of doctors Gross and Agnew in the middle of their comparably demanding manual performances. The deliberate placidity of Eakins' composition is such that the rowers look as if they were standing still in the water (the mistaken conclusion many a casual viewer has drawn from the compositional stillness of the work).

The water in front of the Biglins is as calmly reflective as their minds, yet as I have suggested, brain and brawn are always interrelated in Eakins' work. Two small dimples in the river, the contrasted positions of the Biglins' bodies, the flex of the muscles in their arms, and the angles of their oar blades (their degree of "feather" and "catch") all tell us that this moment of mental poise is simultaneously one of tremendous physical exertion. The bow rower (on the right) is pulling backward on his oar with full force while the stern or "stroke" rower is counterpoising his oar with equal force against the movement, employing the resistance of the water to pivot the boat clockwise. (At the moment Eakins has imagined, the boat has all but completed its pivot around the stake and is just about to begin another lap.)

Yet, as I have already suggested, the work being done by the Biglins is mental as much as physical. Even as they are exerting themselves physically, both rowers are making a series of calculations: the bow rower calculating the distance of the stern rower's oar from the stake, making sure it clears it and will continue to clear it on the stroke that is about to begin; the stern rower meanwhile monitoring the boat's alignment with respect to the shore (using a preselected object on the shore to line up the boat), preparing to call out and initiate the regular stroke in unison with the bow rower once the boat is lined up properly to begin the next leg of the course. Eakins imagines a moment of contemplative calm, just prior to a furious unleashing of brute force. Mental and physical turns are one.

The point of going into this much detail is to suggest not only how much interrelated thinking and doing Eakins has depicted, but how much interrelated thinking and doing the depiction itself involved. Thinking and doing are inseparable for both the rowers and the artist. Just as it is impossible to say where the Biglins' mental prowess (their calculations of distances, timing of the pivot, and pacing of the strokes) ends and their physical prowess begins, it is impossible to say where Eakins' draftsmanship (his study of perspective, his calculations of angles, sizes, distances, and reflections, and his knowledge of details of rowing) ends and his artistry begins. That is precisely what interested Eakins about this moment—for both the Biglins and himself. As in the clinic and hunting paintings, at a time like this, hand and mind, art and science merge.

That is what it means to say that the events and figures in Eakins' work are surrogates for the representational achievement of the painter himself, who is not merely depicting Agnew's, Gross's rail hunters', or the Biglins' challengingly coordinated acts of thinking and doing, but is enacting his own course of coordinated thinking and doing as he creates such spatially and temporally detailed works. His art is the doing of thinking.

Evidence that Eakins thought of his athletes and other figures as alter egos is that so many of them seem to be holding brush-like implements. Eakins repeatedly includes veiled representations of his own painting activity in his works. We have already seen brush-like shapes in the form of the scalpels in the two clinic paintings (in *The Gross Clinic*, with a paint-like splatter of blood on its tip and on the doctor's fingers). *The Concert Singer* contains another example of Eakins' depiction of a brush-shape in his work in the form of an orchestra conductor's baton. (In the Philadelphia Museum sketch that precedes the final version, the *trompe l'oeil*-like impression that the baton is Eakins' own brush painting the work is unusually striking.) In the rowing paintings, the shape and size of the oars also repeatedly evoke images of artists' brushes. Even the hunters in *Pushing for Rail* may be viewed as miniature miniaturists, manipulating objects that resemble the tiny brushes that Eakins used to paint them. It should not be surprising that we should find images of painters in these paintings. The skills that Eakins' surgeons, hunters, and rowers display are clearly related to the skills he displays in creating them.

The portrait of *Professor Henry A. Rowland* is the next to last work I shall consider. It falls into the fairly large group of Eakins' paintings that deals with scientists and inventors—another set of figures who move from thinking to doing and back again, marrying the work of the mind and hand. Rowland invented the ruling machine that made possible the creation of diffraction gratings. (A diffraction grating simulates the effect of a prism by creating a spectrum. It was a scientifically important invention because spectra display what are called absorption or Fraunhofer lines, allowing a scientist to study the chemical properties of the material emitting the light. Thus Rowland was the inventor of a machine that made possible a new way of understanding matter, upon which most of modern physics and chemistry are based.)

As should by now be familiar, Rowland's portrait highlights both the professor's intellect and his practical skills, and explores the connection of the two. While the overall visual effect is quite subdued (rendered as it is almost entirely in earth tones), and the room Rowland sits in is quite dark and shadowy, just as he did in the clinic paintings, Eakins uses pools of light to draw the viewer's attention to specific aspects of Rowland's life and work.

The brightest light illuminates Rowland's face and prominent, veined forehead. Similar to what we have seen in other works, Eakins not only dramatically positions Rowland's head against a flatter background, but angles his body and directs his gaze away from the viewer and the other figure in the work. The effect is to prevent a social interpretation of the relationship of Rowland and his assistant (or a social interpretation of Rowland's body language), and to encourage a reading of Rowland's expression as a state of thoughtfulness.

From the *Louis Kenton, Letitia Wilson Jordan, and Amelia Van Buren* portraits to *The Portrait of Maud Cook* and *John H. Brinton,* many of Eakins' portraits focus on this precise imaginative moment—the moment in which a formal, social relationship with one's surroundings gives way to an unposed, meditative one. It is as if—as he explicitly does in the various works about the sculptor William Rush—Eakins aspired to depict his sitters at the instant they cease to be sitters—to capture them the way they are *just prior to* or *just following* the formal occasion of being painted, as they are when they don't realize anyone is looking at them and stop "posing." The goal is to represent some deep part of the person separate from and more important than his social self.[14]

What further links the Rowland painting with the clinic paintings is its two other pockets of light, which emphasize Rowland's practical relationship to his surroundings. A dim light in the background displays the slowly moving wheels and shining gears of Rowland's ruling machine being operated and adjusted by his lab assistant. Like Rowland, the assistant is granted a double depiction that emphasizes both mind and hand. Mindfulness is depicted by having his head bowed (always an indication of thought in Eakins' work), and handiness in terms of the brawniness of his right arm, the prominence given to the shining shank of his screwdriver, and the alluringly blurred wheels and gears of the machinery.

The final area of illumination falls in Rowland's lap. In the only area of the painting as brightly lighted as Rowland's face and forehead, Eakins displays two things that (even more than the machinery in the background) refer us to Rowland's life of practical accomplishment. We see the product of Rowland's research, his diffraction grating, which he holds in his left hand; and we see the professor's right hand—with its obvious strength and heavy veining, clearly the hand of not just a thinker but a doer. As in the Biglins' performance on the water or Gross' and Agnew's performances in their operating theaters, the combination of delicacy, sensitivity, and strength in Rowland's hand beautifully suggest that fine knowledge can be blended with the capacity for fine action. Along with the other doublings in the painting, it suggests a perfect unity of thought and action.

Rowland's left hand holds the most visually arresting presence in the painting, one of the diffraction gratings his machine produces. Not only does the sky-tinctured polychrome of its brilliant rainbow coloration place it uncannily outside the earth-toned monochrome of the rest of the painting, but, like a real diffraction grating (especially a concave one, as Rowland's was), the light it gives off seemingly floats somewhere above the surface of the work (a visual effect partially achieved by its being framed

Thomas Eakins, *Professor Henry A. Rowland,* 1891 (oil on canvas),
© Addison Gallery of American Art, Phillips Academy, Andover, Massachusetts.
All rights reserved. Gift of Stephen C. Clark, 1931.5.

with a black background as if it were a separate painting within the painting). It glows in spectral splendor, as if the process of imbuing matter with spirit, the process by which thought is transmuted into object and event were a kind of magic. When we look at the shimmering spectrum, it is as if the spirit that informed it still vibrated within the trembling skin of its being—suspending it half in the world of objects and half beyond it, as if the power of thought on matter created a third element—numinous and intangible—somehow mysteriously beyond both thought and matter. (The spinning, glowing wheels in the background repeat the effect in monochrome, in a minor key as it were.)

There is an even more spectral aspect of Rowland's portrait which, though it is the painting's most prominent feature in life, is occasionally omitted from reproductions of it in books: its handpainted frame. Eakins frames the portrait with a golden nimbus (rectangular as befits a living figure) of thoughts, calculations, and insights taken from the professor's experimental notebooks (written in a facsimile of Rowland's own handwriting).

Eakins' father was a "writing master" who made his living by copying and inscribing a wide range of official and unofficial documents—from deeds to diplomas to birth, death, and marriage certificates. We do not have to look further than this frame to be certain that, probably dating from Eakins' earliest conversations with his father as a boy, the painter had thought deeply about what various writing styles "meant"—and about the act of writing itself as the place where the human spirit most intimately impinges upon the world of concrete objects. The pen, is, as it were, the place where the mind and the hand meet. It is where idea becomes event.[15]

The writing on the frame explores the relation of theory and practice in ways that parallel the linkages of vision and execution within the painting. Mind is felt equally on both sides of the frame, but in moving from left to right, we move from a realm of abstract ideas to one in which ideas express themselves in actions and events. On the left panel is a differential equation that defines one of the fundamental principles of Rowland's work. Both its form and content express the energy and emotion of a grand conceptual insight. It is written in a large, fluent, sweeping style. Its scrawl is free and impassioned—easy, rapid, and exuberant—as it unfurls expansively from the bottom of the frame to the top.

In going from the left side of the frame to the right, Rowland comes down from the heights of mathematical abstraction and purity to grapple with a thousand practical details. He shifts from the heady realms of physics to the grind of practical engineering. The content of this writing is not grand and theoretical, but detailed, practical, and specific. It consists of rough drawings of planned inventions, wiring diagrams, and columns of experimentally determined coefficients and graphed approximations based on a series of meticulous observations and minute calculations. We have left the beauty and scope of general insights to grapple with the nitty-gritty ordeal of lab experiments. Inspiration gives way to perspiration. The grand sweep of an informing idea must come to grips with the technicalities of execution. Just as it did on the left side of the frame, the form of the writing reflects its meaning. The penmanship is tiny, crabbed, and pinched. Squeezed horizontally into a series of short, confined lines, its style is careful, niggling, and crowded.[16]

In short, the movement from the frame's left to its right side enacts the drama that Eakins himself participated in every time he painted: the drama of an idea finding a way to express itself in the forms of actual life. As the cramped style tells us, the translation from one realm to the other is never easy. All of Eakins' work demonstrates the effort the movement from mind to world requires. The doings in Eakins' paintings above everything else require *work* to be successful. The achievements of the "heroic mind" require enormous energy and discipline. The paintings show us over and over again that whether we are surgeons, athletes, seamstresses, inventors, or artists, the act of expressing our souls in the forms of everyday life costs us labors of effort.

I would note in passing that even a painting like *The Pathetic Song*, which features not a scientist, surgeon, or athlete, but a female singer, and clearly depicts a state of imaginative exaltation, does not let us forget the *work* that underpins the apparently effortless spiritual expression it depicts. The stunning detail of the singer's dress emphasizes the time and labor that she must have put into every stitch; the treatment of her hair makes us aware of the effort that she must have spent braiding every strand. Eakins is showing us that no spiritual expression, no act of "realization" comes easily, automatically, or effortlessly. There is always a price to pay, frequently an enormous one—in time, pain, work, or suffering (which we can read on the faces of his sitters)—in making the spirit flesh.

My metaphors are intended to evoke one final Eakins painting, *The Crucifixion*, surely one of the greatest of his explorations of the potentially difficult, pained relation of the soul and the world. There is a deliberately unresolved quality to many aspects of the work. Eakins suspends his Christ figure uneasily between the dust and dirt of the world (visible in the figure's feet, fingernails, and uncut and broken toenails) and a state of sublime spiritual calm beyond earthly concerns and contingencies (felt in the elegant lines of the figure's body and the serenity of his delicately bowed head). The viewer is similarly placed in an unresolved, in-between position as a result of the low angle at which Christ is presented. Rather than standing below Christ approximately at the level of his feet, where crucifixion altarpieces customarily locate the spectator, we are positioned approximately half-way up his body, encountering him not distanced from us, floating over us as a God, but with an uncomfortable intimacy and equality. Adding to the effect, the boyish grace of the frail body defines the figure neither as entirely man nor God, but at an unresolved in-between point.

As in so many of Eakins' other works, the hands are the place where the contrasting pulls of the body and the spirit are felt. As our eyes move around the edges of the painting from one limb to another in a counter-clockwise direction—from the figure's tortured left hand (which recalls the mother's hands in *The Gross Clinic*), to the slightly more relaxed right hand, to the calmly grounded feet, and then up along the delicate legs and serene body, Eakins, the devotee of time-lapse photography, presents us with the equivalent of a time-lapse photograph of Christ's migration from the travails of the flesh to the composure of the spirit as one nail after another is pounded into him. It is as if we are watching Jesus gradually lose consciousness on his way to death, as if his spirit were in the process of releasing itself from his body before our eyes. (The absence of a sword mark in the figure's side is another sign that Eakins has chosen to focus precisely on the moment in which Christ hovers in transition between life and death.)[17]

It is critical to the meaning of the painting that Christ's state of spiritual composure and elevation is achieved against the ground of the physicality and earthy ordinariness in his situation. For all of the ultimate spirituality of the depiction, this is an emphatically *human* Christ, with realistically untanned skin, displayed in the full harshness of early afternoon sunlight, the weight of whose upper body is truly felt to be hanging from a cross-beam. Eakins uses the weave of the canvas (visible through the rocks and sky) and the materiality of the paint itself (crudely applied with a pallet knife in the same areas) to further de-idealize the depiction. The combination of the graininess of the canvas and the scuffed, unfinished treatment of the pallet-knife passages gives the work a material tactility and tangibility—even as Christ's state of repose commemorates his power to make those physical realities bear spiritual meanings.

This emphasis on the materiality of the painting (and the materiality of the persons, events, and objects depicted) is one of the most important

Thomas Eakins, *The Crucifixion,* 1880 (oil on canvas), Philadelphia Museum of Art, Gift of Mrs. Thomas Eakins and Miss Mary Adeline Williams, 1929-184–24.

aspects of Eakins' greatest work. He frequently painted on untreated or burlap canvas with somewhat thinned-down pigments to allow the grain of the canvas to show. He used the technique especially in his depictions of men's clothing to create the effect that the viewer is not looking at an idealized, oil-painted *representation* of cloth, but at actual cloth itself (as in his *Portrait of Leslie Miller*). He often posed his sitters in chairs with worn lacquer and frayed upholstery (as in his *Portrait of Amelia Van Buren*). The shoes of many of his sitters are scuffed or beat-up (as in *The Dean's Roll Call*). Their clothes are baggy from use, wrinkled, or creased from storage (as in the *Portrait of Letitia Wilson Jordan* and the *Portrait of a Lady with a Setter Dog*). The presence of these mundane realities is central to the meaning of Eakins' work.

The deeply pragmatic implication is that our most profound imaginative attainments take place *within* the materiality of the world—not as an escape or vacation from it. Rather than leaving material experience behind even briefly, we must shape our destinies *inside* it. That, I take it, is the deepest meaning of the Gross and Agnew portraits (and of all the other works I have examined). Gross' and Agnew's intellectual poise and balance are not states of detachment from but *engagement with* the welter, mess, and confusion of the practical events around them. Eakins aspires to take his art a least a little down off the wall and bring it into contact with the world, taking its interests and forms of expression from everyday life. To paraphrase a line from Robert Frost, the pragmatist (whether surgeon or artist) understands that the best way out is always *through*. As Eakins' Christ demonstrates, our supreme spiritual performances are staged, not as a release from, but as an expression of our loving *immersion in* and *embrace of* the contingencies and pains of human experience. To invoke James' metaphor one last time, we must shape our performances *within* the "barbed-wire complications."

As he did in the Rowland painting, Eakins uses handwriting in *The Crucifixion* to communicate the quality of the principal figure's mind—though, in this case, by contrasting the central figure's physical and spiritual state with the physical and spiritual state of those doing the writing. Christ's imaginative achievement is brought home to us by the difference between his sublime calm and composure and the hysteria of the handwriting on the signage above him. The smooth cleanness of his bodily line is visually played off against the physical crudity of the inscription's Greek and Roman characters (whose irregular zig-zags are visually echoed and reinforced by the crown of thorns immediately under them). I would note parenthetically that, as on the Rowland frame, the style of the writing matches its content: The agitation and ugliness of its scrawl parallel its taunting, snidely sarcastic message. The clumsiness, ignorance, and lack of composure of the minds and hands that made the placard contrast with the sensitivity and grace (in both the physical and spiritual senses of the word) of Christ's expression of himself.

If writing is the place where mind most visibly becomes hand (in Emerson's metaphor) or verb (in Dewey's)—the line where idea and action meet—there may be said to be a kind of writing in each of these paintings, pen and ink being only one of the forms it takes. In Eakins' view, we write our intentions and meanings on the world in many different ways. Christ "writes" his state of grace in his physical deportment, and more generally by acting out his destiny in the world. Rowland "writes" his ideas not only in his formulas and calculations, but in the rulings his machinery inscribes on pieces of glass (like a painter writing his ideas in light), and in the focus and firmness of his posture and pose. The rowers "write" their identities in the large shapes of their overall performances and in the smaller forms of the whorls and ripples that mark the paths they take.[18] The hunters in the shooting paintings "write" their intentions and knowledge in their shifting acts of coordination and balance. Gross and Agnew "write" their wisdom and skill in many different ways: in the effect of their words on their students (and on the recording secretary who is prominently featured in the Gross portrait), who themselves then go on to write their remarks down. They also "write" their ideas in the form of their actions on their patients (cuts inscribed on them with pen-like scalpels).[19] For Eakins, as for all pragmatists, the unexpressed impulse or feeling is a fiction. Ideas and emotions only exist to the extent that we "realize" them. Our inner states only count when they enter the world, when we "write" them in space and time. Our meditative turns must yield wordly returns.

But I have omitted what is arguably the most important aspect of the acts of writing in these paintings (and the most important aspect of the acts of writing they depict): their temporality, evanescence, and mutability. For Eakins, the writing we do in both life and art—whether we construe the concept literally or metaphorically—is constantly decomposing, melting, and transforming. It is always being superseded by new acts of writing. It is in motion.

Eakins' interest in the study of motion is well documented. It is generally acknowledged that his study of the photography of Eadweard Muybridge and his photographic experiments with the Marey wheel and rotating camera shutters (both of which produce a series of rapid exposures on a single photographic plate) informed a number of his paintings of human and animal bodies in motion—*The Freeman Rogers Four-in-Hand*

and *The Swimming Hole,* for example. But what has been less commented upon is the consciousness of time and change displayed by virtually all of Eakins' work. Whether his figures are moving or still, Eakins' work, like that of the pragmatists in this respect as well, is deeply committed to honoring the flow of experience.

It is more than a pun on the subject matter of many of his outdoor paintings to say that the meanings and relationships in Eakins' work are written in water. There is a profound awareness of the fugitiveness of experience at the center of each of the works I have discussed. In the hunting and rowing paintings, birds are on the wing, a gun is being aimed, a second or two more or less and everything and everyone will have changed. One hunter will have fired his shot; others will be raising their guns to fire theirs; and every hand, arm, foot, and boat will be in a slightly different position, rebalanced and recoordinated with every other one. In *Turning the Stake,* only a split second after the moment imagined, the Biglin brothers will have completed the turning movement, changed their postures entirely, and begun pulling upstream on the next leg of the race.

Though the fugitiveness of experience may be less obvious in the other paintings I have considered, it is equally present. I already pointed out the implicit temporality of *The Crucifixion*—the time-lapse aspect of its understanding of experience. In the clinic paintings, a minute more or less and each of the positions will have shifted. Gross and Agnew will be at different points in their operations and lectures. Even the portrait of Professor Rowland, apparently so much more static in its presentation, registers motion and change—not only in the surprising lightness and animation of Rowland's right hand and the flicker of the rainbow that floats above his left, or in the whirl of the equipment behind him and the activity of his assistant, but, even more importantly, in the movements of mind melting and dissolving one into the other on the frame. The dynamism of the writing captures the flow and revision of the experimental process itself, as if Eakins were presenting motion-study snapshots of Rowland's brain in action. It displays the partial, provisional, ineluctably temporal unfolding of an unending process of scientific exploration and discovery. To paraphrase Emerson at a thoroughly pragmatic moment, what Eakins' frame depicts is not "thoughts" but the drama of "Man Thinking." Eakins' interest is not in product, but process.[20]

The point is the tentativeness, partialness, and incompleteness of *all* acts of "writing" in Eakins' work—both the actual and the figurative, both the artist's and the ones he depicts. William James appreciated this aspect of "writing" (both his own and others') when he talked about the provisionality of all acts of intellectual codification. At one point in *A Pluralistic Universe,* in an attempt to verbally capture the flowingness of experience, he even unleashes a cascade of metaphors that find coincidental echoes in Eakins' water pictures and motion studies: "abstract concepts are but as flowers gathered, they are only moments dipped out from the stream of time, snap-shots taken, as by a kinetoscopic camera, at a life that in its original coming is continuous."[21]

In an earlier essay, using a metaphor that deliberately calls attention to the fugitiveness and evanescence of all writing, James compares his own work to a series of "blazes" or "spots" through a pathless wood or, in terms that take us back to the frame of the Rowland painting, "a few formulas, a few technical conceptions, a few verbal pointers," which only indicate the outline of a provisional and constantly adjusted course of action:

> Philosophers are after all like poets. They are path-finders. What every one can feel, what every one can know in the bone and marrow of him, they sometimes can find words for and express. The words and thoughts of the philosophers are not exactly the words and thoughts of the poets—worse luck. But both alike have the same function. They are, if I may use a simile, so many spots, or blazes,—blazes made by the axe of the human intellect on the trees of the otherwise trackless forest of human experience. . . .
>
> No one like the path-finder himself feels the immensity of the forest, or knows the accidentality of his own trails. Columbus, dreaming of the ancient East, is stopped by pure pristine simple America, and gets no farther on that day; and the poets and philosophers themselves know as no one else knows that what their formulas express leaves unexpressed almost everything that they organically divine and feel. So I feel that there is a center in truth's forest where I have never been: to track it out and get there is the secret spring of all my poor life's philosophic efforts; at moments I almost strike into the final valley, there is a gleam of the end, a sense of certainty, but always there comes still another ridge, and so my blazes merely circle towards the true direction; and although now, if ever, would be the fit occasion, yet I cannot take you to the wondrous hidden spot to-day. To-morrow it must be, or to-morrow, or to-morrow; and pretty soon death will overtake me ere the promise is fulfilled.
>
> Of such postponed achievements do the lives of all philosophers consist. Truth's fulness is elusive; ever not quite, not quite! So we fall back on the preliminary blazes—a few formulas, a few technical con-

ceptions, a few verbal pointers—which at least define the initial direction of the trail.[22]

The most pragmatic aspect of Eakins' work is his understanding of all action and expression as ineluctably rough, imperfect, and partial. Painting after painting tells us that the transactions between the mind and the hand are denied finality or perfection. As *The Gross Clinic* shows us, there will always be messy spatters of blood (or paint) where there shouldn't be, and hesitant, uncertain pauses while we deliberate what to do or say next. James wrote that "we realize this life as something always off its balance, something in transition," and D. H. Lawrence continued his thought with a phrase that unconsciously echoes James' formulation: "we must balance as we go."[23] It is a metaphor that might be applied literally to Eakins' hunters, sailors, and rowers, and figuratively to all of his depictions. There is no goal to reach, no end to the process of balancing and rebalancing (or turning and re-turning, to cite another process-oriented Jamesian metaphor Eakins employs. Where mind is a verb, there can be no resting place, no end to the activity of expressive realization. Meditative turns out of the world are succeeded by practical returns to it in an unending cycle of forever unfinished acts of expression.

As every artist (and writer) knows, the process of moving from abstract conception to practical execution, of translating from mind to hand, of making mind a verb, inevitably involves accepting the imperfection of enacted truth. There is no pure truth, no complete truth, no eternal truth in the world of practical expression. There is no rising above the partialities of space and time. Meanings made in space and time are forever subject to decay in space and time.

The mind may be able to imagine meanings that rise above spatial imperfection and temporal contingency, but the meanings made by the hand are irredeemably spatially imperfect and temporally contingent. They are partial, provisional, and (in James' favorite term) "fluxional." The movement from mind to hand and back to mind that Eakins depicts is itself forever on the move. It will not sit still to have its picture painted, and when it is arrested pictorially, it reminds us of how experience keeps moving beyond any particular pictorial expression of it. There are few artists who more instinctively understood life as an endless, imperfect transaction between elegant, orderly ideas and unresolved, imperfect practices. The truth of the mind can stand still, but for Eakins, as for Emerson, James, Dewey, and all pragmatists, the truths of the hand must remain in motion.

Notes

1 My book *The Films of John Cassavetes: Pragmatism, Modernism, and the Movies* (New York: Cambridge University Press, 1994) constituted a similar extended experiment—a test of the extent to which a filmmaker's oeuvre could be treated as a philosophical text. My "Two Forms of Modernism: Notes Towards a Pragmatic Aesthetic," in *Modernism in the United States*, ed. Townsend Ludington (Chapel Hill: University of North Carolina Press, 1999) represents a large-scale attempt to define an "aesthetics of pragmatism."

2 There are slightly fuller discussions of art's distinctive ways of knowing in my review of *The Johns Hopkins Guide to Literary Theory and Criticism*, "A Yellow Pages of Criticism," *Partisan Review* 62, no. 1 (Winter 1995): 138–43, and in the 1996 Preface of my *American Vision: The Films of Frank Capra* (Hanover: University Press of New England, 1996), pp. xi–xviii.

3 William James, *Writings, 1902–1910* (New York: Library of America, 1987), p. 934.

4 *Ibid.*, pp. 951, 745–46.

5 *Ibid.*, p. 741.

6 The imaginative stances of Eakins' surgeons and their states of slight meditative withdrawal from (or mastery of) a complex situation have many echoes in American culture—extending from Whitman's "Apart from the pulling and hauling stands what I am. . . . Both in and out of the game and watching and wondering at it" to the imaginative positions (and physical postures) of Method actors like Brando, Clift, and Dean in films almost a century later.

7 There is probably an autobiographical reference (and a bit of a joke) embedded in this part of the painting. Like Gross and Agnew, Eakins had spent a lot of time talking to groups of students and undoubtedly had many experiences with students too bored or insouciant to bother taking notes.

8 My argument will be recognized as a reply to one of the common criticisms of *The Gross Clinic*: namely, that the physical clutter and near illegibility of the visual space of the radically foreshortened operating table is a flaw or miscalculation on Eakins' part. (Note, most egregiously, the unattached hand and arm of an almost invisible fifth surgical assistant sitting behind Gross.) My point is that the incoherence of the group around the table is essential to Eakins' meaning insofar as it presents a visual contrast for Gross to establish the coherence of his own identity against.

9 James, *Writings, 1902–1910*, p. 509.

10 See Elizabeth Johns, *Thomas Eakins: The Heroism of Modern Life* (Princeton: Princeton University Press, 1983).

11 The "heroic mind" is from Ralph Waldo Emerson, *Essays and Lectures* (New York: Library of America, 1983), p. 60; and William James, *Writings, 1878–1899* (New York: Library of America, 1992), p. 425. (As an illustration of the degree of James' indebtedness to Emerson, even beyond his borrowing of this particular phrase, compare page 65 of the Emerson text with page 425 of the James.) I would note in passing that the belief that the movements of the imagination can make themselves felt in practical social and ethical expressions is the deepest connection between the work of William James and that of his novelist brother Henry. To cite only one example, Maggie Verver is a pragmatic "American heroine" in the sense the present essay develops.

12 A letter written in May 1874 from Eakins to his teacher Gérôme goes into detail about the specific acts of balance and coordination involved in the hunters' performances. See

Lloyd Goodrich, *Thomas Eakins* (Cambridge: Harvard University Press, 1982), vol. 1, p. 320.

13 The color scheme of this painting is characteristic of much of Eakins' work. He frequently employs hot colors (and red in particular) to signify some degree of unstable movement, explosiveness, or imbalance (which is why the central shooter in both hunting paintings wears a bright red shirt); while cool colors (blues and greens) and earth tones (burnished browns and blacks) are his preferred way of rendering states of contemplation, calm, poise, or concentration (which is why the pole-pusher in the Will Schuster painting wears blue jeans). Eakins uses blue for a similar expressive effect in *The Biglin Brothers Racing.*

14 For more on this issue as well as discussions of several of the paintings mentioned in this paragraph, see my *American Vision,* pp. 8–13, 161–70.

15 Michael Fried focuses on Eakins' interest in writing in the first part of *Realism, Writing, Disfiguration* (Chicago: University of Chicago, 1987), pp. 1–90. I should note, however, that Fried not only takes an entirely different tack than I do, but has little to say about the Rowland work (or the work that follows in my discussion: *The Crucifixion*). For more on the relation of my approach to Fried's, see my review of his book: "Crane and Eakins," *Partisan Review* 55, no. 3 (Summer 1988): 464–73.

16 The top and bottom of the frame present a slightly different contrast, involving the difference between relative (experimentally determined) values and absolute (intellectually obtained) ones. For more technical information on Rowland's work in general (and a fairly cursory treatment of the meaning of some of the symbols on the frame), see A. D. Moore, "Henry A. Rowland," *Scientific American* 246, no. 2 (February 1982): 150–61.

17 I would like to thank Douglas Paschell of the Philadelphia Museum of Art for a conversation that shaped my understanding of certain aspects of this work.

18 *Max Schmitt in a Single Scull* is the best illustration of Eakins' interest in this sort of writing. The work is a tour de force of watery dimples, ripples, and wakes that "write" a mini-history of the present and past paths and relationships of the two boats present in the painting. *The Chess Players* does something similar by documenting the entire history of a chess game in terms of the current positions of the pieces. Even Eakins' interest in wrinkles and other signs of aging in his sitters' faces, bodies, and clothing may be understood in terms of an interest in time's and nature's "writing" on them.

19 I am indebted to Michael Fried's *Realism, Writing, Disfiguration* for the comparison of the scalpels with pens, though again I would emphasize that he draws quite different conclusions from the analogy than I do.

20 Eakins deliberately took the examples he used to decorate the frame from entries in Rowland's journals made years apart and at vastly different points in his research. The drawing of the circle in the upper right corner of the frame, boyish in its clumsiness, was made by a twenty-year-old Rowland just starting out in his professional scientific career. In style and content it is light years away from the authority and panache of the differential equation on the left side of the frame.

21 James, *Writings, 1902–1910,* pp. 735–36.

22 From "Philosophical Conceptions and Practical Results" (1898), in James, *Writings, 1878–1899,* pp. 1078–79.

23 James, *Writings, 1902–1910,* p. 759; D. H. Lawrence, *Phoenix* (New York: Viking Press, 1968), p. 529.

Religion and the Recent Revival
of Pragmatism

GILES GUNN

Religion, it must be said, has not played a very significant role, except perhaps negatively, in the recent renewal of pragmatism. There are no doubt many reasons for this, but none is more important than the responsibility that Richard Rorty deservedly bears for helping to promote this revival and the connection he has made between the development of pragmatism and liberalism's project of disenchanting the world religiously.

Rorty has actually come up with two different genealogies for pragmatism, both of which narrativize its development as a secular coming-of-age story. In the first, which is to be found in *Consequences of Pragmatism,* pragmatism lies at the end of a process of de-divinization that began with metaphysical idealism's attempt to relocate the sphere of ultimate reality within human experience rather than beyond it, then led to Romanticism's claim that if ultimate reality is now immanent rather than transcendent, its meanings can be described in more than one vocabulary, and finally wound up with pragmatism's assertion that these different vocabularies are ultimately no more than different ways of expressing what we need and sometimes get.[1] In the second genealogy, which appears in his *Contingency, Irony, and Solidarity,* this sequence of historical transformations follows a course charted in Hans Blumenberg's *The Legitimacy of the Modern Age,* where the love of God gave way, first, in the seventeenth century to the love of truth, then the love of truth gave way, by the end of the eighteenth century, to the quasi-divinity of the self, and eventually the idealist or Romantic love of the self succumbed, toward the end of the nineteenth century and the beginning of the twentieth, to the realization, variously phrased by Nietzsche, Freud, and Wittgenstein, that we now do not need to worship anything at all as divine, whether God, the world, or our own spiritual nature, since, as we can presently see, "everything—our language, our conscience, our community—is a product of time and chance."[2] In short, Rorty has traced a history linking the emergence of pragmatism with the arrival of a new antireligious dispensation in the West that has in effect emptied the world of intrinsic significance.

If Rorty is now prepared in "Pragmatism as Romantic Polytheism" (this volume) to revise, or at any rate to modify, this liberal agenda, it should not go without notice that several of his own heroes within liberalism would have viewed his proposal to cure us of our dependence on metaphysics so that we can be freed to grapple with the real contingencies of our existence as, in any event, going too far. Most conspicuous in this regard is, perhaps, Sir Isaiah Berlin who, while sharing Rorty's suspicions of religious authoritarianism, has nonetheless always conceded the validity of humanity's "deep and incurable metaphysical need" for greater moral and spiritual assurance. Using language similar to Rorty's but with a different intent, Berlin acknowledged that this no doubt basic human desideratum often masks a deep and potentially dangerous "moral and political immaturity," but he went on to observe that this only makes it that much more incumbent on us to see to it that this immaturity does not get the better of us.[3] Berlin's pragmatic circumspection is a reminder, to paraphrase William James, that there are no intellectual methods to assist one in navigating between the opposite dangers of believing too little and of believing too much; there is only, James added, the intellectual responsibility to face such dangers and try to hit the right balance between them.

In sounding this theme, James expressed what was in different terms to become, more than half a century later, a leitmotif in the writing of a number of thinkers from Rorty's own generation, thinkers who struggled to prevent pragmatism from suffering a complete eclipse during the long period when linguistic analysis held complete sway in American philosophy. Easily effaced because the texture and tone of their work was conciliatory, generalizing, and melioristic in an academic environment where asperity, exactitude, and an uncompromising professionalism were much in fashion, philosophers like John E. Smith, Richard J. Bernstein, and John McDermott viewed pragmatism not only as a philosophical theory in need of defense but also as an intellectual method capable of keeping open the lines of communication between philosophy and some of the other departments of the intellectual life. Thus Bernstein, for example, was out to explore, in a series of studies seeking to press "beyond objectivism and relativism," as he titled his third book, the ethical, political, and metaphysical horizons that defined the modern and the postmodern.[4] Smith, for his part, took it upon himself in *Reason and God* to stage encounters between philosophy and religion and also to historicize pragmatism by constructing a central place for it within a cultural narrative seeking to define, as he called his most widely read book, "the spirit of American philosophy."[5] And McDermott not only compiled important anthologies that became in the 1970s and 1980s, and still remain in the 1990s, the chief resource for teaching James and Dewey (as well as Josiah Royce), but also produced two collections of his own essays designed to test the ontological and moral reach of a pragmatist notion of experience.[6]

Without such work—and this is only the tip of the iceberg—it would have been much more difficult than it has proven to be for certain contemporary thinkers to reintroduce the subject of religion into a discussion of pragmatism itself. Yet even now, when the wall of separation has been breached again and again, it still remains the case that many intellectuals continue to persist in the opinion that pragmatism is at the very least indifferent to religion and more likely inhospitable to it, if not downright incompatible with it. An interesting version of the latter view is to be found in *The Promise of Pragmatism*, where John Patrick Diggins has recently declared pragmatism to be on balance intellectually shallow, politically naive, and spiritually empty. Like secular modernism generally, of which it is one variant, Diggins contends that pragmatism has served up for us an eviscerated world of felt absences: "knowledge without truth, power without authority, society without spirit, self without identity, politics without virtue, existence without purpose, history without meaning."[7] Interestingly enough, Diggins finds the antidote to this bleak, even repugnant, prospect not in the world Dewey described for us, where unity and coherence is sought without the appeal to anything transcendent, but rather in the kind of world that Henry Adams delineated, where the futile search for meaning and wholeness is replaced by the attempt to establish the limits of the known and the limitations of the knower.

Not least among the problems with this critique is that when the classical pragmatists turned their attention, as they so often did, to such limits and such limitations, they were frequently brought up against all that apparently exceeds them. How else to explain what James was doing phenomenologically in *The Varieties of Religious Experience,* or Dewey was undertaking aesthetically in *Art as Experience,* or, for that matter, Peirce was up to semiotically in essays like "A New List of Categories," "Some Consequences of Four Incapacities," and "The Architecture of Theories"? But communication between religious thought and pragmatic philosophy has been reviving since the 1970s when, quite apart from the work of such philosophers as Smith and McDermott, theologians like Bernard Meland, in *Realities of Faith,* Joseph Haroutunian in *God With Us: A Theology of the Transpersonal Life,* and, later, Gordon S. Kaufman, in *An Essay on Theolog-*

ical Method, began to reappropriate pragmatism as a model for testing the validity of theological and moral claims.[8] Kaufman put it characteristically by pointing out that if theology begins with images and notions of the world that are inherited from the past, it ends with the attempt to determine what difference a theistically revised notion of the world may make to the kinds of activity and forms of life that are possible within it. He thus concludes, "the criteria for assessing theological claims turn out in the last analysis . . . to be pragmatic and humanistic . . . not because theologians are necessarily committed to pragmatic or utilitarian conceptions of truth in general but rather because such considerations—when understood in the broadest possible sense—are the only ones by which a way of life, a worldview, a perspective on the totality of things, a concept of God, may ultimately be assessed."[9]

By the late 1980s and 1990s, intellectual commerce between religion and pragmatism had expanded still further. In *The American Evasion of Philosophy,* for example, Cornel West found it necessary to supplement the "prophetic pragmatism" he refashioned from Emerson, Du Bois, and Dewey with the personally meaningful Protestant neoorthodoxy he found in Reinhold Niebuhr.[10] At roughly the same time, the philosopher of religion Jeffrey Stout offered as his own candidate for, as his title phrased it, *Ethics After Babel,* what he called a "moderate pragmatism."[11] But perhaps the most dramatic rapprochement between religion and pragmatism was effected by the religious historian Henry Samuel Levinson who, in a book that succeeded in restoring George Santayana to the pragmatist tradition, produced a full-blown theory of what he subtitled "pragmatism and the spiritual life."[12]

But the recent story of pragmatism's associations with religion does not stop here. If, for example, one adopts a somewhat broader view of the historical development of pragmatism of the sort, say, that Joseph Brent brings to his biography of Charles Sanders Peirce, or that Alan Ryan takes in his book on John Dewey, or, for that matter, that Bruce Kuklick assumed in *From Churchman to Philosophers,* one can easily see that religion played a not inconsiderable, if not always obvious, role in the thinking of the founding generation, and that it was also a factor in inducing others, such as W. E. B. Du Bois, and perhaps even Alain Locke, to embrace their own version of pragmatism.[13]

Indeed, by taking a less philosophical and more broadly intellectual and cultural approach to the evolution of American pragmatism, one can readily discern its inflections with the religious in the writing of a long line of American thinkers and writers from Emerson and Thoreau to Wallace

Stevens and Elizabeth Bishop. This is not, of course, to pretend that these exchanges have always been smooth or unvexed but merely to observe that, despite the widespread impression to the contrary, created by the work of intellectuals like Stanley Fish, Barbara Herrnstein Smith, and, until recently, Rorty himself, that pragmatism is relentlessly secular, it has not always proved insensible of, much less hostile to, religious interests. Nor should this come as much of a surprise. William James originally offered pragmatism as "a method of settling metaphysical disputes that otherwise might be interminable," and there is no reason to think that we cannot still employ pragmatism—precisely because in numerous instances it is already being so used—to sort out and assess the comparative merits of religious perspectives, or "world-formulas," as James elsewhere called them, in the new globalized world in which we now find ourselves, a world where none of us, as Clifford Geertz has pointed out, can any longer manage to get out of each other's way.[14]

Though Rorty himself has comparatively little to say about such matters in "Pragmatism as Romantic Polytheism," his new conviction that pragmatism and theism do in fact mix is an encouraging development. It is, however, a development not without problems of its own because of Rorty's continuing attachment to several general assumptions to which I can only allude here before passing on to other issues. The first of these assumptions has to do with the nearly absolute distinction Rorty makes between the individual and the social, between realms of personal choice and public responsibility. In addition to compelling Rorty to argue almost as though history and culture did not matter—in other words, as though people everywhere, and in all times, have been able to keep this distinction as pure as it remains in the pages of *On Liberty*—the wall he erects between the private and the public condemns him to repeat the same mistake Alfred North Whitehead made when he maintained, against all evidence, that religion is chiefly concerned with what we do with our solitariness rather than with our sociality.

The second of the problematic assumptions that Rorty makes throughout this new paper is that the will to truth is the same as the will to happiness and that their unity therefore leaves us with no way of differentiating either between the cognitive and the noncognitive or between the serious and the nonserious. Unless this sweeping claim is intended to reduce the will to truth to utter banality, hasn't the history of religions, along with the history of art, provided us with abundant testimony to the contrary? Don't they both show that under certain circumstances the will to truth decisively overrides the desire for happiness? If this were not the case, what sense could one otherwise make of the meaning of the Crucifixion for Christians, or of living in *galut* for Jews, or of the nature of suffering (*dukkha*) for Buddhists? The stock of happiness being, as it were, in such comparatively short supply, is not most of the rhetorical and ritual machinery of the world's great religions designed precisely, as the majority of their modern interpreters have informed us, to cope with this unpleasant fact? As in the mithridatic techniques of classical tragedy and modern psychoanalytic theory, the will to happiness in most religions takes a back seat to the will to truth in the hope that the homeopathic administration of the pain of truth will partially insure us to the greater truth of life's pain.

These problematic assumptions have in turn created what appear to me to be several difficulties with the five theses Rorty has advanced in behalf of a pragmatist philosophy of religion, and in the remainder of this paper I would like to turn to three of them. Let me begin with Rorty's preference for Dewey's view of religion over James' on the grounds that, if I understand Rorty correctly, Dewey defined pragmatism's relation to religion principally in terms of the notion of tolerance. To be sure, Dewey often invoked this notion to underline the fact that pragmatism views religion without prejudice, but the reduction of their relationship essentially to one of toleration places it on too weak a footing even for Dewey. Clearly, Dewey never went as far as James did in the apologetic "Conclusion" to *The Varieties of Religious Experience*, where, as Rorty quotes him, he asserts that "the conscious person is continuous with a wider self through which saving experiences come." But James himself pulled back from this essentializing claim in *Pragmatism* and simply asserted that, except to morbid minds that desire nothing less than absolute religious certainty, a universe with a fighting chance of security is a more interesting, if not more potentially uplifting, moral prospect than one without it. And in the famous pet analogy, James then went on to posit the high probability that our own relation to the universe may be analogous to the relation that our canine and feline friends presumably have to the things that go on in our own living rooms. Just as they participate with us in actions whose full meaning is completely beyond their ken, so we likewise probably take part ourselves in scenes of whose "cosmic" significance we have only the vaguest clue.

In "The Will to Believe," written well before the religion sections of *Pragmatism*, James had been even more circumspect about these matters by avoiding all talk about "higher powers," though Rorty rather curiously deflates the argument of this essay to the assertion "that we have a right to believe what we like when we are, so to speak, on our own time." The essay actually refrains quite pointedly from privatizing or personalizing the religious will in this fashion, maintaining instead that belief becomes compelling only when it presents us with an option that strikes us as unavoidable, genuine, and serious. There's no mention here of, as Rorty implies, the right to believe anything we like so long as we don't let it interfere with the business of anyone else. By James' reckoning, any option that confronts us with a momentous choice that we cannot put by because it is living and inescapable invokes what he might otherwise have called "the right to believe."

Long before his own summarizing remarks about religion and the religious in *A Common Faith,* Dewey gave some consideration of his own to those conditions that warrant "the right to believe." This topic comes up, for example, in *Human Nature and Conduct* in connection with a discussion of the mind's sense of the totality that surrounds it and defines the horizon of meaning beyond the reach of current formulations toward which the implications of any given act potentially extend. Confronted with the prospect of this unthinkable totality, Dewey postulated that the mind comes up against a sense of the whole that it cannot conceptualize but can nevertheless dimly imagine or conceivably intuit. But Dewey was not for long comfortable with the Hegelianism of these formulations and eventually exchanged them for the aesthetic idioms he adopted in *Art as Experience.* It is here, and not in *A Common Faith,* that Dewey makes his strongest case for the right to believe, but it is a case that holds little interest for Rorty because he sees Dewey's entire project to ground the aesthetic in the natural rhythms of ordinary experience as a form of outworn metaphysics.

Were Rorty not so quick to write off the whole of *Art as Experience* because of the traces of transcendentalism that shadow some, but by no means all, of its pages, he might well have found there a pragmatist attempt to reformulate the case for belief in relation to the aesthetic drive that converts obstacles and impediments to further growth into instruments for the creation of a new, if only temporary, balance of forces. That is, as Dewey understands it, art's juxtaposition of the actual with the imaginative, of the given with the potential, not only inscribes the critical within the aesthetic—"it is by a sense of possibilities opening before us that we become aware of constrictions that hem us in and of burdens that oppress"—but also opens the aesthetic to the possibility of continuously transcending itself by producing in response the desire to create more things like it.[15]

This leads to the second issue I want to raise in connection with Rorty's pragmatist philosophy of religion, which has to do with his desire to make religion more like art. Rorty intends to make religion more like art by dissociating his understanding of both from morality and from science alike. Thus the pragmatist understanding of religion is less like morality and more like art, Rorty contends, in that it exhibits no interest in the ranking—I'm not sure what he means by the "commensuration"—of needs, and it is less like science and more like art, he goes on, because religion is not involved in the prediction of consequences. But remove from art and religion alike the obsession with hierarchy, with ranking and valuation, as well as the preoccupation with projection, forecasting, and prognostication, and the question then becomes whether you are left with anything that can be recognized as either art or religion? Rorty seems to be involved here in what can only be described as a kind of category mistake. As it happens, almost everything that goes by the name art—and this applies to most postmodernist art as well—is concerned with scarcely anything besides the ranking of human needs, though it refuses for the most part to undertake this task, as religion does, in a normative or prescriptive manner. And while all of the valuational procedures within art are equally dependent on the estimation of results, effects, and implications, most art goes about the business of predicting outcomes not, as in religion, on the basis of prophecy or proclamation, but rather on the basis of inference, conjecture, hypothesis, and speculation.

If Rorty were not so attached to a Romantic aesthetic that views art, as in John Stuart Mill or even Matthew Arnold, as a substitute for religion, he might see more clearly the virtues of a pragmatist aesthetic that views art, as in Henry James, Kenneth Burke, and, most recently, Richard Poirier, as a complement to, sometimes even a corollary of, religion. Poirier's theory of literature is particularly instructive on this last point just because its recent developments have occurred in such close conversation with post-structuralist theories of literature. Starting with Emerson's statement that the poet "uses forms according to the life, and not according to the form," Poirier has retrieved for us an Emerson who is the originator of a tradition of literary and intellectual pragmatism in American writing that, in addition to being underappreciated (where it has been recognized at all), constitutes an alternative to our conventional view of modernism, and casts modernism's relation to postmodernism in an entirely different light. Poirier sees this pragmatist tradition as one held together by its aversion to absolutes and foundationalism, its fascination with contingency and process, its emphasis on the relationality of the real, its respect for the ordinary, and its delight in moments when the ordinary becomes "other" and the habitual suddenly unfamiliar. In *Poetry and Pragmatism* Poirier associates this tradition with the discoveries afforded by a self-conscious linguistic skepticism.[16]

This is a skepticism linked to the deconstructive mechanisms within language itself but one that also rethinks those mechanisms as tropological instruments capable of empowering language to resist the self-reflexivity of its own inherited meanings and thus points beyond those meanings toward possibilities for renewal that are at once personal and cultural as well as semiotic. Poirier insists that to follow this movement within language, as it were, beyond language requires that we begin to think very differently about words and the things that can be done with them. Where the conventional way of thinking about such matters associates words with things, language with reference, verbal signs with substantive entities, Emerson, anticipating the nomenclature that William James would later employ to give this linguistic skepticism its first philosophical elaboration in the United States, showed us more than a century in advance of speech act theory that words have more to do with actions and events, language with processes and power, verbal signs with transitives and connectives.

If this linguistic skepticism were merely another way of maintaining that "words," as T. S. Eliot said in "Burnt Norton," "will not stay in place,/ Will not stay still," such a demonstration would merely reinforce the appeal of deconstruction itself, with its summary rejection of the Eliotic quest for "the still point in the turning world" and its conviction that the instability of language points to the indeterminacy of its reference. But Emerson and James, together with Poirier, intend to say something quite different than this. In opposition to Eliot's attempts to evade such issues by positing the possibility of their transcendence in some larger "idea of order," and in contradistinction to deconstruction's tendency to identify these problems with something flawed and treacherous about the nature of language itself, Poirier, James, and Emerson all insist that the obstacles language places in the way of what Dewey called the "quest for certainty" afford significant opportunities, both cognitive and affective, for further knowledge, for the revelation of what Wallace Stevens meant by "ghostlier demarcations, keener sounds." William James himself formulated this proposition most simply when, as he says somewhere, what "these [verbal] formulas express leaves unexpressed almost everything that they organically divine and feel." Poirier has in turn followed James by referring to this element of the "unexpressed" and the verbally inexpressible simply as "the vague" and by urging its recovery in criticism just as James urged its reinstatement in philosophy.

"The vague," and for Poirier its cognate "the superfluous," are to be associated with what James elsewhere called the "Sense of the More." This was James' rather crude, but nonetheless operative, description for that surplus of intelligibility that attends all acts of understanding, the remainder that is always left over, so to speak, when we try to calculate their sum. In this sense, vagueness is far more than a mere constituent of perception. It is also, as Poirier brings out more effectively than James ever did, the only guarantee that perception contains within itself a potential for criticizing some of its own cognitive deliverances. Requiring, as Poirier calls it, "a disciplined resistance" to the seductions of habit as well as to the desire for closure, vagueness functions simultaneously as a kind of Burkean counterforce to dogmatization and as an incitement to the exploration of new truths. Often conveyed in writing by nothing more concrete than voice and sound, vagueness derives, so Poirier maintains, from the failure that language continuously experiences in its effort to represent its own understanding in words. If most postmodernist criticism typically reads this failure as the death knell of logocentricism, pragmatism reads it as representing potentially a "saving uncertainty."[17]

In this pragmatist understanding of language, then, the words are there—in Charlotte Perkins Gilman's "The Yellow Wallpaper" or Robert Frost's dramatic dialogues, Gertrude Stein's *Tender Buttons* or Wallace Steven's "The Snow Man"—to point to, or, better, to lead toward, insights, intuitions, intimations situated on the horizon of consciousness that would either be lost if in fact they were named or lack any placement within our current hierarchies of understanding. Thus for pragmatism art is important not because it designates, as in the monumentalist or high canonical view, somewhere to get to, but rather because it suggests, as in a more democratic or populist view, somewhere to depart from. The arts, as Emerson said, are initial, not final. It is what they aim at, not what they achieve, that matters. Hence even when they claim to furnish their readers with what Thoreau described in *Walden* as "a hard bottom and rocks in place, which we can call *reality,* and say This is, and no mistake," that "bottom" or "*reality,*" as Thoreau characteristically added in further elaboration and pragmatist critics like Burke, Trilling, Poirier, and Posnock would agree, is merely another "*point d'appui.*"[18]

Because it is difficult to imagine how human needs can be hierarchically rearranged, or at least imagined and represented as being amenable to such rearrangement, without producing, as one of its consequences, some noticeable alterations in our sense of community (the community between text and reader, the community between one reader and another, the community between readers and non-readers), I want to take up as my third issue the definition of the ideal of human fraternity that pragmatism, like democracy, according to Rorty, supposedly takes over from Christianity. As Rorty phrases it, this is the belief that every human need should be satisfied unless doing so causes too many other human needs to go unsatisfied.

Here again I find that Rorty's preference for the minimalist case may encourage him to put the matter too weakly. If democratic pragmatism can be said to have inherited any conception of solidarity from Christianity, it has a lot less to do with the belief that we should get what we want so long as it does not prevent others from getting what they want and a lot more to do with the belief that no human being is an island unto itself because all human beings have to consider the needs of at least some others in order to satisfy their own. Although this certainly does not go as far as someone like Emmanuel Levinas—and his claim that the self is thus constituted as a human being by means of its encounter with an "other" who is then experienced as the ground of the self's own ethicality—pragmatism does take over from Christianity, both in Dewey's theory of the Great Community (itself possibly influenced by Josiah Royce's theory of the Beloved Community) and in aspects of George Herbert Mead's theory of the social self, a much stronger version of human fraternity than any with which Rorty seems to credit it.

Of particular relevance in this connection, since its influence on democratic pragmatism is less well known or fully appreciated than Dewey's, is the work of George Herbert Mead. Mead's theory of society turns on the role played by significant symbols in permitting individuals to communicate with one another. Significant symbols enable the communication between and among individuals by permitting the self to adopt the subject position of the other with respect to itself. In this model of social construction and interaction, democratic individuality is not based, as Rorty maintains, on the limited compatibility between the desires of the self and the desires of others but on the practical intersubjective demands whereby the self is compelled to adopt the point of view of the "other" to know itself, much less to communicate with the "other." Rorty's resistance to this kind of thinking points up the fact that, despite his deep social conscience, he may well be more interested in liberty than in solidarity. This would help explain his preference, when it comes to religion, for freedom over commitment. But if Rorty remains a liberal, and a Romantic one at that, all the way down, he nonetheless runs the risk of forgetting that even the more socially radical of the Romantic liberals, such as Shelley and Whitman, were in the main less interested in the recreation of the self than in the rebirth and reform of community.

Dewey, of course, was prepared to say exactly the same thing, and even went so far as to define his own democratic and social ideal in *Art as Experience* by quoting Shelley on love, or "*a going out of our nature* and the identification of ourselves with the beautiful which exists in thought, action, or person, not our own."[19] But if Dewey's image of the democratic embrace of the actual and the ideal attested to the importance of mutuality and fellow feeling, his notion of the interpersonal as well as the transpersonal nonetheless suffered from certain lacuna of which Rorty remains curiously silent. Not only did Dewey fail to account for most of the complications of the subjective life, and particularly for the whole realm of sexual relations, as Alan Ryan has recently noted, but he also paid comparatively little attention to the bureaucratic obduracy of large institutions and the mysteries of social change. Lacking a sufficiently subtle theory either of the private or of the institutional, Dewey's theory of democracy may therefore prove too fragile a political foundation to support the edifice of Romantic polytheism without considerable shoring up. Such shoring up would require that Rorty look beyond the tradition of the "founders" of pragmatism to such thinkers in the pragmatist grain as W. E. B. Du Bois, Kenneth Burke, Lionel Trilling, and Ralph Ellison, all of whom could suggest ways of complicating his Romantic polytheism with a richer sense of the duplicities of, and disturbances within, the self and a deeper grasp of the dangers of bureaucratizing the imaginative.

But Rorty's Romantic polytheism creates further problems for a democratic pragmatist because of the way he conflates it with a celebrationist reading of America's religious destiny. By linking Dewey's pantheism with Whitman's—and thereby associating the unity of poetry and religious feeling with the creation of a community of free individuals—Rorty foresees Romantic polytheism completing itself in the construction of "the United States of America," an entity which, for both Whitman and Dewey, represented what Rorty calls "the possibility of as yet undreamt of, ever more diverse, forms of human happiness." Over against this triumphalist image of American futurity, I would place an altogether different religious prospect envisioned by a pragmatist, or at least pragmatist sympathizer of another stripe.

When at the end of *The American Scene* Henry James was confronted with a similar temptation to link the nation with its visionary ambitions, he found himself thinking instead not of undreamt of forms of human felicity yet to be achieved but of historical obligations and commitments continuously deferred and of social and political potentialities habitually postponed. That is, when Henry James looked at his country pragmatically through the eyes of its own religious sense of itself, what he saw was not a blank check on the future that the United States had written to legitimate its present but rather the bill of arrears that the United States had already accumulated on its past. A bill of arrears that revealed the inconsistencies, lapses, and contradictions inherent from the beginning within America's own religious imagination of itself, it encouraged Henry James to believe that this debt cannot, and will not, be settled without a full accounting of its costs to the treasury of national values and a full assessment of its consequences for a redefinition of national purpose. A task we have yet to fulfill, it is a project in which James could imagine the pragmatic serving as the perfect ally of the religious.

Notes

1 Richard Rorty, *Consequences of Pragmatism* (Minneapolis: University of Minnesota Press, 1982), pp. 143–55.

2 Richard Rorty, *Contingency, Irony, and Solidarity* (Cambridge: Cambridge University Press, 1989), p. 22.

3 Isaiah Berlin. *Four Essays on Liberty* (London: Oxford University Press, 1969), p. 172.

4 Richard J. Bernstein, *Beyond Objectivism and Relativism: Science, Hermeneutics, and Praxis* (Philadelphia: University of Pennsylvania Press, 1982); *The New Constellation: The Ethical-Political Horizons of Modernity/Postmodernism* (Cambridge: MIT Press, 1992).

5 John E. Smith, *Reason and God: Encounters of Philosophy and Religion* (New Haven: Yale University Press, 1961); *The Spirit of American Philosophy* (New York: Oxford University Press, 1963).

6 John E. McDermott, ed., *The Writings of William James: A Comprehensive Edition, including an Annotated Bibliography Updated through 1977* (Chicago: University of Chicago Press, 1977); *The Philosophy of John Dewey* (New York: Putnam Sons, 1973); *The Culture of Experience: Philosophical Essays in the American Grain* (New York: New York University Press, 1976); *Streams of Experience: Reflections on the History and Philosophy of American Culture* (Amherst: University of Massachusetts Press, 1986).

7 John Patrick Diggins, *The Promise of Pragmatism* (Chicago: University of Chicago Press, 1994).

8 Bernard Meland, *Realities of Faith* (New York: Oxford University Press, 1962); Joseph Haroutunian, *God With Us: A Theology of the Transpersonal Life* (Philadelphia: Westminster Press, 1965); Gordon S. Kaufman, *An Essay on Theological Method* (Missoula: Scholars Press, 1975).

9 *Ibid.*, p. 76.

10 Cornel West, *The American Evasion of Philosophy: A Genealogy of Pragmatism* (Madison: University of Wisconsin Press, 1989).

11 Jeffrey Stout, *Ethics After Babel: The Languages of Morality and Their Discontents* (Boston: Beacon Press, 1988).

12 Henry Samuel Levinson, *Santayana: Pragmatism and the Spiritual Life* (Chapel Hill: University of North Carolina Press, 1994).

13 Joseph Brent, *Charles Sanders Peirce, A Life* (Bloomington: Indiana University Press, 1993); Alan Ryan, *John Dewey and the High Tide of Liberalism* (New York: W. W. Norton, 1995); Bruce Kuklick, *Churchmen and Philosophers: From Jonathan Edwards to John Dewey* (New Haven: Yale University Press, 1985).

14 William James, *Pragmatism* (Cambridge: Harvard University Press, 1978), p. 28.

15 John Dewey, *Art as Experience* (New York: G. P. Putnam Sons, 1934; Perigee Books Edition, 1980), p. 346.

16 This tradition originates in Emerson, the elder James, and his son William, and includes Whitman, Frost, Stein, and Stevens, while also conceding a place to a host of other writers from Thoreau, Dickinson, Pound, and a part of T. S. Eliot (I would add Robinson and a bit later Cather) through Fenellosa, William Carlos Williams, and Kenneth Burke to contemporaries, or near contemporaries, like Frank O'Hara and John Ashbery.

17 Richard Poirier, *Poetry and Pragmatism* (Cambridge: Harvard University Press, 1992) pp. 42, 4.

18 Henry David Thoreau, *Walden,* ed. J. Lyndon Shanley (Princeton: Princeton University Press, 1971), p. 98.

19 Quoted in Dewey, *Art as Experience,* p. 349.

Afterword

Truth and Toilets: Pragmatism and
the Practices of Life

STANLEY FISH

I have been assigned the job of summing up or wrapping up or mopping
up. I could do the short version and just say that Tom Grey gets it right
when he declares that no result we reach in philosophical investigation will
"undermine the working standards by which we assess claims based on
evidence and argument," and adds that the pursuit of philosophical explanations is not compulsory on pain of having one's character impugned
(254). The first statement puts philosophy—pragmatist or any other—in
its place as a special activity whose successes or failures do not entail or
even make more likely successes or failures in activities other than the
activity of doing philosophy; the second statement refuses to confer a
superior moral status on those who engage regularly in this odd pursuit.
Some people do philosophy, some people (lots more) don't and those who
do have not ascended to some rarified realm of reflection or critical self
consciousness from which they bring back the news to their less enlightened brethren; they merely have the knack of doing a trick some others
can't do and the competence they have acquired travels no further than the
very small arenas in which that trick is typically performed and rewarded.

I take Hilary Putnam to be saying something like that when he asks,
"what if all the philosophers are wrong, and the way it seems to be is the
way it *is?*" (40). Or, if I might rephrase, what if the answers philosophers
come up with are answers only in the highly artificial circumstances of the
philosophy seminar where ordinary reasons for action are systematically
distrusted and introduced only to be dismissed as naive? And what if, once
the philosopher goes away or ceases himself or herself to be a philosopher,
those ordinary reasons return *without* a vengeance and action is just as it
was before, if not unproblematic, at least not mysterious. This is one of the
lessons pragmatism teaches, and because it is, Putnam's other question—
"how can a pragmatist be a realist?" (38)—might appropriately be answered, "how could a pragmatist be anything else?" For after all, a prag-

418

matist believes in the sufficiency of human practices and is not dismayed when those practices are shown to be grounded in nothing more (or less) than their own traditions and histories; the impossibility of tying our everyday meanings and values to meanings and values less local does not lead the pragmatist to suspect their reality, but to suspect the form of thought that would deny it. When the formalist dream of finding invariant meanings underwritten by God or the structure of rationality is exploded, what remains is not dust and ashes but the solidity *and* plasticity of the world human beings continually make and remake.

In short, in the wake of formalism's failure, everything remains as it was. It is true that once you start going down the antiformalist road (with pragmatism or any other form of antifoundationalist thought) there is no place to stop; once contextualism is given its head and apparently firm meanings are made to shift and blur whenever a speaker is reimagined or a setting varied, no mechanism, not even the reification of context itself, will suffice to put on the brakes. But it is also true that when you come to the end of the antiformalist road what you will find waiting for you is formalism; that is, you will find the meanings that are perspicuous for you given your membership in what I have called an interpretive community, and so long as you live and move and have your being in that community (and if not that one, then in some other), those meanings will be immediately conveyed by public structures of language and image to which you and your peers can confidently point (of course members of other communities will not see what you point to or will see something else, but that's life). It is only if you expect those meanings to survive every sea change of situation that you will be tempted to declare them insubstantial, mere constructions; but that temptation and worry is one you should no longer feel if you have taken the antiformalist road all the way to its last stop.

In saying this I affirm what many in this volume have already said: philosophy should underwrite our ordinary ways of talking and our common sense experience of the world; I would only add that our common sense experience of the world doesn't need to be underwritten by philosophy, even by pragmatist philosophy which can no more shore up the world of common sense than analytic philosophy can break it down. If pragmatism points out that its rivals cannot deliver what they promise— once and for all answers to always relevant questions—pragmatism should itself know enough not to promise anything, or even to recommend anything. If pragmatism is true it has nothing to say to us; no politics follows from it or is blocked by it; no morality attaches to it or is enjoined by it. I typically make this point by distinguishing between a pragmatist account and a pragmatist program. A pragmatist account is an account of decision making and change that dispenses with decision procedures, hard and fast rules, and comprehensive theories, and emphasizes instead hunches, luck, creative opportunism, being in the right place at the right time with the right resources. A pragmatist program is what might follow if, once you had a pragmatist account, you could do something with it except prefer it to other accounts urged by Realists or proponents of natural law. But there is nothing you could do with it, for like the accounts it would dislodge, a pragmatist account has traction only in the context of the competition it seeks to win; in any other context, it is more or less useful depending on the purposes you are pursuing. Moreover, not only is there nothing you can do with a pragmatist account, there is nothing it makes *you* do; it doesn't commit those who are persuaded by it to any particular course of action or way of proceeding. (As Judge Posner observes, a pragmatist account of judging doesn't direct judges to be pragmatists.) If I am a pragmatist and hold that beliefs are internal to practices and cannot be justified by independent and general criteria, *this* belief will not lead me to lose confidence in my other beliefs or inhabit them more loosely than would be the case if I had another account of them. A belief about the source of my beliefs will have scope only over the matters it pronounces on and commits me only to rejecting alternative pronouncements on those same matters. If you know that someone has a pragmatist account of belief, you know nothing about what he or she will do in a moment of crisis or decision.

Indeed, this is true of all epistemological accounts, whether they be pragmatist or not. The way you are in the world of practices is independent of the account you might give of those practices, be it realist, rationalist, pragmatist, or whatever; your preferred vocabulary of explanation will not in and of itself either gift you or burden you with the certainties or uncertainties it proclaims; your preferred vocabulary of explanation will take you neither to heaven or hell. That's the bad news, at least for those who either harbor high hopes or entertain dark fears. The good news is that because your preferred vocabulary will not take you either to heaven or hell you are free to deploy it (or not) when the occasion suggests it would be good to do so. And this holds, too, for vocabularies you do not prefer, because they won't commit you to acting in any particular way, you can traffic in them without worrying that some bad residue will be left on your skin. In the past few years, I have spent a good deal of time arguing that the vocabulary of mainstream First Amendment jurisprudence—made up of words and phrases like autonomy, freedom, the marketplace of ideas, individual self-improvement—is either empty and incoherent or filled with a coherence I don't like. But I would never urge that this same vocabulary be abandoned, only that it should not be worshiped. If we worship it we shall find ourselves saddled with things we don't want; but if we avail ourselves of it—with a lightness that will be bearable in that it does not penetrate to our being—it can be put in the service of what we do want. As Richard Rorty puts it, vocabularies with philosophical pretensions are fine as long as they are regarded as helps to our practices "rather than as foundations for them."[1]

In this volume David Luban and Michel Rosenfeld take the opposite view when they argue that law cannot do without first philosophy (indeed, Luban seems at times to believe that to think something is to do philosophy), that when cases involve the issue of teaching creationist science, or the protection of artistic expression, or the justice of affirmative action, there is no agreement on ends and we must fall back on foundations. No, we will fall back and deploy rhetorics—highly charged vocabularies and formulas like the fact-value distinction, reverse racism, the independence of art from politics—and what we will do with these rhetorics is use them as clubs against our opponents all the while daring them to deny the force of a way of talking that has captured the heart and mind of America. The advantage of vocabularies or rhetorics over foundations is that they are already available in a storehouse of stock arguments, a storehouse Aristotle first furnished in his *Rhetoric* and one we have been adding to ever since. Foundations have to be sought, and as pragmatism tells us, they are never found. Rhetorics in long short and middle versions are already there for the quarrying and, what is even better, using them in a moment of need commits you to nothing, necessarily, in the next moment. After you have gotten from one what you want, you can just put it back on the shelf. (I know from long experience that this will be heard as cynicism or something worse, but it would be cynicism only if I were recommending something as opposed to describing something, describing what we all do unreflectively and quite sincerely: look around for ways of conveying and making attractive the points in which we fervently believe.)

I would say as much about any rhetoric and vocabulary, except for the vocabulary of religion, which seems to me to be quite another kettle of fish. When Richard Rorty wants to de-devinize philosophy, I say go to it—God speed—but when he wants to de-devinize theology, something doesn't ring true because theology doesn't seem to be the kind of thing you can de-devinize and still have anything left. As Giles Gunn observes, if you remove from religion "the obsession with . . . ranking and evaluation, . . .

the question becomes whether you are left with anything that can be recognized as . . . religion" (411). One knows what Rorty has in mind; it is what Locke had in mind when he announces in the first paragraph of the *Letter Concerning Toleration* that the true characteristic of any church is tolerance, and what Mill had in mind when he commends religious sentiments so long as they do not smack of the doctrinal, so long as Christians, for example, take care to be "just to infidelity."[2] But I confess that I have never been able to understand these assertions, except as a determination to retain the name of something even after you've cut its heart out. It's like *Hamlet* without the prince or like veggie-burgers. Where's the beef? Religions are not tolerant; that's why they are religions and not philosophical systems. Rorty is perfectly comfortable with Christianity "as a strong poem, one . . . among many" (27), but Christianity's claims are more exclusive. A religion without doctrine? To quote Grey again, "Philosophy is not compulsory, in the way religion is in the eyes of a . . . believer" (268). I take that to mean that you can walk away from a philosophy, even from one to which you have been persuaded; and you can do that because the answers you give in the very special situation of a philosophy seminar have very little purchase on the situations of ordinary life in relation to which they are either too remote or too specialized, not to the point. You can't, however, walk away from your religion, if it is really yours and not a collection of sentiments trotted out for special—and intermittent—occasions. Your religion is always to the point: you shall love the Lord thy God with all thy heart and all thy soul and all thy might, not just on Friday evenings or Sunday mornings, when you'd rather be reading Wallace Stevens. Religious claims do not relax, nor do they respect any line between the private and the public.

That is why liberalism cannot tolerate them; they violate its religion of tolerance, the religion instituted by Locke three hundred years ago. Grey reports Rawls (Locke's heir) asking "how is it possible for those affirming a religious doctrine . . . based on religious authority . . . also to hold a reasonable political conception that supports a just democratic regime?" (254). That's the easy end of the question and it is answered by Grey's report of the degree of agreement about the law and social life he is able to reach with an evangelical friend. The hard end is "how is it possible for a political conception centered on reason and democracy to do justice to those uninvested in either the reasonable or the democratic?" The answer is that it isn't possible. In the eyes of a democratically reasonable person what is owed to the strong religious believer is fairness, but fairness is not what the strong religious believer wants; what he wants is a world ordered in accordance with the faith he lives by and would die for, and liberal democracy (or pragmatism) isn't going to give him that, ever. When Grey tells us that his evangelical friend "turns out to be a pragmatist for legal purposes" (267), I conclude that he isn't really a committed believer because he has allowed secular authorities to tell him when and in what precincts he can invoke and act on his religious convictions. My diagnosis is confirmed when this same supposed fundamentalist is prepared to respect the diversity of conceptions of the good "even if he and his co-religionists become politically dominant" (269). Why would he be prepared to do that unless respect for diversity had become his religion and what he likes to call his religion has become that set of pieties he rehearses at catechism? In his *Areopagitica* Milton pokes fun at a merchant who "finds religion to be a traffic so entangled, and of so many piddling accounts" (you have to keep it in mind all the time) that he simply cannot keep a stock going in that trade. Wearied by religion's demands, he hits upon the device of hiring someone who will take on the burden of his religious duties and thereby allow him to have the "name" of being religious without any of the work. In the person of this proxy his religion "comes home at night, is liberally supped, and sumptuously laid to sleep; rises, is saluted and . . . better breakfasted than he whose morning appetite would have gladly fed on green figs between Bethany and Jerusalem, his religion walks abroad at eight, and leaves his kind entertainer in his shop [or is it in his law office] trading all day, without his religion."[3]

As Grey describes him, his friend sounds a lot like Milton's merchant and not at all like Vicki Frost, a real evangelical Christian and a plaintiff in a recent cause of action (*Mozert v. Hawkins*) directed at public schools because they were teaching her daughter tolerance and respect for the viewpoints of others, values subversive to her religious beliefs and likely, in her opinion, to corrupt her child by diverting her from the one true way. To the argument that her daughter was not being indoctrinated into alternative viewpoints but merely exposed to them, she replied that exposure is precisely what she feared (the point was a winner in the Amish case, *Wisconsin v. Yoder*, largely because the Amish wanted nothing more than to be left to themselves) and that the distinction between indoctrination and exposure was an artifact of the very liberalism that was oppressing her. It is the voice of someone like Vicki Frost, of someone who thinks that diversity, freedom of expression, fairness, and dialogue are bad ideas which pave the road to hell, that should stand in for Tom Grey's oh so reasonable friend. What does liberalism, and the pragmatism that is its philosophical support, say to her? What it will usually say is that we of course respect your religious views and will not be a party to their silencing, but you must understand that we cannot allow those views to spill over into the public sphere where they might succeed in enacting themselves into law and thereby disenfranchising or marginalizing the views of others. In short Vicki Frost will be read the lesson Madison read to the nation in the *Remonstrance*—that religion is after all a wholly private matter. But that is precisely what Vicki Frost does not believe—she believes that her religious commitments extend to every aspect of her life and to *yours*, too—and she will be understandably frustrated when she is told not that her religious views are false (that at least would be a challenge she could pick up) but that they are beside the point.

One might think I exaggerate the tension between Vicki Frost and the tolerant society in whose many mansions she is what Stanley Hauerwas has called a resident alien; after all she lived in that society quite comfortably (we can presume) before she decided to file her suit. True, but then the pinch came, and she realized what was really at stake, and at that moment the accommodations she had no doubt previously made became experienced as intolerable burdens. Liberalism in general and pragmatism in particular (at least when it takes the form of tolerance and the enlargement of sympathy) are dedicated to warding off that moment, to doing everything possible to make sure that the pinch doesn't come and that we have as relaxed and expansive a relationship to our convictions as we can manage. That is why one of pragmatism's strengths is what has often been cited as one of its weaknesses. Pragmatism—as Ruth Anna Putnam, Richard Bernstein, Richard Posner, and Nancy Fraser observe in their different ways—has no firm outline, is vague, and means many things to many people. But as the wolf said to Little Red Riding Hood, "the better to eat you with my dear." A pragmatism so amorphous and omnivorous has the two advantages of (1) being a very bad target—you feel that there is nothing to hit—and (2) being a very bad substitute for the absolutes it tilts against—if you don't know exactly what it is, it is hard to march under its banner. Pragmatism may be the one theory—if it is a theory—that clears the field not only of its rivals, but of itself, at least as a positive alternative. Once you see this, Michel Rosenfeld's complaint that pragmatism is of no help to someone trying to figure out "which of the available alternatives ought to be pursued" (324) in a particular situation can be heard as a compliment to a pragmatism that is being true to itself by being very little. This is not to say, as Richard Weisberg seems to, that pragmatism commits you to being very little, to being morally small. Although Weisberg is right to point out that nothing in pragmatism keeps us from sliding back into the model of European law during World War II or from indiscriminately attaching ourselves to the latest "fashionable movement" (312), he is mistaken when he suggests that pragmatism pulls us in those directions. It pulls us in no direction, neither does it bar any.

This parsimonious view of pragmatism's imperatives is not one shared by most self-identified pragmatists, who tend to turn the pragmatist withdrawal from strong claims into a strong claim of their own, the claim that pragmatism, if adhered to, leads to forms of behavior that make the world a better place and you a better person: kinder, gentler, more respectful of others, and less likely to hold it against someone that his beliefs are not yours. In this volume that claim takes the form of linking pragmatism to democracy and to poetry. The hinge that supposedly ties the three together is a distrust of received views, unimpeachable authorities, and unexamined dogma. The idea is that democracy, rather than being monistic and theocratic, is pluralist and secular; holding no ideas sacred, it is open to all ideas so long as they are willing to subject themselves to the scrutiny of public reason. What democracy requires, says Richard Bernstein, is "the cultivation of critical habits of deliberation" (147), and, according to Richard Poirier (as reported by Luke Menand), those same habits are what is cultivated by poetry; a word in a poem, says Poirier, is "alert to the constraints of its own doubleness, combining and contending with other elements in the poem in an ongoing process of inflection and change." Being faithful to that process is the "central work" of the pragmatist-poet who turns away from "already familiar and knowable forms of life" and opts instead for "the continuous creation of truth, an act that must be . . . never ending" (347). In short, poetry (here in the position reserved in earlier versions of the pragmatist story for science) schools one in the habit of resisting the temptations of closure and dogma.

It is all very neat and seems to hang together nicely: if you read a lot of poetry you will be in rehearsal for the work of rejecting the lure of final solutions (even when, especially when, they are your own); you will then perform that work in the public forums of democracy where you will be slow to insist on the primacy of your own interests and open to considering the interests of others; and underwriting both your life as a reader and your life as a citizen will be the pragmatist distrust of "all forms of foundationalism, all attempts to establish philosophy on unchanging *a priori* postulates" (Kloppenberg, p. 84). Now I don't doubt that there are some people whose aesthetic political and philosophical inclinations dovetail in this way, but the convergence in them of parallel dispositions would be fortuitous and neither necessary nor even likely. The reason is one I have already given: your philosophical views are independent of your views (and therefore of your practices) in any realm of life other than the very special and rarified realm of doing philosophy. If you believe that your convictions have their source not in ultimate truths or foundations, but in contingent traditions of inquiry and are therefore revisable, that belief, in and of itself, will not render you disposed to revise your convictions or turn you into a person who enters into situations provisionally and with epistemic modesty. You can give all the standard answers to all the pragmatist questions and still be an authoritarian in the classroom, a decided conservative in cultural matters or inclined to the absolutes of theology. (I am, in differing degrees, all three.)

Nor will your pragmatism—or, more properly, the fact that you will give pragmatist-type answers to some traditional questions about truth, objectivity, language, and reference—especially fit you for participation in democracy, if only because democracy is grounded not in philosophy (although philosophy may be called on to shore it up or perform the work of public relations), but in a set of political arrangements laid down in the *Federalist Papers* and enacted in the Constitution—checks and balances, divided government, mechanisms for orderly change, obstacles to hasty change, all devices designed to keep at bay the conflicts that tore English society apart in the seventeenth century. They do that job not by making people less aggressive in holding their beliefs, but by making it more difficult (although not impossible) to use those beliefs as the occasion for, and justification of, oppression. Provisionality, openness, and toleration are not what the mechanisms of democracy generate, but what they *enforce* against the inclinations of citizens who remain as dogmatic, closed minded, and bigoted as they were before democracy emerged. These virtues (if they are virtues; there is a powerful antiliberal argument always in the course of being remounted) are the properties of the system, not of those who live under it. If democracy has to some extent worked, it is because certain political structures are firmly in place and not because its citizens have internalized the sayings of Emerson, Dewey, and James. Pragmatism may have emerged under democratic conditions (although its basic tenets were long ago articulated by Cicero and Machiavelli), but it neither produces nor necessarily accompanies democracy. And if pragmatism has no special affinity for democracy, neither does it have any special relationship to the positions you might take on the issues that turn up in the democratic landscape. Your political allegiances are more likely to be a function of whether repeal of the capital gains tax will benefit you than of your epistemology, should you be a person so odd as to have one.

And reading poetry? Well that's something I do for a living, and as it happens I do it in pretty much the way Poirier and Menand urge, attending to the meanings sense hurries past in its rush to completion and univocal coherence. I read that way because I was taught to do so by my instructors at Yale and by the writings of William Empson. My reading style, in short, is a *professional* practice, something I picked up in the course of an apprenticeship designed to prepare me for performances in the classroom and learned journals; its relationship to any of my other performances (as a father, citizen, consumer, press director) is entirely contingent and in my case almost nonexistent. The only carryover I'm aware of are those moments when I annoy someone by detecting in his perfectly straightforward speech meanings he did not intend and (quite reasonably) finds distracting. Just as you can have a pragmatist position in philosophy and have any number of political views (or have none) so you can be an Empsonian reader of poetry and be a straight-on literalist, looking neither to the semantic left or right, when you set out to do other jobs of work.

Indeed, I would go further: you had better be such a literalist when you argue a case or talk to your Dean or bargain with a car dealer or give directions to someone trying to get to your house. Ruth Anna Putnam criticizes philosophers "who lead one life in their studies and another outside" and argues for a philosophy "that enables us to lead one life, to be as consistent as is humanly possible" (62). I suppose that one could achieve that consistency but I'm not sure how human it would be and I suspect that the result would be something akin to insanity. We laugh at the plumber who tours Europe and comes back talking of nothing but the primitive state of showers and the absence of copper piping. Why should we not laugh equally hard at the philosopher who tours the world and finds nothing to remark on but fallacies, category mistakes, and insufficiently nuanced modals? The answer is that while we don't think that a focus on toilets is appropriate to any and all situations, we do think that a focus on philosophical puzzles can never be beside the point; but we think so only because we mistake a professional practice—and a professional conversation we may decline to join and be none the worse for it—for life itself. (The thesis that toilets are more central to life than philosophy seems to me self-evident, perhaps only because I am the son, brother, and nephew of plumbers.)

The truth is that neither the benefits nor the troubles of professional practices come along with us when we leave their precincts and enter another. It is the failure to understand this truth that leads people to worry about the effect of postmodernist or pragmatist philosophy on their ability to do things other than philosophize. Kloppenberg for example, wonders "how history written by 'new' pragmatists could contribute anything distinctively different from novels or poetry to helping us to understand experience." The answer is that a history written by a new pragmatist would be just like any other history and subject to the usual evaluations, so long as the new pragmatist were really writing a history and not interrogating the assumptions within which history is written. If he were doing the latter he would not be a historian at all but a metahistorian, and he would be engaging in a practice with its own traditions, exemplary achievements, authoritative forbearers, and influential contemporaries. The mistake is to think that news from the one practice can either authorize or deauthorize the other, to think that if your meta-theory puts into question the basic components of historical work—facts, evidence, agency, cause and effect—you would no longer be able to do it (or would do it in some odd and self defeating way, perhaps by tagging every assertion with a warning that it is unsupportable and the mere product of social construction). I understand the reasoning: it asks, if you don't believe in the hardness of fact, how can you write history? But the question assumes that before you lost your epistemological innocence to the new pragmatism, you went around *actively* believing in fact, and that having had that active belief taken away from you, fact now seems like quicksand. But in fact (if you will pardon the phrase) in ordinary life we don't believe in facts, we encounter them. If issues of belief arise, it is in equally ordinary situations of doubt and they are resolved (when they are resolved) by ordinary methods—getting more information, searching archives, employing finer instruments of measurement, and so on. Moreover, you will encounter facts in the same ordinary (which is not to say indisputable) way after you have learned how to deconstruct the ordinary from Rorty or Derrida or me.

That deconstructive lesson, after all, is a special one, involving the deliberate bracketing and interrogation of the familiar world of phenomena, events, actors, consequences; and when you are not learning it or teaching it, that world has all the solidity it ever had. It is in that solid world that historians work—the assumption of its solidity is a prerequisite of historical thinking—and just as they didn't need an actively willed belief to encounter facts, so will they not be deprived of those encounters because they have been introduced to a form of thought that aggressively suspends the very conditions of historical experience. That form of thought—call it new pragmatist, or postmodern, or antifoundationalist—tells us that if you look underneath our everyday ways of knowing you will find that they are unanchored by anything but contingent and revisable traditions of inquiry; but contingent and revisable conditions of inquiry are what historians traffic in, and the news that they are supported by nothing firmer than themselves will not at all be disabling (although it may be of interest) since the firmness they provide is all the historian needs to do his work and to do it without any metaphysical doubts. Metaphysical doubts are what you don't entertain while doing history; they don't even *occur* to you. As Westbrook observes, glossing Putnam, practitioners "begin investigations . . . within the context of a body of warranted assertions . . . they have no reason to doubt" (131).

This doesn't mean that historians have no decisions to make; it is just that what they will decide between are the alternative perspectives (economic, ecological, dynastic, top-down, bottom-up) from which one might make historical sense; they will not be deciding whether historical sense can or cannot be made. Kloppenberg is exactly wrong when he says that "Historians face a choice . . . between newer varieties of pragmatism that see all truth claims as contingent and older varieties of pragmatism descended directly from James and Dewey" (116). The choices historians face are historians' choices, choices of method, bodies of evidence, authoritative sources, and so on. Historians can take pragmatism—old, new, conservative, radical, democratic, visionary—or leave it. In fact they can be new pragmatists, preaching the contingency of all truth claims, in the morning, and be good historians, on the scent of fact, in the afternoon. No matter how radical the thoughts about foundations and indeterminacy historians entertain in their metacritical moods, the documents they look into will yield up meanings, patterns, explanations, and conclusions aplenty. The conclusion by now should be expected and familiar; no practice of history either follows from or is blocked by pragmatism.

In the end—and this has been my single note—nothing follows from pragmatism, not democracy, not a love of poetry, not a mode of doing history. (As Sidney Morgenbesser remarks, "the relevant theses are independent" [54].) It is true that these things come together in the lives of some, who have called themselves pragmatists, and this is a fact worth noting. However, it is a sociohistorical fact about a bunch of guys, mostly eastern, who went to the same schools, were published in the same magazines, read the same books, taught in the same universities where they produced a generation of students who followed pretty much in the same paths (except that these days some of them are Jews). To make this accident of geography, education, and progressive politics into something inevitable, into a flowering of deeply related truths, is to turn pragmatism in the direction of the foundationalism (and eschatology) it tilts against.

Turning into just another would-be-foundation is always the danger pragmatism courts when it becomes too ambitious, as it does when pragmatists begin to talk about and proclaim the advent of something called "undistorted communication." Undistorted by what? Undistorted, says Richard Bernstein, by our "individual biases," those "prejudgments and . . . prejudices" that "prevent us from knowing what is real" (142). But I thought that in the pragmatist view the real is not to be opposed to interested human behavior but identified with it, and that our prejudices—a pejorative term for what appears to us to be true given our histories, education, institutional affiliations etc.—are what we must go along with in the absence of some final truth or self-declaring reality. What is a philosophy that begins with James' declaration that "the trail of the human serpent is . . . over everything"[4] doing with notions of the really real and with a program for transcending our biases?

The answer returns us to the supposed connection between pragmatism and democracy, joined in Bernstein's arguments by a regimen of "self-correcting critical habits" (142). The idea is that if we keep in mind the fact of our fallibility, and are open to the views of other equally fallible men and women, we can together fashion a society populated by individuals with a capacity to "assume the attitudes and roles of other" and in this way move toward the "ideal of a universal democratic community" (150). This formulation has its analogues in Roberto Unger's hope for the emergence of a "community of sympathy" and Rorty's program of "redescription" in the service of expanding "our sense of 'us' as far as we can."[5] But whatever form it takes, the project is an instance of what I call the critical self consciousness fallacy or antifoundationalist theory hope, the fallacy of thinking that there is a mental space you can occupy to the side of your convictions and commitments, and the hope that you can use the lesson that no transcendent standpoint is available as a way of bootstrapping yourself to transcendence (on the reasoning that because we now know that "we cannot hope to escape from" our prejudices, we can be on guard against those prejudices and better able to see things clearly). The fallacy would not be one if it were put forward by a foundationalist who begins with a faith in Rationality and the possibility of correcting belief by standards external to it; but it is surely a fallacy when put forward by an antifoundationalist, for given the antifoundationalist account of how we reason and reach conclusions (by following this or that trail of the human serpent) there would seem to be no room for a faculty—critical, reflective, aggressively, as opposed to ordinarily, aware—to which our beliefs could be referred in the way of a caution.

This is not to say that in an antifoundationalist world one lacks mechanisms for confirming or disconfirming beliefs, or hunches. It is just that such mechanisms (authoritative documents, the pronouncements of revered authorities, standards of measurement, etc.) do not stand apart from the structure of one's belief *but are items within it.* I once heard Rorty hold his ground in the face of a hostile question, but then immediately add, "still, I hear that Davidson is developing an argument contrary to mine, and anything Davidson says I will take seriously." What Rorty was doing is what Bernstein recommends—engaging in the self-correction of his present beliefs; but what corrects his belief (at least potentially) is another of his beliefs, the belief that if Davidson disagrees with him about something, he should take a second look. Someone with a different relationship to Davidson (opposition, indifference, ignorance) could not have the same self-correcting experience, although no doubt there would be something or someone that would cause him to pause and reflect. Pausing and reflecting are always possibilities; but they are internal to our "prejudgments and prejudices" and not checks against them.

In short, even when self correction has occurred you are as much inside what Bernstein calls your "biases" as you were before, and you stand in the same relationship to the biases of your fellows, a relationship either of accidental (and temporary) agreement or unresolvable (because deep) disagreement. This, of course, tells against the achievement of anything like a "universal democratic community" (141), which is unavailable exactly in the measure that the critical space of reflection and distance from one's beliefs is unavailable. Both pragmatist philosophy and democratic process begin in a recognition of the intractability of difference and it would be a contradiction to turn that recognition into a method for eliminating (or even ameliorating) difference. Democracy (*pace* Bernstein) is not a program for transforming men and women into capacious and generous beings but is a device for managing the narrow partialities that (as Hobbes saw so clearly) will always inform the activities of human actors. And by the same reasoning, communication is not a vehicle for harmonizing those partialities; not, as Habermas would have it be, a cooperative venture, rather it is a competitive one, and the prize in the competition is the (temporary) right to label your way of talking "undistorting," a label you can claim only until some other way of talking, some other vocabulary elaborated with a superior force, takes it away from you.

This is finally the only sense I am able to make of the idea of the strong poet. The strong poet is someone whose vocabulary dislodges the vocabulary of his or her predecessors and, for a while at least, establishes the distinctions, hierarchies, slogans, and binaries that will carry the day in most conversations. The strong poet, in short, is a rhetorician, and if pragmatism is anything (some of its detractors, including Ronald Dworkin, would say it is not), it is an up-to-date version of rhetoric, that account of thought and action anchored in two famous pronouncements of Protagoras': "About the gods I cannot say either that they are or that they are not" and "Man is the measure of all things." It's all there—the bracketing of ontological questions, and the location of knowledge, certainty and objectivity (of a revisable kind) in the ways of knowing that emerge in history. That is the lesson pragmatism teaches, that we live in a rhetorical world where arguments and evidence are always available, but always challengeable, and that the resources of that world are sufficient unto most days. It is neither a despairing nor an inspiring lesson, and it doesn't tell you exactly how to do anything (it delivers no method) although it does assure you that in ordinary circumstances there will usually be something to be done. This may not seem much, but it is all Bernstein is able to offer when he identifies pragmatism's imperative: "we should try to support our conclusions with the best available evidence and reasons" (154). True, no doubt, but, one might ask, as opposed to what? No one offers evidence and reasons he thinks inferior; everyone is already doing what Aristotle advises in the *Rhetoric*, looking around for the available means of persuasion.

Now, whenever someone says that we live in a rhetorical world, someone else will immediately say what Kloppenberg says in a snippy little note directed at me: this means " 'anything goes' " (125 n.58). No, what it means is that *anything that can be made to go goes,* at once a tautology and acknowledgment of the difficulties James acknowledges in the second half of the oft-quoted sentence: "The true is the name of whatever proves itself to be good in the way of belief, and good, too, for definite, assignable reasons."[6] What James tells us when he adds "and good, too, for definite, assignable reasons" is that we neither believe nor persuade others to believe by an exercise of the will. Rather, we come to beliefs by virtue of our situations and our histories in relation to which certain routes of evidence and persuasion are already part of the structure of our understandings (as the authority of Davidson is part of Rorty's). And we disseminate our beliefs—fit them into the relays of public truth—by connecting them up, if we can, with the routes of evidence and persuasion constitutive of the understandings of others. *If we can.* Success is not assured, definite, assignable reasons are not always at hand, and loudly proclaiming that you have them will not do any good, will not prove anything in the way of belief. But successes do happen; obstacles are sometimes overcome; new and hitherto unthinkable links are forged. That is the world pragmatism describes and the world we inhabit independently of its description. Pragmatism is the philosophy not of grand ambitions but of little steps; and although it cannot help us to take those steps or tell us what they are, it can offer the reassurance that they are possible and more than occasionally efficacious even if we cannot justify them down to the ground.

Notes

1 "Does Academic Freedom Have Philosophical Presuppositons?," in *The Future of Academic Freedom*, ed. Louis Menand (Chicago: University of Chicago Press, 1996), p. 24.
2 J. S. Mill, *On Liberty*, ed. D. Spitz (New York: Norton, 1975), p. 49.
3 Milton, *Areopagitica*, in *Areopagitica and Other Prose Works* (London: J. M. Dent, 1927), p. 28.
4 William James, "What Pragmatism Means," in *Pragmatism: A Contemporary Reader*, ed. Russell B. Goodman (New York: Routledge, 1995), p. 60.
5 Roberto Unger, *Knowledge and Politics* (New York: Free Press, 1975); Richard Rorty, *Contingency, Irony, and Solidarity* (Cambridge: Cambridge University Press, 1989).
6 William James, "What Pragmatism Means," p. 63.

Selected Bibliography

Anderson, Charles W. *Pragmatic Liberalism*. Chicago: University of Chicago Press, 1990.

——. *Prescribing the Life of the Mind*. Madison: University of Wisconsin Press, 1993.

Anderson, Quentin. *Making Americans: An Essay on Individualism and Money*. New York: Harcourt Brace Jovanovich, 1992.

Apel, Karl-Otto. *Charles Sanders Peirce: From Pragmatism to Pragmaticism*. Trans. John M. Krois. Amherst: University of Massachusetts Press, 1981.

Barzun, Jacques. *A Stroll With William James*. New York: Harper & Row, 1983.

Bernstein, Richard J. *John Dewey*. New York: Washington Square Press, 1966.

——. *Beyond Objectivism and Relativism: Science, Hermeneutics, and Praxis*. Philadelphia: University of Pennsylvania Press, 1982.

——. *The New Constellation: The Ethical-Political Horizons of Modernity/Postmodernity*. Cambridge: MIT Press, 1992.

——. "The Resurgence of Pragmatism." *Social Research* 59 (Winter 1992): 813–40.

Bourne, Randolph. *The Radical Will: Selected Writings, 1911–1918*, ed. Olaf Hansen. New York: Urizen, 1977.

Brent, Joseph. *Charles Sanders Peirce: A Life*. Bloomington: Indiana University Press, 1993.

Brint, Michael, and William Weaver, eds. *Pragmatism in Law and Society*. Boulder: Westview Press, 1991.

Campbell, James. *The Community Reconstructs: The Meaning of Pragmatic Social Thought*. Urbana: University of Illinois Press, 1992.

——. *Understanding John Dewey: Nature and Cooperative Intelligence*. Chicago: Open Court Press, 1995.

Carney, Ray. "Two Forms of Modernism: Notes Towards a Pragmatic Aesthetic." In *Modernism in the United States*, ed. Townsend Ludington. Chapel Hill: University of North Carolina Press, 1999.

——. *The Films of John Cassavetes: Pragmatism, Modernism, and the Movies*. New York: Cambridge University Press, 1994.

Cavell, Stanley. *The Senses of Walden: An Expanded Edition*. 1979. Chicago: University of Chicago Press, 1992.

——. *The Claim of Reason: Wittgenstein, Skepticism, Morality, and Tragedy*. New York: Oxford University Press, 1979.

435

——. *In Quest of the Ordinary: Lines of Skepticism and Romanticism.* Chicago: University of Chicago Press, 1988.

——. *This New Yet Unapproachable America: Lectures after Emerson after Wittgenstein.* Albuquerque: Living Batch Press, 1989.

——. *Conditions Handsome and Unhandsome: The Constitution of Emersonian Perfectionism.* Chicago: University of Chicago Press, 1990.

Commager, Henry Steele. *The American Mind.* New Haven: Yale University Press, 1950.

Cotkin, George. *William James, Public Philosopher.* Baltimore: Johns Hopkins University Press, 1990.

——. *Reluctant Modernism: American Thought and Culture, 1880–1900.* New York: Maxwell Macmillan International, 1992.

Coughlan, Neil. *Young John Dewey: An Essay in American Intellectual History.* Chicago: University of Chicago Press, 1975.

Croce, Jerome. *Science and Religion in the Era of William James, Volume One: The Eclipse of Certainty, 1820–1880.* Chapel Hill: University of North Carolina Press, 1995.

Depew, David, and Robert Hollinger, eds. *Pragmatism: From Progressivism to Postmodernism.* Westport, Conn.: Praeger, 1995.

Dewey, John. *Reconstruction in Philosophy.* Boston: Beacon Press, 1957 (originally published 1920).

——. *The Public and Its Problems.* 1927. Denver: Alan Swallow, 1954.

——. *Art as Experience.* 1934. New York: Capricorn Books, 1958.

——. *A Common Faith.* 1934. New Haven: Yale University Press, 1991.

——. *The Philosophy of John Dewey,* ed. John J. McDermott. Chicago: University of Chicago Press, 1981 (originally published 1973).

——. *The Essential Writings,* ed. David Sidorsky. New York: Harper & Row, 1977.

Diggins, John Patrick. *The Promise of Pragmatism: Modernism and the Crisis of Knowledge and Authority.* Chicago: University of Chicago Press, 1994.

Feffer, Andrew. *The Chicago Pragmatists and American Progressivism.* Ithaca: Cornell University Press, 1993.

Feinstein, Howard M. *Becoming William James.* Ithaca: Cornell University Press, 1984.

Fisch, Max H. *Peirce, Semeiotic, and Pragmatism,* ed. Kenneth Laine Ketner and Christian J. W. Kloesel. Bloomington: Indiana University Press, 1986.

Fish, Stanley. *Is There a Text in This Class?: The Authority of Interpretive Communities.* Cambridge: Harvard University Press, 1980.

——. *Doing What Comes Naturally: Change, Rhetoric, and the Practice of Theory in Literary and Legal Studies.* Durham: Duke University Press, 1989.

Fraser, Nancy. *Unruly Practices: Power, Discourse and Gender in Contemporary Social Theory.* Minneapolis: University of Minnesota Press, 1985.

——. *Justice Interruptus: Critical Reflections on the "Postsocialist" Condition.* New York: Routledge, 1997.

Goodheart, Eugene. "The Postmodern Liberalism of Richard Rorty." In *The Reign of Ideology.* New York: Columbia University Press, 1997, pp. 44–61.

Goodman, Russell B., ed. *Pragmatism: A Contemporary Reader.* New York and London: Routledge, 1995.

Gouinlock, James. *John Dewey's Philosophy of Value.* New York: Humanities Press, 1972.

Grey, Thomas C. "Holmes and Legal Pragmatism." *Stanford Law Review* 41 (1989): 787–870.

Gunn, Giles. *Thinking Across the American Grain: Ideology, Intellect, and the New Pragmatism.* Chicago: University of Chicago Press, 1992.

Haack, Susan. " 'We Pragmatists . . .': Peirce and Rorty in Conversation." *Partisan Review* 64, no. 1 (1997): 91–107.

Habermas, Jürgen. *Knowledge and Human Interests.* Boston: Beacon Press, 1971.

———. *The Theory of Communicative Action,* trans. Thomas McCarthy. Boston: Beacon Press, 1984.

Hollinger, David A. "The Problem of Pragmatism in American History." *Journal of American History* 67 (June 1980): 88–107.

———. *In the American Province: Studies in the History and Historiography of Ideas.* Bloomington: Indiana University Press, 1985.

Hook, Sidney. *John Dewey: An Intellectual Portrait.* New York: John Day, 1939.

———. *Pragmatism and the Tragic Sense of Life.* New York: Basic Books, 1974.

James, William. *Varieties of Religious Experience.* New York: Modern Library, 1994 (originally published 1902).

———. *Pragmatism: A New Name for Some Old Ways of Thinking.* 1907. Cambridge: Harvard University Press, 1975.

———. *Letters of William James,* 2 vols., ed. Henry James, Jr. Boston: Little, Brown, 1920.

———. *The Writings of William James: A Comprehensive Edition,* ed. John J. McDermott. Chicago: University of Chicago Press, 1977 (originally published 1967).

———. *Writings, 1878–1899.* New York: Library of America, 1992.

———. *Writings, 1902–1910,* ed. Bruce Kuklick. New York: Library of America, 1987.

Jay, Paul. *Contingency Blues: The Search for Foundations in American Criticism.* Madison: University of Wisconsin Press, 1997.

Joas, Hans. *G. H. Mead: A Contemporary Re-Examination of His Thought.* Cambridge: MIT Press, 1985.

———. *Pragmatism and Social Theory.* Chicago: University of Chicago Press, 1993.

———. *The Creativity of Action,* trans. Jeremy Gaines and Paul Krest. Chicago: University of Chicago Press, 1996.

Kloppenberg, James T. *Uncertain Victory: Social Democracy and Progressivism in European and American Thought, 1870–1920.* New York: Oxford University Press, 1986.

———. "Democracy and Disenchantment: From Weber and Dewey to Habermas and Rorty." In *Modernist Impulses in the Human Sciences, 1870–1930,* ed. Dorothy Ross. Baltimore: Johns Hopkins University Press, 1994, pp. 188–90.

Kuklick, Bruce. *The Rise of American Philosophy.* New Haven: Yale University Press, 1977.

———. *Churchmen and Philosophers: From Jonathan Edwards to John Dewey.* New Haven: Yale University Press, 1985.

Levinson, Henry Samuel. *The Religious Investigations of William James.* Chapel Hill: University of North Carolina Press, 1981.

———. *Santayana: Pragmatism and the Spiritual Life.* Chapel Hill: University of North Carolina Press, 1994.

Lewis, R. W. B. *The Jameses: a Family Narrative*. New York: Farrar, Straus and Giroux, 1991.

Livingston, James. *Pragmatism and the Political Economy of Cultural Revolution, 1850–1940*. Chapel Hill: University of North Carolina Press, 1994.

Lovejoy, Arthur O. *The Thirteen Pragmatisms, and Other Essays*. Baltimore: Johns Hopkins University Press, 1963.

Luban, David. *Legal Modernism*. Ann Arbor: University of Michigan Press, 1994.

Mailloux, Steven, ed. *Rhetoric, Sophistry, Pragmatism*. Cambridge: Cambridge University Press, 1995.

Malachowski, Alan, ed. *Reading Rorty*. Cambridge, Mass.: Basil Blackwell, 1990.

Margolis, Joseph. *Pragmatism Without Foundations: Reconciling Realism and Relativism*. Oxford: Blackwell, 1986.

McDermott, John J. *The Culture of Experience: Philosophical Essays in the American Grain*. New York: New York University Press, 1976.

——. *Streams of Experience: Reflections on the History and Philosophy of American Culture*. Amherst: University of Massachusetts Press, 1986.

Menand, Louis, ed. *Pragmatism: A Reader*. New York: Vintage, 1997.

Mitchell, W. J. T., ed. *Against Theory: Literary Studies and the New Pragmatism*. Chicago: University of Chicago Press, 1985.

Morgenbesser, Sidney, ed. *Dewey and His Critics*. New York: Journal of Philosophy, 1977.

Mouffe, Chantal, ed. *Deconstruction and Pragmatism*. London and New York: Routledge, 1996.

Mulvaney, Robert J., and Philip M. Zeltner, eds. *Pragmatism: Its Sources and Prospects*. Columbia: University of South Carolina Press, 1981.

Mumford, Lewis. *The Golden Day*. New York: Boni & Liveright, 1926.

Murphy, John P. *Pragmatism: From Peirce to Davidson*. Boulder: Westview Press, 1990.

Myers, Gerald E. *William James: His Life and Thought*. New Haven: Yale University Press, 1986.

Nagel, Thomas. *Mortal Questions*. New York: Cambridge University Press, 1979.

——. *The View from Nowhere*. New York: Oxford University Press, 1986.

Orrill, Robert, ed. *The Condition of American Liberal Education: Pragmatism and a Changing Tradition*. New York: College Entrance Examination Board, 1995.

Peirce, Charles S. *Philosophical Writings of Peirce*, ed. Justus Buchler. New York: Dover, 1955.

——. *Charles S. Peirce: Selected Writings*, ed. Philip Wiener. New York: Dover, 1966.

——. *The Essential Peirce, Selected Philosophical Writings*, vol. 1, *1867–1893*, ed. Nathan Houser and Christian Kloesel. Bloomington: Indiana University Press, 1992.

Perry, Ralph Barton. *The Thought and Character of William James*, 2 vols. Boston: Little, Brown, 1935.

Poirier, Richard. *The Renewal of Literature: Emersonian Reflections*. New York: Random House, 1987.

——. *Poetry and Pragmatism*. Cambridge: Harvard University Press, 1992.

Posner, Richard. *The Economics of Justice*. Cambridge: Harvard University Press, 1981.

——. *The Problems of Jurisprudence*. Cambridge: Harvard University Press, 1990.

——, ed. *The Essential Holmes*. Chicago: University of Chicago Press, 1992.

——. *Overcoming Law.* Cambridge: Harvard University Press, 1995.

Posnock, Ross. *The Trial of Curiosity: Henry James, William James, and the Challenge of Modernity.* New York: Oxford University Press, 1991.

Putnam, Hilary. *Reason, Truth and History.* Cambridge: Cambridge University Press, 1981.

——. *The Many Faces of Realism.* LaSalle, Ill.: Open Court, 1987.

——. *Realism With a Human Face,* ed. James Conant. Cambridge: Harvard University Press, 1990.

——. *Renewing Philosophy.* Cambridge: Harvard University Press, 1992. See especially "A Reconsideration of Deweyan Democracy," pp. 180–200.

——. *Words and Life,* ed. James Conant. Cambridge: Harvard University Press, 1994. See especially "Pragmatism and Moral Objectivity," pp. 151–81.

——. *Pragmatism: An Open Question.* Cambridge: Basil Blackwell, 1995.

Quine, Willard van Orman. "Two Dogmas of Empiricism." In *From a Logical Point of View.* Cambridge: Harvard University Press, 1953, pp. 20–46.

Rajchman, John, and Cornel West, eds. *Post-Analytic Philosophy.* New York: Columbia University Press, 1985.

Rockefeller, Steven. *John Dewey: Religious Faith and Democratic Humanism.* New York: Columbia University Press, 1991.

Rorty, Richard. *Philosophy and the Mirror of Nature.* Princeton: Princeton University Press, 1979.

——. *Consequences of Pragmatism.* Minneapolis: University of Minnesota Press, 1982.

——. *Contingency, Irony, and Solidarity.* Cambridge: Cambridge University Press, 1989.

——. *Objectivity, Relativism, and Truth.* Cambridge: Cambridge University Press, 1991.

——. *Essays on Heidegger and Others.* Cambridge: Cambridge University Press, 1991.

——. "Trotsky and the Wild Orchids." *Common Knowledge* 1 (1992): 140–53. Also in *Wild Orchids and Trotsky,* ed. Mark Edmundson. New York: Penguin, 1993, pp. 31–50.

——. "Dewey Between Hegel and Darwin." *Modernist Impulses in the Human Sciences, 1870–1930,* ed. Dorothy Ross. Baltimore: Johns Hopkins University Press, pp. 54–68.

——. "Putnam and the Relativist Menace." *Journal of Philosophy* 90 (1993): 443–61.

——. "Does Academic Freedom Have Philosophical Presuppositions?" in *The Future of Academic Freedom,* ed. Louis Menand. Chicago: University of Chicago Press, 1996, pp. 21–42.

Rosenthal, Sandra B. *Speculative Pragmatism.* Amherst: University of Massachusetts Press, 1986.

Ross, Dorothy, ed. *Modernist Impulses in the Human Sciences, 1870–1939.* Baltimore: Johns Hopkins University Press, 1994.

Ryan, Alan. *John Dewey and the High Tide of American Liberalism.* New York: Norton, 1995.

Saatkamp, Herman J., ed. *Rorty and Pragmatism: The Philosopher Responds to His Critics.* Nashville: Vanderbilt University Press, 1995.

Scheffler, Israel. *Four Pragmatists: A Critical Introduction to Peirce, James, Mead, and Dewey.* New York: Routledge, Chapman, and Hall, 1986.

Seigfried, Charlene Haddock. *Chaos and Content: A Study in William James.* Athens: Ohio University Press, 1978.

——. *William James's Radical Reconstruction of Philosophy.* Albany: SUNY Press, 1990.

——. *Pragmatism and Feminism: Reweaving the Social Fabric.* Chicago: University of Chicago Press, 1996.

——, ed. *Hypatia,* 8, no. 2 (Spring, 1993). Special issue on "Feminism and Pragmatism."

Shusterman, Richard. *Pragmatist Aesthetics: Living Beauty, Rethinking Art.* Oxford: Blackwell, 1992.

Simon, Linda, ed. *William James Remembered.* Lincoln: University of Nebraska Press, 1996.

——. *Genuine Reality: A Life of William James.* New York: Harcourt Brace, 1998.

Sleeper, R. W. *The Necessity of Pragmatism: John Dewey's Conception of Philosophy.* New Haven: Yale University Press, 1986.

Smiley, Marion. *Moral Responsibility and the Boundaries of Community.* Chicago: University of Chicago Press, 1992.

Smith, Barbara Herrnstein. *Contingencies of Value.* Cambridge: Harvard University Press, 1988.

Smith, John E. *The Spirit of American Philosophy.* New York: Oxford University Press, 1963.

——. *Purpose and Thought: The Meaning of Pragmatism.* Chicago: University of Chicago Press, 1984.

Stout, Jeffrey. *Ethics after Babel: The Languages of Morals and Their Discontents.* Boston: Beacon Press, 1988.

Strout, Cushing. "The Legacy of Pragmatism," *Intellectual Life in America,* vol. 2, ed. Cushing Strout. New York: Harper and Row, 1968.

Sunstein, Cass R. *Legal Reasoning and Political Conflict.* New York: Oxford University Press, 1996.

Symposium on the Renaissance of Pragmatism in American Legal Thought, *Southern California Law Review* 63 (1990): 1569–1854.

Thayer, H. S. *Meaning and Action: A Critical History of Pragmatism.* Indianapolis: Hackett, 1981.

——, ed. *Pragmatism: The Classic Writings.* Indianapolis: Hackett, 1982.

West, Cornel. *The American Evasion of Philosophy: A Genealogy of Pragmatism.* Madison: University of Wisconsin Press, 1989.

Westbrook, Robert B. *John Dewey and American Democracy.* Ithaca: Cornell University Press, 1991.

White, Morton. *Social Thought in America: The Revolt Against Formalism.* 1949. Boston: Beacon Press, 1976.

——. *Toward Reunion in Philosophy.* Cambridge: Harvard University Press, 1956.

Wilson, Daniel J. *Science, Community, and the Transformation of American Philosophy, 1860–1930.* Chicago: University of Chicago Press, 1990.

Wittgenstein, Ludwig. *Philosophical Investigations,* trans. G. E. M. Anscombe. New York: Macmillan, 1953.

——. *On Certainty,* ed. G. E. M. Anscombe and G. H. von Wright, trans. Denis Paul and G. E. M. Anscombe. New York: Harper & Row, 1972.

Contributors

MORRIS DICKSTEIN is Distinguished Professor of English at the Graduate School and Queens College, CUNY, and the Director of the Center for the Humanities at the CUNY Graduate School. His books include *Gates of Eden: American Culture in the Sixties* (1977) and *Double Agent: The Critic and Society* (1992). He is co-author of a forthcoming volume of the *Cambridge History of American Literature* dealing with postwar fiction and drama.

RICHARD J. BERNSTEIN is Chairman and Vera List Professor of Philosophy at the New School for Social Research. His early work on Dewey preceded the recent pragmatist revival. He is author of *John Dewey* (1966), *Philosophical Profiles* (1986), and *The New Constellation: The Ethical-Political Horizons of Modernity/Postmodernity* (1992).

DAVID BROMWICH, Professor of English, Yale University, is the author of *A Choice of Inheritance: Self and Community from Edmund Burke to Robert Frost* (1989) and a widely discussed study of culture and education today, *Politics by Other Means: Higher Education and Group Thinking* (1992).

RAY CARNEY is Professor of Film and American Studies at Boston University and teaches courses on the relation of various forms of American artistic expression. He is the general editor of *The Cambridge Film Classics* series. His most recent books are *American Vision: The Films of Frank Capra* (1986) and *The Films of John Cassavetes: Pragmatism, Modernism, and the Movies* (1994).

STANLEY CAVELL is Walter M. Cabot Professor of Aesthetics and the General Theory of Value, Harvard University. His many books on philosophy and the arts include *The Claim of Reason* (1979), *This New Yet Unapproachable America: Lectures after Emerson after Wittgenstein* (1989), *Conditions Handsome and Unhandsome: The Constitution of Emersonian Perfectionism* (1990), and *A Pitch of Philosophy* (1994). Other books include *The Senses of Walden* (1972) and *Pursuits of Happiness* (1981), a study of what he calls "comedies of remarriage" among the films of the thirties and forties.

JOHN PATRICK DIGGINS is Distinguished Professor of History at the CUNY Graduate School. A prolific intellectual historian, he is the author of *The Lost Soul of American Politics* (1984), *The Rise and Fall of the American Left* (rev. ed., 1992), and *The Promise of Pragmatism:*

441

Modernism and the Crisis of Knowledge and Authority (1994). His most recent book is entitled *Max Weber: Politics and the Spirit of Tragedy* (1996).

STANLEY FISH is Arts and Sciences Professor of English and Professor of Law, Duke University, and Executive Director of Duke University Press. He established his own distinctive brand of pragmatism in *Is There a Text in This Class? Interpretive Communities and the Sources of Authority* (1980), and *Doing What Comes Naturally: Change, Rhetoric, and the Practice of Theory in Legal and Literary Studies* (1989). His most recent works include *There's No Such Thing as Free Speech* (1993), and *Professional Correctness: Literary Studies and Political Change* (1995).

NANCY FRASER, Professor of Political Science at The New School for Social Research, has written on French feminism and on the necessity of expanding the public sphere to include women. She is the author of *Unruly Practices: Power, Discourse and Gender in Contemporary Social Theory* (1989) and *Justice Interruptus: Critical Reflections on the "Postsocialist" Condition,* 1997.

THOMAS C. GREY is Nelson Bowman Sweitzer and Marie B. Sweitzer Professor of Law at Stanford University. Grey has written a number of articles published in the *Stanford Law Review,* including "Holmes and Legal Pragmatism" (1989). He is also the author of *The Legal Enforcement of Morality* (1983) and *The Wallace Stevens Case: Law and the Practice of Poetry* (1991).

GILES GUNN is Chair and Professor of English at the University of California, Santa Barbara. He is the author of, most recently, *The Culture of Criticism and the Criticism of Culture* (1987) and *Thinking Across the American Grain: Intellect, Ideology, and the New Pragmatism* (1992). Currently he is working on a book on the nature of human solidarity.

HANS JOAS is Professor of Sociology, Free University of Berlin/John F. Kennedy Institute. He is the author of *G. H. Mead: A Contemporary Re-Examination of His Thought* (1985), *Social Action and Human Nature,* with Axel Honneth (1988), *Pragmatism and Social Theory* (1993), and *The Creativity of Action,* (1996).

JAMES T. KLOPPENBERG is Professor of History at Brandeis University. He is coeditor, with Richard Wightman Fox, of *A Companion to American Thought* (1995), and the author of *Uncertain Victory: Social Democracy and Progressivism in European and American Thought, 1870–1920* (1986), and *The Virtues of Liberalism,* forthcoming.

DAVID LUBAN is the Frederick Haas Professor of Law and Philosophy at the Georgetown University Law Center. His books include *Lawyers and Justice: An Ethical Study* (1988), *Legal Modernism* (1994), and *The Ethics of Lawyers* (1994).

LOUIS MENAND, Professor of English at the CUNY Graduate School, is the author of numerous articles in *The New Republic, The New Yorker,* and *The New York Review of Books,* of which he is a contributing editor. He has edited *The Future of Academic Freedom* (1996) and *Pragmatism: A Reader* (1997).

SIDNEY MORGENBESSER is John Dewey Professor of Philosophy Emeritus at Columbia University and a legend in American philosophy. He is the editor of *Philosophy, Morality, and International Affairs* (1974) and *Dewey and His Critics: Essays from the Journal of Philosophy* (1977).

RICHARD POIRIER, Marius Bewley Professor of American and English Literature at Rutgers University, is the editor of *Raritan* and chairman of the board, Library of America. His books include *The Performing Self* (1971), *Robert Frost: The Work of Knowing* (1977), *The Renewal of Literature: Emersonian Reflections* (1987), and *Poetry and Pragmatism* (1992).

RICHARD A. POSNER is a judge at the U.S. Court of Appeals for the Seventh Circuit, and a prolific writer on legal and social subjects. He is the editor of *The Essential Holmes* (1992) and the author, among many other books, of *Law and Literature: A Misunderstood Relation* (1988) and *Overcoming Law* (1995).

ROSS POSNOCK, Hilen Professor of American Literature at the University of Washington, has recently completed a book on black intellectuals and pragmatism and is the author of *The Trial of Curiosity: Henry James, William James, and the Challenge of Modernity* (1991).

HILARY PUTNAM, Cogan University Professor at Harvard University, is one of the outstanding philosophical proponents of pragmatism. He is the author of *Reason, Truth, and History* (1981); *The Many Faces of Realism* (1987); *Realism with a Human Face* (1990); *Renewing Philosophy* (1992); and, most recently, *Pragmatism: An Open Question* (1995).

RUTH ANNA PUTNAM is Professor of Philosophy at Wellesley College. Trained in the sciences as well as in philosophy, she has written on William James and ethics, and edited *The Cambridge Companion to William James* (1997).

RICHARD RORTY is Professor of Comparative Literature at Stanford University and is one of the figures most responsible for the current revival of pragmatism. He previously taught at Princeton and the University of Virginia. His books include *Philosophy and the Mirror of Nature* (1979), *Consequences of Pragmatism* (1982), *Contingency, Irony, and Solidarity* (1989), and *Achieving Our Country* (1998).

MICHEL ROSENFELD is Professor of Law at the Benjamin N. Cardozo School of Law, Yeshiva University. He is the author of *Just Interpretations: Inquiries Across the Boundaries of Law, Ethics and Politics* (1998); the editor of *Constitutionalism, Identity, Difference and Legitimacy: Theoretical Perspectives* (1994); and coeditor with Andrew Arato of *Habermas on Law and Democracy: Critical Exchanges* (1998).

RICHARD H. WEISBERG is Walter Floersheimer Professor of Constitutional Law at the Benjamin N. Cardozo Law School of Yeshiva University. His books include *The Failure of the Word: The Protagonist as Lawyer in Modern Fiction* (1984), *Poethics, And Other Strategies of Law and Literature* (1992), and *Vichy Law and the Holocaust in France* (1996).

ROBERT B. WESTBROOK is Chair and Professor of History at the University of Rochester. His intellectual biography, *John Dewey and American Democracy* (1991), was a major contribution to the revival of interest in Dewey's relation to American political thought.

ALAN WOLFE is University Professor and Professor of Political Science and Sociology at Boston University. His many articles have appeared in *The New Republic, Lingua Franca,* and *The New Yorker.* He has edited *America at Century's End* (1991), and his books include *The Human Difference: Animals, Computers, and the Necessity of Social Science* (1993); a collection of essays on social criticism, *Marginalized in the Middle* (1996); and, most recently, *One Nation, After All* (1998), an ethnographic study of middle-class morality.

Index

Library of Congress Cataloging-in-Publication Data
The revival of pragmatism : new essays on social thought, law,
and culture / edited by Morris Dickstein.
Includes bibliographical references and index.
ISBN 0-8223-2228-5 (cloth : al. paper).
ISBN 0-8223-2245-5 (paper : alk. paper).
1. Pragmatism.   2. Social sciences—Philosophy.
3. Culture.   I. Dickstein, Morris.
B832.R43   1998   144'.3—dc21   98-2992 CIP